Clinical Pharmacology

Edited by
Ronald H. Girdwood

President of the
Royal College of Physicians of Edinburgh

TWENTY-FIFTH EDITION

Baillière Tindall   London Philadelphia Toronto
Mexico City Rio de Janeiro Sydney Tokyo Hong Kong

Baillière Tindall   1 St Anne's Road
Eastbourne, East Sussex BN21 3UN, England

West Washington Square
Philadelphia, PA 19105, USA

1 Goldthorne Avenue
Toronto. Ontario M8Z 5T9, Canada

Apartado 26370—Cedro 512
Mexico 4, DF, Mexico

Rua Evaristo da Veiga, 55–20° andar
Rio de Janeiro—RJ, Brazil

ABP Australia Ltd, 44 Waterloo Road
North Ryde, NSW 2064, Australia

Ichibancho Central Building, 22–1 Ichibancho
Chiyoda-ku, Tokyo 102, Japan

10/FL, Inter-Continental Plaza, 94 Granville Road
Tsim Sha Tsui East, Kowloon, Hong Kong

First published 1884
Twenty-fourth edition 1979
Twenty-fifth edition 1984

Typeset by Herts Typesetting Services Ltd, Hertford
Printed in Great Britain at the University Press, Cambridge

British Library Cataloguing in Publication Data

Clinical pharmacology.—25th ed.
  1. Pharmacology
  I. Girdwood, R. H.
  615'.7   RM300

ISBN 0-7020-0974-1

Contents

Contributors

I. W. Campbell, BSc, MB, ChB, FRCPE
Consultant Physican, Victoria Hospital, Kirkcaldy; Honorary Senior Lecturer in Medicine, University of Edinburgh.

J. A. J. H. Critchley, BSc, PhD, MB, ChB, MRCP (UK)
Lecturer, Department of Therapeutics and Clinical Pharmacology, Univeristy of Edinburgh; Honorary Senior Registrar, Royal Infirmary, Edinburgh.

R. H. Girdwood, MD, PhD, PRCPE, FRCP (Lond.), Hon. FACP, FRCPath, FRSE
President of the Royal College of Physicians of Edinburgh; Professor (Emeritus) of Therapeutics and Clinical Pharmacology, University of Edinburgh.

J. A. Gray, MB, ChB, FRCPE
Consultant in Communicable Diseases, Infectious Diseases Unit, City Hospital, Edinburgh; Part-time Senior Lecturer, Department of Medicine, University of Edinburgh.

R. C. Heading, BSc, MD, FRCPE
Senior Lecturer, Department of Therapeutics and Clinical Pharmacology, University of Edinburgh; Honorary Consultant Physician, Royal Infirmary, Edinburgh.

J. G. McVie, BSc, MD, FRCPE
Consultant Physician and Head of Clinical Pharmacology Unit, Netherlands Cancer Institute, Amsterdam.

J. Nimmo, BSc, MB, ChB, FRCPE
Consultant Physician, Eastern General Hospital, Edinburgh; Part-time Senior Lecturer, Department of Therapeutics and Clinical Pharmacology, University of Edinburgh.

W. S. Nimmo, MD, MRCP (UK), FFARCS
Senior Lecturer, University Department of Anaesthesia, Western Infirmary, Glasgow.

A. Pottage, BSc, MB, ChB, MRCP (UK)
Director of Clinical Research, Astra Clinical Research Unit, Edinburgh.

J. S. A. Sawers, BSc, MB, ChB, MRCP (UK)
Senior Registrar in Clinical Pharmacology, Royal Infirmary, Edinburgh.

A. D. Toft, BSc, MD, FRCPE
Senior Lecturer in Medicine, University of Edinburgh; Honorary Consultant Physician, Royal Infirmary, Edinburgh.

Preface

Major alterations have been made in the text of this book which has now reached a hundred years of continuing publication. By chance, too, it appears exactly fifty years after the editor commenced his studies as a medical student, and it is during this latter period that most of the drugs in use today have been marketed for the first time. Each year about forty completely new products appear, to which must be added many others that are fairly similar to those already available.

In this edition, the chapter on Antimicrobial Drugs has been completely rewritten by Dr J. A. Gray, an expert in this complex area of therapy. Three new authors, Drs A. D. Toft, I. W. Campbell and J. S. A. Sawers, have combined their specialist knowledge to rewrite the chapter on The Pharmacology of the Endocrine System. Dr J. A. J. H. Critchley, another new author, has written the section on Heavy Metals. Many readers have suggested that it is not necessary for a book of this nature to commence with an introductory chapter on such general subjects as pharmacodynamics (the mode of action of drugs), pharmacokinetics (the absorption, distribution, metabolism and elimination of drugs) or other matters with which they are already familiar. It is likely, however, that this view is not universally shared and that many readers welcome basic information. Accordingly, Dr A. Pottage's general chapter (now retitled General Aspects of Drug Action) has been included as Appendix 1. It is probable, too, that important though it is to know about adverse drug reactions, this section should not come before consideration of the individual therapeutic agents and hence the subject is dealt with towards the end of the volume.

Our knowledge of drug therapy changes rapidly and all the authors have found it necessary to discard information about substances no longer in common use and to add sections dealing with agents that have been recently introduced. Reference has also been made to new techniques such as the use of medical genetic engineering and the possible practical value of monoclonal antibodies. Few pages remain unchanged since the 24th Edition was produced, but some of the substances mentioned have been introduced so recently that their true place in therapeutics is, as yet, uncertain. This creates problems for the reader and on many occasions the editor has been asked to provide a much shorter list of preferred drugs. Unfortunately, there is no general agreement as to which medicinal agents should be included in such a list and preferences may depend on many factors such as the geographical area concerned, the teachings of local specialists, the age of the majority of patients being treated, the degree of persistence of the attentions of company representatives, the amount of cost consciousness and the information provided by local hospital pharmacists. In Appendix 2 there is given a list of 200 medicinal agents, selected after much discussion amongst physicians and pharmacists in a large teching hospital in Scotland that deals with adult patients. Agreement was not unanimous and, although most of the substances required for specialized units have been omitted, a few remain, usually at the request of authors. The numbering employed is that of the *British National Formulary* No. 5 (1983). It may be of interest to note that of the 709 different medicinal agents listed in the index of the 1884 edition of this book, only six are included in Appendix 2, not necessarily in exactly the same form. These are digitalis, atropine, nitroglycerin, morphine, ferrous sulphate and calcium. (In AD 43 the Romans in Britain were using belladonna, opium and iron salts). By 1934 a further 17 substances still considered to be basic necessities today were included, namely adrenaline hydrochloride, aspirin, codeine phosphate, dextrose solution, diamorphine hydrochloride, glycerin suppositories, insulin, kaolin, parathyroid extract, phenobarbitone, sodium chloride, thyroxine, vitamins A, B, C, D and G (riboflavin). As a student, the editor heard with much interest about the introduction of the new substance sulphanilamide, which was said to be able to control certain infections. Some clinical teachers of the time were very doubtful about this claim. By the time of his graduation in 1939, there was not yet a suitable drug to arrest the progress of pulmonary tuberculosis. In the First Edition of this book the author, Dr J. Mitchell Bruce, wrote 'Phthisis is rarely benefited by iodides, unless there be a syphilitic taint present'. So far as drug therapy is concerned, there was no true progress until 1945.

In a hundred years we have passed from volatile oils and infusions to the products of complex industrial procedures and to substances prepared or extracted as a result of detailed knowledge of physiological and pathological processes in the body. Individuals may have ideas, but large teams are usually now required to give us the finished product. The initial cost in money terms may be enormous, but the benefits to mankind are great.

The medical student and practitioner of 1884 or 1934 had difficulty in remembering the names and doses of drugs used empirically and often chosen for no obvious reason. In 1984 the problems are of keeping up to date as new products appear, and appreciating sufficient of the detailed knowledge that is available about modes of action and side-effects of the various therapeutic agents to make understanding and learning possible. In the First Edition of this book Dr Bruce wrote in the Foreword 'In using the book the first year's student is recommended to confine his attention to the Materia Medica proper; and under the action and uses of the drugs to read only the words printed in thick type'. Thus, under the heading *Digitalis*, only forty words out of 1500 are marked in this way. It was reasonable to suggest that it was not necessary to read about the action of a drug when this was not understood, but things are very different now, and the student of today would find it tedious and difficult to adopt such an approach. It is hoped that this Centenary Edition will provide the student with sufficient information to understand the action in man of the drugs now in common usage.

The editor has travelled widely abroad in recent years, particularly in eastern countries, and has obtained helpful advice from doctors, students, hospital pharmacists and medical librarians; hence the problems of the overseas reader have constantly been borne in mind, in addition to those of his or her counterpart in the British Isles.

The editor and contributors are again most grateful to Miss Elspeth R. Shields for typing the manuscript in her leisure hours, and to Dr M. E. Jones for helpful discussion relating to the use outside Britain of certain drugs mentioned in Chapter 1. They are also grateful to Messrs David Dickens and Peter Gill of Baillière Tindall, who have been most co-operative in ensuring that the Centenary Edition was produced with the minimum of delay, so that it would, indeed, appear at the correct time.

Ronald H. Girdwood

1 Antimicrobial Drugs

J. A. Gray

ANTIBACTERIAL AGENTS

The dramatic decline in mortality from communicable diseases in the past 50 years has been variously attributed to improved nutrition, housing and sanitation, to immunization, international programmes for disease surveillance and control, and to the natural waning in virulence of certain micro-organisms. In addition, antimicrobial drugs have played a significant part. From the discovery of the antimalarial properties of Peruvian bark early in the 17th century to Ehrlich's magic antisyphilitic bullet, salvarsan, in 1909, little progress in antimicrobial therapy was made. Then the era of synthetic antibacterial drugs opened with the development of Prontosil by Domagk in the early 1930s; next, during the 1940s, penicillin was developed as the first of the naturally occurring antibacterial substances, following Fleming's discovery of the bactericidal property of the mould *Penicillium notatum* in 1929.

Subsequently a plethora of antibiotics has been discovered, many, like penicillin, initially derived from mould or fungi. Once the nucleus of the natural compound was identified, numerous semisynthetic substances were produced by manipulation of the side chains, so altering the antibacterial and pharmacokinetic properties of the parent drug. Alongside the development of antibacterial agents, the past 50 years have also seen the production of drugs effective against some fungi, protozoa, helminths and viruses.

Wisely applied, these antimicrobial drugs have an enormous potential for good in human and veterinary medicine and animal husbandry, but they are often misused with disastrous results. Many organisms against which these drugs are effective are shared by man and animals either as commensals or pathogens. Consequently, the use of an antimicrobial agent in a member of one species may have unpredictable results extending far beyond the initial site where it was first employed.

The prescriber of antimicrobial drugs rarely appreciates the enormous responsibility he assumes. Firstly, the drug may be toxic to the host's tissues as well as to the pathogen against which it has been directed. The host's commensals may be inhibited along with the target organism, leaving an ecological vacuum into which opportunists may be drawn. Alternatively, the commensals and pathogens may not be killed, but may acquire multiple

1

resistance both to the drug being used and to several others in addition. This sinister property can be transferred from the micro-organisms of the host to those of his fellows, to those of other species and then to the environment at large, leading to a microflora largely insensitive to many of the previously effective drugs.

The model described applies mainly to antibiotics and bacterial infections which have been extensively studied. The use of antibacterial substances to accelerate fattening of livestock for the market has rightly been condemned. Antibiotics should only be given to animals for therapy under the direction of a qualified veterinary surgeon. Otherwise a reservoir of resistant micro-organisms will grow up and the usefulness of the antibiotics will fast diminish. Similarly, in human medicine and dentistry, antibacterial drugs must be cherished and only prescribed by qualified doctors and dentists when genuinely indicated. The availability of antibacterial agents is all too easy in some countries and often leads to self-medication, widespread antibiotic abuse and high levels of multiple antibiotic resistance amongst dangerous bacterial pathogens. Prolonged or repeated therapy and low dose suppressive antibacterial prophylaxis are most likely to induce drug resistance amongst bacteria. Although less is known about the development of resistance amongst non-bacterial micro-organisms, it is likely that the same trends will occur. An example of protozoal resistance is the chloroquine insensitivity of malarial parasites already found in many different parts of the world. Similar problems may develop amongst viruses and fungi if proper control is not exercised in the use of antimicrobial agents.

Before any antibacterial drug is prescribed, it is important not only to be sure that an infection is present, i.e. that the tissues have been successfully invaded by the micro-organism, but also that the bacteria are doing harm or are likely to do harm if left untreated. Antibiotics are often wrongly given simply because some potentially pathogenic organisms have been isolated even though they are not making the patient ill or are sufficiently trivial for the patient's own defence mechanisms to deal with them unaided. Ideally, when an infection is to be treated, the organism should first be isolated and its sensitivity determined. Some bacteria, such as *Streptococcus pyogenes*, are always sensitive to penicillin, so assessment of sensitivity need not be routinely requested. Others may be variably resistant to antibiotics, in which case laboratory help is essential in determining the antibiogram, as it is now called.

Whenever possible, a bactericidal drug should be used, especially in the immunocompromised patient. The spectrum should be narrow to avoid interference with commensals. It is equally important to ensure that the chosen drug will penetrate to the site of the infection. Thus orally administered antibiotics must be well absorbed from the intestine if they are to provide adequate antibacterial concentrations in infected tissues. Pyogenic meningitis, for example, can only be successfully treated other than by direct intrathecal or intraventricular injection if the antibacterial drug crosses the blood–brain barrier and enters the CSF in sufficient amounts.

The pharmacokinetics of the drug must therefore be understood and caution exercised in very ill or elderly patients who cannot metabolize or excrete these drugs efficiently because of hepatic or renal functional impairment. Special care must be observed during pregnancy and lactation and in the newborn, whose immature handling of certain drugs may be quite different from that in the older child or adult. In these circumstances, certain antimicrobial drugs should be avoided altogether or else their dosage modified.

Sometimes it is important to monitor drug concentrations in body fluids to ensure that an adequate antibacterial concentration has been achieved. In the context of toxic antimicrobial drugs, monitoring is essential to prevent the drug level rising excessively, which could lead to tissue damage unless a reduction is made in the dose or the interval between doses is prolonged. It is occasionally difficult to find the right balance between the therapeutic and toxic doses in acutely ill patients whose pharmacological handling of the drug may fluctuate rapidly due to hypotension, reduced renal clearance or hepatic insufficiency.

Another reason for limiting the use of antimicrobial agents for genuine therapeutic indications is their ability sometimes to induce severe or fatal adverse reactions. A history of previous drug sensitivity must be sought and the same drug or a closely allied one should be avoided if a reaction has been recorded before. Certain drugs are more liable to be toxic when used in particular disease states. Ampicillin and amoxycillin skin eruptions are more common when lymphoid tissue is exuberant, as in lymphomas or glandular fever. Chloramphenicol is more likely to induce aplastic anaemia if long or repeated courses are given. Some drug combinations increase the risk of reactions, such as the nephrotoxicity associated with the combination of an aminoglycoside with certain cephalosporins, or the use of cephaloridine or cephalothin with frusemide or ethacrynic acid. Interference with the anticoagulant action of warfarin can be a dangerous side-effect of various antimicrobial drugs, notably the sulphonamides. The low oestrogen pill may lose its contraceptive effect if taken with rifampicin or other drugs that induce liver enzymes (pp. 37, 425).

In general, a single antimicrobial agent should be employed, depending on the known or expected sensitivity of the pathogen causing the infection. Antibacterial drug combinations are only justified in three circumstances: (i) for the blind treatment of the severely ill septicaemic patient whose infecting agent has not yet been identified and who urgently requires antibiotic cover for Gram-positive and -negative bacteria and also possibly anaerobes, (ii) to prevent the emergence of resistance, as in the management of tuberculosis, where three drugs may be initially used until the sensitivity of the tubercle bacilli is known, whereupon they should be replaced by two effective drugs, or in chloroquine-resistant malaria, where a combination of pyrimethamine with sulfadoxine or dapsone is advocated, and (iii) where the synergism occurs as with co-trimoxazole, whose two components, sulphamethoxazole and trimethoprim, sequentially interfere with bacterial folinic acid synthesis. Disadvantages of combined therapy include the increased risk of toxicity by the use of more than one drug, the difficulty of assaying drug concentrations in tissue fluids, the greater chance of superinfection because of the broader overall spectrum of activity, and, not least, the cost.

Penicillins

1: Thiazolidine ring
2: β – Lactam ring

BENZYLPENICILLIN

The number of penicillins continues to increase from Fleming's original crystalline, benzylpenicillin (penicillin G), which remains a very effective antibiotic, to the highly sophisticated broad- and narrow-spectrum penicillins now produced from the original fermentation product nucleus by semi-synthetic processes. The penicillins are a particularly valuable group of antibiotics, being relatively non-toxic and so therapeutically very useful.

Description and General Properties
The 6-aminopenicillanic acid (6-APA) nucleus, from which all penicillins are derived, is a thiazolidine ring fused to a β-lactam ring. Different and often lengthy side-chains added to this basic structure confer different antibacterial and pharmacokinetic properties. One disadvantage of penicillin G is its inability to resist gastric acid, making the drug effective only after parenteral administration. Adding phenoxyacetic acid instead of phenylacetic acid during the fermentation process results in the production of phenoxymethyl-penicillin (penicillin V), which is acid stable, unlike the original penicillin G.

    Organisms such as *Staphylococcus pyogenes* and certain coliforms produce β-lactamase (penicillinase), an enzyme which disrupts the β-lactam ring of the 6-APA nucleus and renders the drug pharmacologically inert. A heavy side-chain added to 6-APA, as shown originally with methicillin, confers β-lactamase stability. The isoxazolyl penicillins, like cloxacillin, flucloxacillin and oxacillin, also possess heavy β-lactamase resisting side-chains, but, unlike methicillin, they are also acid resistant and so can be given by mouth as well as by injection. The substitution of a single chlorine atom by fluorine on the side-chain confers on cloxacillin an enhanced degree of absorption from the gut as flucloxacillin.

    Until the arrival of ampicillin, which is active against many of the

Enterobacteriaceae, the penicillins were mainly effective against Gram-positive cocci and bacilli and only a few Gram-negative species, like gonococci and meningococci, were sensitive to it. Various esters of ampicillin have been developed with enhanced absorption from the gastrointestinal tract, but the closely related compound, amoxycillin, which differs from ampicillin only by the addition of a hydroxyl radical on the side-chain, is particularly well absorbed and gives higher serum concentration than ampicillin after a similar oral dose.

The amidino-penicillins, injectable mecillinam (p. 8) and the orally acceptable pivmecillinam (p. 8) have a similar, but not identical, spectrum to ampicillin and this includes activity against salmonellae. The amidino-penicillins have a single attachment site to the bacterial cell wall at protein binding site 2, thus differing from other penicillins which can attach at various different sites. Although their action is different because of the formation of easily ruptured bacterial spheroplasts, the therapeutic value of the amidino-penicillins on their own is not superior to that of other penicillins; used in combination with other antibiotics, they may have more than an additive antibacterial effect.

Carbenicillin was the first penicillin active against *Pseudomonas aeruginosa*, but, being acid labile, it had to be given by injection and in very high i.v. doses in order to be effective. The orally administered carbenicillin derivatives, carindacillin and carfecillin, are therapeutically disappointing for use in serious pseudomonas infections. One new development from carbenicillin, ticarcillin, however, has a better spectrum of activity than carbenicillin against Gram-negative bacilli, including *Ps. aeruginosa*, and the recently introduced piperacillin is even more active in vitro. The ureido-penicillins, mezlocillin and azlocillin, are also particularly effective anti-pseudomonas drugs. These valuable agents with special properties must be safeguarded and only used when specifically indicated. Ticarcillin, piperacillin and the ureido-penicillins are acid labile like carbenicillin and must be given parenterally. They are all sensitive to β-lactamase to a variable degree.

One discovery running parallel with the development of the newer penicillins has been the production of two β-lactamase inhibitors, clavulanic acid and sulbactam. Although they only have weak antibacterial properties on their own, a small amount of these new agents will render β-lactamase sensitive drugs, like ampicillin, resistant to enzymatic degradation. The exact therapeutic place of these new preparations is still unclear, despite intense marketing pressure by the pharmaceutical companies.

Mode of Action
Penicillins interfere with bacterial cell wall synthesis and render the bacterium unable to withstand changes in osmotic pressure which cause it to swell up and rupture. Penicillins bind at one of several sites on the cell wall, except the amidino-penicillins, which only bind to protein binding site 2. Bacterial cell

walls consist of long glycopeptide and peptidoglycan chains. Penicillins prevent the formation of the cross linkages between these chains by interference with the enzymes transpeptidase and endopeptidase, but do so only when the bacteria are dividing. Long filamentous forms result if end-wall synthesis is disrupted, as with ampicillin, or spheroplasts result if side-wall synthesis is inactivated, as with amoxycillin and the amidino-penicillins. As peptidoglycan is common to all bacteria but is not found as such in human cells, the penicillins can be used almost with impunity, thanks to the exploitation of a basic biochemical difference between host and pathogen.

Pharmacokinetics

The acid stable penicillins, like penicillin V, ampicillin, amoxycillin, isoxazolyl penicillins (pp. 7,9), carindacillin, carfecillin and pivmecillinam, are absorbed variably in the upper small intestine. Amoxycillin is better absorbed than ampicillin, so that higher blood levels are reached. Accordingly, 8-hourly rather than 6-hourly administration can be used. Amoxycillin penetrates into sputum better than ampicillin. Various ampicillin esters, like talampicillin, have been developed. They have no pharmacological action on the gut flora before absorption, but are rapidly hydrolysed to ampicillin and esters on crossing the gut wall. Higher serum ampicillin concentrations result on a weight for weight basis than with the non-esterified drug.

After injection i.v. or i.m., the acid labile penicillins are handled similarly to the orally administered acid stable compounds. Serum levels rise steeply and tissue diffusion is good, except to the cerebrospinal fluid, where therapeutic concentrations of penicillin are only achieved when the meninges are inflamed. Protein binding of some penicillins is high, especially the isoxazolyl penicillins. Some biliary excretion occurs with all the penicillins, but particularly with ampicillin, where bile levels of ampicillin may be 300 times greater than the serum concentration. Very little penicillin is metabolized. Most is excreted in the urine by renal tubular mechanisms within a few hours, necessitating repeated administration of any penicillin several times in 24 hours to maintain therapeutic concentrations. Probenecid interferes with the tubular excretion of penicillins and may be used to achieve very high tissue concentrations of the antibiotic.

Preparations

Benzylpenicillin (penicillin G; Crystapen). This drug remains the least toxic of the family and has been used safely in extremely high doses. It is usually prepared for i.m. injection in a concentration of 150 mg/ml in water and does not keep for longer than a day at room temperature. The usual dose range is from 300 to 600 mg 6-hourly, although an insensitive organism may only be eradicated with doses of 6 g or more given 6-hourly.

Procaine penicillin (Depocillin). A relatively insoluble preparation, procaine penicillin is slowly released from the injection site, and it therefore takes longer for high blood levels to be achieved. It is less painful for the recipient than is benzylpenicillin. The dose is 600 mg and this is required only once a day. Procaine penicillin may be mixed with benzylpenicillin (Bicillin) to achieve fast mobilization to the tissues and less frequent dosage.

Benzathine penicillin (Penidural). This pink *suspension* is given in adult doses of 458 mg every 6–8 hours (229 mg in 5 ml) or as *paediatric drops* in lower doses according to body weight (115 mg in 1 ml).

Benethamine penicillin (Triplopen). This is available as a powder in a vial which contains 475 mg of benethamine penicillin, 250 mg of procaine penicillin and 300 mg of sodium penicillin. When water for injections is added, a suspension for i.m. use is formed. One vial is given every two or three days.

Phenoxymethylpenicillin (penicillin V) (Aspin VK, Crystapen V, Distaquaine V-K, Econocil VK, Icipen, Stabillin V-K, V-Cil-K). Tablets (usually 125 or 250 mg) of phenoxymethylpenicillin are stable in gastric acid and one is taken every 4–6 hours. Absorption is delayed by food, so doses should be given prior to meals.

Phenethicillin (Broxil) and *Propicillin*. These drugs are less active than phenoxymethylpenicillin, but are better absorbed. Propicillin is tightly bound to protein in the plasma and is therefore distributed less well in the tissues and is less active. Phenethicillin is similar in efficacy to phenoxymethylpenicillin and the dose is identical. The amount usually given is 250 mg 4–6 hourly on an empty stomach.

Methicillin (Celbenin). While being useful against penicillinase-producing bacteria, methicillin is unstable in gastric acid. It is best given by injection i.m. or i.v. in a dose of 1 g 4–6 hourly. It is approximately one-fiftieth less active against Gram-positive bacteria than benzylpenicillin, though higher concentrations are attainable free in plasma owing to lower binding to protein.

Cloxacillin (Orbenin) and *Flucloxacillin* (Floxapen). These penicillins combine the properties of penicillinase resistance and acid stability. Accordingly, they may be given orally, and flucloxacillin achieves particularly satisfactory plasma levels at a dose of 250 mg 6-hourly. The same dose may be used for the i.m. preparation. Cloxacillin may also be given orally or i.v., the dose being 500 mg 6-hourly. Both drugs surpass methicillin in antibacterial action, although neither gives results comparable with those obtained when benzylpenicillin is used against organisms that are sensitive to it.

Ampicillin (Amfipen, Penbritin, Vidopen). Ampicillin, a widely used drug, can be given orally, i.m. or i.v. in a dose of 250 mg 6-hourly. It has a broad range of activity, but many bacteria quickly form resistance to it. Like benzylpenicillin, it is not found in high concentration in brain tissue, though bactericidal levels reach the CSF in purulent meningitis. Combinations of 250 mg of ampicillin with 250 mg of cloxacillin (Ampiclox) or of 250 mg ampicillin with 250 mg of flucloxacillin (Magnapen) are available for parenteral and oral use, respectively. These are combined in an effort to produce broad spectrum properties and at the same time have penicillinase resistance. Sulbactam, a β-lactamase inhibitor, combined with ampicillin renders the ampicillin resistant to enzyme destruction, but it is not yet available for general use.

Amoxycillin (Amoxil). This is twice as well absorbed as ampicillin and so can give therapeutic serum levels after 250 mg capsules are given at 8-hourly intervals. Although not a penicillin, clavulanic acid, a β-lactamase inhibitor, combined with amoxycillin, confers resistance to the enzyme. An adult dose of 125 mg of potassium clavulanate with 250 mg amoxycillin (Augmentin) is given 8-hourly or may be doubled in severe infections.

Talampicillin (Talpen). This is one of several ampicillin-ester preparations which has no pharmacological activity against gut flora, but which is rapidly de-esterified in the gut mucosa or liver to release ampicillin to the systemic circulation. Absorption is good and 250 mg 8-hourly (or 125 mg 8-hourly for children over 2 years) gives good serum concentrations.

Carbenicillin (Pyopen). This was the first penicillin to be effective against *Ps. aeruginosa*. For suspected or proven pseudomonas septicaemia up to 30 g daily was necessary in 4–6 hourly divided doses i.v. It has now been supplanted by ticarcillin, the ureido-penicillins, and piperacillin. It is acid labile and β-lactamase sensitive. Two oral derivatives can be used for pseudomonas urinary infection without systemic involvement. They are carindacillin (Geocillin — USA only), 500 mg to 1 g 6-hourly, or carfecillin (Uticillin in the UK), 500 mg 8-hourly. Note that in the USA, Uticillin VK is a proprietary name for phenoxymethylpenicillin (p. 7).

Ticarcillin (Ticar). Ticarcillin is chemically closely related to carbenicillin, but much more active against *Ps. aeruginosa*. It is acid labile and β-lactamase sensitive. For septicaemias, 5 g may be given intravenously every 6 hours.

Mezlocillin (Baypen) and *Azlocillin* (Securopen). These ureido-penicillins should be reserved for serious infections with Gram-negative species, especially *Ps. aeruginosa*. They are less active against Gram-positive organisms. They are acid labile and variably β-lactamase sensitive. In septicaemic adults 2–5 g may be required i.v. every 6–8 hours.

Piperacillin (Pipril). This is very active against *Pseudomonas* spp. and sufficiently broad-spectrum to include many Gram-positive and Gram-negative bacteria, except some staphylococci and klebsiella organisms. For seriously ill bacteraemic adults 3–4 g may be given i.v. 6-hourly.

Mecillinam (Selexidin) and *Pivmecillinam* (Selexid). These amidino-penicillins are β-lactamase sensitive. Mecillinam is acid labile and is given i.m.

or i.v. in doses of 5–15 mg/kg body weight every 6 hours in serious infections. Pivmecillinam is acid stable and is given orally in doses ranging from 600 mg to 2.4 g daily in 3 or 4 divided doses.

Indications

The earlier penicillins are most effective against Gram-positive cocci and bacilli. Streptococci, pneumococci, corynebacteria, listeria, meningococci and most gonococci remain sensitive, but some β-lactamase resistance has developed amongst gonococci, making penicillin no longer the drug of first choice for treating gonorrhoea. Meningococci, however, remain fully sensitive. Syphilis may still be safely treated with procaine penicillin injected once daily for 10–20 days.

The versatility of dosage of the penicillins is illustrated by the comparison of prophylaxis in a patient with rheumatic heart disease and intensive treatment of streptococcal endocarditis. In the former case, as little as 125 mg of phenoxymethylpenicillin twice a day by mouth will suffice. For eradication of endocarditis, on the other hand, up to 18 g of benzylpenicillin daily i.v. may be used. High doses are also required to treat pneumococcal meningitis, owing to the limited concentration of drug traversing the blood–brain barrier. Many staphylococcal strains, particularly in hospitals, are resistant to penicillin. The drug of choice for oral medication in infections involving those bacteria is flucloxacillin, owing to its superior absorption. The same drug may be given to a very ill patient parenterally, or, alternatively, the other penicillinase-resistant drugs, cloxacillin and methicillin, may be used. The latter is associated with more side-effects, so cloxacillin is generally employed.

Less frequently seen are meningococcal meningitis, actinomycosis, gas gangrene, anthrax, and erysipelas, all of which respond to narrow-spectrum penicillins.

Often broad-spectrum penicillins, ampicillin, its esters and amoxycillin, are usually effective against *Haemophilus influenzae*, common Gram-positive cocci and *Escherichia coli* and so are often successful in the treatment of respiratory and urinary infections. In serious salmonella infections, amoxycillin is a safer alternative to chloramphenicol and co-trimoxazole, though many still prefer chloramphenicol for the management of typhoid fever. The more widely these drugs are used, however, the greater the risk of resistance developing. Prior knowledge of the sensitivity pattern of the pathogen is becoming increasingly important.

Carbenicillin, one of the first effective non-toxic drugs for pseudomonas septicaemia, has largely been supplanted by the newer penicillins, ticarcillin, mezlocillin, azlocillin and piperacillin, to which *Ps. aeruginosa* is much more susceptible. Like the new anti-pseudomonas cephalosporins, cefotaxime and ceftazidime, these drugs should be used only for Gram-negative septicaemia where pseudomonas infection is likely. Combinations with an aminoglycoside may be justified until the pathogen is isolated on blood culture and its sensitivity determined.

Although effective against salmonellae, pivmecillinam is best reserved for urinary tract infections with Gram-negative bacilli. Clavulanic acid and sulbactam combinations can be very effective, but their exact role outside the treatment of urinary infections has yet to be decided.

Adverse Effects

Toxicity. The penicillins are remarkably free from toxic effects. Occasionally neurotoxicity, myoclonic movements, and loss of consciousness have been reported in patients who have had renal impairment delaying excretion and who have received large doses of parenteral penicillin.

Gastric intolerance and mild diarrhoea may sometimes be caused by phenoxymethylpenicillin, ampicillin, or amoxycillin. Skin rashes are fairly frequent, and, indeed, a maculopapular rash is almost invariable when ampicillin or amoxycillin is given to a patient who has either infectious mononucleosis or lymphatic leukaemia.

Numerous types of skin raction have been alleged to be due to the administration of penicillin, but sometimes the evidence is scanty. It has been cited as the cause of erythema nodosum, erythema multiforme, anaphylactoid purpura, Henoch–Schönlein purpura, exfoliative dermatitis, bullous conditions, and the Stevens–Johnson syndrome. This last consists of severe erythema multiforme with bullous lesions and involvement of the mouth, upper respiratory passages, and external genitalia. In high doses, methicillin has been associated with nephritis, this usually, however, being reversible.

Allergy. Penicillin has been blamed for hypersensitivity reactions of most types, including those classified by many as Types I, II, III, and IV, though some authorities consider that this classification is an oversimplification (p. 551). If this approach is used, however, by far the most life-threatening reaction is Type I anaphylactic shock. This occurs immediately after a re-exposure to penicillin, and consists mainly of severe bronchospasm and hypotension. It may be almost instantaneously fatal if not relieved by a rapid subcutaneous injection of 1 in 1000 adrenaline or by the infusion of i.v. hydrocortisone. A localized form of Type I hypersensitivity may lead to angioneurotic oedema in certain sensitized individuals and to urticaria in others. Type II allergy is due to cytotoxic antibodies and may be part of the explanation of penicillin-induced thrombocytopenia and haemolytic anaemia. The latter occurs only after high doses of penicillin. Serum sickness (p. 551) has been well documented following penicillin therapy and is insidious in that it may take 10 days to develop. Although skin tests have been attempted, they cannot be depended on to predict whether or not a given patient is at risk to this complication. In contrast, a 'patch' test will reliably select those prone to contact dermatitis, a cell-mediated delayed Type IV hypersensitivity to penicillin. None of the family of penicillins is recommended for topical use, so those employed to handle penicillin in industry are at risk to contact dermatitis.

Desensitization of patients who urgently require penicillin is tedious, dangerous and often fruitless. Antihistamines and steroids provide unreliable protection when given with penicillin to sensitized individuals. Wherever possible, an alternative antibiotic should be tried. As with all adverse reactions to drugs, it is essential that the patient at risk is aware of the nature of his allergy and knows the names of all substances which may contain penicillin or a cross-reacting antibiotic. In this context, it is worth warning of the presence of traces of the drug in milk or butter when cattle have been undergoing medication.

Contraindications

The main objection to using penicillin in the treatment of a sensitive organism is a history of previous allergy. As mentioned before, a repeat challenge with penicillin will commonly cause distress and may occasionally be fatal.

Cephalosporins

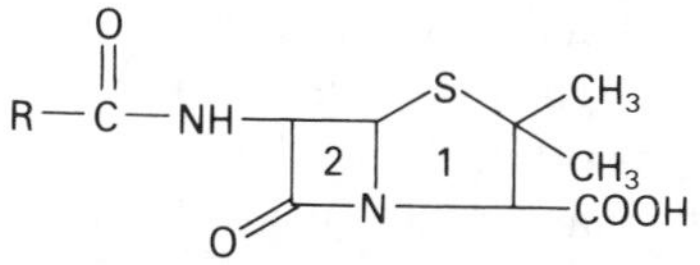

1: Thiazolidine ring
2: β-Lactam ring

PENICILLIN NUCLEUS (6-APA)

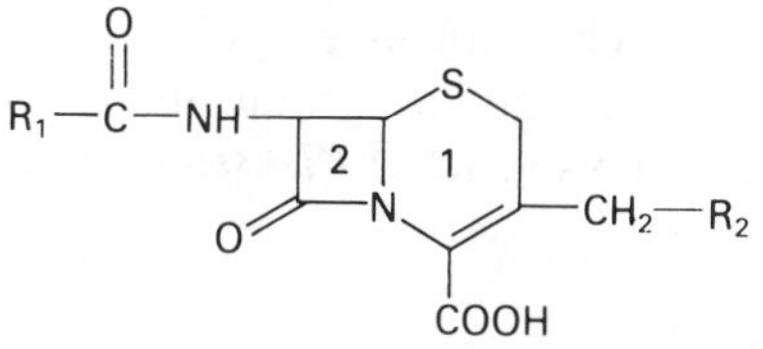

1: Dihydrothiazine ring
2: β-Lactam ring

CEPHALOSPORIN NUCLEUS (7-ACA)

Mould from Mediterranean sewage provided the original source of Cephalosporin C from which the ever growing family of semi-synthetic cephalosporin antibiotics has been derived. The earlier cephalosporins were spelt with an initial *ceph-*, as in cephaloridine, cephalothin, cephalexin and cephradine, and those developed later were given an initial *cef-*, as in cefuroxime and many others. The cephalosporins are now so numerous that only some representative drugs can be described in this chapter.

Description and General Properties

The basic nucleus is 7-aminocephalosporanic acid (7-ACA), a dihydro-thiazine ring fused, as with the penicillins, to a β-lactam ring which must remain intact to preserve the antibacterial action. If not protected by appropriate modification of one of the two side-chains, 7-ACA can be destroyed by β-lactamases. The earlier cephalosporins were β-lactamase sensitive, but some of the later compounds are highly enzyme stable. The addition of a methoxyl group to the nucleus created the first cephamycin, cefoxitin, whose broad spectrum includes anaerobes.

Because of the similar starting point in the fermentation process leading to 6-APA and 7-ACA, some of the original cephalosporins may have contained sufficient traces of penicillin to induce allergic reaction suggesting a degree of cross-hypersensitivity. The compounds are basically so similar, however, that it is considered unwise to prescribe either group of drugs to a patient who has had a severe (particularly Type I) reaction to a penicillin, cephalosporin or cephamycin.

The earlier cephalosporins, cephalordine and cephalothin, are effective against Gram-positive and -negative bacteria, but are less powerful than the penicillins and aminoglycosides against sensitive organisms and are destroyed by β-lactamase. The oral cephalosporins are convenient, but, with the exception of cefaclor, they are also β-lactamase sensitive. The later cephalosporins are generally less toxic, diffuse better and have enhanced activity against Gram-negative bacilli. Thus cefuroxime, cefamandole, cefotaxime, ceftazidime and the cephamycin, cefoxitin, do not cause renal damage like cephaloridine or cephalothin. Some of the newer cephalosporins penetrate the CSF in amounts that should make them effective in the treatment of meningitis caused by sensitive bacteria. In addition, cefuroxime, cefamandole and cefoxitin are β-lactamase stable. Of the latest generation of cephalosporins, cefotaxime and ceftazidime, although rather less active against Gram-positive cocci, are highly effective against Gram-negative bacilli, including *Escherichia coli*, indole producing *Proteus* spp., *Pseudomonas aeruginosa* and opportunists such as *Klebsiella* spp. and *Serratia marcescens*.

Mode of Action
Although the cephalosporins do not necessarily bind to the same bacterial cell wall proteins, their action is similar to that of other β-lactam antibiotics, such as penicillin. They prevent the formation of the cross-bridges on the glycopeptan chains of actively dividing bacteria by interfering with transpeptidase and endopeptidase activity.

Pharmacokinetics
Few orally acceptable cephalosporins have been developed and a disadvantage of the newer broader spectrum compounds is that they must be given by injection. The earliest cephalosporin that was acid resistant and well absorbed was cephalexin and this, with cephradine (which can be given orally or parenterally) and cefaclor are the only widely used oral cephalosporins.

The serum half-life of cephalosporins is about one hour. There is a wide variation in the degree of protein binding from about 10 % with cephradine to 80 % with cephazolin. Diffusion is usually good except into the CSF, where only the newer cephalosporins, especially latamoxef disodium, can be relied upon to achieve therapeutic concentrations. Cefuroxime penetrates well into sputum, pleural and peritoneal fluids and also CSF. Except for cephalothin, cefotaxime and, to a lesser extent, cefoxitin, which are partly metabolized, cephalosporins tend to be excreted as such by glomerular filtration and tubular secretion. Probenecid assists in achieving high tissue levels of cephalosporins by blocking their excretion. In renal failure, the dose of cephalosporins should be reduced, since serum and tissue concentrations rise steeply. Cephaloridine and cephalothin, which can both be nephrotoxic, should be avoided in uraemic patients.

Preparations

So many cephalosporins are now available that a description of each cannot be given, but rather a representative list. The earlier compounds, with their potential for kidney damage, have now been largely supplanted, but are still included for comparison. Only the adult doses are quoted, but infants and children tolerate the cephalosporins well.

Cephaloridine (Ceporin). Up to a maximum of 6 g daily may be given i.m. or i.v. in 6–8-hourly divided doses. Nephrotoxicity may result from higher doses. Cephaloridine is β-lactamase sensitive.

Cephalothin (Keflin). Up to a maximum of 12 g daily may be given i.v. in 4-hourly divided doses. I.m. injections are painful. The dose should not be exceeded to avoid nephrotoxicity. Cephalothin is β-lactamase sensitive.

Cephradine (Velosef). Up to a maximum of 8 g may be given daily by i.m. or i.v. injection in 6-hourly divided doses. Usually 2–4 g daily is sufficient. Cephradine is the only cephalosporin available for parenteral and oral use. Capsules of 250 or 500 mg and a syrup containing 125 or 250 mg in 5 ml are available. The adult oral dose is 500 mg 6-hourly or double if indicated. Cephradine is variably β-lactamase stable.

Cephazolin (Kefzol). This may be given in a dose of 500 mg to 1g i.m. or i.v. every 6–12 hours, depending on the severity of the infection. I.m. injections may be painful. Cephazolin is variably unstable to β-lactamase.

Cephamandole (Kefadol). 500 mg to 2 g may be given i.m. or i.v. every 4–8 hours. I.m. injections are occasionally painful. Cephamandole is β-lactamase stable.

Cefuroxime (Zinacef). 750 mg to 1.5 g may be given i.v. every 6–8 hours or lower doses i.m. Cefuroxime is β-lactamase stable and mainly active against Gram-negative bacilli and Gram-positive cocci.

Cefotaxime (Claforan). 1 g may be given i.m. or i.v. every 12 hours or in severe infections 3 g 6-hourly, i.v. The spectrum includes *Pseudomonas* spp. and some anaerobes. *Ceftazidime* has a very wide spectrum, again including *Pseudomonas* spp.

Cefoxitin (Mefoxin). This β-lactamase stable cephamycin has a broad spectrum, including *Legionella* spp. and anaerobes. 1–2 g may be given i.m. or i.v. every 8 hours. I.m. injections tend to be painful.

Latamoxef disodium (Moxalactam). From 250 mg to 3 g 12-hourly may be given i.v. or deep i.m., and the dose may be increased in severely ill adults to 4 g every 8 hours. The spectrum is broad and covers β-lactamase producing organisms, some *Pseudomonas* spp. and anaerobes. Tissue diffusion is good, including the CSF, and the drug can be used in meningitis, except for neonatal Group B streptococcal disease. Latamoxef is available as a powder in vials of 500 mg, 1 g and 2 g.

Cephalexin (Ceporex, Keflex). The first oral cephalosporin is given in doses of 250–500 mg every 6 hours. It is β-lactamase sensitive.

Cefaclor (Distaclor). This oral cephalosporin is variably β-lactamase stable and is given in doses from 250 mg every 8 hours up to a maximum of 2 g daily in divided doses.

Indications
Until the arrival of the β-lactamase stable cephalosporins and those with activity against *Ps. aeruginosa* and anaerobes, there were rarely clinical indications for making these compounds drugs of first choice. Their weaker activity against staphylococci compared with the penicillins and their inability to combat *Streptococcus faecalis* made them less attractive. In acute urinary infections, the newer cephalosporins can be valuable and are less toxic than aminoglycosides, being safer in the uraemic patient. Cefotaxime and the new ceftazidime are both effective against *Ps. aeruginosa*. For lung infections with mixed organisms, including *Haemophilus influenzae*, cefuroxime is effective, but less so than penicillin G in pure pneumococcal pneumonia. The cephalosporins effective against *Ps. aeruginosa* may be indicated in cystic fibrosis, though less active against staphylococci if these are the major pathogens. Septicaemias with unknown bacteria may be an indication for using a cephalosporin-containing antibiotic combination, but amino-glycosides with cephalosporins tend to be more nephrotoxic than aminoglycosides with penicillins. In abdominal or pelvic sepsis, where anaerobes are suspected, cefoxitin may be valuable. Some of the newer drugs such as cefuroxime, cefotaxime. latamoxef disodium and ceftazidime cross the blood–brain barrier well enough to be effective in *Haemophilus influenzae* meningitis or in neonatal meningitis and septicaemia caused by Gram-negative bacilli. In acute gonococcal infections, the newer cephalosporins are effective. In non-invasive urinary infections, cephalexin and cephradine can be given orally or cefaclor, which is also useful in both urinary and respiratory infections, may be used.

Adverse Effects
Hypersensitivity reactions to cephalosporins are similar to those produced by

the penicillins and range from immediate Type I reaction to serum sickness 10 days later. A proportion of penicillin-allergic patients will react to cephalosporins, so some cross-hypersensitivity does occur. Proximal tubular damage results from high doses of cephaloridine and cephalothin, especially if these drugs are given during renal failure or combined with aminoglycosides or frusemide. The later cephalosporins are not nephrotoxic. CNS disturbances may occur if very high serum concentrations of any of the cephalosporins are achieved, as with the penicillins. Other side-effects of cephalosporin therapy include eosinophilia, neutropenia, thrombocytopenia, a positive Coombs' test and transient elevations of liver enzymes. Even latamoxef disodium has already been associated with bleeding diatheses possibly due to hypoprothrombinaemia or thrombocyte dysfunction. Although antibiotic-associated colitis may occur with cephalosporin treatment, diarrhoea is an uncommon side-effect.

Aminoglycosides

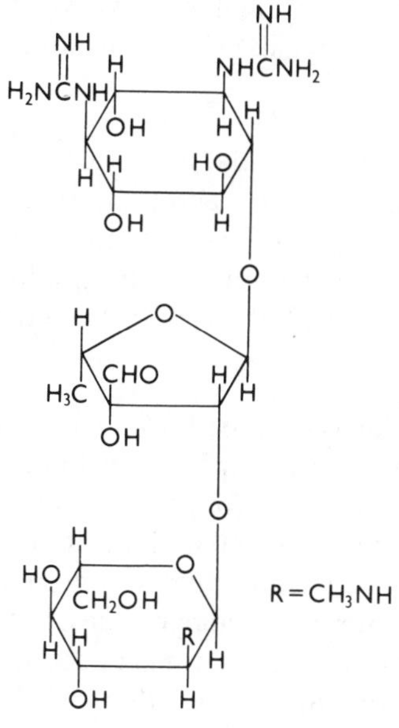

STREPTOMYCIN

The aminoglycosides, originally derived from *Streptomyces* fungi, are all true antibiotics with a similar antibacterial spectrum. Streptomycin, in combination with isoniazid and para-aminosalicylic acid, was for a long time the standard treatment for tuberculosis. Now the main indication for aminoglycosides is for treating Gram-negative bacillary sepsis. Although their spectrum of activity also includes Gram-positive cocci, there are safer and more effective agents available against staphylococci and streptococci. The earlier aminoglycosides were active against *Escherichia coli*, *Proteus* spp., *Klebsiella* spp. and *Haemophilus influenzae*, but not *Pseudomonas aeruginosa*. Some of the more recently developed aminoglycosides, such as gentamicin, tobramycin, amikacin and netilmicin, are relatively resistant to inactivating enzymes such as acetyl, adenyl- and phospho-transferase and so also include *Pseudomonas* spp. in their spectrum. All the aminoglycosides can damage the eighth cranial nerve and the kidneys and some, like neomycin, paromomycin and framycetin, are so toxic that they should never be given by injection.

This worrying toxicity of aminoglycosides, together with the recent introduction of certain cephalosporins, ticarcillin, piperacillin and the ureido-penicillins, all with excellent and relatively safe action against a wide range of enzyme-producing Gram-negative bacilli, suggests that the previous important therapeutic role of the aminoglycosides may not last indefinitely. None the less, newer, perhaps less toxic but more enzyme resistant aminoglycosides, such as netilmicin, may be developed and, in combination with appropriate penicillins or cephalosporins, will continue in the meantime to be a formidable weapon against Gram-negative bacillary septicaemia.

Mode of Action
The aminoglycosides are bactericidal and interfere with ribosomal protein synthesis at the 30S subunit. In addition, their interference with cell permeability and respiration may explain their bactericidal action compared with the bacteriostatic action of erythromycin and chloramphenicol, which act similarly on protein synthesis, but at the 50S subunit of the ribosome.

Pharmacokinetics
Little or no aminoglycoside is absorbed from the healthy gut. Enough may be absorbed, however, from topical applications to the peritoneum, wounds or burns or the external ear to cause ototoxicity. Peak serum levels are achieved within 1 hour of an i.m. injection and antibacterial concentrations persist for 6–8 hours. Monitoring of peak and trough serum concentrations is mandatory in all patients given parenteral aminoglycosides, but especially the elderly or uraemic. The therapeutic and toxic serum concentrations must be familiar to the prescriber if infections are to be effectively treated without toxicity. Except for penetration into CSF and tuberculous abscesses, tissue diffusion is good after injection. Excretion is by glomerular filtration and creatinine clearance estimations help in calculating the dose.

Preparations

Streptomycin sulphate. Adult doses vary from 250 mg 6-hourly by i.m. injection to 1 g twice weekly, as in some antituberculous combinations, with a reduction in dose for patients older than 40 years. Dihydrostreptomycin is more liable than streptomycin to cause deafness and it should not be used.

Kanamycin sulphate (Kannasyn, Kantrex). Assuming normal renal function, the adult dose is 250 mg 6-hourly i.m. or i.v. The peak serum level should be measured and should not exceed 32 mg/l and preferably be 16 mg/l or less.

Gentamicin sulphate (Cidomycin, Garamycin, Genticin). The standard adult dose in patients with good renal function is 2–5 mg/kg body weight per day given in 8- or 12-hourly divided doses. The peak serum level must not exceed 10 mg/l, nor the trough level 2 mg/l. Monitoring of renal function and serum concentrations is important and a nomogram can be helpful in determining the dose. In neonatal meningitis, 1 mg gentamicin may be given intrathecally every 24 hours. A special preparation is available.

Tobramycin sulphate (Nebcin). The daily i.m. or i.v. dose for adults with normal renal function is 3–5 mg/kg body weight, given in divided doses 6–8-hourly. Vials containing 10 mg/ml or 40 mg/ml are available. Monitoring is essential and the peak serum level should not exceed 8 mg/l.

Amikacin sulphate (Amikin). 15 mg/kg body weight per day in two divided 12-hourly doses is the standard adult dose when renal function is normal, increasing to 7.5 mg/kg body weight every 8 hours in life-threatening infections. The peak serum level should not exceed 15–20 mg/l and the trough should remain less than 4 mg/l.

Netilmicin (Netillin). Although claimed to cause less ototoxicity and nephrotoxicity than other aminoglycosides, monitoring should be carried out. The daily adult dose is 4–6 mg/kg body weight in patients with normal renal function, given in 8–12-hourly divided doses i.m. or slowly i.v.

Neomycin (Mycifradin, Nivemycin), *Framycetin* (Soframycin) and *Paromomycin*. These drugs must never be given parenterally. Neomycin or framycetin can be used topically for eye and external ear infections and for skin sepsis, though care should be taken to avoid absorption if a large burned area is being treated. Paromomycin, neomycin and framycetin have been used to alter bowel flora in patients with hepatic failure, to reduce the amount of ammonia produced. They should not be used for gastrointestinal infections nor for sterilizing the bowel before colonic surgery. Paromomycin has a minor degree of activity against *Entamoeba histolytica*, but other drugs are more efficient amoebicides.

Indications
Apart from the topical and oral administration of neomycin, framycetin and paromomycin, all the other aminoglycosides are given parenterally. In combination with isoniazid and *p*-aminosalicylic acid (PAS), streptomycin was one of the standard antituberculous drugs until the arrival of rifampicin, ethambutol and pyrazinamide and it can still be useful. It must always be used in combination to prevent resistance developing.

Gentamicin is so effective against Gram-negative bacilli that it should be reserved for serious sepsis with these organisms and used, perhaps in combination, with a ureido-penicillin or cephalosporin which broadens the spectrum against Gram-positive cocci if the causative organism is unknown. The newer drugs, tobramycin, amikacin and netilmicin, should be kept for septicaemias in which an enzyme producing *Ps. aeruginosa* is thought a likely possibility. Other indications for aminoglycosides include enterococcal septicaemia and brucellosis.

Adverse Effects

Toxicity. Eighth nerve damage is common to all aminoglycosides if over-dosage occurs and this also applies to the safer drug, netilmicin. Kanamycin and amikacin (and dihydrostreptomycin) cause deafness, whereas gentamicin, tobramycin and streptomycin damage the vestibular portion of the nerve. These adverse reactions may be permanent. They are more likely to occur in the elderly, in the presence of renal failure or when aminoglycosides have been used previously. The fetal ear may be damaged by an overdose given to the mother. Nephrotoxicity is more likely to occur if cephaloridine or cephalothin are combined with the aminoglycoside. Agranulocytosis and aplastic anaemia have occurred after streptomycin therapy. The injections may be painful.

Allergy. Drug fever (type III immune complex hypersensitivity) and skin rashes are seen occasionally after streptomycin therapy, but desensitization is possible. Contact dermatitis (type IV reaction) may occur in nurses or pharmacists who are often handling the drug.

Interactions

Aminoglycosides can potentiate neuromuscular blocking agents, leading to respiratory arrest often during anaesthesia. Antidotes include calcium gluconate and neostigmine.

Chloramphenicol

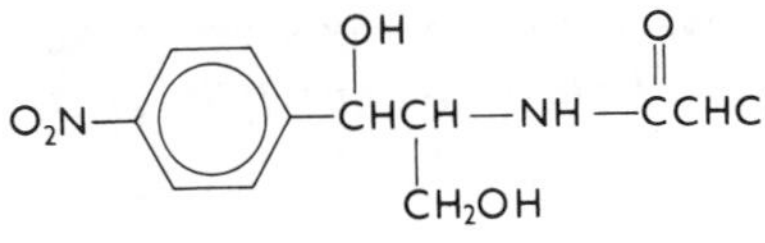

CHLORAMPHENICOL

First found in a compost heap, and grown from *Streptomyces venezuelae*, chloramphenicol is easily produced synthetically. It tastes very bitter and is a stable acid in aqueous solution, even withstanding boiling. It is a broad-spectrum bacteriostatic antibiotic more active against *Haemophilus influenzae*, *Bordetella pertussis*, *Salmonella typhi*, and *Salm. paratyphi* than almost any rival product. Rickettsiae, Gram-positive cocci and many

Gram-negative organisms including some anaerobes are susceptible to the drug, but its efficacy is less marked on them.

Mode of Action

Chloramphenicol has a similar action to erythromycin (p. 24) and lincomycin (p. 26), blocking protein synthesis at the ribosome. Each of these drugs will bind competitively against one another for the 50S subunit of the ribosome and then block amino acid uptake on the growing peptide chains that are to become proteins.

Pharmacokinetics

Good absorption takes place from the gut, peak plasma levels being reached in 2 hours and halving in 6 hours. Absorption from an i.m. injection can be unpredictable and an antimicrobially inactive unhydrolysed ester accounts for one-third of the dose, so serum concentrations are less, dose for dose, than from orally administered chloramphenicol. The sodium succinate preparation may be given i.v. without hydrolysis occurring. Part of the drug circulates bound to proteins, but, despite this, distribution is good and levels in the cerebrospinal fluid are as high as, if not higher than, those achieved by other antibiotics, particularly in meningitis. The liver conjugates chloramphenicol to a glucuronide which is non-toxic and is excreted by the kidney. The urine may contain about 10% of a given oral dose in an unaltered state. Excretion by bile is insignificant.

Preparations

Chloramphenicol palmitate (Chloromycetin) and *Chloramphenicol sodium succinate* (Kemicetine). Capsules of 250 mg are available for adults, but children require a less bitter form of the drug and a suspension of chloramphenicol palmitate is used. The active antibiotic is split by hydrolysis in the gut prior to absorption. A similar process occurs at the injection site when the parenteral preparation, chloramphenicol sodium succinate, is instilled; the powder ready for dissolving is prescribed in vials of 1 or 1.2 g. Usual adult doses are 1 g 6–8 hourly. Great care must be taken in calculating children's doses, particularly for infants, who are easily poisoned by chloramphenicol. Premature infants and neonates must not be given more than 25 mg/kg body weight per day, in divided doses.

Topical preparations are available for use on skin and conjunctivae, and are widely used.

Indications

Use of chloramphenicol is now severely limited in the UK because of rare but serious toxic reactions, particularly blood dyscrasias. The outstanding use for the drug is in *Haemophilus* meningitis and in enteric fever. In both instances, chloramphenicol is superior to ampicillin, but this is not so in relation to many other less dangerous Gram-positive or Gram-negative infections. *Salmonella typhi* cannot always be guaranteed sensitive to chloramphenicol. Widespread resistance was reported in Central America in 1972. Chloramphenicol with an aminoglycoside can be lifesaving in severe pneumonias caused by *Klebsiella pneumoniae*. Combinations containing chloramphenicol are valuable in brain abscess treatment. Resistance or hypersensitivity to ampicillin and its analogues is a less frequent reason for using chloramphenicol, although in many other countries it is more freely employed. Safety in renal insufficiency is a useful attribute as long as there is no accompanying hepatic embarrassment. Topical chloramphenicol rarely produces side-effects, but, being bacteriostatic only, it may not thoroughly eradicate sensitive bacteria.

Adverse Effects

Idiosyncrasy. The main reason for limiting the applications of chloramphenicol is its association with aplastic anaemia. The incidence is small but many cases are fatal and totally unpredictable. There is no evidence to support the view that this is a form of allergy, and, as two sets of twins have suffered the side-effect, it may be that a genetically determined idiosyncrasy to chloramphenicol exists in some members of the population.

Toxicity. A separate dose-related, reversible, toxic effect of chloramphenicol on the blood is well described. The pathogenesis in this case is related to the inhibition of protein synthesis, the mechanism by which the drug is antibacterial. Mammalian cells do not have 50S subunits or 70S ribosomes, but have 80S ribosomes. Mammalian mitochondria, however, do have 70S ribosomes similar to those in bacteria and chloramphenicol exerts an inhibitory effect on them. The clinical effect may be mild anaemia, leukopenia or thrombocytopenia. In this instance, the marrow is not aplastic and blood counts recover after the drug is stopped.

Premature infants develop the 'grey syndrome' if large doses of chloramphenicol are administered. The grey colour of the children is due to cyanosis, and this is accompanied by abdominal distension, hypothermia and circulatory failure. The immature liver cannot conjugate chloramphenicol, and high plasma levels persist for days, aggravated by inadequate renal excretion of the unaltered drug.

In children with cystic fibrosis, optic neuritis has been attributed to chloramphenicol given in several courses for bronchiectasis. Other toxic effects are minor and include soreness of the mouth due to stomatitis, glossitis or candidiasis, and also nausea, vomiting and diarrhoea. Deficiency of riboflavine or nicotinic acid was once thought to account for the oral symptoms and, indeed, the drug is marketed freely in combination with seven vitamins of the B complex.

Allergy. Urticarial rashes are seen, and the Herxheimer reaction is reported during treatment of syphilis, brucellosis, and typhoid. This reaction consists of a rise in temperature, a rapid pulse, general constitutional upset and aggravation of signs of the disease.

Tetracyclines

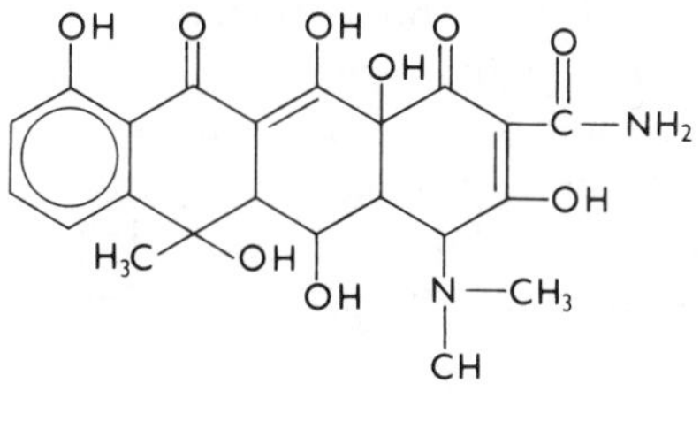

OXYTETRACYCLINE

Another product of *Streptomyces* is the large group of polycyclic naphthacene carboxamides. The varieties marketed in the UK are tetracycline, chlortetracycline, demeclocycline, oxytetracycline, methacycline, doxycycline, minocycline, lymecycline and clomocycline. They have the broadest spectrum of all antibiotics, since they have an action not only against Gram-positive cocci and Gram-negative bacilli, but also against rickettsiae, *Coxiella burneti*, chlamydia including *C. psittaci* and *C. trachomatis*, *Mycoplasma pneumoniae* and *Ureaplasma*. *Leptospira* and *Treponema* spp., *Entamoeba histolytica* and *Mycobacterium tuberculosis* are susceptible to tetracycline, but, as this is a bacteriostatic drug, it is not commonly used in these infections.

Mode of Action
Tetracyclines exert inhibitory effects on protein synthesis at the ribosome, and, to a lesser extent, interfere with oxidative phosphorylation, glucose oxidation and cell membrane permeability. The actual site of tetracycline interference on bacterial ribosomes is not clear, though it results in the blocking of the link of transfer RNA to messenger RNA essential for the transmission of accurate coding of new protein structure.

Pharmacokinetics
Incomplete absorption of oral tetracyclines leads to significant residual gut levels and deleterious effects on local flora. If the oral dose is increased, the proportion of the drug reaching the blood is lowered. Ions such as calcium, iron, and aluminium bind the drug and inhibit absorption. Citric acid, which binds calcium, will neutralize its delaying effect. Highly soluble forms, such as lymecycline and clomocycline, are said to be absorbed well and higher plasma and tissue levels are achieved. Protein binding is variable among the

group, and the more completely bound varieties, such as demeclocycline and doxycycline, are consequently more slowly excreted by the kidney. Doxycycline is also excreted to a large extent by the liver. Less frequent dosage is therefore possible than with the original tetracycline and chlortetracycline. Distribution patterns are similar among the members of the group. They reach serous cavities, brain and fetus with ease, and are, unfortunately, deposited in new bone and teeth, causing yellow staining. CSF penetration is at the highest one-tenth of the simultaneous serum concentration. Excretion occurs in bile and reabsorption into the entero-hepatic circulation is proved. Urine contains about 20% of an oral dose and 50% of a parenteral dose of tetracycline. The discrepancy reflects the inefficient absorption alluded to above.

Preparations

Tetracycline (Achromycin, Achromycin V, Deteclo (with chlortetracycline and demeclocycline), Sustamycin, Tetrabid, Tetrachel, Tetrex), *Chlortetracycline* (Aureomycin) and *Oxytetracycline* (Abbocin, Berkmycen, Chemocycline, Galenomycin, Imperacin, Oxymycin, Terramycin, Unimycin). Each of these is made up in 250 mg tablets or capsules; the dose is 250 mg 6-hourly.

Demeclocycline (Ledermycin). One 300 mg tablet 12-hourly suffices, since this is a more active compound than the drugs referred to above and it is more slowly excreted.

Doxycycline hydrochloride (Vibramycin). This tetracycline is excreted even more slowly than the last-mentioned. Tablets of 100 mg are given once daily. High tissue levels are claimed even at such a dose. A syrup containing 50 mg in 5 ml is recommended for children if it is considered essential to use a tetracycline in this age group.

Clomocycline (Megaclor). This is available in tablets that contain 170 mg. The dose is one tablet 6-hourly.

Minocycline (Minocin). The tablet sizes are 50 and 100 mg of the hydrochloride. A loading dose of 200 mg is usually followed by 100 mg 12-hourly. A single dose of 200–300 mg is consistently effective in gonococcal urethritis in the male. Females require more extended therapy.

Methacycline hydrochloride (Rondomycin). This is prescribed in capsules of 150 mg, one to be taken 6-hourly.

Lymecycline (Tetralysal). Two capsules of 204 mg should be taken 12-hourly.

Tetracycline and procaine injection, BPC. A dose of 40 mg of local anaesthetic is included with 100 mg of tetracycline hydrochloride in an attempt to lessen the pain of i.m. injection. A total daily dose of 200–400 mg is advisable. Care must be taken to avoid accidental i.v. injection.

Oxytetracycline ointment. Several forms of application exist, not only for use on skin, but also for instillation into the ears, eyes and nose. Combinations with nystatin, hydrocortisone acetate and polymyxin B sulphate are variously computed in an attempt to provide blanket treatment for several eventualities. Few of these variations have outstanding advantages.

Indications

The wide spectrum of the tetracycline group has led to over-use of the drugs and consequent development of numerous resistant species. Cross-resistance between the tetracyclines was absolute until the advent of minocycline, which is the most active of the family, in addition to retaining an effect against tetracycline-resistant organisms. The main use is in treatment of acute and chronic upper respiratory infections in general practice. Indeed, many bronchitics receive a tetracycline continuously each winter. This practice is not without hazards and expense. Brucellosis is a good indication for using tetracycline, although, once again, protracted therapy may be required. Less common indications are acne vulgaris, rickettsial infections including Q fever, mycoplasma infections, psittacosis, lymphogranuloma venereum, granuloma inguinale, leptospirosis, typhus, cholera, tularaemia and trachoma. *Shigella sonnei* infections are often resistant to sulphonamides and although sometimes sensitive to tetracyclines, the temptation to use any antibiotic in uncomplicated bacillary dysentery should be resisted. Nevertheless, this policy should not be carried to extremes, particularly in the very young or in frail elderly patients. In anthrax, treponemal infections and actinomycosis, the drug may be used as a second choice to penicillin. Minocycline can be used to protect contacts of meningococcal infection. Topical applications are successful in treating susceptible dermatological infections, but resistant organisms are again the main deterrent to wider use.

Breakdown Products

Stored tetracyclines are often broken down to toxic products such as epianhydrotetracycline. A Fanconi-like syndrome affecting the kidneys is attributed to such substances, though alterations of the types of excipients employed are thought to have solved this difficulty.

Adverse Effects

Toxicity. Gastrointestinal symptoms occur frequently and include stomatitis, glossitis, nausea, vomiting and diarrhoea. Malabsorption, sometimes secondary to superinfection of the small bowel with abnormal flora, is a disadvantage of long-term tetracycline therapy. Candidiasis may spread to involve any part of the gastrointestinal tract. The superinfection may be with a more virulent organism such as *Staphylococcus aureus*, resulting in acute enterocolitis, a life-threatening condition. All of the antibiotics in the group are incorporated into children's teeth, and may cause yellow discoloration. They are deposited in bones and may cause some inhibition of growth.

Oxytetracycline is believed to be less prone to have these effects. Tetracyclines given in pregnancy may damage the child's primary dentition. They should not be used either in pregnancy or in children under 7 years of age. Hepatic necrosis, occasionally fatal, has been reported after i.v. therapy, especially in pregnancy, but the mechanism is not understood. Demethylchlortetracycline may cause photosensitive rashes, but this is rare with other members of the group. Exceptionally, neurotoxicity and blood dyscrasias are said to have followed the taking of tetracyclines. Vertigo limits the usefulness of minocycline.

Allergy. Skin rashes are common and hyposensitization to prevent them frequently unsuccessful.

Interactions

Tetracyclines bind metal ions, as mentioned above. Antacids containing magnesium or aluminium, milk or ferrous sulphate will make satisfactory absorption of tetracyclines unlikely. On i.v. injection, tetracycline will interact with most fluids, and if given with penicillin in the same container, will inactivate it. Great care must be taken in preparing injection fluids; it is recommended that tetracyclines should be given in a 'bolus' i.v., since they may precipitate or break down on standing, even in a bottle of normal saline or dextrose.

Doxycycline has been shown to have a half-life of 15 hours except when given with phenobarbitone or other hepatic enzyme inducers such as diphenylhydantoin or carbamazepine. Dosage must be more frequent, therefore, if it is given with these drugs.

Contraindications

Tetracyclines should be avoided in pregnancy and in young children if possible. Combinations of tetracycline with other antibiotics or antifungal agents are to be discouraged.

With the possible exceptions of doxycycline and minocycline, tetracyclines should be avoided in uraemic subjects since they may aggravate pre-existing renal failure.

Macrolides

Erythromycin

Thirty or so drugs form a group called the macrolides. They include erythromycin, oleandomycin and spiramycin, of which only the first maintains a regular place in therapeutics. Structurally they consist of a large lactone ring to which numerous sugars are attached. They are freely soluble in various solvents but not in water. Erythromycin readily forms esters, or may be used as the basic stearate. Antibacterial activity is most consistent in the Gram-positive organisms, including penicillin-resistant staphylococci.

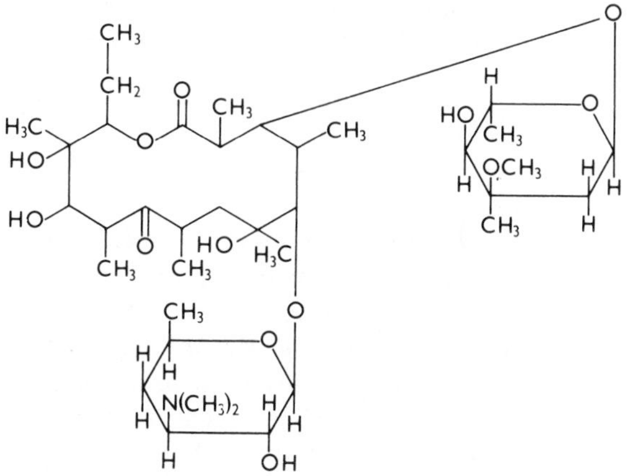

ERYTHROMYCIN

Haemophilus influenzae, *Neisseria* spp., Legionnaires' bacillus, campylobacters and chlamydiae are also sensitive.

Mode of Action
Erythromycin is one of the many bacteriostatic drugs which delay or disrupt protein synthesis in bacterial ribosomes. It probably binds to the 50S subunit of the ribosome and blocks the execution of instructions coded by messenger RNA.

Pharmacokinetics
Esters of erythromycin are well absorbed, but the stearate requires an enteric coat to resist digestion by gastric acid. Peak plasma levels occur 2 hours after ingestion and distribution follows into most tissues except CSF within 6 hours. Only 20% is excreted by the kidneys; the remainder is metabolized or appears in bile, where it is highly concentrated.

Preparations

Erythromycin (Ermysin, Erycen, Erythromid, Ilotycin, Retcin). 250 or 500 mg tablets are available. The usual adult dose is 250–500 mg 6-hourly.

Erythromycin stearate (Erythrocin). 250 mg tablets are available. The usual adult dose is 250–500 mg 6-hourly. A suspension containing 100 mg in 5 ml is available for children.

Erythromycin ethylsuccinate (Arpimycin, Erythroped). Granules are available for suspension in water, giving strengths of from 125 to 500 mg per 5 ml. Adult doses vary from 250 to 500 mg 6-hourly.

Erythromycin lactobionate (Erythrocin). Vials of 300 mg or 1 g are available containing powder for reconstitution and i.v. use. Standard adult doses are 300 mg 6-hourly or 600 mg 8-hourly by slow i.v. injection or infusions.

Erythromycin estolate (Ilosone). Capsules of 250 mg are available for adults, in whom the dose should be 250–500 mg 6-hourly.

Indications

Penicillin-resistant Gram-positive infections or penicillin sensitivity are the main reasons for employing erythromycin. Unfortunately some hospital staphylococci are known to be resistant. Erythromycin is also useful in primary atypical pneumonia caused by *Mycoplasma pneumoniae* and in syphilis or infections with *Haemophilus influenzae*. New indications for erythromycin include Legionnaires' Disease, which requires high parenteral doses, and severe campylobacter enteritis, where a 3-day course of oral erythromycin may sometimes be justified. In unimmunized infants who are contacts of whooping cough, a 10-day course of oral erythromycin may modify or even prevent pertussis. Erythromycin is valuable in the treatment of chlamydial pneumonia in infants and pelvic sepsis in pregnancy. It is also used for clearing diphtheria carriers.

Adverse Effects

Toxicity. Children tolerate the drug well and serious toxicity is uncommon in treatment of minor upper respiratory ailments over short periods. Nausea, diarrhoea, vomiting and abdominal pain may follow large dosage, and occasional superinfection by *Candida albicans* is reported on lengthy exposure.

Allergy. A delayed hypersensitivity type IV reaction is probably the cause of cholestatic jaundice, which is now well established as occasionally being due to erythromycin estolate if given for more than 14 days. Allergic skin rashes also are more common with the ester than with alternative forms.

Lincomycins

Lincomycin is a naturally occurring product of *Streptomyces lincolnensis*. A synthetic variant has been marketed and is called clindamycin. Either drug will be effective against Gram-positive cocci and *Bacteroides* spp. but less so in *Haemophilus* and *Neisseria* infections. Penicillinase-producing staphylococci are usually sensitive, though several studies have reported strains with a natural resistance to lincomycin. Acquired resistance develops predictably on prolonged treatment of staphylococci, haemolytic streptococci and pneumococci.

Mode of Action

Protein synthesis is inhibited in the same way as with erythromycin, at the level of the ribosome; some cross-resistance may occur between the two groups of drug for this reason.

Pharmacokinetics

Lincomycin is not completely absorbed from the gut and low plasma levels occur if food is taken with the drug. On the other hand, food only decreases the rate of absorption of clindamycin, without affecting the eventual amount of drug reaching the plasma. Accordingly, plasma levels are superior to those obtained after the identical oral dose of lincomycin. Distribution of both drugs is comparable and good except in the cerebrospinal fluid. High levels are found in bone, and this has led to widespread use of these antimicrobial substances in osteomyelitis. Excretion occurs in the urine after parenteral administration but not following ingestion.

Preparations

Lincomycin hydrochloride (Lincocin). This is available in 500 mg capsules and a 250 mg in 5 ml syrup. The dose is 500 mg 6–8-hourly. An injection of 600 mg in 2 ml is also available and is usually given 12-hourly.

Clindamycin hydrochloride (Dalacin C). This is available in 75 and 150 mg capsules and a 75 mg in 5 ml syrup. The dose is 150–300 mg 6-hourly for adults. Clindamycin phosphate is marketed for injection (150 mg/ml).

Indications

Although the lincomycins are effective against streptococci and pneumococci outside the meninges, they should be reserved for severe staphylococcal infections or *Bacteroides fragilis* septicaemia. They can conveniently be given parenterally at first and then by long-term oral administration in the treatment of staphylococcal osteomyelitis, assuming no gastrointestinal toxicity occurs.

Adverse Effects

The major drawback to lincomycin or clindamycin therapy, whether given parenterally or orally, is the frequent occurrence of diarrhoea. As with other broad-spectrum antibiotics, toxin-producing *Clostridium difficile* organisms may be encouraged and trigger off either mild diarrhoea or fulminating pseudomembranous colitis. Proctoscopy shows elevated, cream coloured plaques with microscopically diagnostic 'summit lesions' superimposed on inflamed, oedematous friable mucosa. If colitis occurs, the lincomycin must be discontinued at once and oral vancomycin given (125 mg 6-hourly) to destroy the *Cl. difficile*. Rarely jaundice or granulopenia complicate lincomycin or clindamycin therapy.

Fusidic Acid

The salt sodium fusidate is a useful antistaphylococcal steroidal antibiotic. It is

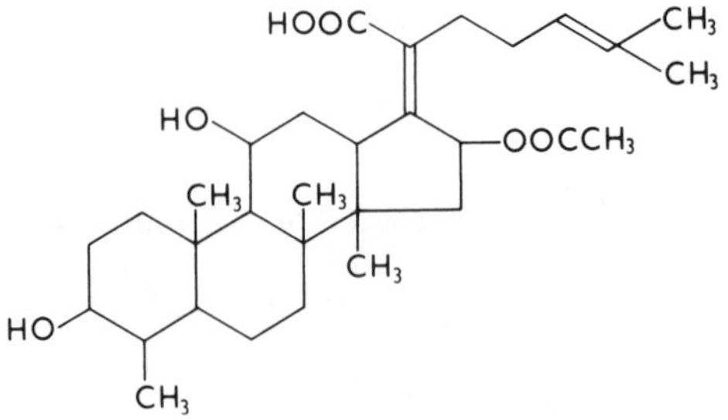

FUSIDIC ACID

used against penicillinase-producing staphylococci, and cross-resistance with other drugs does not occur. The concentration required to inhibit growth of *Staphylococcus aureus* is about 0.03–0.12 mg/l and bacterial killing is shown with very similar levels. Streptococci and pneumococci and most Gram-negative bacilli resist fusidic acid. Sensitive organisms in addition to staphylococci are *Neisseria* and *Clostridia* spp., *Corynebacterium diphtheriae* and some mycobacteria. Mutant strains exist among each of these groups, but seem more significant in vitro than in clinical practice.

Mode of Action
Fusidic acid acts in a similar way to erythromycin. It affects the synthesis of protein by bacterial ribosomes. The exact molecular level of interference is not conclusively proved, but the end result is a block of translocation of messenger RNA, leading to misdirection of amino acid sequences in the growing peptide chain. Whereas erythromycin is bacteriostatic, fusidic acid is bactericidal if sufficient concentrations are reached.

Pharmacokinetics
Absorption of an oral dose of sodium fusidate is efficient and levels in the plasma reach a peak at 2–4 hours. In the plasma, most of the drug is reversibly bound to protein, but, nevertheless, diffusion into tissues is thorough. Brain does not achieve inhibitory levels, but lungs, kidney, bone, and serous cavities do so. Passage across the placenta to the fetus occurs. The antibiotic is broken down to ineffective derivatives in the tissues, particularly in the liver, and slow excretion occurs in bile and faeces. The drug does not appear as such in the urine.

Preparations

Sodium fusidate (Fucidin). Capsules and enteric-coated tablets of 250 mg and a mixture containing 250 mg in 5 ml are the common forms of the drug, 500 mg being prescribed 8-hourly. A 2% ointment or gel is used topically, and tulle dressings impregnated with the ointment are recommended for serious skin infections such as burns.

Diethanolamine fusidate (Fucidin). A dose of 580 mg of diethanolamine fusidate is equivalent to 500 mg of sodium fusidate, and it is dispensed in a dry powder form to be dissolved in a phosphate–citrate buffer and then diluted in 300–500 ml of normal saline. The main parenteral application is slow i.v. infusion.

Indications

The sole indication for fusidic acid is staphylococcal infection. It is particularly valuable in patients hypersensitive to penicillin or whose staphylococci produce β-lactamase. As penetration into tissues is good, osteomyelitis, bronchiectasis, endocarditis and deeply buried abscesses are vulnerable to its effect.

Adverse Effects

Toxicity. Mild gastrointestinal upset occurs after oral administration on occasion. Despite the fact that the drug has a steroid structure, no obvious metabolic effects have been reported. Allergy is not a problem.

Interactions

There is a synergistic effect between fusidic acid and erythromycin and between fusidic acid and novobiocin. With penicillin, however, an ambivalent interaction is seen. In a colony of penicillin-resistant staphylococci, fusidic acid will kill the majority of bacteria. The remainder may often be sensitive to penicillin, which, if given alone, would be inactivated by the concentrations of penicillinase produced by the fusidic acid-sensitive bacteria. Thus the two antibiotics are exerting an additive and co-operative effect, not truly a synergism. In contrast, fusidic acid, given with penicillin in an infection caused by penicillin-sensitive staphylococci, antagonizes the bactericidal activity of the penicillin. A similar detrimental result is obvious when fusidic acid is mixed with cloxacillin or methicillin to treat penicillinase-producing organisms. In summary, penicillin-resistant bacteria should be treated with flucloxacillin alone, or by fusidic acid and penicillin together. Naturally enough, infections due to penicillin-sensitive staphylococci are best treated with penicillin.

Contraindications

Fusidic acid crosses the placenta and is best avoided in pregnancy. As it is inactivated in the liver and excreted in bile, it should not be given during hepatic failure.

Vancomycin

Vancomycin is produced by *Streptomyces orientalis*. It has unique activity against staphylococci, but is a second-choice drug owing to toxicity when parenterally administered. Oral vancomycin, however, is valuable in controlling *Clostridium difficile*-associated diarrhoea. Gram-negative bacteria are resistant.

Mode of Action
The cell wall of the bacterium is constructed from basic phospholipid units linked together with bonds attached to the peptidoglycan moieties. Vancomycin inhibits the synthesis of the peptidoglycan from lipid intermediates. Bacitracin (p. 41) acts a stage earlier on the formation of these lipids. Like cycloserine and penicillin, vancomycin inhibits only bacteria actively engaged in building cell walls for multiplication.

Pharmacokinetics
No absorption of note takes place in the gut. I.m. injection may lead to necrosis locally, so the route of administration for systemic infections is i.v. Blood levels fall off slowly, and distribution is good, except to the cerebrospinal fluid and bile. Serum concentrations peak at 20–50 mg/l and troughs are between 5 and 10 mg/l. Almost all of the drug is excreted by the kidney and impaired renal function may cause accumulation in the blood.

Preparations

Vancomycin (Vancocin). Ampoules of 10 ml are available, each containing 500 mg for i.v. injection. The usual dose is 1 g 12-hourly. The dose by mouth for adults with *Cl. difficile*-associated diarrhoea is 125 mg 6-hourly.

Indications
The main use of vancomycin is the eradication of resistant staphylococci, especially in serious situations such as endocarditis, pneumonia and septicaemia, when no other safer drug can be used. Enterococcal endocarditis and resistant *Streptococcus viridans* or *Streptococcus faecalis* infections have also responded well. Given orally in a dose of 500 mg 6-hourly, vancomycin will sterilize the bowel of Gram-positive cocci and in a quarter of that dose it destroys *Cl. difficile*. It may therefore be used to treat staphylococcal enterocolitis or antibiotic-associated colitis.

Adverse Effects
Tinnitus, nerve deafness, renal failure, drug fever, urticaria and eosinophilia may occur especially in the elderly or already uraemic subject. Serum levels should not exceed 25 mg/l and strict monitoring is advised. Local necrosis at injection sites can occur.

Metronidazole and Tinidazole

These are considered on p. 77.

Cycloserine

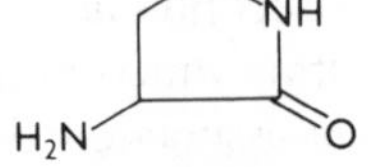

CYCLOSERINE

Streptomyces orchidaceus and *S. garyphalus* are the sources of cycloserine. Its chemical structure is D-4-amino-3-isoxazolidone and it is a small molecule. *Escherichia coli* and other coliforms are usually sensitive and to a lesser extent *Mycobacterium tuberculosis*. Most *Proteus* spp. are resistant.

Mode of Action

Cycloserine attacks the bacterial cell wall but in a different way from penicillin and the cephalosporins. It resembles D-alanine structurally, and competes with alanine racemase and synthetase to block the formation of the basic units of the cell wall. This failure of cell-wall synthesis takes place inside the bacteria at a stage before penicillin has any effect. Cycloserine has a minor effect on inhibition of protein synthesis.

Pharmacokinetics

Absorption of the drug is good when it is taken by mouth. It diffuses freely throughout the body fluids, including the CSF, and is excreted unchanged by the kidneys, where antibacterial concentrations are easily achieved.

Preparations

Cycloserine. This is available in 250 mg tablets, and 125 mg and 250 mg capsules. The usual eradicative dose for *E. coli* and coliform urinary tract infections is 250 mg 12-hourly, and long-term treatment doses are 125–250 mg on alternate days.

Indications

Cycloserine has a useful role in the elimination of stubborn *E. coli* urinary infections. It is a minor second-line drug in the treatment of tuberculosis, for which higher and potentially toxic doses are required.

Adverse Effects

Toxicity. Significant and serious CNS involvement accompanies dosage higher than 1 g daily. Symptoms range from drowsiness and headache to epileptiform fits and psychoses. All of the effects are reversible after withdrawal of the drug and may be aggravated by concurrent alcohol ingestion or by renal failure.

Allergy. Allergic skin rashes are occasionally reported.

ANTITUBERCULOUS DRUGS

DRUG TREATMENT OF TUBERCULOSIS

The corner-stone of antituberculous treatment is combination chemotherapy. One by one, the traditional principles such as bed rest, isolation and good diet have been overshadowed by the overwhelming evidence in support of appropriate, correctly given antimicrobial drugs. This is not to say that the other aspects of therapy can be ignored. The trio of streptomycin, sodium aminosalicylate and isoniazid remained for many years the group of drugs most commonly employed in the first instance, but now a satisfactory combination is that of isoniazid, rifampicin and ethambutol. Some recommend the addition of pyrazinamide to this regimen till sensitivity results are known. With this regimen, many patients may start treatment at home and soon return to normal duties. Alterations may be required if the culture of organisms and their sensitivities suggest endemic strains of resistant organisms. The likelihood of a patient's organisms withstanding the attentions of two or all of the drugs in these combinations is remote, except in some parts of the developing world, where improper chemotherapy has led to the development of primary drug resistance.

More likely is the development of side-effects due to toxicity or allergy to one or more of the drugs. The incriminating agent should be identified by test dose techniques and either replaced or raised in gradual increments from a low non-toxic dose. Less toxicity may be achieved in a twice weekly intermittent schedule employing two or three drugs. Two drugs, if appropriate, suffice for maintenance after 3 months or so of triple or quadruple therapy. The classical Madras scheme was designed to improve the reliability of administration of the two drugs streptomycin and isoniazid, with pyridoxine added to lessen the toxicity of the latter.

It has been usual to stress that continuous therapy will only achieve a cure if continued for 18–24 months, but many patients have been successfully treated with the combination of isoniazid, rifampicin and ethambutol for only 6 months.

The choice of agents depends on the sensitivity of the organisms and on the reaction of the patient to the drugs, and several alternatives remain on trial. Prednisolone may cause deterioration of untreated disease, but in combination with treatment as outlined above it is indicated in the therapy of tuberculous pleural effusion, in renal involvement, or where there is tuberculous meningitis or miliary disease.

*Para-*Aminosalicylic Acid (PAS)

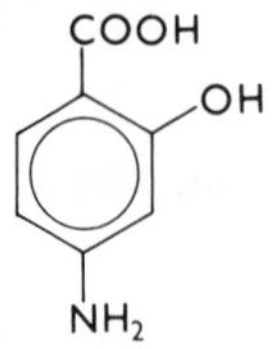

PARA–AMINOSALICYLIC
ACID

PAS is a structural analogue of *para*-aminobenzoic acid (PABA). Its sodium, potassium or calcium salts have a bacteriostatic action against tubercle bacilli, but their main function, when used in combination with other antituberculous drugs, is to prevent the emergence of resistant organisms. Since the development of rifampicin, ethambutol and pyrazinamide, PAS is much less used, particularly in view of the frequent side-effects it can cause.

Mode of Action

Like sulphonamides, PAS acts as a competitive inhibitor to the formation of folic acid from PABA. The resultant defect in purine synthesis paralyses the mycobacteria, but PAS does no harm to human cells, which derive folic acid by a different mechanism.

Pharmacokinetics

Sodium PAS is better absorbed than calcium PAS from the gut. Peak serum levels are achieved 2 hours after oral administration. Diffusion even into tuberculous abscesses is good, but CSF is not penetrated. The acetyl derivative is excreted by glomerular filtration and tubular secretion and high serum levels may be achieved after the blocking of renal excretion with probenecid (pp. 6, 13).

Preparations

Cachets of sodium or calcium PAS of 1.5 g or tablets of 500 mg and a variety of PAS–isoniazid combinations (e.g. Inapasade), are available. Adult doses of 10–20 g daily or approximately 300 mg/kg body weight per day, usually in a single dose, are given. The drug must never be given alone. Even in combination a year's chemotherapy is desirable or, if the combination contains rifampicin, a 9-month course may suffice.

Indications

The only indication is in the treatment of tuberculosis resistant to the first-line drugs and then only in a suitable drug combination.

Adverse Effects

These are sufficiently numerous and frequent to limit the use of PAS to special circumstances. Severe gastrointestinal upset with salt and water depletion, hepatitis, renal damage and psychoses may occur. PAS blocks the incorporation of iodine in tyrosine to form thyroxine and may result in goitre formation, reversible with thyroxine treatment. Long-term PAS treatment can so interfere with gut flora that hypoprothrombinaemia can result from impaired synthesis of vitamin K in the gut. Type III hypersensitivity with drug fever also occurs.

Interactions

Acetylation of PAS is by the same enzymic pathways as that of isoniazid.

When both drugs are given together, PAS is preferentially metabolized, leading to a relative increase in plasma levels of isoniazid. PAS interferes with the absorption of rifampicin and if given together orally, the administration of each should be separated in time.

Contraindications
Care must be taken when PAS is given to a patient who has impaired renal function, as accumulation of the drug leads to excess toxicity.

Isoniazid

ISONIAZID

Isonicotinic acid hydrazide was synthesized 40 years before the discovery of its antituberculous properties in 1952. It is a crystalline compound, is soluble in water, and has a bitter taste. It is very active as a bactericidal agent against tubercle bacilli only. Unfortunately, resistant species evolve even more rapidly on exposure to isoniazid than to PAS or streptomycin.

Mode of Action
Although isoniazid interferes with an enzyme, mycolase synthetase, which is unique for mycobacteria and required for the formation of mycolic acids, it is not known if this is the mechanism responsible for its bactericidal action.

Pharmacokinetics
Isoniazid is well absorbed from the gut and diffuses well into the tissue fluids, including the CSF, where the concentration is similar to that in the serum. It also penetrates phagocytes, killing mycobacteria which they have ingested. Acetylation of isoniazid occurs at one of two rates, genetically determined. The slower inactivation characteristic is inherited as a recessive trait and rapid acetylation is dominant. As alluded to before, acetylation is inhibited competitively by PAS, leading to higher plasma levels of active isoniazid. The acetylated form, the active drug, and isonicotinic acid hydrazones appear in the urine in varying proportions, according to the degree and rate of acetylation. Thus the plasma half-life of isoniazid in a patient who acetylates slowly is about 3 hours compared with 1 hour in a rapid acetylator.

Preparations

Isoniazid. Tablets of 50 and 100 mg are dispensed and a dose of 200–300 mg daily is customary. An elixir, available for children, contains 50 mg in 5 ml.

The paediatric dose is 3 mg/kg body weight daily. I.m. isoniazid (Rimifon) is available in ampoules containing 50 mg in 2 ml for the unconscious or vomiting patient, but intrathecal isoniazid is unnecessary because of the excellent CSF penetration of the drug even after oral administration. Combination with PAS in cachets and granules has been mentioned (p. 33). The most convenient variation contains 1.5 g of sodium aminosalicylate and 33 mg of isoniazid in a rice-paper envelope. A granule form is marketed in an attempt to cut down gastric irritation, which either drug may cause. A standard dose is 6 g of sodium aminosalicylate with 150 mg of isoniazid taken twice daily. Combinations with rifampicin or ethambutol or both are today preferred to PAS-containing regimens.

Indications

The sole use of isoniazid is in the eradication of tuberculosis. It is never employed alone, owing to the ease with which bacilli form resistant mutants. A combination of streptomycin by injection and large doses of isoniazid given twice weekly has been adopted by some physicians to make prolonged treatment more palatable. Isoniazid has successfully been combined with rifampicin (p. 36) to greater effect than the pairing of isoniazid and ethambutol (p. 38). A particular advantage of isoniazid is its penetration into the CSF and hence its value in the treatment of tuberculous meningitis.

Adverse Effects

Toxicity. Of all the antituberculous agents, isoniazid is probably the least troublesome to the patient. CNS complaints are reported, such as insomnia, difficulty in concentration, impairment of memory, inco-ordination, epileptiform seizures and alcohol intolerance. Peripheral effects, such as neuritis, difficulty with micturition, and muscle twitching, are also bothersome, particularly in slow inactivators or where there is impaired renal excretion. Pyridoxine deficiency (p. 453) is the aetiology of many of these complaints, produced by interference with pyridoxine metabolism. This effect of isoniazid is sometimes reversed by oral pyridoxine in a dosage of 50–100 mg daily.

Allergy. Drug-related hypersensitive reactions are infrequent, but, unfortunately, are similar to some of those caused by PAS. Type III hepatitis, fever, lymphadenopathy, eczema and occasionally marrow hypoplasia are seen after treatment commences, and, as PAS and isoniazid are commonly given concomitantly, the causative agent may be difficult to elucidate. Test doses of the drugs must be given separately and with great care so that the offender may be omitted from further combinations.

Interactions

Plasma levels of free isoniazid are elevated if sodium aminosalicylate (PAS) is given concomitantly, as the latter competitively inhibits acetylation of isoniazid.

Contraindications

Isoniazid must only be given as a last resort to mothers who are breast feeding, since it appears in milk in concentrations similar to those in the plasma.

Rifampicin

Rifamycins are a group of antibiotics from which rifampicin is synthetically derived. The latter has a similar spectrum to the parent group but a much more efficient action, since it can destroy bacteria even if the plasma level is very low. Streptococci, staphylococci, clostridia, *Mycobacterium tuberculosis* and *M. leprae* are the main organisms against which rifampicin has proved its potency. Among each of these organisms are found resistant mutants, which, unfortunately, tend to be selected out on lengthy contact with the drug. Given with an antibiotic that will deal with the residual bacteria, rifampicin is an important therapeutic agent.

Mode of Action

Rifampicin is known to kill micro-organisms by restraining the synthesis of RNA at its earliest stages. The main mechanism is by binding the β subunit to the enzyme RNA polymerase at its core. Mutant bacterial RNA polymerase does not bind rifampicin, nor does the equivalent enzyme in human cells. The last property is the key to the excellent selectivity of the drug. Rifampicin inhibits growth of pox viruses, not by an anti-RNA effect but by preventing assembly of virus components into mature virions.

Pharmacokinetics

Oral administration is a particular advantage in the long-term treatment of tuberculosis. Absorption is good, and peak blood levels may be found after 2 hours. Microbiocidal concentrations are still in evidence 12 hours from an oral dose. Excretion is mainly in bile and thereafter some reabsorption and recycling takes place.

Preparations

Rifampicin (Rifadin, Rimactane). Capsules of 150 and 300 mg are dispensed to be taken in a single dose of about 450–600 mg before breakfast. There is a syrup containing 100 mg in 5 ml. As referred to earlier, combination with at least one other antibiotic is essential, to prevent resurgence of mutant bacteria. Rifampicin- and isoniazid-containing preparations include Rifinah and Rimactazid.

Indications

With isoniazid or ethambutol, rifampicin is a good antituberculous agent. It is speedy, acts in small concentrations and has relatively little toxicity. Rifampicin is more active against the leprosy bacillus than dapsone, but, if used for leprosy, treatment may need to be given for several years or a combination used for a shorter time. Rifampicin plus erythromycin is a good second-line antistaphylococcal combination. It is recommended that if PAS and rifampicin are both included in the same treatment regimen, they should be given not less than 8 hours apart, to ensure satisfactory blood levels. In general, however, rifampicin is so valuable in the treatment of mycobacterial diseases that it should not be used for other infections without good reason.

Adverse Effects

Toxicity. As rifampicin is excreted in bile, patients with liver disease may be at risk from toxicity. Although direct hepatotoxicity has been reported, it is uncommon and the drug has been taken in deliberate overdose without upsetting liver function. The sweat and urine become reddish in colour and plasma bilirubin estimations may be recorded erroneously high in patients taking rifampicin.

Allergy. Skin rashes, mild leucopenia, thrombocytopenia, haemolytic anaemia and occasional renal failure are other side-effects known to be particularly prevalent in intermittent schedules – e.g. when using the drug with isoniazid twice weekly. Anti-rifampicin antibodies have been characterized as either IgG or IgM and they adhere to red cells or platelets and bind complement.

Enzyme induction. Rifampicin is a potent inducer of enzymes in the liver and these may increase the metabolism of endogenously produced hormones and of certain administered drugs. Patient response to enzyme induction may vary, but it is recommended that:
1. Those taking one tablet daily of an oral contraceptive should increase this to two daily or seek alternative contraceptive methods.
2. Those requiring treatment with corticosteroids should have a substantial increase in dose.
3. Those receiving oral anticoagulants, digitalis preparations or oral hypoglycaemic agents may require an increased dose.

When the administration of rifampicin ceases, the dosage of these other drugs will probably have to be reduced.

Contraindications
A reduced dose of rifampicin should be employed when a patient with liver disease is treated, to avoid accumulation of the drug.

Ethambutol

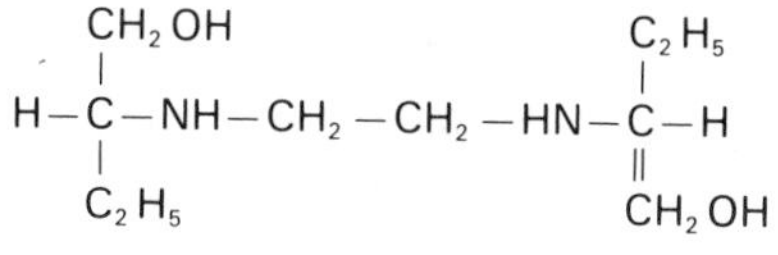

$$H-\underset{\underset{C_2H_5}{|}}{\overset{\overset{CH_2OH}{|}}{C}}-NH-CH_2-CH_2-HN-\underset{\underset{CH_2OH}{\|}}{\overset{\overset{C_2H_5}{|}}{C}}-H$$

ETHAMBUTOL

This synthetic drug, discovered in 1961, passively enters mycobacteria without accumulation and probably exerts its antibacterial effect as an antimetabolite interfering with RNA synthesis. It is now regarded along with rifampicin and isoniazid as a first-line antituberculous drug, but it has no activity against non-mycobacterial species.

Pharmacokinetics

Ethambutol is well absorbed from the gut and peak serum levels are reached in 4 hours. It does not accumulate in the body if there is normal renal function. Eight per cent is excreted in the urine, the remainder via the faeces or as inactive metabolites in the urine. The drug probably penetrates most tissue fluids, except the CSF. It is concentrated in erythrocytes, which may help to act as a slow-release reservoir of the drug, permitting a once daily dosage.

Preparations

Ethambutol hydrochloride (Myambutol). Tablets of 100 and 400 mg and combined preparations (Mynah) of ethambutol with isoniazid, in varying doses, are available. Ethambutol doses should not exceed 15 mg/kg body weight per day in adults or 25 mg/kg body weight per day in children for the first 60 days' treatment, followed thereafter by 15 mg/kg body weight per day. In general, antituberculous drugs other than ethambutol are preferred for young children. The quantities and proportions of ethambutol and isoniazid make Mynah an unsuitable preparation for children. Ethambutol must always be combined with at least one other reliable antituberculous drug, such as isoniazid or rifampicin.

Adverse Effects

Toxicity. Retrobulbar neuritis with central scotomata, colour blindness, and constriction of visual fields is the most serious toxic effect of ethambutol and is related more to the acute dosage and serum levels than to the total amount of drug administered in a course. Patients must be asked to report any visual symptoms and stop the drug immediately if they occur. Most ocular toxicity is reversible if the drug is stopped at once. Peripheral neuritis and interstitial nephritis may also occur. So far, it has not been shown to be a drug that is unsafe to use in pregnancy.

Ethionamide

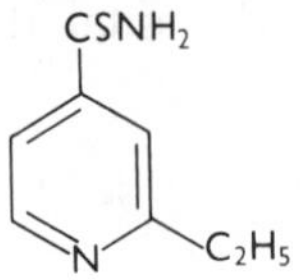

CSNH$_2$

C$_2$H$_5$

N

ETHIONAMIDE

Ethionamide is derived from nicotinic acid and is a synthetic 'second-line' antituberculous drug, since, despite its good activity against mycobacteria, it is poorly tolerated because of gastrointestinal side-effects. After an oral dose of 1 g of non-enteric coated ethionamide, a serum level of 20 mg/l is reached in 3 hours and all of the drug is not eliminated till 24 hours after administration. It is probably metabolized by unknown enzyme systems and little appears in the urine. It penetrates tissue fluids, including the CSF, very well. Despite this, other antituberculous drugs are preferred.

Preparations

Ethionamide (Trescatyl). Tablets of 125 mg were formerly readily available and an adult dose was 750 mg to 1 g once daily, assuming satisfactory hepatic function. It should always be given in combination with other active antituberculous drugs. A similar drug, *prothionamide* (Trevintix), was given in a single daily adult dose of 500 mg to 1 g, but was not significantly less toxic than ethionamide and so had no major advantage.

Adverse Effects

Both ethionamide and prothionamide can cause nausea, vomiting, depression, deafness, visual disturbances and acne.

Pyrazinamide

Pyrazinamide is derived from nicotinic acid, as are isoniazid and ethambutol. It was a 'second-line' antituberculous drug, though of particular value both for intensive short-course therapy in the developing world, where resistance to 'first-line' drugs is common, and for treating tuberculous meningitis. Some now advocate an initial regimen containing rifampicin, isoniazid, ethambutol *and* pyrazinamide until the sensitivity of the tubercle bacilli is known. In vitro, its antimycobacterial activity is not good, but in vivo, perhaps where pH is lower, it has bactericidal properties. It is well absorbed from the gut and peak serum levels are reached in 2 hours. Its presence in the serum continues for nearly 24 hours, whilst it is slowly excreted in the urine and bile mainly as pyrazinoic acid. Hepatic metabolism probably also occurs, the drug accumulating in patients with liver dysfunction. It diffuses in body tissues and enters the CSF in therapeutic concentration when the meninges are inflamed.

Preparations

Pyrazinamide (Zinamide). Tablets of 500 mg are available and a single daily adult dose of 20–30 mg/kg body weight (maximum 3 g daily) is given. It should not be given in presence of liver dysfunction. Other suitable antituberculous drugs must be given similtaneously to prevent resistance developing.

Adverse Effects
Pyrazinamide-induced liver damage is related to the dose and duration of treatment. It has been suggested that this toxicity has been exaggerated because the drug is often given with other potentially hepatotoxic agents such as rifampicin and isoniazid or to elderly patients who may already have impaired liver function. Other side-effects include gastrointestinal disturbances, allergic drug rashes and even gout, possibly induced by the suppression of uric acid excretion by the metabolite, pyrazinoic acid.

Capreomycin

This aminoglycoside is effective against some streptomycin-resistant mycobacteria and so can be used as a 'second-line' antituberculous drug in combination with other suitable agents. A single daily adult dose of 1 g, or not more than 20 mg/kg body weight per day, is given i.m. (Capastat), this being equivalent to 1 000 000 units of capreomycin sulphate, and it results in peak levels in the serum of 20–35 mg/l. Approximately 50 % is excreted by the kidneys unchanged. It should not be used in patients with severe renal or hepatic impairment, nor simultaneously with other potentially ototoxic or nephrotoxic drugs. Adverse reactions include damage to the liver, kidneys and eighth cranial nerve, as well as skin rashes and pain at the injection site. Safety in pregnancy and infancy has not been established.

ANTILEPROTIC DRUGS

Dapsone

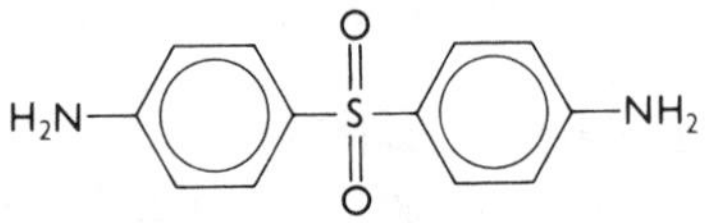

DAPSONE

The sulphones, including dapsone or diaminodiphenylsulphone, are chemically related to the sulphonamides. Dapsone was first tested as a tuberculostatic drug and later was noted to be effective in leprosy. As with the drugs mentioned earlier, its advantage is limited by development of bacterial resistance.

Mode of Action
Dapsone acts in a similar way to the sulphonamides by virtue of their common chemical structure. Thus dapsone competitively inhibits utilization of PABA in the synthesis of folate.

Pharmacokinetics
Dapsone is rapidly absorbed after ingestion. Adult plasma concentrations 24

hours after 100 mg is taken by mouth range from 0.41 to 1.2 mg/l, due to the genetically determined variable rate of acetylation in different individuals. Irrespective of this variation, levels well above the minimum inhibitory concentration of the organism are achieved. The drug is slowly excreted in the urine and very high plasma levels are reached in renal failure if the dose is not reduced. The drug is well distributed in body tissues, including the nerves and skin, but it does not penetrate the CSF well.

Preparations

Dapsone. Tablets of 50 and 100 mg are available.

Indications and Control of Dosage

It is recommended that in the UK advice on treatment of leprosy should always be obtained from the Panel of Leprosy Opinion. It appears that dapsone resistance only occurs in lepromatous leprosy, though persistence of sensitive *Mycobacterium leprae* organisms can occur even after 10 years of adequate treatment, presumably because some bacilli lie dormant and metabolically inactive. Although it was previously taught that lepromatous leprosy should be treated for life, a triple agent approach for as short a period as 2 years may suffice with dapsone 100 mg daily combined with clofazimine (Lamprene) 100 mg daily or three times weekly and rifampicin 600 mg monthly. The dosage does not require to be built up slowly and has the advantage that infectivity stops within two weeks. Lepra type 2 reactions should not interfere with treatment and do not appear to depend on the dose of dapsone used. Clofazimine dosage can be increased, anti-inflammatory agents used and in all but the female of childbearing age, thalidomide used in divided doses of 400 mg daily with great effect in lepra reactions.

For tuberculoid leprosy, dapsone 100 mg daily and rifampicin 600 mg monthly is recommended for 6 months, this dose being used throughout the treatment period.

The antimalarial drug, Maloprim, contains 100 mg of dapsone and 12.5 mg of pyrimethamine (p. 76).

Adverse Effects

Toxicity. Overdose of dapsone is easily achieved due to the accumulation of the drug, particularly if renal excretion is diminished. Haematological toxicity is common, taking the form of mild anaemia and methaemoglobinaemia. Patients with glucose-6-phosphate dehydrogenase deficiency may develop haemolytic anaemia. Anorexia, nausea and vomiting are transient early accompaniments.

Bacitracin

Certain strains of a species of Gram-positive spore-bearing bacilli (*Bacillus licheniformis* and *B. subtilis* var. *Tracy*), when grown in liquid culture, synthesize this antibiotic. The name 'bacitracin' was concocted by fusing the word 'bacillus' with 'Tracy', the surname of a young girl whose osteomyelitis provided the first culture. There are three closely related polypeptide variants: A, B and C. The group is useful with the same range of bacteria as penicillin, so the drugs are effective against Gram-positive cocci and bacilli. Moreover, they have an action on penicillinase-producing staphylococci. Resistance to this drug has evolved very slowly and is practically of no significance. It is not commonly used, however, because of its effects on the kidney.

Mode of Action
Bacitracin destroys cell walls by inhibiting synthesis of the lipid precursors of peptidoglycan. It also binds to the inner cell membranes of bacteria and will kill protoplasts. The latter property is shared by all the peptide antibiotics, whereas the effect on cell wall synthesis is akin to the mode of action of penicillin.

Pharmacokinetics
Absorption from the gut is negligible, and parenteral use has proved unacceptable owing to toxicity. Topical application is the only practical use and absorption has occurred from the skin.

Preparations
Bacitracin is available in an ointment, solution or aerosol, either alone or in combination with another drug such as neomycin or polymyxin. A preparation suitable for application to the eye is also marketed.

Indications
Pyogenic Gram-positive infections of the eye, ear, mouth or skin, especially burns, may be treated successfully. Postoperative wound infections which may be due to combined infection with a Gram-negative organism and a Gram-positive one are better treated with the combined preparation neomycin and bacitracin. Bacitracin may be instilled intrathecally, but this is seldom necessary, and it is difficult to foresee a reason for giving it i.m.

Adverse Effects

Toxicity. Acute tubular necrosis has made parenteral bacitracin unacceptable except in extreme circumstances. Even small doses cause albuminuria, with granular casts and cellular elements in the urine.

Allergy. It is seldom that sensitization follows on local application to the skin, but dermatitis may be precipitated. Anaphylaxis, however, has been reported, presumably due to absorption of small amounts of drug through damaged epidermal tissue.

Polymyxins

Several polymyxins, labelled A to E, have a basic structure similar to that of bacitracin. They are basic polypeptides with antibacterial activity. Polymyxin B and colistin (which is polymyxin E) are the only variations that are not too toxic to the kidneys to be suitable for clinical use. The drugs have a narrow spectrum limited to action against Gram-negative species (excluding *Proteus* and *Neisseria*). At least half of their activity in vitro is inhibited by inclusion of high concentrations of serum in the growth medium. Polymyxins are bactericidal near the minimum inhibitory concentration for many bacteria and resistance to them has not become a clinical problem as yet.

Mode of Action

The main site of bacterial interference is association of the polymyxin with the bacterial cell membrane. This has been shown by fluorescence studies, which, however, have not elucidated the character of the molecular attractions between the drug and the membrane. In particular, the extraordinary preference of interaction with Gram-negative cells to the complete exclusion of Gram-positive membranes may hold the key to the design of further narrow-spectrum antimicrobial agents. After this specific binding has taken place, leakage of small molecules from the bacteria is evident, suggesting an increase of membrane permeability. This view is supported by fluorescent dye experiments, which show subsequent leakage in the opposite direction too, with resultant death of the bacteria.

Pharmacokinetics

Little or no absorption of polymyxins takes place from the gut and, indeed, they may be digested. Peak levels are low, owing to inactivation by serum, but are achieved in 2 hours from an i.m. injection. Distribution is widespread, except to brain, although intrathecal installation is feasible, if not without hazard. Excretion is slow through the kidneys and there is no significant loss in the bile.

Preparations

Polymyxin B sulphate (Aerosporin). An ampoule for injection i.m. contains 500 000 units, which can be given as often as 8-hourly. There are several topical preparations of polymyxin, including one with bacitracin in an eye ointment, and bacitracin and neomycin are combined in an aerosol (Polybactrin).

Colistin sulphate, BP (Colomycin). This is a preparation for oral administration consisting of tablets of 1500 000 units each or it can be obtained in the form of a syrup containing 250 000 units in 5 ml.

Colistin sulphomethate sodium (Colomycin). The colistin for parenteral use is made up in strengths of 500 000 or 1 000 000 units per vial, to be given i.m.

or i.v. in a dose of 50 000–100 000 units/kg body weight. The intrathecal dose is one-hundredth of the i.m. dose. Care must be taken over the accuracy of the proprietary names of the colistins. Colomycin is the version sold in the UK, and that preparation differs in toxicity from the American counterpart, Coly-Mycin, which is said to be more active and more toxic. To add further to the possible confusion, there is an aminoglycoside known as Colimycin available from the USSR. It has no chemical relationship to colomycin and its activity is similar to that of neomycin.

Indications

The polymyxins are second-choice therapeutic agents in *Pseudomonas* infections, except where the skin is affected, when they are the drugs of choice. Coliform urinary pathogens are killed adequately, but the drug has to be given by injection and there are numerous equally efficient drugs available for oral administration. Polymyxins given by mouth are of doubtful efficacy because of the likelihood of destruction of the drug and survival of the bacteria. However, some bacteria may be affected in the bowel flora, and colistin may be used in preference to neomycin to alter the gut flora during the management of acute hepatic failure.

Adverse Effects

Toxicity. I.m. injection of the unaltered polymyxins is painful and a local anaesthetic has been added to some of the preparations that are commercially available. After injection, paraesthesiae are invariably noted in the extremities and around the mouth. The polymyxins are toxic to renal tubules at high levels. Colistin does less damage than polymyxin B on a weight for weight basis, but, as the former must be used in much higher doses to achieve the same MIC, the two are equally nephrotoxic in practice.

Interactions

Polymyxins must not be mixed with cephalosporins, chloramphenicol, heparin or tetracyclines when given i.v.

Contraindications

Renal failure is likely to cause accumulation of the drug due to failure of excretion. However, it is possible to use the polymyxins provided that the dose is fashioned according to the creatinine clearance.

Sulphonamides

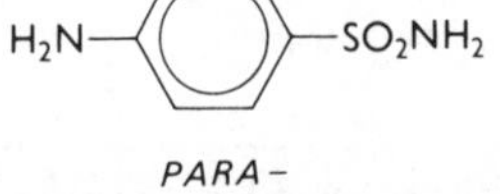

$$H_2N - \bigcirc - SO_2NH_2$$

PARA-
AMINOBENZENESULPHONAMIDE

Para-aminobenzenesulphonamide is the parent of several thousand very similar offspring. They are all structural analogues of *para*-aminobenzoic acid (PABA), having variance at the sulphonamide (SO_2NH_2) group. Without exception, they are bacteriostatic, and widespread resistance has caused them to be largely superseded by modern antibiotics. The spectrum of activity includes action against Gram-positive cocci, Gram-negative bacilli, *Pasteurella pestis*, psittacosis, lymphogranuloma inguinale organisms and trachoma. Marked improvement in therapeutic efficacy and range of activity has been achieved by the combination of trimethoprim (p. 51) with sulphamethoxazole (co-trimoxazole), or with sulphamoxole (co-trifamole, Co-Fram). Co-trimoxazole (Bactrim, Chemotrim, Comox, Nodilon, Septrin) has been shown to be useful against meningococci, pneumococci, *Haemophilus influenzae*, brucellae, *Escherichia coli*, *Klebsiella* spp. and many Enterobacteriaciae.

Mode of Action

The sulphonamides are antimetabolites. They inhibit synthesis of DNA and therefore prevent certain bacteria from replicating; they have no effect on resting bacteria. DNA synthesis requires thymidine, which is formed with the help of folinic acid. Folinic acid is a reduced form of folic acid (p. 465), which, in turn, has as a constituent *para*-aminobenzoic acid. As mentioned above, sulphonamides are analogues of PABA and competitively inhibit its incorporation into folic acid. No folinic acid, thymidine or DNA should then result should there be no alternative pathways.

Man's cells depend on a chain of events very similar to that which occurs in the bacteria. Where they differ is in the source of folic acid. The bacteria make it from PABA because they cannot transport it across their cell membranes from their environment. Certain human cells are more sophisticated and have developed a membrane pump to transfer folic acid into their cytoplasm, where it is reduced to folinic acid and allows DNA synthesis to take place. The subtle difference between cells and bacteria means that sulphonamides are active against many bacteria in the body, without harming the host's cellular mechanisms.

The mode of action of trimethoprim–sulphonamide combinations is a double attack on the synthesis of folinic acid and, although each constituent is bacteriostatic, the combination may be bactericidal in some instances. The sulphonamide constituent acts on the first step in the chain of reactions – to inhibit incorporation of PABA into folate. Trimethoprim inhibits the next step – namely, enzymic reduction of folate to folinic acid by dihydrofolate reductase (p. 465). There is evidence that the two drugs combined in the above way are synergistic, in that the resultant fall in bacterial DNA synthesis is greater than what might be predicted by adding the advantages of each used separately.

Human cells contain dihydrofolate reductase and theoretically trimethoprim and, hence, co-trimoxazole might damage them by causing depletion of folinic acid. In practice, this rarely occurs, since there is a differential sensitivity of the enzyme to the drugs, so that bacterial dihydrofolate reductase is approximately 50 000 times more inhibited than mammalian reductase. There is a practical problem only when the patient is already folate-deficient from another cause (p. 466).

Pharmacokinetics
Most sulphonamides are well absorbed from the upper gastrointestinal tract and peak blood levels are achieved about 4 hours after oral administration. Succinylsulphathiazole and phthalylsulphathiazole are not absorbed and were used against bacteria affecting the bowel. After absorption, a variable concentration of sulphonamide becomes bound to plasma albumin. The bond is loose and reversible, so drug attached to protein may still become available in its free form for diffusion into tissues and for glomerular filtration. Most organs are reached by bacteriostatic levels of drug, and this includes the brain and placenta. Indeed, sulphonamides cross the latter and reach the fetus.

Several of the group displace bilirubin from albumin, thus raising the plasma bilirubin level. In this regard, they are dangerous to the fetus and may cause kernicterus secondary to a high bilirubin concentration. Sulphadimidine is highly protein bound, as are the long-acting drugs such as sulphadimethoxine, sulphamethoxypyridazine, sulphaphenazole and sulphamethoxydiazine. The sustained effect of these preparations may not be due entirely to high protein binding and subsequent slow excretion, since some of them are very efficiently excreted. A more likely explanation for prolonged plasma levels is a high degree of tubular reabsorption from the glomerular filtrate. Just as sulphonamides are variably protein bound, so are they conjugated, usually by acetylation, to differing extents at the *para*-amino grouping. Sulphasomidine is hardly acetylated at all, whereas sulphadimidine is halved in efficacy by this means. Conjugated drug is not active against bacteria and is excreted in urine under different conditions from the intact drug.

Yet another variable that affects the plasma levels of sulphonamides, independent of any property of the drugs themselves, is genetic variation in patients. There is a bimodal distribution in any population as regards the rate of acetylation of drugs such as sulphonamides and isoniazid. One group of individuals conjugates rapidly and the other does so slowly.

All absorbable sulphonamides are excreted in the urine by glomerular filtration and variably by tubular secretion. Mention has been made already of the differing efficiency of tubular reabsorption among the group. In the presence of kidney malfunction, excretion may be impaired and toxic plasma levels may ensue. Many of the early sulphonamides are insoluble in urine, and as they reach high concentrations there, crystals may develop, leading to obstructive uropathy (p. 573).

An alkaline urine may be achieved when administering these drugs by giving bicarbonate or potassium citrate at the same time and ensuring a high fluid intake. Alternatively, low dosages of three sulphonamides, for instance, used to be advocated on the grounds that their antibacterial effect was additive but their solubility was not. A suitable combination was thought to be sulphathiazole, sulphadiazine and sulphamerazine. Recently developed drugs, such as sulphamethizole, are highly soluble, even in acid urine, and avert the danger of renal damage. When choosing a trimethoprim–sulphonamide preparation to treat a urinary infection, it should be realized that there are differences in the solubility and degree of metabolization of the sulphonamides which may influence therapeutic efficacy and toxicity.

Preparations

Calcium sulphaloxate (Enteromide). This poorly absorbable sulphonamide is given in adult doses of 1.5 g 12-hourly. The tablets contain 500 mg.

Sulfametopyrazine (Kelfizine W). This highly protein-bound long-acting absorbable sulphonamide is used for urinary infections in oral adult doses of 2 g weekly. For children, a suspension of 500 mg in 5 ml is available to be taken once weekly in a dose of 30 mg/kg body weight.

Sulphacetamide (Albucid, Bleph-10, Isopto Cetamide, Minims Sulphacetamide, Ocusol). A variety of eye drops and ointments containing different strengths of sulphacetamide is available for topical use in ocular infections, although many regard antibiotic containing preparations as safer and more effective.

Sulphadiazine (Streptotriad – with streptomycin, sulphadimidine and sulphathiazole. Sodium sulphadiazine is available for i.m. or i.v. injection in 4 ml ampoules containing 250 mg/ml and is given in doses of 1–1.5 g every 4 hours. Sulphonamides must *never* be injected intrathecally. Oral sulphonamide or sulphonamide–streptomycin combinations do not offer major advantages and the risk of toxicity can be greater even though the theoretical risks of crystalluria are reduced by the lower dose of each constituent sulphonamide in the preparations.

Sulphadimethoxine (Madribon). 500 mg tablets of this absorbable sulphonamide are available and are given for urinary and respiratory infections in adult doses of 1–2 g initially, then 500 mg to 1 g daily.

Sulphadimidine (Sulphamezathine). The sodium salt is available in 3 ml ampoules containing 333 mg/ml for i.m. or i.v. injection in adult doses of 2 g initially, followed by 500 mg to 1 g every 6–8 hours for urinary infections. If used in meningococcal meningitis, the dose is 3 g, then 1–1.5 g every six hours; but the organisms may be insensitive. It must *never* be given intrathecally.

Sulphafurazole (Gantrisin). This absorbable sulphonamide for urinary infections is available in 500 mg tablets or a syrup containing 500 mg in 5 ml. The adult dose is 2 g initially, followed by 4–6 g daily in divided doses.

Sulphamethizole (Urolucosil). Tablets of 100 mg or a suspension of 100 mg/5 ml are available of this absorbable sulphonamide for urinary infections. 200 mg 5 times daily is recommended for adults and smaller doses for children.

Sulphamethoxypyridazine (Lederkyn). Tablets of 500 mg of this absorbable sulphonamide are given in a loading dose of 1–2 g to adults, followed by 500 mg daily. (A single daily dose is employed because of the long half-life of the drug.)

Sulphapyridine (M&B 693). Used only in dermatitis herpetiformis unresponsive to dapsone, this drug is given in doses of 3–4 g daily with 500 mg to 1 g daily for maintenance. The tablets contain 500 mg.

Sulphasalazine (Salazopyrin). This sulphonamide-like drug is helpful in the maintenance of remission of non-infectious inflammatory bowel disease such as Crohn's disease and ulcerative colitis (p. 348).

Sulphathiazole (Thiazamide). 500 mg tablets are available of this absorbable sulphonamide and after a loading dose of 2 g adults receive 1 g every 4–6 hours.

Sulphaurea (Uromide). This sulphonamide is absorbable and has been specifically synthesized for the treatment of urinary infections. The adult dose is 2 tablets three times daily, each containing sulphacarbamide 500 mg and an anaesthetic agent, phenazopyridine hydrochloride 50 mg.

Indications
The development of more effective and safer antibacterial agents, especially antibiotics, has reduced the indications for using sulphonamides. Besides, over the years, many organisms have become resistant. Apart from their value in urinary tract infections, especially in general practice, where the flora are more likely to be sensitive, there is now little place for the absorbable sulphonamides on their own. In the next section, their use with trimethoprim is discussed, but the latter drug is now frequently given without sulphonamides for the treatment of urinary infections, often with as good an effect as the combination and with less risk of toxicity. In the management of chronic chest infections, especially bronchitis, and in the treatment of some specific infections like typhoid, co-trimoxazole and related combinations may have a real advantage. Although soluble sulphonamides penetrate the CSF very well, too many meningococci and pneumococci are sulphonamide resistant for sulphonamides to be used today. Penicillin is safer and more effective. For sterilizing the large intestine before colonic surgery, the insoluble, non-absorbable sulphonamides have largely been replaced by metronidazole and antibiotics. Their use in the management of travellers'

diarrhoea, possibly due to enteropathogenic or enterotoxigenic *Escherichia coli*, and in bacillary dysentery is highly controversial, even if the pathogens are shown to be sensitive in vitro. Sulphonamide-containing topical applications for the eyes may induce sensitivity reactions and chloramphenicol- or aminoglycoside-containing drops and ointments are often preferred. Sulphapyridine in dermatitis herpetiformis and sulphasalazine in inflammatory colonic disease have a definite role to play.

Administration

It is customary to give a loading dose of sulphonamides by mouth to establish a high plasma and tissue level prior to continuation with therapy as suggested above. I.v. sulphonamides must be given very slowly, preferably diluted in a solution of normal saline. Most i.m. preparations are also irritants. Intrathecal administration *must never be carried out*, since there is intense irritation, with the possibility of nerve injury and collapse.

Adverse Effects

Toxicity. Crystalluria is discussed above; it arises as a consequence of the insolubility of many sulphonamides in acid urine and their concentration by the kidney. Acute tubular necrosis, independent of crystal formation, is also described, particularly when a poor fluid intake has accompanied the ingestion of a sulphonamide. Blood dyscrasias of almost every variety have been noted, ranging from marrow depression, agranulocytosis, aplastic anaemia or thrombocytopenic purpura to haemolytic anaemia, with Heinz body inclusions in the red cells. Sulphasalazine administration is well known in association with the last, and sulphamethoxypyridazine with the others. An acute form of haemolysis follows ingestion of sulphonamide by a susceptible individual who suffers from glucose-6-phosphate dehydrogenase deficiency. A severe and sometimes fatal illness may ensue due to rapidly developing anaemia and it is therefore wise to check for the enzyme defect prior to any sulphonamide therapy, especially in negroid subjects. Methaemoglobinaemia and sulphaemoglobinaemia are reversible if exposure to sulphonamides is halted.

Hepatitis, acute and chronic, occurs rarely after sulphonamides. Mention was made above of the danger of kernicterus to the fetus and premature infant secondary to a displacement of bilirubin from protein into plasma by any member of the group. Other non-specific yet common toxic effects are headache, depression, sometimes frank psychosis, nausea, vomiting and diarrhoea.

Allergy. Skin reactions of several kinds have been caused by sulphonamides. Morbilliform rashes, eczema, urticaria or bullous or exfoliative dermatitis may occur after a week or so of treatment. Topical application almost invariably induces Type IV contact sensitivity and cross-resistance is absolute between individual drugs, with the exception of mafenide. This is available as a cream to prevent infection of burns under the proprietary name Sulfamylon and for superficial eye infections as Sulfomyl.

Polyarteritis nodosa, drug fever, erythema multiforme, or the Stevens–Johnson syndrome (p. 569) may occur, and a systemic progression of the last is seen, particularly after the long-acting drugs. Type III hypersensitivity is thought to be the main mechanism of action, damage being done after antibody–antigen complexes have formed in the circulation.

Contraindications

Pregnancy, premature infancy and glucose-6-phosphate dehydrogenase deficiency are absolute contraindications. Acute intermittent porphyria is another inherited disease in which attacks may be precipitated by sulphonamides. There is abdominal pain, vomiting, peripheral neuropathy and possibly mental abnormalities. Renal impairment and dehydration are conditions in which sulphonamides should only be used as a last resort, and even then with adequate supervision. A history of reactions in the past is a reason for not giving sulphonamides.

Trimethoprim and Trimethoprim–sulphonamide Combinations

TRIMETHOPRIM

The 2,4-diamino-pyrimidines include trimethoprim, a drug which was originally tried alone in the treatment of malaria and then marketed for a number of years as an antibacterial agent in combination with sulphamethoxazole, as co-trimoxazole. Subsequently, trimethoprim has become available both on its own and in combinations containing sulphonamides other than sulphamethoxazole. Trimethoprim is bacteriostatic against a number of Gram-positive and Gram-negative bacteria and is also active against some protozoa.

Mode of Action

Trimethoprim inhibits the enzyme dihydrofolate reductase (pp. 465–7) in all cells, but it displays a preferential selectivity for bacteria or certain parasites such as plasmodia. The factor involved is commonly many thousandfold, so that human tissues are not injured despite the effect on micro-organisms. Absence of dihydrofolate activity in the latter leads to failure of folinic acid synthesis from folate and consequent loss of purine manufacture. Sulphonamides act on the same metabolic pathway at an earlier stage (p. 45).

Pharmacokinetics

Absorption of trimethoprim is rapid and the peak plasma level is achieved in 3–4 hours. The plasma half-life ranges from 6 to 12 hours, according to the degree of protein binding and the rate of urinary excretion. About half of the drug is protein-bound and some of the free drug becomes conjugated prior to excretion. Almost all of it will be retrieved in the urine up to 5 days after administration. The kidney excretes trimethoprim by glomerular filtration at an increasing rate as the urine pH falls. It is thought that at least some of the drug is secreted by the tubules.

Preparations

Trimethoprim alone (Ipral, Monotrim, Syraprim, Trimopan) is available in tablets of 100 or 200 mg and in suspensions containing 50 mg in 5 ml. Standard adult doses are 200 mg every 12 hours or 300 mg once daily, or for prophylaxis 100 mg every night. An i.v. preparation (Syraprim) is also available as the lactate in 5 ml ampoules containing 20 mg/ml and should be given slowly in adult doses of 150–250 mg every 12 hours.

Trimethoprim–sulphonamide combinations.

Co-trifamole (Co-Fram). Tablets containing 400 mg of sulphamoxole and 80 mg of trimethoprim are given in adult doses of 960 mg of the combination initially, followed by 480 mg every 12 hours.

Co-trimoxazole (Bactrim, Chemotrim, Comox, Nodilon, Septrin). This was the first trimethoprim–sulphonamide combination. It is available in tablets of 400 mg sulphamethoxazole and 80 mg trimethoprim, the standard adult dose being 2 tablets every 12 hours. Paediatric tablets and syrup are available and also double strength adult tablets. I.m. injections are also available, there being 800 mg of sulphamethoxazole and 160 mg of trimethoprim in each 3 ml ampoule. For i.v. infusion there are 5 ml ampoules containing 400 mg of sulphamethoxazole and 80 mg of trimethoprim. This must be diluted to 125 ml for infusion purposes. For adults, the standard dosage of the i.m. preparation is 3 ml, and of the i.v. form 10 ml, diluted to 250 ml 12-hourly.

Indications

Only time will tell if significant resistance will develop to trimethoprim used alone without the in vitro demonstrable synergistic co-operation of the sulphonamide component in trimethoprim–sulphonamide combinations. In some instances of urinary tract infection, the enterobacteria are sensitive only to trimethoprim and not to sulphonamides. So far, trimethoprim seems to be active on its own in treating sensitive infections and the attraction of using the single drug in vivo is that sulphonamide toxicity problems can be forgotten. The main indication for trimethoprim alone remains urinary tract infection, both as short-term therapy and long-term prophylaxis. Respiratory infections may also respond, but mycoplasmas and tubercle bacilli are resistant and

probably other drugs are in general more effective, including trimethoprim–sulphonamide combinations.

The combined drug is widely prescribed, especially in general practice, for
urinary and respiratory infections. Immunocompromised patients have been
protected from infections by the use of co-trimoxazole. Co-trimoxazole is a
standard alternative to chloramphenicol and amoxycillin for the management
of invasive salmonella infections, including typhoid fever. Prostatitis and
acute brucellosis are well-proven indications for the drug in long-term dosage.
Pneumocystis carinii pneumonia and toxoplasmosis will sometimes respond
to high parenteral dosage of co-trimoxazole.

Adverse Effects

Toxicity. Nausea and vomiting are the only common complications
attributable to trimethoprim. Skin rashes occur occasionally. Folate
deficiency has been sporadically reported after trimethoprim and co-
trimoxazole, but in most instances there have been other reasons for folate
depletion, such as dietary deficiencies or malabsorption. Trimethoprim might
then just tip the balance. Almost all the micro-organisms that are inhibited by
trimethoprim are unable to utilize preformed folic acid or folinic acid if either
of these is given to the patient. These drugs should not be given during
pregnancy.

Interactions
In addition to a synergistic effect with sulphonamides, trimethoprim enhances
the antibacterial ability of the polymyxins.

Nalidixic Acid

Nalidixic acid is a 1,8-naphthyridine, synthesized in 1962. It is antibacterial in
the Gram-negative range, particularly against *Escherichia coli* and *Proteus*
species when they invade the urinary tract. Resistant organisms emerge in a
variable time after exposure to the drug.

Mode of Action
Nalidixic acid probably interferes with DNA synthesis from precursors. It
seems to have little detrimental action on RNA or other cell proteins.

Pharmacokinetics
Absorption from the gut is dependable, and plasma levels of free drug fall
steadily after an hour, owing to reversible protein binding and rapid excretion
by the kidney. Antibacterial concentrations are not achieved in the plasma.
Some of the drug is altered in the liver, but several of its derivatives have been
found to retain their antibacterial ability, even in the urine. Concentrations of
unaltered drug in the urine are enhanced by a high pH.

Preparations

Nalidixic acid (Negram). Tablets of 500 mg and a suspension of 300 mg in 5 ml are dispensed. An adult dose is 500 mg to 1 g 6-hourly, and children over the age of 3 months may be given 150–600 mg 6-hourly, according to weight and age. Mictral contains 660 mg of nalidixic acid with 3.75 g of sodium citrate in a sachet.

Indications

Acute and chronic urinary infections usually respond to nalidixic acid, assuming that the offending organisms are sensitive. *E. coli* and *Proteus* organisms are well eradicated, whereas the various strains of *Pseudomonas* are resistant. Long-term therapy for urinary tract infections should be in low dose, to reduce the likelihood of cumulative neurotoxicity.

Adverse Effects

Toxicity. Nausea, vomiting and diarrhoea are reported in 10% of patients on the drug. More serious are the neurological effects, particularly after prolonged administration and if there is renal impairment. These include severe headache, epileptiform fits and hallucinations.

Interactions

Nalidixic acid and nitrofurantoin negate the antibacterial properties of each other and they should never be used concomitantly.

Contraindications

Premature infants cannot metabolize or excrete nalidixic acid efficiently. In addition, it is transferable in breast milk, so should not be given to nursing mothers.

Related Compounds

Compounds chemically similar to nalidixic acid and also used for treating urinary infections include oxolinic acid and cinoxacin (Cinobac); two others, pipemidic acid and flumequine, show some activity against *Pseudomonas aeruginosa*.

Nitrofurantoin

Nitrofurantoin is one of three nitrofuran compounds that have antibacterial activity. It is a yellowish compound which must be protected from the light, otherwise it turns brown. It is bactericidal against most urinary pathogens, particularly Gram-negative organisms, except some *Proteus*, and almost all *Pseudomonas* species. Resistant forms appear in vitro and in the patient as the drug becomes more commonly used.

Mode of Action
There is no known mechanism to account for the bactericidal properties of this drug, though it does produce various biochemical anomalies in organisms exposed to it.

Pharmacokinetics
Oral administration is suitable, since absorption is good. The concentration is highest at 2 hours and half is excreted quickly in the urine, while the remainder is equally rapidly metabolized. The plasma half-life is therefore short, being about 20 minutes. No tissue levels of note (except in the kidney) are recorded after oral dosage and very little of the drug is found in cord blood or breast milk. Renal excretion is by glomerular filtration and tubular secretion and some reabsorption is said to take place from alkaline urine.

Preparations
Nitrofurantoin (Berkfurin, Ceduran, Furadantin, Macrodantin). Tablets of 50 and 100 mg of the drug are marketed and a suspension of 25 mg in 5 ml is also available. Usual doses recommended are 50–100 mg 6-hourly.

Indications
The sole use of nitrofurantoin given by mouth is in the treatment of coliform lower urinary tract infections.

Adverse Effects
Toxicity. Gastrointestinal side-effects are so predictable that several alterations in particle size and the coating of the drug (for instance, with liquorice) have been attempted. Peripheral neuropathy is well documented, particularly when renal disease has impaired excretion of the substance.

Allergy. Anaphylactic episodes (Type I hypersensitivity) have occurred after nitrofurantoin, as have allergic skin rashes. Long-term administration may be associated with the development of acute pulmonary infiltrates often with eosinophilia or a separate, insidious dyspnoea associated with pulmonary fibrosis.

Interactions
Nitrofurantoin should not be given with nalidixic acid, since they cancel each other out in practical antibacterial terms.

Contraindications
Renal failure is an absolute contraindication to the use of nitrofurantoin, because of the consequent accumulation in the body of the drug and its metabolites, several of which are toxic. Haemolytic anaemia occurs in patients who have glucose-6-phosphate dehydrogenase deficiency and are given nitrofurantoin. The enzyme defect is rare in Caucasians (p. 564).

Hexamine Hippurate and Hexamine Mandelate

Methenamine or hexamine was first used before the turn of the century in the form of its salt. Hexamine hippurate (Hiprex) 1 g 12-hourly and hexamine mandelate (Mandelamine) 1 g 6-hourly are both well absorbed from the gut and excreted mainly unchanged in the urine. No antibacterial activity occurs in blood or tissues, but in the urine with a pH below 6 or 5.5, formaldehyde is liberated. Providing the concentration is sufficiently high, no micro-organisms can survive. The drugs are relatively ineffective against urea-splitting *Proteus* spp., which thrive in an alkaline urine where the pH is too high for the production of formaldehyde. Some have, therefore, recommended the addition of an acidifying agent to lower the urinary pH and so make the drugs more effective. The only indication for the use of hexamine salts is for the long-term management of urinary infections. Side-effects, such as gastrointestinal upsets and bladder irritation, limit their value.

Noxythiolin

This is hydroxymethyl-methyl-thiourea. It is used to prevent or eradicate infection from the body surface and accessible cavities. For example, it is employed when catheterization is done. It is active against Gram-negative and Gram-positive organisms, fungi, and flagellates. In diseased bladders, it may cause pain. A proprietary name is Noxyflex.

Chlorhexidine

Chlorhexidine hydrochloride is an antibacterial agent which is bactericidal to a wide range of Gram-negative and Gram-positive organisms. It is designed for incorporation into topical preparations such as antiseptic dusting powders, creams, ointments and surgical dressings. The acetate, suitably diluted, can be used for urethral disinfection, catheter lubrication and bladder and body cavity irrigation. There is also a gluconate.

ANTIFUNGAL AGENTS

Yeasts and fungi are common commensals, but may act as opportunists and take advantage of a compromised patient, causing severe or even fatal infection. Antibacterial treatment often encourages the multiplication of yeasts and fungi. Candida vulvitis can be the presenting symptom in obese maturity-onset female diabetics. Parenteral drug abusers are candidates for systemic mycoses and right-sided endocarditis. Fungal infections derived from animals often recur even after adequate treatment, because of re-exposure to the source of infection. Antifungal drugs fall into several groups, the polyenes, flucytosine, the imidazoles and griseofulvin.

Polyenes

It is, perhaps, not surprising that antibiotics synthesized by fungi are usually inactive against micro-organisms similar to their parents. Penicillin itself is one exception to the rule, in that it can kill *Actinomyces israelii*. The numerous polyenes are the other exceptions, but most of them are too toxic for any therapeutic application. Nystatin, amphotericin B and natamycin are all products of *Streptomyces* species and have useful antifungal properties, but are not antibacterial. Their chemical structure is not fully determined, but they are large cyclic lactones boasting lipophilic and hydrophobic portions, making solubility in water difficult.

Mode of Action
The two portions mentioned above are essential for the specific hydrophobic interaction of the polyenes with the fungal cell membranes. Sensitive fungi have ergosterol in their plasma membranes, to which the polyenes have a greater binding affinity than to the cholesterol which is the predominant sterol in the plasma membrane of mammalian cells. A selective action is developed against the fungi, whose cytoplasmic membranes quickly develop holes and leak intracellular potassium, leading to a breakdown of their essential respiratory and metabolic processes. Some of the resistant fungi appear to have altered sterols to which polyenes may not so readily bind. The toxicity of amphotericin B to human cells does, however, appear to be caused by damage to plasma membranes as well and, in vitro, amphotericin B can be shown to bind to the surface sterols of human erythrocytes, leading to cell death.

Pharmacokinetics
Nystatin is not absorbed and is so insoluble that it is primarily used orally for gut infections or else topically. Amphotericin B is commonly given i.v., since little or no absorption is possible from the gut. Slow depletion of plasma levels takes place over a day after injection. Diffusion is good, except to the CSF, but intrathecal injection can remedy this. Bioassay of the drug is difficult, owing to inhibitory sterols being present in the serum and because of a variable degree of protein binding. Excretion is slow and is only partly carried out by the kidney.

Preparations

Nystatin (Nystan, Nystaform). Numerous forms, such as ointment, powder and pessaries, are marketed for topical use. Tablets of 500 000 units strength are available, and a suspension containing 100 000 units/ml is used for paediatric infections. Combinations of nystatin and broad-spectrum antibiotics such as tetracyclines, which may in themselves cause fungal superinfection, produce added side-effects and are of questionable value.

Amphotericin B (Fungilin, Fungizone). Amphotericin B deoxycholate is a dry powder, 50 mg of which is dissolved in sterile water and then administered diluted in 5% dextrose. A precipitate forms if it is added to saline. The dose ranges from 0.25 to 1 mg/kg body weight/day by slow infusion. A mixture, lozenges and an ointment are useful in dealing with topical and oral infections.

Natamycin. Topical, including vaginal, preparations are marketed, but unique to natamycin is a 2.5% suspension (Pimafucin) which is inhaled into the respiratory tract.

Indications
Fungal infections such as candidiasis, involving skin, eyes, mucous membranes and gut are adequately eradicated by the variety of topical preparations. Natamycin by inhalation is recommended for broncho-pulmonary aspergillosis and candidiasis. Deep-seated fungal infections such as cryptococcal meningitis, systemic aspergillosis, histoplasmosis, coccidioidomycosis, blastomycosis or candidal endocarditis leave no alternative but i.v. amphotericin, or in the insensitive infections, amphotericin in combination with flucytosine. In the first-mentioned infection, intrathecal administration may be needed. Treatment may require to be continued for some weeks and toxicity may frequently interrupt the course.

Adverse Effects

Toxicity. Oral polyenes may cause nausea, vomiting and diarrhoea. I.v. amphotericin invariably causes some side-effects. Local pain and phlebitis at the injection site is common, as is abdominal or chest pain, headache, nausea, anorexia and vomiting. Transitory radiculitis follows intrathecal administration. Nephrotoxicity and marrow depression follow prolonged exposure to amphotericin, and hypokalaemia, hypomagnesaemia, uraemia and anaemia are expected.

Interactions
Amphotericin precipitates if added to normal saline prior to infusion.

Contraindications
Renal failure is an absolute contraindication to amphotericin, since aggravation will be automatic. Amphotericin should only be used in pregnancy if a life-threatening fungal infection is present and no less toxic agent available.

Flucytosine

Flucytosine (5-fluorocytosine) is a fluorinated pyrimidine originally developed unsuccessfully as an antimetabolite for treating malignant disease. Later it was shown to have activity against certain yeasts and yeast-like fungi, including *Candida* spp., *Cryptococcus neoformans* and *Torulopsis glabrata*. *Histoplasma* and *Blastomyces* spp. are always insensitive. Unfortunately, acquired resistance can develop to flucytosine and some prac' .ioners therefore recommend a synergistic combination with amphoterici B. The amphotericin renders the yeast cell membrane permeable so i, at more flucytosine is taken up.

Mode of Action
Flucytosine is rapidly deaminated in the fungal cell by cytosine deaminase to the antimetabolite 5-fluorouracil. This then becomes incorporated instead of uracil in the RNA of the fungus, which stops growing. As cytosine deaminase is not found in the host's cells, flucytosine acts selectively against the fungus and is relatively non-toxic to man.

Pharmacokinetics
Flucytosine is well absorbed from the gut and achieves peak serum concentrations 2–6 hours after oral dosing. It is excreted as flucytosine by glomerular filtration, so the normal serum half-life of 3–4 hours is prolonged in renal failure. Tissue levels of the drug are good and about 50% of the serum concentration is achieved in the CSF.

Preparations

Flucytosine (Alcobon). Tablets of 500 mg and an i.v. infusion containing 10 mg/ml made up to 250 ml are available and the dose for adults with normal renal function is 100–200 mg/kg body weight per day in 4 divided doses.

Indications
This drug should only be used in systemic yeast infections or the management of candida or cryptococcal meningitis because of its good CSF penetration. In life-threatening infections, combined therapy with amphotericin B may be justified, as in the treatment of candida endocarditis or cryptococcal meningitis where the combined regimen sterilizes the CSF more quickly than amphotericin B alone.

Adverse Effects
Gastrointestinal upset, skin rashes, liver enzyme derangement, leucopenia and thrombocytopenia may occur. The dose must be reduced in uraemic patients. Its safety in pregnancy has not been established.

Imidazoles

Ketoconazole is potentially the most useful new anti-fungal agent because it is well absorbed after oral administration. It joins the imidazole group, which includes clotrimazole, miconazole and econazole, all of which are effective against a wide range of fungal infections.

Mode of Action

The imidazoles damage the cytoplasmic membrane and cell walls of yeasts, making them leak intracellular contents. This action involves peroxidase and catalase enzymes in the yeast cell so, although the end result is similar to that produced by the polyenes, the mechanism is different. It is thought that ketoconazole inhibits the conversion of lanosterol to ergosterol in the cell wall.

Pharmacokinetics

Ketoconazole is well absorbed from the gut, and peak serum concentrations are reached 2–3 hours after oral administration, with therapeutic concentrations lasting for up to 8 hours. Ketoconazole is best absorbed in an acid environment and should be taken with meals and separate from concomitant antacid or cimetidine administration. Metabolism occurs in the liver and very little is excreted in the urine. Poor concentrations are found in CSF and peritoneal fluid.

Clotrimazole and miconazole are very poorly absorbed from the gut. Miconazole can be given i.v., but does not diffuse into tissues very well. For adequate CSF penetration intrathecal miconazole would be required. Econazole is rather better absorbed, but is only available in topical form at present.

Preparations

Ketoconazole (Nizoral). The adult dose is 200–400 mg daily taken with a meal. The tablets contain 200 mg.

Clotrimazole (Canesten). One and two per cent topical applications and 100 and 200 mg vaginal tablets are available.

Miconazole (Daktarin). Tablets of 250 mg, oral gels and a solution for i.v. administration are available. The adult oral dose is 250 mg 6-hourly. The i.v. solution contains 10 mg/ml and adults can be given 600 mg every 8 hours.

Econazole (Ecostatin). This is available as a 1% cream, lotion, powder or spray solution. Vaginal pessaries contain 150 mg of econazole nitrate.

Indications

The main uses of these drugs are for candidiasis, especially of the skin, mucosa and genital tract, but dermatophyte infections will respond. Oral miconazole and the better absorbed ketoconazole can be used for local or systemic fungal infections, especially when these have failed to respond to topical treatment. Ketoconazole is valuable in oral thrush, mycoses of the hair and skin, systemic candidiasis, coccidioidomycosis and histoplasmosis. Prophylactic imidazole therapy is often justified in immunocompromised patients for up to 6 months.

Adverse Effects
Oral ketoconazole and miconazole can both cause itchy skin rashes and nausea. I.v. miconazole may cause phlebitis and a transient normochromic, normocytic anaemia. Both drugs should be avoided in pregnancy. The local application of clotrimazole, miconazole or econazole to the genital tract may sometimes cause local irritation. There may be a transient abnormality of liver function tests with ketoconazole.

Griseofulvin

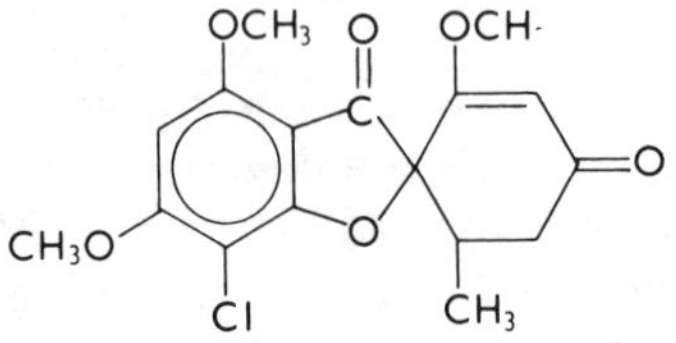

GRISEOFULVIN

Penicillium moulds produce, among other useful antibiotics, griseofulvin, which kills growing fungi. It has little or no effect on static organisms.

Mode of Action
Although morphological changes can be ascribed to griseofulvin and many biochemical changes may be related to its use, the exact mode of action of the drug awaits elucidation.

Pharmacokinetics
Griseofulvin is insoluble, but a preparation of fine particles facilitates absorption in the bowel. A fatty meal is said to increase the efficiency of uptake of the drug into the circulation. It is distributed evenly and is laid down in growing epidermis of skin and nails in particular. Metabolism and inactivation by demethylation takes place in the liver. Most of an oral dose of griseofulvin appears unchanged in the faeces.

Preparations

Griseofulvin (Fulcin, Grisovin). Tablets of 125 mg and 500 mg allow a simple dose schedule of 250–500 mg 12-hourly. The paediatric dose is 10 mg/kg body weight daily, and a suspension of 125 mg in 5 ml is marketed for use in children.

Indications
Ringworm and fungal infections (excluding *Candida*) involving skin, hair and nails are indications for the use of griseofulvin. *Microsporum audouini*, tinea and *Trichophyton rubrum* infections do very well, whereas *Trichophyton mentagrophytes* is more resistant. Skin infections require therapy over at least

1 month, afflictions of the finger nails 3–6 months and of the toe nails 12 months.

Adverse Effects

Toxicity. Few serious hazards have been reported after prolonged treatment with griseofulvin. Occasional skin rashes and photosensitivity occur, and an increased bowel habit is invariable. Headache, mild memory difficulties and impairment of judgement are common but not to an extent that the drug has to be withdrawn. Porphyria may be precipitated (p. 596) and the effect of alcohol may be potentiated. In high doses, it acts like colchicine on human cells grown in vitro, arresting mitosis at the metaphase. No such interference has been reported in vivo, but it is wise to withdraw the drug in early pregnancy.

Interactions

As griseofulvin is demethylated in the liver, it is predictable that phenobarbitone, an enzyme inducer, might increase the metabolism of griseofulvin. In rats, that very sequence has been proved, but not so in man. Phenobarbitone given by mouth, while lowering griseofulvin levels, does not do so by any hepatic interaction, because the same drug given i.v. is ineffective. It appears that phenobarbitone has this action because it inhibits absorption of griseofulvin from the gut, and to do this, it must be given orally along with the antifungal agent. Griseofulvin may decrease the response to oral anticoagulants, and the latter may reduce the effectiveness of the former.

Contraindications

It is advisable to avoid the use of griseofulvin in pregnancy. It should not be given to those with acute intermittent porphyria, since the drug induces the enzyme δ-aminolaevulinic acid synthetase, which is essential in porphyrin metabolism. It should be used with caution in hepatic disease.

ANTIVIRAL AGENTS

A few antibacterial drugs, such as fusidic acid and rifampicin, inhibit viruses, but the doses required are so high that toxicity to the host is likely to occur. One problem in the development of antiviral agents lies in the close relationship between viruses and host cells which often share the same proteins; this leads to difficulty in exploiting any differences between the pathogen and host through chemotherapy. Some antiviral drugs protect the host cell from attachment or penetration by the virus, while others attempt selectively to disrupt viral protein synthesis within the host cell.

Another difficulty associated with antiviral chemotherapy is for the clinician to be in a position to use the drug before it causes cell damage. This is rarely possible because the symptoms of viral infection are due to the inflammatory response by the tissues to the virus and this may occur too late for any antiviral agent to be effective. This has prompted attempts to enhance host resistance or to use antiviral chemotherapy more for prophylaxis than treatment.

The antiviral agents discussed here are the interferons, methisazone, amantadine and the anti-DNA replicating drugs idoxuridine, cytarabine, vidarabine and acyclovir.

Interferons

Interferons are proteins of different sizes which are remarkably stable, except to the action of proteolytic enzymes. They are produced by the host cells that harbour replicating viruses and they appear to protect other cells from attack, not only by the virus initially inducing their production, but also by other viruses, irrespective of their nucleic acid composition. Their exact mode of action is unclear. It appears to be unrelated to virus invasion, but occurs very early on in the attempts by the virus to reproduce once within the host cell.

Interferons are expensive to produce from human white blood cells and fibroblasts, but, with the advent of genetic engineering (p. 393), clones of bacterial cells may be persuaded to manufacture therapeutic amounts of interferon more economically. So far, interferons have been used topically for herpes simplex keratitis and systemically in herpes simplex and zoster, hepatitis B virus infections and cytomegalovirus infections. They can ameliorate or delay the symptoms of influenza B infections and the common cold. Adverse reactions appear to be few to date.

Two interferon inducers, helenine and statolon, both derived from penicillin moulds, have been used prophylactically to prevent respiratory virus infections. Double-stranded RNA may be the active substance in the interferon inducers and the results of further studies are awaited.

Interferons are also under trial in the management of malignant disease.

Methisazone

METHISAZONE

Several thiosemicarbazones are antituberculous agents and methisazone (Marboran) was developed as a drug with additional characteristics, such as the inhibition of multiplication of vaccinia viruses. It is a β-thiosemicarbazone and probably acts late in virus replication by selectively interfering with viral messenger RNA. Resistance easily develops. The drug has been used with apparent success as a prophylactic against smallpox during outbreaks and for the prevention and treatment of generalized vaccinia or vaccinial encephalitis, especially in immunocompromised patients. There appear to be few uses for it today. Its value was diminished by the frequent occurrence of gastrointestinal side-effects. The dose range was from 200 mg to 400 mg/kg body weight daily by mouth.

Amantadine

AMANTADINE

Amantadine hydrochloride (Symmetrel) is solely effective against RNA viruses — particularly, in vitro, influenza A_1 and A_2, parainfluenza 1, and rubella. Practically, however, it is of value in the prophylaxis of influenza A_2 (Asian) infection. It is ineffective in preventing influenza B. Several clinical trials have reinforced its validity, but none show an obvious ameliorative effect on the established disease. The latter failure is probably explained by the proposal that amantadine acts by preventing adsorption of a virus on to a cell wall or by stopping the uncoating of viruses at the entry site. Thus, the drug is ineffective against intracellular replicating viruses. It is given orally in a dose of 100 mg twice each day as a syrup or in capsules and is well absorbed within 4 hours. No metabolism is obvious in the tissues and excretion of the unaltered drug is by the kidney. The only side-effects are mild lethargy, drowsiness, depression and occasional tremors. In a patient who suffered from Parkinson's disease, however, chance remission of rigidity and tremor was reported. A widespread application in that disease has since evolved.

Inhibitors of Viral DNA Replication

Idoxuridine, cytarabine, vidarabine and the more recently developed acyclovir all have antiviral activity through interference with DNA replication. Each has a slightly different mode of action. So far, most experience has been gained with idoxuridine in the treatment of herpes virus infections, but acyclovir promises to be more effective and less toxic.

Idoxuridine

Idoxuridine (Dendrid, Herpid, Iduridin, Kerecid; IDU) is a pyrimidine analogue and therefore a nucleoside. It antagonizes thymidine competitively, since it differs from it merely in the halogen grouping. As a result, DNA in a virus may lack precursor molecules of thymidine and growth will be stunted,

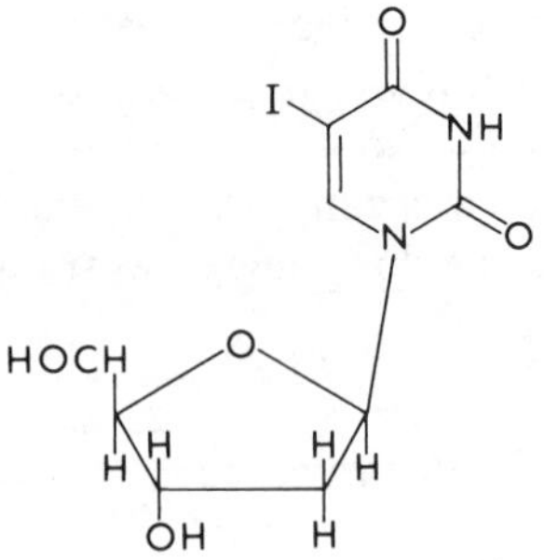

IDOXURIDINE

or IDU may become incorporated by polymerization into DNA in lieu of thymidine and thereafter inhibit its coding efficiency. The latter mode of action is more important in the treatment of herpes simplex infections, though resistant herpes has unfortunately been noted. Local application to the eye (0.1% drops) and skin (5% ointment) are its principal uses. Formerly i.v. infusion (220 mg/kg body weight daily) for the treatment of herpes encephalitis was recommended. Herpes zoster infections of the skin, especially in immunocompromised hosts, can be halted by the early application of 40% idoxuridine in dimethylsulphoxide, which acts as a penetrating agent. Lower concentrations of IDU (5%) are less effective. Systemic therapy is accompanied by marrow depression and hepatocellular damage. Local treatment sometimes causes itching and oedema, and, on application to the conjunctiva, photophobia. IDU has an unpleasant cloying smell.

Cytarabine

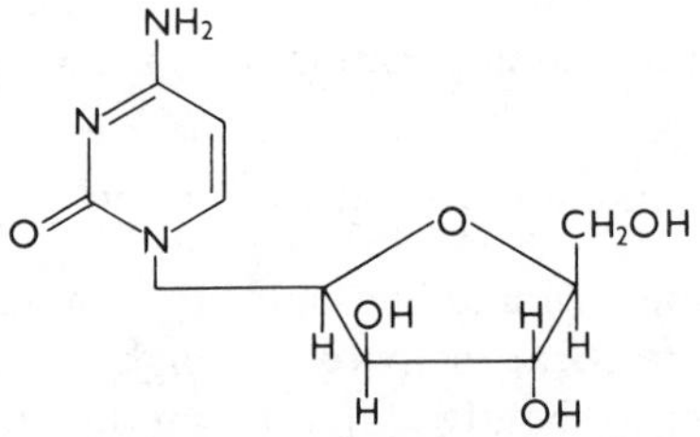

CYTARABINE

Cytarabine (cytosine arabinoside; Cytosar) inhibits the reduction of cytidilic acid to deoxycytidilic acid and so decreases the amount of phosphorylated products of deoxycytidilic acid available for incorporation into viral DNA. It may also interfere with the action of DNA polymerase. Although it has been used topically in the eyes for herpes keratitis, it may be irritating. I.v. use is associated with nausea, vomiting, blood dyscrasias, skin rashes and damage to the liver and kidneys and is no longer recommended.

Vidarabine

This purine nucleoside analogue (adenine arabinoside; Vira-A), originally developed for managing malignant disease, is derived from a Streptomyces fungus and is effective against DNA viruses. It apparently acts through its triphosphate metabolite, which may inhibit DNA polymerase or ribonucleotide reductase. Host-cell DNA synthesis is selectively less inhibited than the viral DNA and it is less toxic than idoxuridine or cytarabine. In herpes keratitis, the active metabolite of vidarabine penetrates the eye and causes less irritation than idoxuridine, to which it is preferred. It has also been used in herpes simplex encephalitis and severe herpes zoster infections in i.v. doses ranging from 5 to 15 mg/kg body weight per day. It may also have activity in cytomegalovirus infection and in type B virus hepatitis, where it decreases the viral DNA polymerase concentration.

Acyclovir

Acyclovir (acycloguanosine; Zovirax), a cyclic nucleoside, is a relatively new agent active against types 1 and 2 herpes simplex and herpes zoster infections, whether used topically in the eye, on the skin or genitalia, or i.v. for disseminated herpes infections. Recently oral acyclovir has been used for genital herpes and is now available on prescription. Acyclovir is more active than cytarabine and is particularly valuable for the treatment of immunocompromised patients.

Acyclovir is taken up by infected cells better than uninfected cells. Under the influence of virus specific thymidine kinase, acyclovir is converted into active acyclovir triphosphate. This then competes with deoxyguanosine triphosphate as a substrate for viral DNA polymerase. If acyclovir triphosphate is incorporated in the viral DNA, the normal replication ceases. It is much more active against the DNA polymerase of herpes viruses than the DNA polymerase of the host cells, making it overall a highly selective antiviral agent. Toxicity, so far, seems low. Local irritation and ulceration at the injection site can occur as the preparation is very alkaline. A sudden increase in blood urea and creatinine levels and in liver enzymes can occur and occasional skin rashes are found, though it is difficult to dissociate these effects from those of the disease process itself. I.v. acyclovir is given by slow infusion of 5 mg/kg body weight over one hour, every 8 hours for a 5 day course. The drug is eliminated in the urine and has a half-life of 3 hours in patients with normal renal function. Dose reduction is required in kidney failure.

Acyclovir may also be used topically in genital herpes, though the i.v. or oral route may be more effective. Very recently, trials of orally administered acyclovir suggest that a five-day course is valuable in the management of genital herpes simplex infection, for which 200 mg of acyclovir is recommended to be given by mouth every 4 hours, omitting the night-time dose. In ocular herpes infections, 3% acyclovir ointment appears to be effective and penetrates the aqueous humour. Further studies are required to establish the place of acyclovir in the therapy of herpes infection and its possible value in Epstein–Barr and cytomegalovirus infections remains to be determined.

ANTIMALARIAL DRUGS

A single substance, dicophane (DDT), has prevented many outbreaks of malaria by killing *Anopheles* mosquitoes and their larvae. It can be assumed that the mosquito vector will not be entirely eradicated by DDT, and failing the emergence of a method of immunization against malaria, the numerous antimalarials are of considerable clinical importance. Infestation by protozoal sporozoites of *Plasmodium vivax*, *P. malariae*, *P. ovale*, or *P. falciparum* will follow a bite from an infected mosquito. No symptoms occur while the sporozoites settle in the patient's liver and propagate. After a variable interval (dependent on the type of malaria), merozoites are released into the blood stream, where they may infect erythrocytes or recycle to the hepatocytes. There is very little persistence of *P. falciparum* in the liver, but the illness is a more serious one. The erythrocytes that are involved will rupture when the parasites have developed and increased in number. Fresh merozoites are released, and this gives various clinical features and perpetuates the infection. The continued life cycle of the plasmodia elsewhere depends on sexually dividing forms of parasites (gametocytes) arising in the course of development in red cells and being ingested by a new vector, the female *Anopheles* mosquito. Completion of the cycle is the stockpiling in the mosquito's salivary glands of sporozoites, the progeny of gametocyte fertilization in its stomach. The mosquito then bites man and spreads the disease. The only other mode of transmission is by blood transfusion. The antimalarials act at different arcs of the orbital scheme condensed above and, accordingly, may either suppress the disease or nullify it.

DRUG TREATMENT OF MALARIA

PROPHYLAXIS

No drug kills sporozoites, so the term 'prophylaxis' is not an absolute one. The aim is to eradicate any infection after it has entered the body. For long-term administration, daily proguanil is the safest and most effective drug, assuming that the parasites are sensitive. Alternatives are chloroquine or pyrimethamine given weekly, but the taking of these drugs is more likely to be forgotten by the patient because of the less frequent dosage. Where the parasites are chloroquine-resistant, Fansidar or Maloprim are advised in weekly doses, Maloprim being preferred in pregnancy and for individuals who may be sulphonamide sensitive.

As the annual notification rate of malaria in the UK is about 2000 and several deaths are recorded each year, it is important that the travelling public should be better educated about antimalarial prophylaxis. Advice is available from Community Health Centres regarding the geographical distribution of malaria and the sensitivity or resistance of the local parasites, something which can change quite quickly. With the exception of proguanil, which can be taken the day before entering the malarious area, all the other antimalarial drugs should be started one week before travel. All prophylactic drugs must be continued for a minimum of four weeks after leaving the malarious zone. Malaria can occur in those apparently receiving adequate prophylaxis, so any fever developing abroad or shortly after return should be investigated with repeated blood smears.

TREATMENT

Acute malaria must be urgently treated with fluid replacement and blood transfusion if severe haemolysis complicates the presentation. The drug of choice is chloroquine, given orally, i.m. or even i.v. (except in infants) where the parasites are known to be sensitive. For *P. falciparum* infection in non-immunes in East Africa or the Far East, quinine is advised. Amodiaquine is another first-line drug. Coma should be treated by quinine in an initial i.v. dose of 20 mg/kg body weight given over 4 hours, then 10 mg/kg body weight as a 4-hour infusion every 8 hours (for usual doses see p. 73) and supportive measures. Infections resistant to chloroquine may be susceptible to quinine, which should be given i.v. in cerebral or severe forms of falciparum malaria, or with the combination of pyrimethamine and sulfadoxine (Fansidar), but the danger of using sulphonamides in glucose-6-phosphate dehydrogenase deficiency has to be remembered after a malarial attack. Mild infections with chloroquine-resistant parasites have been successfully treated with Fansidar alone in a single dose of 3 tablets. Mefloquine and qinghaosu may be developed as drugs effective against chloroquine-resistant *P. falciparum*. A single oral dose of 1 g of mefloquine appears to make a radical cure and two oral or i.m. doses of qinghaosu clear parasites extremely quickly.

SUPPRESSION

Malarial attacks may be suppressed in those who have just been treated for the disease, even if the patient remains in an endemic area. It is necessary to prevent further erythrocytic infestation. Chloroquine given weekly is usually sufficient in a dosage equivalent to 300 mg base, together with 45 mg of primaquine base for 8 weeks, but drug resistance has to be taken into account, and the regular taking of prophylactic antimalarials will be required thereafter.

RADICAL CURE

Sensitive strains of falciparum malaria will be eliminated if suppressed with chloroquine for up to 2 months after leaving an endemic area. Because of the exoerythrocytic persistence in liver cells, other forms of malaria will require eradication with primaquine used twice daily for 2 weeks (7.5 mg base per dose) after the initial course of chloroquine or other agent. Alternatively, chloroquine together with primaquine can be used as indicated above. Occasional relapses have been noted 6 months after such a regimen, and if this occurs, the course should be repeated. Patients should be screened for glucose-6-phosphate dehydrogenase and if found deficient, they should only receive primaquine in low doses with careful monitoring to detect haemolysis.

4-Aminoquinolines

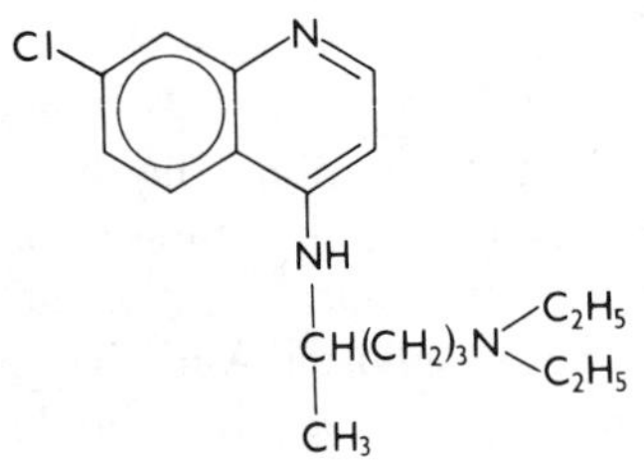

CHLOROQUINE 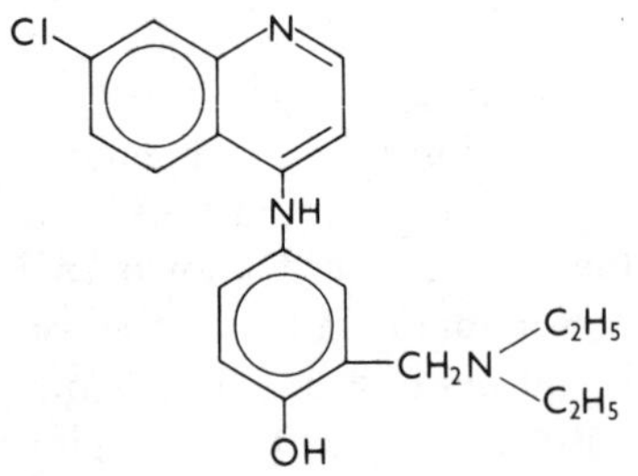   AMODIAQUINE

Chloroquine and amodiaquine are useful drugs for the treatment of symptomatic, clinical malaria, because they are active against erythrocytes containing asexual forms of all types of malaria. Lately the evolution of falciparum protozoa resistant to the 4-aminoquinolines has unfortunately reached a significant magnitude in South America and South-east Asia, and some African countries as well. Strains of *P. falciparum* resistant to chloroquine are also resistant to other 4-aminoquinolines and usually to mepacrine. Some are resistant to proguanil and pyrimethamine. Chloroquine is active in giardiasis, and is an efficient amoebicide in hepatic, but not intestinal, amoebiasis.

Mode of Action
Experimental evidence supports a common mode of action between the 4-aminoquinolines and the cinchona alkaloids (p. 72). The parasitized erythrocyte concentrates chloroquine to over 100 times the plasma level. The drug proceeds to bind to the purines of DNA and inhibits nucleic acid and protein synthesis in the parasite, leading to its death. Binding also occurs to tissue DNA, and the selective toxicity for the parasite is possibly dependent

on the concentration properties of the erythrocyte. Resistance to chloroquine and amodiaquine may be due to a failure of this concentrating ability.

Pharmacokinetics

Both chloroquine and amodiaquine are absorbed well from the alimentary tract. Distribution is widespread, and serum protein and tissue binding are significant. The half-life of chloroquine is several days, owing to slow release from the binding sites, so much so that the drug is suppressive on a once weekly schedule. Accumulation becomes a hazard in the long term, particularly because of effects on the retina, iris and cornea. Metabolism of a certain amount of free drug is undertaken by liver microsomes and the products are excreted by the kidney along with the remnants of the unchanged substance. An acid urine enhances elimination.

Preparations

Chloroquine. Two oral preparations are available in tablet form – the phosphate (250 mg; Avloclor) and the sulphate (200 mg; Nivaquine). Chloroquine phosphate is also available as a syrup with 80 mg in 5 ml (Malarivon). Saturation of tissue binding sites requires a loading dose of four tablets, followed by two tablets daily for 2 days. Urgent treatment is possible with 200 mg chloroquine sulphate (Nivaquine) given slowly i.m. or i.v., and in serious illness further such doses may be required by the same route. Chloroquine given i.v. is contraindicated in infants who may develop cardiovascular complications. In an emergency it is important to know that Nivaquine for injection is a proprietary preparation of chloroquine. The manufacturer's instructions about dosage in relation to age and body weight should be followed. The adult prophylactic dose of either drug is two tablets weekly.

Amodiaquine hydrochloride. Tablets containing 200 mg are an alternative to chloroquine; 600 mg is sufficient as an initial dosage, followed by 400 mg daily for 2 days, for the subjugation of a malarial attack. As with chloroquine, two tablets weekly provides prophylaxis.

Indications

Malaria. Acute symptoms occur when merozoites in sufficient numbers are liberated from dividing schizonts into the plasma. The 4-aminoquinolines only have effect on the parasites while they inhabit the red cells, so they are ineffective in the eradication of hepatic plasmodia. On the other hand, symptoms of an attack rapidly subside, and treatment of this phase is complete in 3 days. For cure of non-falciparum malaria, a course of primaquine is needed to eradicate parasites from exoerythrocytic sites. In falciparum malaria, the hepatic phase is self-limiting, so chloroquine will eventually eradicate this variant. In the Middle East and the Indian subcontinent west of Bangladesh and in most African countries except Kenya and Tanzania, chloroquine prophylaxis is satisfactory. Chloroquine no longer gives reliable protection in South-east Asia, Kenya, Tanzania, and South America, where a pyrimethamine-containing combination sometimes with chloroquine in addition is needed to prevent falciparum malaria and either this or quinine is needed for treatment. Expert up-to-date advice is important regarding the changing patterns of malarial resistance.

Other conditions. Chloroquine has other varied uses, as in the treatment of amoebic liver disease, giardiasis, rheumatoid arthritis, and photosensitive dermatitis, including that associated with systemic lupus erythematosus.

Adverse Effects

Toxicity. Accumulation of chloroquine in the eye leads to retinal damage and corneal opacities. A total dose of 60 g chloroquine may cause irreversible retinopathy, although many have taken more without ill effect. The standard prophylactic dose is seldom associated with ocular toxicity. Headache, nausea, vomiting, pruritus, lichenoid dermatitis, alopecia and leucopenia are occasionally reported. It is possible that chloroquine and amodiaquine may be mutagenic and carcinogenic, since they resemble the acridine dyes in structure and mode of action by adsorption to DNA. Amodiaquine causes neutropenia if employed in large doses. Rarely, haemolytic anaemia may be precipitated in an individual who has a genetic deficiency of glucose-6-phosphate dehydrogenase. Hypotension may occur when chloroquine is given i.v. and it should not be used except to save life in a serious plasmodial infection. It should never be given i.v. to infants.

8-Aminoquinolines

PRIMAQUINE

As is obvious from the structure of this series, the resemblance to the 4-aminoquinolines is close. Primaquine is the principal member useful in antimalarial therapy. Its site of action is completely different from that of chloroquine, since it acts only on exoerythrocytic parasites. In practice, this means that it eradicates them from the liver, an important consideration in the treatment of vivax, ovale or quartan malaria. The parasites within erythrocytes are immune, except that sexually dividing erythrocytic forms are killed as if they were in the liver.

Mode of Action

It is known that primaquine binds to DNA in a fashion not dissimilar to that of chloroquine. The exact mechanism by which this binding then kills the parasite is unknown. Tissue culture studies merely indicate that mitochondrial damage may be a significant factor.

Pharmacokinetics

Primaquine is well tolerated orally and quickly absorbed into the blood. Metabolism takes place rapidly and several of the degradation products are considered to be more lethal than the parent substance. This may explain the discrepancy between the peak plasma level of primaquine, which is 6 hours, and the peak therapeutic effect, which is 12 hours after administration. No tissue binding of note occurs and renal excretion of the drug is speedy.

Preparations

Primaquine phosphate. Two tablets each containing 7.5 mg are taken daily for a fortnight following initial chloroquine therapy as above, or the drugs may be given concurrently in the first 3 days, primaquine alone being used thereafter.

Indications

Primaquine is effective as a prophylactic drug, but is too toxic for prolonged ingestion. It is therefore most commonly employed to eradicate liver infestation in established vivax, ovale or quartan malaria, after treatment of the symptomatic disease with chloroquine. It has to be remembered that falciparum malaria may coexist with one of the other forms.

Adverse Effects

Toxicity. Abdominal pain and leucopenia are common dose-related consequences of lengthy primaquine ingestion. Methaemoglobinaemia and haemolytic anaemia follow administration to patients with glucose-6-phosphate dehydrogenase deficiency.

Interactions

Proguanil (p. 74) and mepacrine (p. 76) interfere with the degradation pathways of primaquine and may lead to its accumulation if given concomitantly. Toxicity is likely to follow. Mepacrine stains skin for some weeks after an i.m. injection or oral administration for any length of time, and interaction with primaquine is possible for that period.

Contraindications

Primaquine is contraindicated in severe glucose-6-phosphate dehydrogenase deficiency, for which patients should be screened before primaquine is prescribed (p. 564), although, with care, low-dose primaquine can be given in mild G-6-PD deficiency.

Cinchona Alkaloids

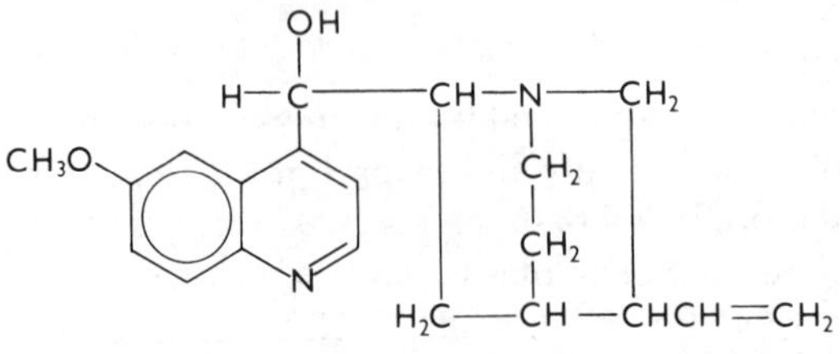

QUININE

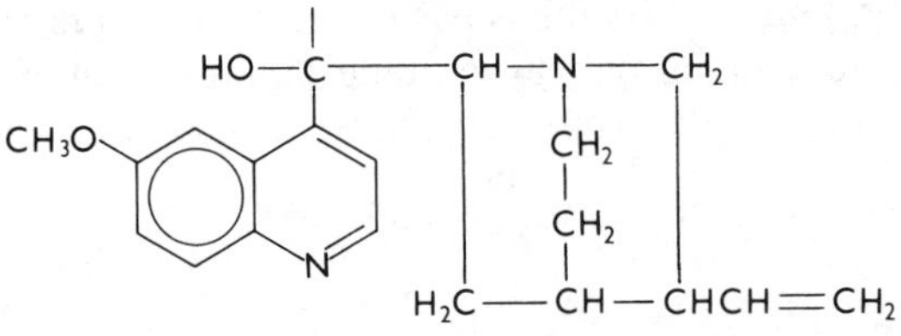

QUINIDINE

The bark of the cinchona tree has been known for several centuries to yield antimalarial substances. Quinine salts are well known for their bitter taste, widely exploited in the manufacture of aperitif waters. The main antimalarial properties are on the erythrocytic phase of the disease, which implies that quinine is useful for treatment of the symptomatic disease. It is less potent as a prophylactic agent.

Mode of Action
Quinine acts like the 4-aminoquinolines by binding to DNA, thus preventing nucleic acid synthesis. The molecular level of interference is not identical, but the end result is similar. In contrast to chloroquine, quinine does not bind to tissues.

Pharmacokinetics
Quinine salts may cause mild gastritis, but if tolerated are absorbed well and distributed widely. Most of the drug is hydroxylated in the liver and the resultant substances are excreted in the kidney within 6 hours of ingestion. I.m. injection is not recommended, though slow i.v. administration is effective in dehydrated, vomiting patients.

Preparations

Quinine bisulphate. A dose of 600 mg (two tablets) 8-hourly is required to maintain plasma levels of quinine. The tablets may be better tolerated if dissolved before ingestion.

Quinine dihydrochloride. Oral preparations are used in the same strength as the bisulphate. An ampoule of 600 mg in 2 ml of water is available for *slow* i.v. injection, preferably in 500 ml of physiological saline. No more than 5–10 mg/kg body weight should normally be given, the maximum dose i.v. being 500 mg, except in cerebral malaria (p. 67).

Indications

Quinine is less potent than chloroquine in the treatment of exacerbations of malaria. In the light of recent chloroquine-resistant strains of *P. falciparum* becoming more significant, quinine salts remain important therapeutic agents. They have not produced resistance in any of the malaria parasites so far, except in certain parts of South East Asia and Africa, where tetracycline-Fansidar combinations may be used. Prophylactic therapy is possible utilizing 600 mg daily from the day prior to exposure to at least a month after departure from an endemic area.

Quinine has a variety of pharmacological actions, some of which have been harnessed to advantage, while others are detrimental. It has an effect on the cardiovascular system comparable with, though less than, that of its optical isomer, quinidine, which is much more active against malarial parasites than quinine itself. Thus, it suppresses excitation and may prevent cardiac dysrhythmias, especially arising in the atria. It prolongs the refractory period in myocardial and skeletal muscle, and has been used for the treatment of cramp and myotonia congenita.

Adverse Effects

Toxicity. Cinchonism is the name given to the effects of high doses of quinine. It resembles salicylism in that patients complain of tinnitus, ataxia, deafness, nausea, headache and blurred vision. The principal damage, which may be permanent, is to the second and eighth cranial nerves. In high concentrations, quinine depresses myocardial contractility and causes vasodilatation by a direct action on small vessel musculature. A profound hypotension results and must be anticipated if a fast i.v. infusion is given. It can cause cardiac arrest. Quinine causes abortion by stimulating contraction of the muscle of the gravid uterus. Haemolysis may occur in those with glucose-6-phosphate dehydrogenase deficiency, but primaquine is more likely to cause it.

Allergy. Quinine, like quinidine, occasionally precipitates allergic thrombocytopenic purpura. Antibodies to quinine complexed with plasma protein are formed some days after exposure to the drug. On reintroduction of quinine, it complexes with plasma protein and an antibody–antigen reaction rapidly follows, with binding of the complement. The reaction takes place in the region of platelets by incidental attachment of either the antigen or the antibody. Destruction of the platelets results. Non-thrombocytopenic purpura may also be produced.

Contraindications
Pregnancy, unless no substitute drug is available and the patient's condition is critical, optic neuritis and allergy to quinine are contraindications to the drug. In addition, it aggravates myasthenia gravis and should be avoided in this condition. If possible, alternative drugs should be used in heart failure.

Proguanil

Proguanil hydrochloride is a biguanide which is lethal to *P. falciparum*. It not only attacks parasites in the human liver, but also renders the carrier mosquito non-infectious. Some falciparum strains are commonly resistant to proguanil in South-east Asia, Kenya, Tanzania, and Central and South America. Cross resistance exists with pyrimethamine-resistant strains of *P. falciparum*.

Mode of Action
Proguanil is an antimetabolite after the fashion of trimethoprim and pyrimethamine. All three drugs inhibit folate utilization in the synthesis of essential cell proteins.

Pharmacokinetics
Slow absorption follows oral ingestion of the salt. Some of it is bound to tissue such as kidney and liver, but the majority is attached to plasma proteins. The concentration of drug in erythrocytes is about six times greater than it is in plasma. Excretion of at least half of the drug is known to take place in the urine, the remainder being metabolized.

Preparations

Proguanil hydrochloride (Paludrine). Tablets containing 100 mg are marketed. The usual suppressive dose is 100–200 mg daily. *Cycloguanil embonate* (Camolar), the embonate of the dehydrotriazine metabolite of proguanil, gives long-term protection, and is given i.m. as a suspension in oil, in a dose of 5 mg/kg body weight. A single dose can protect against *P. falciparum*, *P. vivax*, or *P. malariae* for 3–4 months provided the parasites are sensitive to it, but the drug has gained only limited acceptance in malaria. It can be used in leishmaniasis (p. 84).

Chlorproguanil (Lapudrine). One 20 mg tablet weekly provides adequate prophylaxis.

Indications

Proguanil now has no place in the treatment of malaria. As a prophylactic agent against sensitive strains of malaria, it is efficient if taken daily as above, or weekly in the form chlorproguanil. It is one of the safest antimalarial prophylactic drugs for use in pregnancy.

Adverse Effects

Toxicity. Minor gastrointestinal complaints have been reported following proguanil but no serious side-effects.

Interactions

Proguanil must not be given with primaquine, since it inhibits the metabolism of the latter, aggravating possible toxicity.

Pyrimethamine and Pyrimethamine Combinations

PYRIMETHAMINE

This antifolate drug resembles trimethoprim, as a 2,4-diaminopyrimidine. It is used both alone and in combination for the prevention of malaria and in combination for the treatment of resistant malaria.

Mode of Action

Pyrimethamine is a competitive inhibitor of dihydrofolate reductase. It therefore diminishes formation of tetrahydrofolate, essential for thymidine synthesis. Resistant plasmodia have been shown to contain increased levels of dihydrofolate reductase, which lessen the efficacy of pyrimethamine.

Pharmacokinetics

Pyrimethamine is well absorbed from the gut and tissue binding is more marked than with proguanil. Metabolism accounts for the disappearance of most of the drug from the plasma and the remainder is excreted by the kidney.

Preparations

Pyrimethamine (Daraprim). 25 mg tablets are available. One or two tablets weekly are sufficient to provide prophylaxis against susceptible parasites.

Pyrimethamine 25 mg, *sulfadoxine* 500 mg (Fansidar). Used after quinine treatment of resistant malaria in a single dose of 3 tablets, it may be curative. For the prophylaxis of resistant malaria, one tablet is taken weekly.

Pyrimethamine 12.5 mg, *dapsone* 100 mg (Maloprim). Adult prophylaxis of chloroquine-resistant malaria is achieved with one tablet weekly.

Indications

Pyrimethamine acts on dividing schizonts, but its action on ring forms is too slow for it to be used alone for the treatment of an acute attack. As it will inactivate the pre-erythrocytic stage of falciparum parasites, it is a causal prophylactic of this kind of malaria and a suppressive prophylactic of non-falciparum malaria. Used with other drugs, such as sulfadoxine or dapsone, it is a valuable prophylactic for chloroquine- and proguanil-resistant parasites and, with sulfadoxine, it can be used for treating resistant malaria and also toxoplasmosis. Already certain areas have shown some malarial parasites to be pyrimethamine-resistant. There is usually some cross-resistance with proguanil-resistant parasites. Pyrimethamine alone has been helpful in the treatment of polycythaemia rubra vera resistant to standard therapy and in the prevention of meningeal relapse in childhood leukaemia.

Adverse Effects

Toxicity. Low doses may cause gastrointestinal upset. High doses have been reported to precipitate convulsions. It may induce folate deficiency, since it does not spare mammalian dihydrofolate reductase to the same extent as trimethoprim. If folate deficiency occurs, it is reversible with folinic acid. Those who are already folate-deficient can have this depletion corrected with folic acid (p. 467) before pyrimethamine is given. High dose Maloprim may rarely cause agranulocytosis.

Contraindications

Pyrimethamine should not be administered to a pregnant patient if other suitable safer drugs are available. If there is no alternative, folic acid supplements should be given. The pyrimethamine–dapsone combination (Maloprim) is preferable to the pyrimethamine–sulfadoxine combination (Fansidar) in pregnancy. Fansidar should not be given to sulphonamide-sensitive patients.

Mepacrine

Mepacrine hydrochloride is now almost completely outmoded as an antimalarial agent, though it was given to allied troops in the Far East during World War II so successfully that it became a court-martial offence to develop malaria. It remains valuable as one of the few drugs in the group that may be given i.m. The dose is 100–300 mg 6-hourly and it is used in acute falciparum crises when other drugs are not available. It cannot be given i.v. It has no place in prophylaxis, since it may stain skin, induce gastritis, dermatitis and psychosis, and it interferes with the metabolism of primaquine. It has a small place as an anthelmintic against tapeworms and in giardiasis.

AMOEBICIDES

The protozoan *Entamoeba histolytica* is responsible for the disease called amoebiasis. The portal of entry of the encysted organisms is the mouth and digestion of the encasement occurs in the small intestine. The amoebae are released and divide to form motile trophozoites which attack the bowel mucosa and sometimes follow the enterohepatic circulation to infect the liver. Thus syndromes which include forms of dysentery, bowel granuloma, hepatitis and hepatic abscess may follow amoebic infestation. A minor bout of diarrhoea may be the only sign of amoebiasis, or, indeed, there may be no clinical features whatsoever. It is not surprising, therefore, that there are many carriers of the disease in certain countries. Trophozoites are not readily purged from the bowel and may re-encyst in colonic mucosa. New cysts are then shed into the bowel and form a reservoir for reinfection by the orofaecal route.

Because of the trophozoite and cyst forms of infestation and the variety of pathological conditions that can be caused by *Entamoeba histolytica*, a bewildering number of different drugs has been advocated for amoebiasis. Direct-acting amoebicides include di-iodohydroxyquinoline (Diodoquin) and diloxanide furoate (Furamide), but these only attack the intraluminal amoebae (particularly cysts) and do not significantly affect gut-wall-situated amoebae. Tetracyclines will affect amoebae in the lumen and wall of the bowel, but do not penetrate the liver. Emetine hydrochloride and the less toxic dehydroemetine control amoebae both in the gut wall and liver. Chloroquine is highly concentrated in the liver, but is less effective against amoebae situated elsewhere. The use of metronidazole in amoebiasis has revolutionized therapy because this reasonably safe drug is effective against the vegetative forms and penetrates the tissues, including the liver. It is the drug of choice for dysenteric and hepatitic forms of amoebiasis, but is relatively ineffective against cysts for which diloxanide furoate may be used. Tinidazole, by contrast, is effective in all forms of amoebiasis, including the treatment of cyst passers.

Metronidazole and Tinidazole

METRONIDAZOLE

The 5-nitroimidazoles are a fascinating antimicrobial family. Metronidazole was originally developed as an anti-trichomonas agent and was subsequently shown to be effective against *Entamoeba histolytica, Giardia lamblia* and *Balantidium coli*. It has more recently been recognized as an important antibacterial agent whose spectrum includes obligate anaerobes only. Tinidazole is a closely related drug with a longer half-life and higher plasma concentrations. It is as effective on initial trials as metronidazole in amoebiasis and anaerobic bacterial infections and it may have advantages in less frequent dosing and even loss toxicity. Unlike metronidazole, tinidaxole is effective in treating cyst passers. Other 5-nitroimidazoles will doubtless be developed.

Mode of Action
The 5-nitroimidazoles are taken up equally well by aerobic and anaerobic bacteria. In anaerobes, however, metronidazole is reduced, whereas in aerobes it is not. The reduced metronidazole forms metabolites which probably interfere with the ability of the anaerobic bacterium to synthesize nucleic acids. The presence of oxygen impairs the antibacterial action of metronidazole. It is thought to act in a similar fashion against anaerobic protozoa.

Pharmacokinetics
The drug is usually absorbed well from the gut, whether given orally or by suppository, though some variability has been noted. Diffusion is good and therapeutic concentrations are achieved in bile, CSF and in abscesses caused by anaerobic bacteria or amoebae. The half-life of metronidazole is about 8 hours and for tinidazole 12 hours after oral administration.

Preparations

Metronidazole (Flagyl, Vaginyl). Tablets of 200 or 400 mg are available, a suspension (Flagyl S) with 200 mg in 5 ml and metronidazole suppositories (Flagyl) containing either 500 mg or 1 g. For i.v. use, Flagyl is available in 20 ml ampoules or bottles of 100 ml containing 5 mg/ml.

Amoebic dysentery and hepatitis may be treated with oral metronidazole in divided doses of 1.2 g daily for 6–8 days or 2.4 g daily for 5 days. Cyst carriers receive orally 1.2–1.6 g daily for 5–10 days or 1.6–2.4 g on 2 successive days. Tinidazole is now the preferred therapy for cyst carriers. These are the doses for adults.

Giardiasis is treated by 2 g daily for 3 days by mouth.

Urogenital trichomoniasis is treated with a single oral dose of 2 g, 200 mg 8-hourly for 7 days or a 2-day regimen with 800 mg in the morning and 1.2 g at night.

Ulcerative gingivitis is treated by 200 mg 8-hourly for 3 days.

Anaerobic bacterial infections. For treatment, adults should receive 400 mg every 8 hours by mouth and children 7.5 mg/kg body weight every 8 hours. Adults may receive a 1 g and children a 500 mg suppository inserted rectally every 8 hours as a temporary expedient. I.v. dosage is 500 mg by slow infusion in adults every 8 hours and 7.5 mg/kg body weight 8-hourly for children.

For prevention of anaerobic infections before gynaecological surgery, a 1 g oral loading dose and then 200 mg 8-hourly by mouth are given preoperatively (except when oral medication is temporarily discontinued). For elective colonic surgery, a variety of oral dose regimens is available (with oral kanamycin or a non-absorbable sulphonamide) and metronidazole suppositories are given when oral medication is discontinued. For appendicectomy, 8-hourly insertion of a suppository is recommended until oral medication can be taken again. I.v. metronidazole may be used in emergency situations perioperatively where mixed or anaerobic sepsis is likely. In all instances the drug should not be started earlier than 3–4 days before surgery.

Tinidazole (Fasigyn). Routine dosage schedules have now been recommended for use in anaerobic bacterial infections and the longer half-life of tinidazole allows less frequent administration than for metronidazole. Oral tinidazole is given during a meal in doses of 2 g initially, followed by 1 g daily or 500 mg twice daily for 5 or 6 days in anaerobic infections; for prevention of postoperative infections, a single 2 g oral dose is given with the last permitted oral intake and similarly for treating ulcerative gingivitis, 2 g is given. I.v. tinidazole is given as a single initial dose of 800 mg, followed by 800 mg daily until it can be taken by mouth. The i.v. route by slow infusion can also be used immediately before surgery to prevent perioperative sepsis.

Tinidazole may become the drug of choice in amoebiasis and giardiasis, but at present there is less information about its safety in children or pregnant women.

Indications

Metronidazole was first employed in urogenital trichomoniasis, where it has proved very successful as long as consorts of the patients are also treated. It is amoebicidal in the intestine and liver and is now the drug of choice in treating amoebiasis. It can be employed in invasive intestinal disease, amoebic hepatitis and amoebic liver abscess, but for symptomless cyst carriers tinidazole is better. Both are effective in giardiasis and acute ulcerative gingivitis.

In anaerobic infections, metronidazole is employed when bacteria have been identified or are suspected as pathogens, particularly *Bacteroides fragilis*, other forms of bacteroides, fusobacteria, eubacteria, clostridia and anaerobic cocci. It has been used successfully in septicaemia, brain abscess, necrotizing pneumonia, osteomyelitis, puerperal sepsis, pelvic cellulitis, pelvic abscess and postoperative wound infection with appropriate organisms. It is also employed to prevent postoperative infections, which often contain anaerobic bacteria together with aerobes. Although metronidazole has no effect on aerobes, mixed infections frequently respond.

Presumably the anaerobes are destroyed first and then the body's own defences clear the aerobic pathogens.

The i.v. preparation is used in patients with severe anaerobic infection for whom oral medication is not possible and in patients needing surgery who are believed to have anaerobic sepsis such as septicaemia, peritonitis, or subphrenic or pelvic abscesses, or who have ulcerative bowel disease.

Adverse Effects

Toxicity. Nausea, vomiting, diarrhoea and headache are the principal complaints associated with metronidazole. Rarely, stomatitis, leucopenia, rashes, pruritus and paraesthesiae have been reported. High doses of metronidazole may impair judgement sufficiently to make driving dangerous.

Interactions

Metronidazole should not be taken after the ingestion of alcohol. Numerous unpleasant effects have been reported and, indeed, the drug has been applied in aversion therapy for alcoholism. Large doses of the drug certainly inhibit alcohol dehydrogenase, thus lessening the metabolism of alcohol, but the mechanism of interaction at low doses is unknown. Combination of metronidazole with disulfiram, much used in aversion therapy, may lead to acute psychosis, again by an unexplained mechanism.

Emetine

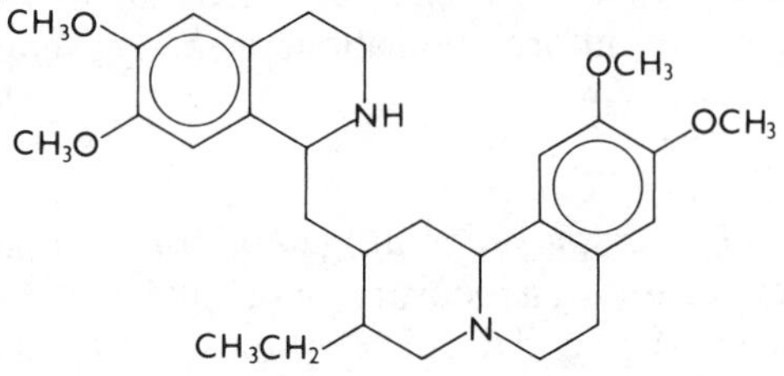

EMETINE

Emetine and dehydroemetine are toxic amoebicides which are used less today than formerly. They are derived from ipecacuanha. The name emetine is derived from the Greek ἕμετος, meaning vomiting, whereas ipecacuanha is a Portuguese word derived from other languages and said to mean 'low or creeping plant causing vomiting'.

Mode of Action

Tissue culture experiments, using human cell lines, hint at an early suppression of RNA synthesis by emetine and this is followed by, or perhaps induces, a fall in DNA synthesis. Emetine structurally resembles cycloheximide, which has the above effects on yeasts and protozoa in culture. Whether emetine harms amoebae in that fashion remains uncertain. What is known is that most damage is done to trophozoites and minimal change is seen in the encysted parasites in the gut. Emetine is concentrated preferentially in the liver and is rapidly effective in the treatment of hepatic amoebiasis unless abscess formation has already occurred.

Pharmacokinetics

Oral administration of emetine hydrochloride is not feasible, because of the immediate regurgitation which is produced. Dehydroemetine, however, is better tolerated by mouth, but should be given with meals. I.m. or deep s.c. injection of either emetine or dehydroemetine is advisable, since the i.v. route is likely to give rise to cardiotoxicity and may cause death. Absorption from the injection site is rapid, but excretion, probably by the bowel, is slow and gradual cumulation may develop. Dehydroemetine is less cumulative and less cardiotoxic, but may be less effective than emetine. The late release form of dehydroemetine has given excellent results in acute amoebic dysentery either above or following parenteral treatment. The oral preparation, emetine and bismuth iodide, is marketed in a gelatin capsule to lessen gastric irritation and to release emetine gradually into the bowel lumen. Variable absorption then takes place, so it is not dependable in the treatment of hepatic infestation and is not used in the initial treatment of intestinal infection. It has few uses today.

Preparations

Emetine hydrochloride. Ampoules containing 30 or 60 mg/ml are marketed. The substance should be protected from the light. A useful dose guide is 1 mg/kg body weight up to a maximum of 65 mg in one daily injection, treatment being continued for a week. A watchful eye must be kept for signs of cumulative toxicity. Repeated courses are inadvisable.

Dehydroemetine hydrochloride. This is used in a similar fashion to emetine, with identical recommendations for i.m. injection. It can also be used orally as the resinate in divided doses of 1 mg/kg body weight/day or as the late release formulation in a daily dose of 60 mg, also given in divided doses.

Emetine and bismuth iodide. Tablets of 60 mg and coated capsules of 200 mg are the main forms of the drug. A nightly dose of 200 mg is best given after the evening meal, but it may be necessary to give an antiemetic at the same time.

Indications

In the treatment of amoebiasis, the imidazoles have almost completely replaced emetine. However, emetine hydrochloride still has a place in treating severe hepatic amoebiasis and its action is improved by concomitant or subsequent chloroquine sulphate therapy in a dose of 400–800 mg daily. Encysted amoebae are immune to emetine hydrochloride, dehydroemetine hydrochloride and chloroquine. Emetine and bismuth iodide does kill the encysted gut forms and is a reasonable cure, provided it is tolerated for a full course of 12 days.

Adverse Effects

Toxicity. The most threatening sequelae are cardiac and they include tachycardia, dysrhythmias and hypotension. At least half of all patients taking emetine show some alteration of the electrocardiogram, such as T-wave flattening and inversion, and prolongation of the P–R and Q–T intervals. These changes do not necessarily constitute grounds for stopping the drug, but must be taken in the context of the clinical situation.

Minor side-effects, apart from the gastric intolerance mentioned already, include muscular weakness, faintness, headache, tremor, paraesthesiae and pain at the site of injections.

Contraindications

Emetine hydrochloride is not advisable in pregnancy or old age, or in patients suffering from cardiac impairment. Even in otherwise fit people, bed rest is advised during treatment, and regular scrutiny of pulse and blood pressure assists early diagnosis of side-effects on the myocardium.

Diloxanide Furoate

Diloxanide (Furamide) is a safe, well-absorbed amoebicide, useful in chronic gut disease in a dose of 500 mg 8-hourly for 10 days. It is present in serum as the glucuronide, which is almost entirely excreted by the kidney. Side-effects are occasional flatulence and nausea.

Di-iodohydroxyquinoline

By contrast with diloxanide furoate, this 8-hydroxyquinoline, di-iodohydroxyquinoline (Diodoquin), is minimally absorbed and kills amoebae locally in the intestine. It is used in mild or asymptomatic disease in a dose of 600 mg 8-hourly for 21 days. Side-effects are not common, but include mild goitre, nausea, diarrhoea and skin rashes. Allergy to iodine is an obvious contraindication.

OTHER ANTIPROTOZOAL DRUGS

Antimonials, pentamidine isethionate, suramin, arsenicals and nitrofurazone are discussed.

Antimonials

Salts of antimony may be trivalent or pentavalent. The latter are the drugs of choice in treating leishmaniasis; the former used to be employed in the therapy of schistosomiasis, but there are now safer drugs available. There is evidence that only the trivalent preparations are active and that pentavalent compounds must be broken down into the trivalent form prior to protozoal killing. Inorganic metals tend to be irritant to the host, so several organic salts have been prepared in order to minimize the effects produced by antimony.

Mode of Action
Trivalent antimonials are known to inhibit the enzyme phosphofructokinase. This prevents the protozoa from completing the anaerobic metabolism of glucose, essential for their survival. The exact mode of interference with phosphofructokinase is not known, but the effect on the organism is predictable, since paralysis occurs and then death. A much higher dose of antimonial is required to alter glucose metabolism in the human host, allowing a reasonable margin of safety between therapeutic and toxic levels of the drug. The mode of action of pentavalent compounds is not yet clear.

Pharmacokinetics
Antimony causes irritation on local application and, predictably, is not suitable for oral ingestion. Most preparations are given i.m., with the exception of sodium antimony tartrate, which causes tissue necrosis and must be administered i.v. The trivalent drugs bind to tissues and especially to red cells; subsequent excretion is slow and is by the kidneys. Antimony may be recovered in the urine up to 3 months after a course has finished. Pentavalent compounds are excreted more rapidly, owing to their lower affinity for cells.

Preparations: Pentavalent

Sodium stibogluconate (Pentostam). This contains 100 mg/ml pentavalent antimony for i.m. or i.v. use. Adults receive 6 ml (600 mg pentavalent antimony or 2 g sodium stibogluconate) daily. For kala-azar in adults, this dose should be given for 7–10 days, but two or three further courses, separated by 10 day intervals, may be required. Recent studies on kala-azar in Kenya suggest using a daily dose of sodium stibogluconate (20 mg i.m./kg body weight per day) for 2–4 weeks, which appears to give a faster clinical and parasitical response. Similar dosage may be given in cutaneous leishmaniasis, possibly combined with oral rifampicin and isoniazid. In diffuse cutaneous leishmaniasis 2% chlorpromazine in a keratolytic ointment may be applied topically. In the muco-cutaneous form, 6 ml sodium stibogluconate daily for 10 days can be repeated, if necessary, on two occasions at monthly intervals. Cutaneous lesions of leishmania may be individually injected with 0.6 g in 5 ml of water infiltrated circumferentially around the bite or sore.

Meglumine antimonate. Ampoules containing 1.5 g in 5 ml of a 30% solution are dispensed. The usual dose range is 0.2–0.3 ml/kg body weight daily for 10 days by i.m. injection. Repeated cycles should not be given until 4 weeks free of treatment have elapsed.

Preparations: Trivalent

Stibocaptate (Astiban). This compound comprises about 27% antimony. It is presented lyophilized in 2 g vials. Immediately before use, the material is dissolved in 20 ml of water and given by deep i.m. injection in a total dose up to a maximum of 2.5 g. The total may be divided into five daily injections, or, more acceptably, may be given twice weekly over 3 weeks. Some preparations include 2 ml of 2% procaine to minimize the pain at injection sites.

Antimony sodium tartrate. Stable 6% solutions are available, or, alternatively, the white powder is readily soluble in water. The compound contains 40% of antimony and must be given very slowly i.v., for, though the most potent of the group, it is also the most irritant. A small dose of 30 mg is injected initially and then 60 mg two days later, and 120 mg two days after that. If that dose is tolerated, it is persevered with to a total dose of 1.5–2 g. The more protracted the course of injections, the fewer the side-effects.

Indications

Leishmaniasis may be restricted to the skin in one area (oriental sore) or the distribution may be widespread (American mucocutaneous leishmaniasis). Kala-azar is a widely accepted name for visceral leishmaniasis. All forms of the infestation are likely to be susceptible to sodium stibogluconate in most areas. Meglumine antimonate is used primarily in Latin America and in French-speaking countries. The limited cutaneous oriental sore may not require treatment with anything other than an antibiotic, though eventual direct infiltration with antimony may be required.

Pentamidine isethionate (p. 85) should no longer be used in leishmaniasis. It may have an occasional role in treating *Pneumocystis carinii* infection in patients intolerant to co-trimoxazole.

Alternative drugs useful in mucocutaneous and cutaneous leishmaniasis are amphotericin B (p. 56), a toxic parenteral antifungal agent, and cycloguanil, mentioned earlier (p. 74), in the consideration of antimalarial chemotherapy. The trivalent antimonials used to be the main drugs for the treatment of schistosomiasis. Since the advent of oral alternatives such as niridazole and praziquantel, the more toxic parenteral antimony drugs have been demoted to the reserve choice, especially in *Schistosoma haematobium* infections.

Adverse Effects

Toxicity. Local tissue necrosis may be caused by any of the antimonials, but sodium antimony tartrate is a particular offender. Given i.v., phlebitis is common and may lead to difficulties in finding sufficient peripheral veins for subsequent infusions. Cardiotoxicity is important and may be manifested by bradycardia, dysrhythmias and circulatory collapse. Electrocardiographic changes occur frequently and persist for some months after cessation of therapy. Strenuous exercise is contraindicated and hospital supervision, though not always practicable, is preferred.

As excretion of antimony salts is by glomeruli, renal disease leads to marked prolongation of tissue levels, so that subsequent injections rapidly induce toxicity. Common effects are abdominal pain, nausea and vomiting, joint and muscle pains, headaches, pruritus, and a maculopapular rash. Rare unrelated sequelae are haemolytic anaemia, hepatitis and lobar pneumonia.

Antidotes. Dimercaprol by i.m. injection reverses the effects of antimonials, and *dimercaptosuccinic acid* orally is suitable for treating toxicity due to stibocaptate.

Contraindications

Pre-existing cardiac, renal or hepatic insufficiency is the principal contraindication to the use of these drugs. Dosage should be reduced and caution exercised when the patient is young or suffering from malnutrition.

Pentamidine Isethionate

$$HN=C(H_2N)-\langle\rangle-OCH_2(CH_2)_3CH_2O-\langle\rangle-C(=NH)(NH_2)$$

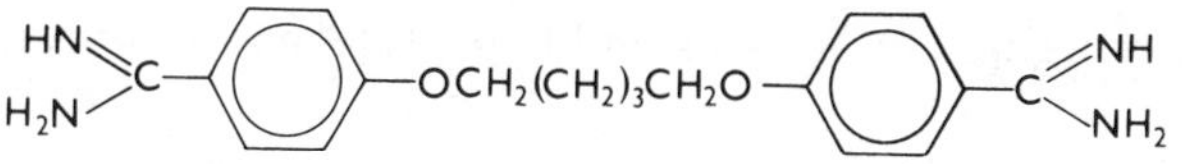

PENTAMIDINE

Pentamidine is a diamidine antiprotozoal compound. It was previously used as a second-line drug for visceral kala-azar and for African trypanosomiasis that had not yet invaded the brain. Now its main indication is in treating *Pneumocystis carinii* infection in immunocompromised patients who cannot tolerate co-trimoxazole. It acts by interfering with either the glucose metabolism or the liposomal enzymes of the trypanosome.

Pharmacokinetics

Pentamidine isethionate is injected i.m., or i.v. in a slow infusion. Distribution is good, except to the cerebrospinal fluid, so the drug is ineffective in late trypanosomiasis involving the CNS. It is bound and excreted, mostly unaltered, very slowly by the kidneys, so a single injection gives adequate protection for several months.

Preparations

Pentamidine isethionate (Lomidine). The drug is dispensed as a white powder, 200 mg being in each ampoule, for dissolving in water. The usual dose range is 300–400 mg daily for 10 days, and it is given by i.m. injection. As a prophylactic against trypanosomiasis, the dose was 300 mg two or three times each year.

Indications

The main use of the drug was previously in the prevention of trypanosomiasis. It was of no value in established disease involving the nervous system, but could be curative if utilized early, particularly in the West African variety. The East African strain of trypanosome was more resistant to pentamidine, and suramin is the drug of choice in early infection. Central nervous involvement in East or West Africa demands treatment by an arsenical or by nitrofurazone (p. 89).

Pentamidine is effective in the treatment of pneumonitis due to *P. carinii*, which is rarely seen other than in primary immunodeficiency in children or following immunosuppression by drugs or radiotherapy as a complication of lymphoproliferative disease. Co-trimoxazole (p. 51) has now been shown to be a safer alternative for treating *P. carinii* infections.

Adverse Effects

Toxicity. Immediate effects are notably pain at the injection site, fall in blood pressure, tachycardia, nausea and vomiting. Adrenaline injections (p. 223) will reverse the cardiovascular effects and may be held in readiness. Rare toxicity in the form of peripheral neuritis and hypoglycaemia has been recorded.

Suramin

The sodium salt of 8-naphthalene-1,3,5-trisulphonic acid is an effective trypanocide. It also has a part to play in treating some filarial diseases. It is a dye derivative and its mechanism of action is unknown.

Pharmacokinetics

Administration is by the i.v. route, since absorption from the gut is unreliable. In the circulation it binds to protein of plasma and tissue, but is slowly released, so that it persists in the body for several weeks. Like pentamidine (p. 85), it does not penetrate to the CNS. Excretion is slow and is by the kidneys. Some of the drug may be retained in renal tissue, giving rise to albuminuria.

Preparations

Sodium suramin (Antrypol). The white powder will dissolve to form a 10% solution in water. Ampoules of 1 g are usually dispensed and a convenient dose for trypanosomiasis is one ampoule on days 1, 3, 7, 14 and 21, or alternatively, 1 g weekly for 5 weeks. A prophylactic regimen involves giving the same or a smaller dose fortnightly. Suramin is moderately active against the microfilariae and kills the adult worms of *Onchocerca volvulus*, but because of its toxicity should only be used if ocular involvement has occurred. First, diethylcarbamazine is used to destroy microfilariae, then suramin may be cautiously employed. A 100 mg test dose of suramin is given i.v. and then 1 g weekly for 5 weeks. Some weeks later a further course of diethylcarbamazine is recommended.

Indications

Suramin is a first-line drug in the eradication of African trypanosomiasis, provided that central nervous invasion has not taken place. It may be used as a pretreatment drug before melarsoprol is given in meningoencephalitic trypanosomiasis (p. 88). It is also useful in the filarial infestation caused by *Onchocerca volvulus* when the eye is involved.

Adverse Effects

Idiosyncrasy. Approximately 1 patient in 4000 has an anaphylactoid reaction after his first exposure to suramin. For this reason a test dose of 100–200 mg is advisable prior to infusion of the total dose. It is recommended that drugs be available for immediate resuscitation.

Toxicity. Albuminuria may be accompanied by haematuria and serious renal damage. Rather obscure reactions have been reported, such as tenderness of the palms and the soles, chronic mouth ulcers, exfoliative dermatitis, diarrhoea, agranulocytosis and haemolytic anaemia. In addition to these drug-related side-effects which may occur in the management of trypanosomiasis, the treatment of onchocerciasis by suramin frequently gives side-effects such as deep abscesses, arthropathy and urticaria due to the death of the adult worms. Some weeks later, the destruction of microfilariae may cause dermatitis, pruritic vesicular eruptions, fever, bronchitis, iritis and further arthropathy.

Contraindications

Renal insufficiency is an absolute contraindication, and so too is known idiosyncrasy to suramin. Cautious administration is advisable in seriously ill, debilitated patients.

Arsenicals

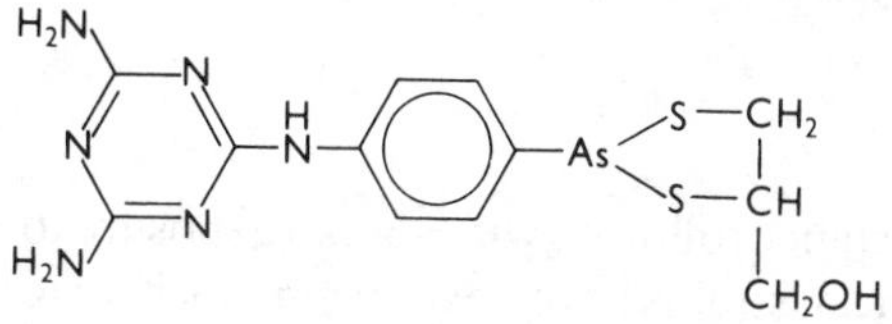

MELARSOPROL

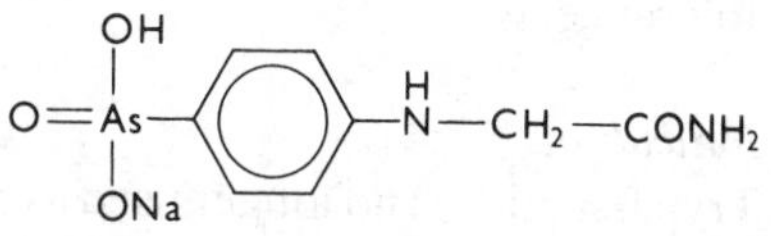

TRYPARSAMIDE

Trivalent and pentavalent arsenic compounds are available. As occurs with the antimonials, the pentavalent drug is believed to be altered to a trivalent arsenical in the body, thus increasing the trypanocidal effect of the drug. The use of arsenicals in the treatment of syphilis, something that was formerly widely practised, is now outmoded and their main application is in the therapy of African trypanosomiasis involving the nervous system.

Mode of Action

The arsenic derivatives broadly inhibit cellular enzyme reactions involved in the metabolic and respiratory pathways in protozoa. The exact site of interference is not clear, though it may be at the sulphydryl groups on the enzymes. It is probable that such an indelicate non-specific interaction does not occur in the host cells, because of a block at the human cell membrane which keeps arsenic from contact with cytoplasmic structures. Certainly the parasites are penetrated by the drug to a greater degree than the host cells.

Preparations

Melarsoprol (Mel B). This compound consists of trivalent melarsen oxide and dimercaprol (BAL). It is given i.v. with caution, and ampoules are marketed as a 3.6% solution in propylene glycol. The dose varies according to the part of the world in which the substance is used. For instance, in West Africa it is 3.6 mg/kg body weight (up to 5 ml) daily for 3 days, repeated 1 week later if required. The course may be escalated more gradually if necessary, and, certainly, less toxicity will then accrue. Particular caution is recommended in planning treatment of the same disease in East Africa. An initial dose is often 0.5 ml, and increments of 0.5 ml are added each day, treatment being given on three consecutive days with rests of 1 week being observed. The dose used in West Africa (5 ml) may not be reached until the last course, at least 1 month after initiation of injections. There are genetically determined variations in toxic reactions to drugs. Melarsoprol is effective, therefore, in both East and West African trypanosomiasis, but because of its toxicity it should probably be reserved for infestations with CNS involvement.

Melarsonyl potassium (Mel W). This trivalent analogue of melarsoprol is less irritant and may be injected i.m. Vials consist of 200 mg of a white powder which may be dissolved in water. A dose of 3–4 mg/kg body weight daily up to 200 mg is injected for 4 days. No drugs are then given for 2 weeks, and thereafter the cycle is repeated. As indicated above, melarsonyl may be given in small doses expanded more gently according to the individual patient's tolerance.

Indications

Tryparsamide is no longer used as resistance followed widespread exposure to the drug in West Africa. The East African strains have never been sensitive to tryparsamide. Melarsoprol is the drug of choice in either variety of trypanosomiasis which has progressed to established neurological complications. Melarsonyl potassium is useful because it can be given i.m., but its efficacy in the East African disease is under question. To reduce the likelihood of an allergic encephalopathy to arsenicals, it is recommended that pretreatment with a non-arsenical trypanocide such as suramin be given in patients with meningoencephalitic as opposed to haematolymphatic trypanosomiasis.

Early trypanosomiasis may be eradicated by a single exposure to melarsoprol, but, owing to the danger of serious toxicity, this drug is reserved for patients who cannot tolerate suramin or who have CNS involvement.

Adverse Effects

Toxicity. A wide range of destructive properties are attributed to the arsenicals. Among the most serious are encephalopathy of varying degrees, agranulocytosis, peripheral neuropathy and albuminuria. The risk of encephalopathy is reduced by pretreatment with a non-arsenical drug. Varied skin reactions include desquamation over the legs, hyperkeratosis of the feet, exfoliative dermatitis and angioneurotic oedema. The Jarisch–Herxheimer reaction may accompany the death of large numbers of trypanosomes and frequently leads to coma.

Antidotes. Dimercaprol in a dose of 3 mg/kg body weight i.m. 4-hourly may reverse some of the toxicity due to overdosage of arsenicals. *Melarsoprol* (Mel B) already contains dimercaprol. Large doses of ascorbic acid have been claimed to lessen toxic effects and may be given along with melarsoprol as a prophylactic measure.

Nitrofurazone

Nitrofurazone is an oral trypanocide as effective as the arsenicals, but very toxic and therefore used after the latter drugs have failed. The dose is 500 mg daily for 3 days, then 500 mg 8-hourly for a week, repeated three times with a week's rest between each course. The predictable side-effects are a polyneuropathy which is said to be prevented to a certain extent if thiamine (p. 448) is given, and acute haemolysis in patients who lack glucose-6-phosphate dehydrogenase (p. 564). Numerous less toxic symptoms may be expected, such as vomiting, headache, urticaria, hyperpigmentation and excitability.

ANTHELMINTICS

A wide choice of agents is available for the control of worm infestation. Although several are discussed in this section, mention should first be made of six of the safest and most effective anthelmintics. Most are not listed in the

Data Sheet Compendium of the Association of the British Pharmaceutical Industry, 1983–84.

Praziquantel has no equal at present in efficacy, safety and convenience in the treatment of the three main types of schistosomiasis. It is superior not only to the antimony compounds, but also to lucanthone, hycanthone, metrifonate, niridazole and oxamniquine.

For ascariasis and most hookworm infestations, *levamisole hydrochloride*, *pyrantel embonate* and *mebendazole* are the drugs of choice. Bephenium hydroxynaphthoate is useful for some hookworm diseases, but is now a 'second-line' drug. Mebendazole is also used for whipworm and threadworm eradication rather than viprynium embonate, hexylresorcinol or piperazine salts. *Thiabendazole* is preferred for strongyloidiasis. For the destruction of tapeworms, *niclosamide* is the most effective and safe agent, but should be followed by purgation in the case of *Taenia solium* disease.

In this section some of the drugs mentioned are not those of first choice, but they are still widely used, especially overseas, their being relatively inexpensive compared to some of the more recent preparations.

Praziquantel

Originally developed as a veterinary taeniacide (Droncit), this pyrazino-isoquinalone will soon become available as the first-line drug for managing schistosomiasis, having an effect against all three species, *Schistosoma haematobium*, *S. mansoni* and *S. japonicum*. It also acts on the liver flukes *Clonorchis sinensis*, *Opisthorchis viverrini* and *felineus* and the lung flukes *Paragonimus* spp. The parasites quickly contract and become immobile in contact with the drug. Vacuoles develop in the tegument of the worm and its glucose metabolism is also upset by praziquantel. The drug is well absorbed after oral administration and is best taken as unchewed tablets with water after a meal. The maximum serum concentration is reached between 1 and 3 hours later and the serum half-life is between 1 and 1.5 hours. The drug is metabolized and the metabolites are excreted in the urine mostly the same day.

Preparations

Praziquantel (Biltricide). This is available in lacquered tablets of 600 mg. For *S. haematobium*, *S. mansoni* and *S. intercalatum*, a single oral dose of 40 mg/kg body weight is given. For *S. japonicum*, 30 mg/kg body weight is given twice on the same day, the doses 4–6 hours apart. For *Clonorchis sinensis*, 25 mg/kg body weight is given three times on the same day, the doses 4–6 hours apart, and for *Paragonimus westermani* infestation, the same dose as for *Clonorchis* is given, but spread over 2 days.

Adverse Effects

The drug is well tolerated, but occasionally causes mild, transient abdominal pain, nausea, headache, dizziness, fever and rarely urticaria.

Oxamniquine

This anti-schistosomal drug is a yellow dye, originally given by i.m. injection, but replaced now by oral therapy because the parenteral route was very painful. It is active only against *Schistosoma mansoni*, which limits its usefulness. Some parasites are relatively resistant and in Zimbabwe and Egypt the standard dose of 15–30 mg/kg body weight given at night for 2 days may require to be doubled. It is available as Vansil in 500 mg capsules. Side-effects include sleepiness, but are minimal if the drug is given on retiring.

Niridazole

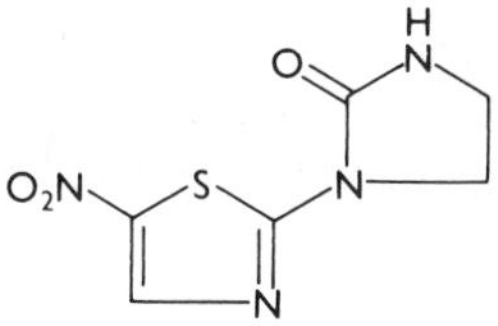

NIRIDAZOLE

Niridazole is a nitrothiazole administered orally for the treatment of schistosomiasis. It is safer than the antimonials and particularly suited to children. It is also effective in amoebiasis and guineaworm infestation.

Mode of Action

The drug selectively induces breakdown of glycogen stored in the parasite and not in the host. Other than that effect, little else is known of the mode of action on carbohydrate metabolism. There is an arrest of eggshell formation by the female worms, and spermatogenesis is inhibited in the male parasites. The effect on spermatogenesis is also reported to occur in animals; human studies are not yet conclusive.

Pharmacokinetics

Absorption after oral ingestion is good and the drug is quickly metabolized in the liver. The metabolites are excreted by the kidney and may lead to a brown discoloration of the urine. It is unlikely that any of the breakdown products are active against schistosomes.

Preparations

Niridazole (Ambilhar). The tablet size is 500 mg. The drug is given with food in a dose of 25 mg/kg body weight in divided daily doses for 1 week.

Indications

Niridazole was the drug of choice in infections caused by *Schistosoma haematobium* or *S. mansoni* without significant hepatic involvement, but it has been replaced by oxamniquine and more recently by praziquantel. If there is considerable hepatic involvement, niridazole is poorly tolerated and the incidence of psychiatric symptoms is very high. *S. japonicum* has not often been exposed to niridazole in clinical trials, though the same caveat obtains as for *S. mansoni* infestations when the liver is involved.

Adverse Effects

Toxicity. Gastritis is so frequent that the drug should be taken with food in an attempt to make it more acceptable. Headaches and maculopapular rashes are commonplace. Of greater note is the accumulation of unmetabolized drug when the liver is compromised by the infestation. Behaviour disorders will then develop and are likely to be followed by severe emotional disturbances and eventual exhaustion going on to coma or, in children, convulsions. Electrocardiographic changes may be noted, but are not, per se, grounds for discontinuing treatment. The drug is not suitable for patients who have glucose-6-phosphate dehydrogenase deficiency, in whom it may induce haemolysis.

Interactions

Phenobarbitone induces metabolism of niridazole by the liver and may lessen the risk of CNS toxicity due to liver infection by *S. mansoni* or *S. japonicum*.

Contraindications

The drug is not advised in pregnancy, because of possible teratogenicity.

Hycanthone

The orally acceptable antischistosomal drug *lucanthone* (Nilodin), derived from a yellow dye, was effective against *S. haematobium*, but its side-effects of vomiting and skin staining limited its use. Its analogue, *hycanthone*, also a yellow dye, was derived as a metabolite of the action of *Aspergillus* spp. on lucanthone. Although it can be given orally, i.m. hycanthone is preferred in a single dose of 1.5–2.0 mg/kg body weight (maximum total adult dose 100 mg). Side-effects, including vomiting and, rarely, hepatic necrosis, are encountered if the dose is increased. Hycanthone is more effective against *S. mansoni* than *S. haematobium*. Both lucanthone and hycanthone may have a limited role to play in certain parts of the world, although other drugs are now usually preferred.

Metrifonate

Metrifonate (Dipterex, Bilarcil). This organophosphorus compound is effective against *S. haematobium* and some intestinal nematodes. The worms are paralysed by metrifonate which inhibits cholinesterase. Rectal schistosomiasis is resistant to metrifonate treatment. The dose is 10 mg/kg body weight up to a maximum adult dose of 600 mg, given orally on three occasions with a three-week interval in between doses. Tablets of 100 mg are available. Side-effects are unusual, but nausea, vomiting and abdominal pain occur if the dose is exceeded. The sperm count is depressed. Plasma cholinesterase concentrations remain low for two weeks after treatment.

Levamisole Hydrochloride

Levamisole hydrochloride (Ketrax) is not easily available as an anthelmintic in the UK. When it is used as an immunostimulant drug for long periods of time, side-effects can occur, but used in a single oral dose of 3 mg/kg body weight, it is safe and highly effective against ascaris worms and to a lesser extent against hookworms. In many countries tablets of 40 mg and a syrup containing 40 mg in 5 ml are available. When side-effects do occur, they include gastrointestinal upset, rashes and neutropenia.

Pyrantel Embonate

Pyrantel embonate (Combantrin, Cobantril) acts as a neuromuscular blocking agent by depolarization and it also inhibits cholinesterase. It is effective against *Ascaris lumbricoides*, hookworms and threadworms. Very little is absorbed after oral administration and the only frequently encountered side-effect is mild gastrointestinal upset. A suspension of 250 mg pyrantel base in 5 ml is available and a single oral dose of 20 mg/kg body weight is all that is required (1 g base is equivalent to 2.9 g pyrantel embonate). It should not be given with piperazine.

Mebendazole

Mebendazole (Vermox) is effective against hookworms, roundworms (with the possible exception of *Strongyloides stercoralis*) and threadworms; even some cestodes such as *Taenia saginata* and *T. solium* are sensitive. The drug is poorly absorbed from the gut, so is mainly active against worms in the intestinal lumen. A small amount is absorbed, however, giving enough tissue penetration to have possible effects on hydatid disease for which only surgical or symptomatic treatment is otherwise available. The drug is available as tablets of 100 mg and a suspension of 100 mg in 5 ml (Vermox). Side-effects are rare if 100 mg is given, a single dose for *Enterobius vermicularis*, or if 100 mg is given daily or twice daily for 3–4 days as a standard dose against luminal worms. Some abdominal pain and gastrointestinal upsets have been reported with large doses. The drug should not be used in pregnancy.

Piperazine

PIPERAZINE

Ascariasis is due to the worm *Ascaris lumbricoides*. The disease is worldwide and frequently asymptomatic. Piperazine will invariably cure ascariasis if given in a single dose of 4 g. It is presented in numerous salts such as the phosphate, adipate, tartrate and citrate, all equivalent in efficacy. Liquid preparations are available for paediatric use. Children under the age of 2 should receive 2 g and children between 2 and 5 years of age should receive 3 g. Purgation is not required and, indeed, is contraindicated in the presence of massive infestation, which may lead to intestinal obstruction. Piperazine is well absorbed and excreted by the kidneys. Its effect on the worm is to paralyse the neuromuscular junction, whereupon worm loses its ability to remain in situ in the bowel lumen. Side-effects are few, but include rashes and transient neurological symptoms. The more disturbing reactions are convulsions, hypotonia, inco-ordination and difficulty in focusing. Inadequate creatinine clearance is a contraindication to piperazine therapy. This drug is also used to treat threadworm infestation in adult doses of 2 g daily for one week. All members of the family should be treated simultaneously. Various preparations are available in tablets, syrups or powders. Piperazine hydrate (Antepar, Ascalix) 100 mg is equivalent to 125 mg piperazine citrate or 104 mg piperazine phosphate (Pripsen). Antepar elixir contains both piperazine hydrate and citrate.

Viprynium Embonate

The cyanine dyes include the red-coloured viprynium embonate (pyrvinium pamoate), a useful anthelmintic, particularly in enterobiasis. It may act by inhibition of oxidative enzymes in the threadworm. It is given orally in a single dose of 5 mg/kg body weight of viprynium base. Tablets contain 50 mg each and a suspension of 10 mg/ml is used in children. Side-effects are not prominent. Occasional gastric irritation and, rarely, photosensitization have been noted. Alarm has been caused by redness of the stool, so patients should be warned of this occurrence.

Hexylresorcinol

This is 1,3-dehydroxy-4-hexylbenzene and it is a broad-spectrum anthelmintic particularly used in trichuriasis. It may be given orally, ten 100 mg tablets being swallowed on one occasion, or as a retention enema diluted 1:1000 in water. Hexylresorcinol irritates the buccal mucosa if sucked or chewed. It also irritates the gastric mucosa, and so the drug is gelatin-coated. It is contraindicated in peptic ulcer. It has been almost completely supplanted by mebendazole.

Bephenium Hydroxynaphthoate

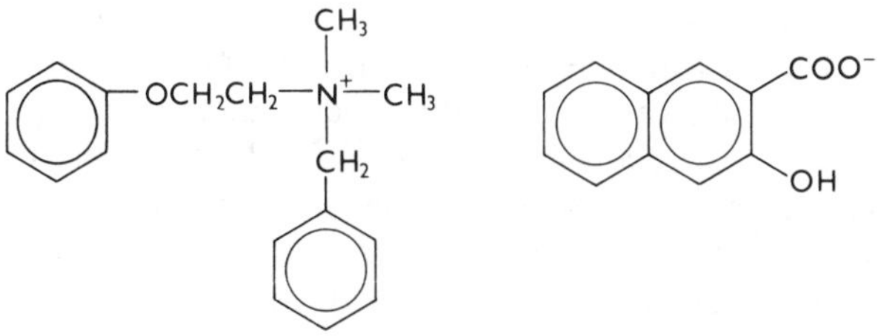

BEPHENIUM HYDROXYNAPHTHOATE

As will be noted from the formula, bephenium (Alcopar) is a quaternary ammonium compound. It acts as a neuromuscular blocking agent. Hookworms such as *Ancylostoma duodenale, Ascaris* and *Trichuris* are all susceptible. It is less effective in *Necator americanus* infestation. A dose of one 5 g sachet is sufficient to eradicate ancylostomae; 3 days of the same dose is required to treat *Necator* infestations successfully. Few side-effects may be expected, since little of the drug is absorbed. Vomiting and diarrhoea do occur and the drug is less pleasant to take than pyrantel embonate and mebendazole, either of which should be used first for hookworm disease, in preference to bephenium.

Thiabendazole

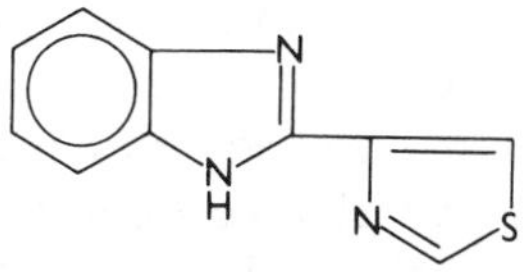

THIABENDAZOLE

Thiabendazole (Mintezol) is a very useful broad-spectrum anthelmintic. It is effective by an unknown mechanism against strongyloidiasis, ancylostomiasis, ascariasis, dracunculiasis, trichuriasis and enterobiasis, but should be reserved for treating strongyloides infestations. It is available as a suspension of 500 mg in 5 ml or as tablets of 500 mg which should be well chewed to aid absorption. The oral dose is 25 mg/kg body weight twice daily for 3 days. Neither fasting nor purgation is necessary. It is well absorbed, quickly metabolized or conjugated, and excreted in the urine. Numerous side-effects are associated with the taking or thiabendazole. These include vomiting and diarrhoea, dizziness, collapse, bradycardia and hypotension, enuresis, paraesthesiae, yellow vision, crystalluria, altered smell of the urine, angioneurotic oedema, and perianal rashes. Albendazole may ultimately replace thiabendazole.

Albendazole

This drug, like mebendazole, belongs to the benzimidazole group, but is better absorbed from the gut and its active metabolite albendazole sulphoxide is concentrated about 100 times more than mebendazole in the blood. A daily oral dose of 10–14 mg/kg body weight appears to be well tolerated, giving good tissue levels, especially in hydatid cysts. It is excreted in bile. The treatment may be repeated several times after intervals of two weeks in patients with hydatid disease. Albendazole may well become the accepted (and at present is the only potentially effective) drug for *Echinococcus granulosus* infestation.

Niclosamide

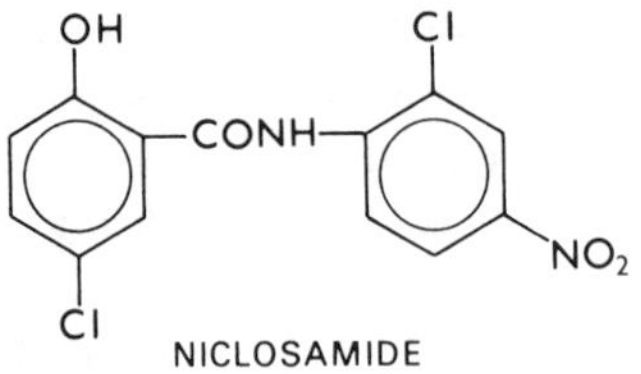

NICLOSAMIDE

Two drugs, niclosamide and dichlorophen, can be used in the treatment of all tapeworm infestations. The dose of niclosamide is 2 g (four vanilla-flavoured tablets) taken as a single oral dose in the morning on an empty stomach. Adults and children receive the same dose. The drug is not absorbed, and few, if any, side-effects occur. The mode of action of niclosamide is by inhibition of the anaerobic metabolism, on which tapeworms rely. The site of interference is thought to be the synthesis of ATP. Some 80–90% of *Taenia saginata* and *Diphyllobothrium latum* infestations are eradicated by this regimen and equally good results are obtained in the treatment of intestinal flukes. Even better results are obtained in treating other tapeworms, including *Taenia solium*. Although certain authorities warn that the dispersal of larval forms throughout the tissues after niclosamide administration could lead to cysticercosis, this does not appear to happen in practice. Nevertheless, it is recommended that an anti-emetic be given an hour before niclosamide, and purgation two hours after. Niclosamide is, therefore, the drug of choice for all human tapeworm infestations, even though the worms cannot then be identified by their scolices. The scolex is digested, so proof of cure is not available after treatment.

Dichlorophen

Structurally similar to niclosamide, dichlorophen has two relative disadvantages. It may lead to abdominal pain and diarrhoea after ingestion of the accepted dosage, which is 6 g on two successive days. This adult dose is three times that of niclosamide. Further purgation is recommended to ensure expulsion of worms from the gut. Partial digestion of the worms after dichlorophen treatment means that identification of their scolices may be impossible, so proof of cure is not obtained. Occasional jaundice has been reported after dichlorophen and it is, therefore, not advisable to use the drug in the presence of pre-existing liver disease. Both niclosamide and dichlorophen outdate substances such as mepacrine and male fern extract or desaspidin, all of which are considerably more toxic drugs.

FILARICIDES

Destruction of adult worms with suramin, antimony or arsenic compounds may result in severe toxicity, but such treatment is usually recommended only when eye involvement has occurred in *Onchocerca volvulus* infection. Microfilaricides control symptoms and reduce the human reservoir of infection, so are most often employed.

Diethylcarbamazine

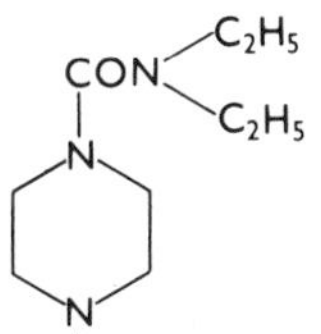

DIETHYLCARBAMAZINE

Diethylcarbamazine (Banocide, Hetrazan, Notézine) is a synthetic derivative of piperazine which, unlike the parent, has a destructive effect on the microfilariae of *Loa loa*, *Wuchereria bancrofti*, *W. malayi* and *O. volvulus*. In this last infestation, results of treatment are improved by subsequent suramin administration when there is ocular involvement. Diethylcarbamazine is mainly effective against microfilariae, but has a slower action on the adult worms. The mode of attack on microfilariae is not understood, but diethylcarbamazine renders them susceptible to phagocytosis.

Absorption from the gut is efficient, and excretion is by the kidneys, predominantly during the day after ingestion. The dose of diethylcarbamazine citrate is 5 mg/kg body weight daily for 21 days, depending on the filarial disease being treated. The initial dose is best kept low and escalated, since the ensuing death of numerous microfilariae may produce unpleasant symptoms such as headaches, rigors, back pain, oedema of the skin and lymph nodes, and even encephalopathy in the case of loiasis. Toxic side-effects of the drug itself are nausea and vomiting, weakness, and sleepiness: none of these are serious contraindications to its use. Repeated courses may be required and, in onchocerciasis, 50 mg doses can be given weekly to suppress symptoms.

LIST OF COMMON PATHOGENS AND APPROPRIATE ANTIMICROBIAL AGENTS

The list which follows can at best only suggest which is the most appropriate drug to use. It should be consulted with reference to the text and the following points should be borne in mind. The sensitivity of micro-organisms frequently changes. The first choice listed may not always be the most effective for infections situated in tissues where drug penetration is poor or very high concentrations required. The occasional use of drug combinations cannot be included. The very young, the pregnant or lactating woman, the elderly or immunocompromised and those with hepatic or renal dysfunction always require special consideration. Previous toxicity with the same or a related drug may prevent its use again. Racial groups may react to drugs in different ways. Finally, the demonstration of a microbe does not necessarily indicate that chemotherapeutic agents should be directed against it.

Organisms	Diseases	Drugs of choice*
Actinomyces (spp.)	actinomycosis	benzylpenicillin lincomycin clindamycin tetracyclines
Ancylostoma duodenale	hookworm infestation	levamisole pyrantel embonate mebendazole
Ascaris (spp.)	ascariasis	levamisole pyrantel embonate mebendazole piperazine
Aspergillus (spp.)	aspergillosis	amphotericin B natamycin
Bacillus anthracis	anthrax	benzylpenicillin clindamycin tetracyclines

*In order of preference at time of going to press.

Organisms	Diseases	Drugs of choice*
Bacteroides (spp.)	respiratory, alimentary, and wound infections	metronidazole or tinidazole clindamycin cefoxitin
Blastomyces (spp.)	blastomycosis	amphotericin B hydroxystilbamidine
Bordetella pertussis	whooping cough	erythromycin ampicillin
Brucella (spp.)	brucellosis	co-trimoxazole tetracyclines streptomycin
Campylobacter (spp.)	enteritis	erythromycin

Candida albicans	candidiasis (thrush)	topically: nystatin
		systemically:
		  amphotericin B
		    plus flucytosine
		  miconazole
		orally: ketoconazole

Chlamydia (spp.)	trachoma lymphogranuloma venereum psittacosis	tetracyclines erythromycin sulphonamides
Clostridium difficile	pseudomembranous colitis	vancomycin (oral) metronidazole

Clostridium perfringens	gas gangrene	benzylpenicillin
		  ± streptomycin or
		  tetracyclines

Clostridium tetani	tetanus	benzylpenicillin (high doses) erythromycin
Coccidioides immitis	coccidioidomycosis	amphotericin B miconazole
Corynebacterium diphtheriae	diphtheria	specific antitoxin, then benzylpenicillin or erythromycin
Cryptococcus neoformans	cryptococcosis	amphotericin B plus flucytosine miconazole
Entamoeba histolytica	amoebiasis	metronidazole emetine chloroquine
Enterobius vermicularis	threadworm infestation	mebendazole pyrantel embonate viprynium embonate piperazine
Epidermophyton	ringworm	griseofulvin ketoconazole

*In order of preference at time of going to press.

Organisms	Diseases	Drugs of choice*
Escherichia coli	urinary, alimentary and wound infections	ampicillin or ureido-penicillins co-trimoxazole gentamicin cephalosporins cycloserine and nitrofurantoin only in urinary infections
Filariidae	filariasis loiasis onchocerciasis	diethylcarbamazine (suramin in special circumstances)
Francisella pestis	bubonic plague	streptomycin tetracyclines sulphonamides chloramphenicol
Francisella tularensis	tularaemia	streptomycin tetracyclines chloramphenicol
Fusobacterium fusiforme	Vincent's angina	benzylpenicillin erythromycin
Giardia lamblia	giardiasis	metronidazole
Haemophilus ducreyi	chancroid	tetracyclines sulphonamides co-trimoxazole
Haemophilus influenzae	bronchitis meningitis	ampicillin co-trimoxazole erythromycin chloramphenicol streptomycin
Histoplasma capsulatum	histoplasmosis	amphotericin B ketoconazole
Klebsiella aerogenes	urinary, alimentary and wound infections	gentamicin chloramphenicol polymyxins
Klebsiella pneumoniae	respiratory, urinary and bone infections	gentamicin chloramphenicol co-trimoxazole
Legionella pneumophila	legionnaires' disease	erythromycin rifampicin cefoxitin
Leishmania (spp.)	leishmaniasis	pentavalent antimonials
Leptospira (spp.)	leptospirosis	benzylpenicillin erythromycin
Listeria monocytogenes	skin, CNS and blood infections, especially in infants	ampicillin benzylpenicillin
Microsporum (spp.)	tinea capitis, tinea circinata and tinea cruris	griseofulvin ketoconazole

*In order of preference at time of going to press.

Organisms	Diseases	Drugs of choice*
Mycobacterium leprae	leprosy	dapsone rifampicin clofazimine

Mycobacterium tuberculosis	tuberculosis	combinations
		  of rifampicin with
		  ethambutol and isoniazid,
		  pyrazinamide or
		  ethionamide

Mycoplasma pneumoniae	'atypical' pneumonia	tetracyclines erythromycin
Necator americanus	hookworm infestation	mebendazole pyrantel embonate
Neisseria catarrhalis	upper respiratory infections	ampicillin cephalosporins tetracyclines
Neisseria gonorrhoeae	gonorrhoea conjunctivitis	benzylpenicillin cephalosporins ampicillin erythromycin minocycline spectinomycin
Neisseria meningitidis	meningitis conjunctivitis	benzylpenicillin cephalosporins erythromycin

Nocardia asteroides	nocardiosis	streptomycin plus dapsone
		  or co-trimoxazole;
		  or streptomycin plus
		  sulfadoxine and
		  pyrimethamine;
		  or streptomycin plus
		  rifampicin

Plasmodium (spp.)	malaria	*see text*
Pneumocystis carinii	lung and brain abscesses	co-trimoxazole pentamidine

Proteus (spp.)	infections of any system,
	  especially urinary
		gentamicin
		ureidopenicillins
		  or cephalosporins
		ampicillin
		nalidixic acid
		co-trimoxazole

Pseudomonas aeruginosa	urinary, respiratory,
	  biliary, CNS and
	  wound infections
		gentamicin
		cefotaxime or
		  ceftazidime
		ureido-penicillins
		azlocillin
		tobramycin
		amikacin

Rickettsia (spp.)	Q fever typhus tick-borne fever Rocky Mountain spotted fever	tetracyclines chloramphenicol

*In order of preference at time of going to press.

Organisms	Diseases	Drugs of choice*
Salmonella paratyphi	paratyphoid fever	amoxycillin chloramphenicol co-trimoxazole
Salmonella typhi	typhoid fever	chloramphenicol amoxycillin co-trimoxazole
Schistosoma (spp.)	schistosomiasis	praziquantel niridazole
Shigella (spp.)	bacillary dysentery	tetracyclines ampicillin oral neomycin (usually no antibiotic needed)
Sporothrix schenkii	sporotrichosis	potassium iodide amphotericin B

Staphylococcus albus	wound, respiratory,
	   bone and eye
	   infections, especially in
	   neonates
	endocarditis
		benzylpenicillin
		cloxacillin
		lincomycin

Staphylococcus aureus	infections of any
	   system
		benzylpenicillin
		erythromycin
		If penicillinase-producing:
		   flucloxacillin
		   clindamycin
		   erythromycin
		   fusidic acid
		   vancomycin

Streptococcus faecalis
   (Enterococcus)
	urinary and alimentary
	   infections
	endocarditis
		ampicillin or
		   gentamicin with
		   benzylpenicillin

Streptococcus pneumoniae (Diplococcus)	pneumonia conjunctivitis meningitis	benzylpenicillin erythromycin clindamycin cefuroxime co-trimoxazole
Streptococcus pyogenes	upper respiratory, skin and bone infections scarlet fever erysipelas meningitis endocarditis	benzylpenicillin phenoxymethylpenicillin ampicillin cephalosporins clindamycin erythromycin
Streptococcus viridans	endocarditis	benzylpenicillin, often with gentamicin
Strongyloides stercoralis	strongyloidiasis	thiabendazole mebendazole
Taenia (spp.)	tapeworm infestation	niclosamide dichlorophen

*In order of preference at time of going to press.

Organisms	Diseases	Drugs of choice*
Toxoplasma (spp.)	toxoplasmosis	pyrimethamine plus sulphadiazine trimethoprim
Treponema pallidum	syphilis	benzylpenicillin erythromycin tetracyclines
Trichomonas vaginalis	trichomoniasis	metronidazole or tinidazole
Trichuris	whipworm infestation	mebendazole thiabendazole
Trichophyton (spp.)	tinea barbae, capitis, cruris and pedis	griseofulvin ketoconazole
Trypanosoma (spp.)	trypanosomiasis	suramin melarsoporol nitrofurazone
	Chagas' disease	nitrofurazone primaquine
Vibrio cholerae	cholera	tetracyclines sulphonamides neomycin (oral) chloramphenicol
Viruses	influenza A_2 or A/New Jersey	amantadine (for prevention)
	common-cold virus	interferons
	herpes zoster ⎫ herpes simplex ⎭	acyclovir idoxuridine
	variola ⎫ vaccinia ⎭	methisazone

*In order of preference at time of going to press.

FURTHER READING

Anabwani G.M., Ngira J.A., Dimiti G. & Bryceson A.D.M. (1983) Comparison of two dosage schedules of sodium stibogluconate in the treatment of visceral leishmaniasis in Kenya. *Lancet*, i: 210.

Ball A. P. & Gray J. A. (1983) *Antibacterial Drugs Today*, 3rd edn. Balgowlah, Australia: Adis; and Bristol: John Wright.

Beeching N. J. & Ellis C. J. (1982) Leprosy and its chemotherapy. *J. antimicrob. Chemother.*, 10: 81.

Bell D. R. (1982) Anthelmintic drug therapy. In Reeves D. S. & Geddes A. M. (eds), *Recent Advances in Infection – 2*, pp. 179–84. Edinburgh: Churchill Livingstone.

Cohen J. (1982) Antifungal chemotherapy. *Lancet*, ii: 532.

Davis A. & Wegner D. H. G. (1979) Multicentre trials of praziquantel in human schistosomiasis: design and techniques. *WHO (Bull.)*, 57: 767.

Davis A., Biles J. E. & Ulrich A. M. (1979) Initial experiences with praziquantel in the treatment of human infections due to Schistosoma haematobium. *WHO (Bull.)*, 57: 773.

Foulkes J.R. (1981) Human trypanosomiasis in Africa. *Br. med. J.*, 283: 1172.

Garrod L. P., Lambert H. P. & O'Grady F. (1981) *Antibiotic and Chemotherapy*, 5th edn. Edinburgh: Churchill Livingstone.

Geddes A. M., Acar J. F. & Knothe H. (eds) (1980) Cefotaxime: a new cephalosporin antibiotic. *J. antimicrob. Chemother.*, 6: Suppl. A.

Howells R. E. (1982) Malaria: advances in chemotherapy. *Br. med. Bull.*, 38: 193.

Jackson D. & Phillips I. (eds) (1982) From penicillin to piperacillin. *J. antimicrob. Chemother.*, 9: Suppl. B.

Jiang J-B., Li G-Q., Guo X-B., Kong Y.C. & Arnold K. (1982) Antimalarial activity of mefloquine and qinghaosu. *Lancet*, ii: 285.

Knight R. (1982) *Parasitic Disease in Man*. Edinburgh: Churchill Livingstone.

Kucers A. & Bennett N. McK. (1979) *The Use of Antibiotics*, 3rd edn. London: William Heinemann.

Leading article (1981) Acyclovir. *Lancet*, ii, 845.

Leading article (1982) Interferon and the common cold. *Lancet*, ii: 369.

Leading article (1982) Ketoconazole. *Br. Med. J.*, 285; 584.

McGill J. (1981) Topical acyclovir in herpes zoster ocular involvement. *Br. J. Ophthalmol.*, 65: 542.

Manson-Bahr P. E. C. & Apted F.I.C. (eds) (1982) *Manson's Tropical Diseases*, 18th edn. London: Baillière Tindall.

Morris D.L. (1983) Chemotherapy of hydatid disease. *J. antimicrob. Chemother.*, 11: 494.

Neu H. C. & Wise R. (eds) (1982) Mezlocillin. *J. antimicrob. Chemother.*, 9: Suppl. A.

Nilsen A. E., Aasen T., Halsos A. M., Kinge B. R., Tjotta E. A. L., Wikström K. & Fiddian A. P. (1982) Efficacy of oral acyclovir in the treatment of initial and recurrent genital herpes. *Lancet*, ii: 571.

Nord C. E. & Phillips I. (eds) (1982) Anaerobic infections: the role of tinidazole. *J. antimicrob. Chemother.*, 10: Suppl. A.

Peters W. (1982) Malaria: antimalarial drug resistance: an increasing problem. *Br. med. Bull.*, 38; 187.

Reeves D. (1982) Sulphonamides and trimethoprim. *Lancet* ii: 370.

Robertson D.H. (1963) The treatment of sleeping sickness (mainly due to *Trypanosoma rhodesiense*) with melarsoprol. *Trans. R. Soc. trop. Med. Hyg.*, 57: 122.

Saimot A.G., Meulemans A., Cremieux A.C., Giovanangeli M.D., Hay J.M., Delaitre B. & Coulaud J.P. (1983) Albendazole as a potential treatment for human hydatidosis. *Lancet*, ii: 652.

Saral R., Burns W. H., Laskin O. L., Santos G. W. & Leitman P. S. (1981) Acyclovir prophylaxis of Herpes-simplex-virus infections. *New Engl. J. Med.* 305: 63.

Williams J. D. & Casewell M. W. (eds) (1981) Ceftazidime. *J. antimicrob. Chemother.*, 8: Suppl. B.

Williams J. D., Geddes A. M. & Nevu H. V. (eds) (1978) Cefoxitin: microbiology, pharmacology and clinical use. *J. antimicrob. Chemother.*, 4: Suppl. B.

WHO (1982) Study Group. Chemotherapy of leprosy for control programmes. *Techn. Rep. Ser.*, No. 675.

2 Analgesics

R. H. Girdwood

The word 'analgesia', meaning insensibility to pain, comes from the Greek word ἀναλγησια.

There are very powerful analgesics, such as the opium derivatives, which have numerous actions in man but, unfortunately, may lead to serious problems of addiction (p. 193). Accordingly, they cannot be used freely. Other milder analgesics are numerous, and some have antipyretic and anti-inflammatory actions in addition to being what is often referred to as 'pain killers'. It should be realized that it is extremely difficult to design a satisfactory comparative trial of the relative therapeutic efficacy of analgesics and that animal studies, though possible, may give little guidance.

PAIN

In general, pain arising from the viscera is most readily ameliorated by narcotics such as morphine or pethidine, which reduce the patient's ability to experience pain, but may also affect his emotional state. Frequently, but not always, it is possible to control pain from skin, muscle, joints or even bones by non-narcotic analgesics which vary in the extent of their antipyretic and anti-inflammatory actions. There are particular conditions such as migraine, trigeminal neuralgia or painful spasm of the colon, where an entirely different approach to the control of symptoms may be necessary.

In order to understand the ways in which analgesics are believed to act, it is necessary to consider some aspects of what is known about the probable mechanism of arousal of pain sensation.

PERIPHERAL FACTORS IN PAIN SENSATION

Histamine, 5-hydroxytryptamine and kinins
The sensory nerve endings which, when suitably stimulated, lead to the sensation of pain (the nociceptors) may be activated by mechanical, chemical or other stimuli. Soon after injury, histamine, 5-hydroxytryptamine (serotonin) and the peptide, bradykinin, are released. The first two of these are widely distributed in platelets, basophils, mast cells and various tissues, and histamine is believed to play a part in the early stages of an acute inflammatory response (p. 554). Serotonin can cause pain locally and, in

addition, it may be the substance which causes vasospasm in migraine attacks.

The formation of bradykinin (so called because it causes a slow contraction of isolated guinea-pig ileum) is a complex matter, and there are other kinins produced in mammalian tissues. It is believed that injury or other activation causes the formation of kallikrein from kallikreinogen and that kallikrein then liberates bradykinin from bradykinogen, though the exact mechanism of activation is uncertain. The kallikrein system is to be found in plasma, urine, saliva, cerebrospinal fluid (CSF), lymph, sweat and tears, in all of which the substance normally present is the readily activated kallikreinogen. Kinins are believed to be of importance in pain due to inflammation. Moreover, bradykinin is the most potent permeability factor known and is capable of causing vasodilation and increased vascular permeability, in addition to pain. Antagonists to kinins have not been developed, and the limited value of antihistamines is referred to elsewhere (p. 555).

Prostaglandins

In the cell membranes of all tissues investigated to date, there are phospholipids which, with suitable stimuli (e.g. pathological changes, mechanical causes, bradykinin, hormones), give rise to arachidonic acid (eicosa-5,8,11,14-tetraenoic acid; $C_{20} H_{32} O_2$) or related substances. The formula of arachidonic acid is shown below.

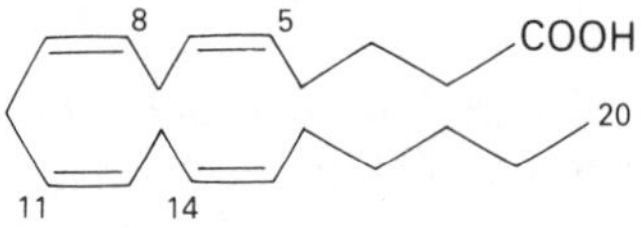

Under the influence of cyclo-oxygenase (sometimes called prostaglandin synthetase), unstable endoperoxides are formed, and these are then converted by further oxygenation into a variety of local hormones known as prostaglandins, which are long-chain fatty acids, varying slightly in structure according to the tissue involved. For instance, there is prostaglandin E_2 (PGE_2):

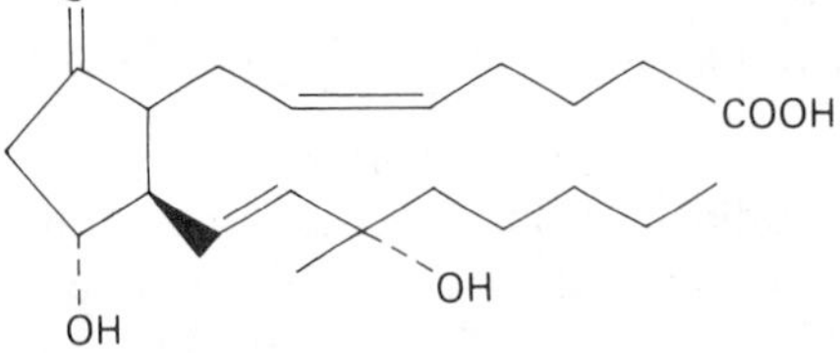

Migrating leucocytes are a major source of prostaglandins in inflammatory exudates. Many authorities believe that prostaglandins can potentiate the pro-inflammatory response of other mediators such as histamine and kinins, and that pain produced by kinins is enhanced by prostaglandins. When prostaglandins are injected into tissues they may cause pain, erythema and swelling, and PGE_1 is a potent endogenous pyretic agent, apparently through an action on the central nervous system (CNS). (The subscript 1 indicates derivation from 8,11,14-eicosatrienoic acid, 2 derivation from arachidonic acid and there are a very few prostaglandins with a subscript 3 to show that they are derived from 5,8,11,14,17-eicosapentaenoic acid.) $PGF_{2\alpha}$ causes pyrexia, but to a lesser extent than does PGE_1. There is evidence that PGE_1 and PGE_2 stimulate the release of histamine from mast cells, but that this is opposed by the action of $PGF_{2\alpha}$.

Non-steroidal anti-inflammatory drugs and the prostaglandins. Many non-steroidal anti-inflammatory drugs are believed to act by inhibiting the biosynthesis of prostaglandins from arachidonic acid, this being due to inhibition of cyclo-oxygenase and occurring at the nociceptor level. They may prevent prostaglandin from sensitizing pain receptors to other endogenous pain-producing substances. Since it is believed that prostaglandins acting on the brain may cause fever, this may explain why certain anti-inflammatory agents are also antipyretics. Aspirin is both anti-inflammatory and antipyretic, whereas paracetamol is antipyretic but not anti-inflammatory. It is no doubt significant that the latter is much more effective in preventing prostaglandin formation in the brain than in the tissues.

Corticosteroids

Corticosteroids are thought to produce their anti-inflammatory and analgesic effects by interfering with the production of arachidonic acid from phospholipids.

Substance P

There is a polypeptide neurotransmitter known as substance P or SP present in primary sensory neurons both at nerve endings just under the skin and at presynaptic neurons in the spinal cord. It is also present in the brain and intestinal tract. SP is possibly associated with pain fibres and perhaps acted upon by local anaesthetics, though its exact role remains obscure. The subject of brain peptides is a complex one.

CENTRAL REGULATORS

Endogenous Opioids

Morphine and related opioids are relatively specific in their actions, in that vision and hearing are not affected by normal doses. This is because of the distribution of opioid receptors in the dorsal horn of the spinal cord, the hypothalamus and various areas of the brain. They also occur in the small intestine and hence morphine causes constipation.

There are endogenous substances known as enkephalins and endorphins which are sometimes described as the 'brain's own opiates'. In the earlier work in this field, brain extracts were found to produce analgesia and to compete with the opiate antagonist naloxone (p. 114) for brain receptor sites. Similar extracts were obtained from the pituitary and gut. The substances concerned are peptides.

Enkephalins are highly unstable in vivo because of rapid enzymatic hydrolysis. The natural substance methionine-enkephalin (met-enkephalin) has the following amino-acid sequence:

$$H_2N\text{-tyrosine-glycine-glycine-phenylalanine-methionine-OH}$$

This is the same amino-acid sequence as the terminal 5 amino-acids of beta-lipotrophin. There are other natural enkephalins such as leucine-enkephalin, and stable analogues have been prepared. In the United States there have been clinical trials of an enkephalin, metkephamid, and, given i.m. for postoperative pain, it was about as active as pethidine (p. 116), but had unexpected side-effects, such as heaviness of the extremities and nasal congestion. Others are under investigation.

The beta-endorphin molecule is larger and it contains the terminal 31 amino-acids of beta-lipotrophin. It is thought that there is a glycoprotein named pro-opiocortin and that it is a precursor common to ACTH and the lipotrophin peptides including beta-endorphin. Synthetic beta-endorphins have been prepared and found to give prolonged and long lasting analgesia when given intrathecally for pain due to disseminated cancer. Unfortunately, all synthetic opioids produce tolerance and addiction.

Enkephalins occur in various parts of the brain, in areas of the spinal cord involved in the transmission of pain sensation and in the gastrointestinal tract. In the pituitary there are beta-endorphins, but not enkephalins, and the former is less widespread than the latter in its distribution in the brain. It has been suggested that the enkephalins have a local (neurotransmitter-like) action, whereas beta-endorphin acts more generally. It is likely that the receptors for natural opioids are not identical with those for opiates such as morphine, but it is suggested that the natural substances formed in the body modulate pain and have various cerebral functions. If opiates, which have similar effects, are taken, it may be that less of the endogenous substances are produced and withdrawal symptoms (p. 193) may be, in part, due to lack of the natural opioids.

It may be that individual variations in sensitivity to pain depend on the levels of endogenous opioids. In addition, it is believed that in acupuncture there is a release of the natural substances into the CSF. Direct measurement has shown a rise in beta-endorphin, but not met-enkephalin levels in human CSF after acupuncture for recurrent pain. It has been suggested that in acupuncture with electrical stimulation analgesia may be mediated by at least two pain-relieving mechanisms. One, produced by low-frequency acupuncture, is related to endorphins and is reversible by naloxone (p. 114). The other, involved in high-frequency acupuncture, is not reversed by this drug and is believed to be serotonin related.

Ectopic beta-endorphin and met-enkephalin have been found in tumour tissue. If this is a common finding, these substances may automatically subdue pain in certain malignant diseases and these or other unknown substances may cause psychological changes in the sufferer.

OPIUM AND SIMILAR AGENTS

Opium

The taking of opium, a juice obtained from the unripe seed capsule of the poppy, *Papaver somniferum*, has been known from ancient times as a way of obtaining pleasurable sensations. The word 'opium' is derived from the Greek ὀπός, meaning juice, and 'narcotic' comes from the Greek ναρκοῦν, meaning to benumb or stupefy. Laudanum is an old name for opium tincture, BP. The name 'morphine', given to an alkaloid of opium, is derived from the Latin poet Ovid's hypothetical name for the Greek god of dreams, viz. Morpheus or Μορφεύς.

The juice of the poppy is allowed to dry in the air and in due course a powder is obtained. This is standardized to contain 10% morphine. The alkaloids constitute about 25% of the weight of opium, and they have two distinct chemical forms, which differ in their pharmacological properties. These are the phenanthrenes and the benzylisoquinolines. Of the first group, the alkaloids of possible medical usefulness consist of morphine 10%, codeine 0.5% and thebaine 0.2%. The isoquinolines include noscapine 6.0% and papaverine 1.0%. In each instance the figure given refers to the percentage weight in opium. The formula for morphine is given below.

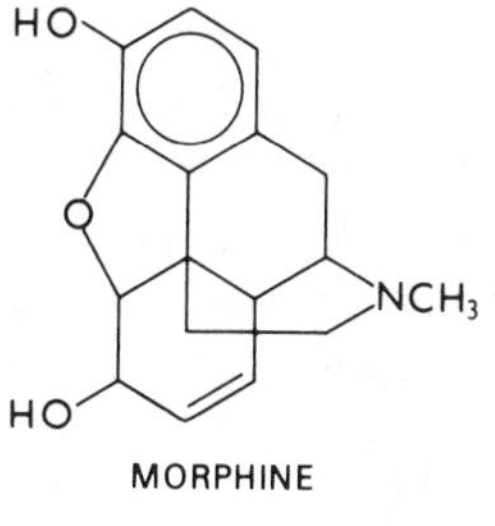

MORPHINE

Codeine is methylmorphine, the methyl substitution being at the phenolic –OH shown at position 3 above. Heroin (p. 114) is not a natural substance, but is semi-synthetic, being derived from morphine by the acetylation of the phenolic and alcoholic –OH groups at positions 3 and 6. Hence it is diacetylmorphine. An important substitution, the clinical importance of which was overlooked for many years, was that of the allyl group ($CH_2CH=CH_2$) for the methyl group attached to the nitrogen, which gave a narcotic antagonist. The substance used is naloxone (p. 114), which is a derivative of oxymorphone (dihydrohydroxymorphinone), an allyl group being substituted.

Preparations of Opium that are in Use

Papaveretum tablets, BPC, and *Papaveretum injection*, BNF. These are preparations of opium alkaloids which have no particular advantage over morphine. They are usually used in the proprietary forms of Omnopon (10 mg tablets), Omnopon injection (20 mg/ml), or, for premedication, Omnopon with scopolamine (20 mg and 0.4 mg/ml, respectively). Tincture of opium is used in doses of from 0.25 to 2 ml to treat diarrhoea or cough. It should not be given for prolonged periods.

Squill opiate linctus, BPC. This consists of equal parts of camphorated opium tincture, oxymel of squills, and syrup of tolu. It is known as Gee's linctus, contains 800 μg of anhydrous morphine in 5 ml, and has been extensively used for coughs. There is also a squill opiate linctus paediatric, BPC. The squill is included as an expectorant, but is of doubtful efficacy.

Morphine

Analgesic Effects
Morphine is a most satisfactory analgesic and analgesia is its greatest therapeutic effect. Reference has already been made to specific receptors and to natural opioids (p. 107). In addition, it causes clouding of thought, reduced mental ability and an increase in reaction time. In small doses (e.g. 10 mg), consciousness is not impaired and the patient is content, free of disturbing emotions and in a state of euphoria. However, judgement is likely to be impaired and movements slow.

With larger doses, the subject is drowsy and apathetic, and if undisturbed may fall asleep. A dose of 30 mg the normal person is likely to cause sleep without euphoria. As in in normal sleep, an electroencephalographic record shows an increase in voltage and decrease in frequency of the wave patterns. Sleep is due to a reduced response of the brain to input stimuli and to depression of the reticular activating system that controls consciousness. The relief of pain is also likely to be a factor. A toxic dose of morphine leads to coma with shallow breathing, and death may occur from respiratory paralysis.

In addition to the depressant effect, there is some evidence of excitation, in that nausea and vomiting frequently occur. In the occasional patient, there is not only euphoria, but also excitement and even mania.

The pupils are small (miosis), but the reason for this is not certain. It may be due to depression of supranuclear inhibition of pupillary constrictor tone. If asphyxia occurs, the pupils dilate. Unlike man, certain species of animal are normally excited by morphine, and in them the drug causes dilatation of the pupil.

Actions on the Respiratory System

In man, morphine depresses the 'respiratory centre' of the brain stem. This centre is a physiological entity rather than an exact anatomical one. The depression occurs even with small doses and the degree is proportional to the amount of the drug that is given. The rate of respiration is first diminished and the amplitude of respiratory movement increases. At higher doses there is periodic breathing and then apnoea. The respiratory centre becomes less responsive to $PaCO_2$ and the main stimulus to the cells in the respiratory centre is then anoxaemia. Accordingly, high dosage of oxygen is likely to lead to respiratory failure, whereas low concentrations may be beneficial, causing recovery of the sensitivity of the cells to the stimulus of carbon dioxide. Sleep also decreases the sensitivity of the respiratory centre to CO_2, and when morphine is used, this action is additive.

The voluntary control of breathing is retained in the conscious patient. The cough reflex is depressed.

It is dangerous to use morphine in patients with respiratory insufficiency or bronchial asthma, because of the diminished response of the respiratory centre to CO_2. Morphine may also cause constriction of bronchial smooth muscle. After operation, its use may lead to collapse of the lungs, because breathing is shallow. However, morphine is very useful in controlling paroxysmal nocturnal dyspnoea, partly because it relieves anxiety and partly because there is an indifference to respiration, so that the patient ceases to struggle to breathe and this reduces the work of the heart. The precise mechanism of this beneficial action is not clear, and it may be that peripheral vasodilatation plays a part.

Actions on the Cardiovascular System

Peripheral vasodilatation may cause venous pooling. In the supine position, a therapeutic dose of morphine has no major effect on blood pressure or heart rate, and the vasomotor centre is little affected. When the patient moves to the upright position, however, the peripheral vasodilatation may cause hypotension and fainting. It is thought that morphine causes histamine release and that this leads to vasodilatation, but that there are other factors.

It is important to use morphine and other narcotics cautiously in patients with a decreased blood volume or with hypotension, and there is danger in giving such drugs concurrently with phenothiazine derivatives or antihypertensive drugs. On the other hand, it is possible to make use of the potentiating effect of phenothiazines and to give a smaller dose of morphine by administering chlorpromazine (p. 165) at the same time. This is important in treating painful terminal illness. Morphine should be used very cautiously if at all in those with cor pulmonale, since death may occur even with therapeutic dosage.

Actions on the Gastrointestinal Tract

Tincture of opium (p. 109) and certain preparations containing morphine

(p. 113) are used to treat diarrhoea. Morphine diminishes peristaltic waves in the colon and increases muscle tone considerably. The tone of the anal sphincter is also augmented. Motility in the stomach is decreased and the secretion of hydrochloric acid diminished. In the small intestine, propulsive contractions are considerably lessened (p. 346). Biliary and pancreatic secretions are diminished. There is a marked increase in biliary tract pressure, with constriction of the sphincter of Oddi. Biliary colic may be made more severe and there may be interference with exocrine pancreatic secretions. Morphine should not be used in acute pancreatitis. Some patients are troubled with vomiting if morphine is given (p. 110), whereas others do not suffer in this way. Vomiting is particularly unfortunate if it is induced after a haematemesis or coronary thrombosis. In an attempt to prevent this, cyclizine is usually given simultaneously.

Actions on the Genitourinary System
There may be difficulty in micturition because of spasm of the sphincter of the bladder, but the tone of the detrusor muscle may also be increased. Accordingly, there can be increased frequency or retention, the latter being made worse because central cerebral effects may lead to inattention. The tone of the ureters is said to be increased, so that, although the actual pain caused by calculi passing along the ureters is relieved, their passage is impeded unless atropine is given simultaneously. It is now believed, however, that the effects of both morphine and atropine on the ureters in man are very variable. Experiments that measure ureteric pressure under anaesthesia may not reflect exactly what occurs in the non-anaesthetized patient.

Morphine causes a reduction in urinary output by increasing the release of antidiuretic hormone.

Large doses of morphine prolong labour, but the mechanism is uncertain.

Actions on the Skin
The face may become flushed and there may be pruritus and sweating.

Pharmacokinetics
There is absorption from the gut, but morphine sulphate tablets are not used extensively. This preparation is usually given s.c., i.m. or i.v. Morphine is rapidly absorbed after injection, the effects appearing 10–20 minutes after s.c. injection and lasting for about 4 hours. Free morphine is concentrated in liver, lung, kidney, spleen, and skeletal muscle, but it does not accumulate in tissues. The primary site of action is the CNS, but little passes the blood–brain barrier. Peak brain levels are found some 30–60 minutes after s.c. injection. Morphine is conjugated with glucuronic acid in the liver. Some free morphine is found in the urine, but it is mainly excreted in the conjugated form. Up to 10% of administered morphine appears in the faeces, there being conjugated morphine excreted in the bile. Morphine and other narcotic analgesics pass across the placenta. Morphine given to a mother before delivery may cause

respiratory depression in a newborn infant because of its immature blood–brain barrier. The half-life of morphine in the body is said to be 10–44 hours.

Preparations

Morphine sulphate injection, BP. This is available in 1 ml ampoules containing 10, 15, 20 or 30 mg. The usual dose is 10–20 mg s.c., i.m. or i.v.

Morphine and atropine injection, BPC. This contains morphine sulphate 1% w/v (10 mg/ml) and atropine sulphate 0.06% w/v (0.6 mg/ml). The usual dose is 0.5–1 ml s.c.

In the UK, under the Misuse of Drugs Act of 1971, these and other opiates come into Schedule 2, and, under the Pharmacy and Poisons Act of 1933, they come into Schedule 4. These two regulations govern permitted availability and specify the form of prescription writing that is necessary. Further information is given on p. 195.

Kaolin and morphine mixture, BPC. This contains light kaolin 2 g, sodium bicarbonate 0.5 g, chloroform and morphine tincture 0.4 ml, and water to 10 ml, which gives 700 μg of anhydrous morphine. The preparation is used for the treatment of diarrhoea. The content of morphine is sufficiently small for it to come under Schedule 1 of the 1971 Act, with consequent freer availability.

Cyclimorph. This is a proprietary preparation, available in two strengths. In a 1 ml ampoule there is either 10 or 15 mg of morphine tartrate together with 50 mg of cyclizine tartrate.

Morphine is also available in controlled release tablets (MST Continus, 10 mg and 30 mg strengths) and in suppository form.

Indications

To relieve severe pain.

To relieve the dyspnoea of paroxysmal nocturnal dyspnoea in left ventricular failure (but *not* in cor pulmonale or bronchial asthma).

To relieve pain and anxiety prior to general anaesthesia in surgery.

To give relief to the dying.

To relieve anxiety where there is distress after haematemesis or other frightening disease (but the possibility of causing vomiting or hypotension should be remembered).

To control restlessness when there is no contraindication such as liver failure.

The use of kaolin and morphine mixture in diarrhoea has been referred to above.

Adverse Effects

Many of these have been referred to already. The dangers of addiction are referred to on p. 193. Tolerance to morphine readily develops on repeated administration of the drug. Other possible adverse effects are nausea, vomiting, tremor and urticaria. Patients with liver disease or hypothyroidism tolerate morphine badly, and if the drug has to be used, the dose should be reduced. The dangers of hypotension and of respiratory failure have been referred to (pp. 111 and 110). In diverticular disease morphine has been known to cause rupture of the abnormal pouches in the large bowel.

Antidotes.

Naloxone hydrochloride injection (p. 528) is a specific antagonist which is available in ampoules at a concentration of 0.4 mg/ml. It also reverses the actions of pentazocine (p. 117) and dextropropoxyphene (p. 119). The adult dose is 0.4 mg i.v., repeated at 2–3 minute intervals as necessary. It can be used in respiratory depression of unknown cause which is suspected of being produced by a narcotic drug. The usual initial dose in children is 0.005–0.01 mg/kg body weight. For neonatal use, an adequate airway should be established before naloxone is given in a dosage of 0.01 mg/kg body weight, s.c., i.m. or i.v.

Interactions

The depressant effects are potentiated by phenothiazines, monoamine oxidase inhibitors, tricyclic antidepressants, and neostigmine.

Diamorphine Hydrochloride (Heroin)

This semi-synthetic substance is structurally closely related to morphine (p. 109). It is hydrolysed to monoacetylmorphine and then to morphine in the body. Both diamorphine and monoacetylmorphine pass the blood–brain barrier more easily than does morphine. Heroin is more potent and therefore more easily transported in illegal drug trafficking. It is said to cause not only less sedation, but also less nausea, vomiting and/or constipation than does morphine; this may be important in treating patients with severe pain or ministering to the dying. It is shorter-acting and is generally considered to be even more addictive. The antidotes, in the event of overdosage, are those referred to above.

Preparations

Diamorphine injection, BP. This is prepared in vials of 5, 10, or 30 mg; the s.c., i.m. or i.v. dose is 5–10 mg.

To ease the suffering of the dying, the following may be administered: diamorphine and cocaine elixir, BPC, containing 5 mg of diamorphine hydrochloride and 5 mg of cocaine hydrochloride in 5 ml, and diamorphine, cocaine and chlorpromazine elixir, BPC, which has, in addition, 6.25 mg of chlorpromazine hydrochloride in the same total volume. As with morphine

(p. 111), the simultaneous administration of chlorpromazine may diminish the amount of diamorphine that requires to be given.

All these preparations come into Schedule 2 of the Misuse of Drugs Act Regulations in the UK (p. 195). In many countries, including the USA, its manufacture or importation is illegal.

Codeine

Codeine is methylmorphine. It has actions similar to those of morphine, but is much less effective as an analgesic, though it has some action in this respect. It has less depressant effects on the respiratory centre and it is very rare for it to lead to dependence. Nausea and vomiting seldom occur. The drug is used effectively in treating cough and as an antidiarrhoeal agent. It is combined with aspirin or paracetamol in many proprietary preparations. Codeine is taken by mouth, and a suitable dose is 10–60 mg of codeine phosphate.

Preparations
Preparations include *codeine linctus*, *BPC, codeine linctus paediatric, BPC, codeine phosphate tablets, BP* (15, 30 or 60 mg), *codeine and paracetamol tablets* (8 mg and 500 mg, respectively), and *codeine and aspirin* (8 mg and 400 mg, respectively).

Dihydrocodeine (DF 118). This is a suitable analgesic for treating moderate pain. Dependence has been known to occur. Dihydrocodeine tablets, BP, are in 10 and 30 mg strengths, and there are dihydrocodeine and paracetamol tablets (containing 10 mg and 500 mg of each, respectively). Dihydrocodeine injection contains 50 mg/ml, and is included in Schedule 2 of the Misuse of Drugs Act Regulations (p. 195).

Oxycodone (dihydrohydroxycodeinone). This is a Schedule 2 drug which is sometimes given as the pectinate, by suppository, in the treatment of severe pain associated with terminal carcinoma. In some countries it is marketed under the proprietary name of Proladone. Each suppository has the equivalent of 30 mg of oxycodone.

Other Drugs

Phenazocine hydrobromide

Phenazocine hydrobromide is a synthetic analgesic with similar actions to those of morphine, and it also is in Schedule 2. It can be given i.m. or can be taken by mouth or sublingually. It acts rapidly and has a longer action than morphine. Proprietary names are Narphen in the UK and Prinadol in the USA.

Buprenorphine

Buprenorphine (Temgesic) is an ethanonormorphine derivative that can be used effectively for pain in association with terminal malignancy, postoperative pain and pain after mycocardial infarction, provided that facilities are available to deal with respiratory failure. It has both narcotic agonist and antagonist properties, and naloxone (p. 114), is not therefore effective as an antidote. The respiratory stimulant doxapram (p. 178) should be used if required.

Temgesic is available in ampoules containing 0.3 mg of buprenorphine per ml. It is for use in adults only, in a dose of 0.3–0.6 mg by i.m. or slow i.v. injection 6- or 8-hourly. It is also available in 0.2 mg tablets for sublingual administration, one to two tablets being dissolved under the tongue 6- or 8-hourly.

Butorphanol

Butorphanol (Dorphanol, Stadol) is a synthetic compound of the nalorphine–cyclazocine series of narcotic agonist–antagonist drugs. It is intended for parenteral use in acute pain.

'Brompton mixture'

Brompton mixture is the term used, particularly in London, for a mixture suitable for administration in inoperable cancer. However, the name 'Brompton mixture' has had more than one meaning and should not be employed. It often refers to a mixture of morphine and cocaine, but there are suitable BPC preparations, named, respectively, morphine and cocaine elixir, and morphine, cocaine and chlorpromazine elixir. It is sometimes possible to add to the effectiveness of morphine or diamorphine without increasing the dose by giving increasing amounts of chlorpromazine.

Pethidine (Meperidine, USP)

Pethidine is a synthetic derivative of piperidine which differs in its structure from morphine and atropine, but has some of the actions of each. It is used as an analgesic, particularly for visceral pain, but is less effective than morphine. It has little hypnotic effect and in toxic doses causes tremors and convulsions. It depresses the respiratory centre less than morphine, but an overdose may cause respiratory failure. It has mild effects in causing relaxation of the smooth muscle of bronchi and of the alimentary tract, but spasm of the sphincter of Oddi is produced, so this is an unsuitable drug for treating biliary colic. The effects on the ureter are similar to those of morphine (p. 112). It is a good analgesic to use in labour, since it has no harmful effects on the uterine muscle at term and has relatively little effect on respiratory function in the newborn.

It does not suppress cough satisfactorily and does not cause constipation or miosis. Hypotension can follow its use, but this is not marked. Vomiting may occur, and in large doses there is unpleasant nausea, dizziness and sweating. It is antagonized by naloxone.

Unfortunately, pethidine dependence occurs and this drug comes under Schedule 2 (p. 195). Tolerance develops.

Pethidine is readily absorbed from the small intestine and rapidly inactivated in the liver, only about 10% being excreted in the urine. It crosses the placental barrier.

Preparations

Pethidine injection, BP. This contains 50 mg of pethidine hydrochloride per ml and the dose is 25–100 mg s.c. or i.m., or 25–50 mg i.v.

Pethidine tablets, BP. These contain 25 or 50 mg and the recommended adult dose is 50–100 mg.

Equagesic is a proprietary preparation containing ethoheptazine citrate 75 mg, meprobamate 150 mg and aspirin 250 mg. Ethoheptazine appears in the US National Formulary as an analgesic that is chemically related to pethidine. The advantages are not obvious.

Methadone (Amidone)

Methadone (Physeptone) is a synthetic analgesic with chemical and pharmacological similarities to morphine. It is firmly bound to tissue protein and there is gradual accumulation of the drug, with slow excretion of metabolites in the urine and faeces. It causes as much respiratory depression as does an amount of morphine that would have similar analgesic effects and is unsuitable for use in obstetrics, since it passes through the placenta. Nausea and vomiting may occur and there is biliary tract spasm and miosis. The drug would be valuable in treating cough were it not for the fact that dependence may occur. This is less severe than with other narcotics and the withdrawal of morphine or heroin is sometimes made easier by the giving of methadone orally in the early stages of treatment.

When it is used as an analgesic, the dose is 5–10 mg (methadone tablets, BP, contain 5 mg). Methadone injection, BP, contains 10 mg/ml and the dose is 5–10 mg s.c.

Pentazocine

Pentazocine (Fortral, Talwin) is a synthetic *N*-allyl derivative of the narcotic analgesic phenazocine and it is a strong analgesic that has weak opiate antagonist properties. It obviously has a chemical similarity to morphine. Its peak analgesic effect occurs about 1–3 hours after an oral dose, depending on

PENTAZOCINE

the amount given and other factors, while after an i.v. injection, the peak effect is in about 15 minutes, and, when given i.m., the most benefit is after about an hour. It is not fully controlled under the Misuse of Drugs Act in the UK, but there have been reports of dependence, problems of withdrawal, development of tolerance and habitual taking of the drug because of its ability to cause euphoria.

Pentazocine is perhaps less likely to cause respiratory depression than equianalgesic doses of morphine, but there is dispute about this and certainly such depression can occur and may be reversed by naloxone. The drug differs from morphine in that it causes slight hypertension and tachycardia rather than hypotension and bradycardia. These effects are associated with increased plasma catecholamine levels. Pentazocine should be used with caution in acute myocardial infarction, since it causes an increase in mean aortic pulmonary artery pressure, in mean aortic pressure, and in total peripheral resistance if an effective dose is given i.v.

Pentazocine given during labour provides relief from pain without having detrimental effects on mother or fetus, but should not be given more frequently than 2-hourly by injection, or late in labour. It crosses the placental barrier, but to a lesser degree than pethidine. However, it may cause nausea and vomiting.

Pentazocine does not cause a feeling of mental detachment, and in severe pain this is a disadvantage. One problem about its use is that it may cause unpleasant and disturbing hallucinations, whether it is given by mouth or by injection. The cause of these hallucinations is not always obvious to the doctor if he does not know of this possible adverse effect. The drug should be given with caution to patients with severely impaired renal or hepatic function, and ambulant patients should not drive cars or operate machinery, because of its sedative effects.

Pharmacokinetics

Absorption from an oral dose is usually good, but there is considerable individual variation. In addition, there is variation in the ability to metabolize the substance in the liver. It is excreted in the urine, partly unchanged, but largely as glucuronide conjugates.

Preparations

Pentazocine injection, BNF. This is available in ampoules containing 30 mg in 1 ml, as pentazocine lactate. It can be given s.c., i.m. or i.v. For severe pain in the adult, the dose is 40–60 mg, and for moderate pain 30 mg. The dose can be repeated every 3 or 4 hours.

Pentazocine tablets, BNF. These contain 25 mg and the dose is 25–100 mg every 3 or 4 hours. Capsules and suppositories are also available.

Dextropropoxyphene

[This drug is also available in combination with other drugs as Cosalgesic, Dolasan, Distalgesic, Napsalgesic.]

Dextropropoxyphene (Depronal SA, Doloxene) is a synthetic analgesic drug structurally related to methadone. It is widely prescribed in the UK, particularly as Distalgesic. Each tablet of this contains 32.5 mg of dextropropoxyphene hydrochloride, BP, with paracetamol, BP, 325 mg (p. 128). Soluble tablets contain 50 mg dextropropoxyphene napsylate, BP, with 325 mg of paracetamol. There is no obvious advantage in giving the drug as an analgesic either alone or combined with other agents and there is concern about the effects of overdosage. Admittedly, it is unlikely to cause alimentary bleeding. Dextropropoxyphene may cause respiratory depression, while paracetamol overdosage can cause acute hepatic failure. Death from respiratory failure has been reported to have occurred within an hour when an estimated 15 tablets of Distalgesic were taken together with much alcohol. Pulmonary oedema has been found. Other adverse effects of dextropropoxyphene are nausea, dizziness, headache, rashes, gastrointestinal disturbances, jaundice and drug dependence. The drug crosses the placental barrier. The antidote is naloxone (p. 114).

NON-NARCOTIC ANALGESICS, ANTIPYRETICS AND ANTI-INFLAMMATORY DRUGS

Some drugs, such as aspirin (p. 122), relieve pain, lower a raised temperature and diminish inflammatory reactions in conditions such as rheumatoid arthritis. The mode of action of many of them has been discussed (p. 107). Others, such as paracetamol (p. 128), do not appreciably share this anti-inflammatory action. Corticosteroids (p. 405) and corticotrophin (p. 373) have an anti-inflammatory effect, but are not considered in this chapter. Very many new preparations are being marketed, and most are included in Table 2.1. There is doubt about their relative efficacy, concern about the adverse reactions produced in a small proportion of patients by some of them and only time will tell whether the newer preparations are safer than the older ones. No medical practitioner is likely to be in the habit of prescribing more than one or two of them and in some countries (such as the USA) a number have not been passed for clinical use by the regulatory authorities. The cost of the product must always be taken into account.

Table 2.1   *Non-steroid anti-inflammatory drugs*

Approved name (UK)	Proprietary names (mainly UK)	Type of drug
Aloxiprin	Palaprin Forte	O-acetyl salicylic acid derivative
Amidopyrine	Not on sale in UK	Pyrazole derivative
Aspirin	Numerous	Acetyl salicylic acid
Azapropazone	Rheumox	Pyrazole derivative
Benorylate	Benoral	O-acetyl salicylic acid derivative
Benoxaprofen	Opren (withdrawn)	Substituted phenyl propionic acid
Chloroquine	Avloclor Nivaquine	Substituted quinoline
Diclofenac	Voltarol	Substituted phenylacetic acid
Diflunisal	Dolobid	Salicylic acid derivative
Dipyrone	Note on sale in UK	Pyrazole derivative
Fenbufen	Lederfen	Biphenyl substituted butyric acid
Fenclofenac	Flenac	Dichlorophenoxy substituted acetic acid
Fenoprofen	Fenopron Progesic Nalfon (USA)	Phenoxyphenyl substituted propionic acid
Feprazone	Methrazone	Pyrazole derivative
Flufenamic acid	Meralen	Substituted anthranilic acid
Flurbiprofen	Froben	Substituted phenyl propionic acid
Hydroxychloroquine	Plaquenil	Substituted quinoline
Ibuprofen	Brufen Ibu-Slo Motrin (USA)	Substituted phenyl propionic acid
Indomethacin	Indocid Imbrilon Indocin (USA) Mobilan	Substituted indole acetic acid
Indoprofen	Flosint	Substituted phenyl propionic acid
Ketoprofen	Alrheumat Orudis	Substituted phenyl propionic acid
Meclofenamic acid	Meclomen	Substituted anthranilic acid
Mefenamic acid	Ponstan Ponstel (USA)	Substituted anthranilic acid
Mofebutazone	Not on sale in UK	Pyrazole derivative
Naproxen	Naprosyn Synflex	Substituted naphthyl propionic acid
Oxyphenbutazone	Tandacote Tanderil Tandearil (USA) Tandalgesic (with paracetamol)	Pyrazole derivative

Approved name (UK)	Proprietary names (mainly UK)	Type of drug
Penicillamine	Cuprimine Distamine Pendramine	Dimethyl cysteine
Phenazone (named Antipyrine in USA)	Auralgicin Auraltone Sedonan (ear drops)	Pyrazole derivative
Phenylbutazone	Butacote Butazolidin Butazone Parazolidin	Pyrazole derivative
Piroxicam	Feldene	An oxicam
Salsalate	Disalcid	Salicylic acid derivative
Sodium aurothio-malate injection	Myocrisin	Gold injection
Sulindac	Clinoril	Indene acetic acid derivative
Sulphinpyrazone	Anturan	Pyrazole derivative
Tiaprofenic acid	Surgam	Substituted propionic acid
Tolmetin	Tolectin	Pyrrole acetic acid derivative
Zomepirac	Zomax (withdrawn)	Pyrrole acetic acid derivative

The probable action of many of these substances on the biosynthesis of prostaglandins has already been discussed (p. 107).

SELECTION OF SUITABLE THERAPEUTIC AGENTS

Although this book deals with clinical pharmacology rather than the management of individual patients, it must be accepted that there is a practical problem in deciding which drug to choose from, particularly in treating rheumatoid arthritis. Huskisson, in a report published by the Arthritis and Rheumatism Council, points out that there are five groups of suitable drugs. These are (1) simple analgesics (paracetamol, codeine, aspirin in doses of less than 2 g daily, and Distalgesic); (2) analgesics with minor anti-inflammatory properties (ibuprofen, ketoprofen, mefenamic acid, and naproxen: since his report, there can be added numerous chemically related substances); (3) analgesics with major anti-inflammatory properties (aspirin in full dosage of at least 3.6 g daily, indomethacin, phenylbutazone and related substances); (4) 'purely' anti-inflammatory drugs (corticosteroids and corticotrophin); (5) 'slow-acting' drugs (4-aminoquinolines, gold, penicillamine, and immunosuppressives: levamisole (p. 93) given by mouth may be added to this group).

Some patients respond to aspirin alone. Others require either a group (2) drug or indomethacin. Phenylbutazone and other pyrazole derivatives are widely used, but all the drugs listed above have their dangers (p. 131). Group (4) and (5) drugs are for more seriously inconvenienced patients.

Aspirin

Originally, aspirin was a trade name for acetylsalicylic acid, but later became the approved name. In some countries it is still a proprietary name. The word 'salicylic' itself came from the Latin *salix*, meaning a willow, and from ancient times willow bark has been used to relieve the symptoms of a feverish illness.

The active principle of willow bark was found to be salicin, a crystalline β-glucoside, but in due course it was displaced as a therapeutic agent by synthetic salicylic acid for external use, and by sodium salicylate and aspirin for oral therapy. For most purposes, aspirin is employed rather than sodium salicylate, and it is probably the most commonly used of all therapeutic agents. The formulae for salicylic acid and for aspirin are as follows:

SALICYLIC ACID   ACETYLSALICYLIC ACID (ASPIRIN)

Aspirin is an analgesic that is not habit forming, except that patients may continue to take tablets of the drug daily for years, but without developing dependence in the accepted sense of the term (p. 182). It is also antipyretic and anti-inflammatory. Aspirin and other drugs with similar effects increase heat loss by an action on the temperature-regulating centre in the midbrain, setting this 'thermostat' at a lower level. The possible ways in which they may exercise their anti-inflammatory effects have already been discussed (p. 107). Aspirin is not effective when pain is severe, but gives relief in aches of the musculoskeletal structures, in mild headache and in dysmenorrhoea. It is not in any way a hypnotic, though many patients firmly believe that it helps them to sleep.

Actions on the Respiratory System

The effects of salicylates require careful consideration for full understanding of the metabolic disorders that occur from overdosage. Salicylates stimulate the respiratory centre directly and by an increased production of CO_2 peripherally. The consequent steps with a high dose are as shown in Fig. 2.1.

It will be seen that toxic doses of salicylates first cause respiratory alkalosis and later can cause both metabolic acidosis, and even what is commonly referred to as respiratory acidosis, because of paralysis of the respiratory centre.

It is not uncommon for aspirin to induce attacks of asthma (p. 573), and this is important to know, because the cause of the attacks may be overlooked. These patients may then be sensitive to other non-narcotic analgesics and to the food-colouring dye tartrazine.

A. CAUSATION OF COMPENSATED RESPIRATORY ALKALOSIS

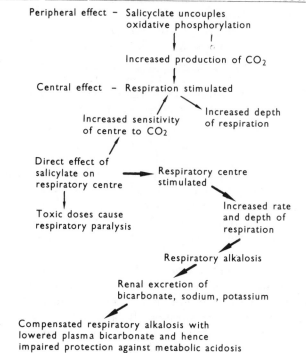

Peripheral effect – Salicyclate uncouples
oxidative phosphorylation

Increased production of CO_2

Central effect – Respiration stimulated

Increased sensitivity of centre to CO_2

Increased depth of respiration

Direct effect of salicylate on respiratory centre

Respiratory centre stimulated

Toxic doses cause respiratory paralysis

Increased rate and depth of respiration

Respiratory alkalosis

Renal excretion of bicarbonate, sodium, potassium

Compensated respiratory alkalosis with lowered plasma bicarbonate and hence impaired protection against metabolic acidosis

B. CAUSATION OF ACIDOSIS

This occurs with very large doses, especially in children

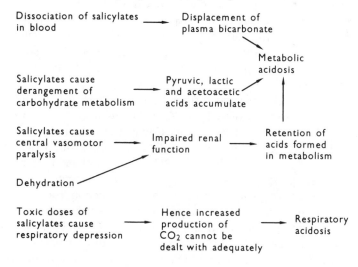

Dissociation of salicylates in blood

Displacement of plasma bicarbonate

Metabolic acidosis

Salicylates cause derangement of carbohydrate metabolism

Pyruvic, lactic and acetoacetic acids accumulate

Salicylates cause central vasomotor paralysis

Impaired renal function

Retention of acids formed in metabolism

Dehydration

Toxic doses of salicylates cause respiratory depression

Hence increased production of CO_2 cannot be dealt with adequately

Respiratory acidosis

Fig. 2.1 Effects of high doses of salicylates on metabolism and respiration.

Actions on the Cardiovascular System
There is no problem with therapeutic doses, but large amounts may cause peripheral vasodilatation and toxic doses lead to central vasomotor paralysis. However, in acute rheumatic fever, doses of salicylates large enough to produce 'salicylism' (p. 128) are often given, and for some reason this causes an increased plasma volume, with consequent increase in cardiac work. In cardiac failure or active carditis, it is wise not to use *sodium* salicylate, as was done in the past, since this introduces an unnecessary increase in sodium intake.

Uricosuric Action
Salicylates have been used to treat acute or chronic gout, but there are better methods of therapy (p. 137). They inhibit both tubular secretion and reabsorption of uric acid, but the latter action is more important. Salicylates should not be given, even in small doses, to those receiving treatment with modern uricosuric drugs, since they antagonize their action.

Effects on Blood Coagulation and on Thrombotic Incidents
Large doses of salicylates prolong the 'one-stage prothrombin time' (p. 482), possibly by interfering with prothrombin synthesis. There is also said to be a decrease in factor VII concentration. If salicylates are given to patients receiving oral anticoagulants, the dosage will probably require to be reduced. Aspirin also inhibits the release by platelets of various compounds derived from special granules within them. The substances normally released include adenosine diphosphate (ADP), serotonin, cationic proteins, prostaglandins E_2 and F_2, and also hydrolytic enzymes, including phospholipase A_1. During prostaglandin formation in platelets (as in a thrombus), thromboxane A_2, which has a half-life of 30 seconds, appears in them and is a powerful stimulator of platelet aggregation. Aspirin interferes with the production of cyclic endoperoxides from arachidonic acid (p. 107) and hence diminishes the formation of thromboxane A_2, thereby inhibiting platelet aggregation. It may be for this reason that aspirin prolongs the bleeding time andicauses a mild haemostatic defect.

The matter is complicated further by the finding that, in the walls of arteries and veins in several species, including man, the prostaglandin endoperoxide derived from arachidonic acid gives rise to a derivative named prostacyclin (PGI_2), which has very different properties from those of thromboxane A_2. The way in which PGI_2 inhibits platelet aggregation is discussed later (p. 484). PGI_2 is also said to have a protective action on the gastric mucosa. Perhaps interference with its production is a reason why so many non-steroidal anti-inflammatory drugs are gastric irritants.

It is difficult to predict whether aspirin may have beneficial effects in the management of cerebral thrombosis, venous thrombosis or coronary thrombosis and we have even less knowledge about the possible effects of other non-steroidal anti-inflammatory drugs. However, it seems that a *low* dose of aspirin preferentially blocks platelet thromboxane A_2 generation, whereas a *high* dose blocks PGI_2 production as well. The clinical application of this and the possible individual variation in what constitutes a high or a low dose remains to be explored. It must be realized that a thrombus in a blood vessel differs structurally from a blood clot in vitro (p. 474).

The action of another substance used to inhibit platelet aggregation may be mentioned in parentheses here. *Sulphinpyrazone* (Anturan) is a uricosuric agent closely related to phenylbutazone. Under certain conditions it inhibits platelet release (p. 474), but does not prolong the bleeding time. Unlike aspirin, it inhibits platelet function only for as long as it is present in the circulation. However, since it inhibits platelet aggregation and adhesion and inhibits the synthesis of prostaglandins by plates, this and the results of some clinical trials have led to it being promoted for the prevention of cardiac mortality following recent myocardial infarction. However, beta-adrenergic blocking agents (p. 310), which have a totally different and little understood mode of action, are also under trial for this. The evidence for their efficacy is possibly more convincing.

Dipyridamole (Persantin), which is used with aspirin to prevent thrombotic incidents, is considered elsewhere (p. 485).

Actions on the Kidney

As will be mentioned later, large doses of phenacetin taken for a prolonged period lead to renal papillary necrosis and eventual renal failure. Salicylates increase the number of red cells and tubular epithelial cells in the urine. Those who have taken phenacetin for long periods have frequently used it in combination with aspirin and it cannot be said with certainty that the long-term continuous use of aspirin does not contribute to analgesic nephropathy or that the danger does not lie in using the two together.

Actions on Endocrine Glands

High doses of salicylates cause release of adrenaline from the adrenal medulla and very large doses stimulate corticotrophin secretion by an action on the hypothalamus. The plasma protein-bound iodine level is decreased by constant taking of aspirin, and in diabetics, the blood sugar level is lowered, perhaps by an increased peripheral utilization of glucose. With large doses, the release of adrenaline may lead to hyperglycaemia.

Actions on the Gastrointestinal Tract

Salicylic acid itself dissolves the cells of the stratum corneum and is used to destroy corns and warts, a suitable preparation being salicylic acid collodion, BPC, which is a 12% w/v preparation in flexible collodion. Obviously salicylic acid cannot be taken by mouth and has to be given as a salicylate. If free salicylic acid were to be liberated in the stomach, it might be expected to be irritant. Aspirin in high doses causes nausea and vomiting by a central effect, but it and other salicylates taken by mouth also have a local irritant action.

The most common effect is increased exfoliation of gastric mucosal cells. There is individual variation in symptoms, but gastroscopic examination of the stomach shows that particles may cause haemorrhagic areas or superficial ulceration. In many subjects, high doses will cause upper abdominal discomfort and symptoms of a peptic ulcer will be exacerbated; however, some patients find that these disagreeable effects follow the taking of even a single aspirin tablet. About one-third of those taking aspirin have dyspepsia as a result.

Aspirin itself is soluble 1 in 300 parts w/v of water, and it is the insoluble salicylates that are likely to be deposited in gastric mucosal folds, where they cause damage. There is evidence that a true gastric ulcer may sometimes be induced by aspirin and most authorities agree that the taking of aspirin for a number of days causes occult blood to appear in the faeces. Many patients admitted to hospital with a gastroduodenal haemorrhage have taken aspirin just before this has occurred, but there is always the counter-argument that so many people take the substance that this may be coincidental. There are, however, some individuals who suffer from alimentary bleeding whenever they take the drug. A combination of aspirin and spirits may be particularly harmful.

Because of these problems, many preparations of aspirin have been developed in the hope that they will be less irritant. Sodium salicylate itself might be more suitable, but it is less effective as an analgesic. Calcium aspirin is soluble 1 in 6 parts w/v of water, but is best freshly prepared by dissolving aspirin soluble tablets, BP, in water before they are swallowed, since calcium aspirin is readily hydrolysed. The soluble aspirin preparation consists of aspirin 300 mg with anhydrous citric acid, calcium carbonate and saccharin sodium, and, in water, calcium acetylsalicylate forms. This is possibly the best aspirin preparation. Other forms are buffered aspirin, buffered soluble aspirin, effervescent buffered aspirin, enteric-coated aspirin, slow-release forms, and an aluminium–aspirin compound (aloxiprin) which is said to liberate aspirin slowly in the stomach, but rapidly in the small intestine. Aspirin can be given as a suppository and occasionally patients with rheumatoid arthritis who cannot tolerate preparations taken by mouth find that this has beneficial effects.

Pharmacokinetics
What happens when tablets of aspirin or sodium salicylate are taken depends in the first instance on the dissolution rate of the tablets and on the gastric emptying time. Both aspirin and sodium salicylate are rapidly absorbed from the stomach and small intestine, the latter drug entering the blood stream more speedily than the former. At the low pH normally found in the gastric juice, aspirin and sodium salicylate are poorly ionized, are lipid-soluble and diffuse through cell membranes. Once in the gastric mucosal cell, they are in a more ionized form and are therefore less diffusible. In the treatment of acute rheumatism, sodium bicarbonate used to be given with sodium salicylate, to

minimize the amount of irritant salicylic acid free in the stomach. In the presence of alkalis, aspirin is more soluble, and this compensates for it being more slowly absorbed through less being in the non-ionized form. In any event, much of the absorption continues in the small intestine. (Aspirin cannot be kept in solution with alkalis for therapeutic administration, since there is rapid hydrolysis to acetic and salicylic acids.)

Aspirin is absorbed as such, but much is hydrolysed fairly rapidly to salicylic acid in the gastrointestinal mucosa, plasma, red cells, liver and synovial fluid. Although this hydrolysis to salicylic acid occurs, aspirin itself is pharmacologically active. Salicylic acid is bound to plasma proteins up to as much as 80%, but little aspirin as such is bound in this way. After a single dose of 600 mg, the half-life in the body is about 3 hours (i.e. half the amount of the drug in the body is eliminated every 3 hours). If a very large dose is taken, the glycine conjugation mechanism is saturated and the half-life may be as much as 24 hours. Prolonged administration of the same dose of aspirin is often associated with a fall in plasma concentration, perhaps because of hepatic enzyme induction.

The urine usually contains mainly salicyluric acid (a conjugate with glycine), together with salicylic glucuronides, some gentisic acid and a variable amount of free salicylate. In alkaline urine, most of the excretion is as free salicylate, and the amount put out in this form may be eight times as much as in acid urine. This is important in practice, in that forced alkaline diuresis may be effective in treating salicylate poisoning. Sodium bicarbonate given with sodium salicylate promotes its excretion.

Salicylates readily cross the placental barrier.

Preparations
Aspirin tablets, BP, contain 300 mg; *aspirin soluble tablets, BP*, contain 300 mg aspirin with suitable added materials; *aspirin and codeine tablets, BP*, contain 400 mg aspirin and 8 mg codeine phosphate; and *soluble aspirin and codeine tablets, BP*, also contain these proportions.

Aspirin, paracetamol and codeine tablets contain aspirin 250 mg, paracetamol 250 mg and codeine phosphate 6.8 mg; and *aspirin and caffeine tablets* contain 350 mg aspirin and 30 mg caffeine.

In addition, there are many proprietary preparations, some of which contain aspirin in combination with various other substances, occasionally for no very obvious reason. Those who are believed to be sensitive to aspirin should carry a list of preparations that should be avoided and this list may include certain pick-me-ups and powders sold to make substitute fruit drinks. *Benorylate* is an ester of aspirin and paracetamol that is believed to cause less gastric irritation and blood loss than aspirin itself. It is available as a 40% suspension or in sachets or as tablets. *Diflunisal* (Dolobid) is 5-(2,4-difluorophenyl) salicylic acid. It has no effect on platelet aggregation and it is claimed that it has no significant effect on gastrointestinal blood loss. It is said that it is not metabolized to salicylic acid. The Stevens–Johnson syndrome (p. 569) has been reported after its use. Choline magnesium trisalicylate (Trilisate) is available, but is expensive and has no obvious advantage.

Mention has been made of the use of sodium salicylate in treating rheumatic fever. Sodium salicylate mixture, BPC, includes in its formulation 500 mg in a total fluid volume of 10 ml, and sodium salicylate mixture, strong, BPC, has 1 g in 10 ml.

In acute rheumatism, when aspirin is used, the daily dose in children should not exceed 80 mg/kg body weight or less if the child is overweight. In adults with this condition, the dose is 6–10 g/day, and if sodium salicylate is used the quantity should not exceed 120 mg/kg body weight.

Adverse Effects
Mild salicylate intoxication is known as salicylism. There is deafness, ringing in the ears, dizziness, and headache. The skin then becomes flushed, and there is vomiting, restlessness, confusion, and hypernoea. With large overdoses, there is hyperpyrexia, mania, convulsions, coma, ketosis, and respiratory failure.

Reference has already been made to possible alimentary bleeding with normal doses and to renal irritation. Aspirin can cause bronchial asthma, vasomotor rhinitis, or urticaria.

Salicylic acid is used as a 2% lotion or ointment because of its keratolytic activity in psoriasis and certain other skin diseases. If the area is large it can have toxic effects, and even death from salicylism has been reported.

Paracetamol (Acetaminophen, USP)

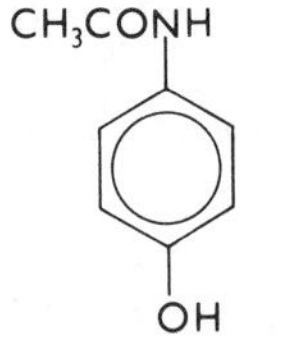

PARACETAMOL

For many years the aniline derivatives acetanilide and phenacetin (acetophenetidin) were used for their analgesic and antipyretic actions, but acetanilide has ceased to be given, since it causes cyanosis from methaemoglobinaemia. This is because a small amount of acetanilide is converted into aniline and this gives rise to a metabolite that somehow produces methaemoglobin, a pigment which is no longer able to participate in the transport of oxygen. In addition, some sulphaemoglobin is found.

Phenacetin is not now in use in the UK, because of the adverse effects it has on the kidneys. If large amounts are taken for a prolonged period, necrosis of the renal papillae occurs (analgesic nephropathy) and in due course renal failure is likely. Pyelonephritis is often associated with this. Carcinoma of the renal pelvis may also occur. It should be added that it is not yet certain that phenacetin is the only drug to cause renal papillary necrosis, since the patients who develop it have often been taking a combination of analgesics, and there is uncertainty about the role of aspirin in producing such changes (p. 125).

Paracetamol is *N*-acetyl-*p*-aminophenol, the major metabolite of phenacetin, and it has similar analgesic and antipyretic actions, but does not have anti-inflammatory activity. For this reason it is not included in Table 4.1. It has replaced phenacetin in compound tablets of aspirin (p. 127). It has advantages in that it does not cause gastrointestinal ulceration or alimentary bleeding, and it has not been shown to lead to renal papillary necrosis. It does not cause methaemoglobinaemia or haemolysis, and thrombocytopenia is very rare. It is largely conjugated in the liver, predominantly with glucuronic acid. However, with a therapeutic dose, less than 10% is converted into a toxic metabolite and this is rapidly inactivated by conjugation with reduced glutathione in the liver. With a large overdose of paracetamol, glutathione becomes depleted and the metabolite causes acute centrilobular hepatic necrosis. What is formed is a highly reactive alkylating metabolite that binds irreversibly to hepatic macromolecules. Hepatotoxicity is enhanced by the previous consumption of barbiturates, ethyl alcohol and other microsomal inducing agents. The clinical features are not clear-cut at first, consisting of vague abdominal symptoms, followed by definite abdominal pain, tenderness over the liver, jaundice and hepatic coma. Glutathione precursors and SH donors, such as cysteine, cysteamine, and methionine, may prevent hepatotoxicity. Therapeutic trials with cysteamine or *N*-acetylcysteine administered i.v. have given promising results, but some authorities consider that methionine given by mouth is as effective (2.5 g, then further doses according to the plasma paracetamol concentration). The dosage of *N*-acetylcysteine recommended is 150 mg/kg body weight in 200 ml 5% dextrose over 15 minutes then 50 mg/kg body weight in 500 ml 5% dextrose over 4 hours and 100 mg/kg body weight in 1 litre 5% dextrose over the next 16 hours. Possibly cysteamine inhibits the oxidation of paracetamol by microsomes, but the mechanism by which these agents prevent hepatic necrosis is uncertain. The action may be multifactorial, with restoration of glutathione and with these substances acting as alternative substrates for the toxic metabolite. To be effective, therapy *must* be commenced within 10 hours of injection: after 12 hours, this treatment may have detrimental effects. In children, methionine or cysteamine is sometimes given by mouth for paracetamol poisoning.

Another possible consequence of an overdose is acute tubular necrosis.

Paracetamol has a half-life of about 2 hours. It crosses the placental barrier, but is not a hazard to the fetus in conventional dosage. Its mode of action in relieving pain seems to be central. Excretion of the conjugates, together with a small amount of free paracetamol, is in the urine.

Preparations

Paracetamol tablets, BP. These contain 500 mg and the dose is 0.5–1 g up to four times daily. Reference has been made to benorylate (p. 127) and to the problems that can arise if dextropropoxyphene is formulated with paracetamol (p. 119). Another combination that is marketed is paracetamol together with the minor tranquillizer chlormezanone under the proprietary name of Lobak. This does not have an anti-inflammatory action and has no direct action on muscles. Paracetamol is also combined with phenylbutazone under the proprietary name of Parazolidin.

Pyrazolone Derivatives

The formulae of three derivatives of phenylpyrazolone used for their analgesic and antipyretic actions are given below:

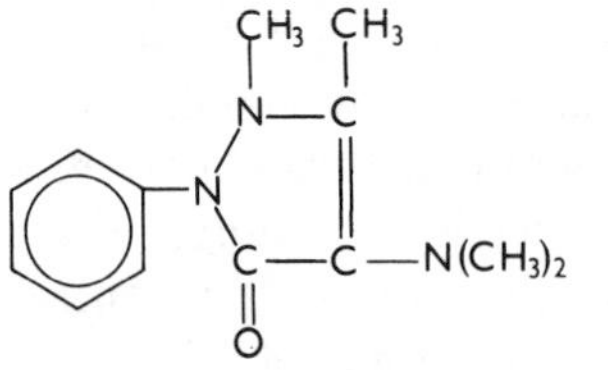

AMIDOPYRINE

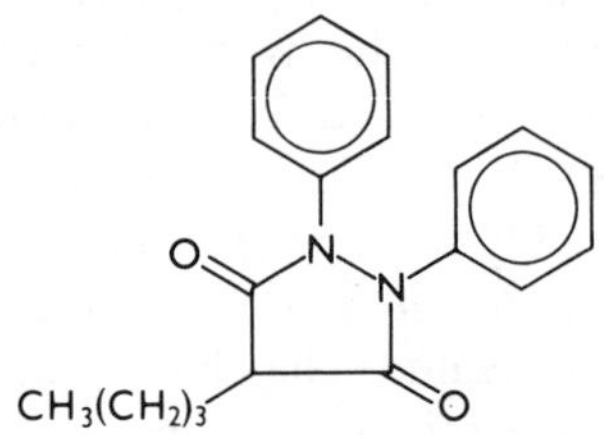

PHENYLBUTAZONE

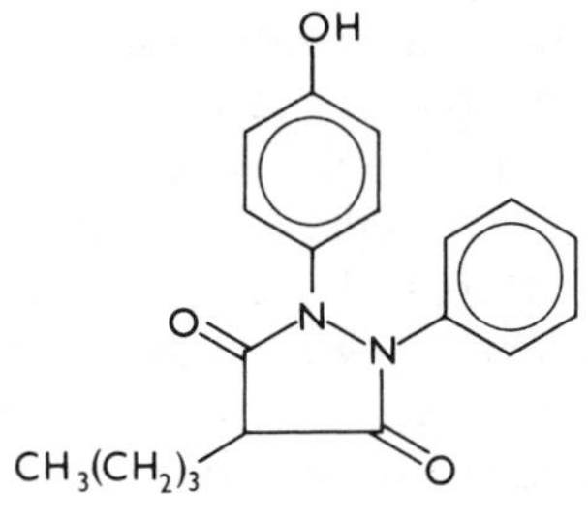

OXYPHENBUTAZONE

Amidopyrine (aminopyrine, pyramidon)

Amidopyrine is still used in some countries, but seldom in the British Isles or North America, because of the number of instances in which it has caused agranulocytosis, aplastic anaemia or thrombocytopenia. The mechanism of this adverse effect is not known.

Phenylbutazone

Phenylbutazone (Butacote, Butaphen, Butazolidin, Butazone, Parazolidin) is available in 100 or 200 mg tablets, and also in 250 mg suppositories and ampoules containing 600 mg in 3 ml with 1% lignocaine. It is used in rheumatoid arthritis, ankylosing spondylitis, osteoarthrosis and a variety of musculoskeletal disorders. It may give relief in superficial phlebothrombosis, and although it has some uricosuric action, the benefit obtained in acute gout is more from its anti-inflammatory properties. It is normally taken by mouth, but suppositories can be used to avoid gastric irritation. It is rarely given by injection, but if this is done, it has to be administered carefully i.m. and never i.v. Its possible mode of action as an anti-inflammatory agent has already been discussed (p. 107).

Dosage
In the first instance, the patient is given 400–600 mg daily in divided doses with meals, this being reduced to half the amount or less if possible. Regular blood counts may be done, but if a blood dyscrasia occurs rapidly, this precaution may not be helpful.

Adverse Effects
Phenylbutazone is well absorbed from the small intestine and almost all is normally bound to plasma proteins. Here it may compete for binding sites with other drugs and have serious results. Thus it displaces warfarin and related drugs (p. 482) and may cause bleeding. It also displaces tolbutamide (p. 395), chlorpropamide (p. 395), thus interfering with diabetic control, and sulphonamides.

Phenylbutazone causes significant retention of sodium and chloride, with an associated reduction in the urinary output. The plasma volume increases and this is important since it can produce cardiac failure, particularly in patients who already have heart disease. The uptake of iodine by the thyroid gland is reduced, and enzymes in the Krebs cycle are inhibited. Liver enzymes are induced and this may affect the concentration of other drugs in the body. The hepatic microsomes almost completely metabolize phenylbutazone, giving oxyphenbutazone and γ-hydroxyphenylbutazone. However, only a small amount is excreted as either of these forms or as phenylbutazone itself.

Phenylbutazone is a potent drug, but in addition to the side-effects indicated above, it has other actions which should make the doctor think very carefully before using it. Thus it should not be given for vague musculoskeletal aches, and, as it is used for conditions that are painful but not potentially fatal, the author feels that patients should be warned that it can cause dangerous or even fatal adverse reactions. Certainly in the UK reports of fatal blood dyscrasias, including aplastic anaemia, are more commonly attributed to phenylbutazone or oxyphenbutazone than to any other drug. Such effects are found more commonly with prolonged usage, but may occur after a short course.

Other adverse effects include gastric irritation with gastrointestinal bleeding, perforation of a duodenal ulcer, and the occurrence of various skin rashes. Fluid retention is mentioned above. Less commonly, jaundice and perhaps renal tubular necrosis have occurred. Insomnia, blurring of vision and even leukaemia have been reported, though this last event may be coincidental.

Contraindications
Phenylbutazone should be avoided if there is oedema, hypertension, or danger of cardiac failure; in renal or hepatic disease; after hepatitis; if there is peptic ulceration, dyspepsia, or hiatus hernia; or if the drug itself or any other pyrazole derivative has caused trouble. It should be avoided by those who have had skin rashes or blood dyscrasias. The possibility of interaction with other drugs, particularly anticoagulants, must also be remembered.

Oxyphenbutazone

Oxyphenbutazone is the hydroxy analogue of phenylbutazone and a product of its metabolism (above), but is also marketed as a therapeutic agent in 100 mg tablets (Tanderil). It is used for the same conditions as phenylbutazone and can produce similar adverse reactions. It has no obvious advantages. It is available as a 10% eye ointment for certain inflammatory conditions in the eye and in 250 mg suppositories.

Other pyrazolone derivatives in general use are azapropazone and feprazone. Both may give rise to serious adverse reactions. Mention is made of sulphinpyrazone on pp. 125 and 485, and its uricosuric activity is referred to on p. 139.

Substituted Phenylpropionic Acids

The formulae of four of these are as follows:

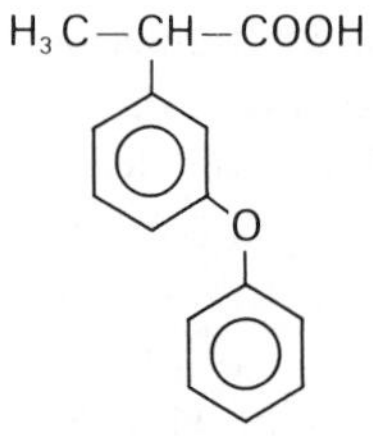

FENOPROFEN 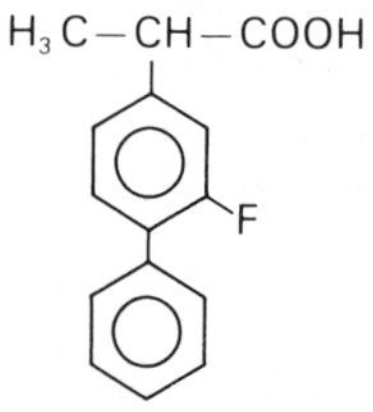   FLURBIPROFEN 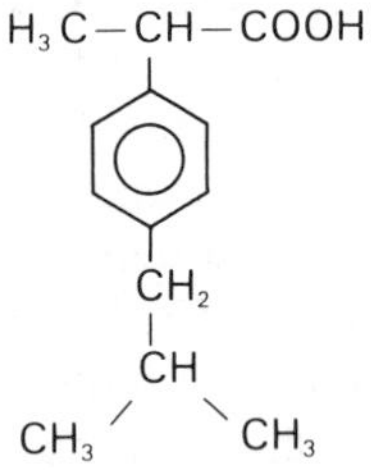   IBUPROFEN 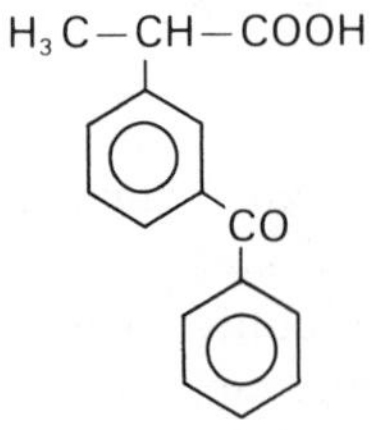   KETOPROFEN

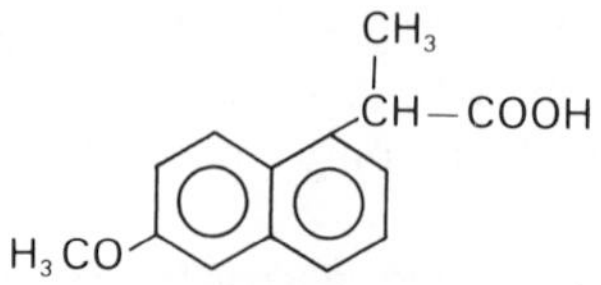

NAPROXEN

The names of others are included in Table 2.1. In addition, the formula of naproxen, a substituted naphthyl propionic acid, is shown. Another commercially available substituted propionic acid is tiaprofenic acid (Surgam).

Unfortunately, each of this group of compounds has been found to have adverse effects in a small number of patients. These include rashes, alimentary bleeding, aplastic anaemia, agranulocytosis and thrombocytopenia. Symptoms of peptic ulceration may be aggravated. Their safety in pregnancy is uncertain.

Benoxaprofen

Benoxaprofen (Opren), another substituted propionic acid, had the advantage that it could be used to treat rheumatoid arthritis or osteoarthrosis in a single dose at bedtime, but was withdrawn because of adverse reactions which included, in many patients, a photo-chemically induced form of skin response.

Substituted Anthranilic Acids

Flufenamic acid, meclofenamic acid and mefenamic acid

The fenamates flufenamic acid (Meralen), meclofenamic acid (Meclomen) and mefenamic acid (Ponstan) are chemically related to the salicylates, but, in addition to inhibiting prostaglandin synthesis, they appear to antagonize certain effects of formed prostaglandins. They are analgesics with antipyretic and anti-inflammatory activity. They bind strongly to plasma proteins and so should not be used with oral anticoagulants. They have effects on the alimentary tract similar to other analgesics already considered, may cause diarrhoea and sometimes lead to rashes. Haemolytic anaemia may occur with mefenamic acid. Bronchospasm has been reported.

Substituted Indole Acetic Acid

Indomethacin

Indomethacin (Indocid, Imbrilon, Mobilan) has the following formula:

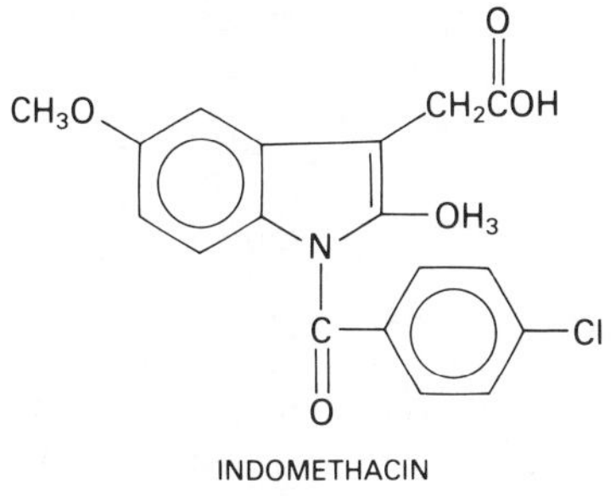

INDOMETHACIN

Indomethacin has analgesic, anti-inflammatory and antipyretic effects and is one of the most potent inhibitors of cyclo-oxygenase and hence of prostaglandin formation. It may also have a central effect as an analgesic. It also inhibits the mobility of polymorphonuclear leucocytes. It is about 90% bound to plasma proteins and extensively bound to tissues, but is largely converted to inactive metabolites.

Indomethacin is of value in rheumatoid arthritis, ankylosing spondylitis and conditions such as bursitis and capsulitis. It also gives relief in acute gout, though not because of an uricosuric action. Like many other drugs, it is employed in osteoarthrosis, but without being strikingly effective, since neither inflammation nor local cellular interactions are the main problems in this condition. For some reason it may give relief in dysmenorrhoea, but, otherwise, should not be used as a simple analgesic.

Adverse Effects
Indomethacin causes alimentary disturbances, including gastrointestinal haemorrhage, and also may rarely depress the production of various formed elements of the blood. Rashes and asthmatic attacks have been reported. It is important to realize that it can cause severe frontal headache, dizziness, vertigo, hallucinations and mental confusion. There may be severe depression and even suicide. Occasionally patients, particularly elderly ones, have been admitted to mental hospitals because it has not been realized that their abnormal mental state has been a temporary result of treatment with indomethacin . Epilepsy and Parkinsonism may become worse. Indomethacin is said not to modify the effect of oral anticoagulant drugs, but, nevertheless, laboratory control should be carefully carried out.

Indomethacin is available as 25 or 50 mg capsules, in 75 mg sustained-release capsules, as a fruit-flavoured suspension (25 mg in 5 ml) and as 100 mg suppositories.

The initial dose is 25–50 mg two or three times daily with food.

Sulindac

Sulindac (Clinoril) has a closely related structure to indomethacin. It is less potent than indomethacin, but has a considerably longer plasma half-life. The indications for its use are similar and it has many of the same side-effects, but whether or not it is a superior therapeutic agent is not yet clear. Twice daily therapy is possible.

Other Drugs

Phenylacetic acid derivatives

Diclofenac (Voltarol) and **fenclofenac** (Flenac). These are substituted phenylacetic acid derivatives. Fenclofenac has a much longer half-life (12–20 hours) than diclofenac and this is an advantage when renal function is good. Adverse reactions are as with other non-steroidal anti-inflammatory drugs.

Pyrrole acetic acid derivatives

Tolmetin sodium (Tolectin). This drug is said to be similar to indomethacin in efficacy, but to have fewer of its side-effects. It is said that it does not interact with anticoagulant drugs or with drugs used to treat diabetes.

Zomepirac sodium (Zomax). This drug is closely related chemically to tolmetin. It has voluntarily been withdrawn from sale at present because of five deaths in the USA. These were thought to be due to anaphylaxis, and two of the incidents occurred in patients known to be sensitive to aspirin. If the substance becomes available again, it should not be given to aspirin-sensitive individuals.

Oxicams

Piroxicam (Feldene). This is one of a series of *N*-heterocyclic carboxamides of 1,2 benzothiazine 1,1-dioxide which have been named oxicams.

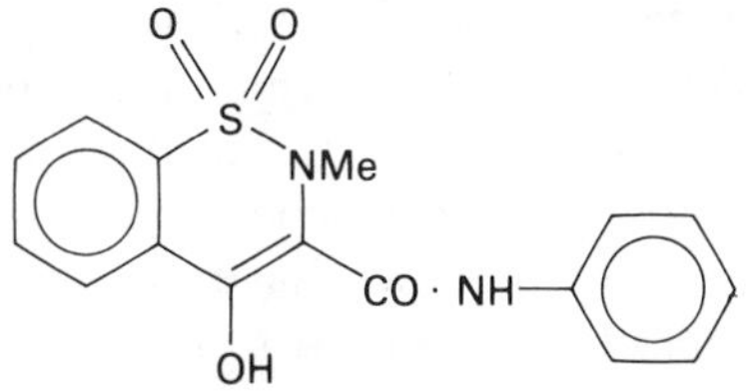

PIROXICAM

It inhibits prostaglandin synthesis and also interferes with chemotaxis of polymorphonuclear leucocytes and the migration of leucocytes. The immune reactions that occur in the inflamed joints in rheumatoid arthritis are a matter of considerable complexity. Thus polymorphonuclear cells in the synovial fluid participate in immune complex reactions and generate mediators of inflammation. Piroxicam has a beneficial effect on these pathological events. In osteoarthrosis it may be that it is the pain associated with a secondary synovitis which is given some relief. In acute gout there may be relief of inflammation.

Unfortunately this drug shares with the other analgesics the propensity to cause gastrointestinal irritation, possibly to a lesser extent than aspirin. Platelet aggregation is decreased (p. 474) and the bleeding time prolonged. The serum transaminase may rise and congestive cardiac failure can be precipitated.

Sodium aurothiomalate injection, BP

Gold (as sodium aurothiomalate, Myocrisin) injections were formerly used extensively for the treatment of rheumatoid arthritis, since they gave benefit to many patients when administered in suitable courses, and are still given by some specialists, particularly when other remedies have failed. They may be administered by deep i.m. injections, at weekly intervals, of 1, 5, and 10 mg to test the patient's tolerance, followed by 50 mg/week to a total of 1 g. Thereafter a maintenance dose of 50 mg/month is given until a total of 3 g has been administered.

Adverse Effects
This form of treatment is used less often than might be anticipated, because of the dangers of skin rashes, blood dyscrasias, nephrotoxicity and hepatic damage. Death may occur. Gold injections should be used with great care and there must be a constant watch for early evidence of adverse reactions. The manufacturer's data sheet should be carefully studied when the substance is used.

Drugs Primarily Used for Other Purposes

Penicillamine

Penicillamine is referred to on p. 526. Because of adverse reactions, it is of only limited value. Chloroquine and hydroxychloroquine have a beneficial effect in the treatment of rheumatoid arthritis, but there may be retinal damage from long-term use. Azathioprine, cyclophosphamide and methotrexate have also been used, but they too may have severe adverse effects. The anthelmintic drug levamisole has been used. How it acts is uncertain. It can be given in doses of 150 mg once a week by mouth, but can cause nausea, fever, malaise, rashes, vasculitis and neutropenia.

Corticosteroids and corticotrophin

These are considered on p. 407. Systemic corticosteroid therapy is used in rheumatoid arthritis only if other agents have failed. Corticosteroids are used, however, in vasculitis, polymyositis and dermatomyositis. Intrasynovial therapy using microcrystalline suspensions of triamcinolone or dexamethasone can be used in rheumatoid arthritis where one joint is particularly resistant, if the disease is very localized and nothing else can be used, or in gout where joint inflammation is not responding to other forms of treatment.

In summary, there are many preparations available for the treatment of rheumatoid arthritis and related conditions. Their effectiveness varies from patient to patient, and, regrettably, the possible drawbacks are numerous and sometimes serious.

Nefopam (Acupan) is marketed as an analgesic for the treatment of a variety of conditions other than the pain of myocardial infarction. It is an analogue of orphenadrine and is not related chemically to other analgesics. Its value has not yet been established.

DRUGS USED IN THE TREATMENT OF GOUT

Mention has already been made of various substances that may be used to treat the symptoms of acute gout. The preparation that is usually given in the acute attack is colchicine (p. 138), phenylbutazone (200 mg four times daily), indomethacin (50 mg four times daily) or naproxen (250 mg three times daily). Alternatively, corticosteroids may be given, though this is seldom necessary. Allopurinol (p. 140) should not be given as treatment for acute gout.

In gout, which may be familial or precipitated in an acute form by various agents (p. 358), there is a high uric acid level in the blood and this is associated with urate crystals in the synovial fluid and an arthritis which is very painful. Urate crystals which are deposited in the joints cause a local inflammatory response. It should be realized that uric acid (not to be confused with urea) is derived from nucleic acids. There may be two pathways, one involving the catabolism of nucleic acids, and the other the early cleavage of nucleotides prior to their incorporation into nucleic acids, with the consequent liberation of purines and thereafter the formation of uric acid. In primary gout, this second pathway may be excessively active, whereas in the hyperuricaemia found in leukaemia and certain other conditions with increased cellular destruction, there is an increased rate of nucleic acid breakdown.

In the process of uric acid formation, the accumulation of purines and pyrimidines in the body is prevented by the action of deaminating and oxidizing enzymes. Adenine and guanine are deaminated to hypoxanthine and xanthine. These last are oxidized to uric acid by *xanthine oxidase*, which is present in liver and kidney. The literature is somewhat confused in that the terms 'uric acid' and 'urate' are sometimes used interchangeably. In tissue fluids and urine, uric acid occurs as monobasic urate and as free acid, solubilized by colloids.

If crystals of monosodium urate are deposited in joints, a local inflammatory response occurs. It is suggested that the crystals are phagocytosed by leucocytes which then produce lactic acid, with consequent urate crystallization leading to further inflammation; hence, a vicious circle. Certainly it has been shown that the injection of sharp urate crystals into a knee joint causes a typical gouty attack, whereas amorphous urate has little effect. In theory, therefore, there are various ways in which to deal with gout:

1. In an acute attack, an analgesic or anti-inflammatory drug will be helpful, as indicated above.
2. Drugs may increase the elimination of urate by the kidney. This will be valuable between attacks. These are known as uricosuric substances (p. 139).
3. A diet low in purines might be helpful. This is not so important in practice, but foods with a very high purine content should be avoided, together with certain substances which the patient may find liable to precipitate attacks. There is also some evidence that fatty foods adversely influence uric acid excretion.

4. A drug that blocks uric acid synthesis is likely to be valuable to prevent attacks. Allopurinol (p. 140) is suitable.
5. Drugs that may interfere with renal excretion of urate should be avoided.
6. Any disease causing secondary gout should be treated if possible, but sometimes this increases the breakdown of abnormal cells.

Colchicine

Colchicine is an alkaloid derived from the meadow saffron, *Colchicum autumnale*, which grew in Colchis in Asia Minor. Colchicine is an antimitotic agent that interferes with cell division.

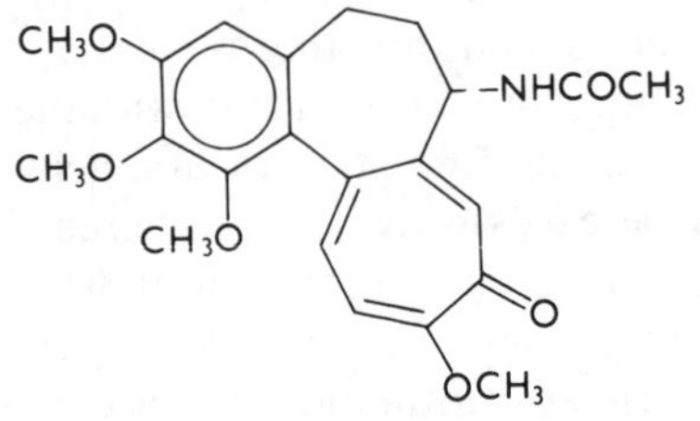

COLCHICINE

The formula of colchicine is given above, but this gives no clue as to its mode of action in acute gout. Suffice it to say that it is usually so effective that it may be given as a test of diagnosis. It is not an analgesic and is of no value in other forms of arthritis. Presumably, as it interferes with cell division, it also has some action on the leucocytes involved in the attack of acute gout referred to above.

Dosage
Colchicine tablets, BP, contain 0.25 or 0.5 mg. The initial dose is 1 mg, followed by 0.5 mg every 2 hours until relief of pain is obtained or vomiting or diarrhoea occurs. It is usual to give a total of 4–8 mg.

Adverse Effects
Colchicine is the traditional remedy for acute gout, but, in addition to vomiting and diarrhoea, it may cause abdominal pain, alimentary bleeding, renal damage, and/or blood dyscrasias. None of this is surprising, since this is an antimitotic agent. It is not given i.v., since local tissue necrosis may occur if there is extravasation. It can be used to suppress gouty attacks, the dose being 0.5–1 mg on alternate days. However, many authorities do not use colchicine even for acute gout, preferring to give non-steroidal anti-inflammatory agents as indicated (p. 141) until pain is controlled. This may occur within 24 hours. Alternatively, corticosteroids may be given.

Uricosuric Drugs

These inhibit the reabsorption of uric acid by the renal tubules and hence it is excreted. The effect is sustained, and with regular treatment, attacks of gout become less frequent and eventually cease. In the early stages it may be necessary to continue with 0.5 mg of colchicine three times daily to prevent acute attacks.

Probenecid

When penicillin was not freely available, probenecid (Benemid) was used to inhibit its secretion by the renal tubules. It is seldom now used for such a purpose, but is sometimes given to maintain a high plasma level of cephalosporins (p. 11). In contrast to this effect on renal tubular excretion, probenecid interferes with the reabsorption of urate, and in the light of these various actions, it must be assumed to have a complex action on renal tubular transport. Salicylates interfere with its uricosuric activity and the two should not therefore be given simultaneously. It does not act satisfactorily if there is renal failure.

Dosage
Probenecid tablets, BP, containing 500 mg, are available. Between attacks of gout the usual dose is 1–2 g daily in divided doses.

Adverse Effects
In the first few weeks of treatment, attacks of acute gout may be precipitated despite the fall in the plasma uric acid level. Nausea, vomiting and minor skin rashes may occur. Patients should drink plenty of fluid to prevent urates crystallizing in the urinary tract and the urine should be kept alkaline with potassium citrate or sodium bicarbonate. Probenecid impairs the metabolism or excretion of heparin.

Sulphinpyrazone

Sulphinpyrazone (Anturan) is an effective uricosuric agent that is structurally related to phenylbutazone. In gout, it is not promoted for purposes other than therapy between attacks. It prevents tubular reabsorption of uric acid, but is said to be antagonized by salicylates but not by probenecid. It potentiates the actions of oral anticoagulants, certain oral hypoglycaemic agents and also sulphonamides. Its actions on platelets and trials of its possible use after myocardial infarction are referred to on p. 125. It is not effective if there is renal failure.

Dosage
Sulphinpyrazone tablets, BP, contain 100 mg. The drug is given initially in a dosage of 1–2 tablets daily with meals, the dose being increased to 600 mg

daily over 2–3 weeks. The aim is to keep the serum uric acid level below 0.36 mmol/l with the smallest possible dose, which may be 200 mg or even 100 mg daily. To prevent an acute attack it is common practice to give 0.5 mg of colchicine three times a day for one to three months at the beginning of treatment. Adequate fluid intake and alkalinization of the urine is important.

Allopurinol

Allopurinol (Zyloric) was developed to protect mercaptopurine (p. 505) against rapid inactivation in the body, but it was found to be very valuable in preventing attacks of gout. It reduces the plasma uric acid level and the urinary output of urates by inhibiting xanthine oxidase (p. 600). Its effect is shown below.

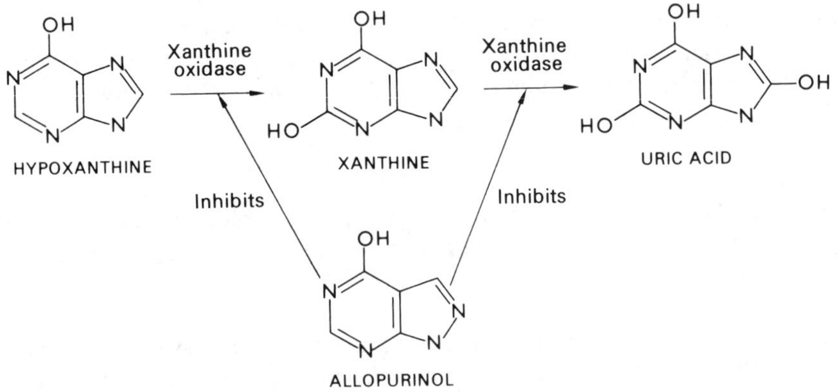

Allopurinol, a potent competitor of xanthine oxidase in low concentrations and a non-competitive inhibitor in higher concentrations, largely prevents the formation of uric acid. It itself is acted upon by xanthine oxidase, and alloxanthine is formed. This, too, is an inhibitor of xanthine oxidase. The result of these actions is that the plasma uric acid level falls, and in the urine the purines and related substances are then a mixture of hypoxanthine, xanthine, urate, allopurinol and alloxanthine, the concentration of urate being less.

Indications
Allopurinol can be used to prevent attacks of gout or is given if there is hyperuricaemia. *Colchicine should be given with it in a dose of 0.5 mg three times a day for at least a month in the early stages of treatment, because an acute attack may be precipitated. Alternatively, a non-steroidal anti-inflammatory drug may be used with it.* Allopurinol can also be given with uricosuric drugs. It is particularly valuable in secondary hyperuricaemia, which occurs in such conditions as myeloid leukaemia, myelofibrosis and multiple myeloma. It will prevent the deposition of urates in tissues and the occurrence of urate renal

stones. Acute uric acid nephropathy may be caused by the excretion of massive amounts of uric acid when leukaemia or lymphomas are treated with cytotoxic drugs, and here allopurinol will give benefit. Indeed, it is wise to start the administration of allopurinol before treatment with cytotoxic drugs is commenced. Gouty tophi may disappear and gouty nephropathy be reversed if the drug is given before renal failure is evident, but it should not be used in the usual dosage if renal function is severely impaired, since it may accumulate in the body.

Dosage

Allopurinol, BP, is available in 100 mg or 300 mg tablets. The initial adult dose is usually 300 mg per day, *not* given during an acute attack of gout. The normal maintenance dose is 200–600 mg daily. Dosage in excess of 300 mg should be given in divided doses. In children, the dose is 10–20 mg/kg body weight per day.

Adverse Effects

Skin rashes, hypersensitivity reactions (fever, lymphadenopathy and arthralgia), nausea and raised levels of serum alkaline phosphatase and transaminase have occurred.

The effects of oral anticoagulants are potentiated, and if mercaptopurine or azathioprine (p. 506) is given simultaneously, the dosage has to be reduced to about one-quarter, since purine analogues are usually inactivated by xanthine oxidase. There is doubt as to whether allopurinol may also increase the marrow toxicity of cyclophosphamide. If so, the reason is not clear.

CONCLUSION ABOUT THE TREATMENT OF GOUT

In the acute attack, colchicine is the traditional remedy, but it is being replaced by non-steroidal anti-inflammatory agents such as indomethacin or phenylbutazone. If these fail, corticosteroids may be effective. Long-term treatment is preferably with allopurinol, but probenecid or sulphinpyrazone may be given to increase renal excretion of uric acid. Treatment can be continued indefinitely, and allopurinol can be given with sulphinpyrazone.

PRECIPITATION OF ATTACKS OF GOUT

Aspirin and other salicylates may interfere with the excretion of urate. Most diuretics may precipitate attacks of gout, but the thiazides are particularly troublesome in this respect, since they inhibit excretion of uric acid in the distal tubules. The active treatment of myeloproliferative disorders such as chronic myeloid leukaemia may produce attacks of gout, and pyrazinamide, sometimes used to treat tuberculosis, may precipitate an attack. If much alcohol is taken, the plasma uric acid concentration may rise. The reason for this is uncertain, though alcohol is a diuretic.

DRUGS USED IN THE TREATMENT OF MIGRAINE

Some patients obtain relief by taking paracetamol or aspirin. In an acute attack, ergotamine (p. 232) should help by constricting large vessels and dilating small ones. Certain amines in food (tyramine and phenylethylamine) stimulate the release of serotonin from platelets and may induce attacks, so the diet may have to be adjusted. Oral contraceptives may precipitate migraine. Clonidine (p. 280) was thought to prevent the harmful effects of serotonin release, but this is doubtful.

For the prevention of attacks, several preparations, including the three described below, are beneficial, but there is great individual variation in response.

Pizotifen

Pizotifen (Sanomigran) has antagonist activity against serotonin, tryptamine, histamine, kinins and acetylcholine. A tablet contains the equivalent of 0.5 mg of pizotifen base and the dose is usually one tablet three times a day, though sometimes this amount has to be doubled. Side-effects are drowsiness, weight gain, increased appetite and dizziness. There may be anti-cholinergic actions.

Propranolol

It is not clear why propranolol (Inderal; p. 234) may be effective, but in some patients there is definite benefit. The dose may be 20 mg three times a day or double that.

Methysergide

Methysergide (Deseril) is a potent serotonin antagonist which can be used to prevent migraine and to control the diarrhoea associated with carcinoid disease. To protect against migraine, the dose should be 1–2 tablets two or three times a day, with meals. Each tablet contains 1 mg methysergide base. There may be nausea, vomiting, drowsiness or abdominal discomfort, but, unfortunately, the drug sometimes causes retroperitoneal fibrosis or fibrosis in the lungs or elsewhere. Arterial spasm can also occur. This drug should be avoided if possible, but, if used, courses should not last for more than three months without full assessment.

TRIGEMINAL NEURALGIA

The treatment of trigeminal neuralgia with carbamazepine is dealt with elsewhere (p. 251).

FURTHER READING

Abel J. A. (1971) Analgesic nephropathy — a review of the literature, 1967–1970. *Clin. Pharmac. Ther.*, 12: 583.

Anturane Reinfarction Trial Research Group Report (1978) *New Engl. J. Med.*, 298:289.

Barrie M. A., Fox W. R., Weatherall M. & Wilkinson M. I. P. (1968) Analysis of symptoms of patients with headaches and their response to treatment with ergot derivatives. *Quart. J. Med.*, 37: 319.

Brogden R. N., Speight T. M. & Avery G. S. (1973) Pentazocine: a review of its pharmacological properties, therapeutic efficacy and dependence liability. *Drugs*, 5: 6.

Calimlim J. F., Wardell W. M., Sriwatanakul K., Lasagna L. & Cox C. (1982) Analgesic efficacy of parenteral metkephamid acetate in treatment of postoperative pain. *Lancet*, i: 1374.

Ciba Foundation Symposium (1982) *Substance P in the Nervous System*. London: Pitman.

Climont-Jones V., McLoughlin L., Tomlin S., Besser G. M., Rees L. H. & Wen H. L. (1980) Increased β-endorphin but not met-enkephalin levels in human cerebrospinal fluid after acupuncture for recurrent pain. *Lancet*, ii: 946.

Cray G. L. & Buchanan W. W. (1980) Antirheumatic drugs: clinical pharmacology and therapeutic use. *Drugs*, 20: 453.

Davis P. & Bleehan S. S. (1976) D-penicillamine in the treatment of rheumatoid arthritis and progressive systemic sclerosis. *Br. J. Derm.*, 94: 705.

Dundee J. W., Clarke R. S. J. & Loan W. B. (1967) Comparative toxicity of diamorphine, morphine and methadone. *Lancet*, ii: 221.

Editorial (1980) Brain peptides — new synaptic messengers? *Lancet*, ii: 895.

Editorial (1980) Opiate peptides, analgesia and the neuroendocrine system. *Br. med. J.*, 280:741.

Editorial (1982) Treatment of migraine. *Lancet*, i: 1338.

Editorial (1982) Endogenous opiates and their actions. *Lancet*, ii: 305.

Editorial (1982) Benoxaprofen. *Br. med. J.*, 285: 459.

Editorial (1983) 'Opren Scandal'. *Lancet*, i: 219.

Editorial (1983) Opiates or Opioids? *Lancet*, i: 687.

Ferreira S. H. (1972) Prostaglandins, aspirin-like drugs and analgesia. *Nature, Lond.*, 240: 200.

Ferreira S. H. & Vane J. R. (1974) New aspects of the mode of action of nonsteroid anti-inflammatory drugs. *Am. Rev. Pharmac.*, 14: 57.

Fletcher J. E., Thomas T. A. & Hall R. G. (1980) β-endorphin and parturition. *Lancet*, i: 310.

Flower R. J. & Vane J. R. (1974) Inhibition of prostaglandin biosynthesis. *Biochem. Pharmac.*, 23: 1439.

Forrest W. H. (1980) Orally administered zomepirac and parenterally administered morphine. Comparison for the treatment of postoperative pain. *J. Am. med. Ass.*, 244: 2298.

Frederickson R. C., Smithwick E.L., Shuman R. & Bemis K. G. (1981) Metkephamid, a systematically active analog of methionine enkephalin with potent opioid α-receptor activity. *Science*, 211: 603.

Hindson T. C. (1983) Panorama on Benoxaprofen, *Lancet*, i: 475.

Huskisson E. C. (1974) *Reports on Rheumatic Diseases* No. 54. London: Arthritis and Rheumatism Council.

Krakoff I. H. (1967) Clinical pharmacology of drugs which influence uric acid production and excretion. *Clin. Pharmac. Ther.*, 8: 124.

Lawson D. H. (1973) Analgesic consumption and impaired renal function. *J. chron. Dis.*, 26: 39.

Loan W. B. & Morrison J. D. (1973) Strong analgesics: pharmacological and therapeutic aspects. *Drugs*, 5: 108.

Medrei V. C. (Ed.) (1973) A symposium on benorylate. *Rheumat. Rehab.*, 12, Suppl.

Moertel C. G., Ahmann D. L., Taylor W. F. & Schwartau N. (1972) A comparative evaluation of marketed analgesic drugs. *New Engl. J. Med.*, 286: 813.

Moncada S. & Korbur R. (1978) Dipyridamole and other phosphodiesterase inhibitors act as antithrombotic agents by potentiating endogenous prostacyclin. *Lancet*, i: 1286.

Moncada S. & Vane J. R. (1978) Unstable metabolites of arachidonic acid and their role in haemostasis and thrombosis. *Br. med. Bull.*, 34: 129.

Morley P. A., Brogden R. N., Carmine A. A., Heel R. C., Speight T. M. & Avery G. S. (1982) Zomepirac: a review of its pharmacological properties and analgesic activity. *Drugs*, 23: 250.

Notification (1983) Zomepirac. *Lancet*, i: 603

Oyama T., Jin T., Yamaya R., Ling N. & Guillemen R. (1980) Profound analgesic effects of β-endorphin in man. *Lancet*, **i**: 122.

Prescott L. F. & Wright N. (1973) The effects of hepatic and renal damage on paracetamol metabolism and excretion following overdosage. A pharmacokinetic study. *Br. J. Pharmac.*, 49: 602.

Prescott L. F., Illingworth R. N., Critchley J. A. J. H., Stewart M. J., Adam R. D. & Proudfoot A. T. (1979) Intravenous N-acetylcysteine; the treatment of choice for paracetamol poisoning. *Br. med. J.*, **ii**: 1097.

Schachter M. (1981) Enkephalins and endorphins. *Br. J. Hosp. Med.*, 25: 128.

Vane J. R. (1971) Aspirin — possible action through inhibition of synthesis of prostaglandins. *Nature*, Lond., 231: 232.

Whittington R. M. (1977) Dextropropoxyphene (Distalgesic) overdosage in the West Midlands. *Br. med. J.*, **ii**: 172.

3 Hypnotics, Sedatives, Tranquillizers and Antidepressants

W. S. Nimmo

Hypnotics, sedatives and tranquillizers all depress the central nervous system (CNS). A *hypnotic* is a drug which produces sleep, whereas a *sedative* is used to quieten a patient and to make him drowsy without actually inducing sleep. A *tranquillizer* (or *anxiolytic*) drug relieves tension and anxiety without noticeably impairing consciousness and, ideally, without producing drowsiness or sleep. However, in clinical practice, this classification is not of great importance, since many drugs produce any one of the effects described when given in the appropriate dose. One may then talk of the hypnotic effect, the sedative effect or the anxiolytic effect of a particular drug.

SLEEP AND HYPNOTIC DRUGS

Normal sleep has two main phases: orthodox and paradoxical sleep.

Orthodox Sleep (non-rapid eye movement, NREM,
or EEG slow-wave sleep)

During orthodox sleep, growth hormone secretion is at its greatest, and this increases the rate of synthesis of protein and ribonucleic acids. Prolactin is also secreted in large quantities during such sleep in both sexes. How hypnotic drugs influence these restorative processes is unknown. Diazepam, in long-term use, causes loss of the large slow electrical waves of sleep, but it is not known whether there is an associated decrease in growth hormone secretion.

Paradoxical Sleep (rapid eye movement, REM sleep)

During paradoxical sleep, brain blood flow is increased; heart rate, blood pressure and respiratory rate fluctuate; and body movements are more pronounced. The increased cerebral blood flow may be required for anabolic processes such as the synthesis of brain proteins.

Most hypnotic drugs tested decrease the proportion of REM sleep. This is

145

not very important in short-term treatment, but, with prolonged therapy (3–14 days of continuous use), tolerance to the effects of the drug on sleep rhythm occurs and in most cases the sleep pattern reverts to normal during continuous treatment. When the drug is stopped serious disturbance occurs, since there is a rebound in the opposite direction and the patient has abnormally long periods of REM sleep. As a result, sleep is disturbed by anxiety, restlessness and vivid nightmarish dreams for two to three months. This is one of the factors that leads to drug dependence.

All drugs with sedative and hypnotic activity act additively with other drugs that depress the CNS. The synergism between the effects of hypnotic drugs and alcohol may be particularly dangerous.

In addition, these drugs cause impairment of judgement or driving skills: this effect may persist for several hours after the sleep-producing effects have worn off.

Hypnotics should not be prescribed indiscriminately and are generally reserved for short courses to alleviate acute insomnia after causal factors have been established and treated.

Hypnotics should not be prescribed to children, apart from occasional use for night terrors or somnambulism. They should also be avoided in the elderly who are at risk of ataxia and confusion.

As well as having effective sleep-inducing properties, a hypnotic must be absorbed rapidly and have a short duration of action. The intermittent type of drug action which is desired means that a hypnotic should be rapidly cleared from the body to prevent accumulation of the drug if it is given every night and to avoid residual CNS depressant effects in the morning.

BENZODIAZEPINES

The benzodiazepine group of drugs has been known for 20 years. There are now some 20 such substances available for use, though many of these are related metabolically. Those of most practical interest are listed in Table 3.1. Of all the drugs that are available, they are the most commonly used. The formulae for three of these are shown below.

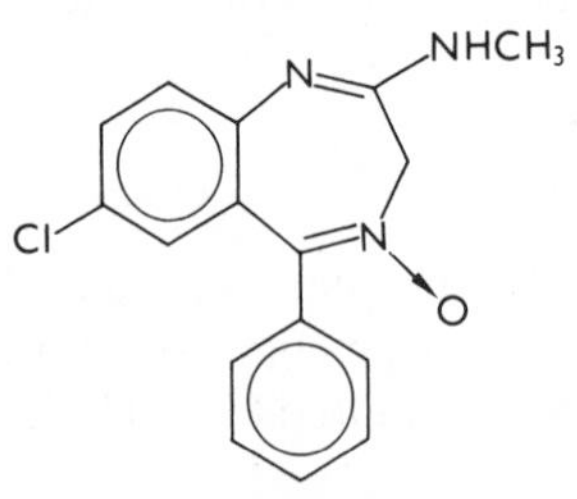

CHLORDIAZEPOXIDE 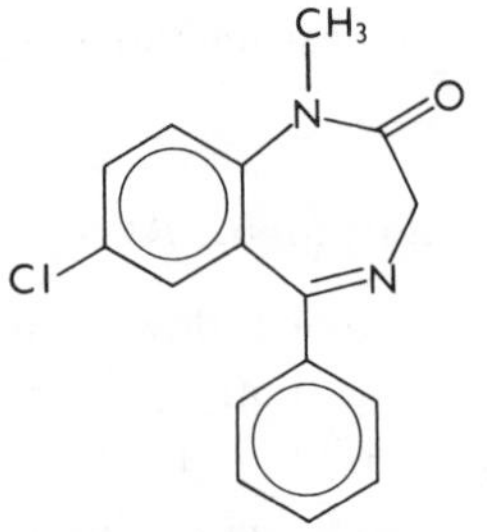   DIAZEPAM 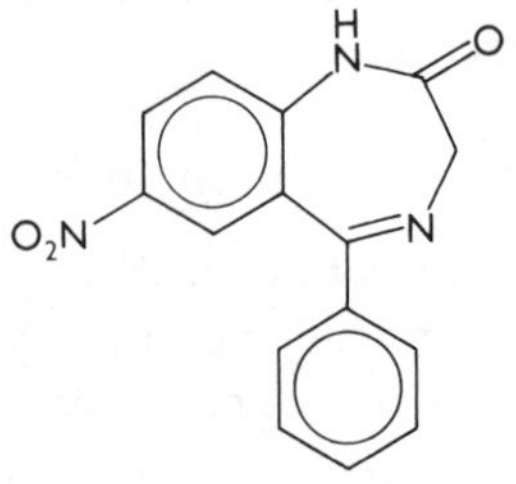   NITRAZEPAM

Benzodiazepines are employed in the treatment of anxiety states and are also effective sedative and hypnotic agents. Their properties include:

1. Anti-anxiety or taming effect and production of amnesia.
2. With increasing doses, production of sedation and hypnosis, and, with i.v. administration, a state of anaesthesia. The relative intensity of these depressant actions in comparison with anti-anxiety activity differs between members of the series: lorazepam and oxazepam produce little sedation in doses exerting good anti-anxiety effect.
3. Marked anticonvulsant action. Abrupt withdrawal after prolonged use may precipitate epileptiform seizures.
4. Depression of polysynaptic reflexes in the spinal cord, producing central muscle relaxation.

Thus benzodiazepines are not general CNS depressants and at first they were thought to be relatively selective for the limbic system (hippocampus, amygdala and hypothalamus), which is concerned with the control of emotions. They probably facilitate the release or the synaptic transmission of the inhibitory neurotransmitter GABA (γ-amino butyric acid).

More recently, it has been demonstrated that benzodiazepines bind with high affinity to a specific site of brain membranes and that this binding site is a physiologically relevant receptor. The highest concentrations of receptors are found in cerebral cortical regions. A specific benzodiazepine antagonist (RO 15–1788) has been identified and in clinical trials it antagonizes all the effects of diazepam.

Some benzodiazepines, such as nitrazepam, are marketed as hypnotics, whereas others, such as diazepam, are sold as sedatives and tranquillizers or as muscle relaxants. As has already been indicated (p. 145), this is a somewhat artificial classification.

Adverse Effects

Following oral administration of any members of the group, there are no significant effects on the cardiovascular or respiratory systems unless the patient is already shocked or in respiratory difficulties (e.g. severe chronic bronchitis), in which case even a small oral dose may have profound effects.

However, unwanted effects of the benzodiazepines are rare, and are extensions of the therapeutic sedative effects. Tiredness, somnolence, ataxia, headache, vertigo, dizziness and confusion may occur, especially in the elderly, and impaired judgement affecting driving has been observed. The drugs potentiate the actions of other centrally acting drugs, and, like all other hypnotics, they can induce dependence, though to a lesser extent than barbiturates. When diazepam is given i.v. in a dose adequate to produce basal sedation, it may depress respiration and lower cardiac output and arterial pressure. It also interferes with normal laryngeal reflexes to allow aspiration. A doctor planning to administer a benzodiazepine i.v. should be capable of cardiorespiratory resuscitation and have the facilities near at hand.

On the question of safety in overdosage, the benzodiazepines are a major advance. Even with a severe overdose, the patients remain rousable, and this fact largely accounts for these drugs being first-choice hypnotics or anxiolytic agents. Recovery has followed the consumption of 10–100 times the recommended doses, but, of course, restraint in prescribing is advisable.

A number of the most important benzodiazepines are related metabolically (Fig. 3.1). Therefore, when their therapeutic use and duration of action are considered, the properties of the pharmacologically active metabolites must be taken into account.

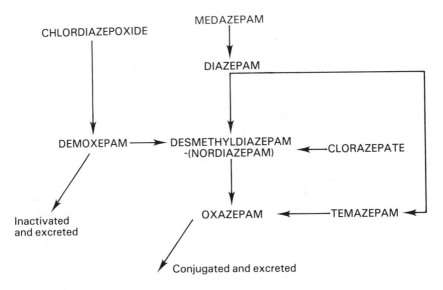

Fig. 3.1 Metabolic pathways of some benzodiazepines.

Benzodiazepines do not induce hepatic microsomal enzymes and so are safer than most other hypnotics or sedatives if oral anticoagulant drugs are administered concurrently.

Within the benzodiazepine group, large differences exist with regard to pharmacokinetic properties and metabolism in man. Some are eliminated from the body at a relatively slow rate (diazepam), while others are metabolized rapidly (temazepam, triazolam, oxazepam). Several have the long acting metabolite N-desmethyldiazepam in common (diazepam, prazepam, clorazepate, ketazolam, medazepam). These factors should be taken into account when prescribing. For example, in anticonvulsant and anti-anxiety therapy, continuous treatment is required and compounds with long half-lives or active metabolites are indicated. However, if the drug is to be given as a hypnotic, and the duration of action is to be restricted to the night, a compound with a short elimination half-life is preferred (Table 3.1). In addition, drugs with a shorter duration of action are likely to have less effect on the total amount of REM sleep.

Table 3.1 *Benzodiazepines and their important active metabolites in healthy adults*

Parent drug	Active metabolite	Elimination half-life (hours)	Dose (adult) Route of administration
Bromazepam (Lexotan)	–	12	3–12 mg orally
Chlordiazepoxide (Librium)		18	10 mg orally, 50–100 mg i.m. or 30–50 mg i.v.
	Desmethyl chlordiazepoxide	10–18	
	Demoxepam	21–79	
	Desoxydemoxepam	44	
Clobazam (Frisium)		18	20–30 mg orally
	Desmethylclobazam	42	
Clonazepam (Rivotril)	–	34	1–8 mg orally (anticonvulsant)
Clorazepate (Tranxene)	Desmethyldiazepam	50–99	15 mg orally
Desmethyldiazepam (not in *British Approved Names*)	–	50–99	10 mg orally
Diazepam (Valium, etc.)		33	10 mg orally, i.m. or i.v.
	Desmethyldiazepam	50–99	
Flunitrazepam (Rohypnol)		15–25	2 mg orally or i.v.
	Desmethyl derivative	31	
Flurazepam (Dalmane)	Desalkylflurazepam	65	15–30 mg orally
Lorazepam (Almazine, Ativan)	–	12	2–4 mg orally, i.m. or i.v.
Lormetazepam (Noctamid)	–	10	1 mg orally
Nitrazepam (Mogadon, etc.)		20–31	5–10 mg orally
Oxazepam (Serenid-D)	–	8–12	15–30 mg orally
Prazepam (Centrax)	Desmethyldiazepam	1.3 50–99	10–30 mg orally
Temazepam (Euhypnos, Normison)	–	8–10	10–30 mg orally
Triazolam (Halcion)		2.2	0.125–0.25 mg orally
	7-α-hydroxy derivative	4.1	

Chlordiazepoxide

Chlordiazepoxide (Librium) is rapidly and completely absorbed following oral administration and this leads to a rapid clinical response. In contrast, i.m. administration results in delayed and possibly incomplete absorption of the parent drug and delayed appearance of the active metabolites. Thus it is probably wise to avoid using this drug i.m. It is metabolized in the liver by demethylation and hydroxylation to pharmacologically active compounds which themselves have a long plasma half-life. Elimination is significantly slower in the elderly.

The dose in mild anxiety states is 10 mg 8-hourly orally, but in severe anxiety with agitation this may be increased to 40–100 mg/day in divided doses. The dose must be reduced in the elderly patient.

Patients taking chlordiazepoxide should be told to avoid alcohol, since its effects will at least be potentiated, and to avoid driving or handling machinery.

Diazepam

Diazepam (Alupram, Atensine, Diazemuls, Evacalm, Solis, Stesolid, Valium, Valrelease) has similar properties to chlordiazepoxide, but is a more potent tranquillizer and a better anticonvulsant (p. 254). Absorption after oral administration is rapid and complete, peak plasma levels being reached in 30–90 minutes. An earlier peak occurs in children; a delayed and lower one is seen in the elderly. Absorption is faster from the suspension than from tablets and there is a very large interindividual variation in plasma concentrations. Following rectal administration, plasma levels are only 50% of those obtained with the same dose by mouth.

Poor and irregular absorption occurs after i.m. administration. Plasma levels are only 60% of those attained with the same oral dose. Following i.v. administration, drowsiness and slurred speech occur in a few minutes, and it is worth noting that there is this short but definite interval between i.v. injection and the appearance of these effects. If the drug is not administered very slowly, titrated against the patient's response, it is easy to give an overdose.

Diazepam is highly bound to plasma proteins and this binding is decreased in the fetus and newborn. The plasma half-life is 1–2 days, but is longer in the elderly. Desmethyldiazepam is the main degradation product. This metabolite is pharmacologically active and has an even longer half-life (50–99 hours) than diazepam. It accumulates with chronic administration of diazepam. Temazepam and oxazepam, the other two active metabolites of diazepam, are only produced in small amounts. Very little parent drug appears unchanged in the urine.

Theoretically, a single daily administration of diazepam at night should be adequate for a prolonged anxiolytic effect over the following day, with no significant accumulation. The oral dose is 2–10 mg.

Diazepam is a drug of choice in the treatment of status epilepticus in a dose of 5–10 mg i.v., repeated if necessary (p. 254).

In the treatment of tetanus, the drug may be given in a dose of 30–40 mg/day in divided doses by mouth or nasogastric tube, or i.v. in 10 mg doses as required. It is used widely as i.v. sedation before and during such procedures as obstetrics, minor surgical procedures, dental procedures, endoscopy and cardioversion. The drug should be administered very slowly until a definite end point is reached – for example, slurred speech, ptosis or disorientation. The dose required varies widely between individuals. It cannot be too strongly emphasized that diazepam given i.v. is an anaesthetic agent and should be used only in a room with resuscitation facilities to hand and by those skilled in its use. It seems likely that newer benzodiazepines with shorter half-lives may replace diazepam for this purpose.

Diazepam potentiates the effects of other drugs which depress the CNS. Patients should be warned to abstain from alcohol while on treatment and to avoid driving vehicles or handling machinery.

When doses of 30 mg are given to women in labour as part of the treatment of pre-eclampsia, there is an association with hypotonia and jaundice in the neonate.

Diazepam readily crosses the placenta and long-term treatment to the mother results in the accumulation of both diazepam and desmethyldiazepam in the fetus. Levels of diazepam in human breast milk are of the order of a tenth of that in plasma. A daily dose of 10 mg to the mother is probably too small to cause untoward effects in the breast-fed infant, but, if higher doses must be given repeatedly, breast feeding should probably be discontinued.

A preparation of diazepam (Diazemuls) has been introduced for i.v. use. It avoids the thrombophlebitis that was a problem after i.v. Valium.

A slow-release preparation of oral diazepam (Valrelease) is now available, but has little to recommend it.

Nitrazepam

Nitrazepam (Mogadon, Nitrados, Somnite, Surem, Unisomnia) is used very widely as a hypnotic rather than as an anxiolytic drug, in a dose of 5 or 10 mg given orally. It rapidly induces sleep, lasting 6–8 hours, but accumulation of the drug occurs, since its plasma half-life is 20–31 hours. It is non-toxic in overdosage and for this reason has become very popular. Minor side-effects such as fatigue and drowsiness may occasionally occur and there is the usual danger of combination with alcohol, having, at the least, an additive effect. A drug with a shorter half-life should replace nitrazepam as the hypnotic of first choice.

Oxazepam

Oxazepam (Serenid-D) is one of the main metabolites of diazepam and it is used as an anxiolytic drug. The oral dose is 15–30 mg. This drug does not undergo hydroxylation or demethylation in the liver, but is conjugated and then excreted. It may be safer therefore, to use in the elderly or in patients with liver disease.

Clorazepate

Clorazepate (Tranxene) is hydrolysed in the stomach to desmethyldiazepam, which is then absorbed. The parent drug is too polar to be absorbed unchanged. Patients with achlorhydria or those taking antacids may not hydrolyse the drug in the stomach and therapeutic failure will result. The oral dose is 15 mg once daily.

Flurazepam

Flurazepam (Dalmane) is used as a hypnotic agent. The dose is 15–30 mg orally at night, after which only trace amounts of the parent drug can be measured in plasma. The major metabolite is the N-1-desalkyl derivative, which is pharmacologically active, with a plasma half-life of 47–100 hours. Significant accumulation of this metabolite occurs during nightly administration of flurazepam.

Lorazepam

Lorazepam (Almazine, Ativan) is one of the newer benzodiazepines, which is effective when given orally, i.m. or i.v. Following oral administration, a peak concentration occurs at 2 hours and this corresponds to the time when clinical effects are maximal. The elimination half-life is 12 hours and conjugation with glucuronide to form an inactive substance is the major mechanism of lorazepam clearance. This seems to be unaffected by the age of the patient. Following i.m. administration, peak plasma concentrations are achieved within 3 hours. After i.v. administration, there is a 'latency of action' of about 5 minutes between the injection and the onset of clinical effects. The oral dose is 2–3 mg/day in divided doses for mild anxiety and 5–7.5 mg for severe anxiety. A dose of 2–4 mg 2 hours before surgery is a useful premedication. The parenteral dose is 0.05 mg/kg body weight.

Lorazepam produces a remarkable degree of amnesia and is very suitable as a premedication for surgery. However, its rather long duration of action makes it unsuitable for out-patient use.

The side-effects and precautions are the same as for diazepam. It is probably a useful drug in the elderly and in liver disease, since it is not hydroxylated or demethylated.

Temazepam

Temazepam (Euhypnos, Normison) is 3-hydroxydiazepam and is available for oral administration only as 10 or 20 mg soft gelatin capsules. It is used as a hypnotic. Absorption is rapid, with peak plasma concentration and clinical effect occurring within 1 hour. The elimination half-life is 8–10 hours and the drug is largely eliminated by conjugation with glucuronide. When administered nightly, therefore, there is no accumulation of active drug, and temazepam would now appear to be a hypnotic of first choice. It may be that this drug will also be a useful premedication for surgery because of its anti-anxiety properties, rapid absorption and short duration of action. The dose is 10–30 mg.

Triazolam

Triazolam (Halcion) is a triazolobenzodiazepine marketed in the UK in 0.25 and 0.125 mg tablets. It has a half-life of 2.2 hours, but it does have an active metabolite. There has been some debate as to its safety, since it may cause depression in some patients.

Lormetazepam

Lormetazepam (Noctamid) differs from temazepam only in the addition of a chlorine atom. It is rapidly absorbed after oral administration and is marketed as a hypnotic since its half-life is short (10 hours) and it has no active metabolite. Ninety-five per cent of the drug is conjugated with glucuronic acid. The oral dose is 1 mg.

Prazepam and Ketazolam

Prazepam (Centrax) and Ketazolam (Anxon) are precursors of desmethyl-diazepam.

Midazolam

Midazolam (Hypnovel) is a new benzodiazepine available for i.v. use. It is given as a water-soluble prodrug and does not damage veins on injection. It has an elimination half-life of 2 hours and no active metabolites. In comparison with diazepam, it has greater amnesic properties. The dose is 2.5–7.5 mg.

BARBITURATES

The use of barbiturates has decreased in recent years, and they are not now drugs of first choice as hypnotics or tranquillizers. Barbituric acid is the parent compound of the series, but is not itself a hypnotic.

The majority of the clinically useful barbiturates are obtained by making

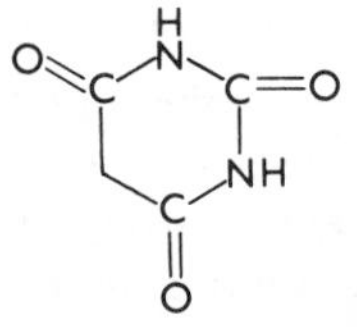

BARBITURIC ACID

appropriate substitutions at position 5 in the molecule – for example, phenobarbitone is ethyl phenylbarbituric acid.

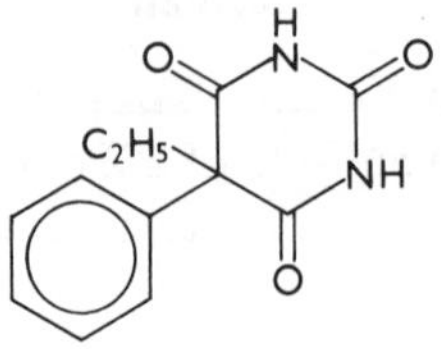

PHENOBARBITONE

An increase in the potency and a decrease in the duration of action can be produced by increasing the length of the alkyl groups on C5, by the substitution of alicyclic, branched or unsaturated side-chains for alkyl groups on C5, and by the attachment of an alkyl group to one of the nitrogen atoms of the ureide. Specific anticonvulsant properties are associated with the presence of a phenyl group on C5 and are more marked in straight-chained alkyl derivatives than in those with branched chains.

For many years the therapeutically useful barbiturates were classifed according to their duration of action, this being based on animal experiments. They were divided up into ultra-short-, short-, medium-, and long-acting barbiturates, but this classification is no longer useful and should be abandoned.

Details of the barbiturates used as hypnotics and sedatives are given in Table 3.2. The very-short-acting barbiturates, such as thiopentone and methohexitone, are used as i.v. anaesthetic induction agents and will be considered on p. 255.

It has been shown that 100 mg doses of quinalbarbitone, pentobarbitone or phenobarbitone are equally effective in inducing sleep and that hangover is not greater with the long-acting phenobarbitone than with quinalbarbitone. Phenobarbitone in daily doses, however, is cumulative because of its very long plasma half-life and its effects will eventually be seen during the day if it is taken on consecutive nights. It is therefore more suitable for continuous sedation than as a hypnotic.

All barbiturates are weak acids that cross biological membranes in their undissociated form at a rate which is a function of their lipid solubility. The variations in absorption, distribution, protein binding, rate of metabolism,

Table 3.2 *Barbiturates used as hypnotics or sedatives*

Drug	Proprietary name (UK)	Dose (mg)	Route of admin-istration	Principal use	Plasma half-life (hours)
Hexobarbitone	Evipan	400	Oral	Hypnotic	4
Heptabarbitone	Medomin	200–400	Oral	Hypnotic	
		50–100	Oral	Sedative	8
Cyclobarbitone calcium	Phanodorm Rapidal	200–400	Oral	Hypnotic	12
Amylobarbitone	Amytal	100–200	Oral	Hypnotic	
		15–50	Oral	Sedative	23
Amylobarbitone sodium	Sodium amytal	60–200	Oral	Hypnotic	
		60	Oral	Sedative	23
Quinalbarbitone	Seconal	50–200	Oral	Hypnotic	25
Pentobarbitone	Nembutal	100–200	Oral	Hypnotic	
		50–100	Oral	Sedative	30
Butobarbitone	Soneryl	100–300	Oral	Hypnotic	
		100	Oral	Sedative	38
Phenobarbitone	Luminal	100	Oral	Hypnotic	
		15–30	Oral	Sedative	50–120
		50–100	i.m.	Anticonvulsant	

Tuinal is a combination of quinalbarbitone and amylobarbitone. The hypnotic dose is 100–200 mg. Evidorm has replaced hexobarbitone alone and contains 250 mg of hexobarbitone and 100 mg of cyclobarbitone.

tissue localization, duration of action and renal excretion are well correlated with the lipid-solubility of the undissociated barbiturate.

Phenobarbitone is relatively slowly absorbed from the gastrointestinal tract and is very slowly metabolized. Thirty per cent of an administered dose is excreted unchanged in the urine because of slowness of metabolism, lack of protein binding, and the small extent of tubular reabsorption after filtration. For barbitone, which is even less lipid-soluble, as much as 65–90% of the administered dose is excreted unchanged in the urine.

The rate of entry into the CNS is strongly influenced by lipid-solubility. For example, thiopentone, when administered i.v., produces an almost immediate onset of anaesthesia, while the effects of phenobarbitone following i.v. injection are not seen for 10–15 minutes. Fat depots are important areas of storage for the thiobarbiturates, because of their high lipid-solubility.

In addition to lipid solubility, the ionization of barbiturates plays a role in their distribution and excretion. This is especially important when the pK_a of the drug is similar to physiological pH. For example, the pK_a of phenobarbitone is 7.3, and small changes in pH significantly affect the ionization. Alkalinization of the plasma produces a move of phenobarbitone from the tissues of the plasma, and alkalinization of the urine increases the excretion of the drug.

The metabolism of barbiturates occurs chiefly in the liver, and metabolic degradation follows four general pathways: (1) oxidation of radicals at C5, (2) removal of *N*-alkyl radicals, (3) conversion of thiobarbiturates into their oxygen analogues, and (4) cleavage of the ring. The first mechanism is most important. Some of the metabolites are hypnotically active. Renal clearance of the products of metabolism is by conjugation with glucuronic acid. All barbiturates appear in the glomerular filtrate, but if they are un-ionized, they diffuse back through the tubule to the circulation. As the drugs are weak acids, the degree of ionization is increased by increasing the pH of the urine, and thus the amount of drug diffusing back across the tubule is decreased. Therefore renal excretion of barbiturates is increased by making the urine alkaline and increasing the urine flow. In practice, so far as barbiturates are concerned, forced alkaline diuresis is of value only in the treatment of phenobarbitone overdosage, when it may shorten the period of unconsciousness.

The main action of the barbiturates is on the nervous system. Following the administration of an appropriate dose, the only significant effect is sleep from which the patient can be roused. In increased dosage, a state of anaesthesia occurs from which the patient cannot be awakened until the drug is distributed, metabolized or excreted. A further increase in dosage results in coma and death due to depression of the respiratory centre.

It has been suggested that barbiturates exert their effects by blocking ascending conduction in the reticular activating system. They also probably increase recovery time and raise the threshold for neurons in general.

Barbiturates are potent anticonvulsants, phenobarbitone being used in the treatment of epilepsy. They do not elevate the pain threshold and a patient experiencing pain may become agitated and delirious if a barbiturate is administered. On the other hand, they modify the reaction to pain and are useful in combination with analgesics.

Hypnotic doses of barbiturates cause minor depression of respiration and larger doses depress the respiratory centre, diminishing its response to an increase in arterial pCO_2. Barbiturates administered i.v. lower arterial pressure by direct depression of the vasomotor centre and can lead to a fall in body temperature as a result of central interference with temperature regulation. Ganglionic transmission may be impaired and urine volume is decreased owing to a release of antidiuretic hormone.

Administration

Only a few barbiturates are suitable for hypnotic therapy and their use as hypnotics or sedatives is no longer justified. Nevertheless, in appropriate doses, heptabarbitone and cyclobarbitone produce a satisfactory plasma concentration profile of the intermittent type during nightly administration.

Rapid absorption and onset of hypnotic action is achieved with barbiturate salts, in contrast to the free acids. Food decreases the rate of absorption but not the amount of drug absorbed.

In patients with severe liver disease, elimination of some barbiturates may be markedly retarded, whereas in renal insufficiency, accumulation of pharmacologically active polar metabolites of some compounds (e.g. amylobarbitone) may occur. In the newborn, the plasma half life of amylobarbitone is 2–5 times as long as in the adult. In the elderly, elimination is also reduced.

For subcutaneous or i.m. administration, a sodium salt is used and the dose is similar to that of the preparation given orally.

Adverse Effects

The serious unwanted effects of barbiturates are almost entirely those of overdosage and consist of loss of consciousness, followed by respiratory and circulatory depression, leading to medullary paralysis and ultimately death. Tolerance that may develop to therapeutic doses is not necessarily accompanied by tolerance to an overdose. The presence of skin bullae may be a useful sign of barbiturate overdosage, but they are seen with other drugs also. Allergic reactions occur occasionally with phenobarbitone and rashes, restlessness and excitement may be seen.

It must be kept in mind that emotional and physical dependence on barbiturates may develop (p. 188). Withdrawal of the drug even after brief use can be difficult because of the insomnia and disturbed sleep that ensues. A single overdose may be followed by disturbed sleep for weeks, even in subjects who have not been in the habit of taking barbiturates. When withdrawal is attempted from dependent patients, it should be done slowly over several weeks, with a reduction of both dose and frequency. The patient should be warned of possible sleep disturbances and nightmares. The elderly may become confused by hypnotics or sedatives and this applies particularly to barbiturates.

With barbiturates, any drug tolerance that develops is at least partly due to a phenomenon known as enzyme induction. These drugs have the ability to increase the production of liver microsomal enzymes over a period of 1–2 weeks, so that they themselves and many other compounds that fit the particular enzyme system are more rapidly metabolized. Knowledge of this ability to induce enzymes is utilized to treat patients who may have defects in their bilirubin-conjugating systems. For example, phenobarbitone may be used to treat neonatal jaundice. Patients who are on prolonged barbiturate therapy will live their lives with highly induced levels of drug-metabolizing enzymes and this becomes very important if other drugs are given concurrently. One particularly striking example concerns the administration of oral anticoagulant drugs (p. 480) and barbiturates. The anticoagulant is metabolized much more rapidly than in a patient who is not receiving a barbiturate, and larger doses of the drug must be given to achieve a therapeutic plasma concentration. If the barbiturate is then withdrawn, enzyme induction ceases and toxic levels of the anticoagulant in plasma may be reached if its dose is not reduced.

There is no true antidote to the barbiturates, but various central nervous stimulants (caffeine, strychnine and bemegride) tend to oppose their actions.

Hepatic and renal disease intensify the action of the barbiturates by interfering with their metabolism or excretion. In severe liver disease, sodium phenobarbitone is the only member that may be used, since it can be excreted unchanged by the kidneys. Some drugs may intensify the action of barbiturates, examples being other hypnotics or tranquillizers, alcohol and antihistamines.

Barbiturates are contraindicated in porphyria, since they may precipitate an acute attack. They should not be used in respiratory insufficiency, since they depress respiration further. In hepatic failure, only phenobarbitone is safe to use.

OTHER HYPNOTICS AND SEDATIVES

Chloral hydrate, paraldehyde, dichloralphenazone and several other non-barbiturate drugs may be used to induce sleep, but once again their popularity is much less than that of the benzodiazepines.

Chloral Hydrate

Chloral hydrate (Noctec), a chlorinated derivative of ethyl alcohol, was introduced into clinical practice in 1869. It is given in solution or as a capsule, since it is irritant to the stomach. It is rapidly absorbed from the small intestine and rapidly reduced in the red cells, liver and kidney to trichlorethanol, which is responsible for the hypnotic action. (Unchanged parent drug cannot be detected in plasma.) This is then conjugated with glucuronic acid to an inert form which is excreted by the kidneys. The average plasma half-life in humans is 8 hours.

Following ingestion, sleep occurs in about 15–30 minutes and lasts from 6 to 8 hours, there then being little hangover. During sleep, respiration is slower than normal and the arterial pressure may fall. The hypnotic dose is 500 mg–1 g orally or rectally.

A derivative of chloral hydrate, named triclofos (trichloroethyl phosphate), is also used as a hypnotic. Like chloral hydrate, it is rapidly metabolized to trichlorethanol. The dose is 1–2 g by mouth.

Adverse Effects

Toxicity. Another metabolite of chloral hydrate is trichloracetic acid, which has a plasma half-life of approximately 4 days and, therefore, will accumulate during nightly administration of the parent drug. It may displace other acidic drugs (e.g. warfarin) from binding sites on serum albumin and thus lead to a potentiation of anticoagulant effect (p. 483). However, chloral hydrate itself may inhibit the anticoagulant action. The net result is unpredictable and therefore chloral hydrate should not be prescribed to a patient receiving anticoagulants.

Concurrent administration of alcohol with chloral hydrate gives rise to an enhanced central depressant effect, since the drugs share the same metabolic pathway. Vasodilatation, hypotension and tachycardia may occur.

Dichloralphenazone

Dichloralphenazone (Welldorm) is a derivative of chloral and phenazone (an obsolete analgesic). It is available as stable tablets and is therefore often preferred to chloral hydrate. It is less irritant to the gastrointestinal tract, but its action is due to the metabolite, trichlorethanol, which is formed in the body. It is contraindicated in acute intermittent porphyria and in patients receiving anticoagulants. Occasionally, skin rashes, nausea and vomiting have been reported following its use. The oral dose is 650 mg to 1.3 g.

Paraldehyde

Paraldehyde is a cyclic ether obtained from the polymerization of acetaldehyde. It is an effective hypnotic but has an offensive smell. It is unique among the hypnotics in that a significant fraction (10–30%) of the administered dose is excreted unchanged in the breath. A patient may smell of it for 24 hours. The remainder of the dose is metabolized in the liver through the stage of acetaldehyde, and a drug which inhibits the oxidation of acetaldehyde (such as disulfiram) elicits severe reactions with paraldehyde.

When administered orally, paraldehyde acts in 15 minutes and lasts 4–8 hours, with little hangover. It may be given i.m. or rectally and the dose by any route is 5–10 ml. When a large dose is given i.m., it should be divided between two sites, to reduce the occurrence of chemical abscesses. When given rectally, it should be diluted in normal saline. Paraldehyde is a safe drug, but, in practice, it is not a drug of first choice.

Paraldehyde decomposes, on standing, to acetic acid and acetaldehyde and so only fresh drug should be used. It is contraindicated in patients with liver disease and this is important in restless patients with liver failure. It may react with plastics and should not be administered in disposable syringes. It must not be given i.v., since fatalities have occurred, and it should be realized that if it is being given i.m., a sterile solution must be used. It is not 'self-sterilizing', as clinicians sometimes think.

Glutethimide

Glutethimide (Doriden), when given orally in a dose of 500 mg, produces sleep lasting about 6 hours. Its absorption rate is variable, however, with the time of peak concentration between 1 and 6 hours after administration. The elimination half-life averages 11.6 hours and so intermittent drug action may be achieved when it is given every night. It is related in structure to thalidomide (p. 561), but it has not been shown to be teratogenic.

Nevertheless, it should not be prescribed for women of childbearing age. Blood dyscrasias and peripheral neuropathy have been reported as side-effects following administration. Liver damage has not been reported and the drug is broken down in the body before excretion.

Meprobamate

Meprobamate (Equanil, Miltown) is a substituted propanediol derivative related to mephenesin and has some muscle relaxant properties. It depresses the CNS and has anticonvulsant properties.

The oral dose is 600–1600 mg/day. It is given as a hypnotic or sedative, but it is not superior to the barbiturates and is much less effective than the benzodiazepines.

Drowsiness and anaphylactoid rashes, purpura, oedema and fever are the commonest unwanted effects. The drug is dangerous in overdosage, and tolerance and psychological and physical dependence occur. It is concentrated in breast milk.

Tybamate is chemically similar to meprobamate, but it is more effective and has fewer unwanted effects.

Bromides

Sodium, ammonium and potassium bromides are general depressants of the CNS with a specific anticonvulsant action. Their hypnotic effect is not great in doses that can be safely given. Large doses produce mental confusion, lassitude, depression, drowsiness, impotence and slowing of respiration, as well as a papular rash.

Absorption following oral administration is rapid, and distribution throughout the body is wide, since the bromide ion replaces the chloride ion. Excretion is slow, only 20% being excreted unchanged in the urine in 24 hours. Complete elimination takes 6 weeks or more and so the action is cumulative.

Bromides should not be given, since more effective hypnotics, sedatives and anticonvulsants with fewer side-effects are available.

Chlormethiazole

Chlormethiazole (Heminevrin) is structurally related to thiamine and has hypnotic, sedative and anticonvulsant properties. It is available as 500 mg capsules of chlormethiazole edisylate, as a syrup containing 50 mg/ml and as an 0.8% solution for i.v. infusion. Absorption after oral administration is rapid, the peak plasma concentration being 1–1½ hours. However, there is extensive first-pass metabolism of this drug in the liver (p. 583) and only 12% of the oral dose reaches the systemic circulation. In liver disease, therefore, and when the drug is given i.v., the dose must be greatly reduced. The plasma half-life of chlormethiazole is 7–8 hours.

Chlormethiazole is given by mouth for the treatment of confusion, agitation and restlessness; for sleep disturbances in the elderly; and to prevent acute withdrawal symptoms in alcoholics and drug addicts. The dose is 2–4 capsules. It may be used by i.v. infusion as a hypnotic and anticonvulsant in status epilepticus and pre-eclamptic toxaemia and to sedate severely agitated patients – for example, in delirium tremens. The dose is 250 mg initially, and then approximately 8 mg/minute, the total dose depending on the patient's response.

Adverse Effects
In large doses, chlormethiazole may produce respiratory depression and hypotension, but the most common side-effects are minor tingling in the nose, sneezing and conjunctival irritation. Thrombophlebitis occurs after i.v. infusion.

The effects are potentiated by phenothiazines and butyrophenones and increased central depression occurs when the drug is taken with alcohol or barbiturates.

Methylprylone

Methylprylone (Noludar), a piperadine, has a moderate hypnotic action comparable with that of pentobarbitone. It acts in 30–60 minutes and lasts about 6 hours. Hangover and side-effects are absent.

The hypnotic dose is 200–400 mg orally.

Chlormezanone

Chlormezanone (Trancopal) has anxiolytic, hypnotic, muscle relaxant and analgesic properties, but is chemically distinct from other anxiolytics. The oral dose is 200 mg three times daily or 400 mg at night.

Hydroxyzine

Hydroxyzine (Atarax) is a diphenylmethane derivative which has appreciable sedative activity, but potentiates the effects of other CNS depressants. It resembles closely the piperazine group of antihistamines in structure and has antihistamine, anti-emetic and local anaesthetic activity.

It is indicated in anxiety, stress related urticaria and dermatoses. The oral dose is 25 mg 3–4 times daily.

Benzoctamine

Benzoctamine (Tacitin) is the first of a new class of chemical compounds that contain four rings and are called tetracyclic tranquillizers. It produces anxiolysis without sedation. It is not a hypnotic and has no anticonvulsant activity. It inhibits polysynaptic reflexes and relaxes muscles.

Benzoctamine is absorbed rapidly after oral administration and has a short half-life of 2–3 hours. The dose is 10–20 mg three times daily. Side-effects include dry mouth.

Propranolol

Propranolol (Inderal) and other β-blockers (p. 234) are effective in alleviating the palpitations, diarrhoea and tremor which accompany anxiety and apprehension.

Many of the drugs considered above may be used in varying doses as hypnotics, sedatives or anxiolytic agents. Some are more suited for one purpose than another, but there is a large overlap. An anxiolytic agent reduces pathological anxiety, tension and agitation, but it does not have a therapeutic effect on disturbances of cognition and perception. It does not deplete amine stores in the nervous system and therefore does not produce extrapyramidal symptoms and signs. It may have anticonvulsant effects and it is liable to induce dependence.

The classification and alternative names for groups of psychotropic drugs are given in Table 3.3.

Table 3.3 *Classification of psychotropic drugs*

Group and alternative names	Classes of drugs	Examples	Therapeutic indications
Tranquillizer Anxiolytic	Benzodiazepine Carbamates Diphenylmethanes Tetracyclic tranquillizer	Diazepam Meprobamate Hydroxyzine Benzoctamine	Anxiety neurosis
Neuroleptics Major tranquilliser Antipsychotic	Phenothiazine Phenothiazine-like Butyrophenones Diphenylbutylpiperidines	Chlorpromazine Fluphenazine Haloperidol Primozide	Schizophrenia, mania, personality disorders
Thymoleptics Antidepressants	Tricyclics	Imipramine Amitriptyline	Psychotic disorders
Monoamine oxidase inhibitors	Hydrazine type Amphetamine type	Iproniazid Tranylcypromine	Depressive reactions
Lithium salts	–	Lithium carbonate	Mania

NEUROLEPTIC OR ANTIPSYCHOTIC DRUGS

The substances often described as major tranquillizers are better considered as neuroleptic or antipsychotic drugs. They produce a specific improvement in the mood and behaviour of psychotic patients without excessive sedation and without causing addiction. They interfere with normal amine transmission in the brain and may produce extrapyramidal symptoms and signs.

THE NEUROCHEMICAL BASIS OF MENTAL DISORDERS

A person's affective state appears to be determined by the balance of activity between central monoamine containing and acetylcholine containing neurones. In depressive illness, there is impairment of noradrenaline-containing systems and overactivity in acetylcholine systems. There may also be dysfunction of serotonin neurones in the limbic system.

Psychotropic drugs used in the treatment of depressive illness result in an increase in the availability of noradrenaline and serotonin as transmitters. In addition, tricyclic antidepressants have a central anticholinergic effect which may give additional benefit.

In mania, there is overactivity in ascending noradrenaline-containing neurones, possibly exaggerated by dysfunction in the cholinergic neurones. Most drugs that are effective in mania decrease the availability of noradrenaline as a transmitter.

Overactivity in dopamine-containing systems in animals underlies compulsive stereotyped behaviour and it is very likely that dopaminergic activity is implicated in the symptoms of schizophrenia. Antipsychotic drugs are dopamine antagonists and thus may give rise to extrapyramidal side-effects and also to hyperprolactinaemia. They affect, to varying degrees, receptors which are cholinergic, α-adrenergic, histaminergic or tryptaminergic.

SIDE-EFFECTS OF ANTIPSYCHOTIC DRUGS

The most troublesome side-effects are extrapyramidal symptoms. These consist of dystonia (abnormal face and body movements), akathisia, which may resemble an exacerbation of the condition being treated, and a parkinsonism-like syndrome.

The symptoms remit if the drug is withdrawn. Parkinsonian effects may be treated by anticholinergic drugs (p. 206), but routine administration of these drugs is not justified, since not all patients are affected and because tardive dyskinesia (p. 168) is worsened by them. Tardive dyskinesia may not be reversible on withdrawing therapy and treatment is difficult. It occurs usually with long-term therapy and high dosage, particularly in the elderly. Hypotension and interference with temperature regulation are dose-related side-effects.

SELECTION OF ANTIPSYCHOTIC DRUGS

Various drugs differ in predominant action and side-effects, but the differences between the drugs are less important than the great variability in patient response. Tolerance to side-effects may occur. There is no evidence that side-effects are minimized by prescribing more than one antipsychotic agent.

Neuroleptic drugs produce a wide range of symptom relief, with diminution of delusions, hallucinations, social inappropriateness and anxiety. Up to 90% of patients diagnosed as schizophrenic are helped by their actions.

Phenothiazines

The development of antipsychotic drugs was an outgrowth of research into antihistamines. The parent drug of the phenothiazines, chlorpromazine (Largactil), was developed as an antihistamine related to promethazine (Phenergan). Once the beneficial effect in psychotic patients was observed, a large number of related compounds were produced. These drugs have a calming effect without excessive sedation; they do not induce dependence and they all have some extrapyramidal effects. Most of the drugs are useful antiemetics and some are antipruritics. All the compounds have blocking actions, to varying extents, at α-adrenergic, dopaminergic, tryptaminergic and cholinergic receptors, as well as having antihistamine properties.

PHENOTHIAZINE NUCLEUS

The phenothiazines are classified on the basis of their chemistry and pharmacology into three groups. The differences result from substitutions on the nitrogen atom in the phenothiazine ring.

Aliphatic or dimethylaminopropyl compounds:
Chlorpromazine	(Largactil)
Promazine	(Sparine)
Promethazine	(Avomine, Phenergan)
Trimeprazine	(Vallergan)

Piperidine derivative:
Thioridazine	(Melleril)

Piperazine compounds:
Prochlorperazine	(Stemetil, Vertigon)
Trifluoperazine	(Stelazine)
Perphenazine	(Fentazin)
Fluphenazine	(Modecate, Moditen)
Thiopropazate	(Dartalan)

The aliphatic and piperidine compounds have greater sedative actions and are more useful in agitated schizophrenics. They have moderate anticholinergic and extrapyramidal side-effects.

The piperidine derivative is less likely to produce parkinsonian symptoms, since it has marked anticholinergic activity.

The piperazine compounds have fewer sedative or anticholinergic effects, but the most marked extrapyramidal effects.

Chlorpromazine

The term 'neuroleptic' was introduced to describe the characteristic emotional quietening indifference and psychomotor slowing produced by chlorpromazine (Largactil). Hyperactive and hypomanic states are controlled without consciousness being seriously impaired and abnormal schizophrenic behaviour is modified. The drug is of no use in the treatment of depression unless agitation is a feature. Normal people feel sleepy and indifferent to their environment following chlorpromazine administration. Large doses produce parkinsonian symptoms. The drug is a powerful antiemetic.

Chlorpromazine has a powerful α-adrenergic receptor blocking effect (p. 230). This results in postural hypotension and vasodilatation leading to a fall in body temperature. Like the benzodiazepines, chlorpromazine potentiates all other cerebral depressants such as alcohol, anaesthetics, hypnotics. Other effects of the drug include a local anaesthetic action, atropine-like, ganglion-blocking and quinidine-like actions.

The mode of action seems to be its ability to block the receptors in the noradrenergic and dopaminergic systems. Its administration is followed by an increase in the cerebrospinal fluid (CSF) concentration of homovanillic acid (HVA), the principal metabolite of dopamine. This is due to the blockade of the postsynaptic dopamine receptors, which results in the presynaptic neuron increasing its synthesis and release of dopamine. Levodopa, therefore, does not ameliorate chlorpromazine-induced parkinsonism. After prolonged use of chlorpromazine, orofacial and other dyskinesias may occur and are often temporarily worsened by stopping the drug. This is due to a compensatory oversensitivity to dopamine, which becomes apparent when the drug-induced dopamine blockade is withdrawn.

Chlorpromazine is well absorbed when given orally, but there is a significant 'first-pass metabolism' which results in very low plasma concentrations of the unchanged drug. Some of the metabolic products are active and some are not. Individuals vary greatly in the way they metabolize chlorpromazine and the drug may induce its own metabolism (p. 587). The number of metabolites of chlorpromazine is very large. Approximately 80 different types of these have been identified in plasma or urine. Very little unchanged drug appears in the urine. The duration of drug action is of the order of 6–8 hours.

The drug may be given orally, rectally, i.m. or i.v., and the dosage varies widely. The starting dose is usually 25 mg orally 6–8-hourly, with an increase every 3 or 4 days until a desired effect is obtained. A maintenance dose of 75–300 mg/day is usual. Patients with psychoses may require much larger doses and in delirium tremens as much as 1000 mg/day may be required parenterally.

Chlorpromazine has been used safely in uraemic patients, but is more potent. It may be dangerous in those with hepatic disease.

The drug is used for many purposes, but the most common use is for calming agitated psychotic, psychoneurotic or delirious patients. As an antiemetic, it is effective against nausea and vomiting produced by drugs and certain diseases, but is not effective in the treatment of motion sickness. It may be used in the treatment of hiccup, vertigo or during drug withdrawal reactions.

Adverse Effects

Chlorpromazine is a potentially dangerous drug and many different adverse effects are seen. Hypotension may be marked, particularly when the drug is given parenterally. Jaundice is seen in 0.5–2% of patients taking the drug, 2–4 weeks after starting therapy. This is due to intrahepatic cholestasis and is an allergic response. The jaundice usually disappears when the drug is stopped. Hypersensitivity dermatitis and light sensitization may occur. Agranulocytosis is rare. Gynaecomastia in males and lactation in females have been reported. Drowsiness, lethargy, dry mouth and parkinsonian symptoms are common. In addition, dystonic movements may occur. Long-continued chlorpromazine therapy leads to a purplish discoloration of the skin. There is increased melanin deposition.

Because of the frequency and the severity of these adverse effects, chlorpromazine should be used only when there are definite indications. It should not be administered if there is hepatic disease, or if the patient has glaucoma or urinary difficulties, because of its atropine-like actions. It must be used with great care when combined with sedatives, hypnotics and anaesthetics, since their effects are enhanced. It should not be used s.c., because of its intense irritant action.

The number of different phenothiazine drugs available is very large, and usually the choice is not critical. A summary of the different drugs and how they differ from chlorpromazine is given below.

Promazine

Promazine (Sparine) is less potent than chlorpromazine and has less anti-adrenergic activity. Indications for its use are the same as for chlorpromazine. It is often given in a dose of 50 mg during labour, in combination with an analgesic. The formula is given on p. 173.

Promethazine

Promethazine (Avomine, Phenergan) is used in a dose of 25 mg orally as sedation or premedication, for travel sickness, and in the treatment of allergic conditions, since it has a more marked antihistamine action than chlorpromazine. It has more marked sedative and hypnotic effects than chlorpromazine, but much less extrapyramidal effects. It is both a phenothiazine and a substituted ethylamine $\left(X{-}CH_2CH_2N{<}^{R_1}_{R_2}\right)$. The latter structure is characteristic of antihistamine drugs, and their actions and uses are considered on p. 555.

Trimeprazine

Trimeprazine (Vallergan) is intermediate between chlorpromazine and promethazine in its effects. It is used as an antipruritic and sedative, as well as being given in premedication for anaesthesia, especially in children. The dose is 10–40 mg orally in dermatological conditions in adults. For premedication in children, the oral dose is 2 mg/kg body weight.

Thioridazine

Thioridazine (Melleril) is used as a sedative, especially in the elderly, in a dose of 60–300 mg/day in divided doses. It has a strong atropine-like action. If given in high dosage, retinal damage may occur.

Prochlorperazine

Prochlorperazine (Stemetil) has a less potentiating effect on hypnotics. It is more effective as an antiemetic and does not produce hypotension. It is used in the treatment of migraine and Ménière's syndrome. The normal daily dose is 15–30 mg orally in divided doses. It is available in 10 and 15 mg sustained-release capsules under the proprietary name Vertigon.

Trifluoperazine

Trifluoperazine (Stelazine) is much more potent than chlorpromazine; it is more rapid in onset of action and has a longer duration of effect. It is a powerful antiemetic and tranquillizer.

The oral dose is 2–4 mg/day as an antiemetic or in mild anxiety states, or 5 mg twice daily in the treatment of the psychoses. It may be given i.m. in a dose of 1–3 mg/day in divided doses.

Perphenazine

Perphenazine (Fentazin) is used for the same reasons as chlorpromazine. The initial oral dose is 4 mg three times daily, which may be adjusted to achieve the desired effect.

Fluphenazine decanoate

An ester of fluphenazine, fluphenazine decanoate (Modecate) is slowly absorbed from the i.m. site of injection and metabolized to fluphenazine in the body. The preparation is useful in the treatment of chronic schizophrenic patients who are unreliable at taking their oral medication. To initiate therapy, an injection of 0.5 ml should be given by deep i.m. injection. Four to seven days later a 1 ml injection is administered. The dosage and frequency of administration is adjusted to obtain the best therapeutic response with the least side-effects. Patients should have received treatment with oral phenothiazines before the long-acting preparation is administered. The concentration is 25 mg/ml.

Extrapyramidal side-effects may cause problems and will require treatment in many cases. These effects can be manifested in four ways: akinesia, acute dystonic reactions, akathisia (restlessness) and tardive dyskinesia. The commonest is akinesia, which often produces a typical parkinsonian state, which responds well to anticholinergic drugs. Akathisia is usually seen as a motor restlessness which is best treated with a benzodiazepine. The other two groups are much less common. Dystonic reactions usually only occur within 72 hours of an injection, and tardive dyskinesia usually appears after prolonged therapy, particularly in the elderly. The latter consists of peculiar abnormal movements of the mouth, tongue, and face. It may persist or worsen when the offending drug is withdrawn, and, in fact, may appear for the first time when the drug is stopped.

The guiding principle in the treatment of side-effects must be to reduce the dose per injection immediately.

Fluphenazine enanthate is available in ampoules of 25 mg/ml and the hydrochloride is marketed in tablets of 1, 2.5 or 5 mg, all under the proprietary name Moditen.

Pimozide

Pimozide (Orap) is a tranquillizer of the diphenylbutylpiperidine series. It is a more selective dopamine receptor blocker than chlorpromazine and, therefore, is less sedative. The adult dose is 2–4 mg once daily orally, increasing to a maximum of 10 mg.

Fluspirilene

Fluspirilene (Redeptin) is similar to pimozide. The recommended starting dose is 2 mg i.m. per week. Extrapyramidal side-effects may occur.

Thioxanthene Derivatives

The thioxanthene derivatives, such as chlorprothixene (Taractan), are very similar chemically and pharmacologically to the phenothiazines. In the thioxanthene drugs, a carbon atom is substituted for the nitrogen in the central ring. Chlorprothixene is used in the treatment of psychosis with agitation and anxiety. The oral dose is 30–45 mg daily in divided doses, although larger doses may occasionally be required.

Flupenthixol

Flupenthixol (Depixol) is available as a tablet or as the decanoate for depot injection. It differs from the phenothiazines in that it has a significant mood-elevating effect. The initial dose is 3 mg twice daily and the maximum is 9 mg twice daily. For i.m. use, the initial dose is 20 mg of the decanoate at 2–4 week intervals. Extrapyramidal symptoms are the commonest adverse effects. It is referred to again on p. 177.

Indole Derivatives

Shortly after the therapeutic efficacy of chlorpromazine had been discovered, it was found that reserpine, a *Rauwolfia* derivative and an indole (p. 236), exerted on schizophrenic symptoms an action similar to that of chlorpromazine. It depletes the brain of 5-hydroxytryptamine, noradrenaline and dopamine. A serious side-effect is mental depression.

Oxypertine

Oxypertine (Integrin) is used as an antipsychotic in schizophrenia, and in low doses to treat mild anxiety. The oral dose for anxiety is 10 mg three or four times daily, but for other conditions it is 80–120 mg daily.

Butyrophenones

The fourth group of antipsychotic drugs is the butyrophenones. It consists of haloperidol (Serenace, Haldol), the prototype of the series, droperidol (Droleptan), trifluperidol (Triperidol) and benperidol (Anquil).

Butyrophenones have, in general, the same properties as the neuroleptic phenothiazines, but are more potent dopamine antagonists, less potent α-receptor antagonists and have only weak atropine-like activity.

Their chemical structure resembles that of γ-aminobutyric acid. They are selectively sequestered in the brain tissue, which takes up about ten times the plasma concentration. Unlike the phenothiazines, they are not sedative and do not reduce REM sleep. They are potent antiemetics.

Haloperidol

Haloperidol (Serenace, Haldol) is a potent neuroleptic agent. It produces a decrease in purposive movements, inhibits learned conditioned behaviour, increases the tendency to maintain an induced posture, inhibits apomorphine-induced vomiting and has an antipsychotic effect like chlorpromazine. In addition, it produces orthostatic hypotension (because of α-adrenergic blockade), hypothermia and a variety of dyskinetic states. It is more potent and more specific in its action than the phenothiazines or the indole derivatives and produces less somnolence.

Haloperidol may be given orally or parenterally in the management of schizophrenia, mania and agitation in psychotic illness. The oral dose varies between 1 and 200 mg/day, depending on the severity of the condition and the individual's response to treatment. The parenteral dose is 5–10 mg.

Haloperidol is metabolized in the liver via oxidative dealkylation to an inactive metabolite. The half-life of elimination ranges from 12 to 38 hours. Approximately 60% of the administered oral dose reaches the systemic circulation.

Side-effects of haloperidol are mostly extrapyramidal. Occasionally, acute administration may lead to a state of mental restlessness and agitation – an 'inner anxiety' which may not be obvious to the prescriber.

Droperidol

Droperidol (Droleptan) is a substituted butyrophenone similar to haloperidol. It produces a state of mental calmness and indifference, but has little hypnotic effect and is a powerful antiemetic. It acts faster than haloperidol, has a shorter duration of action and is less toxic. It does not depress respiration, but has some antiadrenergic activity. Like haloperidol, it is completely metabolized in the liver, but the plasma half-life is only 2.2 hours.

It is used to treat psychoses and as an antiemetic, and is given either alone or with a narcotic analgesic as premedication for surgery, or in conjunction with a narcotic analgesic i.v. in the technique known as neuroleptanalgesia. The i.m. and i.v. dose is 5–10 mg and the oral dose is 5–20 mg.

Droperidol is contraindicated in the depressed patient and should be used with care in patients with liver disease. Extrapyramidal symptoms and dystonia may occur. The drug is known to potentiate other drugs acting on the CNS. Psychomotor performance may be impaired for as long as 10 hours after one dose of 5 mg. This is probably due to accumulation and retention of the drug in the brain.

Benperidol

Benperidol (Anquil) is used in an oral dose of 0.25–1.5 mg daily in divided doses.

Lithium

Lithium carbonate

The monovalent cation lithium, given as the carbonate salt, regulates the mood in the treatment of manic illness and in the prevention of manic and depressive illnesses. It quietens the overactive euphoric patient.

The mechanism of action is not clear. It substitutes for the cations sodium and potassium in cellular transport processes. In the initial stages of therapy, an antipsychotic drug may also be required, since lithium may take a few days to exert its effect. Once started, treatment should be discontinued only if relief is absent or insignificant.

Lithium is absorbed rapidly and completely after oral dosing. It is excreted unchanged by the kidney, the half-life being 20 hours. It is distributed in total body water and reaches steady-state concentrations at around 5 days. The drug has a very narrow therapeutic range (0.6–1.2 mmol/l) and should be prescribed only when facilities for measuring plasma concentrations are available. Since lithium clearance is 0.2 times the creatinine clearance, the dose must be modified in the presence of renal impairment and in the elderly. Diuretic therapy modifies plasma drug concentrations.

Overdosage with plasma concentrations greater than 1.5 mmol/l may be fatal. Toxic effects include tremor, ataxia, dysarthria, nystagmus, anorexia, vomiting, diarrhoea, muscle weakness and fasciculation, and convulsions. With prolonged use, a goitre or nephrogenic diabetes insipidus may occur. Toxicity is worse in dehydration, salt depletion and with diuretic therapy. Because of the dangers of lithium, the need for continued therapy must be reassessed at least every 3–5 years. Different preparations vary greatly in bioavailability. Plasma concentrations should be measured every 10 weeks or more often if changing dose or if toxicity is suspected. Thyroid function should be monitored regularly.

The initial oral dose is 0.5–2 g daily, adjusted to achieve a plasma lithium concentration of 0.6 mmol/l.

ANTIDEPRESSANT DRUGS

Just as drugs such as neuroleptic agents, which deplete monoamine stores in the brain, lead to depression and sedation, drugs which replete the stores (levodopa or L-tryptophan) or those which lead to increased concentrations of free monoamines at the nerve terminals (monoamine oxidase inhibitors and imipramine) antagonize depression and elevate the mood. These drugs are known as antidepressants. Since imipramine (a tricyclic) and iproniazid (a monoamine oxidase inhibitor) were discovered in 1957, many other related compounds have been synthesized for this purpose. They can be divided into four groups:

1. Monoamine oxidase inhibitors (MAOIs).
2. Tricyclics.
3. Sympathetic stimulants.
4. 'Second generation' drugs.

CHOICE OF ANTIDEPRESSANT

Controlled studies have shown that the antidepressants are approximately equivalent in efficacy when given in appropriate doses. Although this is the case for populations, it may not be true for individual patients who may fare better on one rather than another. Often a trial of treatment with different drugs is required. 'Second generation' drugs may reduce troublesome side-effects.

Monoamine Oxidase Inhibitors (MAOIs)

The enzyme monoamine oxidase is widely distributed in the body, its function being the oxidative deamination of biogenic amines. Treatment with MAOIs results in a rise in free amine levels within nerve cells, and, following administration of the drugs, it takes from 4 days to 3 weeks for the antidepressant action to become apparent. At the periphery, there is a fall in sympathetic tone and a lowering of arterial pressure (p. 236), but there is an increase in noradrenaline stores in the adrenergic nerve endings. MAOIs, therefore, potentiate indirectly acting sympathomimetics, and, if foods containing tyramine (cheese, yoghurt, broad beans, Marmite, red wine or beer) are given to a patient receiving an MAOI, there may be a sudden catastrophic rise in arterial pressure owing to the release of amines at the nerve endings and their relatively slow inactivation in the presence of the enzyme inhibitor. Potentiation of directly acting sympathomimetics does not occur.

MAOIs can also be used as hypotensive agents, but their popularity as antidepressants or for the treatment of hypertension has deservedly diminished as newer, safer drugs have been introduced.

They can be divided into two groups:

Hydrazine derivatives:
Phenelzine	(Nardil)	
Isocarboxazid	(Marplan)	Drugs of choice if an MAOI must be used.
Iproniazid	(Marsilid)	

Non-hydrazine derivatives:
| Tranylcypromine | (Parnate) | The most hazardous MAOI, because of its stimulant action. |
| Pargyline | (Eutonyl) | |

Adverse Effects

Unwanted effects of administered MAOIs include postural hypotension, impotence, difficulty in micturition, sweating, restlessness, irritability, gastrointestinal upsets, leucopenia, rashes, convulsions, jaundice and optic nerve damage.

Interactions with other drugs are very common. The interaction with sympathomimetics and some foodstuffs has already been discussed. The drugs also interact with tricyclic antidepressants to produce excitement, and with pethidine to produce respiratory depression. They interact with all CNS depressants, with antihypertensives and with insulin. After the drug is stopped, the effects may take 1–2 weeks to disappear, because of the time taken by the body to resynthesize monoamine oxidase.

Uses

The use of MAOIs is fraught with too many hazards to warrant their use without a very clear indication (such as failed therapy with tricyclics and electroconvulsive therapy), and strict and continuous supervision is necessary. Endogenous depression does not respond well, but more favourable results have been obtained in patients with reactive depression, in whom these drugs may relieve emotional tension and also instability.

Tricyclic Antidepressants

Tricyclic antidepressants, amitriptyline, imipramine, desipramine and nortriptyline, are chemically and pharmacologically related to the phenothiazines.

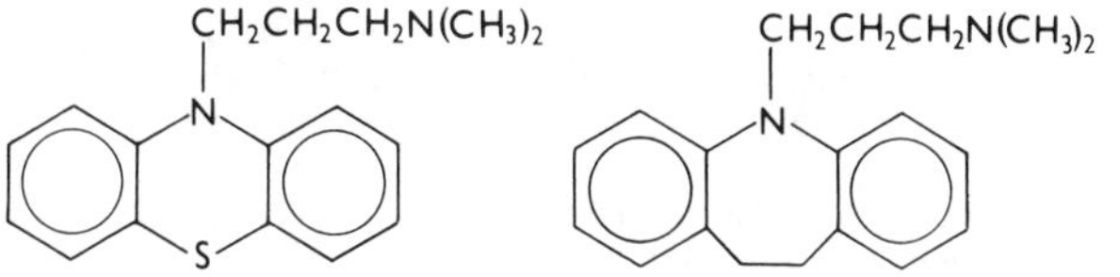

PROMAZINE   IMIPRAMINE

They competitively block neuronal uptake of noradrenaline and serotonin and, in the short term, increase the concentrations of transmitter in the synaptic cleft. This effect on the peripheral amine system is responsible for the interactions with other drugs. In the long term, these agents lead to changes in the number and sensitivity of pre- and post-synaptic α-adrenoreceptors and serotonin receptors in the brain.

Other effects of tricyclic drugs may include α-receptor blockade, an anticholinergic effect and sedation. They potentiate indirectly acting sympathomimetics such as amphetamine and ephedrine by preventing the re-uptake of noradrenaline and this may result in hypertension and excitement. They sensitize the myocardium to endogenous catecholamines and thus may cause ventricular dysrhythmias. They reverse the hypotensive effect of guanethidine, debrisoquine and bethanidine.

The therapeutic response to tricyclic drugs develops over 2–3 weeks, and self-poisoning from overdosage with the antidepressant drug may occur during this period. Electroconvulsive therapy may be required in severe depression when delay is hazardous or intolerable.

Tricyclic antidepressants are extensively metabolized in the liver by two major routes: ring hydroxylation of the tricyclic nucleus and demethylation of the aliphatic side-chain. Metabolites may be active and dosage once daily is usually sufficient with most tricyclic agents. Hepatic metabolism varies as a result of genetic and environmental factors. There are often wide variations in plasma concentrations between individuals after oral administration. There is a narrow therapeutic range of plasma concentrations and monitoring of the concentrations may be useful in difficult cases.

About 10–20% of patients will fail to respond to these drugs.

There are three clinical types of action exerted by the tricyclic antidepressants (Table 3.4).

Table 3.4 *Classification of tricyclic antidepressants*

Type	Action	Drugs
Sedative	Relief of depression Relief of anxiety Relief of restlessness	Amitriptyline Chlorimipramine Trimipramine Dothiepin
Neutral	Relief of depression Slight psychomotor activation	Imipramine Dibenzepin
Stimulant	Relief of depression Marked psychomotor activation (similar to MAOI)	Desipramine Nortriptyline Protiptyline

Patients with agitation or anxiety usually respond best to a sedative, whereas retarded or anergic patients often prefer a neutral drug or stimulant.

Imipramine

Imipramine (Tofranil) is chemically almost identical with promazine. It is well absorbed following oral administration and is largely metabolized in the liver, the major part of an ingested dose being excreted as metabolites within 24–48 hours. One of the metabolites is desmethylimipramine (desipramine).

Imipramine is a drug of first choice in endogenous depression, and although some benefit may be observed in a few days, the relief of symptoms usually takes 2–3 weeks. It is also used in the treatment of enuresis in children after thorough investigation has excluded any organic cause. Imipramine is sometimes useful in the treatment of chronic pain.

The usual oral dose is 75 mg in divided doses or as a single dose at bedtime, increased gradually as necessary to a maximum of 225 mg. In severe cases or in the unco-operative patient, it may be given i.m. In childhood enuresis, the dose is 25–50 mg at bedtime, depending on the size of the child. It should be continued for 6–8 weeks and then withdrawn gradually.

Side-effects include blurred vision, dry mouth, constipation and urinary retention. More rarely, a tremor, skin rash, photosensitization, failure of ejaculation and postural hypotension may be seen. A cholestatic type of jaundice has been reported and very occasionally agranulocytosis occurs. The drug should not be given concurrently with, or within 3 weeks of cessation of therapy with, MAOIs.

Imipramine is contraindicated in patients with glaucoma, prostatic hypertrophy or recent myocardial infarction, and it should not be given to patients receiving guanethidine, bethanidine, methyldopa, anticholinergic drugs, alcohol, or local anaesthetics with noradrenaline.

Amitriptyline

CHCH$_2$CH$_2$N(CH$_3$)$_2$

AMITRIPTYLINE

Amitriptyline (Tryptizol) has similar properties to imipramine, except that it has a greater sedative action. The indications for its use and warnings are the same as for imipramine. The initial oral dose is 30–75 mg (elderly patients 25–50 mg) daily in divided doses or as a single bedtime dose, increasing until the desired therapeutic response is seen. Lentizol is a proprietary name for amitriptyline in a special sustained-release preparation which allows the drug to be released over a period of 12 hours. It should be given in a dose of 50–100 mg at night. *Trimipramine* (Surmontil) is similar to amitriptyline. It also has a sedative effect. The oral dose is 25 mg at noon and 50 mg at night.

Nomifensine

Nomifensine (Merital) is a tricyclic which has dopamine-agonist activity and therefore may be of use if extrapyramidal symptoms are present in the depressed patient. The oral dose is 25 mg twice or three times per day, increasing over 7–10 days. Its use should be avoided in renal impairment.

Other tricyclic compounds used in the treatment of depression include desipramine (Pertofran); nortriptyline (Allegron, Aventyl), which is a partially demethylated metabolite of amitriptyline; iprindole (Prondol), which has less anticholinergic activity and, surprisingly, hardly any effect on amine uptake mechanisms; and dothiepin (Prothiaden).

Doxepin (Sinequan) and protriptyline (Concordin) differ from the other tricyclics largely in having minor modifications of the tricyclic ring structure. Clomipramine (Anafranil) differs from imipramine only in having a chlorine atom at the 3-position of the tricyclic moiety. Trimipramine (Surmontil) has a 2-methylpropyl side-chain rather than the *n*-propyl side-chain of imipramine. Butriptyline (Evadyne) differs in a similar fashion from amitriptyline.

Lack of Response

In patients who do not respond to these antidepressants, the diagnosis, dosage, compliance and social conditions should be reviewed: other drug treatment may be successful. Flupenthixol (marketed for this usage as Fluanxol (p. 177) or an MAOI may be tried. Tryptophan (Pacitron, Optimax) may have some benefit when given alone or as adjunctive therapy.

Sympathetic Stimulants

Dexamphetamine, other amphetamines and amphetamine 'surrogates' such as pipradol or methylphenidate (Ritalin) are occasionally used as antidepressants. They have a limited usefulness and their use should be discouraged since they may cause dependence and psychotic states. Patients with narcolepsy may derive benefit.

'Second-Generation' Antidepressants

This group includes a number of new drugs with different chemical structures.

Usual tricyclic drug

Amoxapine. This drug has a piperazine side-chain. It has many of the pharmacological properties of antidepressants, but retains some of the post-synaptic dopamine blocking action of neuroleptics. The usual dose is twice that of imipramine or amitriptyline and it is equally effective with a more rapid onset of action and less severe side-effects (e.g. sedation and dry mouth). It is not freely available in the UK.

Tetracyclic drugs

Maprotiline (Ludiomil). Maprotiline is similar in efficacy to imipramine and amitriptyline. It may have a more rapid onset of effect. Anticholinergic sedative and cardiotoxic side-effects are less. Rashes may occur and there is an increased risk of convulsions at higher doses. The oral dose is 25–75 mg daily and the plasma half-life is about 2 days. It is eliminated by metabolism and conjugation to glucuronide and does not appear to have active metabolites.

Mianserin (Bolvidon, Norval). This drug has little effect on the uptake of either noradrenaline or serotonin and no central anticholinergic action. It has pre-synaptic α-receptor blocking activities as well as antihistamine properties. Its efficacy is similar to that of the tricyclics. Cardiotoxicity has not been reported. The oral dose is 30–120 mg/day.

Bicyclic drugs

Viloxazine (Vivalan). This drug has effects on the uptake of amines that are similar to, but weaker than, those of desipramine. Unlike the tricyclic drugs which may precipitate convulsions, it has anticonvulsant properties. Although it has some amphetamine-like properties, it has little peripheral anticholinergic effect. The oral dose is 100–300 mg daily. It is as effective as the tricyclic drugs, but causes less sedation, is less cardiotoxic and the anticholinergic effects are not as great. Nausea and vomiting are more common.

Zimelidine (Zelmid). Zimelidine is highly specific in blocking the uptake of serotonin, but it is no longer available because of reports of adverse effects including severe headaches and disturbed liver-function tests.

Monocyclic drugs

Tofenacin (Elamol). This drug is a metabolite of orphenadrine. It has marked anticholinergic effects. The oral dose is up to 240 mg daily in divided doses.

Other structures

Trazodone (Molipaxin). Trazodone is a phenylpiperazine derivative (c.f. oxypertine, p. 169). The triazolo moiety gives it its antidepressant properties. It has efficacy similar to tricyclic drugs, but has less anticholinergic effect and less cardiotoxicity.

Nomifensine (Merital). This drug is a tetrahydroisoquinoline compound. Its principal effects are that it blocks the uptake of noradrenaline and dopamine. It has virtually no effect on serotonin uptake and little anticholinergic effect. It is as effective as amitriptyline and has fewer anticholinergic and cardiotoxic side-effects. It may aggravate schizophrenia or other psychoses. The oral dose is 50–200 mg daily.

Flupenthixol (Fluanxol). Flupenthixol (p. 168) has antidepressant properties. It is a thioxanthene derivative. With the low doses (1.5–3 mg daily) usually employed, it has fewer side-effects than the tricyclic drugs. It should be withdrawn in one week if there is no response.

Tryptophan. This drug may be given alone or as an adjuvant. An antidepressant effect may take up to 4 weeks to develop.

ANALEPTICS

Apart from the antidepressant drugs, there is another group of CNS stimulants which affect mainly the centres in the brain stem. These are known as analeptics. They act either directly or reflexly at various levels, but especially at the medullary respiratory centre and vasomotor centre. They lighten narcosis, but in excessive amounts will produce convulsions.

Analeptics may be classified into two groups:

1. Those acting reflexly through the chemoreceptors in the carotid body – nikethamide.
2. Those acting directly on medullary centres – picrotoxin and leptazol.

They have a limited but useful place in the treatment of ventilatory failure. However, there is no evidence that their long-term use is of any value in chronic respiratory failure. They must be given by i.v. injection or infusion.

Nikethamide

A dose of 4–8 ml i.v. will usually arouse a patient with carbon dioxide narcosis. The drug may be used in the emergency situation of acute respiratory failure, to allow time for mechanical respiratory equipment to be set up. Excessive dosage may lead to convulsions and ultimately death from respiratory failure. The myocardium may also be depressed.

Ethamivan

This is vanillic acid diethylamide and it is closely related structurally and pharmacologically to nikethamide.

Other Drugs

Bemegride

Bemegride (Megimide) was introduced as a specific antagonist to the barbiturates, but it is a general CNS stimulant and has analeptic effect in its own right.

Doxapram

Doxapram (Dopram) has outstanding respiratory stimulant effects compared with its analeptic effects. The margin of CNS safety is good, but it may produce hypertension. It is used to stimulate respiration, in a dose of 1–1.5 mg/kg body weight, i.v. Because of its short duration of action, it must be given by continuous infusion thereafter.

Pentetrazol

Pentetrazol (Leptazol) is a stimulant of the CNS and spinal cord. Respiration is stimulated and blood pressure is increased following its administration. The drug is excreted unchanged in the urine to the extent of 75%. The i.v. dose is up to 50 mg.

Amiphenazole

Amiphenazole (Daptazole) is an analeptic which may be given orally, i.m. or i.v. in the short-term treatment of respiratory depression. Long-term usage has been reported to give rise to bone marrow depression.

In the emergency situation, nikethamide in a dose of 2–10 ml of 25% solution i.v. or doxapram are the drugs of choice.

APPETITE SUPPRESSANT DRUGS

Methylcellulose and Sterculia

Methylcellulose (Cellucon, Celevac, Cologel) and Sterculia (Prefil) act as aids to the losing of weight because they fill the stomach. They are less effective than centrally acting appetite suppressants (anorectics), but they are safe.

Anorectics reduce hunger and suppress food intake in both obese and non-obese subjects. They act in one of two ways:

1. Potentiation of central catecholamine pathways. Accordingly, they are stimulant drugs. They include amphetamine with dexamphetamine (Durophet), diethylpropion (Apisate, Tenuate Dospan), mazindol (Teronac) and phentermine (Duromine, Ionamin).
2. Influencing serotonergic pathways. Accordingly, they are non-stimulant drugs. They include fenfluramine (Ponderax).

The pharmacology of amphetamine will be discussed on p. 228. It is now no longer used for appetite suppression because of its multifarious effects.

Methamphetamine

Methamphetamine is similar to amphetamine, with even more pronounced CNS effects.

Phenmetrazine

Phenmetrazine is related to amphetamine and is used to reduce appetite in cases of obesity. Phentermine and diethylpropion are also related in structure.

They are most effective if taken $1-1\frac{1}{2}$ hours before a meal, when controlled studies have demonstrated that there is a significant reduction in appetite. However, they all have pronounced central effects, causing restlessness, anxiety, insomnia, tolerance or habituation, and they should be used briefly, if at all, as an aid to dietary education.

Fenfluramine

Fenfluramine (Ponderax) is a trifluoromethyl derivative of amphetamine and its effects are different. It is sedative rather than stimulant and it does not reverse the effects of antihypertensive drugs. Moreover, it has a direct peripheral effect on muscle glucose uptake and on fat mobilization and metabolism, as well as a central anorectic effect. It is uncertain whether the peripheral effects contribute to any weight reduction that occurs.

Fenfluramine is given orally in a dose of 20 mg twice daily, this being increased, if necessary, to 120 mg/day total in divided doses. It should be given for up to 3 months and then slowly withdrawn. Physical dependence on the drug occurs and sudden withdrawal may lead to depression. It has been suggested that intermittent therapy, with an interval of not less than 4 weeks between courses, is preferable to continuous treatment. This is effective and less likely to lead to dependence, though this may still occur.

Unwanted effects of fenfluramine include dry mouth, abdominal pain, vomiting, diarrhoea, drowsiness, alopecia, depression, confusion, pulmonary hypertension and impotence. Fenfluramine is the drug of choice if any such drug is to be used in the treatment of obesity. It is contraindicated in patients with depression and in those taking MAOIs, but is an effective though unpredictable weight-reducing drug.

FURTHER READING

Blackwell B. (1981) Adverse effects of antidepressant drugs. *Drugs*, 21, 201, 273.

Bowman W. C. & Rand M. J. (1980) Hypnotics and sedatives. In: *Textbook of Pharmacology*, 2nd edn, p. 8.1. London & Edinburgh: Blackwell.

Bowman W. C. & Rand M. J. (1980) Psychotropic drugs. In: *Textbook of Pharmacology*, 2nd edn, p. 15.1. London & Edinburgh: Blackwell.

Breimer D. D. (1977) Clinical pharmacokinetics of hypnotics. *Clin. Pharmacokinet.*, 2: 93.

Cooper T. B. (1978) Plasma level monitoring of antipsychotic drugs. *Clin. Pharmacokinet.*, 3: 14.

Drug and Therapeutics Bulletin (1981) Appetite suppressants reassessed. 35.

Editorial (1978) Choosing an antidepressant. *Br. med. J.*, i: 128.

Edwards J. G. (1981) Adverse effects of antianxiety drugs. *Drugs*, 22: 495.

Grahame-Smith D. G. (1978) Clinical implications of recent advances in neuropharmacology. In: Weatherall D. J. (ed.) *Advanced Medicine*, p. 311. London: Pitman Medical.

Hollister L. E. (1980) Psychiatric disorders. In: Avery G. S. (ed.) *Drug Treatment*, 2nd edn, p. 1057. Sydney & New York: Adis Press.

Hollister L. E. (1981) Current antidepressant drugs – their clinical use. *Drugs*, 22: 129.

Oswald I. (1976) *Sleep*, 3rd edn. Harmondsworth: Penguin Books.

Shader R. I. & Greenblatt D. J. (1977) Clinical implications of benzodiazepine pharmacokinetics. *Am. J. Psychiat.*, 134: 652.

Simpson G. M., Pi E. H. & Sramek J. J. (1981) Adverse effects of antipsychotic agents. *Drugs*, 21: 138.

4 Dependence on Drugs and Other Agents

R. H. Girdwood

Throughout the world there are many millions of people who habitually ingest tea, coffee, drugs, alcohol or other substances, while a smaller, but very appreciable number smoke tobacco, cannabis or opium, and there are also those who inhale solvents or other volatile substances.

These actions are usually done to provide pleasure or to give relief from anxiety, tension or pain. Some of the more notorious habits are developed as evidence of rebellion against society. There may even be confusion between religious experience and the effects of certain drugs. At one end of the scale there is the old lady with her harmless pleasure in the drinking of frequent cups of tea, and at the other end, the terror of a heroin addict who is unable to obtain the drug on which he is dependent. There can also be unexpected problems, such as the case of a lady, subsequently found to have schizophrenia, who drank up to half a bottle of undiluted Dettol daily for ten years. Dettol contains chloroxylenol, but it appears that the patient was not truly dependent – instead her motive was that she was attempting to purify herself.

Although the expression 'heroin addict' was used in the previous paragraph, it has to be said that the term 'addict' has so often been wrongly used that many authorities and, in particular, World Health Organization (WHO) Committees recommend that it is advisable not to employ this word. The nouns 'addiction', 'abuse', 'habituation' and 'dependence' are those that have caused difficulty because of differences in interpretation and it is now considered better to use only the terms 'abuse' and 'dependence', though the phrase 'deviant drug use' has also been suggested.

DRUG ABUSE

There may be abuse of any drug, but in the present context the term is taken to represent a value judgement of society. What is thought to be abuse by one group of persons may be considered normal by another, and it is here that there is a conflict of opinion — for instance, about cannabis. Nevertheless, the laws of a country should be accepted and must be enforced. With certain drugs, including alcohol, there may be antisocial behaviour that is a hazard to society. In some countries, the taking of alcohol is a criminal offence, and those visiting the Middle or Far East should find out about the local laws before starting their journey. The consequences of attempting to flout these laws may be very serious.

DRUG DEPENDENCE

The term 'drug dependence' means what it says: the person has a continuing desire to take the drug, usually because of having already taken it repeatedly, and so is dependent upon it. There are many patterns of dependence and degrees of its intensity. Dependence may be emotional or physical. If there is physical dependence, this may be because the drug or its metabolite has become necessary for the normal functioning of certain processes in the body. If the drug is stopped, there may be withdrawal effects. The alcoholic, deprived of this substance which is now necessary for the normal functioning of his body's metabolism, develops the psychosis known as delirium tremens, and the person who has become dependent on barbiturates may develop fits.

DEPENDENCE ON ALCOHOL

Ethyl alcohol (ethanol) is a drug with serious problems of emotional dependence and in many people who use it for a prolonged period physical dependence develops.

It is of interest that the word 'alcohol' comes from the Arabic *al-koh'l*, meaning the fine metallic powder used in the East to stain the face and eyelids. The name was later extended to mean any powder produced by trituration or sublimation, and then to a fluid obtained by distillation. It next meant 'pure spirit of wine' and, finally, a distinct class of compounds of this type. Ethyl alcohol is C_2H_5OH. Methyl alcohol (CH_3OH) is produced when the cellulose of wood pulp is fermented, and it is highly toxic to man, causing blindness. As little as 10 ml can cause permanent loss of sight. A fatal dose is 100–200 ml.

Fermented liquors may contain higher alcohols in small quantities and these may be the cause of a 'hangover'.

Ethyl alcohol is a drug with potentially serious effects, but it can be obtained legally without prescription, except in certain areas with prohibition laws.

ALCOHOLIC BEVERAGES

It must have been at a very early stage in his history that man discovered that the fermented juice of fresh grapes had effects other than those of quenching his thirst. This is because the juice pressed from grapes starts to ferment because of yeasts in the bloom of the berry, named saccharomyces. These supply enzymes to start the process of fermentation.

Naturally fermented *wines* usually contain from 8 to 13% of alcohol (exceptionally, 17%) w/v. Fortified wines such as sherry and port have alcohol added to bring the concentration up to about 20% by volume.

In the manufacture of *beer*, the action of fermentation is begun by the enzyme diastase, which is formed in the grains of barley during malting. Distillation is not part of the process. The term 'malting' is applied to the process whereby grain is softened by being soaked in water for about 2 days and then exposed to air until partial germination occurs. Diastase converts starch in the malt to dextrin and maltose. Yeast is then added and maltose is converted to glucose by maltase, while zymase breaks glucose to alcohol and carbon dioxide. Strong ale may contain 6.6% of alcohol w/v.

Whisky is distilled from malted barley and for sale outside Scotland it is usually blended with unmalted grain whisky produced by an apparatus known as the patent Coffey's still. Irish whiskey is made from a mixture that may include malted and unmalted barley, wheat, oats or rye. Rye whiskey is made in North America from a mash mainly from rye, while bourbon is a whiskey originally distilled in Kentucky at Georgetown, Bourbon County, from a mash consisting mainly of maize (corn) grain. Other spirits and their sources of alcohol are brandy (champagne grapes), gin (various sources, but with added juniper and other vegetable agents), rum (molasses), and vodka (fermented rye or potatoes).

A question that is frequently asked concerns the equivalent alcohol content of various beverages. It is difficult to answer this, since there are so many variables. Wine glasses vary in size, measures of the quantities of spirits are not standard, even in different parts of the UK, and there are regional variations in the terminology used for fermented liquors. Half a pint of ale may contain anything from 6.25 to 18.75 g of alcohol, according to the type that is drunk; a glass of wine may have 10–25 g, a glass of sherry or port about 8 g, and an English measure of spirits about the same amount. A Scottish measure is larger. Alcohol has a calorific value of 7 kcals/g.

In many parts of the world, the problem of excessive alcohol consumption is escalating. This is true of the UK and is particularly serious in Scotland. Alcoholism plays a significant role in acts of violence, murder, wife-battering, road accidents, broken homes, inefficiency at work, social degradation and poverty. In a survey in the UK, 24% of men aged 40 to 59 were non-smokers, but only 6% were non-drinkers. Of manual workers, 66% drank only beer, while non-manual workers on the whole preferred spirits, wine or sherry. Manual workers tended to have a pattern of heavier drinking, particularly at weekends. Heavy drinkers were more likely to be heavy smokers.

PHARMACOKINETICS OF ALCOHOL

Alcohol is rapidly absorbed, partly from the stomach but mainly from the small intestine. The absorption is delayed if food is taken or if the alcohol is either in dilute solution or so concentrated that it inhibits gastric peristalsis. After a partial gastrectomy, the alcohol reaches the small intestine rapidly and the patient may very quickly have a high blood level. There is individual variation in the time of absorption, some feeling the effects within a few minutes. The blood level usually reaches its peak in between 30 minutes and 2 hours. Most of the alcohol is metabolized by enzymes in the liver to acetaldehyde, then to acetate, and finally to carbon dioxide and water. Some is excreted in the breath or urine and a proportion in sweat. As tolerance develops, the rate of metabolism increases.

ACTIONS OF ALCOHOL

It will be obvious that alcohol differs from all other drugs of dependence in that mankind throughout the world and down the ages has sought pleasure and solace from its central actions. Like an anaesthetic, it depresses the central nervous system (CNS). There is decreased mental and visual acuity, impaired co-ordination, disturbed hearing, unsteadiness and prolonged reaction time. Ability to make judgements or solve problems is impaired, and this is important in relation to the driving of vehicles, operation of machinery, or participation in decision-making. In the early stages there can be improved performance of certain activities, because of euphoria and release from inhibitions. It is important to remember that, occasionally, abnormal behaviour or a speech problem in a person smelling of alcohol is because he has had some incident such as a mild cerebral thrombosis and has been given, say, a glass of brandy by a friend in the hope that it will be a suitable therapeutic agent.

With increasing doses of alcohol, the individual may become aggressive and obstreperous, may go to sleep and can develop respiratory depression and die. Serious effects are more likely if other depressants are given, and these must be avoided, even if the patient is violent. Synergism is found with barbiturates, narcotics, antihistamines and, to a lesser extent, nitrazepam, but long-continued drinking of alcohol causes the induction of hepatic microsomal enzymes and this increases the clearance of various drugs including warfarin, phenytoin and tolbutamide. Alcohol is a food, and can be given i.v. in solutions containing from 2.5 to 10% of alcohol and about 5% of dextrose in water. It should not be administered at a rate exceeding 15 ml of alcohol per hour.

Alcohol causes peripheral vasodilatation by depressing the vasomotor centre, and although alcoholic drinks can be taken with advantage on coming in from the cold, they should not be taken in a cold environment. It is a cardiac depressant, causing a reduction in myocardial contractility and efficiency. It also increases the secretion of gastric acid and may have deleterious effects on those with a peptic ulcer or a hiatus hernia, because it causes gastritis. Sometimes, however, it relieves the symptoms of a duodenal ulcer when stress is extreme, because of its psychic effects. In large amounts, it leads to vomiting, and alimentary bleeding may occur, particularly if non-narcotic analgesics are taken at or about the same time (p. 119). It inhibits the secretion of the antidiuretic hormone (p. 375) of the posterior pituitary gland and hence has distinct diuretic effects. The blood glucose level rises because of diminished uptake by the tissues and then falls because of an increased secretion of insulin. This causes hunger. It has been found that the i.v. injection of naloxone (p. 114) prevents the impairment of psychomotor performance induced by small amounts of alcohol and suggests that alcohol causes intoxication by stimulating the release of endogenous opioid peptides (p. 107).

CHRONIC ALCOHOL ABUSE

Apart from deterioration in social behaviour, the chronic alcoholic may develop acute hepatitis, chronic hepatitis, portal cirrhosis of the liver, pancreatitis, gastritis and vitamin deficiency states. Such deficiency particularly takes the form of syndromes associated with thiamine depletion (p. 449), such as Korsakoff's psychosis, Wernicke's encephalopathy and even beri-beri, with polyneuropathy or cardiac enlargement and failure. Folate deficiency has been reported and it is suggested that this may be more than a simple nutritional folate depletion (p. 467). Perhaps enzymes that destroy folates are induced. Sideroblastic anaemia may also occur, and here there is a fall in the serum level of pyridoxal (p. 453). Alcoholic cardiomyopathy may occur, because of a direct toxic effect on cells of the myocardium. There may also be ectopic beats, atrial fibrillation and progressive cardiac failure.

The end stage of alcohol abuse may include deterioration of the personality, blackouts, recurrent infections, tuberculosis and, rarely, a transfer to dependence on other drugs, such as heroin. This may be a reflection of the underlying personality. Alcoholism usually starts with social drinking and this is followed by occasional further drinking to obtain relief from stress. This is then done frequently and surreptitiously, more and more alcohol being required to give the same effect as tolerance develops. As the problem becomes more serious, the quantity imbibed daily becomes greater and the alcoholic may sell his possessions or steal to obtain money to satisfy his craving for spirits.

At one time in poor areas in the UK, the drinking of 'red Biddy' or 'red Lizzie', a mixture of methylated spirits and red wine, was common. There are various varieties of methylated spirit, the one sold for usual retail purposes containing ethyl alcohol, wood naphtha, crude pyridine, mineral naphtha and a trace of methyl violet. Industrial methylated spirit, BP, has ethyl alcohol 19 volumes with wood naphtha 1 volume. Wood naphtha is largely the toxic methyl alcohol (p. 182). Surgical spirit, BPC, is industrial methylated spirit with castor oil, methyl salicylate and diethyl phthalate. A tincture is an alcoholic or hydroalcoholic solution of the active principles of drugs. There are proprietary medicines containing alcohol which are advertised for over-the-counter sale to the public. One such is Night Nurse, which has, in 20 ml, 20 mg of promethazine hydrochloride, 15 mg of dextromethorphan hydrobromide, 500 mg of paracetamol and 3.08 ml of alcohol.

WITHDRAWAL OF ALCOHOL

After prolonged heavy intake of alcohol, some alcoholics develop withdrawal symptoms within a few hours. There may be anxiety, coarse tremors, weakness and abdominal cramps. Soon after this, the patient may develop hallucinations, disorientation, and severe tremors, possibly with fits. It is important to remember that an alcoholic may have some of these features from another cause, such as bleeding within the cranium (subdural haematoma) through having fallen when drunk.

When alcohol is withdrawn, there are various ways to handle the situation in addition to psychotherapy. In an inebriated alcoholic who is likely to become delirious, if he is not already so, the best drug to use is chlordiazepoxide (Librium), 50–100 mg being given i.m. This dose is repeated if necessary after 2–4 hours. Dry-filled ampoules containing 112 mg of chlordiazepoxide hydrochloride (equal to 100 mg of chlordiazepoxide) are available together with 2 ml ampoules of a special solvent. Drugs to help withdrawal are disulfiram and citrate of calcium carbonate.

Disulfiram

Disulfiram (Antabuse) prevents completion of the metabolism of alcohol. Acetaldehyde accumulates in the body and the effects are unpleasant. Within a few minutes of taking alcohol, the patient has nausea, vomiting, sweating and headache. There may be cardiac dysrhythmias, hypotension and collapse. Indeed, death may occur if a patient receiving disulfiram takes alcohol. The recommended dose is four tablets, each of 200 mg, the first day, three tablets on the second, two on the third day, and half to one tablet daily for up to a year. Alcohol must not be taken except with this minimal dose and under medical supervision.

Citrated Calcium Carbimide

Citrated calcium carbimide (Abstem) is used for the same purpose as disulfiram. The dose is 50 mg once or twice daily, and the drug is contraindicated in those already in a state of intoxication or where there is heart disease. It may cause hypothyroidism.

Lithium Carbonate

Lithium carbonate (Camcolit, Phasal, Priadel) reduces the drinking and incapacity in depressive alcoholics, but has no significant effect on non-depressed patients. It is available in 250 mg, 300 mg and 400 mg tablets. The blood lithium level should be maintained in the range of 0.6–1.5 mmol/l.

DEPENDENCE ON AMPHETAMINES

In this form of drug dependence there is a desire to continue the dose, tolerance may develop and there is psychic dependence but little evidence of physical dependence. The amphetamines were introduced as antidepressants and then used in the treatment of obesity, since they depress the appetite (p. 179), but their use is now restricted to the treatment of narcolepsy. Amphetamines and the other drugs referred to here are adrenergic CNS stimulants, the basic adrenergic structure being phenethylamine. Amphetamines release noradrenaline from sympathetic nerve terminals, but their central stimulant effects are not blocked by depletion of the granular stores of catecholamine by reserpine. This suggests a direct action by the drugs. There is a structural relationship to dopamine (p. 224) and to the hallucinogen mescaline (p. 191), which is also a phenethylamine but is not an amphetamine type of drug when dependence is discussed. It is classed with the hallucinogens.

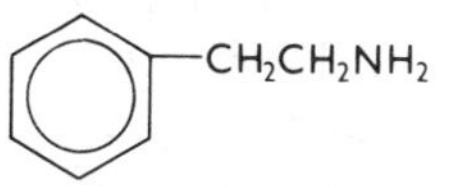

$CH_2CH_2NH_2$

PHENETHYLAMINE

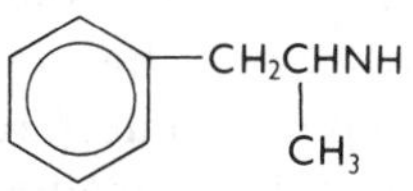

CH_2CHNH | CH_3

AMPHETAMINE

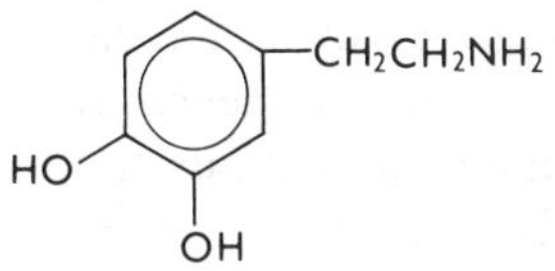

$CH_2CH_2NH_2$, HO—, OH

DOPAMINE

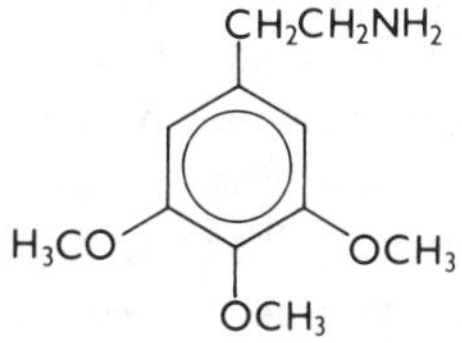

$CH_2CH_2NH_2$, H_3CO, OCH_3, OCH_3

MESCALINE

The racemic amphetamine and its dextro isomer, dexamphetamine, were introduced before World War II, and because they were believed to increase mental activity, were issued to some troops. There is increased confidence, but performance may be less accurate and there may be a feeling of anxiety. Tremors and palpitations occur and backache may be experienced. The appetite is impaired. Sexual function may be depressed, there being transient erections, with failure to ejaculate. Normally, fatigue follows the excitement produced by the drug, but high doses may cause confused actions, hyperpyrexia, hallucinations, paranoia, cardiac dysrhythmias, and sometimes death associated with lactic acidosis.

In addition to the effects described above, the person taking i.v. amphetamines may be suspicious and violent. Compulsive repetitive behaviour may occur. With prolonged use, there may develop a psychotic state that resembles schizophrenia. When treatment of dependence is attempted, many users find it difficult to abstain from this drug-taking habit, but crises may respond to the use of phenothiazine tranquillizers.

AMPHETAMINES AND RELATED SUBSTANCES THAT MAY BE AVAILABLE

These are amphetamine, dexamphetamine, methamphetamine, phenmetrazine and methylphenidate (Ritalin). Amphetamines have been marketed in combination with barbiturates or other drugs such as aspirin or phenacetin.

Colloquial names for some of this group are 'bennies', 'dexies', 'purple hearts', 'black bombers', 'blues' and 'minstrels'. Methamphetamine, the drug commonly injected, is known as 'meth', 'speed' or 'crystal'. Ephedrine is sometimes taken and is known as 'Freddy'.

DEPENDENCE ON BARBITURATES

The barbiturates are discussed elsewhere (p. 153). It is believed that hypnotics act on the ascending reticular formation of the brain stem. Wakefulness is thought to be due to maintained activity within multi-neuronal circuits, and sleep to an interference with this activity. Barbiturates depress the ascending reticular formation without significantly affecting the ordinary afferent nervous pathways. Fortunately, the connections involving the control of respiration are relatively resistant. Many people take barbiturates and experience no problems, but both psychic and physical dependence may occur and the desire to take the drug can be strong. There is a tendency for tolerance to occur and in some patients the dose is progressively increased.

A therapeutic dose causes sedation, slowing of speech and decreased reaction time. With an overdose, there is ataxia, nystagmus and vertigo. The patient may develop diplopia. A large overdose causes respiratory depression. Those who become dependent on barbiturates are frequently middle-aged women who take the drugs orally. Barbiturates are largely being replaced as hypnotics by nitrazepam, and for sedation diazepam is given rather than phenobarbitone. Usually one barbiturate can be substituted for another, though there are differences in metabolism, since barbitone and phenobarbitone are eliminated in the urine unchanged to the extent of about 20%, whereas the others are more extensively metabolized. Tolerance may occur quite rapidly, so that a plasma level that causes drowsiness on the first day of administration may perhaps be increased fivefold after 2 weeks without giving this effect. Tolerance is partly due to the synthesis of enzymes in liver cells and may result in tolerance to other hypnotics, other drugs and alcohol.

Withdrawal Syndrome

There may be anxiety, anorexia, nausea, vomiting, insomnia, muscle twitching, delirium, fits and possibly status epilepticus following withdrawal. However, some patients who have taken barbiturates for many years can cease taking them without having significant withdrawal symptoms.

Other drugs that may lead to dependence include chlordiazepoxide, diazepam, glutethimide, meprobamate, methaqualone and nitrazepam (Chapter 3).

Colloquial names for barbiturates include 'goof balls', 'sleepers', 'red devils' (Seconal) and 'blue heavens' (Amytal).

DEPENDENCE ON CANNABIS

The greek word κάνναβις means hemp and from it is derived the Latin cannabis. Hemp is a plant of the genus *Cannabis*, family Urticaceae, of which *Cannabis sativa* is the only species, though it is sometimes known in the tropics as *Cannabis indica* (Indian hemp) and in North America as *Cannabis americanä*. It is botanically allied to the hop. *Cannabis sativa* grows anything from 1 to 5 m in height and has an erect stalk which is more or less square in cross-section. It has 5–7-fingered leaves with serrated margins. The seed can be used for feeding birds or can be crushed to give an oil. The plant itself secretes a resinous substance which has intoxicating qualities. The fibre is obtained by burying the stems in mud and after they have rooted, taking them out and treating them in such a way that the fibrous material can be separated. Some forms of hemp (such as sisal hemp) are obtained in a similar manner from entirely different plants. Hemp is then used to produce ropes or twine.

The active principle is in the resin of cannabis and there are three principal cannabinoids. These are cannabinol, cannabidiol, and tetrahydrocannabinol. It is said that this last is the only form that is active and that the isomer responsible for most of the psychological effects of cannabis is L-Δ^9-tetrahydrocannabinol (Δ^9-THC). Its formula is given below.

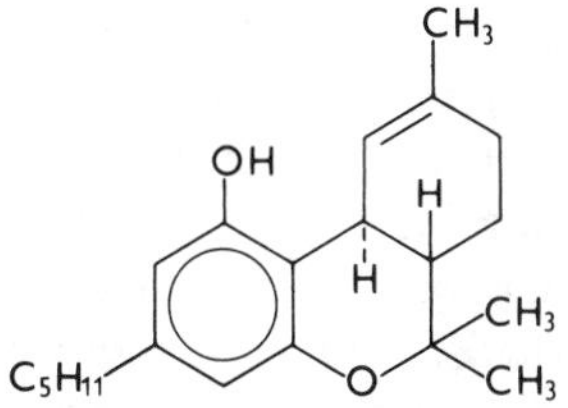

TETRAHYDROCANNABINOL

The flowering heads of the plant contain most of the active material and there is an appreciable amount in the leaves, but little, if any, in the stem. There are male and female forms of flower on different plants, but both contain the active principle. The best-quality resin comes from plants grown in Chinese Turkestan. *Bhang* is the word used on the Indian subcontinent for the dried leaves and flowering shoots, while *bhang ke beej* is the bazaar name for the seeds.

Charas is a name for the resin, while hashish is a powdered and sifted form of this resin. It is of interest that the word 'assassin' is derived from the Arabic *hashashin*, or hashish-eater. These were Moslem fanatics in the time of the Crusades who were sent to destroy the Christian leaders. *Marihuana* is probably a Mexican expression derived from Maria and Juan, and is applied to the group as a whole.

Colloquial names include 'charge', 'daggo' (South Africa), 'guge', 'ganga' (West Indies), 'grass', 'hash', 'hemp Kief' (North Africa), 'pot', 'tea' and 'weed'. Cannabis cigarettes are known as 'joints', 'muggles', 'reefers', 'root', 'split' and 'tuskie'. There are at least 150 other names under which cannabis is known. Many derivatives of tetrahydrocannabinol have been synthesized. The metabolite fate of cannabis is uncertain, but a glucuronide conjugate can be found in the urine.

THE CANNABIS PROBLEM

Cannabis has been used from time immemorial by millions of people, mainly in Eastern countries. The first reference to its use in Europe was given by Herodotus, the Greek historian, about 450 BC. The problem that has arisen is its increasing use in Western society, where it is not socially or legally acceptable. It was formerly provided for medicinal purposes as cannabis tincture, BPC, and cannabis extract, BPC, but was seldom used. It is no longer available. Cannabis is used illegally as resin or dried resin or in a form for smoking. Some persons have attempted to make a decoction in water and to give it i.v., with serious effects. In countries where alcohol is freely available, virtually as a natural substance, most people can see no harm in partaking of alcohol, and in countries where cannabis is freely available, the same applies. However, it is illogical to suggest that, because a drug of dependence already exists in a country, there is no harm in adding another one.

Recently, however, there have been papers published in a number of Western countries suggesting that Δ^9-THC should be made available as an antiemetic for patients receiving chemotherapy for malignant disease. It may cause confusion, depersonalization, hallucinations and hypotension, but in many patients there has been satisfactory antiemetic efficacy. Other synthetic cannabinoids are being tested as antiemetics where this form of chemotherapy is being used. Two that have been the subject of reasonably favourable reports are nabilone and levonantradol. In some states of the USA, legislation now permits this type of treatment and efforts are being made to find structurally related antiemetics that do not have comparable adverse effects.

EFFECTS OF CANNABIS

It is said that the desire to take cannabis is slight, that tolerance is not a great problem, that physical dependence does not occur and that psychic dependence is possibly less than with alcohol. Cannabis causes euphoria, excitement, inner joyfulness (being 'high'), sharpening of vision, sometimes with visual distortions, and difficulty in concentration. There can be depersonalization; drowsiness or depression can occur. Accuracy of performance may be impaired. Cannabis is more often smoked than taken orally and hence the intake is variable and the result unpredictable. A smoker may become 'high' with one or two cigarettes. The effects may occur within a few minutes and are of short duration. If Δ^9-THC is ingested, the effects may be felt after half an hour and may last for about 5 hours. Few would wish to travel in a vehicle driven by someone who had been taking sufficient cannabis to impair judgement, a problem similar to that relating to alcohol. With prolonged use, the person becomes indolent and non-productive. Progression to more dangerous drugs may be an indication of an inadequate personality.

DEPENDENCE ON COCAINE

Cocaine is obtained from the leaves of *Erythroxylum coca*, the coca-tree, which is found in many tropical countries, particularly South America. These leaves are regularly chewed by millions of persons living in Peru and Bolivia.

Cocaine dependence is not common, partly because the drug is so expensive. It can cause euphoria and excitement, even if sniffed, but to sniff it repeatedly may cause ischaemic necrosis, with perforation of the nasal septum. The drug leads to sexual desire and when taken i.v. may in itself give ejaculation and sexual gratification. For this reason it is sometimes given the colloquial name of 'girl'. There may be hallucinations and tremors. High doses lead to pyrexia, dilated pupils and palpitations.

Those who are in the habit of taking cocaine have a desire to continue to do so and there is psychic dependence, but not physical dependence. Tolerance is not a problem.

Colloquial names are 'candy', 'Charlie', 'C', 'big C', 'coke', 'girl' and 'snow'.

Sometimes it is injected with heroin or morphine by those who are drug dependent. The colloquial name 'speedball' refers to a mixture of cocaine and heroin.

DEPENDENCE ON HALLUCINOGENS

Amphetamines and cannabis may cause hallucinations, and passing reference has been made to mescaline (p. 187), an alkaloid from the Mexican cactus, *Lophophora williamsii*. This is cut off and dried to make peyote or mescale buttons, which are eaten by the Indians of the south-western parts of the United States and in Mexico in the conduct of religious ceremonies. Vivid hallucinations are said to occur.

Lysergic Acid Diethylamide

A serious matter is the introduction into society of lysergic acid diethylamide (LSD), an indole-containing hallucinogen related to 5-hydroxytryptamine. The structural relationship is shown below.

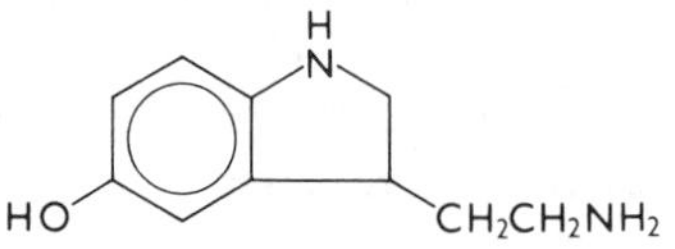

5-HYDROXYTRYPTAMINE

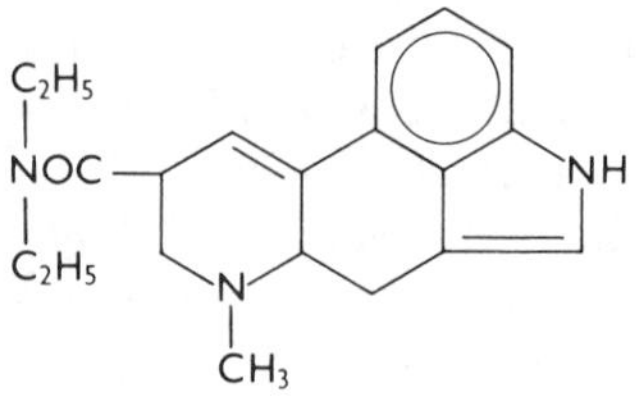

LSD

A fungus that causes a disease of rye is *Claviceps purpurea*, the dried sclerotium of which is often called ergot (p. 232). This contains a number of potent pharmacological agents, many of which are derivatives of lysergic acid. However, LSD does not occur naturally.

LSD is not a therapeutic substance (p. 195). The desire to continue taking it may be slight, physical dependence does not occur, tolerance develops rapidly, but is lost after discontinuance of the drug, and psychic dependence is not usually serious. However, the drug has bizarre effects on the personality akin to madness and many workers believe that chromosomal abnormalities may be induced. This latter subject is a matter of controversy, but there are obvious implications in relation to carcinogenesis and teratogenesis. LSD is usually taken by mouth. It is without odour, colour, or taste and can be administered to others without their knowledge, so is particularly dangerous. Sometimes it is taken i.v. Cannabis can be soaked with LSD in solution and smoked. Chlorpromazine, 50 mg i.m., may counter the psychotic effects of LSD.

Mode of Action
How LSD acts is uncertain. It has an ergot-like effect on smooth muscle and blood vessels, and has sympathomimetic actions, causing a rise in blood pressure, tachycardia, pupillary dilatation and piloerection. There is augmented sensitivity to sensory stimuli, tendon reflexes are increased, nausea and vomiting may be experienced, and tremor occurs. At first there is insomnia, but subsequently REM sleep is enhanced. The nature of the psychic experience varies, but usually the subject has vividly coloured hallucinations and may be overcome by the beauty of life around him. Usually the psychosis is of short duration. Sometimes, however, there is confusion, panic or paranoia, and bizarre reactions may occur weeks or months after the LSD has been taken. The person using the drug may find that his abnormal state of mind persists, so that, in effect, he has been driven mad. There may be

psychotic depression and suicide. It is difficult to understand why any rational being, knowing of these possible effects, would ever wish to take such a substance. Perhaps the person is unbalanced in the first place.

It has been suggested that the central effects are caused by antagonism to 5-hydroxytryptamine (5-HT), and yet 2-bromolysergic acid diethylamide, a more potent antagonist of 5-HT, does not have the same psychic effects. It does seem that LSD can mimic the actions of 5-HT on some receptor sites and interfere with its effects on others, but we do not understand the cause of the hallucinations. Hydrogenation of one of the double bonds of lysergic acid gives dihydroergotamine. If an amine is added to lysergic acid, methylergotamine is produced, while an amine added to N-methyllysergic acid gives methysergide (p. 142).

Other Hallucinogens

Other dangerous psychotomimetic agents are diethyltryptamine (DET), dimethyltryptamine (DMT) and dipropyltryptamine (DPT). The time of onset and duration of action are less with these. Additional hallucinogens are bufotenine, cohoba snuff, daturine, harmaline, harmine, ololiuqui, psilocin and psilocybin, all alkaloids derived from the seeds or leaves of various plants. Lysergic acid itself is part of the structure of all ergot alkaloids. Amides of lysergic acid are found in the seeds of a climbing plant called ololiuqui by the Aztecs, and this is believed to have been *Rivea corymbosa*, a convolvulaceous plant. Moreover, lysergic acid amides are found in the seeds of a certain species of the plant morning glory (*Ipomoea violacea*), but not in the usual *Ipomoea purpurea*.

Colloquial names include 'acid', 'zen' and 'white lightning'. LSD on a sugar lump is known as 'sugar'. Morning glory seeds are called Heavenly Blue or Pearly Gates.

Psilocybin is the main indole alkaloid present in the mushroom *Psilocybe mexicana*, which grows in certain areas of Mexico. It has hallucinatory properties similar to those of lysergic acid and mescaline. Psilocin comes from the same mushroom, but is less stable. The Mexican drug teonanacatl is derived from this and other mushrooms.

DEPENDENCE ON MORPHINE-TYPE DRUGS

The therapeutic use of morphine and related compounds is discussed elsewhere (Chapter 2). The main reason why such substances are not used more freely is that they possess all the worst features that a drug of dependence may have. Thus the desire to continue taking the drug is strong, tolerance develops and there is both psychic and physical dependence. Heroin is more popular with illicit drug users and possibly gives more euphoria than does morphine, though there is doubt about this. On a weight for weight basis, heroin is the more potent drug. Physical and emotional dependence develops rapidly, though the reaction to a first dose may disappoint an experimenter. There may be a transitory 'flush' after an i.v. injection of heroin, morphine or codeine due to histamine release, but the main desire of those who become dependent on heroin or morphine is to escape from anxiety and, hence, to feel that all is well with the world.

As tolerance develops, the craving becomes, largely, part of a desire to avoid the effects of withdrawal. First there may be a feeling of distress and then, after about 8 hours, the dependent person is anxious and restless. Tension builds up. He yawns, sweats and has lacrimation and rhinorrhoea. Sleep may overcome him, but he wakens in a state of extreme restlessness and misery. Tremors occur, and after 48 hours or so, his symptoms become more severe, with added nausea, vomiting and abdominal cramp. Muscle spasms may be observed. As the patient cannot take food, ketosis and dehydration are likely. Even if no treatment is given, provided no further narcotic is taken, the patient may recover within about a week. During a period of withdrawal, the patient can be helped with methadone, perhaps supplemented by a tranquillizer such as chlorpromazine (p. 165).

Other hazards facing those who inject themselves with heroin, apart from overdosage, are hepatitis, cellulitis, thrombophlebitis, septicaemia and tetanus. Deterioration of the personality occurs and there is rejection by society. The patient is not particularly aggressive, but may go to any lengths to obtain his drug.

Registration

In the UK, those dependent on heroin or cocaine can receive it only from specially licensed doctors, and such 'addicts' must be registered. This does not, of course, apply to the temporary therapeutic use of such substances. A doctor who attends a person whom he considers to be an 'addict' must, within 7 days, advise the Chief Medical Officer to the Home Office. The instructions giving details are the Misuse of Drugs (Notification of and Supply to Addicts) Regulations, 1973. The drugs concerned are cocaine, dextromoramide (Palfium), diamorphine, dipipanone (Diconal), hydrocodone, hydromorphone, levorphanol (Dromoran), methadone (Physeptone), morphine, opium, oxycodone, pethidine, phenazocine (Narphen) and piritramide (Dipidolor). Of these, the substances not referred to elsewhere in the book are narcotic analgesics with effects of a morphine type. Between 1977 and 1979, over half the offenders in Scotland found guilty of offences involving controlled drugs not included under the Misuse of Drugs Act, 1971 (p. 195) were using dipipanone. Doctors and others should be suspicious of those who ask for this drug, which is available in the UK in tablet form as Diconal. Some addicts grind up the tablets in water and inject the material i.v., with unpleasant consequences.

Colloquial terms for heroin include 'H', 'horse' and 'jack'.

DEPENDENCE ON OTHER NARCOTICS

As has been indicated elsewhere, there may be dependence on other narcotic analgesics, such as pentazocine and even codeine, together with the substances referred to above.

GENERAL LEGAL CONTROLS

In the UK there are three legal categories of drugs. These are: (1) pharmacy medicines, which may be sold or supplied only in a registered pharmacy by or under the supervision of a pharmacist — all medicines fall into this category unless expressly included by the licensing authority in one of the other two categories; (2) prescription-only medicines, which, in addition, may be sold or supplied only in accordance with a prescription given by an appropriate practitioner; and (3) General Sale List medicines, which may be sold or supplied otherwise than by or under the supervision of a pharmacist as a medicinal product on a general sale list. There are special regulations to deal with the types of drugs under discussion in this chapter.

The Misuse of Drugs Act, 1971, specifies 'dangerous or otherwise harmful drugs' called 'controlled drugs'. Under the Misuse of Drugs Regulations, 1973, these drugs are classified into four Schedules with different levels of control. Schedule 2 (which restricts the manufacture, possession and supply of the substance) applies to morphine, heroin, methadone and major stimulants such as amphetamines. Schedule 1 includes preparations containing very small quantities of certain controlled drugs such as morphine. The sale and supply of Schedule 1 preparations is not restricted, as with Schedule 2 drugs. Some drugs included in Schedule 1 are prescription-only medicines, while others may be sold by a pharmacist.

Schedule 3 to the Misuse of Drugs Regulations, 1973, is of little practical importance, but Schedule 4 requires a special licence from the Home Office for the possession and supply of hallucinogenic drugs such as LSD and cannabis. The list of those entitled to possess such substances does not include medical practitioners in the ordinary course of their work, but would, for instance, include a police officer when acting in the course of his duty. The relevant information is given in the Misuse of Drugs Regulations, 1973. The Misuse of Drugs (Designation) Order, 1973, indicates that the Schedule 4 drugs are bufotenine, cannabinol, cannabinol derivatives, cannabis, cannabis resin, concentrate of poppy straw, lysergamide, lysergide and other *N*-alkyl derivatives of lysergamide, mescaline, psilocin, raw opium, *N,N*-diethyltryptamine, *N,N*-dimethyltryptamine and 2,5-dimethoxy-α-4-dimethylphenethylamine.

CAFFEINE

Tea, coffee and cocoa are drunk throughout the world, but true dependence does not occur. Tea contains both caffeine and theophylline, cocoa has caffeine and theobromine, while coffee owes its stimulant action to its content of caffeine. Caffeine is a methylated xanthine, with the formula given below. Theophylline is usually combined with ethylenediamine as aminophylline (p. 321).

CAFFEINE

The way in which the methylated xanthines act is uncertain, but they inhibit the enzyme phosphodiesterase and hence there is an increase in cyclic adenosine monophosphate (AMP) in the CNS. Catecholamines promote the formation of cyclic AMP, and amphetamines release catecholamines. Both caffeine and theophylline stimulate mental activity and they cause diuresis because of reduced tubular reabsorption. The myocardium is stimulated and there may be palpitations and ectopic beats. Increased coronary blood flow may occur, possibly because of increased myocardial activity.

Caffeine is rarely taken alone except in the treatment of migraine, where it is not very effective, but it is frequently added to analgesic tablets such as aspirin or paracetamol, and codeine may also be included. The intention in adding caffeine is to potentiate the effects of the analgesics. However, the main sources of caffeine are the beverages referred to above. Those who drink them have an increase in mental alertness, but may be kept awake.

The problem of sleeplessness from the drinking of coffee is quite a definite one and many people who suffer from insomnia do not realize that it is self-inflicted. Students who have a sleepless night before an examination may not appreciate that this is due to the coffee that they took as a stimulant for last-minute studying. Some of those who suffer in this way may be affected by a surprisingly small amount of coffee; they may fall asleep initially and then waken in the small hours, restless and perhaps anxious, with a disturbing tachycardia. A smaller number find that it is tea that has this effect. It is said that tea contains higher amounts of caffeine than does coffee, but less is used in making an infusion. Perhaps there is some other factor involved, since some who are sleepless with coffee can drink a surprisingly large amount of tea at night without suffering from insomnia. Instant coffee contains a higher percentage of caffeine than ground coffee beans, but less is used in making a cup of the beverage. The amount of caffeine in powdered instant coffee is between 3 and 4%. Decaffeinated coffee is very palatable and the maximum caffeine content permitted is 0.3%. Coffee and tea form highly insoluble precipitates when mixed with phenothiazines or butyrophenones and this may explain variations in response to these and other drugs between patients or even in the same patient at different times.

SOLVENT ABUSE

There is concern about the practice of solvent abuse (sometimes and often erroneously called glue-sniffing), particularly in the age group 10–19. Substances are sniffed because they give off vapours which, like alcohol, are hydrocarbons. They may cause pleasure and sedation or may lead to aggressive behaviour. The child may sniff the substance until intoxicated and then meet with an accident or drown, may inhale vomitus or possibly suffocate by placing a plastic bag over the head. There is doubt as to whether death has been due merely to fumes.

The substances sniffed include adhesives, aerosol propellants, dry-cleaning fluids, petrol and a variety of other volatile substances.

Control of this habit lies in the hands of parents, teachers and social workers, together with voluntary action by retailers to curb the sale of solvents to young people when they suspect that there may be abuse.

NICOTINE DEPENDENCE

There is a form of chewing gum available, Nicorette, which contains either 2 mg or 4 mg of nicotine. When chewed the nicotine is slowly released into the mouth and absorbed by the buccal mucosa. The substance is intended to help those who cannot give up smoking because of nicotine dependence. In the UK the preparation can be obtained only on prescription. Those who do not inhale when smoking may experience nausea, faintness or headache and a test dose of 2 mg is advised. The maximum suggested is 15×4 mg pieces per day. The fatal acute dose of nicotine is probably about 60 mg, but nausea or vomiting would no doubt prevent fatal poisoning. In the event of overdosage, vomiting should be induced with syrup of ipecacuanha or gastric lavage carried out. A suspension of activated charcoal should be left in the stomach. Artificial respiration with oxygen might be needed.

FURTHER READING

Bateman P. N. & Rawlins M. D. (1982) Therapeutic potential of cannabinoids. *Br. med. J.*, 284: 1211.

Brunt P. W. (1978) Alcoholism as a medico-social problem. In: Vere D. W. (ed.) *Topics in Therapeutics 4*, p. 124. London: Pitman Medical.

Caplin M. & Rehahn M. (1978) Alcoholism and tuberculosis. In: Vere D. W. (ed.) *Topics in Therapeutics 4*, p. 136. London: Pitman Medical.

Department of Health and Social Security (1970) *Amphetamines, Barbiturates, LSD and Cannabis: Their Use and Misuse*. London: HMSO.

Department of Health and Social Security (1973) *Alcoholism*. A Memorandum prepared by the Standing Medical Advisory Committee for the Central Health Services Council. London: HMSO.

Editorial (1974) Recovery from heroin addiction. *Br. med. J.*, 3: 591.

Editorial (1978) Alcohol and the blood. *Br. med. J.*, 1: 1504.
Editorial (1982) Solvent abuse. *Lancet*, ii: 1139.
Editorial (1983) Blood and alcohol. *Lancet*, i: 397.
Editorial (1983) Alcohol and the fetus – is zero the only option? *Lancet*, i: 682.
Edwards G. (1983) Alcohol and advice to the pregnant woman. *Br. med. J.*, 286: 247.
Einhorn L. H., Nagg C., Furnas B. & Williams S. D. (1981) Nabilone: an effective emetic in patients receiving cancer chemotherapy. *J. clin. Pharmacol.*, 21: Suppl. 8–9, 64.
Glatt M. M., Pittman D. J., Gillespie D. G. & Hills D. R. (1967) *The Drug Scene in Great Britain — Journey into Loneliness*. London: Arnold.
Hotchen J. S. (1975) *Drug Misuse and the Law*. London: Macmillan–Winthrop.
Irwin S. & Egozcue, J. (1967) Chromosomal abnormalities in leucocytes from LSD-25 users. *Science*, NY, 157: 313.
Irwin S. T., Patterson C. C. & Rutherford W. H. (1983) Association between alcohol consumption and adult pedestrians who sustain injuries in road traffic accidents. *Br. med. J.*, 286: 522.
Isselbacher K. J. & Greenberger N. J. (1964) Metabolic effects of alcohol on the liver. *New Engl. J. Med.*, 270: 351.
Kahn J. S., Wilson M. C. & Taylor T. V. (1979) A case of Dettol addiction. *Br. med. J.*, 1: 791.
Kulhanek F., Linde O. K. & Meisenberg G. (1979) Precipitation of antipsychotic drugs in interaction with coffee or tea. *Lancet*, **ii**: 1130.
Laszlo J., Lucas V. S., Hanson D. C., Cronin C. M. & Sallan S. E. (1981) Levonantradol for chemotherapy-induced emesis: phase 1–11 oral administration. *J. clin. Pharmacol.*, 21: Suppl. 8–9, 51.
Louria D. B., Hensle T. & Rose J. (1967) The major complications of heroin addiction. *Ann. int. Med.*, 67: 1.
Lucas V. S. & Laszlo J. (1980) Δ⁹-tetrahydrocannabinol for refractory vomiting induced by cancer chemotherapy. *J. Am. med. Ass.*, 243: 1241.
Mott J. & Taylor M. (1974) *Delinquency Amongst Opiate Users*. A Home Office Research Unit Report. Home Office Research Studies, No. 23. London: HMSO.
Sallan S. E., Cronin C. M., Zelen M. & Zinberg N. E. (1980) Antiemetics in patients receiving chemotherapy for cancer. A randomized comparison of delta-9-tetrahydrocannabinol and prochlorperazine. *New Engl. J. Med.*, 302: 135.
Stefanis C., Dornbush R. & Fink M. (eds) (1977) *Hashish – Studies of Long-Term Use*. New York: Raven.
Vincent B. J., McQuiston D. J., Einhorn L. H., Nagy C. M. & Brames M. J. (1983) Review of cannabinoids and their antiemetic effectiveness. *Drugs*, 25: Suppl. 1, 52.
World Health Organization (1973) *Existing Patterns of Services for Alcoholism and Drug Dependence*. Copenhagen: Regional Office for Europe.

5 Drugs Affecting the Autonomic and Central Nervous Systems

W. S. Nimmo

THE AUTONOMIC NERVOUS SYSTEM

The autonomic nervous sytem (ANS) controls the vegetative functions of the body, such as the circulation, respiration, digestion and the maintenance of body temperature. All of the efferent axons which leave the central nervous system (CNS), with the important exception of those which innervate skeletal muscle, belong to the ANS. It may be subdivided on physiological and anatomical grounds into the sympathetic (thoracolumbar) and parasympathetic (craniosacral) systems.

The parasympathetic system is concerned primarily with the conservation and restoration of energy. It slows the heart, lowers arterial pressure, increases gastrointestinal motility and secretion, and empties the bladder and rectum. The sympathetic system is concerned primarily with arousal and has the opposite effects. It elevates the blood sugar concentration, increases the heart rate and causes the vascular response that occurs after haemorrhage and with exercise.

Stimulation of the parasympathetic system results in the release of acetylcholine, which acts on effector cells to elicit their responses. Acetylcholine is also the transmitter at the ganglia in both the sympathetic and parasympathetic systems, at the postganglionic sympathetic nerve endings to sweat glands and blood vessels, at the neuromuscular junction of skeletal muscle, between some neurones within the CNS and at the preganglionic nerve endings to the adrenal medulla. In contrast, noradrenaline is the transmitter released by the postganglionic sympathetic nerves.

It is evident, therefore, that the effects of parasympathetic nervous activity in an organ may be produced either by stimulation of a parasympathetic nerve fibre supplying the organ or by the application of acetylcholine to the effector cell. This is known as 'cholinergic activity'. Similarly, sympathetic nerve activity may be demonstrated by sympathetic nerve stimulation or by the application of noradrenaline or adrenaline ('adrenergic activity'), except in the case of the sweat glands and blood vessels.

CHOLINERGIC DRUGS

An increase in the activity of tissues innervated by cholinergic nerves may be produced by:

1. Acetylcholine itself and its derivatives – methacholine, carbachol, bethanechol.
2. The naturally occurring cholinergic alkaloids – pilocarpine, muscarine, nicotine, lobeline.
3. Inhibitors of cholinesterase (anticholinesterases; p. 203). These inactivate or inhibit the enzyme which normally hydrolyses acetylcholine, thereby allowing acetylcholine to accumulate at the receptor sites – neostigmine, pyridostigmine, physostigmine, edrophonium, organophosphorus compounds.

For convenience, the actions of acetylcholine may be divided into two main groups:

1. Nicotinic actions – those produced by stimulation of all autonomic ganglia and the neuromuscular junction.
2. Muscarinic actions – those produced at postganglionic cholinergic nerve endings (all parasympathetic endings and sympathetic endings at sweat glands and blood vessels).

Nicotinic Actions

Cardiovascular system. Stimulation of sympathetic ganglia and adrenal medulla, with discharge of adrenaline and noradrenaline, results in vasoconstriction, tachycardia and an elevated arterial pressure.

Gastrointestinal tract. Increased tone and peristalsis occurs, due to stimulation of the parasympathetic ganglia.

Glands. There is stimulation of salivary and bronchial secretions.

Central nervous system. There is central stimulation, with tremors and convulsions in large doses, and a release of antidiuretic hormone occurs.

Muscarinic Actions

Cardiovascular system. Vasodilatation and bradycardia results in a fall in arterial pressure.

Gastrointestinal tract. Smooth muscle is stimulated and therefore tone and motility are increased. The tone and motility of gall-bladder and bile ducts are also increased.

Glands. Salivary, lacrimal, gastric, pancreatic, intestinal and bronchial secretory cells are stimulated.

Smooth muscle in bronchi, uterus and bladder is stimulated and bronchospasm may result.

Eye. Pupillary constriction and paralysis of accommodation occurs.

Acetylcholine and its Derivatives

Acetylcholine

Acetylcholine is synthesized from choline and acetylcoenzyme A by choline acetylase and is stored at the nerve endings. When a nerve impulse arrives it is released in quanta and diffuses across the synaptic gap to the specific receptor sites on the postganglionic cell membrane. This leads to depolarization of the postganglionic cell. The duration of action of acetylcholine is very brief (a few milliseconds), since the compound is rapidly hydrolysed by specific cholinesterase to choline and acetate. This enzyme is present at nerve endings and in red blood cells. Pseudocholinesterase is a similar enzyme which is not specific for acetylcholine and is found in the plasma.

Acetylcholine is never used in therapeutics. It is so unstable that it would have to be given i.v. and it would be impossible to judge the correct dose. Also, it produces a huge variety of effects when injected.

Methacholine

Methacholine has both nicotinic and muscarinic actions, but the observed effects are predominantly cardiovascular and last up to 30 minutes after a s.c. dose of 10–30 mg. It is destroyed by cholinesterase much less rapidly than acetylcholine, but it cannot be given orally, since it is largely destroyed by the intestine. Anticholinesterases potentiate its effect.

Carbachol

Carbachol is a choline ester that is not destroyed by pseudocholinesterase. With anticholinesterases there is therefore a summation of effect rather than mere potentiation. Carbachol is more potent and longer-acting than methacholine and its actions are more pronounced on the bladder and bowels. It may be given by s.c. injection, but, unlike methacholine, it is stable in the alimentary tract and thus may also be given by mouth.

Indications
It is used to stimulate micturition following operation and childbirth, if there is no physical obstruction to the outflow of urine.

Carbachol is very dangerous when given i.v.

Dosage
Orally the dose is 1–4 mg. The dose by s.c. injection is 0.25–0.5 mg up to three times daily.

Bethanechol

Bethanechol is a stable choline ester which is not hydrolysed by cholinesterase. It has a weak but prolonged effect and its actions are mainly muscarinic. It may be used for difficulty in micturition and for gastric distension following surgery. Sweating, salivation and flushing of the skin are likely. The dose is 5–30 mg by mouth or 2.5–5 mg by s.c. injection.

Cholinergic Alkaloids

Pilocarpine

Pilocarpine, a naturally occurring alkaloid, acts directly at postganglionic cholinergic end organs to produce sweating, salivation and gastric secretion, and in the bronchial tree it causes mucous secretion. These effects are antagonized by atropine. It also stimulates and then depresses the CNS, but its action on the neuromuscular junction and autonomic ganglia is very slight.

Pilocarpine may be used as a 1% solution which is applied to the eye to produce miosis in glaucoma. Occasionally it is given s.c. or by mouth as a sialogogue in patients with parkinsonism who are taking large doses of atropine-like drugs, but sweating may be excessive as a result. The dose is 3–12 mg s.c. or orally.

Muscarine

Muscarine is of no therapeutic importance, but occasionally cases of muscarinic poisoning occur following ingestion of the fungus *Amanita muscaria*. Its effects are to stimulate all parasympathetic postganglionic fibres and are reversed by atropine.

Nicotine

The alkaloid is obtained from the leaves of the tobacco plant as nicotine. Knowledge of its actions is used in the classification of the actions of acetylcholine. Its actions are:

1. Stimulation of all ganglia of the ANS, followed by a characteristic depolarizing paralysis of ganglia. The cells of the adrenal medulla behave in a similar fashion.
2. Depolarization of the neuromuscular junction, followed by neuromuscular blockade.
3. Stimulant action on the CNS, followed by a depressant action.
4. Release of antidiuretic hormone.

The use of the drug in chewing gum as an anti-smoking aid is described on p. 197. Some of its actions are seen after cigarette smoking or after contact of the skin with some insecticides containing nicotine.

Lobeline

Lobeline, a naturally occurring alkaloid, has actions virtually the same as those of nicotine, but weaker.

Cholinesterase

True or specific cholinesterase is found at nerve endings and in red blood cells, unlike pseudocholinesterase (p. 216), which is found in plasma. Chemicals which inhibit these enzymes are known as anticholinesterases and are used in medical practice as drugs and in agriculture as insecticides. They act by allowing naturally occurring acetylcholine to accumulate instead of being destroyed and their effects are entirely due to the accumulation of acetylcholine. They have both nicotinic and muscarinic actions, and increase the effects of all cholinergic drugs.

Anticholinesterases

The anticholinesterases used in therapeutics inhibit the cholinesterase for a few hours. The organophosphates used as insecticides inactivate the enzyme completely and irreversibly, so that recovery depends on formation of new enzyme, an event which may take weeks. They act by phosphorylating the active centre of the enzyme, and if treatment of organophosphate poisoning is carried out within a few hours using i.v. pralidoxime, a specific reactivator of cholinesterase, the latter either competes for the poison in the body or dephosphorylates the enzyme.

Neostigmine

Neostigmine (Prostigmin), a synthetic anticholinesterase, is a quaternary ammonium compound and a structural analogue of acetylcholine. It forms an alternative substrate for the cholinesterase and is then hydrolysed much more slowly than the acetylcholine–enzyme combination. Its actions are more prominent on the neuromuscular junction and the alimentary tract than on the cardiovascular system or the eye. It is effective when given orally (25–100 mg three times per day) or by s.c. or i.v. injection (2.5 mg), or when used topically on the eye. It is often used in conjunction with atropine, which antagonizes its muscarinic actions and allows the nicotinic actions to become apparent. If neostigmine is given i.v., atropine must always be given at the same time.

Indications

Indications include myasthenia gravis, paroxysmal tachycardia, paralytic ileus, urinary retention and glaucoma (by local application in 3% solution), and it is used to antagonize non-depolarizing muscle relaxants.

Precautions
Care must be taken if the drug is to be administered to patients with bronchial asthma. If overdosage occurs in myasthenia gravis, the condition is made worse, since the anticholinesterase produces neuromuscular blockade in its own right (cholinergic crisis). It should not be used in the presence of intestinal or urinary obstruction.

Adverse Effects
Commonly encountered side-effects are nausea, vomiting, increased salivation, diarrhoea and abdominal cramps due to stimulation of smooth muscle.

Pyridostigmine

Pyridostigmine (Mestinon) is similar to neostigmine, but has a slower onset and slightly longer duration of action. It has only 25% of the potency of neostigmine and is usually taken by mouth in a dose of 100–400 mg three times per day in the treatment of myasthenia gravis.

Physostigmine

Physostigmine (Eserine) is a naturally occurring alkaloid which has been used as an ordeal poison in the past. It readily enters the CNS, since it is not a quaternary ammonium compound. It is a tertiary amine and its degree of ionization depends on the pH of the medium. Physostigmine may be used i.v. in a dose of 1–2 mg to control the CNS manifestations of poisoning with anticholinergic and tricyclic drugs and to reverse ketamine anaesthesia (p. 259). It is also used as eye drops in 0.25% solution to produce miosis. Overdosage produces a stimulant effect followed by a depressant effect on the brain, especially at the respiratory centre. The cause of death in physostigmine poisoning is respiratory failure.

Distigmine

Distigmine (Ubretid) is a variant of pyridostigmine. It is used orally or i.m. to treat urinary retention following surgery or as an adjunct to treatment in myasthenia gravis. It has a much longer duration of action than neostigmine or pyridostigmine.

Ambenonium

Ambenonium (Mytelase) has a slightly longer duration of action than pyridostigmine.

Edrophonium

Edrophonium (Tensilon) is related to neostigmine, but it is very short-acting and has a direct stimulant effect on the neuromuscular junction. Its effects following i.v. injection are over within 5 minutes, but overdosage may cause prolonged neuromuscular block. Autonomic effects are minimal.

Indications

Edrophonium may be useful in myasthenia gravis when it is administered i.v. to distinguish between underdosage and overdosage of anticholinesterase drugs used in treatment of this condition (p. 203). In underdosage, edrophonium improves muscle power while in overdosage, it causes a transient increase in weakness. Similarly, edrophonium i.v. can elucidate a dual block following depolarizing neuromuscular blocking agents. A dual block is reversed by the drug, while a depolarizing block is made temporarily worse. Edrophonium reverses the effect of curariform neuromuscular blocking agents, but its action is too short to be of use. The normal dose is 10 mg i.v.

Ecothiopate

Ecothiopate (Phospholine) is used topically as a long-acting miotic in glaucoma. Enough may be absorbed systemically to potentiate cholinergic drugs and also suxamethonium-induced muscle relaxation.

Demecarium

Demecarium (Tosmilen) is similar to ecothiopate.

Tacrine

Tacrine (THA) is a cerebral stimulant with a marked effect on the respiratory centre. It is a non-specific antagonist to the depressant action of morphine, barbiturates and similar drugs, but has strong anticholinesterase and mild anticholinacetylase activity. It antagonizes the action of non-depolarizing muscle relaxants but potentiates the action of suxamethonium. When given with suxamethonium, a severe bradycardia results and this should be anticipated and pretreated with atropine if both drugs are administered (p. 168).

Indications

Tacrine is used i.v. with suxamethonium to prolong its muscle relaxation from 5 minutes to about 25 minutes. Atropine must always be given beforehand. It has been used in the past to prevent respiratory depression and to promote wakefulness when large doses of morphine are required in the treatment of chronic pain (p. 113). The i.v. dosage is 15 mg.

MYASTHENIA GRAVIS

Myasthenia gravis is a disease of the muscle motor end-plate, in which there circulate antibodies to the cholinergic receptor. The reduction in the number of cholinergic receptors contributes to motor weakness, which may fluctuate.

Treatment consists of increasing the availability of acetylcholine at the motor end-plate by the use of anticholinesterases such as neostigmine or pyridostigmine (p. 203). Care must be taken to avoid the production of weakness due to excess acetylcholine (cholinergic crisis, p. 200).

Weakness may be increased by aminoglycoside antibiotics (p. 15), which inhibit the release of acetylcholine, and also by phenothiazines and phenytoin.

Corticosteroid drugs (p. 404), immunosuppressant therapy (p. 505), plasmapheresis or thymectomy may be necessary in patients who do not respond adequately to anticholinesterase drugs.

DRUGS WHICH BLOCK THE EFFECTS OF ACETYLCHOLINE

Drugs which block the effects of acetylcholine may be divided into three groups:

1. Anticholinergics, which antagonize acetylcholine at postganglionic parasympathetic nerve endings (atropine and related drugs).
2. Ganglion-blocking drugs.
3. Neuromuscular blocking agents.

Anticholinergics

Anticholinergics block the effects of acetylcholine at postganglionic cholinergic endings and also block the direct vasodilator effect of acetylcholine on the blood vessels and in the CNS. In other words, they block the muscarinic effects of acetylcholine. Some of the drugs have a mild ganglion-blocking action, but none affects the neuromuscular junction. In general, the doses required to block the responses to parasympathetic nerve stimulation are greater than those required to block the effects of injected parasympathomimetics.

Atropine

Atropine is the racemic mixture of D- and L-hyoscyamine. The L form is much more potent that the D form, but atropine is more stable chemically than either isomer and so is preferred. It acts by competing for the same receptors as acetylcholine, occupying them and thus rendering the acetylcholine ineffective. Therefore, in general, the peripheral effects of atropine are inhibitory and may be overcome by increasing the amount of acetylcholine reaching the receptors – for instance, by the use of anticholinesterases.

The word 'atropine' is derived from the name of the plant *Atropa belladonna*, the deadly nightshade, from which it can be obtained. Ἄτροπος (Atropos) in Greek mythology was one of the Fates, daughters of Night and of Erebus. She continually cut short the thread of man's existence, regardless of age, quality or sex. The other Fates were Clotho, who presides over mortals at the moment of their birth, and Lachesis, who spins the threads of life and the future. This sister is also commemorated in the BNF, in that lachesine is a mydriatic that can be used to dilate the pupil of a patient sensitive to atropine and homatropine.

Actions on the Respiratory System

Atropine reduces secretions in the respiratory tract and relaxes the smooth muscle of bronchi and bronchioles.

Actions on the Cardiovascular System

Atropine inhibits the vagus, reducing vagal tone, and thus it increases the heart rate and improves conduction in the bundle of His. Transient initial stimulation of the dorsal nucleus of the vagus may lead in the first instance to bradycardia, especially noticeable if a small dose of atropine is given. A therapeutic dose (0.6 mg) of atropine in adults may increase the heart rate by 30 beats/minute, but this effect is less marked in infants and old people. Atropine does not affect the peripheral blood vessels, except in toxic doses, and then vasodilatation occurs. Atropine does not affect the arterial pressure unless there is hypotension as a result of bradycardia, e.g. following myocardial infarction, in which case atropine may return the pressure to a normal value. Large doses of atropine cause vasodilatation of the skin blood vessels, which is unconnected with its antimuscarinic effect. This may be a direct action or may be due to histamine release. This so called 'atropine-blush' is a sign of atropine toxicity.

Actions on the Gastrointestinal Tract

All smooth muscle is relaxed by atropine and this leads to a reduction of tone and motility. Muscle spasm induced by morphine may be reduced. The total volume of gastric juice and the total acid content are decreased. The concentration of hydrogen ions and therefore the pH may be unaltered.

Actions on the Eye

Mydriasis occurs when atropine is administered and therefore the drug should not be used in patients with narrow-angle glaucoma. Intraocular pressure is not increased in normal subjects. Accommodation of the eye is set for infinity and normal pupillary reflexes may not be regained for 2 weeks. These effects can be reversed by pilocarpine or physostigmin. The mydriatic effect occurs no matter how the drug is administered, whether it be orally, topically or parenterally.

Actions on the Exocrine Glands

All secretions except milk are diminished. For instance, volume of saliva is decreased, leading to the characteristic dry mouth.

Actions on the Central Nervous System

There is cerebral stimulation; restlessness, insomnia and excitement occur with large doses. Hyperthermia may occur and this is dangerous because of the lack of sweating, something to be borne in mind in very hot climates. There is a moderate anti-nausea effect and the tremor of parkinsonism is improved.

Smooth muscle tone in the urinary tract is diminished and atropine administration may produce urinary retention.

Atropine is poorly absorbed from the skin and the conjunctiva, but when given orally, it is absorbed rapidly. It may also be given s.c., i.m. or i.v. The drug is destroyed mainly by hydrolysis in the liver, but some is excreted unchanged in the urine. Some tolerance to its actions occurs. It readily crosses the placental barrier to enter the fetal circulation.

The usual dose of atropine is 0.6–1.2 mg by any route. As a mydriatic, 1% eye drops are used.

Indications

The use of atropine is indicated in bradycardia or heart block, as premedication for anaesthesia to dry the mouth and respiratory passages, and to prevent the bradycardia which might result from vagal stimulation.

It is also used to dilate the pupil and paralyse accommodation, to relax smooth muscle spasm (e.g. atropine may be administered with pethidine in the treatment of biliary or ureteric colic; p. 116), as a bronchodilator, as an antiemetic, in parkinsonism, in spasm of bowel, in hyperhidrosis, and in poisoning by cholinergic drugs to prevent muscarinic effects.

Precautions

Patients with narrow-angle glaucoma should not be given atropine. Urinary retention may be precipitated.

Hyoscine (scopolamine)

Hyoscine is chemically and pharmacologically similar to atropine. However, the drug is a CNS depressant and produces drowsiness and euphoria. It is useful in the treatment of motion sickness and is a very efficient premedicant for anaesthesia in a dose of 0.4 mg. It may be given orally, s.c., i.m. or i.v. Eye drop preparations are available in a 0.25% solution.

Hyoscine butylbromide

As well as being antimuscarinic, hyoscine butylbromide (Buscopan) also blocks ganglia. It is less effective if given orally, because of poor absorption. It is a useful drug when given parenterally to relax smooth muscle of the bowel or bladder. It may be used by radiologists for this purpose.

Homatropine

Homatropine is used in a 2% solution as eye drops to produce mydriasis. Its action is shorter than that of atropine and therefore it is less likely to produce a serious rise in intraocular pressure. Its effects wear off in a few days and may be reversed by physostigmine eye drops.

Dicyclomine

Dicyclomine (Merbentyl) is useful in treating infantile colic and functional bowel disorders involving smooth muscle spasm. In certain proprietary preparations it is in combination with other drugs, such as phenobarbitone. The adult dose is 10–20 mg three times per day. Adverse effects include dry mouth, thirst, dizziness, fatigue, blurred vision, nausea and vomiting. Dicyclomine should not be given to patients with glaucoma.

Tropicamide and Cyclopentolate

In 0.5% or 1% solutions, tropicamide (Mydriacyl) and cyclopentolate (Mydrilate) are used topically to produce mydriasis. They have a more rapid onset and shorter duration of action than homatropine.

Atropine methonitrate

Atropine methonitrate (Eumydrin) is a quaternary ammonium derivative of atropine used in the treatment of congenital hypertrophic pyloric stenosis in infants. It is also a potent ganglion-blocking agent.

Propantheline

Propantheline (Pro-Banthine) is a synthetic anticholinergic drug. It has marked peripheral atropine-like actions and weak ganglion-blocking properties. In very high doses it interferes with neuromuscular transmission. It may be given orally or parenterally. The oral dose is 15–30 mg three times per day.

Indications
Propantheline is used as a spasmolytic in diseases of the gut where pain is due to smooth muscle spasm (p. 346). It is used to decrease gastric acid secretion and to delay gastric emptying in patients with a duodenal ulcer. Hyperhidrosis is also an indication for its use.

Adverse Effects
Dry mouth, blurred vision, constipation, retention of urine, postural

hypotension and impotence are relatively common side-effects of propantheline therapy. Symptoms associated with hiatus hernia are sometimes made worse, but the drug may be valuable in the prevention of acid regurgitation at night. If propantheline is administered concurrently with other orally administered drugs, the absorption of the latter will be influenced by the delay in gastric emptying produced by the propantheline. Narrow-angle glaucoma and urinary retention are contraindications to propantheline therapy.

Poldine

Poldine (Nacton) has properties similar to those of propantheline and may be used in the treatment of duodenal ulcer.

Emepronium

Emepronium (Cetiprin) is also similar to propantheline and has been found useful in reducing bladder motility and increasing bladder capacity in cases of urinary frequency and incontinence due to urgency.

Glycopyrronium bromide (glycopyrrolate, USP)

Unlike atropine and hyoscine, which are tertiary amines and therefore readily cross the blood–brain barrier, glycopyrronium bromide (Robinul) is a quaternary ammonium compound and does not enter the brain. Thus it has no central anticholinergic activity and for this reason it may be safer than the other anticholinergic drugs. It is used to reduce acid production in the management of peptic ulcer and in anaesthesia. The dose is 1–2 mg orally three times daily or 0.2–0.4 mg parenterally. The duration of action is longer than that of atropine.

Ipratropium

Atropine-like substances have been used for many years in treating asthma, but side-effects limit their usefulness. They produce bronchodilatation and reduce bronchial secretions, but also increase sputum viscosity.

Ipratropium (Atrovent) (p. 315) is used by aerosol inhalation and may have a more potent bronchodilator effect than adrenergic stimulants. It does not seem to affect sputum viscosity.

Pirenzepine

Pirenzepine (Gastrozepin) is a selective antimuscarinic drug which is used to reduce gastric secretion in the treatment of peptic ulcers. The dose is 50 mg orally night and morning.

The anticholinergic drugs used in the treatment of Parkinson's disease are described on p. 237.

A large number of drugs of other groups also demonstrate atropine-like activity to a varying degree and may produce troublesome side-effects — e.g. dry mouth, blurred vision. They include the tricyclic antidepressant drugs, the phenothiazines, antihistamines, quinidine and procainamide.

Ganglion-blocking Agents

Substances producing selective blockade of the transmission of nerve excitation in autonomic ganglia are called ganglion-blocking agents.

The pharmacologically important ganglion-blocking preparations can be classified as follows:

1. Quaternary ammonium compounds — e.g. hexamethonium.
2. Secondary amines — e.g. mecamylamine.
3. Tertiary amines — e.g. pempidine.

All these drugs act by competing with acetylcholine for receptor sites on the post-synaptic ganglion cell membrane.

The quaternary ammonium compounds are highly ionized and therefore are poorly absorbed through the gastrointestinal mucosa. They are thus unsuitable for oral administration and must be given parenterally for predictable pharmacological effectiveness. Secondary amines are better absorbed, and tertiary amines such as pempidine have a sufficiently large un-ionized fraction at gastrointestinal pH for satisfactory absorption to be achieved following oral administration.

Quaternary ammonium compounds

Hexamethonium.

Actions on the Cardiovascular System
Hexamethonium leads to a reduction in arterial pressure, especially in patients who are hypertensive. Postural hypotension is marked. The reduction in pressure can be attributed to a reduction in the total peripheral resistance due to vasodilation following ganglion blockade. When the patient stands, venous return to the heart is reduced owing to pooling of blood in the lower limbs under the influence of gravity. Cardiac output then falls, producing the phenomenon of postural hypotension. The compensatory vascular adjustments which prevent postural hypotension in the normal person are dependent on an intact sympathetic vasoconstrictor outflow. Ganglion blockade abolishes these sympathetic reflexes at sympathetic ganglion level.

In patients with congestive cardiac failure, hexamethonium lowers the central venous pressure as well as peripheral resistance, and so the drug is very useful in hypertensive heart failure.

Skin blood flow is generally increased and the feet and face become flushed. Muscle blood flow is only moderately affected and splanchnic blood flow is reduced. Renal flow is reduced in the upright posture, but cerebral blood flow is well maintained unless the arterial pressure falls precipitously.

Actions on Other Systems

Hexamethonium produces widespread effects due to autonomic ganglion blockade. They include dry mouth, a decrease in the acidity and volume of gastric secretions, delayed gastric emptying, constipation, paralytic ileus, dilated pupils, lack of tears, loss of accommodation, abolition of sweating, inhibition of adrenal medullary secretion, impotence and urinary retention.

Less than 5% of an oral dose of hexamethonium is absorbed and hence the drug is given parenterally. It is distributed in the extracellular fluid and is excreted unchanged in the urine by glomerular filtration. Excretion is complete in 24 hours.

The dose is 15–25 mg by the s.c. route or 5–15 mg i.v., and this amount may be repeated in 4 hours.

Indications

Hexamethonium was used in the treatment of hypertensive crises or to produce hypotension during anaesthesia, but it has now been largely replaced by drugs with fewer side-effects. It is no longer available in the UK.

Adverse effects include postural hypotension, syncope and all the effects on other systems mentioned above.

Secondary amines

Mecamylamine (Inversine), a secondary amine, has a direct depressant action on heart muscle and on the smooth muscle of the gut, as well as being a ganglion-blocking drug. It is also a local anaesthetic and a neuromuscular blocking agent. It acts in a different fashion from quaternary ammonium compounds in that it readily penetrates cells and alters the physiological state of the ganglion cell and muscle fibre, thus modifying their response to acetylcholine.

Mecamylamine is freely absorbed from the gastrointestinal tract and circulates partly bound to plasma proteins. It readily penetrates cells and crosses the blood–brain barrier. It is excreted unchanged in the urine, and the rate of clearance is slow. In fact, less than 50% is excreted in 12 hours, and the output is reduced if the urine is alkaline.

The initial dosage is 2.5 mg twice daily by mouth, with a rise by 2.5 mg increments every 2–3 days until the desired response is obtained. Tolerance is not a problem. The only indication for use of the drug is as a hypotensive agent in severe hypertension. It was deleted from MIMS* in February 1983.

Side-effects include constipation, which may be severe, coarse tremor, malaise and even psychosis. Postural hypotension is common.

Tertiary amines

Pempidine, a tertiary amine, has similar properties to mecamylamine, but it is excreted more rapidly by the kidney and its excretion is less affected by variation in the pH of urine. Its duration of action, therefore, is shorter. The dosage is 2.5 mg orally twice daily, this being increased incrementally until a satisfactory effect on arterial pressure is obtained. The only indication for its use is hypertension.

Many other pharmacological substances which are used for their effects on the central or peripheral nervous system or for their cardiovascular actions have secondary but well-marked effects on autonomic ganglia. They will therefore potentiate the effects of all the ganglion-blocking drugs described above. These drugs include ether, chloroform, halothane, barbiturates, tricyclic antidepressants, monoamine oxidase inhibitors, local anaesthetics, hyoscine, propantheline, non-depolarizing muscle relaxants, procainamide, quinidine and hydralazine.

Sulphonium compound

Trimetaphan (Arfonad) is a short-acting ganglion-blocking agent, but it also releases histamine and has a direct vasodilator action. These actions reduce arterial pressure by lowering total peripheral resistance and cardiac output. Tachycardia may occur and reduce its effect.

If an i.v. 'bolus' of 50 mg is given, the effects are seen in 1–3 minutes and last for 5–15 minutes. When a 1 in 1000 solution is infused i.v., the rate of infusion should be adjusted to maintain the desired degree of hypotension. When the infusion is stopped, the pressure rises again within 10 minutes. The drug is partly excreted unchanged in the kidney.

Vascular thrombosis may be a side-effect. Anuria, reactionary bleeding and shock may occur with overdosage. The drug should only be used by doctors skilled in its use.

PHYSIOLOGY OF NEUROMUSCULAR TRANSMISSION

At the junction of a motor nerve and the skeletal muscle it supplies, there is a specialized portion of muscle membrane known as the motor end-plate.

---

*MIMS, the *Monthly Index of Medical Specialities*, is published by Medical Publications Ltd, 76 Dean Street, London W1A 1BU.

Under resting conditions, selective permeability of this membrane to ions enables an unequal distribution of ions, and therefore an electrical potential difference, to be maintained between the inside and the outside of the cell. When an impulse reaches the nerve ending, it causes acetylcholine to be released. This modifies the motor end-plate and increases its permeability to some ions, so that polarization occurs and triggers the action potential which is associated with contraction of the muscle.

Acetylcholine is formed at the nerve ending by acetylation of choline with the help of the enzyme cholineacetylase. Electron microscopy has revealed, at the nerve ending, the presence of vesicles which contain molecules of acetylcholine stored after manufacture to await their final release. Even in the resting state, small quantities of acetylcholine are sporadically released from the nerve ending. The arrival of an impulse, however, releases numerous packets of acetylcholine, which cross to the motor end-plate and initiate contraction of the muscle. A fall in calcium concentration or a rise in magnesium concentration will greatly reduce the number of acetylcholine molecules that are liberated from the nerve ending.

Neomycin, streptomycin, botulinus toxin and perhaps procaine all interfere with the release of acetylcholine. The myasthenic syndrome such as is sometimes found in bronchial carcinoma is due to a difficulty in release of acetylcholine.

On leaving the prejunctional area (the nerve ending), the acetylcholine molecules cross the minute gap (1 μm) to the postjunctional area on the muscle membrane, producing a wave of depolarization in the muscle. The acetylcholine molecules are destroyed by the specific enzyme (cholinesterase), giving acetic acid and choline almost as rapidly as the molecules are produced.

Neuromuscular Blocking Agents

The neuromuscular blocking agents used in clinical practice interfere with the process described above, but do not affect muscle or nerve. Nor do they interfere with acetylcholine release.

There are two principal ways of producing neuromuscular block:

1. By a prolongation of the normal depolarization process. Suxamethonium and decamethonium are examples of drugs that act by prolonging the depolarization process. Initially they produce contraction of the voluntary muscle, but as they are not destroyed immediately, as is acetylcholine, the depolarization persists. Anticholinesterases not only are useless as antidotes to depolarizing drugs, but also may increase the paralysis.

2. By the non-depolarizing or competitive inhibition exhibited by tubocurarine and similar drugs. These drugs have an affinity for the protein molecules of the motor end-plate and bind to them loosely. The

liberation and destruction of acetylcholine molecules continues normally, but no muscle contraction occurs. If an anticholinesterase is given, the destruction of acetylcholine is prevented and its concentration at the end-plate rises to overcome the competition from tubocurarine for the receptors. Therefore, anticholinesterases are used as antidotes to competitive neuromuscular blocking agents.

Factors Affecting the Duration or Degree of Neuromuscular Block

1. Blood flow. This is the single most important factor. Muscle groups with a high blood flow have earlier onset and shorter duration of paralysis. In elderly patients or those with serious diseases, neuromuscular block may be prolonged.
2. Body temperature. Hypothermia increases the duration and the magnitude of depolarization block. The effects are reversed by rewarming. In contrast, hypothermia reduces the degree of block produced by tubocurarine but has no effect on its duration.
3. Carbon dioxide tension and pH. The action of tubocurarine is increased by acidosis and decreased by alkalosis. The findings for gallamine are the reverse of those quoted for tubocurarine.
4. Renal excretion. With the exception of suxamethonium, all the muscle relaxants are at least partly excreted in the urine. Gallamine is entirely excreted by the kidney. Eighty per cent of an injected dose of tubocurarine is excreted unchanged by the kidney and 5% passes through the biliary system to the bowel, but in renal failure 40% may leave the circulation by this route. Gallamine does not have this alternative pathway. The new competitive antagonist atracurium (p. 219) undergoes spontaneous hydrolysis in plasma and thus is likely to be safer in renal failure.
5. Antibiotics. Drugs such as streptomycin, neomycin, colomycin and viomycin all prolong the effect of neuromuscular blocking drugs. Calcium chloride reverses this action.
6. Tranquillizers. Diazepam increases the duration of block produced by non-depolarizing relaxants and shortens that of suxamethonium.
7. Potentiation by other drugs. Ether and halothane block neuromuscular transmission by reducing the sensitivity of the postjunctional membrane to acetylcholine. Quinidine and local anaesthetics potentiate neuromuscular block by a presynaptic action.
8. Because of their relatively large extracellular fluid volume, infants require more suxamethonium on a weight basis than adults to produce equal neuromuscular blockade. The duration of action is not altered. However, the newborn infant is very sensitive to tubocurarine.

All the neuromuscular blocking agents in common use have one to three quaternary ammonium groups and are thus ionized and positively charged irrespective of the pH.

Suxamethonium (succinyl dicholine, diacetylcholine)

$$(CH_3)_3 \overset{+}{N}CH_2 \ CH_2 \ O\overset{O}{\overset{\|}{C}}CH_2 \ CH_2 \ \overset{O}{\overset{\|}{C}}OCH_2 \ CH_2 \ \overset{+}{N}(CH_3)_3 \qquad\qquad (CH_3)_3 \ \overset{+}{N}CH_2 \ CH_2 \ O\overset{O}{\overset{\|}{C}}CH_3$$

SUXAMETHONIUM   ACETYLCHOLINE

Suxamethonium is a short-acting depolarizing neuromuscular blocking drug with a molecular structure consisting of two acetylcholine molecules joined together. A typical i.v. dose of 1 mg/kg body weight produces complete neuromuscular blockade with recovery to 50% neuromuscular transmission in about 10 minutes. Muscle fasciculation precedes the paralysis. These fasciculations produce a rise in intraocular pressure and are probably the cause of severe muscle pains which may be noticed by the patient 1–3 days after operation. In ambulant patients the incidence of muscle pains is 60–70%, but if the patient is confined to bed the incidence drops to 10%. If a second injection of suxamethonium is given shortly after the first injection, bradycardia or even cardiac arrest may occur due to vagal stimulation. Atropine prevents this complication. Patients with high plasma potassium (e.g. after burns or trauma) are very likely to develop dysrhythmias following suxamethonium and should not receive the drug.

Following an i.v. injection, nearly all the drug in the plasma is hydrolysed within 1 minute by pseudocholinesterase, a glycoprotein produced in the liver and found in the plasma.

The breakdown of suxamethonium occurs in two stages:

1. Suxamethonium → succinylmonocholine + choline. This reaction is so rapid that less than 5% of the injected dose reaches the peripheral muscles. Succinylmonocholine is a much less powerful muscle relaxant than suxamethonium.
2. Succinylmonocholine → succinic acid + choline. This reaction is extremely slow.

Other methods of elimination of suxamethonium are unimportant in the normal individual. They include alkaline hydrolysis, which is a non-enzymatic process (less than 5% of an injected dose is destroyed per hour) and renal excretion (less than 2% of an injected dose is excreted unchanged). If plasma pseudocholinesterase is deficient (e.g. in liver disease or in malnutrition), or if the enzyme is incapable of hydrolysing the suxamethonium, these methods represent the only route of elimination and recovery from suxamethonium paralysis is prolonged. If the paralysis lasts for hours, there is no effective way of eliminating the drug and intermittent positive pressure ventilation must be instituted. Atypical plasma pseudocholinesterase has been recognized and individuals with this enzyme can lead perfectly normal lives until they receive an injection of suxamethonium. The presence of this atypical enzyme is due to the inheritance of an abnormal gene. This gene appears to be non-sex-linked, since the atypical enzyme is seen in both males and females.

About 96% of the population are normal (i.e. homozygotes for normal enzyme) and nearly 4% are heterozygotes, having a mixture of typical and atypical enzymes. Suxamethonium is metabolized less efficiently in the latter group. However, 1 in 2800 of the population is a homozygote for the abnormal enzyme and will have grossly delayed recovery of muscle power after an injection of suxamethonium.

Dibucaine may be used to inhibit the pseudocholinesterase in plasma in vitro, and the percentage inhibition is called the dibucaine number. Normal homozygotes have a dibucaine number of 70–85. Heterozygotes have a dibucaine number of 50–65. Abnormal homozygotes have a dibucaine number of less than 25.

Suxamethonium is usually given i.v. in a dose of 1 mg/kg body weight, but it may be given s.c. or i.m. Fasciculations are first noted in the eyelids and paralysis lasts 2–6 minutes. The action can be opposed by previous administration of non-depolarizing drugs and can be potentiated by anticholinesterases. Tacrine, an anticholinesterase, may be used clinically to prolong the paralysis. Procaine and propanidid are also metabolized by pseudocholinesterase and may prolong the effects of suxamethonium.

Indications
Suxamethonium is used to produce muscle paralysis just after induction of anaesthesia to facilitate rapid tracheal intubation.

Decamethonium

Decamethonium is also a depolarizing muscle relaxant. There is no evidence that it undergoes any form of breakdown in the body. Of the total dose injected, 80–90% is excreted unchanged in the urine. An i.v. injection of 3–4 mg produces profound paralysis in 2–3 minutes and this lasts 15–20 minutes. Decamethonium is very seldom used in clinical practice.

D-Tubocurarine

D-Tubocurarine (Tubarine) is a monoquaternary alkaloid which produces neuromuscular block and profound muscle relaxation by competition with acetylcholine and its action may therefore be reversed by anticholinesterases.

When injected i.v. its effect is maximal in 4 minutes; the time to 50% recovery of neuromuscular transmission is 51 minutes. Its onset of action is not preceded by muscle fasciculations. It has some ganglion-blocking properties and hypotension occurs following an injection. It does not cause a tachycardia and the hypotension may be due to histamine release by the tubocurarine. There is no effect on the CNS, the effect on the muscles being entirely peripheral.

Following i.v. administration, the kidneys provide the principal route of elimination, with the liver and biliary systems offering an alternative which becomes much more important in renal failure. Tubocurarine is not broken down in the body but is excreted unchanged. Recovery of spontaneous respiration occurs due to redistribution before excretion. In hepatic failure, larger doses of the drug are required owing to variation in the globulin/albumin ratio, and protein binding is increased. Tubocurarine does not affect the fetus and the drug may be used for Caesarean section.

Indications
Tubocurarine is used to produce muscle relaxation during surgical operations. It may also be used in tetanus, in severe status epilepticus and as part of the treatment of crushed chests. Whenever the drug is given artificial ventilation of the lungs must be instituted.

Administration
Tubocurarine may be given i.v., i.m., or dissolved in oil by deep i.m. injection so that its duration of action is prolonged. Absorption after oral administration is poor. The i.v. dose is usually 30 mg for the adult patient to produce paralysis lasting 30 minutes for intra-abdominal operations.

Potentiation of the effects of the drug occurs with chlorpromazine, halothane, ether and antibiotics.

Care must be exercised in patients with myasthenia gravis or low potassium, and in asthmatic patients, who may experience bronchospasm due to histamine release.

Gallamine

Gallamine (Flaxedil) is a synthetic, non-depolarizing muscle relaxant that contains three quaternary ammonium groups. When given i.v., it acts in $1\frac{1}{2}$ minutes and 50% recovery occurs in 23 minutes. As with tubocurarine, there is no effect on the CNS, but gallamine produces a tachycardia, while leaving the arterial pressure unchanged. Gallamine does cross the placenta, but seems to have no effect on the fetus. It is excreted entirely by the kidney and 30–100% of an injected dose is recovered in the urine within 2 hours. Its actions may be reversed by anticholinesterase.

Indications
Gallamine is used in circumstances similar to those in which tubocurarine is used. It is shorter-acting than curare. Artificial ventilation of the lungs must be undertaken.

Dosage
The adult i.v. dose is 80–120 mg, with increments of 20–40 mg as required.

Precautions
Gallamine must not be given to patients suffering from myasthenia gravis or renal failure.

Pancuronium

Pancuronium (Pavulon) is a steroidal bisquaternary ammonium compound. It is a very effective neuromuscular blocking agent without evidence of steroid activity. Like tubocurarine and gallamine, it is a competitive, non-depolarizing muscle relaxant.

It has very little effect on the cardiovascular system and does not affect the CNS. It may cross the placenta, but has no effect on the fetus. About 50% of an administered dose appears in the urine, 20% in a metabolized form. Another 10% is eliminated in the bile.

Indications
The indications for pancuronium are the same as those for tubocurarine. Its action is reversed by anticholinesterase.

Administration
Pancuronium is given i.v. in a dosage of 4–6 mg to produce complete neuromuscular blockade with 50% recovery in 37 minutes.

Alcuronium

Alcuronium (Alloferin) is a derivative of calabash curare alkaloid. It is a non-depolarizing relaxant, twice as potent as tubocurarine, but its duration of action is shorter. As with tubocurarine, hypotension may follow its use.

Indications
The indications for alcuronium are the same as those for tubocurarine.

Administration
The adult i.v. dose is 10–20 mg, with increments of 3–5 mg. This drug is antagonized by anticholinesterase.

Fazadinium

Fazadinium (Fazadon) has a similar duration of action to gallamine. It is largely excreted unchanged in the urine. The dose is 0.75–1 mg/kg body weight.

Atracurium

Atracurium (Tracrium), a competitive neuromuscular blocking agent, has recently been introduced. It has a very rapid onset and short duration of action which is due in part to spontaneous degradation by Hoffman elimination in vivo. This reaction occurs rapidly at pH 7.4 and does not require enzymatic activity. The drug is also excreted unchanged in the kidney. Its effects are reversed by neostigmine. In addition, its actions on the cardiovascular system are less than those of the older drugs.

Thus atracurium is likely to prove very successful in anaesthetic practice, particularly in patients with renal failure. The dose is 0.3–0.6 mg/kg body weight.

Vecuronium

Vecuronium (NC45, Norcuron) is a monoquaternary analogue of pancuronium. It has a shorter duration of action and fewer cardiovascular side-effects than pancuronium.

SYMPATHOMIMETIC DRUGS

As their name suggests, these drugs resemble sympathetic nerve stimulation in their effects. They may be divided into two groups on the basis of their chemical structure and mode of action:

1. Catecholamines, including adrenaline, noradrenaline, dopamine and isoprenaline. These are derivatives of catechol (dihydroxybenzene).
2. Non-catecholamines, including orciprenaline, terbutaline, salbutamol, phenylephrine, methoxamine, metaraminol, ephedrine, amphetamine, methylamphetamine and mephentermine. These all have structural similarity to the catecholamines.

Catecholamines

Catecholamines have a direct action on sympathetic effector cells, interacting with receptor sites on the cell membrane. They are, therefore, effective when the sympathetic nerve has been cut or inhibited pharmacologically. Many of the non-catecholamines exert part of their effect by releasing endogenous catecholamines from the post-ganglionic nerve fibres.

Adrenaline (epinephrine, USP)

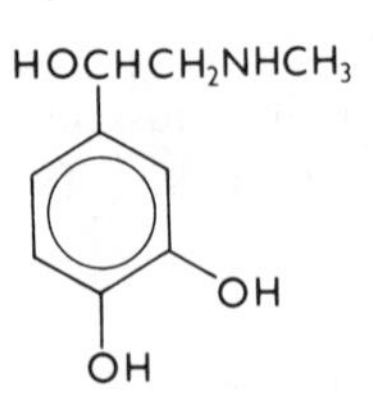

HOCHCH$_2$NHCH$_3$

ADRENALINE
(epinephrine)

Table 5.1 *Classification of sympathomimetic drugs*

Group	Drug	Receptor stimulated	Mode of action	Clinical use	Notes
1. Endogenous substances	Adrenaline	α and β	Direct	Many uses (see text)	
	Noradrenaline	α	Direct	Vasoconstrictor	
	Dopamine	β_1, α, and dopamine	Direct and indirect	Inotropic agent and to increase urinary output	
2. α-receptor agonists	Metaraminol	α	Direct and indirect	Pressor agents and nasal decongestants	
	Phenylephrine	α	Direct and indirect		
	Methoxamine	$\alpha(\beta$ block)	Direct		
3. β-receptor agonists (catecholamines)	Isoprenaline	β	Direct	Inotropic agent and bronchodilator	
	Isoetharine	β_2	Direct	Bronchodilators	
	Rimiterol	β_2	Direct		
	Hexoprenaline	β_2	Direct		
	Dobutamine	β_1	Direct	Inotropic agent	
4. β-receptor agonists (non-catecholamines)	Orciprenaline	β	Direct	Bronchodilators	
	Terbutaline	β_2	Direct		
	Fenoterol	β_2	Direct		
	Salbutamol	β_2	Direct		
	Isoxsuprine	β	Direct	Vasodilator and to delay premature labour	Also used to delay labour
	Ritodrine	β	Direct	To delay labour	Also used to delay labour
5. Sympathomimetics with predominantly indirect action (may have weak direct activity)	Tyramine	α and β	Indirect and weak direct	—	
	Phenylethanolamine	α and β	Indirect and weak direct	—	CNS stimulant
	Phenylpropanolamine (Norephedrine)	α and β	Indirect	Nasal decongestant and anorectic	Not a substrate for MAO
	Ephedrine	α and β	Indirect and direct	Nasal decongestant and vasoconstrictor	Not a substrate for MAO
	Amphetamine	α and β	Indirect	For narcolepsy	CNS stimulant
	Mephentermine	α and β	Indirect	Nasal decongestant and pressor agent	
	Isometheptene	α and β	Indirect only	Pressor agent, a mydriatic and for migraine	No CNS stimulation

Adrenaline is produced in the body by the cells of the adrenal medulla and by chromaffin tissue. Its actions may be divided into two categories, depending on the type of receptor stimulated. Since 1948 these receptors have been classified as α and β. The β receptors were then classified as β_1 (heart) and β_2 (bronchi, uterus, blood vessels). The α receptors also may be subdivided into α_1 and α_2.

The α effects consist of vasoconstriction in skin and viscera, mydriasis, platelet aggregation and some increase in blood glucose. The β effects consist of increased contractility and rate of the heart, with a decreased refractory period (β_1 receptor), vasodilatation in muscles and coronary vessels (β_2 receptor), bronchial relaxation (β_2 receptor), uterine relaxation (β_2 receptor), hyperglycaemia, lactic acidaemia, and increased circulating free fatty acids. Both α and β receptors are involved in producing relaxation of the intestine and contraction of the pylorus. The detrusor muscle of the bladder is relaxed, while the trigone and sphincter are contracted. The splenic capsule is contracted, and the capillaries throughout the body are constricted and have decreased permeability. Even in a small dose, adrenaline produces a feeling of restlessness, apprehension, tremor and headache.

The net effect of adrenaline on the cardiovascular system is that the heart rate and systolic pressure are increased, while the diastolic pressure falls.

It seems likely that the adrenergic receptor is the enzyme adenylcyclase, which catalyses the conversion of adenosine triphosphate (ATP) to cyclic adenosine monophosphate (AMP). The cyclic AMP then produces the observed biological effects.

Adrenaline is rapidly destroyed in the gastrointestinal tract and conjugated and oxidized in the liver. It is, therefore, ineffective when given orally, and should be given s.c. or i.m. Intravenous injection is highly dangerous and is likely to precipitate ventricular fibrillation. The drug may, however, be given by nebulizer for inhalation when its relaxing effect on the bronchi is desired, or it may be applied topically to mucous membranes to produce vasoconstriction. Most exogenously administered adrenaline is metabolized (methylated), chiefly by catechol-*O*-methyl transferase in the blood, but some is metabolized by monoamine oxidase in the liver and nerve endings. The two processes result in the appearance of 3-methoxy-4-hydroxymandelic acid in the urine. A little is excreted unchanged (2%).

Indications
Adrenaline is used to produce vasoconstriction in local analgesia, to produce bronchodilatation in bronchial asthma (p. 315), for topical vasoconstriction, and in the treatment of allergic reactions.

Side-effects include tissue necrosis, which may occur due to intense vasoconstriction. Therefore adrenaline must not be used with local anaesthetic in the base of the finger or the penis. Sudden death due to ventricular fibrillation may occur if it is given i.v.

Great care must be taken if the drug is used in the presence of thyrotoxicosis, hypertension, or ischaemic heart disease. Overdosage produces anxiety, apprehension, pallor and tachycardia.

In patients under general anaesthesia with any of the volatile agents, cardiac dysrhythmias are very likely to occur if adrenaline is administered. Hypercapnia and hypoxia have a potent aggravating effect.

Dosage and Administration

When used with local anaesthetics to prolong nerve block, a 1 in 200 000 or 1 in 400 000 solution is effective. For topical application, a 1 in 1000 solution may be used. In asthma, the patient may inhale the spray of 1 in 100 solution of adrenaline or be given a s.c. injection of 0.2–0.5 ml of 1 in 1000 solution. This dose may also be used in the treatment of various forms of allergy. In anaphylactic shock it may be given i.m. but it should not be given i.v.

Noradrenaline (Levarterenol, L-Norepinephrine)

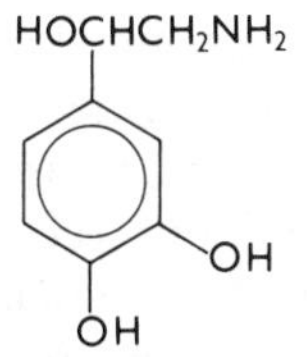

NORADRENALINE

Noradrenaline is the neurochemical mediator released by nerve impulses and various drugs from the postganglionic sympathetic nerves. It also constitutes about 10% of the catecholamine output of the adrenal medulla. It is predominantly an α receptor stimulant, but has mild β stimulating properties.

Actions

Noradrenaline increases peripheral vascular resistance by producing vasoconstriction in most vascular beds, and results in a fall of blood flow through the kidney, brain, liver and splanchnic regions. Coronary blood flow is increased, however. Both systolic and diastolic blood pressures are elevated and compensatory vagal reflexes then slow the heart rate. There is a moderate rise in circulating free fatty acids and in plasma glucose concentration.

Like adrenaline, noradrenaline must be given parenterally, and as intradermal and s.c. injections produce tissue necrosis, it should be given i.v. Its metabolic fate is similar to that of adrenaline: less than 5% is excreted unchanged in the urine.

Indications

In peripheral vasomotor collapse, noradrenaline is used in order to restore the arterial pressure. During infusion the pressure must be monitored closely, and the infusion should be stopped gradually, since sudden cessation may be followed by a catastrophic fall in arterial pressure.

Noradrenaline may be used with local anaesthetics in place of adrenaline.

Dosage
The usual dose is 8–12 μg/minute, diluted in saline or laevulose, by i.v. infusion, but the rate of infusion should be adjusted to the response. A single i.v. dose produces effects lasting only a few minutes.

Adverse Effects
Side-effects include gangrene of the extremities following prolonged infusion and necrotic ulceration of an area around the injection vein. Tolerance to its effects may occur.

Dopamine

Dopamine (Intropin) is the immediate precursor of noradrenaline in man, but has important pharmacological properties of its own. It has weak direct actions on adrenoreceptors and also has indirect sympathomimetic actions: in addition, it acts on specific dopamine receptors of renal and mesenteric vascular smooth muscle to cause vasodilatation. It increases myocardial contractility and heart rate by stimulating the β-adrenergic receptors. It also releases noradrenaline. Dopamine can produce relaxation or contraction of vascular smooth muscle, depending on the vascular bed studied and the dose administered. It produces vasodilatation in renal, mesenteric, coronary and intracerebral arteries by a direct effect on dopaminergic receptors. The effects are not antagonized by β-blockers, but are reversed by phenothiazines and butyrophenones. When large doses of dopamine are used the predominant effect in all vascular beds is vasoconstriction due to α-adrenergic stimulation. Bradycardia often results from its use. It is used to increase arterial blood pressure and urine output in patients who are shocked following surgery or septicaemia.

The dose of dopamine is 2–20 μg/kg body weight per min. by i.v. infusion, this being increased if necessary to maintain arterial pressure and urine flow. The drug is inactivated in alkaline solution. Below 5 μg/kg body weight per min., dopamine increases renal blood flow by stimulation of dopamine receptors. As the dose is increased in the 5–20 μg/kg/min. range, both β_1 and α receptors are stimulated and cardiac output and arterial pressure rise. Above this range, α-receptor effects are more marked, with a further rise in arterial pressure. Dopamine is metabolized by monoamine oxidase and therefore patients taking monoamine oxidase inhibitors (p. 172) should receive a reduced dose of dopamine if they require the drug. Side-effects include peripheral ischaemia and cardiac dysrhythmias. The literature supplied with the drug should be carefully studied when it is used.

Isoprenaline (Isopropylnoradrenaline; isoproterenol, USP)

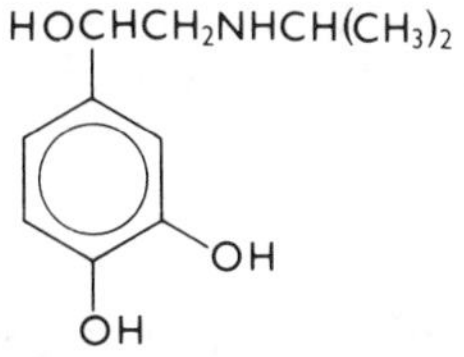

$$HOCHCH_2NHCH(CH_3)_2$$

ISOPRENALINE

Isoprenaline has the most marked β-stimulating activity. It may have very weak α stimulating effects.

Actions

Isoprenaline increases cardiac output by increasing heart rate and force of contraction. Coronary vasodilatation occurs, as well as widespread vasodilatation, especially in skeletal muscles. As a result, diastolic blood pressure falls, though systolic pressure is increased.

Isoprenaline stimulates the respiratory centre to some extent, as well as being a potent bronchodilator. It decreases tone and motility in the gut and the uterus. It produces a rise in circulating free fatty acids and hyperglycaemia. Central stimulation with anxiety and restlessness occurs with its administration.

Although absorption from the gastrointestinal tract is unpredictable, isoprenaline is absorbed sublingually or when given as an aerosol. It may also be given parenterally. Metabolism and excretion occur as with adrenaline. The drug is extensively metabolized in the gut wall.

Indications

The indications for the use of isoprenaline are heart block, bronchial asthma (p. 317), or, by i.v. infusion, for the maintenance of systolic blood pressure. However, alternative drugs are available.

Dosage and Administration

Isoprenaline is given as an i.v. injection of 25 μg, but only for heart block. For other purposes it can be given in a dose of 10–20 mg as a tablet dissolved under the tongue and repeated as necessary or administered as a sustained release preparation (Saventrine) to be swallowed. In bronchial asthma a spray containing 1% or an aerosol for inhalation is often used and is more effective than tablets under the tongue. The effects are noted in 30 seconds, are maximal after 5 minutes and disappear after 1 hour.

Unwanted effects include tachycardia, palpitations, tremor and hyperglycaemia, the last of which may be troublesome in the control of diabetes. Many deaths have been recorded following the excessive use of sprays or aerosols and patients should be warned of the dangers of their too frequent use leading to ventricular tachycardia or fibrillation. The concentration of isoprenaline in such preparations may vary with different manufacturers or alternative strengths may be available. Great care must be exercised when using the drug in patients with thyrotoxicosis or heart disease.

Rimiterol

Rimiterol (Pulmadil) is a catecholamine and a selective β_2-adrenoreceptor agonist. It is available as an aerosol for use as a bronchodilator, but is not effective when given orally because it is conjugated in the gut wall to an inactive compound. Its duration of action is similar to that of isoprenaline and shorter than those of salbutamol or terbutaline, though it acts faster than these last two drugs. It may be used i.v. and has a very short plasma half-life of less than 5 minutes. (See also p. 320).

Hexoprenaline

Hexoprenaline is also a selective β_2-receptor agonist used as a bronchodilator by oral or i.v. routes and by inhalation. It is longer-lasting than isoprenaline and rimiterol, partly because its methyl metabolite is an effective bronchodilator. The drug produces fewer side-effects than isoprenaline and, in particular, produces fewer effects on the heart.

Dobutamine

Dobutamine (Dobutrex) is a β_1 stimulant, but is more effective in increasing the force of the heart than the rate. Thus it is used as an inotropic agent (p. 270) in the management of patients with cardiovascular failure associated with low cardiac output after myocardial infarction or open-heart surgery.

Non-catecholamines

Many sympathomimetics lack the catechol nucleus. They are not substrates for catechol-*O*-methyl transferase. Many of these drugs act on the adrenergic receptor directly, while others enter the adrenergic neurone (usually by an active process) and then displace noradrenaline from its binding sites in the storage vesicles. They are described as acting indirectly (Table 5.1).

Orciprenaline (metaproterenol)

Orciprenaline (Alupent) is a β-adrenergic stimulant that is longer-acting than isoprenaline, probably because it is not a substrate for catechol-*O*-methyl transferase. It stimulates the β_1 and β_2 receptors equally. It is active when swallowed in a dose of 20 mg 6-hourly, but may also be used by inhalation.

The drug is indicated in the treatment of bronchial asthma (p. 318), but, like isoprenaline, is dangerous in overdosage.

Terbutaline

Terbutaline (Bricanyl) (p. 320) is similar to salbutamol (p. 316). The dose is 2.5–5 mg three times daily or by inhalation.

Salbutamol

Salbutamol (Ventolin) is relatively selective for β_2 receptors and should have less effect on the heart than isoprenaline. It may be taken orally in a dose of 2 mg four times daily or by inhalation in the treatment of asthma (p. 319). It is not a substrate for catechol-O-methyl transferase and therefore has a longer duration of action than isoprenaline. Unwanted cardiac effects are sometimes seen following excessive use.

Metaraminol

Metaraminol (Aramine) produces intense vasoconstriction and may be used in an emergency to raise arterial pressure while preparations are being made for more effective therapy such as transfusion.

The danger of vasoconstrictors is that, although they raise arterial pressure, they do so at the expense of perfusion of vital organs such as the kidney. In addition, in many patients with shock, the peripheral resistance is already high and to raise it further is unhelpful.

When metaraminol 1.5–5 mg is given i.v., the effects are seen in 3 minutes and last from 20 to 25 minutes.

Phenylephrine

Phenylephrine is a powerful direct α-receptor stimulant with very little β-receptor activity. Its effects on the cardiovascular system are similar to those of noradrenaline – i.e. it causes vasoconstriction, hypertension, and reflex bradycardia. Renal and skin blood flow are reduced. It is less potent but longer lasting than noradrenaline.

Phenylephrine is used primarily in many nasal decongestant preparations because of its vasoconstrictor action.

Methoxamine

Methoxamine (Vasoxine) has entirely an α stimulant effect and it may also exhibit some β blockade. It acts directly and constricts peripheral blood vessels. Both systolic and diastolic blood pressure are increased. There is no effect on respiratory musculature. Heart rate slows due to vagal reflexes.

Methoxamine is used in the treatment of hypotension associated with circulatory failure and spinal analgesia. As it does not increase the irritability of heart muscle, it may be used during anaesthesia with volatile agents. It may be given i.m. or i.v. When given i.v. in a dose of 5–10 mg, it acts within 2 minutes and lasts 1 hour. It must be used with great care in patients with hypertension, heart disease or thyrotoxicosis.

Ephedrine

Ephedrine has both α and β effects and acts directly and indirectly. Tachyphylaxis is marked. The drug inhibits monoamine oxidase.

Actions
There is considerable stimulation of the cerebral cortex and medulla following ephedrine administration and spinal reflexes are enhanced. Cardiac output and heart rate increase. Vasoconstriction is balanced with vasodilatation and overall resistance is little changed. Diastolic blood pressure is increased more than systolic pressure. Renal blood flow is reduced, but coronary blood flow increases. There is dilatation of the bronchial tree and respiration is stimulated. The drug may cause retention of urine.

Ephedrine is not a substrate for catechol-O-methyl transferase or monoamine oxidase. It is demethylated to norephedrine. Some of the drug is excreted unchanged in the urine.

Indications
Ephedrine is now rarely used for its pressor action or in the treatment of bronchial asthma. It is active when given by mouth, but may also be given i.m.; the duration of action may be 1 hour or more. The oral dose is 30–60 mg, repeated as required, but tolerance develops rapidly. Ephedrine in saline drops may be used to relieve nasal congestion. It may also be employed as a mydriatic, though the action is of short duration. It is used as a 3% aqueous solution for this purpose. There is less of a rise in intraocular pressure following the instillation of ephedrine than there is after homatropine. The beneficial effect of neostigmine in myasthenia gravis can be intensified and prolonged by giving ephedrine. The drug is also of some use in relieving the paroxysms of whooping cough.

Adverse Effects
Side-effects include wakefulness, anxiety, restlessness, tachycardia, palpitations and hypertension. Because of its liability to produce insomnia, ephedrine should not be given after 4 p.m.

Amphetamine and Dexamphetamine

In general, the properties of amphetamines are those of ephedrine, but amphetamine (Benzedrine) has a more powerful effect on the CNS and less effect at all other sites. It has both α and β effects, and acts largely indirectly. It is well absorbed from the gastrointestinal tract and the majority of the administered dose is excreted unchanged in the urine. As it is a weak base, excretion is enhanced in an acid urine. Amphetamine is racemic; dexamphetamine (Dexedrine) is the dextrorotatory form.

Because of the cortical arousal produced by these drugs, they have been used illicitly as stimulants. Although they have been given therapeutically as appetite suppressants, they are seldom used in contemporary therapeutics, because of this abuse.

Methylamphetamine

Methylamphetamine is a derivative of amphetamine and has similar properties, but is more rapid in its onset and acts for a longer period of time. It has α and β effects and its action is indirect. It is used occasionally as a pressor agent in the control of hypotension when both α and β effects are desired. It may be used i.m. or i.v. Side-effects and precautions are the same as for amphetamine.

Mephentermine

Mephentermine is very similar in structure and actions to methylamphetamine. It has both α and β activity and acts indirectly.

Isoxsuprine

Isoxsuprine has been advocated for use in dysmenorrhoea and in threatened premature labour, because of its uterine relaxant action, and also for peripheral vascular disease, because of its vasodilator action. Its value has not been well established.

Ritodrine

Ritodrine also has predominant β_2-mimetic activity, and is used to relax the uterus in premature labour.

Prenalterol

Prenalterol (Hyprenan, Varbian) is a new selective β_1 agonist and is used as an inotropic agent in patients with a low arterial pressure following myocardial infarction, cardiac surgery or overdose of β-blocking drugs. The dose is 500 μg/min. by i.v. infusion, with a maximum total dose of 20 mg.

ADRENERGIC RECEPTOR BLOCKADE

Adrenergic receptor blockade may be considered in two groups:

1. Drugs blocking the α-adrenergic receptors.
2. Drugs blocking the β-adrenergic receptors.

The adrenergic receptor blocking drugs prevent the response of effector organs to adrenaline, noradrenaline and other sympathomimetic amines, whether released in the body or injected. Circulating catecholamines are antagonized more readily than are the effects of sympathetic nerve stimulation. The drugs act by competing with the catecholamines for the α or β receptors on the effector organ. They do not alter the production or release of the substances.

α-adrenergic Receptor Antagonists

All the α-adrenergic receptor blockers produce peripheral vasodilatation. They do not block the metabolic effects of adrenaline or its central actions, but miosis follows their administration. They are used in the investigation and in the preoperative treatment of phaeochromocytoma, which is a rare hyperfunctioning tumour of the adrenal medulla. It is composed of chromaffin tissue and secretes vast quantities of noradrenaline and adrenaline. α-adrenergic blockade transiently lowers the elevated arterial pressure that is characteristic of this tumour. A more common therapeutic application is in the treatment of Raynaud's disease or in arteriosclerotic vascular occlusion and narrowing. The drugs may be of use in glaucoma, and the ergot derivatives (p. 232) are of particular value in migraine.

Phenoxybenzamine

Phenoxybenzamine (Dibenyline) is closely related to drugs of the mustine (nitrogen mustard) group. It is a powerful α blocker but has a slow onset of action, even after i.v. injection. Its effects may last 2 days or more. Active metabolites which act as alkylating agents are formed and have antagonistic actions at histamine, serotonin and muscarinic acetylcholine receptors. The blockade is competitive and may be reversed initially by increasing concentrations of noradrenaline at the receptor site, but when the blockade has been fully established, it is resistant to increasing concentrations of noradrenaline, owing to the formation of a covalent bond between drug and receptor.

Actions
Phenoxybenzamine produces a moderate fall in diastolic blood pressure, but in hypertension or hypovolaemia a marked fall is observed. Orthostatic hypotension is common. Adrenaline should not be given with it or a further fall in arterial pressure may occur.

Miosis is produced, and in glaucoma there is a fall in intraocular pressure. It may have a beneficial effect in vascular spasm due to blockade of vasoconstriction.

This drug is effective when given orally or i.v. and is extensively localized in body fat. It should not be used i.m. because of local irritation. Following i.v. administration, the peak effect is in 1–2 hours, and some effect persists for 3–4 days. Eighty per cent of the dose is excreted in 24 hours, but a little remains in the body for as long as 7 days.

Indications
When a phaeochromocytoma is being removed, the drug is used for preoperative treatment and during operative management. It is also used in the treatment of Raynaud's disease and chilblains.

Dosage
Dosage is 10–70 mg orally twice daily or 10–70 mg i.v. titrated to a response. For simpler conditions the dose is less.

Adverse Effects
Side-effects include postural hypotension, reflex tachycardia, nasal stuffiness, failure of ejaculation, nausea, vomiting and sedation.

Phentolamine

Phentolamine (Rogitine) has similar properties to phenoxybenzamine, but is shorter-acting. It is unreliable when given by mouth, and is usually given in a dose of 5–10 mg i.m. or i.v. Phentolamine has some direct vasodilator properties. It is used in the diagnosis and treatment of phaeochromocytoma, but care must be taken in using it, since deaths have been reported. It has some intrinsic sympathetic activity.

Tolazoline

Tolazoline (Priscol) has a brief and only moderately powerful α-adrenergic blocking effect, but has a direct vasodilator action on peripheral vessels. The drug is therefore of use in peripheral vascular disease (p. 285). It also has some intrinsic sympathetic activity.

It causes tachycardia by direct action on the heart, stimulates the gastrointestinal tract and causes diarrhoea and also increases gastric-acid secretion, thereby activating dormant peptic ulcers. Nausea and vomiting may occur.

Tolazoline is effective when administered orally. The dose is 12.5 mg four times daily.

Thymoxamine

Thymoxamine (Opilon) is a pure α-adrenergic blocking drug. It does not stimulate β receptors as tolazoline does and it does not have a histamine-like action.

It is used orally in the treatment of peripheral vascular disorders such as intermittent claudication. The dose is 40 mg four times daily. It may be used i.v. or intra-arterially.

Nausea, diarrhoea, vertigo, headache and facial flushing may be encountered.

Indoramin

Indoramin (Baratol) is an α-receptor antagonist without effect on β receptors. It has antihistaminic, local anaesthetic and cardiodepressant activity. It produces a fall in arterial pressure without a compensatory reflex tachycardia.

Prazosin

Prazosin (Hypovase) has about 10 times the potency of phentolamine in blocking the classical α_1 vascular receptor. It is used in the treatment of hypertension (p. 293).

Labetalol

Labetalol (Trandate) is unique in that it antagonizes both α and β receptors. It is used in the treatment of hypertension (p. 285).

Ergot

Ergot derivatives raise the arterial pressure due to an action on α receptors of vascular smooth muscle. They act as partial agonists with a very high affinity for the receptors (ergotamine has 300 times the affinity of noradrenaline for α receptors, but the maximal response is only about one-third of that produced by noradrenaline). The agonist effect is followed by blockade of α receptors.

However, ergot administration may result in high arterial pressure, coronary vasoconstriction, vascular insufficiency and even gangrene of the extremities.

Ergotamine

Ergotamine is used as a vasoconstrictor acting on the muscle of vessel walls. It also has some antagonistic activity on peripheral serotonin receptors. When given during the prodromal phase of migraine it can prevent the development of the vasodilator crisis. When given during the crisis it can produce striking relief. Ergotamine tartrate is given in a dose of 0.25–0.5 mg s.c. or i.m., or in 1 mg tablets, which must be taken sublingually.

Side-effects include nausea, vomiting, abdominal cramps and peripheral vasoconstriction. Ergotamine is contraindicated in the presence of coronary, cerebral or peripheral arterial disease, pregnancy, hypertension, and hepatic or renal disease.

Methysergide

Methysergide (Deseril) is a specific antagonist of serotonin. It is useful in the prophylactic treatment of migraine, but should be administered for short periods only.

Unsteadiness, vertigo, nausea, vomiting, water retention, weight gain, peripheral vasoconstriction and retroperitoneal fibrosis have all been reported following its use.

Pizotifen

Pizotifen (Sanomigran) is an antiserotoninergic drug which is structurally related to the tricyclic antidepressants. It has anticholinergic side-effects and may cause weight gain. Drowsiness may be a problem. However, it is now the drug of choice in the prophylaxis of migraine in many patients. The dose is 1.5–3 mg/day orally.

Clonidine

Clonidine is an α_2 receptor agonist used in the prophylaxis of migraine. It is helpful in some 70% of patients, but may aggravate depression and cause insomnia. The dose is 50–100 μg orally per day (see also p. 142). For treating migraine the drug has the proprietary name Dixarit, while for treating hypertension it is Catapres.

MIGRAINE

Migraine is a common and frequently familial form of headache believed to be caused by vascular changes in the brain or perhaps the neck. Characteristically, an attack consists of a prodromal period of listlessness, often with visual disturbances, followed by a unilateral headache spreading from behind the eye. The headache is constant and throbbing and may be accompanied by photophobia, nausea and vomiting. It may last for many hours. Attacks may be quite atypical. The initial aura and warning symptoms are thought to be caused by vasoconstriction of intracranial blood vessels while the later headache results from vasodilatation of extracerebral and intracerebral vessels. It may be that in some instances the vascular changes are secondary to a neurological primary cause. Migraine may be precipitated by vasoactive amines, prostaglandins, oral contraceptives, peptides, tyramine and serotonin, and also by environmental factors such as the flicker on a television set. Attacks can be brought on by excessive mental strain or, sometimes, by the cessation of overwork. The successful management of migraine varies with the individual, but commonly consists of:

1. Avoiding any known precipitating factors.
2. Simple analgesics for a mild acute attack; ergotamine and antiemetics for a more severe attack.
3. Prophylactic treatment with serotonin antagonists such as methysergide or pizotifen or with a β-adrenergic receptor antagonist.

   Migraine is also referred to on p. 142.

β-adrenergic Receptor Antagonists

These drugs are competitive antagonists of the effect of catecholamines on β receptors in the heart and other tissues. Their practical use in the treatment of hypertension is considered on p. 286, in cardiac dysrhythmias on p. 304 and in ischaemic heart disease on p. 309. Their actions will be summarized here.

Blockade of the β_1 receptor leads to bradycardia, a fall in cardiac output and a reduction of heart work and in myocardial oxygen demand. β blockers reduce renin release in the kidney. Blockade of the β_2 receptors in peripheral vessels may lead to cold hands and feet, with consequent exacerbation of peripheral vascular disease.

β_2 blockade may precipitate an acute attack of asthma in a susceptible person. Because of the β receptors in the brain, these drugs may produce nightmares, dreams and hallucinations.

Table 5.2   *Classification of β-blocking drugs*

Drug	*Cardioselectivity*	*Intrinsic sympathomimetic activity*	*Membrane stabilizing activity*
Propranolol	−	−	+
Oxprenolol	−	+ +	+
Pindolol	−	+ +	+
Sotalol	−	−	−
Timolol	−	−	+
Nadolol	−	−	−
Labetalol	−	−	+
Atenolol	+ +	−	−
Metoprolol	+ +	−	+
Acebutolol*	+	+ +	+
Practolol	+ +	+	−

*Acebutolol is metabolized to *N*-acetyl acebutolol which is also a β blocker, but is not cardioselective.

Not all β blockers are identical in their action. Some of the newer drugs are relatively selective for the cardiac β_1 receptor (Table 5.2). Some have intrinsic sympathomimetic activity (partial agonists) and some have a membrane stabilizing (quinidine or local anaesthetic-like) activity. One drug (labetalol) has both α and β blocking properties.

Cardioselectivity may reduce the side-effects of the drug by reducing β_2 blockade, but the other pharmacological differences are not of great therapeutic importance. The drugs with partial agonist activity may produce a less severe bradycardia and reduction in cardiac output.

POSTGANGLIONIC ADRENERGIC NEURONE BLOCKING DRUGS

Postganglionic adrenergic neurone blocking drugs selectively depress the sympathetic nervous system by impairing the function of the postganglionic sympathetic adrenergic nerves. They all lower arterial pressure.

Bretylium

Bretylium (Bretylate) is a quarternary ammonium compound that is concentrated in postganglionic adrenergic neurones and initially causes release of noradrenaline, followed by impairment of neurotransmission. It was first tested for its antihypertensive effects, but was unsatisfactory because of the development of tolerance. It was found to have antidysrhythmic properties (p. 304).

Guanethidine, Bethanidine and Debrisoquine

These drugs inhibit the release of noradrenaline at the neuroeffector junction. All three drugs gain access to the adrenergic neurone by active transport by the 'noradrenaline pump', but guanethidine differs from the other two drugs in that it causes depletion of noradrenaline stores within the nerve terminal. Debrisoquine has some monoamine oxidase inhibiting activity. Guanethidine, bethanidine and debrisoquine are used much less than in the 1950s and 1960s, when they were the mainstay of antihypertensive therapy. Their clinical use and adverse effects are described on page 281.

Methyldopa

Following administration of methyldopa (Aldomet), there is depletion of tissue noradrenaline due to its replacement with α-methyl noradrenaline. The methyldopa is incorporated into the synthetic pathway of noradrenaline instead of dopa.

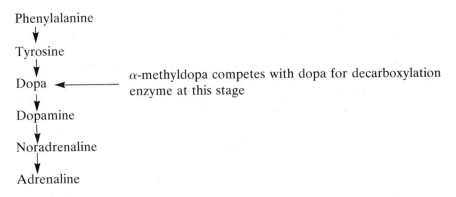

Phenylalanine

Tyrosine

Dopa ← ————— α-methyldopa competes with dopa for decarboxylation enzyme at this stage

Dopamine

Noradrenaline

Adrenaline

α-methyl noradrenaline then becomes a false neurotransmitter. However, there is no evidence that this substance is a weaker pressor agent than noradrenaline. Like clonidine, methylnoradrenaline acts on α_2 receptors in the brain stem to reduce efferent sympathetic tone and arterial pressure.

Methyldopa will be described on page 283.

Reserpine

Reserpine (Abicol, Serpasil) is an alkaloid derived from *Rauwolfia*. It reduces the body's stores of noradrenaline both peripherally and in the CNS. This results in a lowering of arterial pressure. Reserpine depletes the CNS stores of serotonin and dopamine and can cause both depression and parkinsonism. Its use as an antihypertensive agent is described on page 280.

MONOAMINE OXIDASE INHIBITORS

Monoamine oxidase is a widely distributed enzyme which is responsible for the intracellular degradation of adrenaline, noradrenaline, dopamine and 5-hydroxytryptamine. Drugs that inhibit this enzyme lead to an increased concentration of the amines in brain and other tissues. Their major therapeutic use is as antidepressant drugs and they are described with the other antidepressants (p. 172).

DRUGS USED IN THE TREATMENT OF PARKINSONISM

Parkinsonism is the name given to a clinical syndrome comprising tremor, rigidity and hypokinesia. This clinical picture is common to a number of conditions:

1. Idiopathic nigrostriatal degeneration.
2. Postencephalitic parkinsonism.

3. Atherosclerotic parkinsonism.
4. Drug-induced parkinsonism — e.g. from phenothiazines and other antipsychotic drugs (p. 164), methyldopa, reserpine, metoclopramide.
5. Toxic causes — e.g. from deposition of copper in basal ganglia (Wilson's disease) and from poisoning by manganese, mercury or carbon monoxide.
6. Rarer causes, such as trauma, syphilis, cerebral tumour.

Only in the case of drug-induced parkinsonism can the condition be cured (i.e. by withdrawing the drug). In other cases drug treatment is aimed at alleviating symptoms. In all cases a causative factor should be sought (e.g. tumour or syphilis) and should be treated if possible.

In the normal individual, dopamine (a precursor of noradrenaline) and acetylcholine are synaptic neurotransmitters in the CNS and high levels of both substances are found in the basal ganglia. Brains from cases of parkinsonism at necropsy show depletion of dopamine. The cholinergic nerve endings in the corpus striatum have a predominantly excitatory function, while the dopaminergic nerve endings belong to an inhibitory pathway. Antagonism between acetylcholine and dopamine in the striatum is analogous to that between acetylcholine and noradrenaline in the ANS.

Parkinson's syndrome may be caused by any pathological or drug-induced disorder, leading to reduction in activity of the dopaminergic system, allowing cholinergic dominance to emerge. Drug therapy, therefore, is directed towards restoration of the balance between acetylcholine and dopamine. Substances that may be used are anticholinergic drugs (benzhexol, benztropine, orphenadrine) or dopaminergic drugs (levodopa, amantadine). Both of these approaches are useful in therapy and may be combined.

Anticholinergic preparations can reduce tremor and rigidity but do not affect the hypokinesia, whereas the dopaminergic drug levodopa reduces hypokinesia and rigidity substantially, as well as improving tremor. Anticholinergics are of use in the management of drug-induced parkinsonism, whereas levodopa is not.

Levodopa (L-dihydroxyphenylalanine, L-dopa)

Dopamine itself does not penetrate the blood-brain barrier, but its immediate precursor, levodopa, is much more lipid-soluble and readily enters the cerebrospinal fluid (CSF), as well as being absorbed rapidly from the gut. Levodopa is converted to dopamine in peripheral tissue, so that only a fraction of the administered levodopa enters the brain. Levodopa may be given with a dopa-decarboxylase inhibitor, which itself will not enter the brain but will act at the periphery to prevent the decarboxylation of dopa.

Improvement with levodopa may take several months and is rarely obvious during the first few weeks. Eventually, expression, gait, writing and voice all show a marked change for the better. The effect on tremor may be a little less than its effect on other features, but, overall, one-tenth of patients get complete symptomatic relief from levodopa. It is important to persist with treatment. Levodopa cannot be said to have failed until at least 6 months and preferably a year of treatment has been given, but 15% of patients will stop the drug because of side-effects.

The drug is well absorbed orally and is given in a dosage of 500 mg–8 g/day. It is absorbed from the small intestine by active transport. The plasma half-life is 30 minutes and the drug is largely decarboxylated to dopamine, which is a substrate for monoamine oxidase, but is also converted into noradrenaline by dopamine β-hydroxylase. The dose to be aimed at is one producing good therapeutic effect with minimum side-effects. Elderly patients are less tolerant of high doses than are younger patients. Levodopa should be taken after meals initially in small doses (250 mg twice or three times daily) and gradually increased over a period of weeks until a satisfactory clinical response is obtained or side-effects prevent further increments. Deterioration of symptoms after stopping treatment occurs, with a similar slow time course.

Levodopa has severe side-effects and this fact has tempered the initial enthusiasm for the drug. Most patients have nausea initially, but this is improved by giving the drug with meals. Many show persistent vomiting for several months. Severe involuntary movements of various forms frequently limit dosage. Choreoathetosis, twisting movements, oral facial dyskinesia and myoclonic jerks may be troublesome and are present in most patients on optimum therapeutic dosage. Orthostatic hypotension is common. Headaches, sweating, and tachypnoea occasionally occur. Psychiatric disturbances include restlessness, agitation, insomnia, hallucinations and delusions. Dark sweat and urine may be seen. Because of dose-limiting side-effects, levodopa is frequently given together with other drugs (e.g. anticholinergics or amantadine) which produce an additive effect with levodopa.

Pyridoxine (Vitamin B₆), which is commonly included in multi-vitamin preparations, is known to reverse the effects of levodopa by enhancing extracerebral decarboxylation.

Levodopa should not be given in conjunction with monoamine oxidase inhibitors (MAOIs). Moreover, drugs that interfere with central amine mechanisms (e.g. reserpine, phenothiazines, butyrophenones and amphetamines) should be avoided whenever possible.

Levodopa is contraindicated in narrow-angle glaucoma, severe psychoneuroses and psychoses. Great care should be exercised when using levodopa in endocrine, renal, hepatic, pulmonary or cardiovascular disease. Levodopa is not indicated for the treatment of drug-induced parkinsonism, but may be used following surgery. It should not be used in pregnancy.

Clinically, not all patients respond to levodopa and even among those who show a good initial response, some have late treatment failure. This may be due to further irreversible damage to the corpus striatum or perhaps to deficiencies of neurotransmitters other than dopamine — e.g. noradrenaline,

5-hydroxytryptamine. Furthermore, after some years of treatment, the therapeutic response becomes marred by abrupt fluctuations between exacerbations of parkinsonism and severe dyskinesia (on–off phenomena).

Levodopa may have combined with it a dopa-decarboxylase inhibitor such as carbidopa (Sinemet) or benserazide (Madopar). These diminish the extracerebral adverse effects caused by the formation of catecholamines and reduce dysrhythmia, hypertension, nausea and vomiting. The daily dose of levodopa then required is also reduced. Central side-effects, such as choreiform movements and psychiatric features may become more severe.

Bromocriptine

Bromocriptine (Parlodel) is a direct dopamine receptor agonist which has a similar range of actions and at least as severe adverse effects as levodopa. After oral administration, peak plasma concentrations occur at 3 hours and the plasma half-life is about 5 hours.

Side-effects are similar to those of levodopa, but more disturbing are psychiatric disturbances, particularly intense visual hallucinations. Reversible pleuropulmonary changes, including pleural thickening and effusion, have also been described. Erythromelalgia (tender, red, oedematous feet), nasal congestion and digital vasospasm may occur.

Bromocriptine is not a drug of first choice, but it may be used as an adjuvant to levodopa to improve the 'on-off swings'. The dose of levodopa should be reduced. Contraindications include confusion, hallucinations, ischaemic heart disease and peripheral vascular disease.

The dose is 1.25 mg at night, rising over a period of several weeks to a maximum of 60 mg/day. The drug is also used in endocrine disorders (p. 371).

Amantadine

Amantadine (Symmetrel), an antiviral drug, causes a slight improvement in all the symptoms of Parkinson's disease, with a 15–25% reduction in disability. It is capable of mobilizing dopamine and most patients respond to this drug. The effect is rapid, and there are few side-effects. The initial dose is 100 mg daily, rising to 200–400 mg/day. Caution should be exercised if other CNS stimulants are being taken. Side-effects include nervousness, insomnia, dizziness, hallucinations and feelings of detachment. Oedema, livedo reticularis and epilepsy may occur.

Other drugs (e.g. amphetamines and apomorphine) also mobilize dopamine and may have some therapeutic value.

Anticholinergics

Anticholinergics act by blocking the effect of acetylcholine in the CNS (p. 206). Atropine, hyoscine, benzhexol, orphenadrine and benztropine are known to have a central effect as well as an antimuscarinic one on the parasympathetic nervous system.

The therapeutic action of these drugs in parkinsonism is modest and is best seen by an improvement in rigidity. Tremor may be less, but speed of movement is rarely improved. Overall, these drugs give a 15–20% improvement in disability.

Side-effects of anticholinergic drugs may include mental confusion and hallucinations, and all will produce constipation, a dry mouth and difficulty in focusing and in micturition.

Anticholinergics are additive with levodopa. There is very little to choose between the various preparations, but individual patients do better on one than on others. All are contraindicated in glaucoma and should be used with care in urinary retention.

Benzhexol

Benzhexol (Artane) is a synthetic anticholinergic. It is well absorbed orally and is given in a dosage of 2–5 mg three times daily. It may cause excitement and confusion in large doses. It is indicated in all forms of parkinsonism, as well as to prevent extrapyramidal symptoms due to drugs.

Orphenadrine, Procyclidine and Benztropine

Orphenadrine (Disipal), procyclidine (Kemadrin) and benztropine (Cogentin) have both anticholinergic and antihistaminic properties. All have similar properties to benzhexol, but benztropine is less of a cerebral stimulant. Benztropine is a powerful drug and can be used parenterally in the treatment of phenothiazine-induced dyskinesias. Orphenadrine has a euphoriant action.

Other drugs which may suit individual patients as adjuncts to therapy are diphenhydramine (Benadryl), hyoscine, atropine, promethazine (Phenergan), phenindamine (Thephorin) and biperiden (Akineton).

PHYSIOLOGY OF NERVE CONDUCTION

During periods of nerve inactivity a resting potential of 50–70 mV exists across the nerve cell membrane, the inside of the cell being negative. When excitation occurs there is at first a relatively slow phase of depolarization, during which the electrical potential within the nerve cell becomes progressively less negative. When a critical potential difference is reached (the firing level) there is a rapid phase of depolarization, which reverses the electrical potential across the cell membrane (action potential). At the peak of this action potential the interior of the cell has a positive electrical potential of 40 mV. Repolarization then occurs until the resting potential is re-established.

The cytoplasm of the nerve contains a high concentration of potassium ions and a low concentration of sodium ions, whereas the extracellular fluid possesses a high concentration of sodium ions and a low concentration of potassium ions. At rest, the cell membrane is relatively impermeable to these ions, but on excitation, an increase in permeability to sodium ions occurs and these ions rush into the cell, accounting for the depolarizing phase of the action potential. At maximum depolarization the permeability of the cell membrane to sodium ions decreases but the permeability to potassium ions increases. The latter rush out of the cell and account for repolarization. Following this process, sodium ions are extruded from the cell (against a concentration gradient) by active transport (sodium pump). This pump is also responsible for the active transport of potassium ions from the extracellular fluid into the cell.

LOCAL ANAESTHETICS

Local anaesthetic agents may be defined as drugs that reversibly block nerve conduction beyond the point of application when applied locally in the appropriate concentration. They appear to exert this blocking action by interfering with the rate of rise of the depolarization phase of the action potential, so that, after excitation, the cell does not depolarize sufficiently to reach the firing level and a propagated action potential fails to occur. The drugs have been shown to decrease the permeability of the cell membrane to sodium ions and thus to decrease the rate of depolarization. Hence the drugs tend to stabilize the nerve-cell membrane. Most of the clinically useful local anaesthetic agents act by displacing calcium from the receptor site on the internal surface of the cell membrane, resulting in blockade of the membrane sodium channel. These agents may exist in the ionized or unionized form. The unionized form diffuses more readily through the neural sheath, while the ionized form attaches to the receptor. The relative amounts of ionized and unionized drug depends on the pK_a of the drug and the pH of the tissues.

The local anaesthetics in current use have the following structure:

Aromatic lipophilic group—Intermediate chain—Hydrophilic group

The intermediate chain may be an ester (–COO–) or an amide (–NHCO–). Procaine is an example of an ester, while lignocaine is an example of an amide.

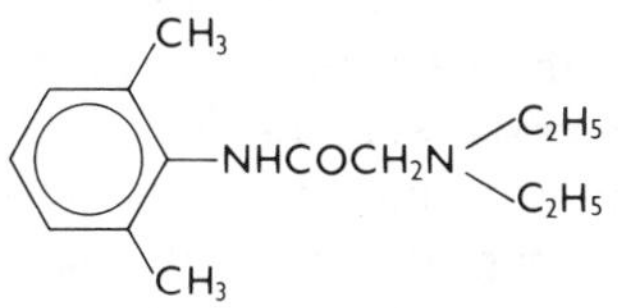

LIGNOCAINE

The hydrophilic group is almost always a tertiary amine. Prilocaine is the only secondary amine in current use. The amine group confers on the molecule the property of a weak base which can combine with an acid to form solutions of a salt (e.g. lignocaine hydrochloride).

This salt can exist both in the form of uncharged molecules (B) and as positively charged cations (BH$^+$). The proportion of each depends on the pH and the pK_a:

$$BH^+ \rightleftharpoons B + H^+$$

$$pH \rightleftharpoons pK_a + \log \frac{[B]}{[BH^+]}$$

In acid conditions more cation will be present than free base, whereas in alkaline conditions more free base will be present. Although both the charged and uncharged forms are involved in the process of conduction block, the uncharged base is important for optimal penetration of the nerve sheath.

Actions

Local anaesthetic drugs have both local and systemic effects. The local effects are due to their action in blocking nerve conduction and are seen in the area supplied by the nerve affected by the block. These effects are loss of pain and sensation, vasodilatation and loss of motor power. Loss of pain is the first effect to appear and occurs at much lower concentrations than is required to produce loss of motor power. The smallest nerve fibres are affected first, probably owing to their high surface area.

Systemic effects occur following absorption from the site of local administration or following systemic administration. These effects result from generalized membrane stabilization and are seen in the cardiovascular and central nervous systems. In the cardiovascular system, cardiac dysrhythmias due to hyperexcitability of the heart are suppressed owing to stabilization of the cell membrane of cardiac tissue. All the local anaesthetics except cocaine produce vasodilatation. In the CNS, all except cocaine are largely depressant in their actions. They initially produce anxiety and excitement, which progresses to sedation, disorientation, restlessness, twitching, tremors, convulsions and unconsciousness. Coma may be accompanied by apnoea and cardiovascular collapse due to medullary depression.

Local anaesthetic agents have no effect on autonomic ganglia and only procaine has any effect on the neuromuscular junction. Whether given locally or applied to mucous membranes, all the local anaesthetics except procaine are absorbed almost entirely into the systemic circulation. The rate of absorption of a particular drug depends on the pK_a and lipid-solubility of the drug and the pH and vascularity of the tissues. The administration of adrenaline with the local anaesthetic causes vasoconstriction, delays absorption of the drug and therefore prolongs its action. Local anaesthetic with adrenaline should not be used at the base of the fingers, in the ear lobe or in the penis, since ischaemia may result from vasoconstriction. Felypressin is a synthetic polypeptide related to vasopressin which may be used as an adrenaline substitute to delay absorption of local anaesthetic drugs. Hyaluronidase may be used to promote spread of the injected drug. It also enhances absorption.

Local anaesthetic drugs are protein bound to a varying extent in plasma and some of the drug concerned enters the red cells. It is rapidly removed from the blood by the tissues and readily crosses the blood–brain barrier to enter the CNS. Local anaesthetic drugs diffuse across the placenta.

With the exception of procaine, these drugs are chiefly metabolized in the liver. *N*-dealkylation of the tertiary amine to produce a more soluble secondary amine which may also be metabolically active is the important route of metabolism. This compound is more susceptible to amide hydrolysis. Hydroxylation of the aromatic nucleus occurs, to produce a more polar compound which is excreted in the urine. Very little of an injected dose of local anaesthetic is excreted unchanged in the urine.

Procaine

Procaine has a short duration of action and extremely poor penetration, because of its marked vasodilator activity and its high pK_a, which makes it highly ionized at physiological pH. It is inactive as a topical anaesthetic. Procaine is hydrolysed in the liver and plasma by pseudocholinesterase to *para*-aminobenzoic acid and diethylaminoethanol. Therefore, it prolongs the effect of suxamethonium, its hydrolysis is delayed by anticholinesterases, it inhibits the effects of sulphonamides because of the production of *para*-aminobenzoic acid, and it potentiates the effects of digoxin because of the diethylaminoethanol produced.

Procaine may be used in a 0.5%, 1% or 2% solution with or without adrenaline to produce very brief local analgesia. The maximum safe dose is 10 mg/kg body weight.

Cocaine

Cocaine is also an ester and is unique in that as well as possessing local analgesic properties, it potentiates the effects of sympathetic stimulation and is a CNS stimulant. It is very toxic when used parenterally and is now used only as a topical preparation to the eye to produce anaesthesia and mydriasis and to the nasal mucosa to produce anaesthesia and vasoconstriction. Because of its amphetamine-like stimulation of the CNS it was formerly a popular drug of abuse (p. 191).

Lignocaine (lidocaine, USP)

Lignocaine (Xylocaine) is an amide of xylidine. It is of moderate potency and duration of action, but has superior penetrative powers and a rapid onset of action. It is effective in topical, local and regional anaesthesia, or may be given systemically. It causes little vasodilatation, but may be used with adrenaline. A 1 or 2% solution is used for local infiltration, regional i.v. or epidural anaesthesia, whereas a 4% solution is used for topical analgesia. The maximum safe dose is 200 mg without adrenaline and 500 mg with adrenaline, but, as with all these drugs, the smallest dose to achieve the desired result should be used. The first effects are noted 5–10 minutes after administration and the duration of action is of the order of 2–3 hours.

Lignocaine may be given i.v. in the treatment of cardiac dysrhythmias, since it possesses Class I antidysrhythmic activity (p. 300). It is metabolized in the liver at a rate which depends primarily on the liver blood flow. If taken orally, only 35% of the administered dose reaches the systemic circulation, because of 'first-pass' metabolism. Two major metabolites, ethylglycine-xylidine (EGX) and glycinexylidine (GX), are pharmacologically active. GX is 10–25% as potent as lignocaine. The plasma half-lives are 120 minutes for lignocaine and EGX, and 10 hours for GX.

Following myocardial infarction, particularly if there is cardiac failure or shock, patients do not eliminate lignocaine or its metabolites normally and hence signs of toxicity are more likely. In such patients it may be useful to monitor the plasma concentration of lignocaine and its metabolites.

The most frequent adverse effects of lignocaine are drowsiness, dizziness, paraesthesiae and euphoria. With higher doses, confusion, agitation, dysarthria, vertigo, visual disturbances, tinnitus, nausea, sweating, muscle tremor, and/or fasciculations may be seen. Severe toxicity may include psychosis, seizures, respiratory depression and coma. In addition, lignocaine is a myocardial depressant and lowers arterial pressure.

Cinchocaine (dibucaine, USP)

Cinchocaine (Nupercaine) is an amide and a very potent local anaesthetic. However, it produces vasodilatation and has a high pK_a and therefore is relatively short-acting. It is used almost entirely for spinal analgesia and in the detection of atypical pseudocholinesterase.

Amethocaine

Amethocaine (Pontocaine), an ester, is a potent, long-acting anaesthetic which is a very effective surface analgesic. It is used in a 0.5% solution in the eye. As it is an ester, it cannot be autoclaved. It is broken down more slowly than procaine.

Prilocaine

Prilocaine (Citanest) is an amide of O-toluidine and is a secondary amine. It is equipotent with lignocaine and can be used for all types of local analgesia. It is less toxic than lignocaine because of its more rapid metabolism and greater degree of tissue uptake. In large or repeated doses it may produce methaemoglobinaemia. It is available in 0.5% and 1% solutions. The maximum dose is 300–400 mg. It is justifiably a very popular drug.

Bupivacaine

Bupivacaine (Marcain) is an amide which is three to four times as potent as lignocaine and considerably longer-lasting. It is particularly useful in local analgesia when a long duration of action is desired. When used in epidural analgesia in labour its duration of action is 2–4 hours, but it has produced postoperative analgesia for 12 hours. Bupivacaine does not produce vasodilatation, but adrenaline prolongs its action. It is bound to plasma proteins and does not produce high fetal blood concentrations.

The solutions in use are of 0.25 and 0.5% concentration, and the maximum safe dose is 150 mg in any 4-hour period.

Indications
Local anaesthesia is generally undertaken for minor operations on a fully conscious patient or as an adjunct in major surgery to avoid deep general anaesthesia. The drugs may be used topically, by local infiltration or to provide regional anaesthesia by i.v. administration to an exsanguinated limb which has an arterial tourniquet applied (Bier's Block), by regional nerve block, or by spinal or epidural blockade.

Overdosage or Excessive Absorption of the Drug
Overdosage results in nervousness, tremors, or even convulsions, with respiratory depression. Nausea, vomiting and abdominal pain may occur, with cardiovascular collapse. Convulsions are treated with barbiturates or diazepam i.v., but apnoea may well result. Because of this any administration of local anaesthetic apart from the simple local infiltration should be carried out by staff skilled in tracheal intubation and resuscitation in a room with facilities close at hand. Special care should be observed in epileptics.

Allergic reactions such as rashes, asthma and anaphylactic shock may occur.

Unfortunately a number of deaths have occurred recently following the inappropriate use of this drug by the i.v. regional technique (Bier's block). It is quite clear that this drug should not be used in this way.

ANTIEPILEPTIC DRUGS

Treatment of epileptic fits depends on accurate diagnostic evaluation and the seeking of specific causes which may be treated directly. For instance, hypoglycaemia, hypocalcaemia, pyridoxine deficiency or toxic states may result in epileptic fits. However, in most cases the basic cause of the seizure cannot be treated directly and it is necessary to administer an anticonvulsant drug.

Epileptic seizures originate from groups of hyperexcitable neurones from which discharges periodically spread either to limited areas, resulting in focal (partial) seizures, or to large areas, resulting in generalized seizures.

SEIZURE CLASSIFICATION

As some seizure types respond best to certain drugs, it is relevant to classify seizures into four groups:

1. *Generalized seizures* (bilaterally symmetrical without local onset)
   (a) tonic–clonic seizures — corresponds to the traditional term of grand mal;
   (b) absence seizures — corresponds to petit mal;
   (c) myclonic and akinetic attacks;
   (d) infantile spasms.

2. *Partial seizures* (often associated with acquired focal brain lesion)
   (a) partial seizures with elementary symptomatology, i.e. without loss of consciousness;
   (b) partial seizures with complex symptomatology which involves impairment of consciousness and disturbances of cognitive, affective and psychomotor or sensory functions (psychomotor or temporal lobe epilepsy);
   (c) partial seizures which become generalized.

3. *Unilateral seizures* (rare).

4. *Unclassified seizures*.

GENERAL THERAPEUTIC PRINCIPLES

1. One fit is an indication for investigation but not for treatment.
2. Treatment should be started after the second seizure.
3. Once drug treatment is started, it should be continued until the patient has been free of fits for 2–3 years.
4. Anticonvulsants should not be stopped abruptly, since status epilepticus may result.
5. A minimum number of drugs should be employed because of the risk of interactions. In fact, with the introduction of plasma concentration monitoring, it is best to use only one anticonvulsant.
6. The choice of antiepileptic drug should be made according to the type of seizure.

MODE OF ACTION

Antiepileptic drugs act by depressing neural excitability, by stabilizing the cell membrane and by modifying synaptic transmission to prevent the spread of seizure discharges. This action is thought to be related to modification of the movements of sodium, potassium and calcium ions across the cell membrane and also to the release or re-uptake of neurotransmitters. For example, phenytoin affects the brain concentrations of γ-aminobutyric acid (GABA), an inhibitory neurotransmitter.

SELECTION OF DRUG

Treatment should begin with a single drug given in a dose which achieves therapeutic plasma concentrations (Table 5.3). If one drug is not successful, a second should be substituted or added.

Table 5.3 *Antiepileptic drugs*

Seizure classification	Drugs of choice	Therapeutic plasma concentration (μg/ml)	Elimination half-life (hours)	Active metabolite
Generalized tonic–clonic	Phenytoin	10–20	9–140	None
	Valproate	50–100	8–15	? None
	Carbamazepine	4–10	8–19	Yes
	Phenobarbitone	15–40	53–140	None
Partial seizures with complex symptomatology (temporal lobe)	Carbamazepine Phenytoin Phenobarbitone Valproate			
Partial seizures becoming generalized (Jacksonian)	Carbamazepine Phenytoin Valproate			
Generalized absence seizures	Valproate Ethosuximide	40–100	60–100	None
Myoclonic attacks	Clonazepam Valproate	30–60	20–60	Yes
Infantile spasms	ACTH Clonazepam			

Phenobarbitone

Phenobarbitone is still the most effective barbiturate anticonvulsant available. However, it is no longer a drug of first choice, because of its adverse

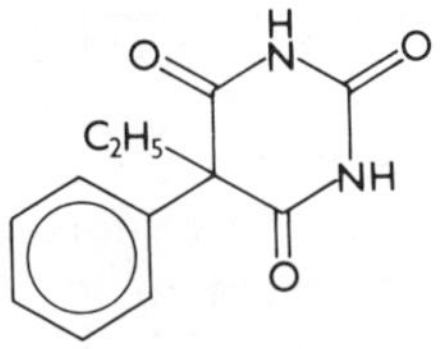

PHENOBARBITONE

effects, and it should be used only when phenytoin, valproate or carbamazepine has been ineffective. Absorption after oral administration is slow, with a peak plasma concentration 6–18 hours after intake. Eighty per cent of the oral dose is absorbed. Forty-five per cent is protein bound in the plasma. Approximately 35% of the administered dose is excreted unchanged by the kidney and this excretion is enhanced by making the urine alkaline to pH 8. The remainder of the drug is metabolized to inactive metabolites in the liver. The half-life of phenobarbitone is 50–140 hours, which means that when it is given daily, there is a cumulative effect. The dose is 100–300 mg/day. The half-life of phenobarbitone is shorter in children. Adverse effects are seen more often in the elderly and in renal and hepatic disease. The dose should be reduced. Because of the very long plasma half-life, steady state is not reached until 2–4 weeks. The therapeutic plasma concentration is 15–40 μg/ml.

The unwanted effects are almost entirely those of overdosage — namely, drowsiness, vertigo, headache and nausea, progressing to coma, with respiratory and cardiovascular depression. Continuous use of excessive amounts may result in ataxia, stupor and delirium. Skin reactions are the most common type of allergic manifestation, but some individuals become restless and excited following administration of the substance.

Phenobarbitone is a potent inducer of hepatic microsomal enzymes. Therefore its dose and that of some other drugs metabolized by the liver will have to be modified during administration if they are given simultaneously (p. 587).

Phenytoin (diphenylhydantoin)

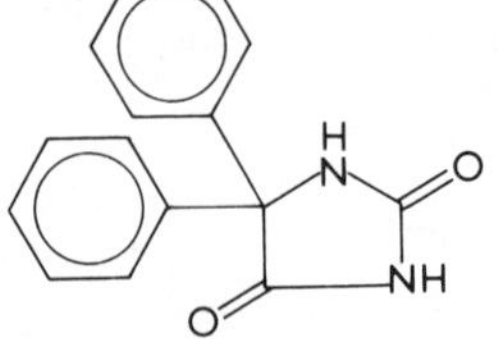

PHENYTOIN

Phenytoin (Epanutin, Dilantin) is the drug of first choice in the treatment of generalized tonic–clonic epilepsy. Unlike phenobarbitone, it does not cause general depression of the CNS, but it is a powerful antiepileptic. Tailoring the dose to achieve an optimum serum concentration allows more than 90% of newly presenting outpatients with major epilepsy to be controlled on phenytoin alone.

Following oral administration, phenytoin is mainly absorbed from the proximal small intestine. The rate of absorption is slow and variable; peak concentrations are attained 4–24 hours after administration. The systemic bioavailability from tablets of different manufacturers varies greatly (20–90%). Difference in particle size seems to be the crucial determinant and the sodium salt seems to be most readily absorbed. Change of brand, therefore, may have a considerable effect on the phenytoin plasma concentration. The drug is 93% bound to plasma protein.

Phenytoin is metabolized predominantly to a parahydroxymetabolite, which is then conjugated with glucuronide. The *p*-hydroxylation is a rate-limiting step, since it may be saturated. Thus phenytoin elimination is subject to dose-dependent kinetics (p. 591) and it is not possible to state precisely what its half-life is in plasma. This also explains the difficulty in adjusting the phenytoin dose to the right level. The average plasma half-life is 20–30 hours.

Children have a higher rate of excretion than adults. During pregnancy, plasma clearance is more than doubled and plasma level monitoring is indicated if the drug is required. There is a rare genetically determined failure of hydroxylation of phenytoin and patients suffering from this defect are intolerant to the drug. The therapeutic plasma concentration range is 10–20 μg/ml. Half the patients with concentrations greater than 30 μg/ml show side-effects.

Dosage

The drug may be given i.v. in the treatment of status epilepticus or acute cardiac dysrhythmias. The dose is 1–3 mg/kg body weight over 5–10 minutes. After i.m. administration, absorption of phenytoin is slower than after oral ingestion. Absorption occurs over 5 days. In addition, i.m. administration produces painful local reactions.

It is usually possible to administer phenytoin as a single daily dose, but if signs of toxicity occur, it may be necessary to give the daily requirements in two or three doses. A nomogram has been devised to enable the clinician to adjust the daily dose to produce the plasma concentration within the therapeutic range. The usual daily dose is 200–400 mg.

Phenytoin is a very potent inducer of hepatic enzymes and has an important interaction with oral anticoagulants (p. 483). Toxic effects are common with phenytoin therapy. The mild effects are dizziness, nausea, skin rashes, insomnia and gastric disturbances. Nystagmus is common, and when accompanied by diplopia and ataxia, the dose must be reduced. Hyperplasia of the gums, tremors, hirsutism, lymphoma-like syndrome, lupus erythematosus, pulmonary fibrosis, and megaloblastic anaemia due to interference with folate absorption or metabolism (p. 467) may occur. There has been some evidence that administration of folic acid to patients receiving phenytoin increases the frequency of fits. It has been suggested that folate deficiency due to the giving of phenytoin to pregnant women may cause fetal deformities, but this view is not yet generally accepted. Hypocalcaemia and osteomalacia may occasionally be found, because of accelerated breakdown of calciferol in the liver consequent upon enzyme induction. Calciferol supplements can correct these disorders.

Phenytoin displaces iodine from its carrier protein, so that measurements of protein-bound iodine may suggest hypothyroidism. In uraemia the unbound fraction of phenytoin in the plasma is higher than in normals and hence lower doses are needed.

Other Hydantoins

Ethotoin

Ethotoin (Peganone) is similar to phenytoin. It also exhibits non-linear kinetics within the therapeutic range, due to saturation of its hepatic metabolism. The half-life is about 5–9 hours. The dose is 1500–3000 mg/day.

Primidone

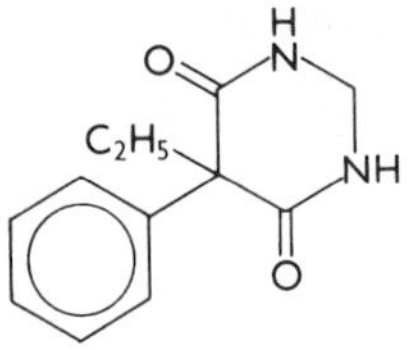

PRIMIDONE

Primidone (Mysoline) is a compound that bears a striking resemblance to phenobarbitone, though it is not in fact a barbiturate. It is a sedative and anticonvulsant, though its anticonvulsant properties are probably entirely due to its conversion into phenobarbitone in vivo.

Initial intolerance, in the form of acute vertigo, ataxia, diplopia and dysarthria, may occur and can be minimized by giving a starting dose of 125 mg daily for 3 days. Thereafter the dosage may be gradually raised to 250 mg four times daily. Rarely, a total daily dose of 2 g may be tolerated. Very rarely, a megaloblastic anaemia responsive to folic acid may occur (p. 467). Following oral administration, peak plasma concentrations occur in about 3 hours, but the range is fairly wide (0.5–9 hours). Plasma protein binding is very low (less than 20%). Primidone is almost entirely converted into two metabolites the plasma half-life being 10–12 hours. The two main metabolites are phenobarbitone and phenylethylmalonamide.

Carbamazepine

Carbamazepine (Tegretol) is an effective drug in generalized tonic–clonic epilepsy and is the drug of choice in partial epilepsy. It is also used in the treatment of trigeminal neuralgia and in other chronic painful conditions.

Absorption from tablets is slow, with maximum concentration at 6–18 hours after the dose; 70% of the oral dose is absorbed and 69–73% of the drug is bound to plasma proteins. After a single dose the plasma half-life is 30–50 hours, but it may be as short as 10–20 hours after chonic use, owing to enzyme induction. Only 2% of an administered dose is found unchanged in the urine. One of its metabolites has anticonvulsant activity (CBZ-10-11 epoxide) and it may account for the side-effects of the drug, since it is to a lesser extent protein bound.

The therapeutic plasma concentration is 4–10 μg/ml.

Dosage

Carbamazepine must be given in two to three divided doses each day because of its short half-life after enzyme induction. The initial dosage is 100–200 mg twice daily orally, increasing as necessary. In some cases as much as 1600 mg per day may be required. Because the drug has first-order kinetics, dose adjustment is easier than for phenytoin.

Side-effects include dizziness, drowsiness, dry mouth, diarrhoea, nausea and vomiting. Idiosyncrasy to the drug may be manifested by a generalized skin rash which disappears on stopping therapy, light sensitivity dermatitis, jaundice, leucopenia and aplastic anaemia. All these idiosyncratic responses are rarely encountered. It is a potent inducer of enzymes and if given concurrently with phenytoin, reduces the plasma concentration of the latter.

Sodium Valproate

Sodium valproate (Epilim) is the sodium salt of di-n-propylacetic acid. It is unrelated chemically to other antiepileptics. It elevates brain concentrations of the inhibitory transmitter γ-aminobutyric acid by preventing breakdown and uptake into nerve terminals. Valproate seems to be effective in all types of epilepsy including generalized absence seizures. It is relatively free from sedative effects.

After oral administration peak plasma concentrations occur in 1 hour and the drug is totally metabolized in the liver, the plasma half-life being 8–15 hours. The usual therapeutic plasma concentration is 50–100 μg/ml and this is associated with an adult daily dose of 1200–1500 mg. Placental transfer occurs, and the drug produces dysmorphogenic effects in animals.

The most common side-effects are nausea, vomiting, abdominal cramps and diarrhoea. Transient drowsiness and sedation have been reported, but most patients feel lively and alert. Prolongation of the bleeding time and thrombocytopenia may occur. A few cases of hepatic failure have been reported. More recently, reports of marrow hypoplasia or leucopenia have been received by the Committee on Safety of Medicines. It is recommended that liver function tests and blood counts are monitored during the first 6 months of therapy.

The dosage is 200 mg orally three times daily, increasing by 200 mg/day at 3 day intervals until control is achieved.

Clonazepam

Clonazepam (Rivotril) is a benzodiazepine closely related to nitrazepam. It is effective in all types of seizures.

Following oral administration, it is rapidly absorbed, with a peak plasma concentration at 2–4 hours; 82% is protein bound. Clonazepam is metabolized in the liver to 3-hydroxyclonazepam, which is active, and to 7-aminoclonazepam and 7-acetaminoclonazepam, which are inactive and are excreted in the urine unchanged or conjugated. The plasma half-life is 19–60 hours. The therapeutic plasma concentration is 30–60 μg/ml, but plasma level monitoring is not indicated for clonazepam. Side-effects include drowsiness, sedation, lack of co-ordination and dysphoria. Very high plasma concentrations result in an increased number of fits.

Dosage
Clonazepam may be used i.v. in a dose of 1–4 mg as the drug of first choice in status epilepticus, according to the manufacturer's instructions. The oral dose is 4–8 mg daily for adults.

Sulthiame

Sulthiame (Ospolot) is a sulphonamide derivative. This drug, when given with phenytoin, will increase the plasma concentrations of the latter and occasionally cause a dramatic improvement in some patients. The drug is well absorbed if taken orally and should be used in a dosage of 100 mg twice daily, rising to 200 mg three times daily. It is probably inactive as an anticonvulsant and enhances the effect of other antiepileptic drugs by inhibiting hepatic mixed function oxidases. Side-effects are usually mild and subside after 8–14 days. Paraesthesiae of the extremities and face is the commonest side-effect. Gastric disturbances, headaches and vertigo have also been reported.

Methylphenobarbitone and Metharbitone

Methylphenobarbitone and metharbitone are converted to phenobarbitone in the body.

Methsuximide and Phensuximide

Methsuximide and phensuximide are useful in partial epilepsy.

Beclamide

Beclamide (Nydrane) is a less powerful anticonvulsant.

Ethosuximide

Ethosuximide (Zarontin) is effective in the treatment of generalized absence seizures, but is now second choice to valproate.

The dosage is initially 250 mg twice daily, rising to 1.75 g/day. Absorption is complete, with maximum plasma concentration 1–2 hours after administration; 10–20% is excreted as unchanged drug and the remainder is metabolized to pharmacologically inactive compounds. The plasma half-life is 60 hours in adults and 30 hours in children. No enzyme induction occurs. The therapeutic plasma concentration is 40–100 μg/ml.

Mild side-effects, which are usually transient, may occur initially. These include apathy, drowsiness, depression or euphoria, headache, ataxia, dizziness, anorexia, gastric upset, nausea and vomiting. Rarely, instances of the occurrence of leucopenia, agranulocytosis and aplastic anaemia have been reported.

Troxidone

Troxidone (Tridione) is a toxic drug, but has a specific effect in the treatment of absence seizures. Like ethosuximide, but unlike phenytoin, it has a marked effect on the EEG. It may aggravate tonic–clonic seizures and should be combined with phenytoin in mixed tonic–clonic and absence seizures. It has no hypnotic action, but has some analgesic effects. It can antagonize convulsions induced by leptazol and picrotoxin.

Troxidone is well absorbed when given orally. It is demethylated in the liver to a substance devoid of anticonvulsant action which is excreted very slowly. Scarcely any unchanged drug appears in the urine.

The dosage is 0.9–1.8 g/day in divided doses for adults and 200–500 mg/day for children.

Side-effects which may occur initially include drowsiness and nausea, but they usually disappear. Photophobia is often seen, with blurring of the vision in bright light. Rarer reactions are skin rashes, blood disorders, hiccup, and the development of the nephrotic syndrome. This is a drug which may cause aplastic anaemia.

Paramethadione

Paramethadione (Paradione) is a closely related drug used to treat patients with absence seizures if they do not respond to troxidone. It has similar side-effects.

The response to the above three drugs should occur within 3 weeks of commencing therapy.

Acetazolamide

Acetazolamide (Diamox), a sulphonamide derivative, may be useful in absence seizures, but is seldom given nowadays, even though short courses are sometimes effective. It is a carbonic anhydrase inhibitor (p. 354) and is used in Ménière's disease, in hydrocephalus, in treating premenstrual tension, as a diuretic, and in glaucoma.

The drug should be given by mouth in a dosage of 250–1000 mg/day. Its action lasts 12 hours.

Overdosage may cause drowsiness, paraesthesia or a hyperchloraemic acidosis.

Side-effects include fatigue, gastrointestinal upsets, polyuria, disorientation, skin rashes, flushing, thirst and the production of agranulocytosis or thrombocytopenia.

DRUG USED IN THE TREATMENT OF STATUS EPILEPTICUS

Status epilepticus is defined as the occurrence of fits in which the patient fails to regain consciousness between attacks. Recurrent or continuous tonic–clonic seizures constitute a medical emergency and require urgent treatment. Control of the fits must be achieved as quickly as possible.

Diazepam

Diazepam (Valium) is a benzodiazepine and is ubiquitous in modern medicine. Its properties are described in detail on p. 150.

For status epilepticus 10 mg should be given i.v. over 1 minute and should be followed by an infusion of 100 mg in 500 ml of saline, administered at a rate just sufficient to control the fits. Particular care must be taken to maintain a clear airway and prevent asphyxia in the unconscious patient. Facilities for resuscitation should be close at hand. Clonazepam (p. 149) may replace diazepam for this purpose in a dose of 1 mg i.v. or up to 3 mg by slow i.v. infusion.

Thiopentone

Thiopentone (Pentothal, Intraval) may be given if other attempts fail. It can be given slowly i.v. (25–100 mg), followed by an infusion of the drug in saline or else rectally.

Very severe status epilepticus may require muscle paralysis with tubocurarine (p. 217) and artificial ventilation of the lungs. This is very rarely required.

Status epilepticus remains a grave medical emergency, with a mortality of 10%.

DRUGS USED IN THE TREATMENT OF MYOCLONIC SPASMS

Clonazepam (p. 252) and sodium valproate (p. 251) are the drugs of first choice in this condition. There have been encouraging results following the use of ACTH (p. 310) or of prednisolone, the latter being given in a dosage of 10–40 mg/day.

GENERAL ANAESTHETICS

Almost all general anaesthetic drugs are given i.v. or by inhalation, since these routes allow the closest control over blood concentrations.

Intravenous Anaesthetic Agents

Intravenous anaesthetic agents produce an extremely rapid induction of anaesthesia, since the blood concentration can be raised very rapidly. Recovery is not so rapid, since the drug must be distributed, or metabolized. However, it is the rapidity of onset and not the brevity of action that is the most desirable property of any drug used primarily for induction of anaesthesia.

Thiopentone

Thiopentone (Pentothal, Intraval) is the most widely used i.v. induction agent in the world. It is the sulphur analogue of pentobarbitone and was first synthesized in 1934.

Thiopentone is a pale yellow powder which is readily soluble in water to provide a strongly alkaline solution (pH 10.6). Solutions for injection should be freshly prepared. It is described as an ultra-short-acting barbiturate, though it is now well recognized that redistribution and not metabolism accounts for the rapid recovery from therapeutic doses of thiopentone. When injected i.v., thiopentone rapidly crosses the blood–brain barrier and the concentration in the CSF reaches a level similar to that of the unbound drug in the plasma. One minute after injection 90% of the injected dose is in the CNS, heart, liver and other richly perfused viscera. These organs are in turn depleted as a result of further distribution. The blood supply of fat is so low, relative to other tissues, that it cannot begin to store thiopentone to any significant degree until the CNS has lost almost all of its peak content. After some hours fat depots contain large amounts of the drug. Metabolism of the drug is very slow. The plasma half-life is 6–8 hours. If repeated doses of thiopentone are given over a short period, a time will come when the rapid distribution of the drug will not result in plasma concentrations low enough for the patient to awaken. Recovery will then occur due to drug metabolism and this takes a very long time.

Thiopentone is almost completely metabolized in the body at a rate of 10–15% of the dose per hour and only 0.3% of the administered dose is excreted unchanged in the urine. The microsomal enzymes in the liver are the main site of metabolism and side-chain oxidation is the main mechanism of inactivation. Patients waken from thiopentone anaesthesia with an appreciable amount of unmetabolized drug still in the body. They should, therefore, be warned against taking any other drugs or alcohol, which might cause hypnosis.

Actions
Thiopentone produces a rapid and pleasant loss of consciousness within 15–30 seconds of i.v. administration and this lasts for 3–5 minutes. The respiratory centre is depressed and there may be a brief period of apnoea following the injection. Laryngeal reflexes are not depressed until deep levels of thiopentone narcosis are reached and stimulation readily provokes laryngeal spasm. There is no analgesia and with small doses there may even be potentiation of painful stimuli.

Thiopentone may cause myocardial depression, but cardiac irritability is unaffected. If dysrhythmias do occur, this is usually attributed to hypoxia and a raised carbon dioxide tension. Peripheral vasodilatation leading to hypotension may occur with large doses. The effects on the kidneys are secondary to the effects on the circulation and to the liberation of antidiuretic hormone. Urine output is decreased. There is some evidence of a weak curare-like action on muscle end plates, but this is clinically unimportant.

In therapeutic doses, thiopentone does not alter the tone of the gravid uterus or the motility of the fallopian tubes. Four minutes after the injection to a woman in labour, there is an appreciable effect on the fetus.

Thiopentone does not alter the blood sugar concentration.

Although active by mouth, thiopentone is rarely given by this route, though it is occasionally used rectally in the treatment of status epilepticus. Mostly it is given i.v. in a 2.5 or 5% solution. The dose varies enormously, according to the age and the degree of fitness of the patient. The smallest dose necessary to produce the desired effect is given, usually 250–500 mg in healthy adults. The more rapidly the injection is given, the quicker and deeper the response and the quicker the recovery will be.

Thiopentone is indicated to induce anaesthesia, to produce anaesthesia for short procedures as in electroconvulsive therapy, to provide light narcosis to cover spinal or other local analgesia and as an anticonvulsant. It may be given rectally to produce basal narcosis in children. It is contraindicated in patients who suffer from porphyria. It should be used with care in patients with respiratory disease and in shocked subjects even a small dose may be fatal. It should not be given to patients in the sitting position.

Adverse Effects
Side-effects of thiopentone administration include respiratory depression,

cardiovascular depression, bronchospasm and laryngospasm. Allergic reactions have been reported rarely. They may be severe. In the event of an extravascular injection, necrosis and ulceration of the s.c. tissues may occur, because of the alkalinity of the solution. If the drug is inadvertently injected into an artery, there is immediate intense pain shooting down the injected limb. This is due to the precipitation of crystals when thiopentone is mixed with blood. Thrombosis eventually occurs and leads to gangrene of the limb. This complication is much more common following the injection of a 5% solution than it is following the injection of a 2.5% solution. It is best avoided by not using veins on the medial side of the antecubital fossa close to the brachial artery and by inspecting the arm after a 1 ml test dose of solution.

Thiopentone has been used extensively for 30 years and has stood the test of time and usage. It is inexpensive, pleasant to use and acceptable to the patient. It is very safe in skilled hands and is the yardstick with which all new induction agents must be compared.

Methohexitone

Methohexitone (Brietal), an oxybarbiturate, is also an ultra-short-acting barbiturate. In man it is three times as potent as thiopentone. At body pH more of this drug is present in the unionized state than after a comparable dose of thiopentone and this contributes to its greater potency. Recovery of consciousness following methohexitone is due to redistribution of the drug from the CNS into the muscles, as for thiopentone. However, unlike thiopentone, methohexitone has an elimination half-life of only 70–125 minutes.

In clinical doses methohexitone produces little effect on arterial pressure, but it causes respiratory depression. It is less likely to produce bronchospasm than thiopentone, but muscular twitching, hiccups and coughing are seen. If injected extravenously, it causes painless erythema, but intra-arterial injection leads to gangrene similar to that produced by thiopentone in equal doses. A 1% solution of methohexitone is usually employed. The i.v. induction dose is 1 mg/kg body weight, which produces sleep lasting 2–3 minutes from which the patient makes a rapid recovery. The onset of sleep occurs within one 'arm–brain' circulation time.

Methohexitone is very useful for short outpatient anaesthetics, as in electroconvulsive therapy or dental extractions, or as an induction agent.

Adverse effects are similar to those of thiopentone.

Propanidid

Propanidid (Epontol), an ultra-short-acting anaesthetic, is not a barbiturate but is a derivative of eugenol. A distinctive property of eugenol anaesthetics is that first there is respiratory stimulation presenting as hyperventilation and this may be followed by a period of hypoventilation or even apnoea lasting for about 30 seconds. Involuntary muscle movements occur in some patients and are common in the absence of premedication. There is usually a transient fall in arterial pressure.

In contrast to thiopentone, propanidid is rapidly metabolized in the blood stream and serum cholinesterase plays a part in splitting the ester linkage. Ninety per cent of the injected dose is eliminated as the inert metabolite in the urine within 2 hours. Thus anticholinesterase administration or low serum levels of pseudocholinesterase may delay the breakdown of propanidid and recovery of consciousness then occurs as the result of redistribution. Propanidid will intensify the paralysing action of suxamethonium.

Recovery of consciousness is normally very rapid (3–6 minutes after a clinical dose) and patients are fit to go home much earlier than following i.v. barbiturates. No hyperalgesia, such as occurs with thiopentone, occurs after small doses of propanidid. In practice, propanidid is rather short-acting, and when used simply as an induction agent there can be no delay in administering supplementary agents or the patient will recover consciousness. It is of use for short surgical procedures on outpatients and as a general induction agent, especially in patients who have history of allergy to barbiturates. The dose is 6–7 mg/kg body weight i.v.

Propanidid has less potentiating effect on alcohol and other CNS depressants than thiopentone, but it prolongs and intensifies the effects of suxamethonium. Its action is prolonged by the administration of anticholinesterases. Injection into arteries has not been followed by vascular complications. Extravascular injection is painless and does not lead to necrosis and abscess formation. The drug has fallen from popularity because of an alarming incidence of anaphylactic reactions following its use.

Althesin

Althesin consists of a mixture of two steroids, *alphaxalone and alphadolone acetate*, solubilized in a ratio of 3 to 1 dissolved in a vehicle containing Cremophor-EL.

Following i.v. injection, the onset of anaesthesia is in one 'arm–brain' circulation time and the patient wakens 5–10 minutes later. Involuntary muscle movements and minor degrees of hypotension may be seen during induction, but there is no undesirable interaction with muscle relaxants or other anaesthetic agents. Recovery of consciousness is smoother and more pleasant than it is following propanidid.

After i.v. administration, Althesin is not stored in fat but is rapidly inactivated by the liver. The metabolites are excreted in the urine.

Each millilitre of Althesin solution contains 9 mg of alphaxalone and 3 mg of alphadolone. The recommended i.v. dose is 0.05–0.075 ml/kg body weight. It is used to provide anaesthesia for short surgical procedures, as in cytoscopy, or can be used as a general induction agent.

Anaphylactic reactions have been reported after Althesin administration. The incidence varies from 1 in 1000 to 1 in 10 000. However, the mortality of these reactions is very low. Althesin may precipitate porphyria (p. 596).

Ketamine

Ketamine (Ketalar) is related to phencyclidine, a drug which was abandoned in anaesthesia 10 years ago because of psychotic effects. It differs from the agents already described in that it can be given i.v. or i.m.

Its site of action is claimed to be the midbrain and this has to be contrasted with that of the barbiturates, which are believed to act on the reticular formation. The property of a drug in affecting one part of the brain and not another earns it the title of a 'dissociative anaesthetic'. Ketamine produces total analgesia, with loss of response to painful stimuli and a form of immobilization, as in catatonic stupor.

When injected i.v., anaesthesia is established in 30 seconds and a single dose lasts 5–8 minutes. The total recovery period after a single dose does not usually exceed 30 minutes. If ketamine is given i.m., skin incision may be made 3 minutes after administration. Recovery time is of the order of 35–150 minutes, but may be prolonged in adults. Children are more resistant to the effects than adults.

The usual dose is 2 mg/kg body weight i.v. or 8–10 mg/kg body weight i.m.

The drug is particularly suitable for the dressing of burns in children and for cardiac catheterization in children. It may be used for vaginal deliveries in obstetrics and for dental extractions.

As with thiopentone, recovery of consciousness following ketamine occurs because of redistribution of the drug. Metabolism occurs in the liver by dealkylation and oxidation. Some of the metabolites are pharmacologically active. Ketamine induces its own metabolism. The elimination half-life is 2.5–4 hours. Diazepam is a competitive inhibitor of the dealkylation of ketamine.

One of the problems of the administration of ketamine is the occurrence of spontaneous muscular movements such as fibrillary movements of tongue, random movements of limbs and clenching of the jaw. The major drawback to its use is dreaming and terrifying hallucinations in the recovery period. These may be controlled by diazepam or simply by allowing the patients to lie quietly without disturbance in the recovery period. Lorazepam premedication abolishes these emergence phenomena.

Salivation is usually excessive unless an atropine type of premedication is given, but the airway is preserved and laryngeal reflexes are not obtunded. Respiratory minute volume is generally maintained. There is a rise in pulse rate and in arterial pressure, but adrenaline-induced dysrhythmias are abolished. There is a rise in blood glucose concentration.

Ketamine is contraindicated in patients who have hypertension or a raised intracranial pressure. It should not be used in subjects who have had a cerebrovascular accident or who are taking thyroxine.

Diazepam

Diazepam (Valium) is a benzodiazepine and a minor tranquillizer (p. 150) rather than an anaesthetic agent. When given i.v. there is a delay of 1–2 minutes before its maximum depressant action becomes evident and there is a great individual variation in response. The period of sleep is long and dizziness may persist for 24 hours after the operation. It has no analgesic actions, but enhances the effect of non-depolarizing muscle relaxants.

Diazepam is most useful in surgery as a sedative or tranquillizer, since it produces amnesia.

Other benzodiazepines with a shorter duration of action are undergoing clinical trials as induction agents. It may be that they will increase in popularity in the future.

Gamma-hydroxybutyric acid

Gamma-hydroxybutyric acid has been studied for almost 15 years, but its place in anaesthesia remains uncertain. It can be converted in the body to gamma-aminobutyric acid, which is a neuroinhibitor. The onset of sleep is unreliable and not smooth, while recovery is prolonged. The drug is more acceptable as a basal narcotic than as an induction agent.

Etomidate

Etomidate (Hypnomidate) is an imidazole derivative. It produces rapid induction of anaesthesia, with minimal cardiovascular and respiratory changes. The dose is 0.3 mg/kg body weight i.v. Distribution results in recovery of consciousness and is very rapid ($T_{\frac{1}{2}}$ 2.8 minutes). The elimination half-life is 4 hours. The major metabolic pathway is hydrolysis in the liver to inactive products.

Etomidate produces pain and involuntary movements on injection. When used, it is often combined with an opioid analgesic drug. It does not release histamine. The drug is no longer recommended for i.v. infusion to maintain anaesthesia or to produce sedation in intensive therapy units because it inhibits cortisol production.

Di-isopropylphenol

Di-isopropylphenol (Diprivan, ICI 35868) is undergoing clinical trials as an anaesthetic induction agent. It has a very high plasma clearance and short metabolic half-life. It may be very suitable for i.v. infusion to maintain anaesthesia.

Inhalational Anaesthetic Agents

The formulae and some physical properties of the commonly used inhalational anaesthetic agents are shown in Table 5.4. At ambient temperature and pressure nitrous oxide and cyclopropane are gases and may be administered as such. The others are liquids and must be evaporated for administration. In other words, they are volatile agents.

Table 5.4 *Inhalational anaesthetic agents*

Agent	Formula	Boiling Point (°C)	Solubility at 37°C Blood/Gas	Oil/Gas
Cyclopropane	C_3H_6	−33	0.42	11.2
Nitrous oxide	N_2O	−89	0.47	1.4
Halothane	C_2F_3HBrCl	43.2	2.4	224
Trichlorethylene	C_2HCl_3	87	9.15	960
Chloroform	$CHCl_3$	61.2	7.3	265
Diethyl ether	$(C_2H_5)_2O$	35	12.1	65
Methoxyflurane	$CHCl_2CFOCH_3$	105	13.0	825
Enflurane	CHF_2-O-CF_2CHFCl	56.5	1.91	98.5

The boiling point of the volatile agents is one factor in determining how readily the agent evaporates at room temperature and, therefore, the theoretical range of concentrations available. Diethyl ether, with a boiling point of 35°C, is more readily evaporated than methoxyflurane, which has a boiling point of 105°C. Thus at a given room temperature and a given carrier gas flow, ether will be present at a higher concentration than methoxyflurane.

The depth of anaesthesia produced by an anaesthetic agent is related to the tension or partial pressure of the agent in the blood. In the lungs the alveolar epithelium presents virtually no barrier to the diffusion of anaesthetic agents. Therefore, the alveolar concentration or partial pressure of the drug in the alveoli is of supreme importance. This is influenced to a great extent by the solubility of the agent in blood.

In a patient breathing his first few breaths of a gas with a low blood solubility (e.g. nitrous oxide or cyclopropane), only a small quantity of gas is absorbed by the pulmonary circulation and the alveolar concentration rises rapidly. These agents, therefore, induce anaesthesia rapidly. A soluble drug such as diethyl ether is absorbed well by the pulmonary circulation and its alveolar concentration rises slowly during induction. Therefore, the blood–gas solubility coefficient is a useful index of how rapidly a drug will induce anaesthesia. Thus, with cyclopropane (0.42) induction is rapid, whereas with diethyl ether (12.1) induction is slow.

Similarly, recovery from anaesthesia produced by a drug soluble in blood is prolonged and recovery following the use of a relatively insoluble drug is rapid.

It follows that an agent in which the blood tension (and therefore the brain and myocardial tension) can only rise slowly (e.g. diethyl ether) has the greatest safety margin in the hands of the inexperienced.

Nitrous oxide, although referred to as a relatively insoluble anaesthetic agent, is 34 times more soluble in blood than is nitrogen. Thus blood can carry much more nitrous oxide than nitrogen. During recovery large amounts of nitrous oxide leave the body by the lungs and may result in dilution of the alveolar oxygen concentration and consequently hypoxia.

The oil–gas or lipid solubility coefficient is a measure of the potency of the anaesthetic agent. The more soluble an agent is in oil, the more potent it is. Also, during long administrations the high oil solubility becomes important, since more of the agent is taken up by the fatty tissues and recovery is prolonged.

The minimum alveolar concentration (MAC) of a drug is the alveolar concentration that produces a state of surgical anaesthesia such that 50% of patients move on skin incision. MAC × oil–gas solubility coefficient for any agent = 200.

There is no metabolic inactivation or destruction of general anaesthetics by nerve tissue and so recovery from anaesthesia is dependent upon a good blood flow from the CNS and elimination from the blood, by excretion, unchanged by the lungs and kidneys, destruction or conjugation in the liver, or temporary storage in the fatty tissues. The inhalational agents described are mostly excreted unchanged by the lungs, which accounts for their acceptability as readily reversible and controlled producers of CNS depression. However, all volatile agents are metabolized to some extent in the liver and the metabolites may account for any toxicity. For instance, the antimetabolite disulfiram prevents both the metabolism and the hepatotoxicity of choloroform in rats, while enzyme inducers such as phenobarbitone increase the hepatotoxicity.

Nitrous Oxide (N_2O)

Nitrous oxide is the only inorganic gas used to produce anaesthesia in man. It is stored as a liquid in blue cylinders in the UK under 50 atmospheres pressure at 28°C, but is administered through flowmeters as a gas at room temperature and pressure. It is neither inflammable nor explosive, but will support combustion.

Since it is a relatively insoluble drug (blood–gas solubility coefficient 0.47), it has a rapid onset of action. It is carried in the circulation in solution and does not combine with haemoglobin or any other chemical combination.

It is a weak anaesthetic which is unable to produce surgical anaesthesia when administered as the sole agent, though it is a very good analgesic. In anaesthesia it is usually administered in a concentration of 50–80% of the inspired gas with oxygen. There are no contraindications to its use in combination with an adequate percentage of oxygen. Present practice suggests that the inhalation should be preceded by the i.v. induction of anaesthesia and that a more potent volatile agent such as halothane should be added to the administration, so that the percentage of oxygen in the inhaled anaesthetic mixture may be at least 30%.

As nitrous oxide is a very good analgesic drug, it has been used in labour, following myocardial infarction, for burns dressings, and by ambulance men at the scene of an accident. For this purpose 50% nitrous oxide and 50% oxygen have been premixed in a cylinder (Entonox) and delivered to the patient via a special high flow on demand valve. In the past, cases have been reported of the nitrous oxide liquefying at $-9°C$ (Poynting effect), but this problem has been eliminated by modification of the cylinder.

Prolonged administration of nitrous oxide (e.g. 48–72 hours) may produce bone marrow depression and hence the agent cannot be used to produce sedation for prolonged intermittent positive pressure ventilation. Chronic exposure to low concentrations may result in peripheral neuropathy, perhaps because nitrous oxide interferes with vitamin B_{12} metabolism.

Cyclopropane

Cyclopropane is a pleasant, sweet-smelling gas which is irritating to the respiratory tract. It is stored in orange cylinders in the UK as a liquid under 517 kPa pressure at 28°C. It is a gas at room temperature and pressure. It is relatively insoluble in blood (solubility coefficient 0.42) and so produces a rapid induction and recovery. It is explosive when mixed with air, oxygen or nitrous oxide.

Cyclopropane, following absorption, is carried in the circulation attached to the red cells. Some is attached to plasma proteins, but little is physically dissolved in plasma. It is excreted almost entirely by the lungs, though a small amount is lost through the skin. Approximately 50% of cyclopropane in the body is excreted within 10 minutes of discontinuing its administration.

Cyclopropane depresses respiration markedly, especially following narcotic premedication. Patients undergoing light anaesthesia have an increased cardiac output, but this falls to normal or below as the depth is increased. The combination of respiratory depression with a subsequent increase in the P_{CO_2} and continued cyclopropane anaesthesia is very likely to produce dysrhythmias, since both are known to increase the rate of noradrenaline liberation from sympathetic nerve endings in the myocardium.

Cyclopropane, unlike most other anaesthetic agents, produces peripheral vasoconstriction. It reduces renal and hepatic blood flow in direct proportion to its concentration. It depresses the contractions of the gravid uterus and increases central venous pressure.

Cyclopropane should be used only in closed circuit, because of its explosive nature. Its principal use is in rapid gaseous induction of anaesthesia as a 50:50 mixture with oxygen. Once anaesthesia is established, 8% in oxygen maintains light anaesthesia. Therefore, cyclopropane is useful where a high concentration of inspired oxygen and maintenance of systolic pressure are desirable.

Diethyl ether

At ambient temperature and pressure, diethyl ether is a colourless, highly volatile liquid with a pungent odour. It is highly inflammable and its vapour is explosive when mixed with air or oxygen. It decomposes on exposure to air, light and heat, and should be stored in sealed opaque containers in the cool.

Ether produces depression of the cerebral cortex and of spinal reflexes. In large doses it depresses the respiratory centre, but paralysis of respiration precedes vasomotor collapse by a considerable margin, making it a safe drug in unskilled hands. The myocardium is depressed by anaesthetic concentrations, but cardiac output is maintained owing to sympathetic overactivity. In light anaesthesia the arterial pressure is maintained, but deeper anaesthesia produces hypotension due to peripheral vasodilatation. There is an increase in coronary blood flow and a rise in CSF pressure. Respiration is stimulated until deep levels of anaesthesia are reached. Bronchial secretions are increased and laryngeal spasm is liable to occur during induction with ether. Salivary and gastric secretions are increased at first and nausea and vomiting are common. Skeletal muscle tone is markedly reduced owing to depression of transmission at neuromuscular junctions by a curare-like action. There is a fall in renal and hepatic blood flow, and hyperglycaemia occurs. During light anaesthesia the pregnant uterus is not affected, but there may be depression of respiration in the infant.

Ether is administered by inhalation, and as it is a soluble compound, it produces slow induction of and recovery from anaesthesia. It may be given by an open mask or any vaporizer in current use with air or a mixture of nitrous oxide and oxygen. Up to a 20% concentration in inspired gas is required for induction, but light anaesthesia can be maintained on a 3–5% concentration.

There is some metabolic breakdown in the body, but 60–80% of the administered dose is excreted unchanged by the lungs. A small quantity is excreted in the urine and secretions. Any metabolism that occurs takes place in the liver, producing non-toxic products, including ethyl alcohol and acetate.

Ether is a very safe drug with a wide safety margin and so it is useful for the occasional anaesthetist and for those working in remote areas.

Unwanted effects include hyperglycaemia and convulsions in febrile patients in hot humid climates. It is very inflammable and should not be used if surgical diathermy is in use.

Chloroform

Chloroform is a colourless fluid with a sweet smell which decomposes on light and heat to form phosgene ($COCl_2$), which is highly irritant to the respiratory tract. It can be used safely with soda lime and is non-inflammable. It is a soluble agent and induction and recovery will be slow, but this is partly offset by its high degree of anaesthetic potency.

Chloroform depresses cardiac muscle, the conducting tissue and the smooth muscle of the peripheral vessels. It sensitizes the heart to the stimulating effects of adrenaline. During induction the pulse rate is slowed, partly owing to vagal stimulation and partly owing to direct depression of the myocardium. This may be overcome by atropine premedication.

Chloroform depresses respiration by a direct effect on the respiratory centre and by depression of the respiratory muscles. It is generally accepted that, following chloroform anaesthesia, there is some degree of centrilobular hepatic necrosis, but there is evidence that this does not occur provided the drug is not given in overdosage, full oxygenation is maintained and there is no carbon dioxide retention. Toxic effects in the form of fatty degeneration may be found in the kidney, pancreas and spleen. Uterine contractions during labour are decreased and nausea and vomiting are common.

Chloroform is seldom used because of its hepatic toxicity, which is due to one of its metabolites.

Halothane

Halothane (Fluothane), a halogenated hydrocarbon, which was introduced into clinical practice in 1956, has deservedly become very popular. It is a heavy colourless liquid which decomposes on exposure to light but which is stable in the presence of soda lime. It is a potent, non-irritant and non-inflammable agent with a blood–gas solubility coefficient of 2.4 (cf. 0.42 for cyclopropane and 12.1 for ether). Therefore induction of anaesthesia with halothane is more rapid than with ether but slower than with cyclopropane.

Halothane is administered by inhalation and 12–20% of the inspired dose is metabolized by hepatic microsomal enzymes to produce products some of which are recovered in the urine over a 13 day period. It undergoes oxidation and reduction. The metabolizing enzymes are induced by barbiturates and by halothane itself. The lungs are responsible for fairly rapid excretion of 80–88% of the administered dose.

Halothane depresses respiration and myocardial performance. It produces a bradycardia which is reversed by atropine. Dysrhythmias are likely to occur if there is retention of carbon dioxide. Halothane produces vasodilatation of skin and muscle vessels, along with a fall in arterial pressure and vascular resistance. It decreases renal and hepatic blood flow and relaxes the uterus in labour. It depresses gastrointestinal motility, but has very little effect on skeletal muscle in therapeutic doses. Cerebral blood flow is increased and intracranial pressure rises. Shivering may occur in the early postoperative period.

Halothane has only minimal analgesic properties, but is a potent anaesthetic agent. Indeed, 0.5–2% of the drug in the inspired gas is sufficient to maintain surgical anaesthesia. It is usually given with an oxygen–nitrous oxide mixture and should be given in a temperature-regulated vaporizer to prevent overdosage.

There has been considerable controversy about the role of halothane in the production of postoperative jaundice. When it occurs, the clinical picture is one of fever, leucocytosis with eosinophilia, and jaundice 5–21 days after anaesthesia; there is also central and mid-zonal hepatocellular necrosis (p. 570). It seems likely that reduction of halothane (a minor metabolic pathway) results in a toxic metabolite that destroys hepatocytes. Patients more likely to suffer from halothane associated hepatitis are elderly obese females with a reason for enzyme induction or those patients with a history of a previous anaesthetic within 6 weeks. Hypoxaemia probably increases the risk. Halothane itself produces microsomal enzyme induction.

Methoxyflurane

Methoxyflurane (Penthrane) is a clear colourless liquid with a boiling point of 105°C. Therefore it is difficult for it to evaporate at room temperature. It is very soluble in rubber and indeed, up to a third of the output of methoxyflurane from the vaporizer can be absorbed by the rubber of the apparatus used in its administration. These facts, combined with the high blood–gas solubility, mean that induction of anaesthesia with this agent is very slow. It is, however, very potent and is a good analgesic drug.

Methoxyflurane depresses respiration but is non-irritant to the airways. The cardiovascular effects resemble those of halothane, but muscle relaxation occurs as a result of a central action. A metabolite of methoxyflurane may produce high output renal failure. Because of this toxicity it is no longer used.

Trichlorethylene

Trichlorethylene (Trilene) is a heavy colourless liquid which contains thymol as a stabilizing agent and an inert blue dye to colour it and to distinguish it from chloroform. It decomposes with heat and light and in contact with soda lime to form phosgene. Accordingly, it must not be used in a rebreathing circuit. It is non-inflammable and non-explosive.

Because of its high boiling point, it is difficult to vaporize high concentrations of trichlorethylene at ambient temperature, but this is offset by the fact that the oil–gas solubility is very high and trichlorethylene is the most potent of all known anaesthetic agents. The blood–gas solubility is 9.15; therefore induction and recovery are slow.

Following administration, some metabolism occurs in the liver, producing trichloroacetic acid and trichloroethanol glucuronide which is excreted in the urine. Almost every type of cardiac dysrhythmia has been reported during trichlorethylene anaesthesia, but always in association with high concentrations of the inhaled vapour. There is no significant alteration of arterial pressure. The agent is non-irritant to airways but causes a tachypnoea in higher concentrations. Cerebral blood flow and intracranial pressure are increased and the contractions of the gravid uterus are depressed by anaesthetic concentrations. In analgesic concentrations, however, the uterine contractions are not affected. In clinical doses no muscle relaxation occurs.

The dose to maintain anaesthesia is usually from 0.5 to 2% in a nitrous oxide–air mixture. To produce analgesia, low concentrations (0.35–0.5%) in air are used.

Trichlorethylene is used as a supplement to nitrous oxide and oxygen to produce anaesthesia for all types of surgical procedures. It is a very potent analgesic and may be used to relieve pain during labour.

Postoperative nausea, vomiting and headache are common. Dysrhythmias are likely to occur with large doses, especially if adrenaline is used or carbon dioxide is allowed to build up. If the drug is used with soda lime, phosgene is produced and cranial nerve palsy is very likely to occur. The trigeminal nerve is most commonly affected.

Trichlorethylene is still available in the UK but is seldom used.

Enflurane

Enflurane (Ethrane) is a fluorinated ether, which is justifiably becoming very popular in the UK as an alternative to halothane. Its basic physical characteristics resemble those of halothane, but it has a lower blood–gas solubility and so induction and recovery of anaesthesia are more rapid. It is only half as potent as halothane and the anaesthetic inspired concentration is 2–3%.

Enflurane produces a fall in arterial pressure due to a reduced peripheral vascular resistance. It depresses cardiac output less than halothane. It is to a greater extent a respiratory depressant and it slows the respiratory rate. It produces good muscle relaxation.

Cardiac dysrhythmias are less likely with enflurane anaesthesia than with halothane. Only 2% of an administered dose is metabolized by the liver and so it is thought that enflurane is less likely to be associated with hepatitis. However, a metabolite of enflurane is epileptogenic and may cause activity of the EEG for days after a single administration.

Isoflurane

Isoflurane (Forane), a chemical isomer of enflurane, is likely to be introduced into anaesthetic practice in the UK in the near future. Its advantages over enflurane are that it is even less likely to provoke cardiac dysrhythmias and that only 0.2% of an administered dose is metabolized in the liver. It is expensive.

FURTHER READING

Bianchine J. R. & Shaw G. M. (1976) Clinical pharmacokinetics of levodopa in Parkinson's disease. *Clin. Pharmacokinet.*, 1: 313.
Black G. W. (1982) Metabolism and toxicity of volatile anaesthetic agents. In: Atkinson R. S. &

Langton Hewer C. (eds) *Recent Advances in Anaesthesia and Analgesia*, vol. 14, p. 31. Edinburgh, London, Melbourne & New York: Churchill Livingstone.

Bowman W. C. & Rand M. J. (1980) *Textbook of Pharmacology*, chapters 9, 10 & 11. Oxford, London & Edinburgh: Blackwell.

Calvey T. N. & Williams N. E. (1982) *Principles and Practice of Pharmacology for Anaesthetists*. Oxford, London & Edinburgh: Blackwell.

Clarke R. S. J. (1982) Biotransformation of intravenous anaesthetic agents. In: Atkinson R. S. & Langton Hewer C. (eds) *Recent Advances in Anaesthesia and Analgesia*, vol. 14, p. 45. Edinburgh, London, Melbourne & New York: Churchill Livingstone.

Covino B. G. (1972) Local anaesthesia. *New Engl. J. Med.*, 286: 975.

Covino B. G. & Vassallo H. G. (1976) *Local Anaesthetics*. New York, San Francisco & London: Grune & Stratton.

Dundee J. W. & McCaughey W. (1980) Drugs in anaesthetic practice. In: Avery G. S. (ed.) *Drug Treatment*, p. 282. Sydney & New York: Adis Press.

Eadie M. J. (1976) Plasma level monitoring of anticonvulsants. *Clin. Pharmacokinet.*, 1: 52.

Ghoneim M. M. & Kottila K. (1977) Pharmacokinetics of intravenous anaesthetics: implications for clinical use. *Clin. Pharmacokinet.*, 2: 344.

Goldberg L. I. (1974) Dopamine — clinical uses of an endogenous catecholamine. *New Engl. J. Med.*, 291, 707.

Hvidberg E. F. & Dam M. (1976) Clinical pharmacokinetics of anticonvulsants. *Clin. Pharmacokinet.*, 1: 161.

Inman W. H. W. & Mushin W. W. (1978) Jaundice after repeated exposure to halothane. *Br. med. J.*, 2: 1455.

Lejkowitz R. J. (1980) Andrenergic receptor regulation. In: Turner P. and Shand D. G. (eds) *Recent Advances in Clinical Pharmacology*, vol. 2, p. 35. Edinburgh, London, Melbourne & New York: Churchill Livingstone.

Reynolds E. H. (1978) How do anticonvulsants work? *Br. J. Hosp. Med.*, 14: 505.

Richens A. (1978) Antiepileptic drugs. In: Turner P. and Shand D. G. (eds) *Recent Advances in Clinical Pharmacology*, vol. 1, p. 147. Edinburgh, London, Melbourne & New York: Churchill Livingstone.

Rowlands D. J. (1980) Choice of a beta-blocker. *Prescrib. J.* 20: 64.

Simpson F. O. (1980) Hypertensive disease. In: Avery G. S. (ed.) *Drug Treatment*, p. 638. Sydney & New York: Adis Press.

Stern G. (1982) Medical treatment of Parkinsonism. *Prescrib. J.* 22: 1.

Turner P. (1969) *Clinical Aspects of Autonomic Pharmacology*. London: Heinemann Medical.

Wingard L. B. & Cook D. R. (1977) Clinical pharmacokinetics of muscle relaxants. *Clin. Pharmacokinet.*, 2: 330.

6 Drugs Acting on the Cardiovascular System

J. Nimmo

DIGITALIS AND OTHER CARDIAC GLYCOSIDES

A large number of plant extracts containing cardiac glycosides have been used for thousands of years to treat human disease. The modern era of treatment with the digitalis glycosides began with the work of William Withering, who published his famous book, *An Account of the Foxglove and Some of Its Medical Uses*, in 1785. Withering was aware that digitalis was effective only in certain forms of dropsy or oedema, and recognized that the drug acted on the heart. During the early twentieth century digitalis was accepted as specific in atrial fibrillation and in the last 50 years it has been firmly established that the main value of digitalis glycosides is in the therapy of congestive cardiac failure associated with atrial fibrillation.

CHEMISTRY OF THE CARDIAC GLYCOSIDES

Digitalis leaf, BP, is the dried leaf of the common foxglove plant, *Digitalis purpurea*. It is also available in powdered form as prepared digitalis, BP. Both contain a number of glycosides, including digitoxin, gitoxin and gitaloxin. The name 'digitalis' is said to be an allusion to the German name *Fingerhut* (thimble), presumably based on the shape of the flower. Numerous other plants, particularly *Digitalis lanata*, strophanthus, sea onion, lily of the valley and yellow oleander, have been used as sources of cardiac glycosides.

Chemically, each glycoside represents the combination of an aglycone or genin, which is a steroid with certain typical structural features, with from 1 to 4 molecules of sugar. The sugar components may be mono-, di-, tri-, or tetrasaccharides. The simplest cardiac genin is digitoxigenin. The pharmacological activity resides in the aglycone, but the particular sugars attached to it enhance water solubility and cell penetration. The number and type of sugar molecules attached to the aglycone may determine the potency and toxicity of the resulting glycoside.

DIGITOXIN = 1 DIGITOXIGENIN + 3 DIGITOXOSE
DIGOXIN = 1 DIGOXIGENIN + 3 DIGITOXOSE

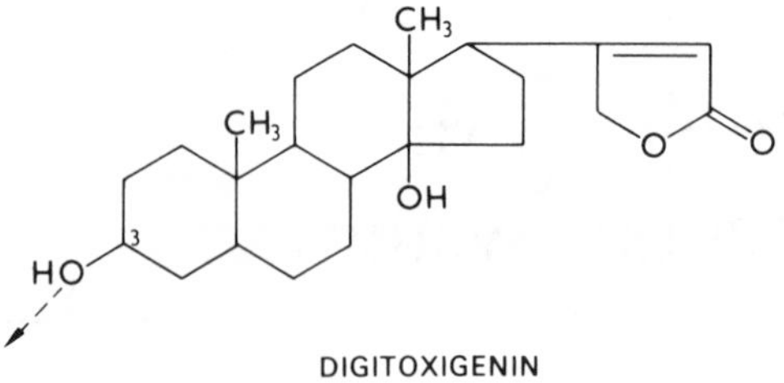

DIGITOXIGENIN

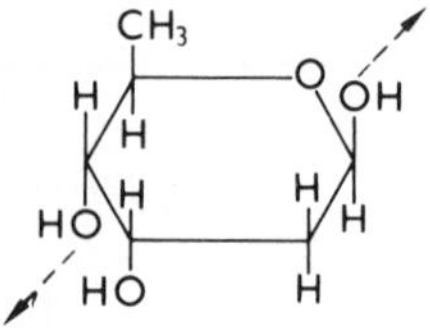

DIGITOXOSE

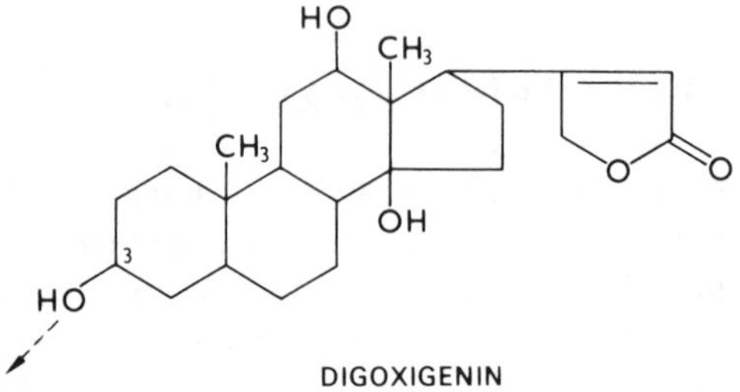

DIGOXIGENIN

CARDIOVASCULAR ACTIONS OF DIGITALIS GLYCOSIDES

Despite the number and diversity of the cardioactive glycosides, they exhibit a common and similar pattern of action. The main actions are:

1. Inotropic effect — the property of inducing increased increment of contractile force from the cardiac muscle.
2. Chronotropic effect — the property of slowing the heart rate.

A most important property of digitalis is its ability to increase the force of myocardial contraction. In congestive heart failure this results in increased cardiac output, decreased heart size, decreased venous pressure and a diuresis with relief of oedema. Digitalis inhibits the sodium pump of the sarcolemma, thus allowing intracellular accumulation of sodium to displace bound calcium ions which, in turn, exert the positive inotropic effect by acting at the actomyosin site.

The slowing effect of digitalis on the heart rate is mediated through at least two mechanisms. These are a stimulatory effect on the vagus which is operative very soon after administration of the drug and a direct effect of digitalis which slows the process of the conduction of impulses through the conducting tissue. Complete suppression of the atrial pacemaker has been described and atrioventricular block is a common manifestation of digitalis toxicity. It must be remembered, however, that congestive failure in patients with normal sinus rhythm is often accompanied by tachycardia as part of the reflex compensation for a reduced cardiac output.

Digitalis, by improving the cardiac output, will reduce the heart rate — i.e. this part of the change in rate is secondary to the improvement in the circulation and not a direct effect of the drug. Although digitalis in therapeutic doses does not greatly reduce the rate of the heart in normal sinus rhythm, it has a pronounced effect on the ventricular rate in atrial fibrillation. Digitalis shortens the atrial refractory period, but it depresses conduction through the atrioventricular node and prolongs the functional refractory period of the atrioventricular transmission system. It also shortens the ventricular refractory period. In atrial fibrillation, therefore, digitalis is not likely to improve the abnormal pattern in the atria, though it reduces the ventricular rate, through vagal and direct influences, both of which cause a delay in atrioventricular conduction.

PREPARATIONS AVAILABLE FOR CLINICAL USE

Many different preparations of digitalis are available and in recent years purified glycosides have replaced the traditional tincture and powdered leaf of digitalis. The practitioner is well advised to become familiar with the use of one preparation, but should be aware of the possible advantages of other preparations in certain situations.

Digoxin

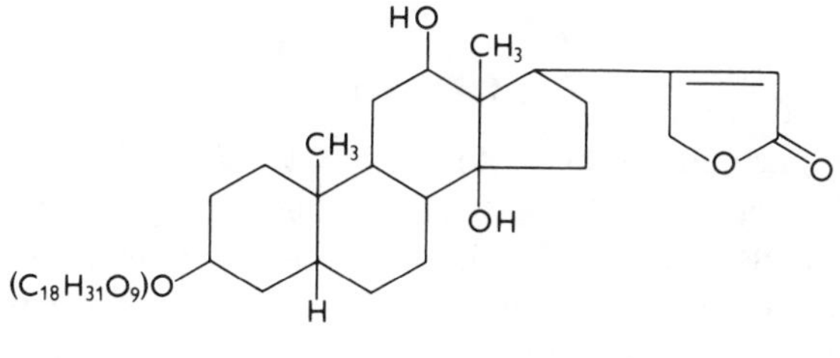

DIGOXIN

Digoxin (12-hydroxydigitoxin), which is derived from *Digitalis lanata*, is by far the most popular glycoside in clinical use. Digoxin in alcoholic solution is absorbed to the extent of 80–85% from the gastrointestinal tract, some 7% undergoing an enterohepatic circulation. Digoxin from the tablet form is probably absorbed to the extent of between 60 and 75%, but there have been considerable problems owing to variation in absorption from tablets marketed by different companies. This matter has been corrected in the UK by stricter instructions on details of preparation.

Digoxin is normally absorbed rapidly in the gastrointestinal tract, with detectable levels appearing in the plasma some 6 minutes after administration and a peak serum level being found at 45–60 minutes. The drug may also be given by i.m. or i.v. injection. The mean plasma half-life for all routes of administration is 34 hours. Regardless of the route of administration, the primary organ of excretion is the kidney, most of the drug being recovered as unchanged digoxin in the urine. Some 10–20% of a single dose may be recovered from the stool. Following a single full digitalizing dose given i.v., the onset of action of digoxin occurs 5–30 minutes after administration. Maximal action is achieved at $1\frac{1}{2}$–5 hours and the total duration of activity is from 2 to 6 days. The drug is available in tablets of 0.25 mg, 0.125 mg, and 0.0625 mg. It is important that the patient should not confuse the tablets of different concentrations. Lanoxin is a proprietary form on sale in the UK which is marketed by the company which first drew attention to variations in generic equivalence (p. 276) and many would regard it as the preparation of choice.

Lanatoside C

Lanatoside C is also derived from *Digitalis lanata*, but it is very poorly absorbed when given orally. It can be given i.v. as the deacetyl derivative deslanoside and its half-life is about 36 hours. The onset of activity with lanatoside C is claimed to be marginally earlier than that with digoxin, in that the maximum effect is reached in 3 hours. The total duration of effect is approximately 5 days. Lanatoside C and deslanoside are available in the UK as Cedilanid.

Digitoxin

Digitoxin is a purified glycoside found in both *Digitalis purpurea* and *D. lanata*. It is absorbed from the gastrointestinal tract almost to the extent of 100% and can also be given i.m. or i.v. After absorption, digitoxin is extensively bound to serum albumin (90–97%). Digitoxin is metabolized prior to excretion; some 8% of the total dose is hydrolysed to digoxin, while the remainder is excreted as metabolites that do not influence the heart. Excretion ultimately takes place by the kidneys, the physiological half-life being 102–116 hours. The onset of action following a single full digitalizing dose of digitoxin given i.v. is 25 minutes–2 hours, but there is little purpose in injecting it unless vomiting or some other reason makes oral administration impossible, since it has an equally rapid effect if taken by mouth. Maximum activity occurs at 4–12 hours and the total activity lasts for 2–3 weeks. Of the cardiac glycosides it is the most cumulative in action. Digitoxin tablets, BP, contain 100 μg and there are proprietary preparations of different strengths.

Ouabain

Ouabain is a pure cardiac glycoside obtained from the strophanthus plant. It is unreliable if given orally, but is used occasionally by the i.v. route for quick effect. Following a full single digitalizing dose given i.v., ouabain starts to act after 3–10 minutes, maximal activity is reached at 30 minutes–2 hours and the total duration of activity is 4 hours–3 days. The dose is 0.12–0.25 mg i.v.

INDICATIONS FOR THE USE OF DIGITALIS PREPARATIONS

Indications for the use of cardiac glycosides are at present contracting. Traditionally these drugs were used in the management of congestive cardiac failure and cardiac dysrhythmias.* However, the introduction of more potent diuretics and vasodilators has decreased the need for digitalis glycosides in heart failure with sinus rhythm. In acute supraventricular tachycardias, cardioversion is employed, or other drugs such as verapamil are preferred.

In the UK it is usually digoxin that is used, principally in the management of cardiac failure with atrial fibrillation and in chronic supraventricular tachycardias. The drug is useful in either right or left ventricular failure. In the past, full digitalizing doses were recommended for congestive cardiac failure of any aetiology. This meant the prescription of increasing amounts of the drug until cardiac or, hopefully, extracardiac signs of toxicity appeared. The drug was then discontinued for a short period and recommenced at a slightly lower dosage. Since digitalis toxicity is associated with a high morbidity and mortality, this was always a cause for concern. The response to digitalis is dose-related until toxicity intervenes and even a small dose improves cardiac performance. It is now common practice to commence treatment with subtoxic doses of digoxin, in combination with diuretic therapy.

It is important to realize that digoxin therapy is indicated in most cases of atrial fibrillation and that the dosage may be adjusted to maintain the ventricular rate in the range of 60–80/minute. The slowing of the ventricular rate is very beneficial. Digoxin is also useful in the management of atrial flutter, but if this occurs in a patient who has not had digoxin therapy and there are no contraindications, DC electric shock is preferable. If not, full digitalization may cause atrial fibrillation, but if the digitalis is then stopped, normal rhythm may ensue. If not, digoxin therapy should be continued. Occasionally atrial flutter is itself due to digitalis poisoning.

Paroxysmal supraventricular tachycardia may respond to carotid sinus pressure or other vagus-stimulating manoeuvres. If not, and if a cardiac glycoside has not already been given, it may respond to the i.v. injection of 0.5 mg of digoxin, followed by 0.25 mg 6-hourly by mouth. No doubt, it has a vagal effect on the sinoatrial node and on the conducting tissue.

*The word 'rhythm' has various meanings. The term 'arrhythmia' is commonly used rather than 'dysrhythmia'. The objection to this is that the ultimate state of arrhythmia is cardiac arrest. It could, however, be argued that atrial fibrillation is a form of arrhythmia, depending on the way in which 'rhythm' is interpreted.

Paroxysmal atrial tachycardia with atrioventricular block, in contrast, is most commonly itself caused by digitalis therapy.

Ventricular ectopic beats or paroxysmal ventricular tachycardia should not be treated with any of the digitalis group of drugs. Indeed, ventricular fibrillation may be induced, with a fatal outcome. Ventricular tachycardia may be best treated by electrical cardioversion, but drug treatment will be described later (p. 300).

Digitalis is contraindicated in heart block, hypertrophic obstructive cardiomyopathy, and some cases of Wolff–Parkinson–White syndrome.

DOSAGE

Full details of the use of digoxin cannot be given here, since management will depend on previous therapy, the type and severity of the illness and the other therapeutic measures employed. Thus morphine may be required in pulmonary oedema (p. 111), oxygen may be needed, and diuretics (p. 352) will be given where necessary by injection or by the oral route.

In very acute illness and if digoxin or an alternative preparation has not already been given, the patient may receive an initial dose of 0.5–1 mg i.v., but this therapy should not be repeated by the i.v. route. In less serious illness the same dose can be given i.m., and in either instance this is followed by 0.25 mg three or four times a day by mouth until the desired effect is achieved or toxic features develop. In some hospitals serum levels can be measured. In the less severe incidents the initial dose can be 0.5 or 1.0 mg by mouth. The maintenance dose usually varies between 0.25 and 0.5 mg daily, but in some patients, especially if they are elderly or if there is renal failure, this may have to be reduced to 0.25 or 0.125 mg on alternate days. Sometimes 0.0625 mg is given daily and, indeed, the difference in required maintenance doses may be considerable, even when the serum digoxin level is being measured. If digitoxin is used, it should be taken that 0.1 mg is approximately equal to 0.25 mg of digoxin. The substance marketed as Digitaline Nativelle is digitoxin. However, digitalin was a standardized mixture of glycosides from the seeds of *Digitalis purpurea*. It is much less potent than Digitaline and is seldom used.

Deslanoside (p. 272) can be given by i.v. injection in a dose of 0.8–1.2 mg and is said to have some action within 10 minutes.

TOXIC EFFECTS OF DIGITALIS

Digitalis intoxication is a common adverse drug reaction with a mortality ranging from 7 to 50% in various series. All cardiac glycosides may produce toxicity and no significant difference in the toxic/therapeutic dose ratio has been reported for different glycosides. Toxic effects are more likely in the elderly and in the presence of hypokalaemia or anoxia.

Gastrointestinal Effects

Anorexia, nausea and vomiting are among the earliest symptoms of digitalis overdose. Anorexia usually occurs a day or so before the nausea and vomiting, but these symptoms are often transient and may be entirely absent in some patients. Therefore they cannot be relied upon to ascertain the presence of digitalis intoxication. Abdominal discomfort or pain and diarrhoea may also occur. When the drug is stopped, the gastrointestinal symptoms disappear in a few days.

Neurological Effects

Headache, fatigue, malaise and drowsiness are common and occur early in the course of digitalis intoxication. Disorientation, confusion, aphasia, delirium and hallucinations may also occur. The vision may be blurred, white borders may appear on dark objects and colour vision can be disturbed with chromatopsia, most commonly for yellow and green. This effect is seldom encountered.

Cardiac Effects

Disorders of cardiac rhythm are the first and possibly the only manifestation of digitalis toxicity in approximately one-third of patients treated. Eighty per cent of patients with digitalis toxicity have cardiac dysrhythmias or conduction disturbances. The commonest dysrhythmias are ventricular tachycardia, multiform ventricular extrasystoles and paroxysmal atrial tachycardia with block. There may be atrioventricular conduction disturbances, including complete heart block.

The concentration of digoxin in the plasma can be measured by a radioimmunoassay technique. Although there are reasonable correlations between response and the plasma concentration of the drug, there are a number of difficulties in interpretation of the findings. Tissue response may not parallel plasma concentration of digoxin, especially in the presence of hypokalaemia. In addition, response to digoxin differs in different patients. Some patients require a higher plasma concentration for therapeutic effect, whereas others tolerate concentrations which would be toxic in most patients. The usual therapeutic plasma concentration for digoxin is 0.5–2.0 ng/ml. Digoxin toxicity may be expected with plasma concentrations in excess of 2.0 ng/ml, but considerable overlap of therapeutic and toxic plasma concentrations has been described.

MANAGEMENT OF DIGITALIS INTOXICATION

Milder toxic manifestations of digoxin can be managed simply by stopping the drug. If dangerous manifestations are present, then more active therapy is indicated and this may involve the use of phenytoin sodium, propranolol, practolol or lignocaine. Reference to these drugs is made later in this chapter. Electrical cardioversion is definitely *not* indicated. Digitalis-induced dysrhythmias are more likely in the presence of hypokalaemia, and potassium should be administered, even if the serum potassium concentration is within normal limits. Potassium effervescent tablets, BPC, should not be given, since they do not contain chloride. Potassium chloride effervescent tablets can be used, but in a serious incident potassium chloride might be given i.v. very slowly, 40–100 mmol at 20 mmol per hour, with careful monitoring of the ECG and serum potassium level. Overdosage must be avoided. Potassium is often effective in abolishing ventricular or supraventricular dysrhythmias or tachycardias, but should not be given in the presence of atrioventricular block. If there is heart block, atropine (p. 206) may be used, since it reduces vagal tone.

GENERIC INEQUIVALENCE OF DIGOXIN PREPARATIONS

Striking differences in the bioavailability of digoxin preparations from different manufacturers have been described (p. 272). These differences appear to be due to different particle sizes of the drug and different dissolution rates, and, indeed, the greatest bioavailability has been shown in preparations with the most rapid dissolution rate in vitro. Difficulty might be experienced when a patient is changed from one manufacturer's preparation to that of another with different bioavailability, but standardization is much improved in the UK.

A recent introduction has been medigoxin (Lanitop), which is claimed to have a greater and more reliable bioavailability than digoxin.

SPECIAL PROBLEMS OF DIGITALIS THERAPY

Digoxin is excreted primarily in the urine. The dosage must be greatly reduced and carefully monitored in the presence of renal failure. Elderly patients show a lower digoxin tolerance and slower excretion of the drug and therefore require lower doses. Following myocardial infarction, it has been claimed that the dose required to produce toxicity is only 60% of that normally expected to do so. Difficulty may also be encountered in patients with thyroid disorders, since those with myxoedema have higher serum levels of digoxin and those with hyperthyroidism lower serum levels after comparable doses of the drug.

It has been claimed that the weight of the patient, the serum albumin level and the results of a creatinine clearance test are of particular importance in determining the dose required to maintain the serum digoxin level in the therapeutic range, which is between 1 and 2 ng/ml.

OTHER DRUGS USED IN CARDIAC FAILURE

In addition to diuretics (p. 352), other drugs used in the management of cardiac failure act either by improving myocardial contractility, i.e. agents with inotropic action (p. 270), or by reducing the load on the left ventricle by vasodilatation.

Drugs Improving Myocardial Contractility

Especially in acute myocardial infarction, drugs causing an increase in contractility and heart rate may have an adverse effect, since they increase myocardial oxygen consumption and thus may lead to an extension of myocardial damage. Initial enthusiasm for the use of noradrenaline to improve myocardial function in shock due to myocardial infarction quickly waned when it was realized that noradrenaline could increase peripheral resistance and increase the load on the heart. The use of drugs designed to improve cardiac failure by increasing contractility is restricted to emergency resuscitation.

Dopamine

Dopamine (Intropin) is a catecholamine-like agent introduced for the treatment of severe heart failure and cardiogenic shock. It is the precursor of noradrenaline and has a direct cardiac action through the local release of noradrenaline. By its action on dopaminergic receptors, it causes dilatation of the renal, mesenteric, coronary and cerebral vascular beds, causing increases in glomerular filtration rate, renal blood flow and urine output. At high doses, dopamine causes peripheral vasoconstriction and the renal blood flow falls.

Dopamine is inactive if given by mouth. I.v. dopamine is metabolized in a few minutes by dopamine β-hydroxylase and monoamine oxidase. It is administered by i.v. infusion and the usual starting dose is 0.5–1 μg/kg body weight per minute. This is increased until the optimum dose for the patient is reached, as judged by urinary flow, blood pressure or heart rate. Vasoconstriction begins at about 15 μg/kg body weight per minute.

I.v. infusions of dopamine may be used in the short-term treatment of refractory cardiac failure, cardiogenic shock, septicaemic shock, after cardiac surgery and in impending renal failure. Any hypovolaemia should be corrected first. Dopamine is contraindicated in the presence of ventricular dysrhythmias and phaeochromocytoma. Dopamine must not be diluted with alkaline solutions. It should not be used together with cyclopropane or halogenated hydrocarbon anaesthetics.

Dobutamine

Dobutamine (Dobutrex) is a synthetic β-adrenergic catecholamine, i.e. an analogue of dopamine. It increases myocardial contractility without any effect on the heart rate. It does not directly release noradrenaline nor affect dopamine receptors.

Dobutamine is given by i.v. infusion at a dose of 2.5–10 μg/kg body weight per minute. The plasma half-life is 2.4 minutes and the therapeutic plasma concentration is 40–190 ng/ml. It may be infused for up to 72 hours.

Dobutamine causes peripheral vasodilatation, but does not dilate the renal arteries. It is indicated when an inotropic effect with reduction of the load on the heart is required, e.g. severe heart failure after myocardial infarction or in cardiomyopathies or after open heart surgery. It should not, however, be used after acute myocardial infarction or in idiopathic hypertrophic subaortic stenosis.

Glucagon

Glucagon, the hyperglycaemic hormone of the pancreas, increases myocardial contractility by increasing cellular cyclic adenosine monophosphate (AMP) levels by a mechanism similar to, but independent of, the actions of the catecholamines. Heart rate is usually increased slightly and there is an increase in splanchnic blood flow. The response to glucagon is lost in chronic congestive cardiac failure and dopamine is preferred in acute heart failure because of its effect on renal blood flow. Glucagon is available in the UK, but is not listed in MIMS.

Vasodilator Drugs

During the past decade the concept that cardiac failure should be treated by reducing the work-load of the heart rather than by attempting to stimulate the failing myocardium has gained increasing acceptance. Vasodilator drugs can be used to reduce the 'afterload'. This is an attempt to reduce aortic impedance and peripheral arteriolar resistance. In contrast, 'preload' is the left ventricular filling pressure and it can be reduced by drugs that dilate the systemic veins and thus reduce venous return to the heart.

Drugs used to decrease the work-load on the heart include sodium nitroprusside given i.v. in acute left ventricular failure and long-acting nitrates and hydralazine for chronic cardiac failure. Further information about these drugs is given when medicinal agents used in the management of angina (p. 307) or hypertension (p. 290) are considered.

DRUGS USED IN THE TREATMENT OF HYPERTENSION

The arterial pressure depends on cardiac output and peripheral resistance. The latter, in turn, is determined by blood viscosity and arteriolar tone. A complex homeostatic mechanism involving central and peripheral sympathetic activity, adrenal cortical and medullary secretions, renal pressor and depressor mechanisms, sodium and fluid balance, and baroreceptor activity exists to maintain the arterial pressure in health within normal limits. In the vast majority of patients suffering from hypertension no specific reason can be found. Causes to be looked for include primary renal disease, endocrine disorders such as phaeochromocytoma or hyperaldosteronism, and a congenital abnormality such as coarctation of the aorta. A great many drugs are available to lower the arterial pressure in the many instances where there is no remediable disorder. The vast majority of these reduce the peripheral resistance by decreasing arteriolar tone, while a few may lower the cardiac output.

While many hypotensive agents exert their effects at more than one site, it is convenient to ascribe to each a primary site of activity. Drugs may, therefore, act at one of the following sites:

1. Afferent nerve endings — i.e. baroreceptors in the left ventricle, lungs, aorta and carotid sinus.
2. Central nervous system (CNS), either at the higher centres or by affecting the hypothalamus and sympathetic vasoconstrictor centre.
3. Sympathetic autonomic ganglia.
4. Postganglionic sympathetic nerve fibres.
5. Sympathetic receptors, blocking the adrenergic transmission.
6. Smooth muscle of the vessel wall.
7. Inhibition of the angiotensin–renin system.

Drugs Affecting Afferent Nerve Endings

Veratrum alkaloids such as protoveratrine are obsolete antihypertensive agents which appear to produce their activity by stimulating the nerve receptors in the left ventricle, lungs, aorta and carotid sinus. Administration of veratrum alkaloids, therefore, results in a bradycardia, mediated via the vagus, and a reduction in arterial pressure due to a decrease in peripheral resistance. The most common toxic effects of the veratrum alkaloids are salivation, nausea and vomiting. Because of the narrow margin between therapeutic and toxic doses, the usefulness of these compounds has been limited and they are no longer used.

Drugs Acting on the Central Nervous System

Higher Centres

Sedative drugs, such as phenobarbitone, are not specifically antihypertensive. They may act by depressing the vasoconstrictor centre in the hypothalamus and can be useful in patients whose anxiety contributes to the high arterial pressure. There is, however, no good evidence that their effect on the pressure is greater than that of a placebo.

Adrenergic Mechanisms in the Hypothalamus

A number of drugs thought to exert some activity in the hypothalamus also act peripherally. These include methyldopa (p. 283) and β-adrenergic blocking drugs (p. 286). Reserpine and clonidine merit discussion.

Reserpine

Reserpine is thought to exert its antihypertensive effect by depleting the *peripheral* stores of catecholamines, with resultant impairment of sympathetic nerve discharge. Reserpine also exerts a *central* action, producing sinus bradycardia, sedation and tranquillization. The antihypertensive effect is thought to be chiefly peripheral. Reserpine is not now widely used because of the toxic effects which are largely due to its central activity. These effects include lethargy, apathy, nasal stuffiness, diarrhoea, dyspnoea, oedema, cardiac failure, depression and even suicide. With large doses an extrapyramidal syndrome resembling parkinsonism occurs. There have been claims that long-term use may occasionally lead to breast carcinoma in women. If reserpine is used, then small doses of 0.3–0.5 mg/day should be given. This dose has a modest hypotensive effect and, if employed, is usually given with a diuretic. In hypertensive crises 5 mg may be given i.m., but it may be about 2 hours before the maximal effect occurs. Almost 50% of patients receiving emergency parenteral reserpine develop gastrointestinal bleeding.

Clonidine

Although the exact mode of action of clonidine (Catapres) is uncertain, it appears to act on the CNS by reducing sympathetic outflow and increasing the depressor effects of baroreceptor stimulation. The acute peripheral effects of the drug are those of vasoconstriction; i.v. administration causes a transient increase in arterial pressure. Clonidine does not appear to interfere with the normal homeostatic mechanisms of blood pressure control and it can be an extremely useful drug for patients who have developed severe postural or exercise hypotension on other antihypertensive therapy. The drug has few side-effects, but may produce sedation or dry mouth. The dose of clonidine required is 0.1–1.0 mg daily in divided doses. Treatment should commence with 0.05–0.1 mg three times per day, increasing every 3 days until control is achieved. Peak plasma levels of the drug are achieved 2–4 hours after oral administration and the plasma half-life ranges from 6 to 24 hours. The duration of action in patients varies from 4 to 24 hours. The tricyclic antidepressant drug, desipramine, interferes with the antihypertensive action of clonidine. Sudden termination of long-term therapy with clonidine may result in a dangerous rebound hypertension. Clonidine has been associated with further episodes of depression in patients with a previous history of that condition. Occasionally a syndrome resembling Raynaud's phenomenon occurs. Constipation and impotence have occasionally been reported.

Drugs Acting at Autonomic Ganglia

Ganglion-blocking agents appear to act through a competitive antagonism with acetylcholine at the cholinergic synapses of autonomic ganglia. Because they are not selective and block both the sympathetic and parasympathetic systems, the ganglion-blockers have largely been replaced in the routine therapy of hypertension by drugs acting on the sympathetic nervous system only. Although some would claim that the ganglion-blockers still have a use in the emergency treatment of malignant hypertension, they are probably best regarded as being obsolete. The ganglion-blocking drugs most commonly used in the past were mecamylamine and pempidine. It is interesting to recall that one of the ganglion-blocking drugs, hexamethonium, was the first clinically useful drug in severe hypertension. The toxic effects of these drugs include postural hypotension, constipation possibly leading to paralytic ileus, dryness of the mouth, blurring of vision, difficulty in micturition, faintness and weakness. Sometimes there is nausea, drowsiness or diarrhoea. Some of these effects can be anticipated from knowledge of the mode of action of the drugs (p. 199).

Drugs Acting on Postganglionic Sympathetic Nerve Fibres or Nerve Terminals

Drugs in this group are taken up into adrenergic nerve endings and reduce the amount of noradrenaline released. There are a number of ways in which they may achieve this, though the differences in mechanism of activity are of little clinical importance. The drugs sensitize vascular musculature to catecholamines and if they are injected, there may be a transient release of noradrenaline. Accordingly, large doses should not be given i.v. in severe hypertension and the drugs must not be used in phaeochromocytoma. The general actions of these drugs are considered on p. 235 and are referred to more briefly in this chapter.

Drugs blocking noradrenaline release

Guanethidine. Guanethidine (Ismelin) is a potent antihypertensive agent whose strongly basic guanidine group prevents entry of the drug into the CNS, so that it lacks many of the central side-effects of reserpine.

GUANETHIDINE

Guanethidine depletes the noradrenaline stores at the sympathetic nerve terminals and blocks the release of noradrenaline that should occur on stimulation of postganglionic adrenergic nerves. Guanethidine therefore produces selective blockade at the sympathetic nerve terminal without any parasympathetic blockade. There is therefore a fall in arterial pressure, partly because of peripheral vasodilatation and partly from decreased cardiac output.

Dosage
Guanethidine is available in 10 and 25 mg tablets. The usual initial dose is 10 mg/day. This can be increased by 10 mg increments every 7 days, until the desired arterial pressure level is attained. The antihypertensive effect of guanethidine may not be seen for 2–3 days and 1 or 2 weeks may be required for the full effect of the drug to be achieved. From 3 to 50 per cent of an oral dose reaches the systemic circulation. Half of the drug is excreted unchanged in the urine and half is metabolized. Following i.v. administration, there are three phases of elimination: a very rapid phase, a second with a half-life of 20 hours, and a third with a half-life of 5 days. If early therapeutic effect is required, a loading dose of about 75 mg orally may be used. Guanethidine is available in ampoules containing 10 mg/ml. If rapid reduction of arterial pressure is required, as in toxaemia of pregnancy, 10–20 mg may be given i.m.

Adverse Effects
The most important side-effects of guanethidine are postural and exercise hypotension, which have limited its usefulness, and there may be diarrhoea because of parasympathetic predominance. Other side-effects are nausea, vomiting, nasal congestion, failure of ejaculation and parotid tenderness. Guanethidine may produce an initial rise of arterial pressure, as indicated above. It should not be used when sudden hypertension is associated with prior treatment with monoamine oxidase inhibitors (MAOIs; p. 172).

BETHANIDINE   DEBRISOQUINE

Bethanidine and **Debrisoquine**. A number of other postganglionic sympathetic blocking agents have been introduced. These include bethanidine (Esbatal) and debrisoquine (Declinax), which block sympathetic transmission at the postganglionic neurone without depleting the tissue stores of catecholamines. The advantage of bethanidine is that it acts for a shorter time than guanethidine, so that the oral dose may be increased more rapidly, thus ensuring earlier control of arterial pressure. Bethanidine is entirely excreted unchanged by the kidney and its plasma half-life is 7–11 hours. It seldom causes diarrhoea. The time of onset and duration of action of debrisoquine lie between those of bethanidine and guanethidine and it has been reported to produce fewer side-effects than the other drugs in this group. If possible, the arterial pressure should be recorded when the patient is standing. The initial dose of bethanidine is one 10 mg tablet three times daily after meals. Where necessary the dosage should be increased by half a tablet three times daily, at intervals. With debrisoquine the dose in mild to moderate hypertension is 10 mg once or twice daily. This can be increased by 10 mg at 3 day intervals. Tricyclic antidepressants antagonize the action of both these drugs. Both bethanidine and debrisoquine may produce postural hypotension, fluid retention, failure of ejaculation and depression. Patients receiving debrisoquine should avoid large quantities of cheese and other amine-containing foods, to avoid the 'cheese reaction'.

False neurotransmitters

METHYLDOPA

Methyldopa. In the postganglionic sympathetic nerve fibre methyldopa (Aldomet, Dopamet) forms the false transmitter α-methylnoradrenaline, which is then released by nerve stimulation, but it is not certain that it is a particularly weak transmitter. The major action of methyldopa is now thought to be on the α-receptors in the medulla oblongata which govern sympathetic outflow to the cardiovascular system. Methyldopa could, therefore, be classified with reserpine and clonidine as drugs acting primarily on the CNS. Methyldopa is a most useful antihypertensive agent and was for many years the drug of choice in moderate to severe hypertension. The effect after an oral dose occurs within 6 hours and the initial dose is usually 250 mg two or three times a day for 2 days. This can then be increased by 250 mg increments every 3 days to a maximum of 2 g/day. If this is not sufficient to control the hypertension, a thiazide diuretic may be added to the regimen. Clinically, the chief advantage of methyldopa is that it produces a fall in the supine blood pressure and much less postural hypotension. If given i.v. in the emergency treatment of hypertensive crises, an effective dose will produce a fall of arterial pressure that may begin in 4–6 hours and be maintained for 10–16 hours.

Adverse Effects
Side-effects include sedation, dizziness, lightheadedness, bradycardia, depression, gastrointestinal difficulties (including sore tongue, nausea, vomiting, flatus, constipation and diarrhoea), nasal stuffiness, impotence,

hepatocellular damage with jaundice (rarely) and agranulocytosis or thrombocytopenia (very occasionally). Haemolytic anaemia, which may be acute, can occur and it is claimed that the drug produces a positive direct Coombs' test in up to 20% of patients being treated. The positive Coombs' test is dose dependent and occurs within 6 months to 1 year from the start of treatment. It may persist from 3 to 17 months after withdrawal of the drug or may revert to normal more rapidly. Patients may require reduced doses of anaesthetics when on methyldopa. Methyldopa should not be used in patients with active liver disease or who are sensitive to the drug. It is contraindicated in phaeochromocytoma, since it produces 'denervation sensitivity' of adrenergic receptors.

Inhibitors of catecholamine synthesis

Postural hypotension has been noted to be a frequent side-effect of MAOIs and consequently these drugs have been studied in the treatment of hypertension. The mechanism of their hypotensive activity is unknown. Only one MAOI, pargyline, is at present used in the treatment of hypertension. The hypotension produced by this drug is mainly orthostatic. Many serious side-effects may occur, however, including the well-known marked sensitivity to foods containing tyramine and the drug is not widely used. It is marketed in the UK as Eutonyl.

Drugs Acting at the Sympathetic Receptors, Blocking Adrenergic Transmission

The response of effector organs to adrenaline, noradrenaline and related substances is blocked by adrenoceptor-blocking drugs. They act by competing with the α- or β-receptors. The actions of adrenaline, noradrenaline and isoprenaline differ according to their selectivity for α- or β-receptors. α affects that are of clinical interest are vasoconstriction in the skin and viscera, and dilatation of the pupil. Accordingly, α-blocking drugs are likely to have the opposite action. β effects include vasodilatation, bronchial relaxation, uterine relaxation and a complex effect on the heart that increases the rate, increases the force of contraction and increases conductivity. The cardiac output is also increased. A β-blocking drug should have the opposite effects. Reference has already been made to the general actions of both α- and β-adrenergic receptor blocking drugs (pp. 230–5). It must be stressed that the classification (p. 222) into α and β_1 and β_2 subgroups is only a general guide. In most cases a catecholamine will possess α, β_1 and β_2 activity to a greater or lesser degree, so large doses of α stimulants will usually exhibit some β stimulation also and vice versa.

α-adrenergic receptor blocking drugs

α-adrenergic receptor blocking drugs by definition prevent the responses that are mediated by the α-adrenergic receptors. When administered to the supine subject they cause little change in systemic blood pressure. However, a sharp fall occurs in any situation involving compensatory sympathetic vasoconstriction, such as hypovolaemia or a return from the supine to the erect position. Such drugs are not of value alone in the management of essential hypertension, though they may have some place in the treatment of peripheral vascular disease, since they increase blood flow in the skin rather than in muscle.

Phenoxybenzamine. Phenoxybenzamine (Dibenyline) is a long-acting α-adrenergic receptor blocking agent that has been used in Raynaud's disease and allied conditions with decreased blood flow in the peripheral vessels. It has been tried in chilblains and hyperhidrosis. It can aggravate symptoms of respiratory disorders, and adrenaline should not be given with it, since phenoxybenzamine causes hypotension, and stimulation of β-adrenergic receptors will further lower the arterial pressure. The drug is considered in more detail on p. 230.

Tolazoline and **Phentolamine**. Tolazoline (Priscol) and phentolamine (Rogitine) produce moderate α-adrenergic blockade, but the effect is relatively transient. Tolazoline is supplied in 25 mg tablets and the dose is 1–2 tablets four times daily. It is marketed for the treatment of peripheral vascular disease, but may activate peptic ulcers. Phentolamine is short-acting and its principal use is in the diagnosis of phaeochromocytoma, as indicated on p. 231.

Ergot alkaloids (p. 232). Ergot alkaloids are α-adrenergic blocking agents, but they are also powerful vasoconstrictors and this action predominates.

Labetalol. Recently the use of labetalol (Trandate), which has both α- and β-adrenergic receptor blocking activities, has been reported in the treatment of hypertension.

Labetalol lowers the arterial pressure primarily by blocking α-adrenergic receptors in peripheral arterioles and thus reducing peripheral resistance. At the same time, it blocks β-adrenergic (cardiac) receptors and prevents the reflex sympathetic cardiac compensation induced by peripheral vasodilatation. It is claimed that labetalol lowers both systolic and diastolic pressure without postural or exercise-induced hypotension. The half-life in plasma is about 4 hours.

The usual recommended dose of labetalol is 100 mg three times daily, increasing to 200 mg three or four times daily after 1 or 2 weeks. Side-effects include nasal stuffiness, vivid dreams and epigastric pain. Postural hypotension, though uncommon, occurs if the initial dose is too high or the dose is increased too rapidly. The drug should not be used in patients with bronchospasm or bronchial asthma.

An injectable form of the drug is available for the rapid control of raised arterial pressure in severely hypertensive patients.

β-adrenergic receptor blocking drugs

Stimulation of the β-adrenergic receptor produces dilatation of arteries and arterioles, increase in the rate and force of contraction of the heart, dilatation of bronchi, renin release and increased glycogenolysis and lipolysis. The sub-division of β effects into $β_1$ (cardiac effects) and $β_2$ (bronchodilatation and vasodilatation) arose as more selective blocking agents were found.

Drugs have been available to produce blockade of β-adrenergic receptors since 1958. The early ones were unsuitable for use in man and the first with practical clinical value was propranolol. Its use in the treatment of hypertension was reported in 1964.

In theory, β-adrenergic blocking drugs might be expected to depress the action of the heart, cause vasoconstriction and lead to bronchospasm.

Since the introduction of propranolol, many β-adrenergic inhibiting drugs have been marketed and as many as 25 such preparations are currently available in the UK. All β-adrenoceptor drugs share the common property of being competitive inhibitors. They have other associated properties, however, and may differ in (1) presence or absence of cardioselectivity, (2) membrane-stabilizing activity (i.e. local anaesthetic effect), and (3) partial agonist activity (i.e. intrinsic sympathomimetic activity, ISA). The associated properties have been used as a basis for classifying β-adrenoceptor blocking drugs into three major divisions.

Division I — Non-selective drugs:
> Group I possess both membrane activity and ISA (e.g. alprenolol, oxprenolol)
> Group II possess membrane activity only (e.g. propranolol).
> Group III possess ISA, but no membrane activity (e.g. sotalol, timolol).

Division II — Cardioselective drugs:
> Group I possess both membrane activity and ISA (e.g. acebutalol).
> Group III possess ISA, but not membrane activity (e.g. practolol).
> Group IV possess neither membrane activity nor ISA (e.g. atenolol, metoprolol).

Division III — β-blocking drugs with α-adrenoceptor blocking properties (e.g. labetalol).

All β-adrenergic receptor blocking drugs have a hypotensive effect, though there is controversy over their exact mode of action. A number of suggestions have been made, including an effect on the CNS, an adrenergic neurone blocking effect, an antirenin effect, an effect secondary to the reduced cardiac output and a mechanism consequent on resetting the baroreceptors. Observations in animals suggest a possible central mode of action for the hypotensive effect. As propranolol and other β-adrenergic receptor blocking drugs control the arterial pressure in man without producing postural hypotension, it seems unlikely that an adrenergic neurone blocking effect is important. β-adrenergic blockade in normal subjects and hypertensives lower plasma renin and it has been claimed that patients with high pretreatment plasma renins show the greatest hypotensive effect. There is, however, substantial evidence against accepting the prime role of renin in the hypotensive effect. The lowering of cardiac output in itself does not appear to be the reason either. There is some evidence that chronic administration of β-adrenergic blocking drugs causes the baroreceptors to generate their inhibitory impulses at a lower level of pressure and hence to lower the arterial pressure. It appears likely that β-adrenergic blocking drugs lower the arterial pressure by more than one mechanism.

β-adrenergic blocking drugs may also be used to treat certain cardiac dysrhythmias, angina pectoris, the tachycardia of mitral stenosis and that of thyrotoxicosis. In the treatment of hypertension these drugs are particularly effective when given with a diuretic and with hydralazine.

I. Non-selective β-adrenergic receptor blocking drugs.

PROPRANOLOL

Propranolol. It was with propranolol (Inderal) that the value of β-adrenergic receptor blockade in hypertension was established. Propranolol is available in 10, 40, 80 and 160 mg tablets. It has a short duration of action and the usual starting dose is 10–20 mg three or four times per day. The dosage is increased every 3 days (in in-patients) or every 2 weeks or so (in out-patients) by increments of about 25% per dose until the arterial pressure is controlled. Doses of 1 g/day are not uncommon and up to 4 g/day have been used. There is a great variation in the dosage of propranolol (and other β blockers) required in different individuals. This is largely the result of difference in absorption, which may vary over a twentyfold range. There is a significant 'first pass' metabolism as the drug is removed by the liver before it reaches the systemic circulation. Some 40–70% of orally administered drug may be removed in a single pass through the liver. The half-life of propranolol is $2\frac{1}{2}$ hours after i.v. administration, 3.3 hours after a single oral dose and $4\frac{1}{2}$ hours after the stopping of chronic oral administration. Plasma protein binding of propranolol varies between 90 and 95% in normal subjects. The half-life is prolonged in hepatic disease.

Although propranolol can be used alone to treat hypertension, it is often given with a diuretic or vasodilator.

Side-effects of propranolol include worsened asthma, heart failure, hypoglycaemia and CNS disturbances, including lethargy, poor concentration, a feeling of coldness, sleep disturbance and vivid nightmares.

It has been claimed that β-adrenergic blockers with partial agonist activity (ISA, p. 286) do not produce excessive bradycardia at rest and may be less likely to provoke bronchospasm or cold extremities.

Oxprenolol. Oxprenolol (Trasicor) is supplied in 40 mg tablets for angina and cardiac dysrhythmias and in 80 and 160 mg tablets for the control of hypertension. The initial dosage is 80 mg twice daily and most patients respond to 480 mg daily or less. Overdosage may lead to excessive bradycardia or hypotension, which can be treated with atropine (1–2 mg i.v.). Sustained-release tablets are available under the proprietary names Slow-Trasicor and Slow-Pren.

Timolol maleate. Timolol maleate (Blocadren, Betim) is promoted for the treatment of angina and hypertension. It is available in 10 mg tablets and the normal dose in hypertension is 30 mg.

Sotalol. Sotalol (Beta-Cardone, Sotacor) is very similar to timolol. It is available in 40, 80 and 200 mg tablets and the usual daily dose in hypertension is 200–600 mg.

Pindolol. Pindolol (Visken) is promoted for the same two purposes and is supplied in 5 and 15 mg tablets. In hypertension the usual daily dose is up to 45 mg.

II. Cardioselective β-adrenergic receptor blocking drugs.

Acebutalol. Acebutalol (Sectral) is available in 100 and 200 mg capsules and in a solution of 5 mg/ml for i.v. injection. It is used in the treatment of angina, hypertension and certain cardiac dysrhythmias. In hypertension the initial dose is 200 mg twice daily and this may be increased to 600 mg twice daily if required. The degree of cardioselectivity of this agent has been disputed recently.

Practolol. Practolol (Eraldin) was not used to treat hypertension, but was employed to treat angina and cardiac dysrhythmias. It was the first of the β-blocking drugs acknowledged to be cardioselective, but has been shown to cause serious adverse reactions in the eye and skin and a sclerosing peritonitis (p. 574). It is not now available for oral administration, but a preparation for i.v. use is available to hospitals.

Atenolol. Atenolol (Tenormin) is promoted for the management of essential hypertension and hypertension of renal origin. It is as cardioselective as practolol in doses producing more cardiac β-blockade. It crosses the blood–brain barrier only to a negligible degree and is less likely to produce side-effects in the CNS. Its longer plasma half-life means it need be given only once or, at most, twice daily. It is available in 100 mg tablets and it is usual to start with a dose of 100 mg daily given in single or divided doses. This may be increased to 200 mg daily after 1 or 2 weeks, if necessary.

Metoprolol. Metoprolol (Betaloc, Lopresor) is also as cardioselective as practolol in equivalent hypotensive dosage. It is available in 50 and 100 mg tablets and the total daily dose in hypertension is 100–400 mg, in either a single or a twice-daily dose. A sustained-release preparation is available.

III. Choice of a β-adrenergic blocking drug. In the face of such a multitude of largely similar drugs, the clinician has considerable difficulty in deciding which preparation to use.

Most adverse effects of β-blocking drugs can be predicted from a knowledge of the functions of the sympathetic nervous system. Some risk of precipitating asthma is inherent in the use of all β-blockers. Patients with a recent history of bronchospasm should not receive drugs that are not cardioselective, but those that are, such as acebutalol, atenolol and metoprolol, may be tried with caution and are less likely to produce bronchospasm.

Cardiac failure may result from the fall in cardiac output produced by β-blocking drugs and the reported incidence of this varies from 1 in 20 to 1 in 300. It is claimed to be less likely to occur with drugs with intrinsic sympathomimetic action (ISA), such as oxprenolol, pindolol and acebutalol. Various psychiatric symptoms may occur with any of the β-blockers, but are less likely with atenolol, which does not cross the blood–brain barrier to any extent. These include strange dreams, hallucinations, insomnia and depression. Various gastrointestinal side-effects, especially nausea, abdominal discomfort and diarrhoea, occur, and an increase in weight has been reported. The unexpected adverse reactions that have occurred with practolol are referred to on p. 574.

There may be some advantage in β-blockers with longer half-lives, since these drugs can be given once or twice daily rather than more frequently, and there is some evidence that patient-compliance increases when dosage frequency is reduced. Examples of drugs that possess this advantage are pindolol, atenolol, metoprolol and perhaps oxprenolol. The presence or absence of membrane-stabilizing effect is probably clinically irrelevant.

Compound preparations. As β-blocking drugs are frequently given with diuretic agents in the management of hypertension, it is not surprising that many preparations combining two such drugs are available. While the administration of fixed-dose drug combinations is to be deplored in hospital usage, they may be of value in general practice, particularly in the elderly where drug compliance can be a problem. Such compound preparations include:

Co-Betaloc	metoprolol 100 mg; hydrochlorothiazide 12.5 mg
Inderetic	propranolol 80 mg; bendrofluazide 2.5 mg
Inderex	propranolol 160 mg; bendrofluazide 5 mg
Lasipressin	*penbutolol 40 mg; frusemide 20 mg
Lopresoretic	metoprolol 100 mg; chlorthalidone 12.5 mg
Moducren	timolol 10 mg; amiloride 2.5 mg; hydrochlorothiazide 25 mg
Prestim	timolol 10 mg; bendrofluazide 2.5 mg
Secadrex	acebutolol 200 mg; hydrochlorothiazide 12.5 mg
Sotazide	sotalol 160 mg; hydrochlorothiazide 25 mg
Tenoret 50	atenolol 50 mg; chlorthalidone 12.5 mg
Tenoretic	atenolol 100 mg; chlorthalidone 25 mg
Tolerzide	sotalol 80 mg; hydrochlorothiazide 12.5 mg
Trasiderex	oxprenolol 160 mg; cyclopenthiazide 0.25 mg
Viskaldix	pindolol 10 mg; clopamide 5 mg

Drugs Affecting the Vessel Wall

Diazoxide

Diazoxide (Eudemine) is a benzothiadiazine derivative, but, unlike the thiazide diuretics, causes salt and water retention. It has only mild hypotensive activity when given orally, but when administered i.v. (300 mg in 10–15 seconds), it produces a marked hypotensive effect by a powerful direct effect on the vascular smooth muscle. This may be mediated by competitive antagonism of calcium. The effect is maximal within about 5 minutes and the duration of activity is from 2 to 5 hours. The drug must be given by the i.v. route and extravasation causes pain. The homeostatic mechanisms of the sympathetic nervous systems remain intact, so there is little or no postural hypotension and cerebral blood flow is not reduced. Diazoxide is a standard therapy in the management of hypertensive crises. Some adult patients will become dangerously hypotensive following a 300 mg 'bolus' of diazoxide. It is safer to give 75 mg i.v. and then 150 mg at 5 minute intervals until control is achieved. It is not suitable for long-term use, since it causes sodium retention and also hyperglycaemia. This last is by inhibition of the release of stored insulin from the β-cells of the islets of the pancreas.

Hydralazine

Hydralazine (1-hydrazinophthalazine; Apresoline) has been used in the treatment of hypertension for more than 30 years. It was not popular in the UK because of its side-effects, but recently it has been found that the drug is particularly effective when combined with other hypotensive agents, particularly β-blockers.

---

*A recently introduced non-selective β-receptor antagonist that is said to have a long-lasting hypotensive effect. This combination is marketed for the treatment of mild to moderate hypertension.

Mode of Action

Hydralazine exerts its action by reducing vascular resistance through direct relaxation of arteriolar smooth muscle. This vasodilatation is not uniform, since vascular resistance in the coronary, cerebral, splanchnic and renal circulations decreases more than in skin and muscle. Hydralazine affects postcapillary capacitance vessels much less than precapillary resistance vessels, producing a rise in cardiac output and a drop in left-sided filling pressure.

Pharmacokinetics

Hydralazine is rapidly and fairly completely absorbed after oral administration. Peak serum concentrations are reached within 1 or 2 hours after an oral dose. The drug is metabolized in the gut wall and there is considerable first-pass effect. It is acetylated in the liver, but slow and fast acetylators exist. About 85% of circulating hydralazine is bound to serum albumin. The plasma elimination half-life is 2–4 hours, but the antihypertensive action persists much longer, perhaps because the drug appears to have a special affinity for the walls of muscular arteries.

Indications

Hydralazine may be given by the i.v. route for the control of severe malignant hypertension. Up to 20 mg may be given by slow i.v. injection until the pressure is controlled.

Hydralazine should not be given by itself in antihypertensive therapy. It should be added to therapy with a β-blocker or diuretic when arterial pressure control is unsatisfactory. The usual dose is 25 mg three times daily and the total daily dose should not exceed 200 mg.

Adverse Effects

Toxicity. Some of the toxic effects of hydralazine are related to its therapeutic action — for example, flushing, nasal congestion, headaches and palpitations. The increases in heart rate and cardiac output augment cardiac work and oxygen consumption, but these problems are minimized if β-blockers are given simultaneously. Chronic administration of hydralazine may be associated with a disseminated lupus erythematosus-like syndrome with circulating antinuclear antibodies. This syndrome is uncommon when the daily dose is below 200 mg. When the syndrome appears (or the antinuclear factor becomes positive), the drug should be withdrawn. The syndrome is almost always entirely reversible.

In chronic left ventricular failure oral hydralazine (50–75 mg six-hourly) is effective for at least 4–6 weeks when added to digoxin and diuretics. There may be longer-term benefit.

Minoxidil

Minoxidil (Loniten) is a newer vasodilator which is likely to be effective in patients whose arterial pressure cannot be controlled on any other oral regimen. It appears to have the same mechanism of action as hydralazine, but is more potent.

Pharmacokinetics
Minoxidil is rapidly absorbed following oral administration and peak plasma concentration is achieved in 1 hour. The plasma half-life is 4 hours, but pharmacological activity decays much more slowly. About 10% of an administered dose is excreted unchanged in the urine, while 85% is excreted as various metabolites.

Indications
Minoxidil is used in the management of severe refractory hypertension and requires concomitant therapy with diuretics to avoid fluid retention and β-blocking drugs to reduce tachycardia. Other antihypertensives should be withdrawn gradually before it is used. The initial adult dose is 5 mg daily in single or divided doses given by mouth. The usual maximum is 50 mg daily.

Adverse Effects

Toxicity. Like hydralazine, minoxidil produces sodium retention and reflex heart stimulation. Minoxidil also stimulates as a reflex the release of renin. The major adverse effect is increased hair growth. Its use is contraindicated in phaeochromocytoma.

Oral diuretics

Chlorothiazide and the other benzothiadiazines have an antihypertensive effect by themselves, but they also enhance the activity of other hypotensive agents. This effect was first thought to be due to sodium and water loss, with a fall in plasma volume and cardiac output. The antihypertensive activity of these drugs persists, however, even when the plasma volume and electrolyte loss are corrected. It has been suggested that these diuretic agents may lower arterial pressure by a direct effect on the smooth muscle of the arteriolar wall. Chlorothiazide, hydrochlorothiazide, bendrofluazide and chlorthalidone are the most useful diuretics in the management of high blood pressure. They are usually used initially in the management of mild to moderate hypertension, but the most beneficial effect is obtained when they are combined with other hypotensive agents. Toxic effects and side-effects are those usually seen with the long-term use of diuretics (p. 356) and include potassium depletion and hypochloraemic alkalosis.

Sodium nitroprusside

Sodium nitroprusside (Nipride) is available for i.v. use in hypertensive emergencies. It is infused by microdrip (0.5–1.5 μg/kg/minute at first) and produces an immediate fall in arterial pressure. This agent is non-specific and causes venous as well as arteriolar dilatation, thus reducing preload as well as afterload. Nitroprusside is metabolized to thiocyanate and hence thiocyanate toxicity may ensue. If a marked reduction of arterial pressure is not obtained with the maximum recommended dose of 800 μg/minute, administration of the drug should cease.

The drug is difficult to use and, rightly, is not popular. If used at all, it should only be until the patient can safely be treated with other oral antihypertensive agents.

Nitroprusside has also been used in refractory cardiac failure, where it may produce a rise in cardiac output.

Prazosin hydrochloride

Prazosin hydrochloride (Hypovase) is available for the treatment of hypertension. It is believed to inhibit the intracellular enzyme phosphodiesterase. This results in an increased level of cyclic AMP which causes relaxation of arteriolar smooth muscle. Prazosin may also have some α-adrenoceptor blocking activity. Levels of cyclic guanosine monophosphate (GMP) in cardiac muscle are elevated and this prevents any reflex increase in heart rate that might arise from the fall in arterial pressure. The drug can cause transient collapse, though this may be avoided if it is introduced at a low dosage, 0.5 mg being given three times daily for at least 7 days before increasing this to 1 mg three times daily. The maximum recommended dosage is 20 mg in divided doses. Fluid and sodium retention may necessitate the addition of diuretics.

Drugs inhibiting the Renin-angiotensin System

Captopril

Captopril (Capoten) is an orally active inhibitor of the angiotensin-converting enzyme. It is a carboxypeptidase (D-2-methyl-3-mercaptopropanoyl-L-proline).

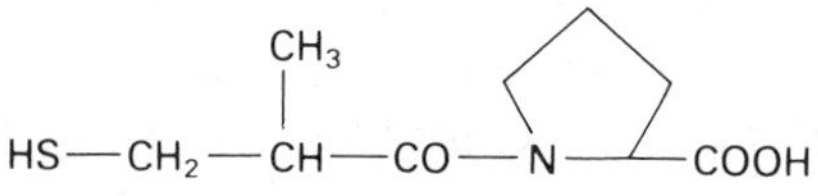

CAPTOPRIL

Mode of Action

Captopril is a potent competitive inhibitor of angiotensin-converting enzyme. The decrease in effective levels of angiotensin II resulting from inhibition of the conversion of angiotensin I is primarily responsible for the antihypertensive action. (The physiological effects of angiotensin II include direct pressor activity and stimulation of aldosterone secretion.) Because angiotensin I-converting enzyme can also degrade bradykinin, it is possible that captopril administration might lead to the accumulation of bradykinin in blood and tissues. There are, therefore, at least two possible antihypertensive mechanisms.

Captopril administration has been shown to cause a sustained fall in plasma angiotensin II with an increase in plasma angiotensin I. Concomitant fall in plasma aldosterone and rise in plasma renin have also been described.

Pharmacokinetics

Captopril is rapidly absorbed after oral administration and peak plasma concentration is reached in 1 hour. Over 75% of an administered dose is absorbed, although the presence of food in the gastrointestinal tract may reduce this significantly. About 25–30% of circulating drug is bound to plasma proteins. The plasma half-life is approximately 4 hours, but this is prolonged in patients with impaired renal function.

Indications

The exact place of captopril in the treatment of hypertension is not yet established. At present its use is indicated in severe hypertension where standard therapy has failed. Captopril has been shown to be of value when given with digitalis and diuretics in severe treatment-refractory congestive cardiac failure.

Dosage and Administration

The usual dosage range of captopril is 25–150 mg three times daily, 450 mg being the maximum recommended daily dose. The initial daily dose is 25 mg three times daily, which should be doubled if a satisfactory response has not been achieved in two weeks. There is a greater tendency to a first-dose hypotensive effect in diuretic pre-treated (i.e. salt and volume depleted) patients. I.v. normal saline infusion may be required to correct this hypotension.

Captopril should be taken one hour before meals. The dose should be reduced in renal insufficiency.

Adverse Effects

Toxicity. Cutaneous reactions occur in 10% of patients given captopril. The rashes are morbilliform or maculopapular, may be associated with fever and usually clear on withdrawal or reduction of the dose. About 6% of patients treated have diminution or loss of taste perception. Proteinuria occurs occasionally and nephrotic syndrome and renal failure have very rarely been attributed to the drug. Serious hyperkalaemia has not been reported, though, in theory, it could occur. Neutropenia and agranulocytosis have occurred, especially in patients with renal failure.

Saralasin

Saralasin is an interesting new compound which acts as a competitive inhibitor with angiotensin II. It is a synthetic eight-chained polypeptide that demonstrates an affinity for angiotensin II receptors of vascular smooth muscle. It has an antihypertensive effect in patients with excessive circulating angiotensin II (i.e. renal artery disease, malignant hypertension). The drug must be given by i.v. infusion and may be of value as a diagnostic agent or for the emergency treatment of patients with angiotensin-II-dependent hypertension.

MANAGEMENT OF HYPERTENSION

There is no clear-cut division between normal arterial pressure and one that would be regarded as being elevated. Statistics from life assurance companies show that even a mild elevation in diastolic pressure is associated with a significant reduction in life expectancy. A number of studies have shown that if the arterial pressure is controlled, then many of the complications of hypertension could be avoided. So many different forms of treatment are now available that confusion might result and the student and practitioner are advised to become familiar with the properties and use of a few drugs. As the vast majority of people suffering from hypertension have no symptoms of their disease, it is reasonable to suggest that drugs used to control hypertension should produce no symptoms and thus have a high patient acceptability. The drugs least likely to cause unacceptable side-effects at the present time are the thiazide diuretics in mild hypertension and β-blocking drugs in more severe hypertension. These two groups of drugs are also effective when used in combined therapy.

DRUGS USED TO TREAT CARDIAC DYSRHYTHMIAS

Treatment of dysrhythmias by drugs should, ideally, be based on an understanding of the electrophysiological basis for the abnormality and the mechanism of action of the drug used. Unfortunately, in most instances these two criteria cannot be satisfied. The electrophysiological background of the normal cardiac impulse and of cardiac dysrhythmias is extremely complex and while many actions of the various drugs used are known, the basis for their therapeutic efficacy in any particular instance is frequently not understood.

CLASSIFICATION OF ANTIDYSRHYTHMIC DRUGS

Antidysrhythmic drugs can be divided into four main groups on the basis of their electrophysiological properties.

Class I Agents slow the phase of rapid ventricular depolarization and reduce the magnitude of the overshoot. Most of these drugs have local anaesthetic properties. Class I is further divided into Group A, consisting of quinidine, procainamide, disopyramide, lorcainide and encainide, which increase the duration of the action potential; Group B, consisting, at present of lignocaine, tocainide, mexiletine and phenytoin which decrease the duration of the action potential; and Group C, aprindine.

Class II Agents are β-adrenergic blocking drugs.

Class III Agents prolong the duration of the action potential and, therefore, the period when a cardiac muscle fibre is effectively refractory to re-excitation. Bretylium and amiodarone are in this group.

Class IV Agents, of which the only example is verapamil, interfere with the inward movement of calcium ions during depolarization and repolarization.

Class I Agents

Quinidine

Quinidine, an optical isomer of quinine, was first prepared and given its present name by Pasteur in 1853. In 1914 Wenckebach reported the effect of quinine alkaloids in certain cardiac dysrhythmias.

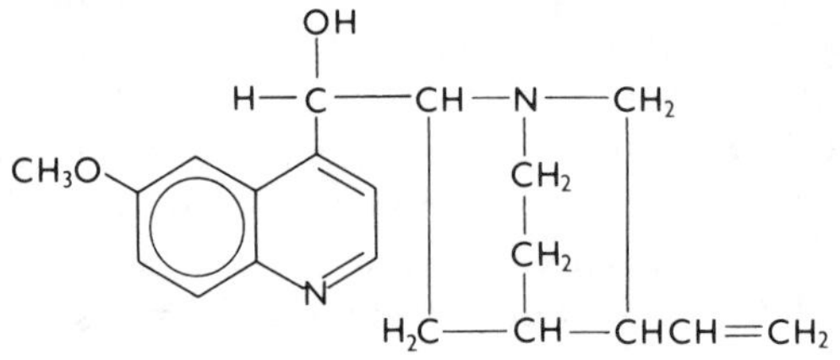

QUININE

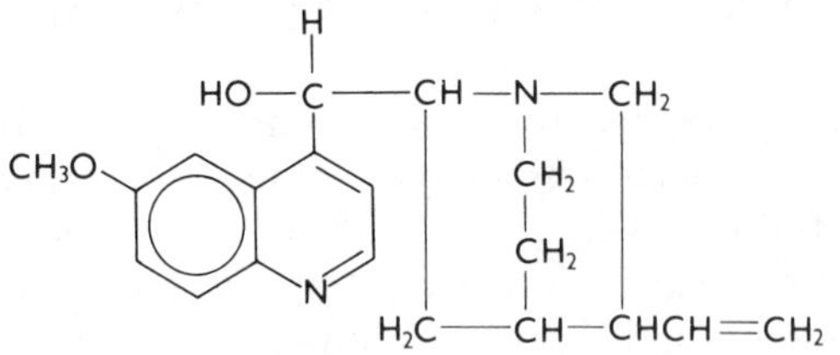

QUINIDINE

Actions

Quinidine has some antimalarial, antipyretic and oxytocic actions, although no clinical use is made of these. It depresses myocardial excitability, conduction velocity and contractility, and may depress or abolish ectopic impulse generation in the myocardium, probably by raising the threshold to electrical stimuli. It also prolongs the effective refractory period of heart muscle, partly by a direct effect and partly by a vagal blocking action. Because of the latter action, quinidine shortens the refractory period of the atrioventricular (AV) node. The most marked effects of quinidine seen electrocardiographically are prolongation of the QRS complex due to a reduction of conduction velocity and an increase in the QT interval due to an extension of the duration of the action potential. The effect on sinus rate and PR interval depends on the interaction of the direct depressant effects and the indirect vagal blocking action of the drug.

Pharmacokinetics

Quinidine is almost completely absorbed from the gastrointestinal tract. Peak plasma levels and maximum therapeutic effects occur within 1–3 hours after a single oral dose and persist for 6–8 hours. Peak plasma concentrations occur a little earlier following i.m. injection, being found after 30–90 minutes. Quinidine is only very rarely given by the i.v. route because of the likelihood of the occurrence of severe hypotension. The drug is extensively bound to plasma albumin; when the total plasma concentration is in the therapeutic range of 3–6 mg/l, approximately 60–80% is bound. Quinidine is primarily metabolized by the liver and has a plasma half-life of 2–3 hours.

Indications

The major clinical uses of quinidine are in the treatment of atrial fibrillation, atrial flutter and paroxysmal supraventricular tachycardia. Quinidine may convert atrial fibrillation to normal sinus rhythm, but attempts to do this should be carried out only in hospital under close supervision. The ventricular rate should be controlled by digitalis therapy prior to quinidine administration. The usual dose of quinidine is 0.2–0.3 g orally every 3–4 hours for 1–3 days.

Adverse Effects

Toxicity. Quinidine is a dangerous drug because of its effects on the heart and deaths have been reported from its use. However, the most common toxic manifestations are diarrhoea, nausea and vomiting. Cinchonism occurs in a dose-related manner and consists of tinnitus, headache and blurring of vision. An idiosyncratic response to quinidine may occur and even small doses may cause tinnitus, vertigo, visual disturbances, headache, confusion, angioneurotic oedema or skin rashes. Thrombocytopenic purpura rarely occurs, and there may be a cross-reaction with quinine. Asthma, depression of respiration and a fall in arterial pressure may be produced. Plasma concentrations of quinidine in excess of 8 mg/l may result in sinoatrial or atrioventricular conduction block. Moreover, ventricular ectopic beats leading to ventricular tachycardia or fibrillation may occur.

Because of the serious side-effects of the drug and the introduction of more effective antidysrhythmic agents, quinidine is now seldom used. DC electrical cardioversion has replaced quinidine in the conversion of atrial fibrillation in most instances.

Procainamide

PROCAINE   PROCAINAMIDE

Procainamide (Pronestyl) differs from procaine merely in the replacement of the ester linkage in the molecule by an amide linkage. The main result of this change is that the drug has greater stability in the body and fewer effects on the CNS. Both drugs have an action on the heart, but procaine itself is not used for this purpose.

Actions
The cardiac actions of procainamide are identical with those of quinidine. Procainamide therefore diminishes excitability, decreases conduction velocity, and prolongs the refractory period to a greater extent in the atrium than in the ventricle. Although, almost by tradition, procainamide is used for ventricular tachycardia and dysrhythmias and quinidine for atrial dysrhythmias, the effectiveness of the two drugs appears to be comparable in either situation.

Pharmacokinetics
Procainamide is rapidly and almost completely absorbed from the gastrointestinal tract. Following oral administration, maximum plasma concentration is achieved in approximately 60 minutes. The drug is slowly hydrolysed by plasma esterases, unlike procaine, which is rapidly hydrolysed. At therapeutic concentrations in the plasma only 15% of procainamide is protein bound. After i.m. injection, peak plasma concentration is reached in 15–60 minutes; the drug may also be given i.v. Nearly 90% of procainamide and its metabolites is excreted in the urine, some 50–60% being excreted unchanged. The plasma half-life of procainamide is 2–3 hours, but this decline is more prolonged if there is renal damage or severe cardiac failure. If renal function is severely impaired, cumulation may occur.

Indications

In general, the usefulness of procainamide parallels that of quinidine and procainamide may be effective in patients who have failed to respond to maximal doses of the former drug. The most favourable results have been reported in ventricular dysrhythmias, except those resulting from digitalis toxicity. Ventricular ectopic beats and paroxysmal tachycardia can be abolished in a large percentage of cases. Larger doses of procainamide may be effective in supraventricular, atrial or nodal dysrhythmias, although the percentage of failures is high. One disadvantage is that because of its short half-life the drug must be given every 4 hours.

Dosage and Administration

Procainamide should be given orally whenever feasible. The i.v. route should be reserved for cases of severe dysrhythmias that are failing to respond to oral or i.m. medication and which are life-threatening. The initial oral dose is 0.5–1 g every 4 hours. Occasionally smaller doses suffice, or larger ones may be required. If used in conjunction with electrical defibrillation, 250–500 mg every 4 hours is likely to prevent recurrences. The i.m. dose is 100–250 mg every 4–6 hours, the usual effective plasma level being 0.4–0.8 mg per 100 ml. For i.v. use 25–50 mg may be given every minute, up to a total of 1 g under ECG control.

Adverse Effects

Toxicity. The effects on the heart are similar to those of quinidine. In atrial fibrillation or flutter the ventricular rate may suddenly increase when the atrial rate is slowed by procainamide or quinidine. Procainamide should not be administered when complete atrioventricular block is present and it should be used only with caution in the presence of partial block. The most frequent side-effects of procainamide are hypotension, anorexia, nausea, vomiting, flushing, diarrhoea, weakness, depression, and confusion or hallucinations. Agranulocytosis has been described. Hypersensitivity to procainamide may occur with chills, fever, joint and muscle pain, angioneurotic oedema and urticaria. Of special interest is the syndrome resembling systemic lupus erythematosus (SLE) which has been reported to occur in almost one-third of patients on prolonged therapy with a dose of more than 2 g/day. This is most likely to occur in slow acetylators. The arthralgia, fever and pruritus of SLE occur, but renal and cerebral involvement have not been observed.

Disopyramide

Disopyramide (Dirythmin, Rythmodan) is an antidysrhythmic drug similar in action to quinidine. It may be given i.v. or orally for supraventricular or ventricular dysrhythmias. It ceased to be marketed in the UK under the proprietary name Norpace in January 1983, but is still available as indicated.

Pharmacokinetics
Disopyramide has 80–90% bioavailability when given orally. About 50–60% of an administered dose is excreted unchanged in the urine. The major metabolite is *N*-deisopropyldisopyramide, which accounts for a further 25% of excretion of the drug in the urine. Therapeutic plasma concentration is 2–7 μg/ml and the plasma half-life is 3.8–4.5 hours.

Indications
Disopyramide is as effective as quinidine in reducing ventricular ectopic activity and ventricular tachycardia. It is effective in preventing recurrent supraventricular tachycardia in about 50% of cases. The claim that disopyramide, given prophylactically after myocardial infarction, may improve long-term mortality rates requires substantiation.

The i.v. dose is up to 150 mg (2 mg/kg body weight) by injection over 5–10 minutes. For oral use a loading dose of 300 mg is given, followed by 100–150 mg every 6 hours. The dose must be reduced in renal insufficiency.

Adverse Effects

Toxicity. The most common side-effects result from the drug's anti-cholinergic activity. Accordingly, there may be dry mouth, urinary retention, obscured vision and constipation. Other side-effects include nausea, vomiting and skin rashes. Disopyramide should not be given in second- or third-degree AV block, in cardiogenic shock or with sick sinus syndrome. Caution is advised in glaucoma, prostatic hypertrophy, uncompensated heart failure or renal failure. The drug should not be given with other Class I antidysrhythmics or with β-blocking agents or anticholinergics. Occasionally disopyramide can precipitate ventricular fibrillation or profound hypotension.

Lignocaine (lidocaine, USP)

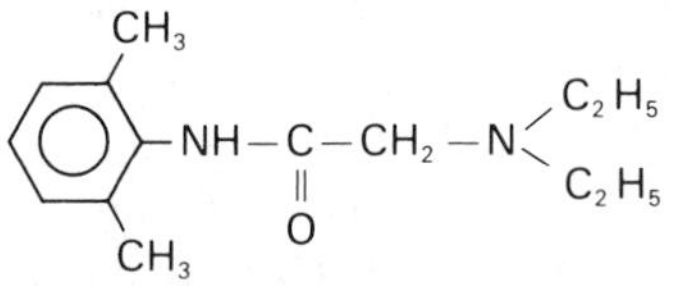

LIGNOCAINE

Lignocaine (Xylocard) is a local anaesthetic which has achieved prominence in recent years for the treatment of cardiac dysrhythmias. It is of particular value in the treatment of ventricular tachycardia and abnormalities of rhythm occurring after myocardial infarction or during cardiac surgery. Lignocaine differs from quinidine and procainamide in its mode of action and in that it decreases the duration of the action potential. Lignocaine usually has no effect on or, indeed, may enhance conduction velocity, and it increases membrane responsiveness. It is said to cause less depression of arterial pressure and of myocardial contractility than does procainamide in equivalent doses.

Pharmacokinetics

Lignocaine is given for this purpose only by the parenteral route and almost always i.v., although adequate blood levels can be achieved by i.m. administration. It is bound to plasma proteins only to a minor extent. The drug is rapidly metabolized in the liver and the plasma half-life following a single injection is of the order of 15 minutes. Lignocaine is therefore usually given by an initial i.v. 'bolus' injection, followed by constant i.v. infusion. With i.v. administration the action develops rapidly and declines quickly when infusion is discontinued.

Indications

Lignocaine is of particular use in the emergency treatment of ventricular tachyarrhythmias, including the development of such complications in patients with suspected or proven myocardial infarcts. An initial loading dose of 100 mg is usually given i.v. over 2 minutes and an i.v. infusion of 500–750 mg per 12 hours commenced. It is possible to relate the ventricular ectopic activity to the rate of lignocaine infusion. The usual therapeutic range of plasma concentrations of lignocaine is 2–5 μg/ml of plasma. Lignocaine is available commercially in the UK in preloaded syringes containing either 20 or 200 mg/ml and also in a solution of 100 mg/ml.

Lignocaine may also be of value in the prophylaxis of ventricular dysrhythmias following myocardial infarction, given by either the i.m. or the i.v. route.

Adverse Effects

Toxicity. Lignocaine is relatively free from cardiac toxicity, but bradycardia or a fall in arterial pressure can occur. The plasma half-life may be prolonged in patients with hepatic disease or in congestive cardiac failure. Toxicity is usually manifested as neurological disturbances, particularly drowsiness, paraesthesia, muscle twitching, disorientation and convulsions. Lignocaine should not be used in third-degree atrioventricular block, other serious conduction disturbances or bradycardia. Naturally, it must be avoided in those known to be hypersensitive to anaesthetics of the amide type.

Tocainide

Tocainide (Tonocard) is a lignocaine analogue effective by the oral or i.v. route. It has been reported to be effective against potentially lethal dysrhythmias.

Pharmacokinetics
Following oral administration, tocainide is almost totally absorbed and peak plasma concentrations are achieved within 30–90 minutes. No significant first pass elimination occurs. At therapeutic plasma concentrations (18–45 μmol/l) about 50% of the drug is bound to plasma proteins. About 40% of an administered dose is excreted unchanged in the urine, the remainder being eliminated by hepatic metabolism. The plasma half-life is approximately 15 hours.

Indications
Tocainide is effective against the same dysrhythmias as lignocaine, its advantages being its long half-life and its use by the oral route.

   In acute situations, tocainide is given by slow i.v. injection, 500–750 mg over 15–30 minutes, followed immediately by 600–800 mg orally. For maintenance treatment, 1.2 g is given orally in divided doses each day. The dosage must be reduced in moderate to severe renal failure.

Adverse Effects

Toxicity. Unwanted effects of tocainide include nausea, lightheadedness, bradycardia and hypotension. A few cases of hepatotoxicity have been reported.

Mexiletine

Mexiletine (Mexitil) is 1-2,6-dimethylphenoxy-2-aminopropane and its formula has a similarity to that of lignocaine. It may be administered orally or i.v.

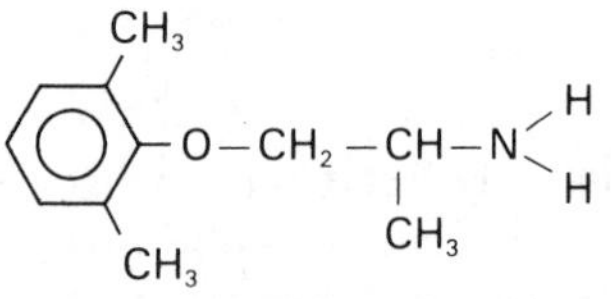

MEXILETINE

Pharmacokinetics
Mexiletine is almost completely absorbed following oral administration and peak plasma concentrations occur within 2–4 hours. The plasma half-life of mexiletine in healthy volunteers is 10 hours and in patients following myocardial infarction is 12–16 hours. After i.v. injection, plasma mexiletine levels fall rapidly and the drug is given by infusion.

Indications
Mexiletine given i.v. is effective in the treatment of ventricular dysrhythmias, ventricular fibrillation, tachycardia and early and multifocal ventricular

ectopic beats following myocardial infarction, cardiac surgery, and digitalis poisoning. The dosage regimen used is complex, the drug is difficult to use and, ideally, plasma concentrations should be monitored. Mexiletine is therefore a second-line drug for i.v. use.

Orally, mexiletine is the drug of choice for ventricular dysrhythmias. It is at least as effective as procainamide, has fewer side-effects and need be given only 8-hourly, the daily dose being 600–750 mg.

Adverse Effects

Toxicity. Mexiletine has similar toxic effects to lignocaine and there is an overlap between effective plasma concentrations (0.5–2 μg/ml) and toxic concentrations (0.8–4 μg/ml). Non-cardiac toxic symptoms include nausea, vomiting, dysarthria, confusion, tremor and paraesthesiae. Cardiac toxicity results in hypotension, sinus bradycardia and transient sinus arrest.

Phenytoin

Phenytoin (p. 248) is structurally related to the barbiturates and is used in the treatment of epilepsy. It has an action on the heart and seems to act on the cell membrane of the myocardial fibres to enhance sodium influx during depolarization and potassium efflux during repolarization. It depresses pacemaker activity in Purkinje tissue, but neither depresses the excitability nor prolongs the refractory period of atrial or ventricular muscle. Phenytoin often enhances atrioventricular conduction and occasionally increases intraventricular conduction.

The pharmacology of phenytoin is considered on p. 249.

Indications

Phenytoin has been used in a wide variety of cardiac dysrhythmias. It is of little value in atrial flutter or fibrillation, but has been employed successfully in the treatment of paroxysmal atrial tachycardia, particularly if associated with digitalis intoxication. Phenytoin depresses the enhanced ventricular automaticity produced by digitalis without adversely affecting intraventricular conduction, and it tends also to reverse the prolongation of atrioventricular conduction induced by digitalis. The plasma levels of phenytoin required to abolish ventricular dysrhythmias are in the range of 10–18 mg/l. The drug is usually administered i.v., 50–100 mg being injected every 5 minutes until a therapeutic response occurs or a maximum of 10–15 mg/kg body weight has been administered. Phenytoin toxicity is uncommon when the drug is given in small incremental doses. When large i.v. doses are given, phenytoin may, paradoxically, produce atrioventricular block, bradycardia or even cardiac arrest.

Class II Agents

β-adrenoceptor blocking drugs

The β-adrenoceptor blocking drugs have already been considered and only their influence on cardiac dysrhythmias will be mentioned here. Propranolol has such activity as a result of inhibition of adrenergic stimulation of the heart and also a direct membrane-stabilizing action on the myocardium, comparable to a local anaesthetic effect. Thus, in the presence of significant adrenergic activity, propranolol reduces the heart rate, prolongs atrioventricular conduction time and reduces contractility. It also acts at the cell membrane to decrease diastolic sodium influx during the spike action potential and increases potassium efflux from the cell during repolarization. The combined effect results in decreased automaticity and conduction velocity, while refractoriness is increased. Practolol (p. 288) does not have a membrane-stabilizing action but is effective.

Indications
Propranolol has been used to control the ventricular rate in supraventricular tachycardia. This action is probably due to prolongation of the atrioventricular nodal refractory period — i.e. an anti-adrenergic action. Propranolol, like phenytoin, is particularly effective in the treatment of digitalis-induced dysrhythmias, both supraventricular and ventricular. It has been particularly successful in converting paroxysmal atrial tachycardia to normal sinus rhythm and is effective in suppressing atrial tachycardia associated with the Wolff–Parkinson–White syndrome. Propranolol may also be useful in controlling the ventricular rate in patients with atrial fibrillation and flutter, where control has not been gained by the use of digitalis alone. It can abolish exercise-induced tachycardia and also reduces the sinus tachycardia due to hyperthyroidism and anxiety states.

Propranolol, oxprenolol and sotalol can all be given by mouth or by i.v. injection. In an emergency 1 mg of practolol may be given i.v. over 1 minute. The dose may be repeated after 2 minutes. The maximum total dose is 10 mg in conscious patients and 5 mg in those under anaesthesia. Atropine should first be given i.v. in a dose of 1–2 mg. The dangers of practolol are referred to on p. 574.

Class III Agents

Bretylium

Bretylium tosylate (Bretylate) is effective against ventricular dysrhythmias refractory to treatment with lignocaine and electrical defibrillation. Bretylium has Class III activity in Purkinje fibres, but less in ventricular muscle.

Pharmacokinetics

Bretylium is poorly absorbed when given orally. After i.v. injection, it is eliminated by excretion of unchanged drug in the urine. However, the drug should not be given i.v. because of nausea and vomiting. The plasma half-life is $7\frac{1}{2}$ hours. Therapeutic plasma levels are 0.5–1 μg/ml.

Indications

Bretylium may be of value in the treatment of patients with ventricular dysrhythmias resistant to conventional therapy. There may be a delay of 20 minutes to 2 hours in the development of antidysrhythmic activity after administration. The initial dose is 5–10 mg/kg body weight i.m. and this may be followed by 5 mg/kg body weight i.m. every 8–12 hours for 48 hours.

Adverse Effects

Toxicity. Hypotension is common as a result of adrenergic neurone blockade. Patients should remain recumbent during treatment. Nausea and vomiting occur occasionally.

Amiodarone

Amiodarone (Cordarone X) was initially introduced as an antianginal drug. It is effective against many dysrhythmias, has a wide safety margin and can be used in the presence of severe congestive cardiac failure.

Pharmacokinetics

Absorption of amiodarone from the gastrointestinal tract is variable. The drug is very slowly eliminated and has an effective half-life of over 30 days. It is strongly protein bound.

Indications

Amiodarone is effective against many dysrhythmias, including supraventricular, nodal and ventricular tachycardias and ventricular fibrillation. It is particularly useful in dysrhythmias associated with the Wolff–Parkinson—White syndrome.

Treatment should be started with 200 mg orally three times daily for at least one week. The drug takes up to 7 days to act and some patients may require up to 4 weeks at this dosage to reach optimal response. When the desired effect is achieved the dosage should be reduced to a maintenance level of about 200 mg per day, but this must be titrated to the individual patient's requirements. Poor cardiac reserve should be controlled with cardiac glycosides and diuretics, since existing heart failure may be made worse by amiodarone. However, this drug may bring about an increase in plasma digoxin levels and precipitate features of digoxin overdosage in those already receiving the glycoside.

Adverse Effects

Toxicity. Amiodarone is contraindicated in sinus bradycardia, all degrees of AV block and in patients with thyroid disease. It should not be given with verapamil or β-adrenergic receptor blocking agents. It may potentiate anticoagulant activity. In long-term use it produces micro deposits on the cornea. Patients on continuous treatment should have regular ophthalmological examination, including by slit lamp. Peripheral neuropathy and extrapyramidal-type tremors have been described. Photosensitization and diffuse pulmonary alveolitis may occur in some patients. Other toxic effects occurring occasionally are nightmares, vertigo, headaches, sleeplessness, fatigue, nausea, vomiting and the development of a metallic taste.

Class IV Agent

Verapamil

Verapamil (Cordilox) is related to papaverine. It acts by blocking the inward movement of calcium ions into cardiac muscle cells, smooth muscle cells of coronary and systemic arteries and cells of the cardiac conduction system. Verapamil, therefore, reduces systemic and coronary vascular resistance and in the heart reduces automaticity, decreases conduction velocity and increases the refractory period.

Pharmacokinetics
Verapamil is well absorbed when given orally, but only 10–20% of the dose enters the systemic circulation, owing to a large first-pass effect. The drug is 90% protein bound in the plasma. The plasma half-life is 3–4 hours. A number of metabolites are pharmacologically active, but less potent than the parent compound.

Indications
Oral verapamil is used in the treatment and prophylaxis of angina and supraventricular tachycardia. The usual oral dose is 80–120 mg three times daily. Poor cardiac reserve should be controlled with digoxin and diuretics, and cardiac depressants should not be given.

In paroxysmal supraventricular tachycardia, i.v. verapamil is very effective in restoring sinus rhythm. I.v. verapamil slows the ventricular rate in atrial fibrillation, and in atrial flutter the degree of block is increased and occasionally sinus rhythm restored. I.v. verapamil should be given only to monitored patients. If the patient has been receiving digoxin or β-adrenergic receptor blocking drugs, i.v. 'bolus' injections of verapamil should not be given, but infusion at a very low dose may be tried cautiously.

The usual i.v. dose is 5–10 mg given over 30 seconds. This may be repeated once, if necessary, 5–10 minutes later. By infusion 5–10 mg per hour is administered, with a total daily dose of 25–100 mg.

Adverse Effects

Toxicity. Side-effects are rare with oral verapamil, but include constipation, flushing, headaches, nausea and vomiting and, rarely, allergic reactions.

I.v. verapamil may cause sinus bradycardia, sinus arrest, hypotension and heart block or even asystole, especially in patients with impaired function of the sinus node or atrioventricular block. I.v. verapamil should not be given to patients with sick sinus syndrome, heart block, hypotension or digitalis toxicity.

DRUGS USED IN THE TREATMENT OF ANGINA PECTORIS

Nitrites and Nitrates

The group of substances including inorganic and organic nitrites (NO_2 compounds) and organic nitrates (NO_3 compounds) is considered. The most commonly used drug in this group is glyceryl trinitrate and the only nitrite in clinical use is amyl nitrite. These two were the first members of this group introduced into clinical practice over one century ago.

The nitrates may be classified into (1) rapidly acting agents for terminating an attack of angina and (2) agents with a greater duration of activity that are used to prevent attacks of angina. Glyceryl trinitrate and amyl nitrite are both rapidly acting agents with a short duration of effect. Erythrityl tetranitrate and pentaerythritol tetranitrate are examples of the second group, having prolonged activity.

Actions

Nitrites and nitrates relax smooth muscle, including vascular smooth muscle. The mode of action at the cellular or membrane level is unknown. There has been considerable discussion as to whether it can possibly be true that nitrites relieve angina by producing coronary artery vasodilatation. It has been demonstrated by coronary angiography that nitrites dilate the large coronary arteries, thus potentially increasing the blood supply to the heart. Studies on total coronary blood flow, however, have provided conflicting evidence. In normal man coronary arterial flow (measured by Fick's principle, using nitrous oxide inhalation) increases following administration of nitrates and nitrites. In patients with coronary artery disease, however, no increase in coronary flow has been produced by doses that abolish angina. It seems likely that both nitrates and nitrites act by reducing systemic blood pressure, pulmonary artery pressure, venous pressure and cardiac output. This diminishes the work load on the heart and reduces myocardial oxygen requirement.

Pharmacokinetics

Most of the nitrites in clinical use are absorbed through the mucous membranes, although gastrointestinal absorption is variable. Amyl nitrite is rapidly absorbed from the lung and is administered by inhalation. Glyceryl trinitrate is quickly absorbed from the mouth and is administered sublingually. Pentaerythritol tetranitrate is the only member of the group not readily absorbed through the buccal mucosa.

The action of amyl nitrite begins almost immediately on inhalation and lasts for about 3 minutes. The action of glyceryl trinitrate begins in 2 minutes and lasts up to 30 minutes. When pentaerythritol tetranitrate is taken orally the action begins in 10 minutes and lasts for about 5 hours.

Nitrite ions and organic nitrates disappear rapidly from the blood. About two-thirds of an administered dose is converted into ammonia and one-third excreted unchanged in the urine.

Indications

The principal use of nitrites and nitrates is in the treatment and prevention of angina pectoris, where coronary artery disease causes myocardial ischaemia and characteristic pain.

Amyl nitrite is no longer used because of the inconvenience (and public spectacle) of having to crush a glass vial containing 0.2 ml and to inhale the vapour. Side-effects are also more prominent with amyl nitrite.

Glyceryl trinitrate is the most useful drug both for the treatment of an attack of angina and also to prevent an attack when exercise is about to be undertaken. The initial dose is 0.5 mg sublingually, but some patients may require more, and up to 6 mg/day may be used. Not more than two tablets should be taken at one time.

There has been considerable controversy over the place of long-acting nitrates in the management of angina. It is currently believed that long-acting nitrates do produce long-lasting haemodynamic effects both in congestive cardiac failure and in coronary artery disease. Isosorbide dinitrate and pentaerythritol tetranitrate have both been claimed to reduce the severity and frequency of anginal attacks, although in some studies they are no better than placebo. Pentaerythritol tetranitrate was in use at least forty years ago. The dose of isosorbide dinitrate is 5–10 mg sublingually or 40–120 mg by mouth daily in divided doses. The dose of pentaerythritol tetranitrate is 20–40 mg three or four times daily.

These long-acting nitrates may also be of value, when given with digitalis and diuretics, in the treatment of cardiac failure. They act predominantly by venous dilatation, thus reducing the afterload on the heart.

Amyl nitrite is also used to induce methaemoglobinaemia in cyanide poisoning and has been employed to reduce the severity of attacks of trigeminal neuralgia. Nitrites may produce transient relief of pain caused by spasm of smooth muscle of the gastrointestinal tract.

Recently novel drug delivery systems have been used in the administration of glyceryl trinitrate. This drug can now be applied to the skin as a 2% ointment (Percutol) three or four hourly, attached as a transdermal patch (Transiderm-Nitro) 5 mg per 24 hours or administered in an aerosol buccal spray (Nitrolingual) 0.4 mg in a metered dose.

Toxicity and Tolerance

The toxic effects of the nitrites are secondary to the generalized vasodilatation they produce and include headache, facial flushing, and postural hypotension with dizziness, weakness and sometimes loss of consciousness. The hypotensive effect of these substances is potentially dangerous in patients with renal insufficiency and they are contraindicated in acute myocardial infarction. This obvious fact is frequently overlooked. High doses of nitrates may lead to methaemoglobinaemia.

Repeated administration of nitrites and nitrates leads to the development of tolerance, when larger doses are required to produce the same effect. The mechanism is unknown. Tolerance develops quickly, even in 2–3 weeks, and also disappears rapidly when the drug is withdrawn. With the usual intermittent therapy in angina, tolerance is not generally a problem.

β-adrenoceptor Blocking Agents in Angina

Cardiac sympathetic nerve stimulation leads to an increase in heart rate, contractile force, and velocity of ventricular muscle fibres, thus increasing cardiac work and myocardial oxygen consumption. As these effects are mediated by the noradrenaline release activating β-adrenoceptors in the myocardium, there are obvious theoretical reasons why the β-adrenoceptor blocking drugs should be effective in preventing angina, especially since increased cardiac sympathetic activity occurs with exercise, emotion, a cold environment and after food, all conditions associated with anginal attacks.

Actions

β-adrenergic blocking drugs reduce heart rate, oxygen consumption at any work load, the rise of arterial pressure on exercise and the velocity of cardiac contraction. All of the many β-blocking drugs already referred to have been shown to increase exercise tolerance in angina. Their possible toxic effects have already been considered and it is important to remember that they may precipitate congestive cardiac failure, particularly in those with poor cardiac reserve. Patients thought to be at risk should first be treated with digitalis and diuretics. Should cardiac failure occur in a patient being treated with β-blocking agents, then the drug should be withdrawn if necessary. Following treatment with digitalis and diuretics, β-blockers can be cautiously reintroduced.

Indications

Many of the β-blocking drugs now available have been discussed, and others are being developed. While various workers have claimed to show the superiority of one preparation over another in decreasing the frequency and severity of anginal attacks, equipotent doses have not always been compared, and it is likely that there is no significant difference in efficacy between the various members of this group. Indeed, none has been shown to be superior to propranolol, one of the earliest β-blockers commercially available.

Patients vary in their response to any given dose of a β-blocking drug and for optimum effect in angina maximum tolerated doses must be used. If propranolol is chosen, it should be introduced at a dose of 20 mg three or four times daily by mouth. This dose can then be increased every few weeks with about 25% increments until the angina is controlled, the supine pulse rate falls to 55 beats per minute or troublesome side-effects occur. For maximum benefit a total of 200–240 mg daily is a likely requirement, but even larger amounts have been given.

Glyceryl trinitrate can be used in the usual way in patients receiving β-blocking drugs and its hypotensive effect is not exaggerated.

Angina of effort has an overall annual mortality of 3–4% and it remains to be established whether control of symptoms with β-blocking drugs is associated with improved prognosis.

A number of trials have shown a favourable effect on mortality when β-blocking drugs were given for one year to patients who had suffered a myocardial infarction. The cumulated mortality was reduced by 26% with propranolol, 39% with timolol and 36% with metoprolol, though the conditions of the three studies were not identical.

Perhexiline

Perhexiline (Pexid) was introduced for the prophylactic treatment of angina pectoris. It produces vasodilatation and is believed to act directly on resistive blood vessels or to produce a non-specific reduction in vasoconstrictor tone. Perhexiline produces a decrease in left ventricular work, index of cardiac energy utilization and myocardial oxygen consumption. Perhexiline also produces a transient depletion of myocardial catecholamines.

Perhexiline has been shown to reduce exercise-induced tachycardia in man. In a number of controlled trials, it was shown to decrease the number of anginal attacks by as much as 80% and to produce a significant decrease in nitroglycerin requirement in patients with angina. It has also been shown to delay exercise-induced angina, partly by reducing myocardial requirements through a decrease in exercise heart rate while ventricular function improves. Perhexiline may also have some antidysrhythmic activity.

Side-effects of perhexiline include dizziness, headache, nausea and vomiting. Other occasional side-effects are nervousness, tremors, gait disorders, fatigue, hypoglycaemia, paraesthesiae, flushing, and rash or urticaria. An elevation in some serum enzymes (SGOT, SGPT, alkaline phosphatase, LDH) has been reported. Papilloedema, loss of vision and weight loss may occur. Peripheral neuropathy is not uncommon.

In view of the frequency and severity of side-effects, perhexiline should not be considered a first-line anti-anginal drug.

Nifedipine

Nifedipine (Adalat) has recently been introduced for the prophylactic treatment of angina pectoris. It is a powerful calcium antagonist which inhibits transmembrane calcium influx into the excited myocardial cells. Accordingly, less phosphate-bond energy is transformed into mechanical work by the calcium-dependent myofibrillar alkaline phosphatase. Thus cardiac oxidative metabolism for muscular activity can be lowered. Nifedipine also causes peripheral vasodilatation, reducing peripheral resistance and, consequently, cardiac work load. The drug may also cause coronary artery vasodilatation.

Pharmacokinetics

Nifedipine is almost fully absorbed after an oral dose. Peak plasma concentration is achieved within 20–45 minutes. The hypotensive effect starts within 20 minutes of an oral dose. Nifedipine is detectable in the plasma for 6 hours after administration and its duration of action is 8–12 hours.

Indications

Nifedipine is effective in the treatment and prophylaxis of angina of effort and Prinzmetal's angina. The usual dose is 10–20 mg three times daily. Nifedipine can be given (10 mg) sublingually in an acute anginal attack.

Nifedipine is an effective hypotensive agent and is marketed for this usage in 20 mg tablets as Adalat Retard. The dose advised is 1–2 tablets twice daily to produce a reduction of blood pressure throughout the 24 hours, without hypotension. Nifedipine has been used sublingually in hypertensive encephalopathy and acute left ventricular failure.

Nifedipine can be used in combination with β-blocking drugs in angina pectoris. It is a most promising therapeutic agent likely to be used increasingly in angina and hypertension.

Adverse Effects

Toxicity. Nifedipine is well tolerated. Peripheral vasodilatation may cause headache, flushing and palpitations. Occasionally angina may be precipitated about 30 minutes after dosing.

FURTHER READING

Hamer J. (1980) Drugs used in cardiac failure: digitalis and vasodilators. In: Turner P. & Shand D. G. (eds) *Recent Advances in Clinical Pharmacology*, Vol. 2, Edinburgh, London, Melbourne & New York: Churchill Livingstone.
Jewitt D. E. (1980) Haemodynamic effect of newer antiarrhythmic drugs. *Am. Heart J.* 100: 984.

Kendall M. J. (1981) Are selective beta-adrenoceptor blocking drugs an advantage? *J. R. Coll. Physicians, Lond.*, 15: 33.

Kumana C. R. & Marlin G. E. (1978) Selectivity of beta-adrenoceptor agonists and antagonists. In: Turner P. & Shand D. G. (eds) *Recent Advances in Clinical Pharmacology*, Vol. 1. Edinburgh, London & New York: Churchill Livingstone.

Lawrie T. D. V. (1980) Comparison of newer antiarrhythmic agents. *Am. Heart J.*, 100: 990.

Leading article (1980) Inhibitors of angiotensin I converting enzyme for treating hypertension. *Br. Med. J.*, 281: 630.

Leading article (1980) Captopril: benefits and risks in severe hypertension. *Lancet*, ii: 129.

Leading article (1981) Beta-blockers after myocardial infarction. *Lancet*, i: 873.

Leading article (1981) Long-term vasodilator therapy for heart failure. *Lancet*, i: 1350.

Opie L. H. (1980) *Drugs and the Heart.* London: The *Lancet*.

Robertson D. & Nies A. S. (1978) Antihypertensive drugs. In: Turner P. & Shand D. G. (eds) *Recent Advances in Clinical Pharmacology*, Vol. 1. Edinburgh, London & New York: Churchill Livingstone.

Ronfeld R. A. (1980) Comparative pharmacokinetics of new antiarrhythmic drugs. *Am. Heart J.*, 100: 978.

Woosley R. L. & Rumbolt T. Z. (1978) Antiarrhythmic drugs. In: Turner P. & Shand D. G. (eds) *Recent Advances in Clinical Pharmacology*, Vol. 1. Edinburgh, London & New York: Churchill Livingstone.

7 Drugs Acting on the Respiratory System

J. Nimmo

A number of drugs used in the treatment of respiratory disease will not be discussed in this chapter. Chemotherapeutic agents used in the treatment of respiratory infections, including tuberculosis, are considered in Chapter 1 and the chemotherapy of bronchogenic carcinoma in Chapter 14.

BRONCHODILATOR DRUGS

One of the most significant advances in the treatment of respiratory disease has been the introduction of agents that are effective in treating reversible airways obstruction. This is the characteristic feature of bronchial asthma, but it often occurs in other respiratory diseases such as chronic bronchitis.

Bronchial smooth muscle tone is controlled by humoral factors and by the autonomic nervous system (ANS). These humoral factors, which include histamine, bradykinin, leukotrienes (formerly named slow-reacting substances) of anaphylaxis (SRS-A), serotonin and prostaglandin F_{2a}, all cause bronchoconstriction. They may influence the calibre of the airways in disease, but in health the calibre is controlled by the ANS, both parasympathetic and sympathetic. The parasympathetic innervation is the primary motor control for the smooth muscle fibres in the wall of bronchi. Parasympathetic stimulation causes bronchoconstriction mediated by the chemical transmitter acetylcholine. Sympathetic postganglionic innervation is the primary motor control to the bronchial vascular smooth muscle. Sympathetic stimulation, acting by virtue of the transmitter noradrenaline on 'adrenergic' tissue receptors, causes increased pulmonary blood flow, vasodilatation of the pulmonary circulation and bronchodilatation.

Sympathomimetic amines produce their effects via the adrenergic receptors. Ahlquist's 1948 studies led to the subdivision of adrenergic receptors into α and β. Alpha responses are mainly excitatory and include vasoconstriction, constriction of sphincters of the gastrointestinal tract, etc; β responses are mainly inhibitory and cause bronchodilatation, vasodilatation, and cardiac stimulation, both inotropic and chronotropic. Following the work of Furchgott (1967) and Lands (1967), it became clear that β-receptors could

313

be further divided into β_1 or cardiac receptors and β_2 or smooth muscle receptors. Specific β_2 stimulants will, therefore, produce bronchodilatation with far fewer side-effects than the less specific sympathomimetic amines. Adrenergic receptor activity is mediated by cyclic AMP. The β-adrenergic drugs increase adenyl cyclase activity, which brings about the conversion of adenosine triphosphate (ATP) to the active cyclic adenosine monophosphate (AMP), and this relaxes bronchial muscle.

There are three groups of bronchodilator drugs: (1) those that are anticholinergic in action, (2) sympathomimetics, and (3) methylxanthines. These groups may be subdivided as follows:

Anticholinergic
    atropine
    ipratropium

Sympathomimetic
    (a) Drugs stimulating α- and β-receptors
         adrenaline
         ephedrine

    (b) Specific β (β_1 + β_2) stimulants
         isoprenaline
         orciprenaline
    (c) Specific β_2 stimulants
         salbutamol
         isoetharine
         terbutaline
         rimiterol
         fenoterol
         hexoprenaline
Methylxanthines (Theophylline derivatives)
    aminophylline
    choline theophyllinate

Anticholinergics

Atropine

The actions of atropine are discussed in detail elsewhere (p. 206). Atropine methylnitrate is more potent than atropine sulphate in producing bronchodilatation. It may be given by aerosol and its peak effect then occurs 30–60 minutes after administration. Side-effects are predictable and include tachycardia, dry mouth, blurring of vision and difficulty in micturition. Atropine also causes increased viscosity of bronchial secretions — a most undesirable effect in bronchial asthma.

Because of its side-effects and slow onset of action atropine has not found a place in the management of bronchial asthma.

Ipratropium

Ipratropium (Atrovent) is 8-isopropyl-noratropine-methobromide and is a synthetic anticholinergic agent.

Mode of Action
The drug is administered by inhalation and is claimed to have some bronchoselectivity, producing bronchodilatation without unwanted anticholinergic side-effects. Ipratropium is a little more active than atropine and has a 30–50% longer duration of action.

Pharmacokinetics
After i.v. injection the plasma level of ipratropium falls rapidly and after 1 hour only a small amount of the administered dose remains in the plasma. The drug is rapidly cleared by the kidney and is also excreted in bile. The substance is poorly absorbed after oral administration.

Indications
Ipratropium is available in a metered dose inhaler delivering 0.02 mg for inhalation. The usual dosage is one or two puffs three or four times daily. The place of this drug is not yet established, but it may be of value in the treatment of chronic airways obstruction, particularly in chronic bronchitis. A combination of ipratropium and a β_2 adrenoceptor agonist produces a greater degree of bronchodilatation than either drug alone. This action appears to be additive rather than synergistic.

Adverse Effects

Toxicity. It is claimed that the anticholinergic type of side-effects are unlikely to occur at therapeutic dosage. Care should be exercised if the drug is used in patients with glaucoma or urinary retention. There is no evidence that in therapeutic dosage ipratropium has any adverse effect on bronchial secretion. Ipratropium bromide is available as a solution containing 0.25 mg/ml for use in a nebulizer, and has occasionally caused bronchospasm.

Sympathomimetics

Adrenaline

Adrenaline has a powerful bronchodilator action and for many years was a drug of choice in the management of acute asthma. However, adrenaline affects both α- and β-receptors, so in addition to bronchodilatation, it produces vasoconstriction and cardiac stimulation. It has the shortest duration of action of the sympathomimetic amines and the maximum potential for harmful cardiac effects. It is now excluded from most therapeutic regimens for asthma, but a single dose in the adult is 0.2–0.5 ml of a 1 in 1000 solution given s.c., *not* i.v.

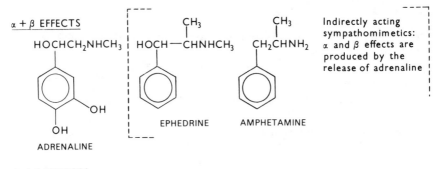

Fig. 7.1 α and β effects of various bronchodilators.

Ephedrine

Ephedrine is structurally very similar to adrenaline (Fig. 7.1) and differs in its pharmacological activity in being effective by the oral route, having a longer duration of activity with more pronounced central actions and having lower potency as a bronchodilator.

Mode of Action
Ephedrine stimulates both α- and β-receptors and also exerts part of its action by stimulating the release of noradrenaline from sympathetic nerve endings.

Pharmacokinetics
Ephedrine is readily and completely absorbed after oral or parenteral administration. Up to 40% of an administered dose is excreted unchanged in the urine. Ephedrine is metabolized by both deamination and conjugation in

the liver. Inactivation and excretion are slow, and the action of ephedrine persists for several hours.

Indications

Ephedrine is used mainly as a chronic medication for mild or only moderately severe bronchial asthma, especially in children. The usual adult dose is 30–60 mg orally, three or four times daily. Resistance may develop, but can often be controlled by discontinuing the drug for a few days. To counteract the central nervous side-effects, ephedrine is often given in combination with a barbiturate, as in Franol. Ephedrine has been replaced to a large extent by newer sympathomimetic drugs with more specific β_2 activity.

Adverse Effects

Toxicity. Side-effects of ephedrine include tachycardia, hypertension, urinary retention, and evidence of central nervous stimulation such as nausea, vomiting, sweating, vertigo, tremor, nervousness and insomnia. There may be extrasystoles and the patient may be irritable and even quarrelsome.

Isoprenaline

Isoprenaline is the parent compound of the newer sympathomimetic amines. Structurally it differs from adrenaline in having an isopropyl group on the amine head.

Mode of Action

Isoprenaline has a powerful action on β-receptors and almost no action on α-receptors. Therefore, in addition to producing bronchodilatation, it causes increased heart rate and cardiac output and slight rise in arterial pressure.

Pharmacokinetics

Isoprenaline is readily absorbed when given parenterally or as an aerosol. Absorption following oral or sublingual administration is unreliable. Isoprenaline undergoes two types of metabolic transformation, since, after oral administration, it is converted to the sulphate conjugate in the gut wall and also, like adrenaline, it is metabolized by hepatic catechol-*O*-methyl transferase to 3-methoxyisoprenaline. Following an i.v. dose 50% appears unchanged in the urine. After an oral dose 8% is excreted unchanged in the urine and 90% is excreted in the conjugated form. Probably only 10% of a dose administered by aerosol enters the airways and so inhaled isoprenaline has the same metabolic fate as the orally administered drug. The bronchodilator activity of isoprenaline is relatively short-lived. An increase in FEV is seen within a few minutes of administration by aerosol and the effect disappears within 60–90 minutes.

Indications

Isoprenaline was for many years a most useful drug in the treatment of bronchial asthma. It was administered by metered aerosol and the recommended dose was 0.08–0.24 mg (one to three puffs) up to eight times daily, with at least 30 minutes separating each administration. Isoprenaline is no longer a drug of choice in bronchial asthma and has been replaced by the more specific β_2-stimulant drugs. It is important to know that some pressurized sprays for inhalation contain even five times the concentration of others and hence are particularly dangerous if over-utilized.

Adverse Effects

Toxicity. The major toxic effects of isoprenaline are related to its β_1 (cardiac) stimulant activity, producing tachycardia, cardiac dysrhythmias and even ventricular fibrillation. Isoprenaline was incriminated in the marked increase in death rate from bronchial asthma in the UK between 1959 and 1966, when isoprenaline inhalers were becoming widely used. A number of mechanisms may have accounted for this:

1. Isoprenaline does cause cardiac stimulation, although it has been claimed that heavy users of isoprenaline aerosols are relatively resistant to this effect.
2. Despite improving airways resistance, isoprenaline may cause a fall in arterial oxygen tension.
3. Paradoxical bronchoconstriction may occur from prolonged high dosage with β stimulants.
4. In dogs isoprenaline produces cardiac depression in the presence of anoxia.

Orciprenaline

Orciprenaline (Alupent) is a long-acting derivative of isoprenaline. Like the parent compound, it stimulates β_1- and β_2-receptors, although it is claimed that it has less activity on heart muscle. Orciprenaline is not readily susceptible to sulphatase enzymes and so is active by the oral route. It is not inactivated by catechol-O-methyl transferase and therefore, is more stable in the body. Side-effects are similar to those of isoprenaline. Given orally, orciprenaline may reduce the frequency and severity of asthmatic attacks. Inhaled as an aerosol, it acts as promptly and efficiently as isoprenaline and remains active for 3–6 hours.

When given orally, the dose is 20 mg every 6 hours. The metered aerosol produces 0.75 mg of orciprenaline sulphate per dose and adults may take up to 12 doses in 24 hours. (One or two doses may be taken separated by 1 minute; then no further dose should be taken for at least 30 minutes.)

Salbutamol and Terbutaline

Salbutamol (Ventolin) and terbutaline (Bricanyl) will be considered together, since there is no significant difference in their pharmacological and therapeutic effects and either may be regarded as a bronchodilator of choice in bronchial asthma. The relative costs should be considered, however, when choosing between them.

Salbutamol is a saligenin derivative with an *N*-tertiary butyl substituent in the side-chain. Terbutaline is the *N*-tertiary butyl homologue of orciprenaline.

Mode of Action

Salbutamol and terbutaline stimulate β_2-adrenergic receptors and have little or no β_1 activity. They therefore produce effective bronchodilatation without cardiac stimulation and acceleration when accepted therapeutic doses are given. Salbutamol also prevents antigen-induced release of histamine and leukotrienes from mast cells in human lung sensitized with IgE antibody. Airways obstruction in asthma is caused by bronchial constriction, mucus inspissation and mucosal oedema. β_2-agonists may help to prevent the development of mucosal oedema. Salbutamol also produces an increased ventilatory response to CO_2 in the presence of hypoxia.

Pharmacokinetics

Both salbutamol and terbutaline can be administered in aerosols or by the oral or parenteral route. Neither is inactivated by catechol-*O*-methyl transferase or sulphatase, which accounts for their long duration of action, both drugs acting for at least 4 hours.

Indications

Salbutamol and terbutaline are good bronchodilator drugs for treating bronchial asthma, but if using them in children read the instructions carefully.

Salbutamol may be given orally in a dose of 4 mg three or four times daily. Absorption is unreliable and may be low by this route. The much preferred route for salbutamol is by inhalation. A metered aerosol delivers 100 μg per inhalation. The usual adult dose is one or two inhalations every 4 hours. An alternative inhalation form (Ventolin Rotacaps) has recently become available for patients who are unable to use pressurized inhalers effectively or who might use them unwisely. Each rotacap contains 200 or 400 μg of salbutamol, and the contents are inhaled, using a device activated by the patient's inspiration. The dose required is slightly higher than that from the pressurized inhaler, 400 μg three or four times a day. Salbutamol may be given s.c. or i.m. in a dose of 500 μg every 4 hours, or i.v., the amount being 250 μg by slow injection. This is very valuable for the treatment of severe bronchospasm and status asthmaticus. Salbutamol is also available as a 'respirator solution' for the management of status asthmaticus or severe reversible airways obstruction. A 0.5% solution is administered in oxygen-enriched air through an intermittent positive pressure ventilator, 2 ml (10 mg salbutamol) being given over 3 minutes. It can also be given in a diluted form by a nebulizer with a suitable face mask.

Salbutamol has also been used with success in the management of uncomplicated premature labour in the last trimester of pregnancy.

Terbutaline is given orally in a dose of 5 mg three times daily. The metered aerosol dose is 0.25 mg and one or two inhalations may be taken when required, the maximum being eight inhalations in 24 hours. Alternatively, 0.25 mg may be injected s.c. up to four times a day and a respiratory solution, giving 2–5 mg, is available for use with a nebulizer or intermittent positive pressure ventilation.

Adverse Effects

Toxicity.   Muscle tremor, usually of the hands, and palpitations have been reported to occur following oral administration of salbutamol and terbutaline, more commonly when higher doses are used. Side-effects are virtually absent when accepted therapeutic doses are given by inhalation.

Although salbutamol has been available in the UK for over 10 years, it has not been approved by the Food and Drug Administration for marketing in the United States. This may be because massive doses of salbutamol and other sympathomimetic agents were said to be associated with an increased incidence of mesovarian leiomyomas in certain strains of rats. It is now claimed that there is no evidence that salbutamol is carcinogenic in any species and no evidence of increased incidence of smooth muscle tumours in women receiving the drug.

A number of highly selective β_2-adrenergic agonists have more recently been introduced. All have actions similar to those of salbutamol. *Rimiterol* (Pulmadil) is available as a metered aerosol inhalation. It has a rapid action, producing effective bronchodilatation within 20 seconds and at the same time it has a shorter duration of activity. *Fenoterol* (Berotec) and *reproterol* (Bronchodil) are available as metered aerosol inhalants and act for 3–5 hours after inhalation. Reproterol is also available in tablet form, as is *isoetharine* (Numotac). Recommended adult doses are as follows:

Rimiterol   0.2–0.6 mg (1–3 puffs), with no more than 8 inhalations in 24 hours.

Fenoterol   0.2–0.4 mg (1–2 puffs) three or four times daily. Maximum in adults 2 puffs four-hourly; In children, 1 puff four-hourly.

Reproterol 0.5–1 mg (1–2 puffs) three times daily. It is not recommended under 6 years of age, and from 6–12 years the dose is 1 puff three-to-six-hourly. The adult oral dose for reproterol is 10–20 mg three times daily.

Isoetharine 10–20 mg three or four times daily. It is not recommended for children.

There is some evidence that tolerance to the bronchodilator response to sympathomimetic agents may develop over some months of chronic therapy. This may be more of a problem with fenoterol.

Theophylline Derivatives

Theophylline derivatives are methylated xanthines structurally related to uric acid. This group includes caffeine, theophylline and theobromine.

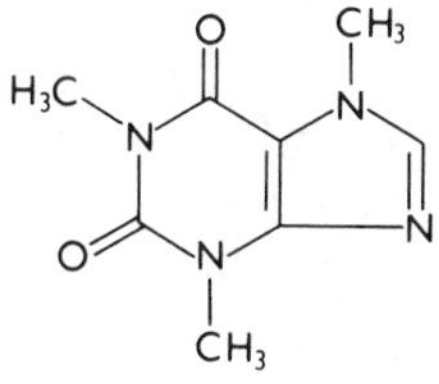

CAFFEINE 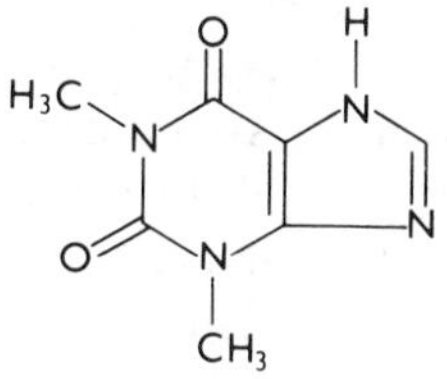   THEOPHYLLINE

AMINOPHYLLINE = 2 molecules THEOPHYLLINE
                + 1 molecule ETHYLENE DIAMINE

Mode of Action

The xanthines have a number of pharmacological actions, including CNS stimulation, myocardial stimulation and bronchodilatation. Theophylline is the most effective xanthine in producing bronchodilatation. It acts directly on the smooth muscle of the bronchi. At a cellular level it may act as a competitive inhibitor of cyclic nucleotide phosphodiesterase, an enzyme that catalyses the inactivation of cyclic 3',5'-AMP by conversion to 5'-AMP, resulting in increased levels of cyclic AMP.

Pharmacokinetics

The xanthine derivatives are absorbed after oral, rectal or parenteral administration. They are, however, poorly water-soluble, and oral administration may cause gastric irritation, nausea and vomiting. For these reasons theophylline is often given in the form of suppositories, whence absorption is likely to be slow and erratic. Choline theophyllinate is more water-soluble and less irritating and can, therefore, be given by mouth. The most widely used theophylline compound is aminophylline, which is a combination of theophylline with ethylenediamine. (The ethylenediamine is inert, but serves to increase the amount of theophylline in solution.) Aminophylline is given by slow i.v. injection.

Xanthines are metabolized by demethylation and oxidation. Theophylline is converted mainly to 1,3-dimethyluric acid, about 10% being excreted unchanged. None of the xanthines is completely demethylated, so there is no increase in uric acid excretion and they are not contraindicated in gout.

There is considerable variation in plasma theophylline half-life in different age groups. In adults the mean plasma half-life is between 5 and 8 hours, in children it is between 3 and 4 hours and in neonates it is 14–57 hours. Plasma theophylline half-life is reduced in heavy smokers and prolonged in hepatic cirrhosis, acute pulmonary oedema and cor pulmonale.

Indications

Aminophylline is often used by slow i.v. injection (250–500 mg) as a first-line treatment in patients with severe asthmatic attacks. It is effective and acts rapidly, but is likely to produce more side-effects than the β_2-adrenergic stimulant drugs. Aminophylline suppositories, BP, are also available in strengths of 50, 100, 150 and 360 mg and are given in this form since given orally, the drug causes nausea. They are useful and have a small prolonged effect in airways obstruction.

Choline theophyllinate (Choledyl) may be used for the relief and prophylaxis of mild to moderate bronchospasm. The adult dose is 400–1600 mg daily in divided doses. It has been suggested that when a maximal bronchodilator response to a β-stimulant drug has been obtained, an additional effect can be achieved by the administration of aminophylline or choline theophyllinate. A microcrystalline form of theophylline (Nuelin) has been claimed to overcome the problems of poor absorption and gastric irritation. The dose is 175–350 mg orally three or four times daily. Each tablet contains 175 mg.

Many compound preparations of various bronchodilator substances are produced. In general, there is no advantage in using such mixtures compared with simple preparations of adrenergic-receptor stimulants, xanthines or ipratropium.

Sodium Cromoglycate

Sodium cromoglycate (disodium cromoglycate; Intal), the sodium salt of 1,3-bis-(2-carboxychromen-5-yloxy)-2-hydroxypropane, is commonly used in the management of bronchial asthma. It is not a bronchodilator and has no anti-inflammatory activity. The trade name varies for different uses.

Mode of Action

The exact mode of action of sodium cromoglycate is unclear, but it appears to act prophylactically, reducing the asthmatic response to allergen. It inhibits the release of histamine and leukotrienes from sensitized human lungs in vitro, thus acting after antigen meets reagin but before release of the chemical mediators. Sodium cromoglycate may act on the mast cells in the bronchial mucous membrane by maintaining membrane stability and inhibiting degranulation of sensitized mast cells, which otherwise occurs after a challenge by antigen.

One puzzling feature of sodium cromoglycate is its prevention of exercise-induced bronchoconstriction in normal and asthmatic subjects.

Pharmacokinetics

Sodium cromoglycate is very poorly absorbed from the alimentary tract, less than 0.5% of an orally administered dose being absorbed. In addition, because of its local action, the most practical way to administer the drug is by inhalation. After inhalation some 5–10% of the administered dose reaches the lungs, the remainder being deposited in the mouth and oropharynx, then swallowed and excreted via the gastrointestinal tract. Sodium cromoglycate is rapidly absorbed from the lungs and is excreted unchanged in the urine and bile.

Indications

Sodium cromoglycate is used most effectively in the prophylaxis of allergic (extrinsic) asthma. It has been particularly useful in young adults and children. The patient should first be made as well as possible with bronchodilators (and even with corticosteroid drugs if necessary) before therapy is started. Many patients who are susceptible to exercise-induced asthma are protected by the use of sodium cromoglycate prior to exercise. Sodium cromoglycate may be beneficial to a small proportion of patients with intrinsic asthma, although in general it is disappointing in such patients. However, a trial of sodium cromoglycate therapy is worth while, since the possibility of a satisfactory response cannot be predicted.

Sodium cromoglycate is also promoted for use in allergic alveolitis, bird fancier's lung, allergic rhinitis, food allergy and allergic conjunctivitis. The initial dose in bronchial asthma is 20 mg four times daily. For bronchial asthma it is a dry powder in a gelatine capsule. A special inhaler (Spinhaler, Fisons Ltd) is required. This contains a mechanism for puncturing the capsule and a turbovibrator constructed in such a way that inhalation is controlled by the patient's own inspiratory effort.

Adverse Effects

Toxicity. No important toxic effects of sodium cromoglycate have been described. Some patients have complained of irritation of the throat with coughing on inhalation of the drug.

Ketotifen

Ketotifen (Zaditen) has been introduced recently as an orally active antianaphylactic agent. It acts by inhibiting the release of histamine and other mediator substances from the mast cell and also exerts a sustained inhibitory effect on histamine receptors.

It has been claimed that ketotifen in an adult dose of 1–2 mg twice daily by mouth, given with food, is effective in reducing the number, severity and duration of asthmatic attacks. This effect may take several weeks to become established.

Ketotifen may cause drowsiness and impaired reactions. Patients should be warned to avoid driving or operating moving machinery until the effect of the treatment is known. They should also be advised to avoid alcohol.

Corticosteroids in the Treatment of Bronchial Asthma

Corticosteroids (p. 406) given by mouth have an established place in the management of bronchial asthma. They may be life-saving in an acute attack or in status asthmaticus and it may be necessary to give 200 mg of hydrocortisone sodium succinate i.v. every 2 hours in the latter condition. In some patients with chronic airways obstruction, their use may be unavoidable, since they may be effective even when there is a failure in response to conventional bronchodilator drugs. It is not known exactly how corticosteroids affect the three major components of reversible airways obstruction, namely bronchospasm, mucosal oedema, and a thickened tenacious sputum. The major effect is probably a non-specific anti-inflammatory one on the mucosal oedema and on the viscous sputum. Some asthmatics may show impaired β-adrenergic receptor responsiveness leading to resistance to inhaled bronchodilator drugs. Responsiveness can be restored by the administration of corticosteroids. In severe acute asthma, corticosteroid drugs in adequate doses are of great importance. Hydrocortisone should be given by continuous i.v. infusion in a dose of 3 mg/kg body weight every six hours, following a loading dose of 3–4 mg/kg body weight i.v. I.v. administration of corticosteroids to patients with acute asthma does not result in improvement in lung function until about six hours have elapsed. It is important, therefore, to continue vigorous bronchodilator therapy, especially during the first few hours of a severe attack.

The long-term use of corticosteroids is associated with a number of serious hazards (p. 408), including suppression of the pituitary–adrenal axis. The introduction of topically acting corticosteroids for bronchial asthma has allowed long-term therapy without the attendant risk of adrenal suppression.

Two such preparations are at present available and will now be considered.

Betamethasone 17-valerate and Beclomethasone dipropionate

The topical activity of anti-inflammatory steroids is well known in dermatological disorders (p. 540). Betamethasone valerate (Bextasol) and beclomethasone dipropionate (Becotide) are anti-inflammatory steroids which act topically when administered into the respiratory tract. They are both synthetic halogenated corticosteroids. Betamethasone valerate (Betnovate) is also available as a preparation for local use in certain skin disorders (p. 541), as is beclomethasone diproprionate (Propaderm, Propaderm-Forte).

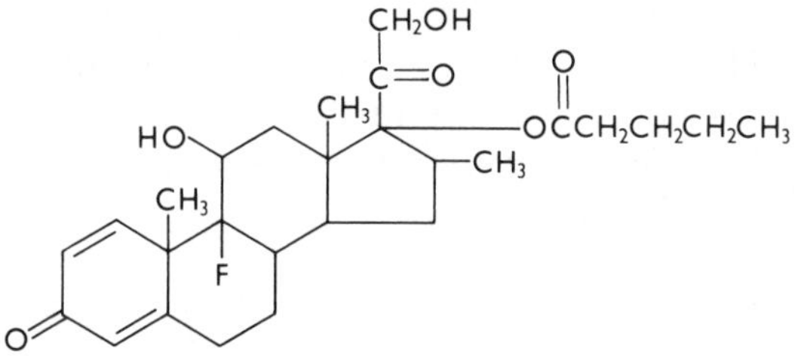

BETAMETHASONE 17-VALERATE

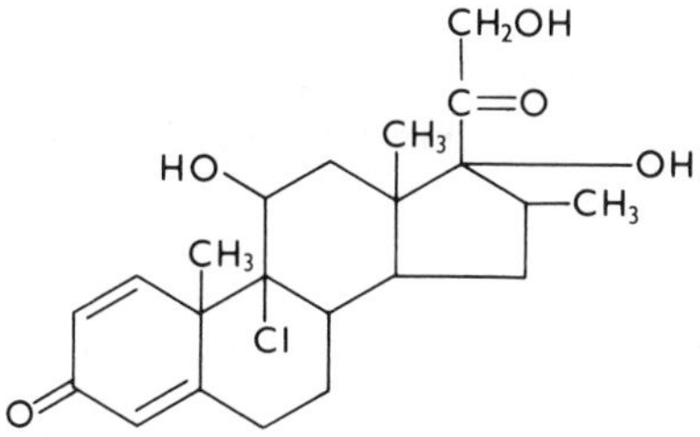

BECLOMETHASONE

Mode of Action

The mode of action of these drugs in asthma is unknown, but it is probably the same as that postulated for systemic corticosteroids. Plasma corticosteroid concentrations are unaffected when betamethasone valerate is given by aerosol at a daily dosage of 1.4 mg/day for 3 weeks. The usual initial therapeutic dose of this preparation is 800 µg/day. Inhalation of 1 mg of beclomethasone diproprionate a day for 4 weeks causes no change in plasma cortisol levels and the usual therapeutic dose is 400 µg/day.

Pharmacokinetics

It has been estimated that 20–25% of an inhaled dose reaches the lungs. No measurable level reaches the systemic circulation.

Indications

Patients may be gradually weaned from oral corticosteroids to these preparations of betamethasone or beclomethasone. This process should be carried out when the patient's asthma is well controlled. Those who have not received prolonged courses of corticosteroids by mouth may respond favourably to the inhaled preparations and the requirement for bronchodilator aerosols is frequently reduced.

Both betamethasone valerate and beclomethasone dipropionate are presented in metered aerosol inhalers. With betamethasone valerate the inhaler delivers 100 µg, and the recommended adult dosage is 200 µg four times daily, this being adjusted, depending on response, to the minimum effective dose. The beclomethasone inhaler delivers 50 μg per dose. The recommended adult dose is 100 μg three or four times daily, with a maximum dose of 600–800 μg/day for those severely affected. Not more than 1 mg should be taken in 24 hours.

Adverse Effects

Toxicity. No systemic side-effects have been reported with the recommended therapeutic doses. Some patients become hoarse or complain of an irritant effect. Localized infection with *Candida albicans* may occur in the mouth and throat.

Although evaluation of the topically acting corticosteroids in bronchial asthma is not complete, they appear to represent a significant therapeutic advance.

RESPIRATORY STIMULANTS

Drugs claimed to act as respiratory stimulants have tended to be disappointing in their clinical effectiveness. This is partly because they have often been used in situations where they cannot reasonably be expected to be helpful, but also because no drug that is available can specifically stimulate the respiratory drive. It is true that the xanthines improve medullary blood flow and therefore may be regarded as respiratory stimulants, but they have many other pharmacological activities and are discussed elsewhere (p. 321).

Analeptics

'Analeptic' is a Greek-derived word and literally means a restorative or strengthening drug. Some analeptics are respiratory stimulants acting directly on the respiratory centre in the medulla. They do not, however, act specifically on this area, and indeed, they stimulate all levels of the cerebrospinal axis, causing what may be described as a general arousal. In large doses they can all produce convulsions.

The two most commonly used such preparations are nikethamide and ethamivan.

Nikethamide

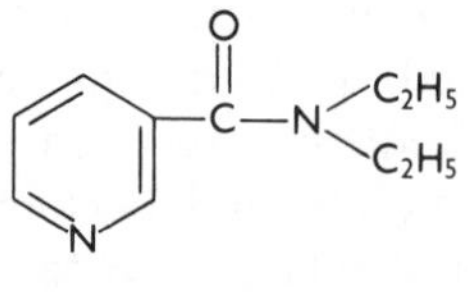

NIKETHAMIDE

Nikethamide is a pyridine derivative and is a synthetic, water-soluble slightly viscous oil.

Mode of Action

Nikethamide stimulates all levels of the CNS, but it produces respiratory stimulation in doses that cause little central excitation. This may be due in part to stimulation of the carotid and aortic chemoreceptors. The drug increases the sensitivity of the respiratory centre to carbon dioxide and acts more powerfully on a depressed respiratory centre than on a normal one.

Pharmacokinetics

Nikethamide is absorbed from all sites of administration, but is usually given i.v. It is converted to nicotinamide (p. 451), which is then excreted as N-methylnicotinamide. Following i.v. injection the action of the drug is over in 2 minutes.

Indications

Nikethamide may be used for treating patients with acute respiratory failure who are hypercapnic, drowsy and unable to cough properly. The level of alveolar ventilation may be temporarily increased and the patient may wake up and co-operate with the physiotherapist by coughing and clearing retained secretions. It may also be used following overdosage with respiratory depressant drugs such as morphine. The usual initial dose is 2 ml of a 25% solution. This may be increased to the optimum dose that will alert the patient without producing side-effects. Administration of the drug is repeated every 4–6 hours if necessary. The drug is suitable for short-term use only. The therapeutic and toxic doses are close and there is inter-individual variation in response. It is mentioned here because it is still used in some countries, though it ceased to be promoted in the UK in 1977.

Adverse Effects

Toxicity. Large doses of nikethamide cause clonic convulsions followed by depression of the central nervous system, including the respiratory centre. Other toxic effects are generalized pruritus, anxiety, and gastrointestinal upsets.

Ethamivan

Ethamivan (Clairvan) is a derivative of vanillic acid. It has similar pharmacological properties to nikethamide and also has comparable therapeutic uses and toxic effects. It has a short duration of action, the effects of an i.v. dose lasting about 10 minutes. Ethamivan may be given in doses of 150–400 mg by i.v. injection. It is supplied in 2 ml ampoules containing a 5% solution of Erthamivan BPC.

Doxapram

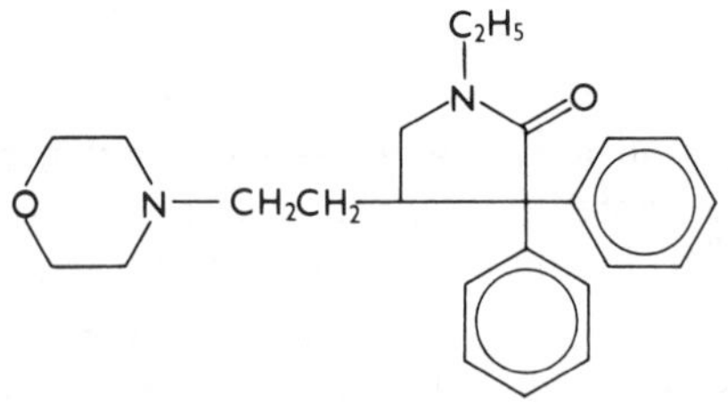

DOXAPRAM

Doxapram (Dopram) is a non-specific analeptic agent used to stimulate respiration. It, too, has a brief duration of activity and is given by i.v. infusion, the initial rate being 5 mg/min., this later being reduced to 2 mg/min. Doxapram has been claimed to have a greater margin of safety than nikethamide or ethamivan, although hypertension, tachycardia, dysrhythmias and vomiting have been reported from its use. Its use is contraindicated in severe hypertension, airways obstruction, coronary artery disease, thyrotoxicosis and status asthmaticus, and if there has been a cerebral vascular accident. The action of doxapram is potentiated by monoamine oxidase inhibitors.

COUGH SUPPRESSANTS

A large number of proprietary cough medicines are marketed. Many of these have little therapeutic effect and will not be discussed here. When it is desired to suppress cough, it is necessary to employ drugs that act on the central mehanism, the so-called 'cough centre' in the medulla. These drugs are mainly opiates and opiate derivatives, and are discussed in Chapter 2. Their approximate equipotent doses in suppressing cough are as follows:

Codeine	15 mg
Dextromethorphan	10 mg
Methadone	2.5 mg
Noscapine	15 mg
Pholcodine	10 mg

These drugs are usually prescribed as syrups or linctuses.

Reference has already been made to the use of codeine (p. 115), and methadone has been mentioned (p. 117). Pholcodine is commonly included in proprietary preparations and is perhaps as effective as codeine without having such a tendency to cause constipation. Dextromethorphan is similar in its

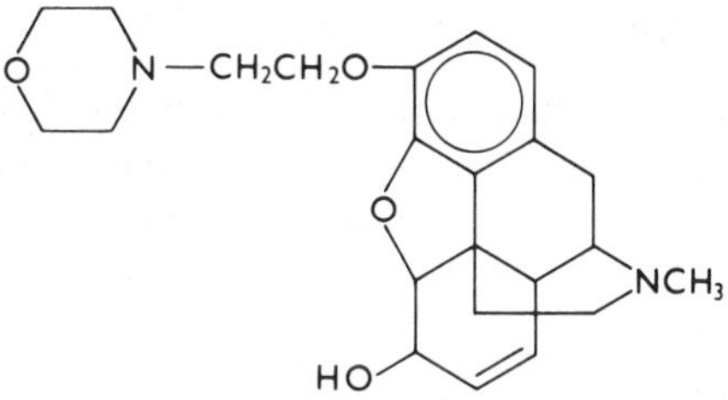

PHOLCODINE

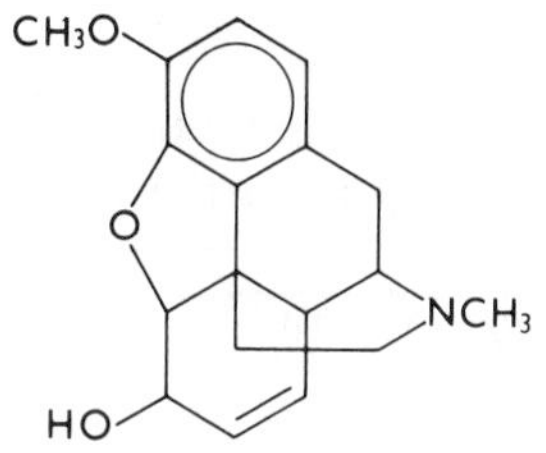

CODEINE

actions, and noscapine is an alkaloid of opium with an antitussive action, but it is little used.

MUCOLYTIC AGENTS

Many patients with chest disease have difficulty in expectorating their viscous sputum. Mucolytic agents are drugs which are claimed to render the sputum less viscous and therefore more easily cleared from the chest. Drugs used for this purpose in the past included ammonium chloride, potassium iodide, ipecacuanha and squill.

Bromhexine

Bromhexine (Bisolvon) is a synthetic derivative of vasicine, an alkaloid derived from the plant *Adhatoda vasica*. Chemically it is *N*-cyclohexyl-*N*-methyl-(2-amino-3,5-dibromobenzyl) ammonium chloride.

Mode of Action
Bromhexine has been shown in vitro to produce rarefaction and fragmentation of mucopolysaccharide fibres in sputum obtained from patients with asthma and chronic bronchitis. If this has any bearing on its action when given to a patient, it may be able to cause a reduction in sputum viscosity. After bromhexine therapy there may be changes in the pattern of sputum immunoglobulins and also alterations in the secretory granules in the glands of the bronchial mucosa, suggesting that clinical improvement might be anticipated.

Indications
Controversy surrounds the possible therapeutic benefit of bromhexine. It probably does cause a reduction in sputum viscosity and an increase in daily sputum volume, but it has not clearly been shown to improve the patient's clinical state or ventilatory function. The usual oral dose is 8–16 mg three times daily, and the manufacturers claim that it is useful in chronic bronchitis, bronchial asthma and mucoviscidosis. No toxic effects have been reported.

Carbocisteine

Carbocisteine (Mucodyne, Mucolex) is a derivative of the sulphur-containing amino acid cysteine, which has been shown to exert a mucolytic action on sputum in vitro or in the lumen of the bronchi when administered as an aerosol spray.

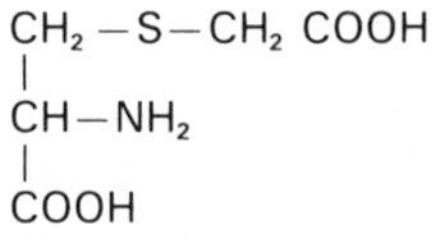

$$
\begin{array}{ll}
CH_2-S-CH_2\ COOH & CH_2-SH \\
| & | \\
CH-NH_2 & CH-NH_2 \\
| & | \\
COOH & COOH
\end{array}
$$

S-CARBOXYMETHYLCYSTEINE 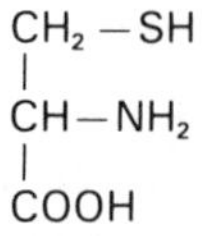   CYSTEINE

Mode of Action

Carbocisteine may exert its effect by one or more of the following mechanisms:

1. Splitting of disulphide bonds linking strands of mucus.
2. Changes in the forces binding large mucoid molecules.
3. Reduction of the mucous gland hyperplasia associated with chronic bronchitis.
4. Correction of the shift towards the sulphomucins with an increase in the sialomucins in the sputum of chronic bronchitics. This would reduce its viscosity.

The sputum of patients with chronic bronchitis is rendered more fluid and as a result the patients are claimed to suffer less disability from their disease.

Pharmacokinetics

Carbocisteine is S-Carboxymethyl-L-cysteine. It is readily absorbed from the gastrointestinal tract and approximately 40% of an orally administered dose can be recovered from the urine in 24 hours.

Indications

Carbocisteine decreases the viscosity and increases the volume of sputum in chronic bronchitis. There is, however, conflicting evidence on whether it improves the patient's clinical state or ventilatory function. It is presented as a syrup (5% w/v) and the adult dose is 15 ml three times daily initially, this being reduced to 10 ml three times daily when a satisfactory response has been obtained.

Adverse Effects

Toxicity. Minor side-effects reported include heartburn, nausea and epigastric discomfort, diarrhoea and headache. Carbocisteine should not be used in patients with peptic ulceration because of possible effects on the mucus-secreting glands of the stomach. The drug should not be given during the first trimester of pregnancy.

The fact that these preparations have a true value has not yet been established.

FURTHER READING

Crofton J. W. & Douglas A. C. (1969) *Respiratory Diseases*. Oxford: Blackwell Scientific.

Hoffbrand B. I. (ed.) (1975) The place of parasympatholytic drugs in the management of chronic obstructive airways disease. *Postgrad. med. J., Suppl.* 7: 51.

Pain M. C. F. (1973) The treatment of asthma. *Drugs*, 6: 118.

Palmer K. N. V. & Petrie J. C. (1980) Respiratory diseases. In: Avery G. S. (ed.) *Drug Treatment*, p. 760. Sydney and New New York: Adis Press; Edinburgh and London: Churchill Livingstone.

Paterson J. W. (1969) Bronchodilator drugs. In: Marsh B. T. (ed.) *A Symposium on Reversible Airway Obstruction*. Allen & Hanbury Ltd.

Pepys J. & Frankland A. W. (eds) (1969) *Disodium Cromoglycate in Allergic Airways Disease*. London: Butterworth.

Rebuck A. S. (1974) Antiasthmatic drugs I: Pathophysiological and clinical pharmacological aspects. *Drugs*, 7: 344.

Rebuck A. S. (1974) Antiasthmatic drugs II: Therapeutic aspects. *Drugs*, 7: 370.

Silverman M., Connolly N. M., Balfour-Lynn L. & Godfrey S. (1972) Long-term trial of disodium cromoglycate and isoprenaline in children with asthma. *Br. med. J.*, 3: 378.

Trembath P. W. (1982) Clinical pharmacology of the respiratory tract. In: Turner P. & Shand D. G. (eds) *Recent Advances in Clinical Pharmacology*, Vol. 2, p. 55. Edinburgh, London, Melbourne and New York: Churchill Livingstone.

Wilcox J. B. & Avery G. S. (1973) Beclomethasone dipropionate inhaler. *Drugs*, 6: 84.

8 Drugs Acting on the Alimentary System

R. C. Heading

ANTACIDS

Antacids are drugs which are taken orally to neutralize the hydrochloric acid secreted by the stomach. By temporarily raising the pH of the gastric contents they relieve the pain of peptic ulcer or oesophagitis and are, therefore, widely used in the treatment of these conditions.

Most currently available antacids are mixtures of several acid-neutralizing substances. It is useful first to consider the properties of these individually.

Sodium bicarbonate

Sodium bicarbonate rapidly neutralizes gastric acid. It is readily available in most homes (as baking soda) and is often taken by patients on their own initiative. However, frequent ingestion of sodium bicarbonate tends to produce a metabolic alkalosis, since bicarbonate in excess of that required for neutralization of the gastric contents is readily absorbed by the alimentary tract. A sustained alkalosis combined with a substantial intake of calcium, as in milk or in calcium-containing antacids, may eventually lead to the development of a hypercalcaemic syndrome (milk alkali syndrome), which in severe forms includes irreversible renal damage. Regular long-term use of sodium bicarbonate in the treatment of peptic ulcer, therefore, is to be avoided.

The other antacids in common use are not absorbed by the gastrointestinal tract and, consequently, do not produce systemic alkalosis.

Magnesium trisilicate

Magnesium trisilicate neutralizes hydrochloric acid by a complex chemical reaction leading to the formation of magnesium chloride, magnesium carbonate and a hydrated silicon dioxide. Some absorption of these products occurs, but is only of practical significance in the presence of renal insufficiency, when magnesium toxicity may develop. Like the other magnesium antacids, magnesium trisilicate tends to produce diarrhoea.

332

Magnesium oxide and Magnesium hydroxide

Magnesium oxide and magnesium hydroxide are also effective antacids, but magnesium carbonate is less potent.

Aluminium hydroxide

Aluminium hydroxide reacts with hydrochloric acid in the stomach to form aluminium chloride, which then reacts further in the small intestine to form insoluble salts, including the phosphate. There is no significant absorption, but the drug increases faecal excretion of phosphate and may rarely lead to phosphate depletion. Aluminium salts cause constipation. Aluminium hydroxide also absorbs bile salts and is sometimes used in place of cholestyramine (p. 350) in the treatment of diarrhoea due to impaired bile salt absorption by the small intestine.

Calcium carbonate and Calcium hydroxide

Calcium carbonate and calcium hydroxide react with gastric acid to form calcium chloride, some of which is absorbed. This is undesirable in the presence of renal insufficiency and even in the absence of pre-existing renal disease it may facilitate development of the milk alkali syndrome.

Absorbed calcium stimulates the release of gastrin and thus ingestion of substantial quantities of the calcium antacids may actually increase gastric acid secretion. This is presumably undesirable, given the circumstances that have led to use of the antacid in the first place.

The calcium antacids have been said to produce constipation, but the evidence is questionable.

PRINCIPLES OF ANTACID THERAPY

The relief of peptic ulcer pain does not require complete chemical neutralization of the gastric contents. It is sufficient to elevate the pH above 3.5 and this is the basis of the symptomatic relief provided by food, something well known by most peptic ulcer patients. Most foodstuffs, but particularly those with a high protein content, have an acid-buffering action and thus raise the pH of the gastric contents in spite of simultaneously stimulating acid secretion. After some time, typically 1–2 hours, the pH falls again as the food is emptied from the stomach, and symptoms may then recur. Neutralization of the gastric contents by antacids is governed by the same factors, and provided an antacid of sufficiently high neutralizing capacity is administered with sufficient frequency, neutralization of the gastric contents can be achieved to a degree that will allow duodenal ulcers to heal. However, the ingestion of such large quantities of antacid is impractical and will often provoke diarrhoea. A more realistic approach is to employ antacids as symptomatic therapy and advise patients to take them (1) when symptoms are present and/or (2) when symptoms may be anticipated — i.e. between meals. A dose of 15–30 ml of most liquid preparations or one or two tablets will usually provide adequate relief of pain.

PREPARATIONS AVAILABLE FOR CLINICAL USE

A great variety of official and proprietary antacid preparations is available, most being mixtures of the individual antacid substances already described. In such mixtures opposing side-effects may sometimes be usefully cancelled out — for example, the constipating effects of aluminium hydroxide may be opposed by the tendency of magnesium trisilicate to produce diarrhoea. In addition, there is considerable variation in the sodium content of the antacid mixtures in common use and for some patients (e.g. those with hepatic cirrhosis or cardiac failure) it may be desirable to choose a preparation that is low in sodium.

Many antacids are available in both liquid and tablet forms. Liquid preparations usually provide more rapid neutralization of gastric acid, but tablets may be preferred for practical reasons. For example, a patient may find a bottle of liquid antacid difficult to carry while at work.

Dimethicone is a surface tension-reducing agent added to some proprietary antacid preparations to coalesce bubbles. Its value is not established.

Alginates are incorporated in some antacid mixtures (e.g. Gaviscon, Gastrocote) and produce a floating viscous gel within the stomach which appears to diminish gastro-oesophageal reflux.

Local anaesthetics have been combined with antacid mixtures (e.g. Mucaine) as a means of providing additional relief from the pain of oesophagitis, but are of questionable value.

Salicylates are best avoided by patients with peptic ulcer disease and their combination with antacids is unsound.

Antipepsins

Reduction in the peptic activity of gastric secretions is inevitably produced by all antacids simply as a consequence of the elevation in pH. However, a more specific reduction of pepsin activity has been suggested as a means of assisting peptic ulcer healing; the practical value of this is doubtful.

Aluminium hydroxide gel adsorbs pepsin in addition to its antacid action.

ULCER HEALING DRUGS

Antacids (in conventional dosage) and most anticholinergic drugs have no significant effects on ulcer healing.

Cimetidine

$$CH_2\ CH_2\ NH_2$$

HISTAMINE

$$CH_3\quad CH_2\,S\,CH_2\ CH_2\ N\,H\,C\,NH\,CH_3$$
$$\|$$
$$N-C\equiv N$$

CIMETIDINE

Cimetidine (Tagamet) was the first histamine H_2-receptor antagonist to become freely available for therapeutic use. Chemically related to histamine, it is a potent inhibitor of gastric acid secretion. For patients with duodenal ulcers, four weeks' therapy with the conventional dosage of 200 mg three times daily and 400 mg at night, or the alternative regimen of 400 mg twice daily, will permit ulcer healing in approximately 60% of patients. After eight weeks of therapy, the corresponding figure exceeds 80%. When healing has occurred, maintenance treatment for up to a year with 400 mg twice daily or even a single dose of 400 mg each evening will prevent recurrence of ulceration in about 70% of patients treated. However, duodenal ulceration will recur in most patients within 6–12 months of stopping maintenance treatment so a permanent 'cure' is not achieved. Many physicians are reluctant to prescribe prolonged periods of maintenance therapy for duodenal ulcer patients and prefer to repeat four or six week courses of treatment as the need arises. If a patient only requires such treatment once or twice a year, he is usually well satisfied.

Cimetidine also appears to be effective in promoting the healing of gastric ulcers. The dosage required is the same as for duodenal ulcers. For the treatment of oesophagitis, a higher dose of 400 mg four times daily is recommended and usually provides excellent relief of symptoms. However, no more than a modest improvement in the condition of the oesophageal epithelium is usually observed, and in such patients a choice may have to be made between continuing therapy indefinitely and resorting to surgery.

I.v. administration of cimetidine (200 mg every four or six hours) is helpful in the treatment of severe haemorrhagic gastritis or stress ulceration. On occasion prophylactic administration of the drug may be of value for patients who are at serious risk of developing such lesions. This is the situation, for example, in the first few days after major trauma or burns, or following renal transplantation. Cimetidine administration has also been advocated in relation to obstetric practice, to minimize the rare but serious acid aspiration syndrome (Mendelson's syndrome), which may sometimes complicate the induction of general anaesthesia.

Approximately 80% of an oral dose of cimetidine is absorbed and the half-time of elimination is just under two hours. Most of the drug is excreted unchanged in the urine. The use of cimetidine in patients with renal failure requires some caution, in view of the renal pathway of elimination. However, it appears that provided an appropriate reduction in daily dose is made, the drug can be used even when renal impairment is severe. Cimetidine is readily removed by haemodialysis.

Possible adverse reactions to cimetidine include diarrhoea, drowsiness and itchy skin rashes. The drug has some anti-androgenic activity, but the relationship of this effect to the occasional development of gynaecomastia and hyperprolactinaemia remains obscure. Impotence has also been attributed to cimetidine, but is uncommon.

By interfering with cytochrome P450 activity, cimetidine prolongs the duration of action of drugs undergoing oxidative metabolism by this enzyme. The effect is seldom of clinical significance, but the fact that cimetidine will potentiate the activity of warfarin and phenytoin should be borne in mind and, if appropriate, the dose of these drugs should be reduced.

There has been considerable publicity about the possible carcinogenicity of cimetidine, should formation of its mononitroso derivative occur within the stomach. At present the evidence suggests that this conversion does not occur.

Ranitidine

Ranitidine (Zantac) is a potent histamine H_2 antagonist, chemically related to histamine. The indications for its use are as for cimetidine and, given in a dose of 150 mg twice daily, its efficacy in the treatment of peptic ulcer and oesophagitis is comparable. Ranitidine does not interfere with the oxidative metabolism of other drugs and does not have the unwanted endocrine effects of cimetidine. No serious side-effects have so far been identified.

Ranitidine is mostly excreted unchanged by the kidney and a reduced dosage is appropriate in patients with renal failure.

Sucralfate

Sucralfate (Antepsin) is an aluminium salt of sucrose octasulphate. When given orally, it adheres to ulcerated gastric and duodenal mucosa, but not to healthy mucosa. The dense, sticky layer that forms in an ulcer crater is thought to provide a physical barrier separating acid and pepsin from the ulcer base, which then has an opportunity to heal. The substance also has some acid neutralizing capacity and is a pepsin inhibitor. Its efficacy in facilitating healing of duodenal and gastric ulcers appears comparable with that of cimetidine. The fact that the drug does not undergo systemic absorption and is thus virtually free of side-effects is an obvious attraction. The recommended dose is 1 g four times daily for 4–6 weeks.

Bismuth

A bismuth compound, tripotassium dicitratobismuthate (De-Nol), promotes the healing of duodenal ulcers. Like sucralfate, it may adhere to necrotic tissue in an ulcer crater, forming a physical barrier between the duodenal lumen and viable tissue so that healing can occur. It is available as a liquid or as tablets.

Pirenzepine

Pirenzepine (Gastrozepin) is an anticholinergic drug which appears to inhibit the secretory actions of acetylcholine more profoundly than other actions. It affects gastric secretion in particular, and a useful inhibition of gastric acid secretion can be achieved without the development of unwanted anticholinergic effects. Treatment for 4–6 weeks with 50 mg twice daily has been shown to promote duodenal ulcer healing. At this dose, anticholinergic side-effects, including a dry mouth and impairment of visual accommodation, have been reported, but are uncommon.

Carbenoxolone sodium

Carbenoxolone (Biogastrone) is a derivative of glycyrrhizinic acid, a constituent of liquorice. It accelerates the healing of gastric ulcers, but the fundamental basis of its action is still controversial. An increased production of gastric mucus and prolongation of the gastric epithelial cell lifespan are recognized.

Carbenoxolone is rapidly absorbed by the gastric mucosa and its effects are believed to result from a topical action. Attempts have been made to formulate a 'position release' capsule which would allow topical application of the drug to a duodenal ulcer (Duogastrone), but these are of doubtful efficacy. Carbenoxolone is given in a dose of 100 mg two or three times daily for 4–8 weeks. The drug promotes retention of sodium and water by the renal tubule, with concomitant potassium loss, and thus weight gain, oedema, hypertension and hypokalaemia are likely complications. These can often be overcome by the administration of a diuretic and potassium supplements. Spironolactone, which would appear to be the logical choice of drug to counteract these effects, also interferes with the desired action of carbenoxolone on the stomach.

Because of its effects on water and electrolyte balance, carbenoxolone is contraindicated in the presence of cardiac failure and in hypertension. Its use in the elderly requires caution.

Pyrogastrone

Pyrogastrone is a combination of carbenoxolone sodium, antacids and alginic acid which is promoted for the treatment of oesophagitis. The value of including carbenoxolone in the mixture is not yet generally accepted.

Deglycyrrhinized liquorice

Deglycyrrhinized liquorice is the residue after removal of carbenoxolone-like substances from crude liquorice. It has also been thought to have an action in promoting ulcer healing, but this has not been confirmed.

Anticholinergics

Anticholinergic drugs such as propantheline reduce gastric acid secretion and might be expected to be of value in the treatment of duodenal ulcer. In practice they proved disappointing and they have now been almost completely superseded by the ulcer-healing drugs described above. However, motility of the stomach and small intestine is suppressed by anticholinergic agents and several have been promoted for the relief of 'gastrointestinal spasm'. Their effectiveness is difficult to assess, not least because the diagnosis is not amenable to precise definition. In some patients, and by a mechanism which is not fully understood, they prevent regurgitation from a hiatus hernia in the night, a dangerous event which could cause asphyxia. Certain patients avert this problem by taking 15 mg of propantheline bromide on retiring at night.

Gastrointestinal Hormones

Pentagastrin

Pentagastrin is the carboxy-terminal pentapeptide of gastrin and is a potent stimulant of gastric-acid secretion. It has no therapeutic application, but is used diagnostically to assess the acid-secretory capacity of the stomach. Pentagastrin is administered s.c. or by i.v. infusion and acid secretion can be quantified after aspiration through a nasogastric tube.

Secretin

Secretin is used similarly in the assessment of exocrine pancreatic secretion, which may be aspirated through a tube positioned in the duodenum. The volume and composition of the secretion are subsequently determined.

EMETICS

An emetic is a drug which is deliberately given to produce vomiting. This may be appropriate after ingestion of some poisons, but has little other application.

A traditional means of inducing vomiting consists of drinking a concentrated solution of common salt, which probably acts as a direct irritant to the gastric mucosa, with vomiting induced reflexly by the vagus. Although simple, this method is unreliable and may lead to serious hypernatraemia.

Apomorphine

Apomorphine is related to morphine. It has a specific action on a chemoreceptor zone in the brain stem, which connects with the vomiting centre. The drug is therefore described as a central emetic and nausea and vomiting develop within a few minutes of s.c. injection of 4–8 mg.

ANTIEMETICS

Antiemetics are substances that counteract nausea and vomiting. Some are believed to act on the chemoreceptor trigger zone, adjacent to the vomiting centre in the brain stem, whereeas others act directly on the vomiting centre itself. The former group are thus antiemetic only in respect of stimuli that activate the chemoreceptor zone, whereas the latter are potentially effective against all causes of vomiting. The trigger zone is thought to be implicated in the vomiting of uraemia, pregnancy, radiation sickness and digitalis overdosage and is not implicated in motion sickness. Its role in most other causes of vomiting is less certain.

Most of the antiemetics that act directly on the vomiting centre are antihistamines that also have anticholinergic activity. As other antihistamines and many anticholinergic drugs have no antiemetic action, there is an intriguing possibility that the antiemetic activity results from a particular molecular structure that can coincidentally combine with both histamine H_1 and acetylcholine receptors. The significance of this, if any, is still unknown.

Several of the antiemetic drugs are phenothiazines. Other uses of phenothiazines and their side-effects are described elsewhere (pp. 164–8).

Chlorpromazine

Chlorpromazine (Largactil) has a powerful sedative and antiemetic action, the latter probably mediated by the chemoreceptor trigger zone. It is of particular value in the treatment of vomiting associated with uraemia, radiation sickness and disseminated malignant disease, where its sedative property may also be appropriate. The usual dose is 25–100 mg by i.m. injection.

Promazine

Promazine (Sparine) is similar in its effects.

Promethazine

Promethazine (Phenergan, Avomine) is another phenothiazine, but, in contrast to chlorpromazine and promazine, it is also a potent antihistamine. It is believed to act directly on the vomiting centre and is effective against motion sickness. If any antiemetic drug is required to treat vomiting in pregnancy, promethazine is effective and as safe as any, although an absolute guarantee of complete safety as regards the fetus cannot be given (p. 565). Like the other phenothiazines, promethazine has a sedative action which in many clinical situations is advantageous. However, sufferers from motion sickness must be advised that after use of the drug they should not drive a car or other vehicle or pilot an aircraft.

Promethazine is given in doses of 25 mg by i.m. injection, or orally as a prophylactic for motion sickness.

Diphenhydramine and Dimenhydrinate

Diphenhydramine (Benadryl) and its derivative, dimenhydrinate (Dramamine), are effective against motion sickness in doses of 100 mg.

Cyclizine

Cyclizine (Marzine) is one of the most widely used antiemetic drugs in clinical practice. It is effective in suppressing nausea and vomiting from a variety of causes. I.m. injections (50 mg) may be repeated 4-hourly. Drowsiness may occur, but other side-effects are rare.

Meclozine

Meclozine (Ancoloxin) also has a low incidence of side-effects and is successfully used against motion sickness. The usual dose, which is 50 mg, has a prolonged action of up to 12 hours.

Hyoscine

Hyoscine, an anticholinergic drug related to atropine, has also been widely used for motion sickness. Its mode of action may differ from that of most of the other antiemetic drugs and may be derived purely from its sedative properties.

Metoclopramide

Metoclopramide (Maxolon, Primperan) is chemically related to procainamide (p. 298). An action on the chemoreceptor trigger zone has been claimed, but the drug also has a direct action on the gastrointestinal musculature, promoting peristalsis, so that gastric emptying is accelerated and small intestinal motility increased. The relative importance of these central and peripheral actions in reducing nausea and vomiting is uncertain. The drug has also been used to facilitate gastrointestinal intubation procedures and by radiologists to hasten the passage of barium through the small intestine. Concurrent administration of anticholinergic drugs will impair or abolish all actions of metoclopramide.

Metoclopramide is given by i.m. or i.v. injection in 10 mg doses. Tablets are also available. The most important adverse reaction is an extrapyramidal syndrome similar to that seen with the phenothiazines. It is uncommon and resolves when the drug is discontinued. Parenteral administration of metoclopramide occasionally produces a sensation of claustrophobia and panic. Metoclopramide increases serum prolactin concentrations, but this is usually of no clinical significance.

Domperidone

Domperidone (Motilium) is a dopamine antagonist which appears not to cross the blood–brain barrier. The mechanism of its antiemetic activity is not wholly clear, but blockade of peripheral dopamine receptors is postulated. The usual dose is 10–20 mg orally, or 5–10 mg by i.m. injection or as an i.v. infusion. The drug should not be given by i.v. bolus injection, since cardiac dysrhythmias may be induced.

PURGATIVES

Purgatives are drugs taken to promote the evacuation of faeces. The term 'laxative', which appears to suggest an agent less drastic in its effects than a purgative, is in practice synonymous.

There are two general categories of purgatives:

1. Those that increase the bulk or water content of the faeces to facilitate easier passage (bulk purgatives, osmotic purgatives).
2. Those that stimulate intestinal motility (stimulant purgatives).

Bulk purgatives

The character of the faeces is in part determined by diet, since foods with a high content of indigestible cellulose and fibre (high-residue foods) tend to increase faecal bulk. Water is then retained within the faecal mass and the stools remain soft. Much attention is now being directed to the significance of this in relation to diverticular disease of the colon and colonic cancer, both of which are particularly common in the Western 'developed' countries, where the diet is generally low in residue.

It follows that most of the so-called bulk purgatives are not purgatives at all, in as much as they do not 'purge' with the dramatic result the term tends to suggest. They are more in the nature of a dietary manipulation with a physiological rather than a pharmacological action.

Methylcellulose (Celevac) absorbs water and swells to form a gel, so that faecal bulk is increased and the stool softened. The usual daily dose is 1–3 g and the substance should be taken with a substantial volume of fluid. Intestinal obstruction is a possible complication, but is rare.

Agar is derived from seaweed and has a similar effect to the above. The dose is 4–12 g/day.

Isogel, **Fybogel** and **Regulan**, preparations of a plant seed husk (Ispaghula husk, BPC), and **Metamucil**, from psyllium seeds, have a similar action.

Dietary modifications, including an increased intake of wholemeal bread, green vegetables and fruit, achieve the same effect. Bran, the residue of husks after the milling of wheat, is also widely taken as a means of 'keeping regular'. Figs and prunes, while providing some bulk effect, also contain organic acids which have a mild irritant action on the colon. Fybranta is a proprietary preparation containing bran in tablet form.

Osmotic purgatives

Certain inorganic salts that are minimally absorbed by the small intestine act as purgatives by virtue of their osmotic effect within the colonic lumen. Water absorption by the colonic mucosa is reduced, with the production of a soft or even a fluid stool.

Magnesium sulphate is a potent means of osmotic purgation. Both the magnesium and sulphate ions are minimally absorbed by the small intestine. It may be used as a means of providing near-complete evacuation of the small and large intestine in patients with chronic liver disease who have suffered a major gastrointestinal haemorrhage and are likely to develop hepatic encephalopathy. The usual dose is 5–20 g.

Magnesium hydroxide (milk of magnesia) has a similar action, but is less potent. It is also a gastric antacid and may offer a means of counteracting the tendency to constipation produced by some other antacids. The usual dose is 10 ml of magnesium hydroxide mixture, BP, one to four times daily.

Sodium sulphate and **Sodium potassium tartrate** are also osmotic purgatives.

Stimulant purgatives

Phenolphthalein is incorporated in many proprietary preparations and is thought to act by direct colonic stimulation. The therapeutic dose is 50–300 mg. Some is absorbed by the small intestine and is then excreted in the bile — an enterohepatic circulation — with the result that the colon is effectively exposed to a second dose. Excretion of absorbed phenolphthalein in the urine will produce a pink coloration if the pH is alkaline and this can be a source of alarm to the patient. The drug may also produce a skin rash.

Phenolphthalein is often implicated in laxative-induced diarrhoea, a condition in which psychologically disturbed patients purge themselves repeatedly, but deny use of any laxative preparation.

Anthraquinone purgatives. The well-known and widely used group of anthraquinone purgatives includes senna, cascara, rhubarb and aloes. The active principles are liberated by hydrolysis of parent glycosides in the small intestine and are all chemically related to anthraquinone. They are absorbed and subsequently re-excreted into the colon, where they are thought to stimulate the myenteric plexus and induce contraction of colonic muscle. There is thus some delay between their ingestion and time of action, and therapeutically they are usually administered late in the evening, so that they may exert their effects the following morning. An advertisement for one American proprietary preparation has attempted to convey this by asserting that 'it works safely and gently while you sleep'.

The anthraquinone purgatives may cause some discoloration of the urine, which can become yellow or red according to the urinary pH. Moreover, their regular use may lead to deposition of pigment in the colonic mucosa (melanosis coli). Neither of these effects need cause concern. However, more serious is the relatively recent suggestion that repeated use of anthraquinone purgatives may eventually cause degeneration of the myenteric plexus and impair normal colonic propulsive activity. In consequence, these purgatives are not to be recommended for long-term use, but for occasional use they are safe and effective. Many proprietary preparations are available. Senokot (dose two to four tablets) is one of the best known, each tablet containing a quantity of sennosides A and B equivalent to 7.5 mg of sennoside B. It is also available as granules or a syrup. Dorbanex contains a synthetic analogue of the natural anthraquinones named danthron and is given in a dose of 5–10 ml.

Bisacodyl (Dulcolax) is a synthetic substance and a derivative of pyridine. Given in tablet form (5–10 mg) or as suppositories (10 mg), it exerts a direct stimulant action on the colonic muscle. It is widely used in current clinical practice. Adverse reactions are rare. It may occasionally cause severe abdominal cramps and suppositories can cause local rectal irritation.

Castor oil is hydrolysed within the small intestine, liberating ricinoleic acid. This is mildly irritant to the small intestine and peristalsis is increased. The absorbed ricinoleic acid probably also modifies motility of colonic muscle. In addition to the stimulant action, some of the oil which escapes hydrolysis acts as a stool lubricant and passage of a soft oily stool generally occurs within six hours of ingestion of the drug.

A traditional remedy of the Victorian era, castor oil has little place in modern medicine.

Other agents

Liquid paraffin is a mineral oil which is minimally absorbed by the alimentary tract. It mixes with and coats the intestinal contents, leading to the formation of soft oily faeces. Some separation of the oil from the faeces may occur in the rectum, this lubricating passage of the faecal mass. It has no other action on the bowel.

Liquid paraffin has for many years been used extensively in the management of constipation, but its use is no longer justified. There is no evidence that it is any more effective than the hydrophilic bulk purgatives and its use is likely to be compromised by the separation of the oil and faeces in the rectum, since the oil may then trickle down to the anal sphincter, where leakage is both messy and embarrassing for the patient. Liquid paraffin also inhibits the absorption of fat-soluble drugs and vitamins. In the very young and in the elderly, there is a particular risk of aspiration which may lead to a lipoid pneumonia.

Docusate sodium (Dioctyl-Medo, Dioctyl-forte and numerous other preparations) is a surface-activating (wetting) agent which softens faeces by increasing their water content. It is safe, effective and especially useful in the treatment of painful anal conditions such as fissures or following haemorrhoidectomy, where the development of hard faecal masses must be prevented. It is available in tablet or syrup form and is used in doses of 40–200 mg three times daily. It may modify the absorption of some other drugs. Sometimes it is combined with the anthraquinone purgative danthron, or with phenolphthalein. It is also used to soften wax in the ear.

Glycerin can be introduced into the rectum as a suppository, and defaecation usually results within 30 minutes. Bisacodyl (p. 343) is more reliable.

Enemas

Enemas, if given to evacuate faeces from the bowl, act (1) by being a distension stimulus to the bowel which promotes evacuation and (2) by simple lavage. Water alone may be used, but slightly soapy water (ordinary household soap) is traditional. A buffered phosphate solution may be preferred.

The fluid (200–250 ml) is instilled into the rectum and evacuation of the bowel generally occurs within a few minutes.

Retention Enemas, as the term suggests, are given in order to be retained within the bowel, usually as a means of giving a drug (e.g. enemas of prednisolone; p. 406).

CONSTIPATION

Constipation is not easy to define. There is a wide individual variation in the normal frequency of bowel evacuation and it is not sufficient to equate constipation with infrequent defaecation. The nature of the stool passed is perhaps more relevant in that hard faecal masses (scybala) are almost always abnormal and are liable to render defaecation painful. As a result, defaecation tends to be postponed and the problem gets worse.

Constipation may be a symptom of many unrelated diseases and clinically it is unforgivable to treat the symptom without consideration of the cause. This is particularly important when a patient indicates that his established normal bowel frequency has altered, since there must be some reason for the change. It is self-evident that when constipation is the consequence of such underlying disease, treatment must often be directed primarily to the cause.

Almost any acute illness will produce temporary constipation. The physical inactivity inevitable when an ill patient retires to bed probably worsens this tendency and the admission of such a patient to hospital with the attendant psychological stress of an unfamiliar environment may make matters worse still. Finally, the embarrassment of the bedpan or bedside commode and the frequently justified uncertainty of privacy while using either must be potent reasons for many patients to postpone defaecation. Clearly the use of purgatives constitutes only part of the management of this problem.

Constipation may be produced by several drugs (e.g. opiates, anticholinergics, or calcium- or aluminium-containing antacids). Appropriate treatment may require the withdrawal of the offending drug or the use of a purgative.

Chronic constipation presents the greatest problem. It may occur in diverticular disease, in the irritable bowel syndrome, or simply as a habit, often developed as a result of childhood resistance to the normal awareness of the need to defaecate. This may lead to a suppression of that awareness, which is normally produced when the rectum is filled with faeces by mass movement from the sigmoid colon. The use of bulk purgatives plays an important part in the management of such chronic constipation. Observance of an appropriate (high-residue) diet and re-establishment of the normal 'call to defaecation' are equally important and, with persistence, a relatively normal bowel habit can be restored. The problem is not easily dealt with, but the temptation to resort to stimulant purgatives is best resisted.

ANTIDIARRHOEAL DRUGS

Several drugs provide symptomatic and palliative therapy for diarrhoea by a variety of mechanisms. Diarrhoea may generally be equated with the production of excessively liquid faeces and the action of many antidiarrhoeal drugs is to diminish the 'free water' content of the stool, either by influencing intestinal (including colonic) motility to enhance water reabsorption by the mucosa or, in the case of non-absorbable agents, by soaking up the free water and thus rendering the faeces more solid. The formerly held belief that diarrhoea of colonic origin, whatever the primary pathology, resulted from excessive colonic motility is now recognized as being quite inaccurate, and some forms of diarrhoea are undoubtedly associated with reduced contractile activity of the colonic muscle. The subject is both complex and controversial, reflecting the reality that diarrhoea is the consequence of a variety of physiological derangements, and the symptomatic treatment of diarrhoea is usually undertaken on an empirical rather than a pharmacological basis. The use of antidiarrhoeal drugs on a symptomatic basis is, of course, only permissible when due consideration has been given to the underlying cause of the diarrhoea and, where appropriate, specific treatment of the cause initiated.

Codeine phosphate

The action of opiates, including codeine, on colonic smooth muscle is complex. Their efficacy in diarrhoea is probably due to an increase in the non-propulsive contractions of colonic muscle, permitting the faeces to be retained longer within the lumen and thus increasing water reabsorption. Codeine phosphate is given as tablets or in syrup in a dose of 30–60 mg three times daily. Although very effective in many forms of diarrhoea, codeine is best avoided when diarrhoea is associated with intestinal colic and in diverticular disease where excessive non-propulsive colonic contractions are believed to be the basis of the disease.

Morphine

Morphine acts in a similar manner to codeine. It is not used alone as symptomatic treatment of diarrhoea, but is often given together with kaolin.

Diphenoxylate

Diphenoxylate is related to pethidine and presumably acts like the opiates. It is available combined with atropine as 'Lomotil', usually given as two tablets four times a day.

Loperamide

Loperamide (Imodium) is similar to diphenoxylate, but does not have sedative or respiratory depressant effects. It is available as capsules or in a syrup and is usually given in divided doses totalling 4–12 mg daily in the adult.

Propantheline bromide (p. 209–10)

Anticholinergic drugs diminish intestinal motility. They sometimes have a beneficial effect on diarrhoea, but are frequently of great value in relieving colicky abdominal pain if this is an accompaniment to the diarrhoea.

Dicyclomine hydrochloride

Dicyclomine (Merbentyl) is an anticholinergic drug frequently used for abdominal cramps, particularly if these are associated with the irritable bowel syndrome. A suitable dose is 10 mg three times daily. It is available in tablet form or as a syrup.

Side-effects of anticholinergics and their contraindications are described elsewhere (p. 206).

Kaolin

Kaolin is a time-hallowed remedy for diarrhoea, but the pharmacological basis for its efficacy is unknown. It has been suggested that it absorbs 'toxins' from the bowel, but the nature of these toxins and their relationship to diarrhoea have not been established. Kaolin is often used combined with morphine in *kaolin and morphine mixture, BPC*, and this is an effective antidiarrhoeal agent. The dose is 15–30 ml 4-hourly.

Methylcellulose

Methylcellulose and other water-absorbing agents (e.g. isogel) provide some help in many cases of diarrhoea by reducing the free water content of the stool. They are especially useful in controlling colostomies and ileostomies when the faeces are excessively liquid. These agents are described under purgatives (p. 341), and their practical value in both constipation and diarrhoea may appear surprising, though it has a rational basis in their hydrophilic nature.

Mebeverine

Mebeverine (Colofac, which should not be confused with Celevac, p. 342) is a derivative of papaverine (p. 109). It has a spasmolytic action on intestinal muscle, but differs from anticholinergic agents in that its action is not one of parasympathetic blockade and appears to involve direct action on the muscle or myenteric plexus. It is thus a drug of considerable pharmacological interest.

Mebeverine is as effective as any drug in the irritable bowel syndrome and is probably the drug of choice for this condition in a dose of 135 mg three times daily. It does not have significant side-effects.

Peppermint oil

Peppermint oil (Colpermin) reduces the contractile activity of the colonic muscle and may also be helpful in treatment of the 'irritable bowel'. The usual dose is two capsules three times daily.

IRRITABLE BOWEL SYNDROME

Irritable bowel syndrome, a very common condition, remains one of the most poorly understood in gastroenterology. It may manifest as constipation or diarrhoea or alternating bouts of each and is believed to be a motility disorder of the colon which, at least in part, has a psychosomatic basis. Sometimes cramp-like pains are a major feature. Drug treatment may form part of the management and antispasmodic agents such as dicyclomine and mebeverine and hydrophilic agents such as bran and methylcellulose are often employed.

DRUGS USED IN THE TREATMENT OF ULCERATIVE COLITIS

Ulcerative colitis is an inflammatory condition of the rectal and colonic mucosa which results in diarrhoea. The cause is unknown.

Prednisolone

Prednisolone (p. 406) (40–60 mg daily, in divided doses) is effective in the treatment of acute attacks. When the condition is less severe, prednisolone or hydrocortisone may be given in a retention enema once or twice daily. Predsol retention enemas contain prednisolone 20 mg (as disodium phosphate) per 100 ml.

Sulphasalazine

Sulphasalazine (Salazopyrin) is a compound molecule of sulphapyridine and 5-aminosalicylic acid which has a specific value in ulcerative colitis. The drug is broken down into its two components by bacterial action within the colon and the sulphapyridine is substantially absorbed. The basis of the action of sulphasalazine in ulcerative colitis is uncertain, but appears to be associated with the aminosalicylic acid moiety.

Sulphasalazine reduces the relapse rate of ulcerative colitis. Its value in the treatment of the acute attack is less certain, but once a remission has been induced, continued treatment with the drug reduces the likelihood of a further acute attack. Sulphasalazine is given in divided doses of 2–3 g daily (plain or enteric-coated tablets) or as suppositories for the treatment of disease confined to the rectum.

Side-effects include nausea and vomiting and haemolysis. Severe haemolytic anaemia (p. 564) is unusual. Skin rashes and leucopenia are also recognized. In males, the drug causes a reduction in the sperm count, which appears to be reversible on cessation of therapy.

MISCELLANEOUS THERAPEUTIC AGENTS

Lactulose

Lactulose is a disaccharide which is not hydrolysed by the enzymes of the pancreatic and intestinal secretions. Taken orally, it passes unchanged to the lower alimentary tract, where it can be hydrolysed by carbohydrate-fermenting bacteria and thus provides an acceptable nutrient for them. The growth of these organisms is then favoured and results in a fall in faecal pH, which is thought to be the basis of the mild laxative action of the drug.

Lactulose is of value in the treatment of hepatic encephalopathy. This is probably an indirect consequence of the lowering of faecal pH, which may inhibit the growth of the micro-organisms that produce ammonia or other nitrogenous substances thought to be implicated in this condition. Lactulose is available as a 50% w/w solution and 50 ml is given two to four times daily.

Vasopressin

Vasopressin (Pitressin) in high dosage lowers splanchnic venous pressure and this effect has led to its use in attempting to arrest haemorrhage from oesophageal varices. It is given by i.v. infusion (20 units at 1 unit/min.), and may be repeated until other effects (colicky abdominal pain or diarrhoea) provide testimony of its action. Since pitressin also diminishes coronary artery blood flow, its use may be hazardous in patients with ischaemic heart disease.

Bile acids

Chenodeoxycholic acid (Chendol) has been shown to be successful in dissolving cholesterol gallstones when given orally in divided doses totalling 10–15 mg/kg body weight per 24 hours. The composition of bile is modified, increasing its capacity to dissolve cholesterol. Use of the drug should be limited to patients in whom gall bladder function is preserved (as judged radiologically) and where gallstones do not exceed 2 cm in diameter. A prolonged period of treatment is necessary, perhaps a year, and gallstone recurrence after completion of therapy is likely unless some maintenance therapy is given thereafter. Thus the drug is unlikely to displace cholecystectomy as the treatment of choice for cholesterol gallstones and has no place in the treatment of other types of gallstones.

Diarrhoea appears to be the only troublesome side-effect of chenodeoxycholic acid.

Ursodeoxycholic acid (Destolit, Ursofalk) is similar to chenodeoxycholic acid but seldom causes diarrhoea. Two doses, each of 4–5 mg/kg body weight, are given daily.

Administration of bile acids would at first sight seem to be appropriate to control the steatorrhoea that occurs in conditions of bile salt depletion that may follow disease or resection of the distal ileum. However, this is usually of little value, since the bile acids cannot then be absorbed by the small intestine and their onward passage into the colon gives rise to a diarrhoea which may be more severe than that of the untreated condition.

Cholestyramine

Cholestyramine (Questran) is an ion exchange resin which absorbs bile salts. Taken orally, it thus prevents their reabsorption by the distal ileum and facilitates depletion of the bile salt pool. This is of particular value in cholestatic syndromes where normal excretion of bile salts into the bile is impaired, since administration of cholestyramine will cause serum concentrations of bile acids to fall and the itching associated with high serum concentrations is thereby relieved.

Cholerrhoeic diarrhoea occurs when excess bile salts reach the colon from the small intestine owing to disease (or surgical resection) of the distal ileum. Cholestyramine, by adsorbing the bile salts, prevents such diarrhoea. The usual dose is 4–16 g daily.

The drug is probably the treatment of choice for Type II hyperlipidaemia, for which it is prescribed together with a diet low in animal fat. Depletion of the bile salt pool diverts hepatic metabolism of cholesterol towards the synthesis of bile acids and thereby assists in the reduction of serum cholesterol.

Cholestyramine adsorbs many substances besides bile acids, including many drugs. On theoretical grounds, the binding of acidic drugs is particularly likely. Caution is therefore necessary when other drugs are also being taken orally and it is wise to separate their administration by at least 1 hour.

Pancreatin

Pancreatin is a preparation containing pancreatic enzymes, principally trypsin and lipases and is used as a form of replacement therapy in cases of pancreatic exocrine insufficiency. Steatorrhoea is reduced and the patient's nutritional state improved. The drug is available as capsules, powder and enteric-coated tablets, but as many as 16 tablets may be required daily, 3 or 4 being taken before or with each meal.

Nutrizym is a proprietary preparation of pancreatin combined with bromelains, which are proteolytic enzymes derived from pineapples.

Medium-chain triglycerides

The triglyceride esters of medium-chain-length fatty acids (8–12 carbon atoms) are used as therapeutic agents. Their absorption by the intestine occurs principally through the portal venous system, in contrast to fatty acids of longer chain length, which are largely resynthesized to triglyceride within the mucosa and transported to the systemic circulation by the lymphatic system. In addition, the greater solubility in water of the medium-chain fatty acids renders their absorption less dependent on bile salts. Thus, in conditions where intestinal disease or inadequate bile salt production compromises absorption of the usual dietary fats, medium-chain triglycerides are more likely to be reasonably well absorbed. Adequate nutrition may therefore be achieved, while steatorrhoea is avoided by prescription of a diet low in normal fat. The usual dose is 30–60 ml three times daily, the preparation being incorporated with other fluids or with food.

Vitamin D

Vitamin D (Calciferol) (p. 440) may sometimes be required by patients with malabsorptive conditions in which the normal absorption of calcium and vitamin D is impaired. As with the dietary vitamin in normal individuals, its efficacy is dependent on conversion into the monohydroxy and dihydroxy derivatives in liver and kidney, respectively, but the impairment in absorption may be overcome by administration of doses many times in excess of normal dietary intake. From 1.25 mg (50 000 international units) twice weekly to 2.5 mg daily may be required, but the dose must be tailored to individual requirements, since overdosage may lead to serious hypercalcaemia.

Special diets

The prescription of particular diets in the treatment of disease lies outside the scope of this book and reference should be made to a textbook of therapeutics. However, it may be noted that in the UK certain products which strictly are foodstuffs may be officially recognized as 'drugs' for the purposes of NHS prescriptions. Gluten-free bread for patients with coeliac disease and lactose-free baby foods for infants with galactosaemia are regarded thus.

FURTHER READING

Albibi R. & McCallum R.W. (1983) Metoclopramide: pharmacology and clinical application. *Ann. intern. Med.*, 98: 86.
Binder H. J. & Donowitz, M. (1975) A new look at laxative action. *Gastroenterology*, 69: 1001.
Bouchier I. A. D. (1983) Gallstone dissolving agents. *Brit. med. J.*, 286: 778.
Conn H.O. (1978) Lactulose: a drug in search of a modus operandi. *Gastroenterology*, 74: 624.
Editorial (1981) Antacids for duodenal ulcer. *Brit. med. J.*, 282: 1495.
Feely J. & Wormsley K.G. (1983) H$_2$-receptor antagonists — cimetidine and ranitidine. *Brit. med. J.*, 286: 695.
Freston J.W. (Ed.) (1979) G.I. pharmacology and current therapy. *Clinics Gastroenterol.*, 8:1.
Langman M.J.S. (1982) Antacids for duodenal ulcer. *Brit. med. J.*, 285: 1520.
Lennard-Jones J.E. (1983) Towards optimal use of corticosteroids in ulcerative colitis and Crohn's disease. *Gut*, 24: 177.

9 Drugs Acting on the Kidney

J. Nimmo

The drugs described in this chapter are those whose prime locus of activity is situated in the kidney or urinary tract. Many of the drugs used to treat renal disorders do not have a specific action on the kidneys and will not be considered here. For example, the chemotherapeutic agents used to treat infections are considered in Chapter 1. Corticosteroids and other immunosuppressive drugs which may be used to treat a number of renal disorders, including the nephrotic syndrome, are also discussed elsewhere.

DIURETICS

The word 'diuresis' really means the excretion of urine, but is usually employed to signify an *increase* in the volume of urine. Moreover, the clinically important diuretic agents produce a net loss of both solute, particularly sodium chloride, and water. Diuretics may act in two principal ways: they may increase the renal blood flow and glomerular filtration rate, or they may augment solute excretion in the glomerular filtrate and tubular fluid. Drugs having the first of these actions are not conventionally regarded as diuretics, but included among them are the cardiac glycosides, certain xanthine derivatives, plasma volume expanders and dopamine. The second group consists of osmotic diuretics and drugs that inhibit sodium reabsorption from the glomerular filtrate. These are able to increase the amount of solute, and thus of water, excreted by the kidneys.

The various diuretics will be considered systematically, but it should be realized that this is not the order of their importance in modern practical therapeutics.

Osmotic Diuretics

Osmotic diuretics are certain substances which are not electrolytes and which are freely filtered at the glomerulus and poorly reabsorbed by the renal tubule. While having a diuretic action, they are otherwise pharmacologically inert.

352

Mannitol

Mannitol, a polyhydric alcohol, is the only commonly used osmotic diuretic, although urea and sucrose were formerly employed for this purpose. High concentrations of glucose in the blood and, accordingly, in the urine are well known to produce polyuria in uncontrolled diabetes mellitus, because the glucose acts as an osmotic diuretic.

Mode of Action

During the infusion of mannitol the fluid throughout the proximal convoluted tubule remains isotonic with the plasma. The unabsorbed mannitol in the tubular lumen limits the diffusion back of water and thus the urine flow is increased. The urinary volume is roughly proportional to the rate of solute excretion and in this instance the solute excreted is largely mannitol. Osmotic diuretics can maintain a good urine flow, even in the presence of a significant reduction in glomerular filtration rate. During mannitol diuresis the tubular reabsorption of sodium is depressed in the proximal tubule and loop of Henle.

Pharmacokinetics

Mannitol must be infused i.v. to produce a diuresis. When given by mouth, it produces osmotic diarrhoea, since it is poorly absorbed from the gastrointestinal tract. Mannitol does not undergo metabolic degradation, is freely filtered at the glomerulus and is not significantly absorbed from the tubule of the nephron.

Indications

The output of sodium promoted by mannitol is insufficient to be of clinical importance and hence the substance cannot be used to increase sodium excretion sufficiently to mobilize oedema fluid. Mannitol should not be given to patients with congestive cardiac failure, since it causes an increase in plasma volume. It has been used in the prophylaxis of acute renal failure, as, for example, after cardiac surgery, severe trauma or severe intravascular haemolysis. In these conditions mannitol will maintain the flow of urine when oliguria would otherwise have been expected. In refractory shock from hypotension mannitol may increase the renal blood flow sufficiently to protect the renal tissue from hypoxia. Another indication for the use of mannitol is the regulation of the osmotic pressure of the plasma. This allows a certain amount of control of the pressure and volume of the cerebrospinal fluid, something that can be of value if there is cerebral oedema after a head injury. Another indication is an intracranial tumour, when surgery is not possible and the patient's life is threatened while investigations are still proceeding.

Dosage

Mannitol must be given i.v., as a 10 or 25% aqueous solution. The dose varies widely, but is usually 25–100 g/day. After a head injury, where appropriate,

500 ml of 25% mannitol may be given over 30–40 minutes as an initial measure.

Adverse Effects

Toxicity. The major potential toxicity of mannitol is related to the increase in plasma volume produced. Thus vascular overfilling with hyperosmolality and cardiac decompensation may occur.

Mercurial Diuretics

Organic mercurials are no longer used as diuretics in clinical practice. They are, however, of historical interest. Calomel (mercurous chloride) was used as a diuretic in the sixteenth century and was later an ingredient of the famous 'Guy's Hospital pills' (digitalis, squill and calomel). Calomel was replaced, because of its toxicity, by the organic mercurials, the most famous of which, mersalyl, was introduced in 1924. The mercurial diuretics of clinical importance were mercuripropanols and mercuripropyl derivatives of organic acids, and mersalyl injection was the sodium salt of mersalyl acid combined with theophylline for i.m. administration. Neptal was a related proprietary product.

The organic mercurial diuretics represented a significant advance in the treatment of oedema. They had many disadvantages, however. They were poorly absorbed from the gastrointestinal tract and had to be given by injection. Toxicity was common and the adverse reactions included sudden death from ventricular fibrillation, acute allergic phenomena, nausea, vomiting, fever, urticaria, and severe haematological disturbances including agranulocytosis. Systemic mercury poisoning was likely if renal function was impaired.

Carbonic Anhydrase Inhibitors

Acetazolamide

A number of aromatic sulphonamides with a free sulphamyl group ($-SO_2-NH_2$) have been known since the 1930s to be specific inhibitors of carbonic anhydrase. The only member of this group with clinical importance as a diuretic is acetazolamide, a 2-acetyl amino derivative of thiadiazole-sulphonamide. The formula for this is shown below, together with sulphanilamide (the therapeutically active moiety of Prontosil).

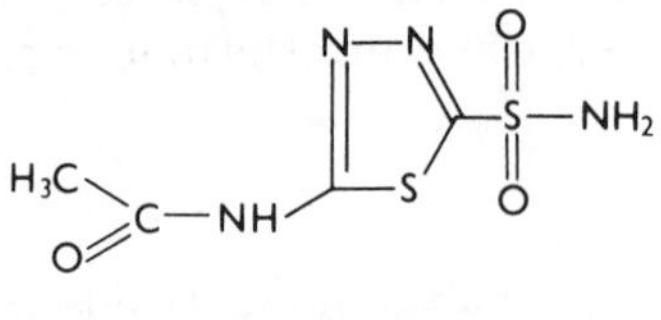

ACETAZOLAMIDE 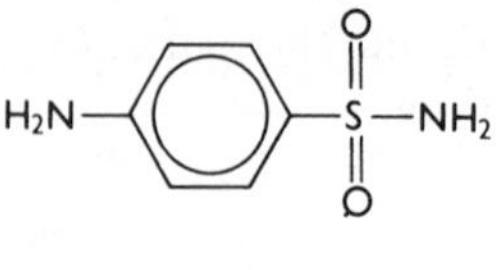   SULPHANILAMIDE

Mode of Action

Carbonic anhydrase catalyses the hydration of carbon dioxide to form carbonic acid, the first step in the production of the bicarbonate and hydrogen ions:

$$CO_2 + H_2O \overset{\text{carbonic anhydrase}}{\rightleftharpoons} H_2CO_3 \rightleftharpoons H^+ + HCO_3^-$$

Acetazolamide acts by a non-competitive inhibition of carbonic anhydrase. Hydration of carbon dioxide proceeds only very slowly in the absence of the enzyme. There is therefore a lack of hydrogen (H^+) ions, which are normally secreted into the tubular fluid in exchange for reabsorbed sodium (Na^+) ions. This inhibition of the $H^+ \rightleftharpoons Na^+$ exchange by the renal tubule leads to increased urinary secretion of sodium, accompanied by biocarbonate ions. Bicarbonate excretion is increased, because the carbonic anhydrase inhibitory effect of the drug also suppresses the reabsorption of carbon dioxide from the tubular fluid.

Following the administration of acetazolamide, therefore, the urine contains increased amounts of sodium, potassium (K) and bicarbonate and, accordingly, the urine volume increases. The urine becomes alkaline, the plasma bicarbonate falls and if therapy is continued, the patient develops metabolic acidosis. In the presence of metabolic acidosis more H^+ ions are available for exchange with Na^+ and K^+, and acetazolamide becomes much less effective in reducing sodium reabsorption.

Pharmacokinetics

Acetazolamide can be taken by mouth and is rapidly absorbed from the gastrointestinal tract: peak plasma levels are reached within 2 hours of administration. Like other sulphonamides, acetazolamide is excreted unchanged in the urine, 80% being excreted within 12 hours. Acetazolamide accumulates within the body in tissues with a high concentration of carbonic anhydrase and these include erythrocytes and cells of the renal cortex.

Indications

Acetazolamide is no longer commonly used as a diuretic agent, since more potent agents are now available and, by producing a metabolic acidosis, the drug induces a form of tolerance to its own activity. Acetazolamide is used in the treatment of glaucoma because it depresses the formation of aqueous humour and thus lowers intraocular pressure. The dosage used in glaucoma is 250–1000 mg in divided doses per 24 hours.

Acetazolamide has also been used as an anticonvulsant, particularly in petit mal epilepsy. It also appears to be beneficial in the management of periodic paralysis.

Adverse Effects

Toxicity. Toxic effects of acetazolamide are not common. Drowsiness, paraesthesiae, headache, dizziness and fatigue may occur. Like other sulphonamides, acetazolamide may cause fever and blood dyscrasias such as leucopenia, agranulocytosis, thrombocytopenia and aplastic anaemia. Allergic skin reactions may develop. Calculus formation and ureteric colic may result, because there is a decrease in urinary citrate with no decrease in urinary calcium.

Thiazide (Benzothiadiazine) Diuretics

This is the group of diuretics most commonly used in clinical practice. The benzothiadiazine diuretics, commonly called thiazide diuretics, were discovered in the 1950s during the search for further carbonic anhydrase inhibitors. Although chemically related to the latter, they are more powerful diuretics and have a totally different mode of action. Nevertheless, most of the thiazide diuretics retain some carbonic anhydrase inhibitory effect in addition.

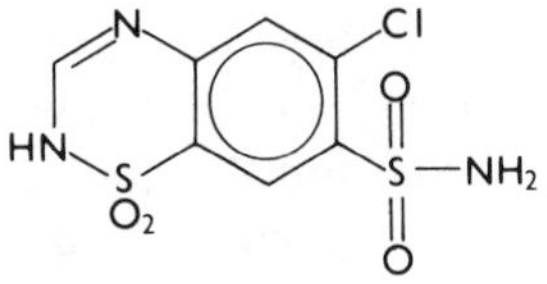

CHLOROTHIAZIDE

The first member of this group found to have diuretic properties was cholorothiazide. Other members include hydrochlorothiazide, flumethiazide, hydroflumethiazide, bendrofluazide and polythiazide. Chlorthalidone and quinethazone are sulphonamide diuretics with a different chemical structure but similar pharmacological activity to the thiazides, so they too are discussed in this group.

Mode of Action

The thiazide diuretics increase the renal excretion of sodium and chloride and of an accompanying volume of water. This is due to inhibition of the tubular mechanisms for electrolyte reabsorption. Their effect is independent of alterations in acid–base balance. Thiazides also produce a significant increase in potassium excretion. There has been considerable controversy over the exact site of their action in the kidney. They are regarded as medium potency agents, acting mainly by inhibition of Na^+ in the cortical diluting segment of the nephron, i.e. the early distal tubule. Certain evidence suggests that they may also act on the proximal tubule.

All thiazides produce increased potassium excretion in the urine. This results from increased potassium secretion by the distal tubule. Since sodium reabsorption is inhibited, there is a higher concentration of that ion in the tubular fluid reaching the distal segment, where sodium is absorbed in exchange for potassium, thereby favouring increased sodium–potassium exchange at that site and an increase in potassium excretion in the urine.

Pharmacokinetics

The thiazides are absorbed from the gastrointestinal tract and are effective when given by this route. Chlorothiazide is relatively slowly absorbed from the intestine and rapidly cleared by the kidneys, so larger doses are required when this particular preparation is used. Hydrochlorothiazide and its congeners are absorbed rapidly from the gastrointestinal tract.

When the thiazides are given orally, diuresis begins in 30 minutes and continues for 12 hours or more. Plasma half-lives vary with the different members of the group, but most thiazides are excreted rapidly, within 3–6 hours. Bendrofluazide, polythiazide and chlorthalidone have a longer duration of activity, because of their slower rate of excretion. Thiazides are excreted primarily by the kidney and to a lesser extent by the liver. All probably undergo tubular secretion in the proximal convoluted tubule, by the same mechanism as the penicillins (p. 6) and certain other substances, including *para*-aminohippurate, a preparation used to measure renal plasma flow. (Inulin clearance is employed to study the glomerular filtration rate.)

Indications

The thiazides are used successfully in the day-to-day management of oedema due to congestive cardiac failure, and of chronic hepatic or renal disease. They also have a useful hypotensive action. Paradoxically, the thiazides can be used to reduce the daily urine volume in diabetes insipidus and hypercalciuria may also respond favourably to thiazide therapy.

The thiazide diuretics are usually given once daily in the morning. The daily doses commonly given are:

Chlorothiazide tablets, BP (500 mg)	500 mg–2 g
Hydrochlorothiazide tablets, BP (25 or 50 mg)	25–100 mg
Hydroflumethiazide tablets, BP (25 or 50 mg)	25–100 mg
Bendrofluazide tablets, BP (2.5 or 5 mg)	5–10 mg
Chlorthalidone tablets, BP (50 or 100 mg)	100–200 mg daily or on alternate days

Adverse Effects

Toxicity. Toxic effects of the thiazides are relatively rare. Unexpected hypersensitivity may occur, resulting in purpura, dermatitis, blood dyscrasias or necrotizing vasculitis. Patients with bronchial asthma may have an attack precipitated. Prolonged therapy may produce mild hyperglycaemia, perhaps due to the suppression of insulin release from the pancreas. Treatment with thiazide diuretics may also cause an increase in the blood uric acid level, since the thiazides decrease urinary excretion of uric acid by inhibiting renal tubular secretion, and an attack of gout may be precipitated. The treatment of gout is considered on p. 137.

In order to avoid potassium depletion, thiazides should be prescribed together with potassium supplements or in association with one of the 'potassium-sparing' diuretics.

Newer compounds

Xipamide (Diurexan) is 4-chloro-5-sulphamoyl-2',6'-salicyloxylidide and resembles chlorthalidone structurally. It is rapidly absorbed after oral administration and is highly protein bound. It is excreted almost entirely by the kidney. Xipamide acts mainly on the proximal part of the distal tubule with perhaps an additional site of action on the distal part of the loop of Henle. It is more potent than the other thiazides and chlorthalidone. The usual dose is 20–40 mg daily.

Metolazone (Metenix) is a quinazolinone derivative. Sixty-four per cent of an orally administered dose is absorbed and 95% is bound to plasma proteins or erythrocytes in the blood. Approximately 80% of the absorbed drug is excreted unchanged in the urine. The usual dose is 5–80 mg daily. Metolazone would appear to have no advantage over the older thiazides.

Indapamide (Natrilix) is a chlorosulphonamide derivative of indoline and is, therefore, chemically related to chlorthalidone. It has been claimed that indapamide lowers the arterial pressure by decreasing peripheral resistance and vascular reactivity with minimal diuretic activity and hence it is promoted as an antihypertensive. The action of indapamide is progressive and the reduction in arterial pressure may not reach a maximum until several months after the start of therapy. The recommended dose is 2.5 mg daily.

Frusemide (furosemide, USP)

FRUSEMIDE

Frusemide is a very potent diuretic that has proved to be a major advance in modern therapeutics. Chemically, frusemide is a monosulphamylanthranilic acid derivative related to the thiazides. It differs from the thiazides in being more powerful and in producing a greater increase in renal chloride excretion.

Proprietary names are Aluzine, Dryptal, Frusetic and Lasix. It is also formulated with potassium salts, other names then being used (p. 362).

Mode of Action

The pharmacological activities of frusemide are confined to the kidney. It acts by inhibiting sodium reabsorption, principally in the ascending limb of the loop of Henle but also in the early distal tubule (cortical diluting segment) and the proximal convoluted tubule. By virtue of its action on the ascending limb of Henle's loop, frusemide interferes with the countercurrent multiplier system and causes excretion of a greater volume of water for a given amount of sodium than diuretics without this locus of activity. The major urinary anion is chloride, and varying amounts of potassium are lost. The diuretic effect is independent of acid–base balance and frusemide does not inhibit carbonic anhydrase. Frusemide has been claimed to produce mild renal vasodilatation and a slight increase in the glomerular filtration rate.

Pharmacokinetics

Frusemide is effective by the oral, i.m. or i.v. route. It is rapidly absorbed from the gastrointestinal tract and a diuretic response should occur 30 minutes after oral administration. Frusemide is strongly bound to plasma proteins. Two-thirds of an ingested dose is excreted through the kidney by glomerular filtration and proximal tubular secretion. A small proportion of frusemide is metabolized by the splitting off of the side-chain; the remainder is excreted in the faeces.

Indications

Frusemide produces prompt diuresis beginning within 30 minutes of administration and this lasts for up to 6 hours. In the severely oedematous patient, massive diuresis occurs and fluid losses of up to 10 litres may occur in 24 hours. Frusemide is extremely valuable in acute pulmonary oedema if given i.v. It is also indicated in oedema due to hepatic or renal disease or in resistant oedema of congestive cardiac failure. It may be used in ascites and toxaemia of pregnancy. Because of its potent action, vast fluid and electrolyte shifts result and it should be reserved for acute or emergency situations, the more gentle thiazides being employed for long-term therapy.

Frusemide has a wide therapeutic range and its effect is proportional to the dosage. The usual oral dose is 40 mg given once daily. This may be increased if necessary. For emergency use, 20–40 mg of frusemide may be injected i.v. or i.m.

Very large doses of frusemide (250 mg–2 g) have been tried i.v. in the management of oliguria due to acute or chronic renal failure. These doses may induce a large diuresis, but there is no evidence that the renal haemodynamic disorder of acute ischaemic renal failure can be influenced by frusemide.

Adverse Effects

Toxicity. The most important toxic effects are due to the powerful diuretic effect of the drug. In particular, when frusemide is administered hypotension and hypovolaemia may occur. Potassium depletion must be prevented by the use of supplements. Chronic dilutional hyponatraemia may also occur. Frusemide may lead to hyperuricaemia and hyperglycaemia. Occasionally skin rashes, thrombocytopenia, neutropenia and gastrointestinal disturbances occur. The use of frusemide in the first trimester of pregnancy should be avoided if possible.

In elderly men with prostatism, the sudden diuresis produced by frusemide may precipitate acute urinary retention.

Ethacrynic Acid

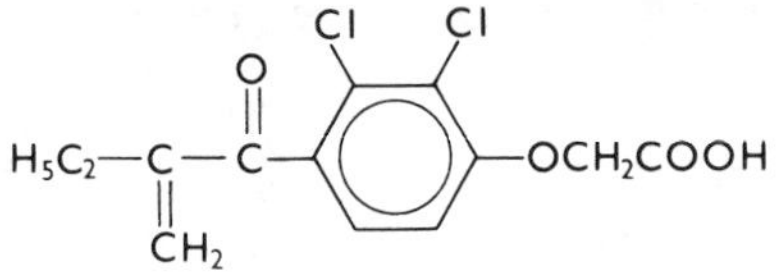

ETHACRYNIC ACID

Ethacrynic acid has very similar pharmacological properties to frusemide and was introduced into clinical practice at about the same time. It is not related chemically to the thiazides, but was developed on the assumption that, as mercurials have a diuretic action since they have an affinity for sulfhydryl groups, the combination of an unsaturated ketone, which has a similar affinity, together with an aryloxyacetic acid, itself concentrated in the kidneys, might be an effective diuretic.

Ethacrynic acid may be given orally or i.v. and it produces a prompt, brisk diuresis. A proprietary name is Edecrin.

Mode of Action
Like frusemide, ethacrynic acid inhibits the absorption of sodium, predominantly in the ascending limb of the loop of Henle. The urine contains chloride as the main anion. Ethacrynic acid does not inhibit carbonic anhydrase and its effect is independent of acid–base balance.

Pharmacokinetics
Ethacrynic acid is readily absorbed from the gastrointestinal tract, and produces a diuretic response within 2 hours of being taken by mouth. After intravenous administration, the plasma half-life is 30–70 minutes, about one-third of the dose being excreted by the liver and two-thirds by the kidney.

Indications

The therapeutic uses of ethacrynic acid are similar to those of frusemide. The initial oral dose in adults is 50 mg once daily. This may be increased by 25 mg/day up to a maximum of 150 mg. The usual adult i.v. dose is 50 mg.

Adverse Effects

Toxicity. The toxic effects of ethacrynic acid are similar to most of those of frusemide. Ethacrynic acid has a narrower dose–response curve than frusemide, and, therefore, adjustment of the dose to achieve the desired therapeutic effect is more difficult.

Bumetanide

Bumetanide (3-n-butylamino-4-phenoxy-5-sulphamoylbenzoic acid; Burinex) is a derivative of metanilamide and is a potent diuretic resembling frusemide both chemically and pharmacologically. It has greater potency than frusemide on a weight basis, in a ratio of about 60:1, and has a rapid onset with a short duration of action.

Mode of Action

Bumetanide acts, like frusemide, by inhibiting sodium reabsorption in the ascending limb of the loop of Henle, the early distal tubule and the proximal convoluted tubule.

Pharmacokinetics

Bumetanide is well absorbed when given orally, and there is an almost equal diuretic response after oral and parenteral administration. The mean plasma half-life is 3.5 hours, and the drug is 95–97% protein bound in plasma. Bumetanide is largely eliminated by renal excretion.

Indications

Like frusemide, bumetanide can be given orally, i.m. or i.v. to produce a prompt and powerful diuresis.

The usual dose by mouth is 1 mg once daily, this being increased if necessary up to 4 mg per day, although doses of 15 mg per day may be required in resistant cases. The i.v. dose is 0.5 mg.

Adverse Effects

Toxicity. Like frusemide, bumetanide may produce hypovolaemia and circulatory collapse or electrolyte disturbances. Bumetanide may cause an increase in the blood uric acid and glucose concentrations. Other reported reactions include skin rashes, muscular cramps, abdominal discomfort, thrombocytopenia and gynaecomastia. Although no teratogenic effects have been shown in animals, bumetanide should not be used in the first trimester of pregnancy.

Combinations of Diuretics and Potassium Supplements

The diuretics described above all cause increased potassium excretion by the kidney, and potassium supplements almost always should be given with diuretics to prevent potassium depletion. A number of proprietary preparations of a diuretic–potassium combination are available. These are widely used in general practice, where there might be the danger of an elderly patient taking a diuretic without potassium supplements, but their use in hospital is deprecated.

Examples of such preparations are Lasikal (20 mg frusemide + 750 mg potassium chloride per tablet), Lasix + K (40 mg frusemide + 750 mg potassium chloride), Diumide K (40 mg frusemide + 600 mg potassium chloride), Burinex K (0.5 mg bumetanide + 573 mg potassium chloride), Neo-NaClex K (2.5 mg bendrofluazide + 630 mg potassium chloride) and Navidrex K (0.25 mg cyclopenthiazide + 600 mg potassium chloride).

Potassium-sparing Diuretics

Potassium-sparing diuretics discussed include spironolactone, triamterene and amiloride.

Spironolactone

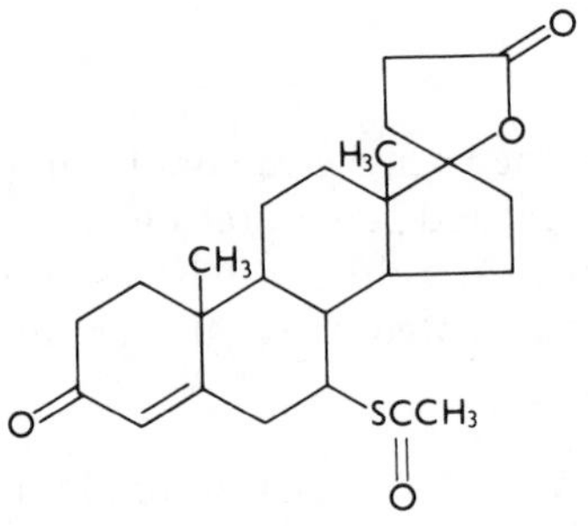

SPIRONOLACTONE

Spironolactone (Aldactone, Diatensec, Spiroctan) is an antagonist of aldosterone, the most potent endogenous mineralocorticoid (p. 408). Spironolactone is a 17-spirolactosteroid with a 7-acetylthio group.

Mode of Action
The renin–angiotensin system has been implicated in the mechanisms of congestive cardiac failure and it has been demonstrated that increased amounts of aldosterone are secreted by patients with heart failure. Spironolactone is thought to act as a competitive antagonist of aldosterone at the renal tubule. It may compete for the receptor site, since it is a homologue

of the hormone. Spironolactone causes secretion of sodium, retention of potassium, decrease in urinary titratable acidity, and increase in urinary pH. There is no alteration in renal blood flow or glomerular filtration rate.

Pharmacokinetics
Spironolactone is given orally. Repeated doses over a period of several days may be necessary before urinary sodium is increased.

Indications
Spironolactone is relatively ineffective if given alone. It has been used in the management of refractory oedema, in conjunction with other diuretic agents. Spironolactone is particularly useful in the treatment of hepatic cirrhosis with ascites and oedema refractory to other treatment. It is effective when given alone to such patients, but efficiency is increased if it is given in combination with thiazide diuretics. Spironolactone diminishes the potassium loss produced by thiazide diuretics and may be of value if hypokalaemia presents a problem. Excessive secretion of aldosterone contributes to the oedema of the nephrotic syndrome and spironolactone may be a useful addition to other diuretics in this condition. Spironolactone is usually given in an oral dose of 25 mg four times per day.

Adverse Effects

Toxicity. Spironolactone is contraindicated in the presence of hyper-kalaemia, since it may cause further elevation in the serum potassium concentration. Diarrhoea and other gastrointestinal disturbances may occur. Lethargy, drowsiness, ataxia, headache, confusion and gynaecomastia have been observed during spironolactone therapy. Androgenic effects of spironolactone include hirsutism, menstrual disturbance and deepening of the voice.

Potassium canrenoate

Potassium canrenoate (Spiroctan-M) is converted in the body to canrenone, the major active metabolite of spironolactone. Its clinical effects are similar to those of spironolactone. It is administered i.v., so its clinical effects are more rapidly apparent. The normal dose is up to 800 mg daily by slow i.v. injection. It is available for use in hospital patients. There are also preparations available for oral administration.

Triamterene

Triamterene (Dytac) is a pyrazine derivative that inhibits sodium reabsorption and promotes potassium reabsorption in the distal tubule. It is a pteridine compound with a certain relationship to folic acid (p. 465) in its chemical structure.

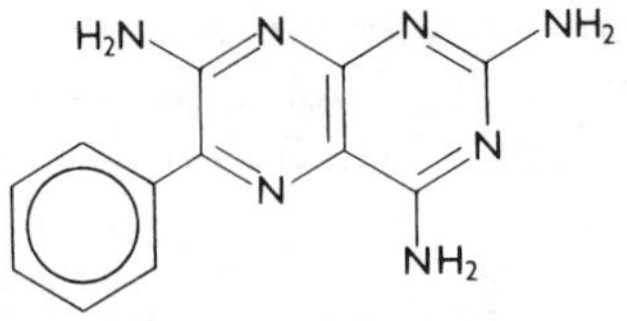

TRIAMTERENE

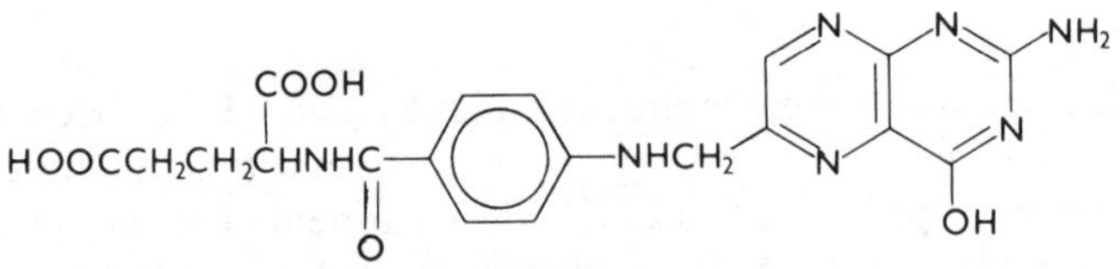

FOLIC ACID

Mode of Action

Triamterene has pharmacological activity only on the kidney. The diuresis produced by triamterene is characterized by increased excretion of sodium and chloride, with slight alkalinization of the urine. There is usually no increase in potassium loss. Indeed, a sharp reduction in potassium excretion is seen when triamterene is given along with another diuretic that itself would cause increased potassium loss, or in circumstances where there is an excess of circulating mineralocorticoid. Triamterene is thought to act directly on the distal tubule, independent of aldosterone and may inhibit secretion of potassium in the distal nephron.

Pharmacokinetics

Triamterene is rapidly absorbed from the gastrointestinal tract. Some 10–88% of the administered dose can be recovered from the urine in 24 hours, this wide range probably reflecting variable absorption. Triamterene is about two-thirds bound to protein in the plasma.

Indications

Although some oedematous patients respond to triamterene given alone, the greatest usefulness of the drug is when it is given with other diuretics such as the thiazides, because it produces greater loss of sodium with less depletion of potassium.

When given alone, the dose of triamterene for the adult is 150–250 mg/day, in divided doses. When administered in combination with a thiazide, the usual dose is 150 mg/day. Patients receiving triamterene must not receive potassium supplements and the serum potassium concentration must be measured regularly.

It is marketed in capsule form with benzthiazide under the proprietary name of Dytide. Each capsule contains 50 mg of triamterene and 25 mg of benzthiazide. Dyazide tablets are another proprietary combination, there being 50 mg of triamterene and 25 mg of hydrochlorothiazide, BP, in each tablet.

Adverse Effects

Toxicity. Side-effects are uncommon, but include nausea, vomiting, cramps and dizziness. Slight elevation in the blood urea may occur. Potassium-conserving therapy should be used with caution in severely ill patients in whom metabolic or respiratory acidosis may occur, because the development of acidosis may cause a rapid increase in serum potassium.

Amiloride

Amiloride (Midamor) is an organic base which is also a pyrazine derivative. Only 15–26% of an orally administered dose is absorbed. Excretion is by the kidney.

The therapeutic usefulness of amiloride is comparable to that of triamterene and its mode of action is believed to be similar. This drug can be used alone or in combination with a thiazide diuretic. Used alone, the dose is 10 mg/day by mouth. When used in combination, the daily dose is 5–10 mg. Amiloride should not be used in the presence of hyperkalaemia, anuria, severe renal disease with uraemia, or diabetic nephropathy. Potassium supplements or other potassium-conserving agents should not be given with amiloride. Hyperkalaemia commonly develops in diabetic patients given the drug. Potassium-conserving therapy should be given only with great caution to patients with metabolic or respiratory acidosis. Amiloride should not be used in pregnancy.

Anorexia, nausea, diarrhoea, skin rashes and confusion may occur. Hepatic encephalopathy may be precipitated in patients with cirrhosis.

It is marketed in 5 mg tablets and also in a combination of 5 mg amiloride hydrochloride with 50 mg hydrochlorothiazide, BP, under the proprietary name Moduretic.

Although it is preferable to prescribe the two types of diuretics separately, the use of fixed combinations of a thiazide with triamterene or amiloride may be justified if compliance is a problem, particularly in the elderly.

ALTERATIONS IN URINARY pH

Acid-forming salts such as ammonium chloride have a transient diuretic action. This is of physiological interest only and has no clinical importance. In contrast, however, it is sometimes possible to reduce irritation in an inflamed urinary tract by making the urine alkaline with sodium bicarbonate, citrate or acetate. These are oxidized and the cation combines with bicarbonate.

Sometimes a potassium salt is used and this is preferable in heart failure. A suitable preparation is potassium citrate mixture, BPC, in a dose of 10–20 ml 6-hourly. Potassium should not be given in renal failure.

Emepronium Bromide

Emepronium bromide (Cetiprin) is a quaternary ammonium anticholinergic drug that blocks peripheral cholinergic nerves and ganglionic transmission. In man it increases bladder capacity, by 20% in normal subjects and by a greater amount in patients with neurogenic bladder disorders. It also delays the first desire to void and decreases voiding pressure.

Emepronium bromide may be of value in urinary frequency, including the nocturnal variety, and incontinence in the elderly. Numerous clinical trials would suggest, however, that the benefit is small. Treatment must continue for three to four weeks to obtain optimal response.

Emepronium bromide may produce ulceration of the mouth or oesophagus so must be taken with an adequate amount of fluid. It is contraindicated in patients with oesophagitis or oesophageal obstruction, with prostatic enlargement and large volumes of residual urine, with gastric retention or glaucoma.

The usual dose is 200 mg three times daily.

USE OF DRUGS IN THE PRESENCE OF RENAL DISEASE

As indicated in Appendix 1, the elimination of many drugs will be impaired in patients with acute or chronic renal failure. This may lead to the accumulation of a drug or its metabolites and result in toxicity or adverse reactions. This obviously applies to those drugs that rely on the renal route of excretion. In general, drugs require to be given in lower dosage or at less frequent intervals in renal failure. Plasma drug concentrations should be monitored whenever possible.

It is impossible to give an exhaustive list of drugs that may accumulate in renal failure. Particular care should be taken with:

Antibiotics — penicillin, the aminoglycosides, tetracyclines
Cardiac glycosides
Procainamide
Insulin and sulphonylureas
Cimetidine

The adverse effects of certain drugs on the kidneys is discussed on p. 571.

FURTHER READING

Anderton J. L. & Kincaid-Smith P. (1971) Diuretics I: Physiological and pharmacological considerations. *Drugs*, 1:54.

Anderton J. L. & Kincaid-Smith P. (1971) Diuretics II: Clinical considerations. *Drugs*, 1:141.

Davies D. L., Lant A. F., Millard N. R., Smith A. J., Ward J. W. & Wilson G. M. (1974) Renal action, therapeutic use and pharmacokinetics of the diuretic bumetanide. *Clin. Pharmac. Ther.*, 2: 141.

Lant A. F. & Wilson G. M. (eds) (1973) *Modern Diuretic Therapy in the Treatment of Cardiovascular and Renal Disease*, p. 97. Amsterdam: Excerpta Medica.

Pitts R. F. (1959) *The Physiological Basis of Diuretic Therapy*. Springfield, Illinois: Thomas.

Reidenberg M. M. (1971) *Renal Function and Drug Action*. W. B. Saunders.

10 The Pharmacology of the Endocrine System

A. D. Toft
I. W. Campbell
J. S. A. Sawers

HYPOTHALAMIC AND ANTERIOR PITUITARY HORMONES

Each of the anterior pituitary hormones is secreted by an individual cell-type, although using conventional staining methods the acidophil cells secrete growth hormone (GH) and prolactin (PRL), and the basophils produce adrenocorticotrophic hormone (ACTH), beta-lipotrophin (β-LPH), thyrotrophin (TSH), follicle-stimulating hormone (FSH) and luteinizing hormone (LH). The chromophobe cells are considered not to secrete hormones. Control of anterior pituitary hormone secretion is multifactorial, but releasing and inhibiting hormones (referred to as factors rather than hormones if the structure is not known) synthesized in the hypothalamus and transported via the hypothalamo-hypophyseal portal system to the anterior pituitary are of major importance in this respect. Three hypothalamic peptides have been characterized and synthesized, namely the tripeptide thyrotrophin-releasing hormone (TRH, protirelin), the decapeptide gonadotrophin-releasing hormone (Gn-RH, gonadorelin) and the tetra-decapeptide growth hormone release-inhibiting hormone (GH-RIH, somatostatin). There is no established role in the treatment of endocrine disorders for any of these hormones, but TRH is a valuable investigative tool.

Thyrotrophin-releasing Hormone (TRH)

TRH (pyroglutamyl-histidyl-prolinamide) causes the release of TSH and PRL from the anterior pituitary gland and has been used in the investigation of suspected hypopituitarism and prolactinoma, but the results obtained are sometimes difficult to interpret. The major value of TRH is in the investigation of suspected hyperthyroidism.

TRH Test
The normal level of TSH in the plasma measured by radioimmunoassay is undetectable to 6.0 mU/l, but reference ranges may vary considerably

368

depending on the specificity and sensitivity of the assay employed. With the exception of TSH-secreting pituitary tumours, which are extremely rare, plasma TSH levels should be undetectable in patients with hyperthyroidism because there is a negative feedback effect of raised thyroid hormone levels on the anterior pituitary gland. However, the current assays for TSH are not sufficiently sensitive to discriminate consistently between euthyroid and hyperthyroid patients and the ultimate diagnosis of thyrotoxicosis depends on a lack of increase of plasma TSH 20 min. after the i.v. bolus injection of 200 μg of TRH. In euthyroid subjects, with the exception of some patients with exophthalmic Graves' disease or nodular goitres, there is always a significant increase in TSH following the administration of TRH. It should be emphasized that in most cases of hyperthyroidism the diagnosis is based on clinical signs and measurement of plasma total thyroxine and tri-iodothyronine, and TRH need only be given when the diagnosis would otherwise be in doubt.

Adverse effects of TRH which are common but persist for a few seconds only include nausea, a desire to micturate, flushing and lightheadedness.

Growth Hormone (GH)

GH is a globular peptide synthesized and secreted by the somatotrophs of the anterior pituitary gland. It has structural similarities to PRL and human placental lactogen. The primary effect of GH is to stimulate protein synthesis and tissue growth, the effects on bone and cartilage being mediated by circulating polypeptides collectively known as somatomedins. GH also has metabolic effects which in general oppose the action of insulin. Thus there is stimulation of hepatic glycogenolysis and gluconeogenesis and of adipose tissue lipolysis.

Pharmacokinetics
Episodes of secretory activity are most marked during the early part of sleep, but also occur in the fasting, resting adult when awake, there also being periods during which plasma levels are undetectable. Plasma GH is increased by exercise, stress, hypoglycaemia and by certain amino-acids, especially arginine. Plasma levels are also increased 2–3 hours after meals. Hyperglycaemia, during a glucose load, and supra-physiological doses of corticosteroids suppress GH secretion.

Control of GH secretion is mediated by the hypothalamus and appears to involve central neural transmitters such as dopamine, noradrenaline and serotonin. Final control of GH release depends on the interrelationship between growth hormone releasing factor and somatostatin (GH-RIH). The plasma half-life of GH is about 20 minutes.

Disorders of Production
Overproduction in children leads to gigantism and, after epiphyseal fusion at

puberty, to acromegaly. This is caused by a GH-secreting eosinophil adenoma of the anterior pituitary. The diagnosis is confirmed by the finding of a high fasting plasma GH level which is not suppressed to less than 2.0 mU/l during a standard oral glucose tolerance test.

Underproduction in children leads to dwarfism but has no demonstrable effect in adults. It is diagnosed by the failure of GH levels to rise after i.v. administration of arginine or with insulin-induced hypoglycaemia.

Treatment
Overproduction of GH is treated by hypophysectomy, pituitary irradiation or suppression of GH secretion by the dopamine agonist drug, bromocriptine (p. 371).

Replacement of GH is only undertaken in children who satisfy certain strict criteria. Human growth hormone is only available at special centres and the daily replacement dose is 0.5–1.0 units i.m.

Prolactin (PRL)

PRL shares some of the structural properties of GH. The most well-defined physiological function of PRL in humans is the initiation and maintenance of lactation.

Pharmacokinetics
In contrast to other anterior pituitary hormones, PRL is under tonic inhibitory control by the hypothalamus. The major prolactin-inhibiting factor is dopamine. There is a nyctohemeral rhythm with highest levels during the early hours of sleep and lowest levels between 09.00 and 12.00. Secretion is increased in response to suckling and physical or emotional stress. Hypoglycaemia and tranquillizing drugs such as chlorpromazine increase plasma PRL, while dopamine agonists lower PRL. The increased levels in subjects taking oral contraceptives, and more markedly raised levels in pregnancy, are oestrogen-dependent. The plasma half-life is about 20 minutes.

Disorders of Production
Hypersecretion of PRL may cause galactorrhoea, oligomenorrhoea or amenorrhoea, and infertility, and, in the male, impotence and occasionally galactorrhoea. High plasma PRL levels may be associated with pituitary tumours, which may be very small (microadenomas) but may also result from treatment with drugs such as phenothiazines, metoclopramide, methyldopa, oestrogens, haloperidol, cimetidine and monoamine oxidase inhibitors. Hyperprolactinaemia and galactorrhoea occasionally occur in patients with primary hypothyroidism. About one-third of patients with acromegaly have hyperprolactinaemia. Like GH and ACTH, PRL levels increase with stress

(e.g. difficult venepuncture), making the interpretation of modest hyperprolactinaemia difficult.

Bromocriptine

Bromocriptine (Parlodel) is a dopamine agonist which stimulates dopamine receptors in the brain and thereby suppresses both physiological and pathological hypersecretion of PRL and also GH release in acromegaly.

Indications

Bromocriptine is of value in the following circumstances:

Parkinson's disease. (See p. 239.)

Prevention/suppression of post-partum lactation. Bromocriptine has superseded stilboestrol for this purpose. The dose is 2.5 mg on the first day and 2.5 mg twice daily for the next 14 days.

Acromegaly. Although bromocriptine causes a significant reduction in plasma GH levels associated with symptomatic improvement (e.g. loss of headache, reduction in soft-tissue thickness) in the majority of patients with acromegaly, normalization of levels rarely occurs and overall the results are not as good as those achieved by successful surgery or radiotherapy. Bromocriptine should therefore be used as an adjunct to hypophysectomy in those patients in whom plasma GH levels have not been reduced to normal or near normal and as an interim measure in patients treated by pituitary irradiation, as the maximum reduction in GH may not occur for up to ten years. Bromocriptine may also produce significant shrinkage of a pituitary tumour, and used preoperatively in patients with major suprasellar extension and visual field defects, may facilitate subsequent surgery. The dose in acromegaly is 5–15 mg four times a day, the initial treatment being with a smaller dose.

Galactorrhoea/amenorrhoea/infertility. In the absence of clear evidence of a pituitary tumour, hypothyroidism or offending drugs, hyperprolactinaemia causing galactorrhoea, menstrual disturbance or infertility can be successfully treated with bromocriptine in a dose of 2.5–7.5 mg daily. Not all patients with symptomatic hyperprolactinaemia require drug treatment and the assurance that mild galactorrhoea or amenorrhoea are not associated with any serious disease may be the appropriate course of action. It must be remembered, however, that some patients with hyperprolactinaemia may have a small pituitary adenoma, which, although not radiologically evident at presentation, may enlarge, especially during pregnancy; regular review is therefore necessary. Hyperprolactinaemic impotence in the male is almost always associated with a large pituitary tumour, which in the first instance should be treated surgically.

Adverse Effects

These include nausea, vomiting, constipation, headache, dizziness and postural hypotension, which can be minimized by starting with a dose of 1.25 mg (half a tablet) or 2.5 mg on retiring at night, the amount being increased by 2.5 mg daily every 2–3 days until the appropriate maintenance dose is achieved. With the large doses used in Parkinson's disease, confusion, hallucinations and dyskinesia have been reported.

The majority of patients with hyperprolactinaemia, whether they realize it or not, are infertile and must be warned that treatment of the acromegaly, galactorrhoea or menstrual disorder will restore fertility.

Gonadotrophins (FSH, LH)

See pp. 411, 429.

Thyrotrophin (thyroid-stimulating hormone, TSH)

TSH is a glycoprotein synthesized and secreted by the thyrotrophs of the anterior pituitary. It stimulates all stages of thyroid hormone synthesis by the thyroid gland.

Pharmacokinetics

There is a slight nyctohemeral rhythm in plasma TSH levels which are highest around midnight and lowest in the early morning. The TRH-induced release of TSH from the pituitary is modulated by the negative feedback effect of free thyroid hormones in plasma, which block the action of TRH on the thyrotroph. Thus increases and decreases in plasma free hormone levels result in reciprocal changes in TSH levels. In primary hypothyroidism, plasma TSH levels are raised, usually in excess of 15.0 mU/l, and in hyperthyroidism, TSH levels are normal or undetectable. The plasma half-life of TSH is about 60 minutes.

Disorders of Production

Excessively rarely hyperthyroidism may be due to inappropriate TSH secretion by the pituitary gland, usually in association with a pituitary tumour. Underproduction of TSH due to hypothalamic or pituitary disease is also rare and is seen much less commonly than primary thyroid failure.

Treatment

Theoretically, secondary hypothyroidism could be treated with TSH, but it is much simpler to use thyroxine replacement therapy. The only preparation of TSH which is available is bovine TSH (Thytropar), which is antigenic and which is used solely to differentiate between primary and secondary hypothyroidism in the absence of a reliable radioimmunoassay for TSH.

TSH Stimulation Test

The radio-iodine uptake by the thyroid gland is measured before and after the i.m. injection of 10 units of bovine TSH on each of three consecutive days. In primary hypothyroidism the initial uptake is low and fails to increase following TSH administration, whereas in secondary hypothyroidism there is a significant increase in iodine uptake as the thyroid gland is inherently normal.

Corticotrophin (adrenocorticotrophic hormone, ACTH)

ACTH is a polypeptide of 39 amino acids secreted by the corticotrophs of the anterior pituitary. The 24 amino acids from the N-terminal end of the molecule are responsible for its intrinsic hormonal activity, the remaining 15 for its antigenicity. ACTH stimulates growth of adrenocortical cells and cortisol biosynthesis.

Pharmacokinetics

There are three mechanisms that regulate ACTH and therefore cortisol production:

Nyctohemeral rhythm. ACTH and cortisol are released in a pulsatile manner, presumably in response to the pulsatile release of corticotrophin-releasing factor (CRF) from the hypothalamus. The frequency and duration of secretory episodes is greatest between 03.00 h and 08.00 h and least between 18.00 h and 24.00 h, giving rise to high levels of cortisol and ACTH during the morning, falling to low levels in the evening.

Negative feedback control. Increasing levels of plasma free cortisol decrease the release of CRF from the hypothalamus and decrease the pituitary ACTH response to CRF. Although the physiological role of this negative feedback effect is not clear, the suppressive effects of pharmacological doses of glucocorticoids on pituitary and adrenal function are well recognized.

Stress response. Stress in the form of anxiety, illness, surgery or even repeated venepuncture is a potent stimulus to ACTH and cortisol release. Plasma ACTH and cortisol levels in acute anxiety can be the same as those after major surgery, or in Cushing's syndrome. The increase in plasma ACTH due to minor stress can be reduced by exogenous corticosteroids, but major stress will override the negative feedback control.

Disorders of Production

Inappropriate excess ACTH secretion arises from pituitary tumours (Cushing's disease) or from a variety of extra-pituitary tumours, most commonly small-cell carcinoma of lung (ectopic ACTH secretion). Although initial therapy is usually by means of surgery or radiotherapy, drugs interfering with the synthesis of cortisol, such as metyrapone (p. 410), aminoglutethimide (p. 411) or trilostane (p. 411), have a supportive role.

The underproduction of ACTH in hypopituitarism could theoretically be treated by ACTH replacement therapy, but it is more convenient to use cortisol.

Therapeutic Uses

There are probably no advantages of ACTH over corticosteroids and ACTH has the disadvantages of parenteral administration and variability in adrenal responsiveness. Of the various preparations available, tetracosactrin depot (Synacthen Depot) is the most appropriate as it is a synthetic preparation of the first 24 amino acids of naturally occurring ACTH and is associated with few if any hypersensitivity reactions. Furthermore, as it is complexed to zinc phosphate, absorption is delayed, giving a duration of adrenocortical stimulation of 24–48 hours. The usual dose is 1 mg intramuscularly 2–3 times weekly.

Investigative Uses

Tetracosactrin (Synacthen) or tetracosactrin depot (Synacthen Depot) are used in the investigation of adrenocortical insufficiency.

Short Synacthen test. This is an effective screening test for patients with suspected Addison's disease. It can be performed at any time of the day without special preparation and is therefore a useful out-patient investigation. Plasma cortisol is measured before and 30 minutes after the i.m. injection of 250 μg of tetracosactrin (Synacthen). The initial level of plasma cortisol should be >140 nmol/l (fluorimetry). The increment at 30 minutes should be more than 200 nmol/l and the actual level should exceed 500 nmol/l. All three criteria should be met before the response to tetracosactrin is considered normal. A normal response excludes Addison's disease. An impaired response does not differentiate between primary and secondary adrenocortical insufficiency and is occasionally found in normal subjects; it indicates the need to proceed with the long Synacthen test.

Long Synacthen test. Plasma cortisol is measured before and 5–8 hours after the i.m. injection of 1 mg of tetracosactrin depot (Synacthen Depot) on each of three successive days. The criterion for the diagnosis of Addison's disease is a failure of plasma cortisol to rise above 690 nmol/l (fluorimetry) 5–8 hours after the third injection. Typically in patients with secondary adrenocortical insufficiency there is little rise in plasma cortisol after the initial injection of tetracosactrin depot but a stepwise increase to normal following the second and third doses.

If a patient has been started on steroid replacement therapy for presumed Addison's disease, prolonged ACTH stimulation remains a valid test of adrenocortical function as long as the medication is changed from cortisol to a synthetic steroid such as prednisolone, betamethasone or dexamethasone, which does not interfere with the measurement of endogenous cortisol. Fludrocortisone therapy can be continued throughout the test.

POSTERIOR PITUITARY HORMONES

The hormones secreted by the posterior pituitary are vasopressin (antidiuretic hormone, ADH) and oxytocin. Both are octapeptides of closely related structure (MW about 1000) and are synthesized in the cell bodies of neurones in the supra-optic and paraventricular nuclei of the hypothalamus. The hormones migrate down the axonal fibres in the form of secretory granules and are stored in the nerve terminals that are found in the posterior pituitary and the median eminence. Vasopressin and oxytocin are each synthesized, transported and stored in association with a neurophysin, which is a protein with a molecular weight of about 10 000. Neural stimuli result in release of the hormone and its associated neurophysin from the nerve terminals.

Vasopressin (antidiuretic hormone, ADH)

The major role of vasopressin is the maintenance of plasma osmolality. Increased plasma osmolality is a powerful stimulus to the release of vasopressin which acts on the renal collecting ducts to increase their permeability to water. The hypertonic environment of the collecting ducts results in water reabsorption, tending to reduce plasma osmolality to normal. Relatively minor increases in vasopressin release are seen in response to a reduction in plasma volume, hypotension, stress, exercise and nicotine. Alcohol reduces ADH secretion.

Pharmacokinetics
ADH is well absorbed from buccal and nasal mucosa and may also be given s.c., i.m. or i.v. Its plasma half-life is about 15 minutes and it is rapidly inactivated by the liver and kidneys. Circulating ADH is largely unbound.

Disorders of Production
Underproduction of ADH causes cranial diabetes insipidus, which is characterized by the passage of large volumes of urine of low osmolality, and polydipsia. Common causes include head injury, hypothalamic metastases from lung or breast cancer and hypothalamic compression by a large pituitary tumour or craniopharyngioma. In 50% of cases the cause is unknown. Treatment is by hormone replacement, although mild cases of cranial diabetes insipidus may respond to chlorpropamide 250 mg daily or carbamazepine 200–400 mg daily. These drugs sensitize the renal tubule to the action of endogenous vasopressin.

In nephrogenic diabetes insipidus the symptoms of polyuria and polydipsia are due to a refractoriness of the kidney to respond to the action of vasopressin. In the absence of a correctable cause such as hypokalaemia or hypercalcaemia, treatment is with a benzothiadiazide such as bendrofluazide. When given in a dose of 5–10 mg daily this drug will often produce a 50%

reduction in urine volume. The mechanism of this paradoxical effect on urine output is obscure.

ADH excess is characterized by a plasma osmolality lower than that of urine, and dilutional hyponatraemia. The symptoms are those of water intoxication and only appear when the plasma sodium level falls to less than 120 mmol/l. Inappropriate secretion of ADH is commonly associated with small-cell cancer of the lung. Treatment is by the removal of the tumour where possible, but unrelated drugs such as demeclocycline 150–300 mg four times daily or lithium carbonate 600–900 mg daily block the renal effects of vasopressin and will restore plasma sodium levels to normal in 5–14 days.

Preparations

Posterior pituitary extract (Di-Sipidin) is given by insufflation but may cause nasal ulceration, rhinitis and allergic alveolitis.

Vasopressin injection (Pitressin) is an aqueous solution with a very brief duration of action (1–2 hours when given i.m.), but it may be given by i.v. infusion.

Lypressin (Syntopressin). This is lysine-vasopressin. It is rapidly absorbed from a nasal spray (2.5 units per spray).

Desmopressin (DDAVP) is a synthetic vasopressin analogue with a long duration of action. It is available for intranasal (100 μg/ml) or parenteral (4 μg/ml) administration.

Diagnostic Uses
In patients with diabetes insipidus a water deprivation test produces no increase in the urine osmolality. If desmopressin is given (20 μg intranasally) and urine concentration occurs, ADH deficiency is confirmed.

Therapeutic Uses
ADH is used in the treatment of diabetes insipidus. Desmopressin is the drug of choice, either intranasally (10–20 μg once or twice daily) or i.m. (2 μg daily). In mild cases Syntopressin spray (two sprays into each nostril as required) may be effective.

When other methods of treatment fail, bleeding oesophageal varices may respond to ADH. Here vasopressin (20 units) is infused over about 5 minutes i.v. and may stop the bleeding by causing constriction of splanchnic arterioles and a reduction in portal venous pressure. Its use may be associated with pallor, abdominal pains, angina and hypertension. Desmopressin also increases factor VIII concentrations and has been used in the control of bleeding in haemophilia and von Willebrand's disease (p. 488).

Oxytocin

See p. 429.

THYROID HORMONES AND DRUGS ACTING ON THE THYROID GLAND

The thyroid gland lies at the junction of the larynx and trachea and secretes the hormones thyroxine (T_4) and triiodothyronine (T_3) under the stimulus of thyrotrophin (TSH). It also secretes calcitonin.

Thyroid Hormones

Thyroxine and triiodothyronine are iodine-containing derivatives of tyrosine.

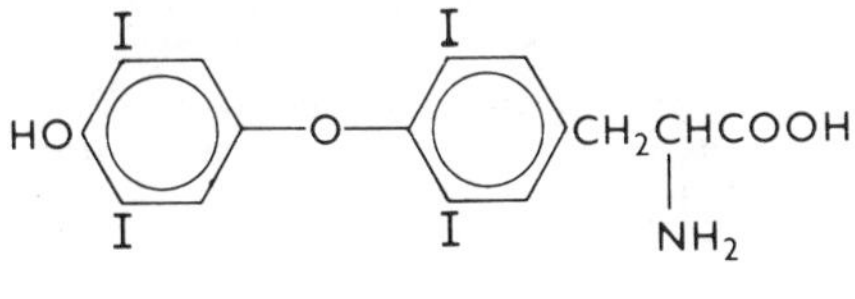

THYROXINE

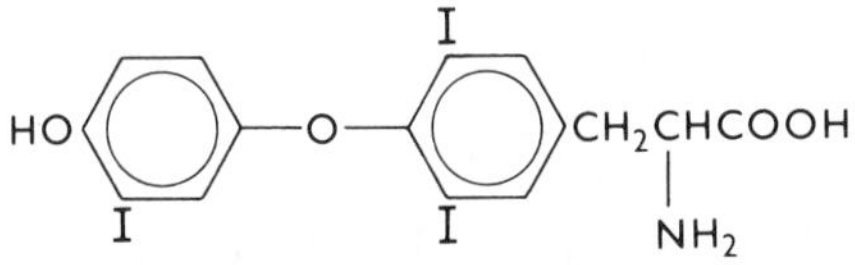

TRIIODOTHYRONINE

Dietary iodine is readily absorbed from the upper gastrointestinal tract and is transported into the gland. There it is oxidized and coupled with tyrosine to form mono- and di-iodotyrosines, which combine to form thyroxine (L-tetra-iodothyronine) and L-triiodothyronine, the active hormones. All are stored combined with a protein as thyroglobulin and this can be hydrolysed to release the active hormones into the blood stream. The iodotyrosines are hydrolysed to tyrosine and iodine, and are stored in the gland. All these processes are stimulated by TSH.

Transport, Metabolic Effects and Metabolism of Thyroid Hormones
More than 99% of both T_3 and T_4 in plasma are bound to plasma proteins, mainly to the specific transport protein, thyroxine-binding globulin (TBG), but also to prealbumin and thyroxine-binding prealbumin. These protein-bound hormones are in equilibrium with the much lower concentrations of non-protein bound (or free) hormones. Only the free hormones, however, can diffuse out of the vascular space and exert the effects on the tissues. These effects include the stimulation of cellular respiration and metabolism especially in immature tissues.

T_3 and T_4 are metabolized and excreted by three main pathways involving (i) hepatic conjugation to yield glucuronide and sulphate esters which are excreted in the bile, (ii) hepatic and renal deamination and deiodination, with recycling of released iodide by the thyroid and (iii) renal excretion of unchanged hormones. Additional quantitative data describing T3 and T4 production and metabolism are shown in Table 10.1. The relatively small size and rapid clearance of the extra-thyroidal T3 pool contrasts with the larger size and slower clearance of the T4 pool. Plasma concentrations of total T4 and T3 reflect the rates of hormone production, the extent of protein binding in plasma and the rate of hormone clearance. Changes in any of these variables may alter the plasma levels of total T4 and total T3, even in the absence of thyroid disease.

Table 10.1 *Quantitative aspects of thyroid hormone metabolism*

	Plasma concentration (nmol/l)		Plasma half-life (days)	Extra-thyroidal pool (nmol)	% pool metabolized daily	Production rate (nmol/day)	Relative biological potency
	Total	Free					
T4	100	0.025	7	1000	10	100	1
T3	1.8	0.005	1	55	75	40	5

From: Toft A. D., Campbell I. W. & Seth J. (1981) *Diagnosis and Management of Endocrine Diseases*. Oxford: Blackwell Scientific Publications.

Plasma total T3, for example, is reduced in many acute and chronic illnesses, probably as a result of decreased conversion of T4 into T3, with a reciprocal increase in reverse T3 (rT3) production. Table 10.2 summarizes some causes of abnormalities in thyroid function tests other than thyroid disease.

Measurement of Thyroid Hormones

Plasma total T4. This is measured by radioimmunoassay and is the most widely used and probably the most valuable single test of thyroid function, as it generally discriminates well between both hyperthyroidism and hypothyroidism and the euthyroid state. The normal range is 60–150 nmol/l (5–12 μg/dl).

Plasma free thyroxine index (FT4I). Plasma levels of free or non-protein bound thyroid hormones reflect tissue exposure to active hormone more closely than plasma total T4. However, the minute concentrations of plasma free T4 require relatively sophisticated techniques for their measurement, although simpler kit methods (e.g. the New Amerlex Free T4 RIA Kit, marketed by Amersham International) are now produced commercially and bring this measurement nearer to routine availability. At present the approach most widely adopted is to calculate a plasma free thyroxine index that is proportional to the free T4 concentration. The calculation involves correction of the plasma total T4 for changes in the binding capacity of TBG.

Table 10.2 *Some causes of abnormal thyroid function tests other than thyroid disease*

Cause	Total T₄	Free T₄-index	Total T₃	Basal TSH	TRH test	Mechanism
Non-thyroidal illness						
Severe infection, chronic and acute	N or ↓	↑	→			1
Post-myocardial infarction, post-surgery	N	N	→			1
Chronic liver disease	↓ or N	↓	→	N	↑ or N	1,2
Chronic renal failure	↓	↓ or N	→	N	→	1,2
Medication						
Oestrogen (oral contraceptives)	↑	N	←	N	←	3
Phenytoin, salicylate, fenclofenac, carbamazepine	→	→ N	→	N	N	2
Propranolol	N	→	→	N		1
Lithium salts, phenylbutazone	→	→	←	↑ or N		4
Physiological						
Pregnancy	←	N	←	N	N	3
Posture (sitting vs supine), or venous stasis (e.g. tourniquet)	←	N	←	N	N	5

Mechanisms
1. Decreased T₄→T₃ conversion
2. Complex effects, probably including increased T₄ clearance and/or decreased protein-binding of T₄ and T₃
3. Increased plasma TBG concentration
4. Inhibition of thyroid secretion
5. Increased concentration of all protein-bound plasma constituents

From: Toft A. D., Campbell I. W. & Seth, J. (1981) *Diagnosis and Management of Endocrine Diseases*. Oxford: Blackwell Scientific Publications.

The latter is simply estimated by one of a variety of in vitro tests collectively termed 'thyroid hormone uptake tests' (e.g. Thyopac-3, also marketed by Amersham International).

The plasma FT_4I is more helpful than plasma total T_4 where TBG levels are abnormal, e.g. in patients who are pregnant or on oral oestrogens. However, the test does not add greatly to the diagnosis in the majority of patients who have normal TBG levels.

Plasma total T_3. Measurement of plasma total T_3 is a valuable investigation in suspected hyperthyroidism where levels are more markedly raised than total T_4 levels. In the relatively rare cases of T_3 hyperthyroidism, plasma total T_3 is raised with a normal total T_4. The test is of little value in investigating suspected hypothyroidism, since the T_3 levels are often normal.

A frequent complication in the interpretation of plasma total T_3 is that levels are often reduced in non-thyroidal illness (Table 10.2) and a low plasma T_3 is therefore not uncommon in euthyroid hospitalized patients.

Disorders of Production
Overproduction of thyroid hormones, either T_4 and T_3 or T_3 alone, causes hyperthyroidism (thyrotoxicosis). The hypersecretion results from the presence in the circulation of stimulating TSH-receptor antibodies (Graves' disease) or from the autonomous production of thyroid hormones by a nodular goitre. Very rarely hyperthyroidism may result from excess TSH production from the pituitary gland. Psychiatrically disturbed patients may present with hyperthyroidism due to the self-administration of excess thyroid hormones.

Underproduction of thyroid hormones usually presents in middle-aged females in whom it is due to autoimmune destruction of the thyroid gland. Thyroid failure may occur in utero and unless diagnosed and effectively treated within a few days of birth may result in mental retardation. Congenital deficiency of one of the enzymes involved in thyroid hormone synthesis, most commonly peroxidase, may result in hypothyroidism which usually presents in the first decade. Hypothyroidism may be drug-induced, usually as a result of treatment with lithium carbonate for manic depressive psychosis. Lithium inhibits the release of thyroid hormones by the gland.

HYPERTHYROIDISM

Hyperthyroidism may be treated by:
1. antithyroid drugs
2. surgery
3. radio-iodine.

Antithyroid Drugs

The choice of treatment in most centres for a patient under 40 years of age presenting with Graves' disease for the first time is an antithyroid drug of the thionamide class. The drug most commonly used in the UK is carbimazole and in the USA methimazole, although propylthiouracil is equally effective.

Mode of Action

These drugs block the formation of di-iodotyrosine and the iodothyronines and to a lesser extent the iodination of tyrosine. Carbimazole and its active metabolite, methimazole, have recently been shown to exert the following immunological effects:

1. Reduction of the extent of lymphocytic infiltration of the thyroid gland in patients with Graves' disease.
2. Inhibition of thyroid autoantibody production by cultured lymphocytes.
3. Reduction in circulating levels of thyroid microsomal antibody in patients with Graves' disease.
4. Reduction in serum levels of stimulating TSH-receptor antibodies.

The relative importance of their biochemical and immunological actions in the initial control of hyperthyroidism of Graves' disease is not known. Although extremely effective in reducing thyroid hormone levels, the antithyroid drugs exert little or no influence on the natural history of the disease, and are given empirically for 12–18 months, in the hope that it will enter prolonged remission spontaneously during the treatment period. Resistance to antithyroid drugs probably never occurs and failure to control hyperthyroidism invariably indicates poor drug compliance.

Preparations

Carbimazole (Neo-Mercazole). This is available as 5 mg tablets. The initial dose is 15 mg orally three times daily. The patient is aware of subjective improvement some 10–14 days after starting drug therapy and is usually clinically and biochemically euthyroid at 3–4 weeks. The dose of carbimazole is reduced to 10 mg three times daily at this stage and maintained for a further six weeks. Further reduction in dosage should be determined by clinical status and ideally by measurement of plasma total T_4 (or FT_4I if appropriate) and TSH. Plasma total T_4 should lie between 80–120 nmol/l, and the TSH level, within the normal range. Once controlled, the patient should attend for review every two months. The maintenance dose is 5–20 mg daily.

Propylthiouracil. This is available as 50 mg tablets. The dose is 10 times that for carbimazole.

Adverse Effects

These are not encountered frequently. Cross sensitivity between carbimazole and propylthiouracil is uncommon, and if an adverse reaction develops while carbimazole is being taken, it is quite acceptable to substitute propylthiouracil. The use of excess doses of thionamides results in goitre formation owing to increased levels of TSH.

Skin rash. The most frequently observed adverse reaction to the antithyroid drugs is a skin rash, which occurs in some 3% of patients. It is usually papular or urticarial, may be transient and is not necessarily an indication for a change in drug therapy.

Agranulocytosis. The most serious untoward reaction is agranulocytosis, which occurs in less than 1 in 500 patients, usually within weeks of starting treatment, and is almost always reversible following withdrawal of the drug. Since the onset of agranulocytosis is rapid, routine measurement of the white blood-cell count is of little value. On starting treatment with one of the thionamide group of drugs the patient should be instructed to consult his medical attendant immediately if a sore throat or fever develops. Leukopenia may occur in the hyperthyroidism itself, but it is also observed not infrequently during antithyroid drug therapy and is not an absolute indication for a change in drug regimen, but indicates the need for careful follow-up.

Rare unwanted effects. These include arthralgia, myalgia, cholestatic jaundice, depigmentation of the hair, psychosis and a lupus-like syndrome.

Contraindications

There are no absolute contraindications to the use of the thionamides, but their long-term administration in the treatment of patients with hyperthyroidism due to nodular goitre is pointless and recurrent thyrotoxicosis will always develop on drug withdrawal. Although thionamides cross the placenta, their use is appropriate in pregnant patients with Graves' disease, as maternal stimulating TSH receptor antibodies also cross the placenta and cause fetal hyperthyroidism. It is extremely important, however, that the minimum dose necessary for control of hyperthyroidism in the mother is used (5–15 mg daily) and is monitored by a monthly measurement of maternal TSH and FT$_4$I. Carbimazole is usually stopped four weeks prior to the expected date of delivery, when fetal brain growth is at a maximum, but if required to be recommenced in the puerperium, breast feeding is contraindicated as the thionamides are excreted in the milk.

Miscellaneous Drugs Used in the Treatment of Hyperthyroidism

Propranolol

This non-selective β-adrenoceptor antagonist (p. 287) alleviates many of the signs and symptoms of hyperthyroidism, such as tachycardia, tremor, sweating, heat intolerance and anxiety. These features are not abolished, however, since the effects of thyroid hormones are not mediated exclusively via the β-adrenoceptors. It follows that β-adrenoceptor antagonists cannot be recommended for the long-term treatment of hyperthyroidism.

An oral dose of 40 mg four times daily achieves symptomatic relief in most patients. There is, however, a marked interpatient variability in circulating propranolol levels and some patients require doses as high as 160 mg four times daily for the effective control of symptoms.

Indications
Propranolol is recommended in the following circumstances:

1. Suspected hyperthyroidism. For symptomatic relief in a patient awaiting confirmatory investigations of hyperthyroidism.
2. Combined with potassium iodide in the preparation of patients with hyperthyroidism for surgery.
3. Adjunct to treatment with ^{131}I. Propranolol can be used to control symptoms for the 4–8 weeks between the administration of ^{131}I and its therapeutic effect.
4. Hyperthyroid crisis. Propranolol is rapidly effective and should be given in a dose of 80 mg orally or 1–5 mg i.v. four times daily, along with carbimazole 15 mg orally three times daily and potassium iodide 1–2 g daily i.v.

Potassium iodide

Potassium iodide prevents the release of thyroid hormones and is of value in the management of a thyrotoxic crisis if given i.v. Since it reduces the vascularity of the thyroid gland, potassium iodide is also used in preparing patients with hyperthyroidism for surgery. The patient having been rendered euthyroid with carbimazole, potassium iodide is substituted in a dose of 60 mg three times a day for 10–14 days prior to surgery. An alternative is to prepare the patient solely with propranolol 160 mg daily and to add potassium iodide 60 mg three times daily for the 10 days prior to surgery.

Potassium perchlorate

Potassium perchlorate (Peroidin) blocks iodine uptake by the thyroid gland but may cause aplastic anaemia and cannot be recommended.

SURGERY

Subtotal thyroidectomy performed by an experienced surgeon yields the best results of all forms of treatment of Graves' disease, as 80% of patients are euthyroid one year after operation. In contrast some 50–70% of patients relapse within 1–2 years of stopping antithyroid drugs and radio-iodine treatment is associated with a high incidence of hypothyroidism.

In the past it has been customary to reserve surgery for those patients with recurrent hyperthyroidism following a course of antithyroid drugs. In recent years, however, an increasing number of newly-diagnosed patients with

Graves' disease have undergone subtotal thyroidectomy as the treatment of choice.

It is essential that patients are prepared prior to surgery either with carbimazole and potassium iodide or, in milder cases, with propranolol and potassium iodide.

Radioactive Iodine (^{131}I)

Indications

The indications for ^{131}I vary from centre to centre but are related largely to the age of the patient and to the ability of the thyroid gland to concentrate iodine.

Age. Although at some clinics in the USA young adults and even children are treated with radioactive iodine, it is generally accepted in the UK that therapeutic ^{131}I should be reserved for patients over the age of 40 years. Exceptions to this age rule are:

1. Serious concomitant disease, e.g. malignancy.
2. Recurrence of hyperthyroidism following surgery, since a second operation is associated with an unacceptably high morbidity.

The reason for this cautious approach is that although an increased incidence of leukaemia or thyroid carcinoma in patients treated with ^{131}I has not been recorded, the follow-up extends for only 25–30 years. In addition, there are other adequate forms of therapy available for those whose life expectancy exceeds this follow-up period. Furthermore, although the radiation dose to the ovaries is small and the incidence of congenital abnormality in children of parents who have been treated with ^{131}I for hyperthyroidism during childhood or adolescence does not seem to be increased, the series are too small to permit definite conclusions.

Iodine uptake. For therapy to be effective, the thyroid gland must be capable of concentrating iodine. Treatment is not usually indicated if the 4-hour uptake of iodine is less than 20%. Because of their effect on iodine uptake, antithyroid drugs like carbimazole must be discontinued at least 48 hours before therapy. If it is necessary to use carbimazole until the ^{131}I has a therapeutic effect, it should not be given for 48 hours after the radioactive iodine has been administered. β-adrenoceptor antagonists do not interfere with iodine uptake.

Dosage

Due to the variable radio-sensitivity of the thyroid, the choice of dose of ^{131}I remains empirical: 200–400 MBq (approximately 5–10 mCi) is given orally, depending on the clinical assessment of goitre size. This regimen is effective in 75% of patients within 4–12 weeks. The initial dose is increased to 600 MBq (approximately 15 mCi) in patients with atrial fibrillation or cardiac failure. Rapid control of hyperthyroidism is important in these patients.

Results of Radio-iodine Therapy

The major disadvantage of ^{131}I therapy is the high incidence of subsequent permanent hypothyroidism, which is greatest, approximately 25%, in the first post-treatment year. The incidence of thyroid failure at this stage is to some extent dose-related. Thereafter, patients continue to develop hypothyroidism at the rate of 2–4% per year, with a cumulative incidence of 80% after 15 years in some centres. The late development of hypothyroidism is not dose-related but probably depends on such factors as auto-immune destruction of the gland and inability of the surviving irradiated cells to replicate.

HYPOTHYROIDISM

Hypothyroidism should be treated with thyroxine. There is no place for treatment with thyroid extract, which is of variable potency and is unreliably absorbed. Tri-iodothyronine and combined preparations of T_3 and T_4 are not recommended for replacement therapy and have no advantage over thyroxine, as administered T_4 is converted to T_3 peripherally.

Thyroxine sodium

Thyroxine (Eltroxin) is available as 0.025 mg, 0.05 mg and 0.1 mg tablets. It is customary to begin T_4 therapy slowly and a dose of 0.05 mg daily should be given for three weeks, this being increased to 0.1 mg daily for a further three weeks and then to 0.15 mg daily. Review should be undertaken three months after starting treatment, plasma total T_4 and TSH estimated and the dose of T_4 adjusted if necessary until both levels are normal. In the absence of a TSH assay, a plasma total T_4 of about 100 nmol/l usually indicates appropriate replacement. Although the mean replacement dose of T_4 is 0.15 mg daily, some patients require 0.2–0.3 mg daily and others as little as 0.05 mg daily. The half-life of T_4 is 7 days and theoretically the drug can be given once each week. However, patient compliance is usually better if the T_4 is taken as a daily dose, though the practice of prescribing T_4 in daily divided dosage is illogical. An improvement in well-being is noticed by the patient 2–3 weeks after starting T_4 treatment. Reduction in weight and in periorbital puffiness occurs early, but restoration of skin and hair texture and resolution of effusions may take 3–6 months.

The patient with hypothyroidism and ischaemic heart disease presents a special problem in clinical management. As T_4 therapy is introduced, the impaired coronary circulation is unable to meet the increased demands of the myocardium for oxygen and angina pectoris may be induced or exacerbated. Myocardial infarction and sudden death are well-recognized consequences. In the presence of angina, a β-adrenoceptor antagonist, such as propranolol 40 mg four times daily, should be prescribed initially with T_4 0.025 mg daily.

The dose of T₄ should be doubled at intervals of not less than four weeks. However, it may not be possible to increase T₄ to the normal replacement dose on account of uncontrolled chest pain. Such patients should be considered for coronary artery surgery.

Liothyronine sodium

Liothyronine sodium (L-tri-iodothyronine sodium) is available as 0.02 mg tablets (Tertroxin) and in 0.02 mg ampoules (Tri-iodothyronine injection). There is no place for tri-iodothyronine tablets, but the injection is the treatment of choice in hypothyroid coma and may be given i.v. as an initial dose of 0.1 mg, followed by 0.025 mg six-hourly and until improvement is noted.

PARATHYROID HORMONE (PTH)

PTH is secreted by the parathyroid glands, which lie close to the thyroid gland. It is a protein of molecular weight 8500. The rate of release of PTH is inversely proportional to the level of free ionized calcium in the blood.

Actions
PTH affects calcium and phosphate metabolism; it increases the rate of resorption of calcium and phosphate from bone, enhances the active absorption of calcium from the upper gastrointestinal tract and increases the renal tubular reabsorption of calcium and excretion of phosphate. All these effects tend to increase the plasma calcium concentration (see also p. 439).

Pharmacokinetics
PTH is destroyed when given orally. After injection, the peak effects of purified PTH are seen in 6 hours. It is bound to plasma proteins, has a plasma half-life of about 20 minutes and is probably destroyed by the kidney; radioimmunoassays are available.

Disorders of Production
Overproduction, usually due to adenoma or hyperplasia of the parathyroid glands, causes hypercalcaemia, bone cysts and renal calculi, the treatment being surgical removal of the affected gland.
    Underproduction is usually due to accidental removal of the glands during thyroid surgery, but hypoparathyroidism may develop spontaneously, usually as a result of autoimmune destruction. Symptoms may be life-threatening and are due to hypocalcaemia, leading to tetany and convulsions.

Preparations and their Use
It is possible to obtain bovine PTH, but because of its slow action and its

antigenicity it is not used in the treatment of hypoparathyroidism. In this condition normo-calcaemia is restored with a vitamin D compound. Alfacalcidol (1α-hydroxycholecalciferol; p. 441) is increasingly favoured on account of its fast onset of action and rapid control of plasma calcium levels.

Calcitonin

Calcitonin is secreted by the thyroid gland and has actions which are in many ways the opposite of those of PTH. It is considered on p. 441.

INSULIN AND HYPOGLYCAEMIC DRUGS

Insulin

Insulin is produced exclusively by the beta-cells of the islets of Langerhans in the pancreas, in response to many stimuli but principally to changes in blood sugar.

In man, insulin is derived from proinsulin and its precursor preproinsulin. Proinsulin (molecular weight 9000) is synthesized in the pancreatic beta cell and cleaved to form insulin and C-peptide (molecular weight 3000) in equimolar amounts. The resulting insulin molecule consists of 51 amino acids and has a molecular weight of 6000. It is made up of two polypeptide chains (designated A and B) linked by disulphide bridges. Insulin release is directly related to the concentration of glucose in blood perfusing the pancreas, but may also be stimulated by ingested amino acids, free fatty acids, ketone bodies, increased vagal activity and several gut hormones including gastric inhibitory polypeptide, gastrin, secretin and glucagon. Its secretion is inhibited by the α-adrenergic actions of adrenaline and noradrenaline. The exact physiological role of these multiple regulators of insulin secretion is uncertain at present.

Actions

Insulin is a major anabolic hormone in man, having metabolic effects on practically all major organic systems but principally those in the liver, muscle and adipose tissue. It probably does not enter cells to bring about its effects, rather it binds to special protein molecules, known as receptors, on the cell surface membrane of target cells and from this insulin-receptor complex arise changes in enzymes within the cells.

The major effects of insulin are on carbohydrate, fat and protein metabolism.

Glucoregulatory effects. Insulin reduces blood sugar concentration by (1) increasing glucose uptake by peripheral tissues, and (2) reducing hepatic glucose release through inhibiting glycogen breakdown (glycogenolysis) and suppressing gluconeogenesis, a process in which pyruvate, lactate and amino acids such as alanine are converted into glucose.

Lipid regulatory effects. Insulin reduces plasma ketone body concentrations by (1) inhibiting from fat cells the release of free fatty acids, the major substrates for hepatic ketogenesis, (2) suppressing hepatic ketogenesis in liver cells.

Protein regulatory effects. Insulin decreases the catabolism of muscle and its release of amino acids, and increases muscle amino-acid uptake and protein synthesis. The cellular uptake of potassium is also enhanced with this positive nitrogen balance effect.

In addition, insulin enhances the renal conservation of sodium, by increasing the renal tubular reabsorption of sodium.

Pharmacokinetics
Following insulin secretion by the beta-cells, the portal vein transports insulin directly to the liver, where 40–50% is extracted in a single passage. The remaining insulin is released from the hepatic vein into the peripheral circulation, from where it exerts its anabolic effects. The half-life of i.v. injected or infused insulin is 5–10 minutes. Insulin is metabolized by the breakdown of the disulphide bridges by an enzyme, glutathione insulin transhydrogenase ('insulinase'), present in high concentrations in the liver and kidneys. The A- and B-chains formed in this process are then broken down by proteases into amino acids. Insulin is excreted in the bile and urine.

Plasma insulin may be measured by radioimmunoassay. Levels vary in relation to changes in blood sugar but in general are less than 10 μu/ml in normal non-obese, fasting subjects and, indeed, are often lower or undetectable.

Disorders of Production

Overproduction. Pancreatic tumours which secrete insulin (insulinomas) are rare. The clinical features of insulinomas are due to hypoglycaemia and include loss of consciousness, drowsiness, confusion, epilepsy, visual disturbances, sweating, palpitations and transient cerebrovascular accidents. The treatment of choice is surgical removal of the tumour. If surgery is unsuccessful or the patient is unfit for operation, diazoxide (p. 290), which inhibits insulin release from the beta-cell, may be used to prevent symptomatic hypoglycaemia. The starting dose is 50 mg orally three times daily and thereafter it may be increased to as much as 1 g daily. Adverse reactions include excessive salt and water retention and hirsutism, especially at high doses. Streptozocin (p. 501), an antibiotic with a toxic effect on the beta-cells of the pancreas, is of value in the management of malignant insulinoma. The drug can be given i.v. or into the hepatic artery via an in-dwelling catheter, since in 90% of malignant insulinomas there are hepatic metastases at the time of diagnosis. It is not listed in *British Approved Names* or in the *Data Sheet Compendium*, but is available in the UK and elsewhere, sometimes under the name streptozotocin.

Underproduction. Diabetes mellitus is caused by a heterogeneous group of disorders which have in common either a deficiency or diminished effectiveness of endogenous insulin. Twenty-five per cent have insulin-dependent (Type I) diabetes mellitus (previously referred to as juvenile onset type), where there is absolute insulin deficiency. Seventy per cent have non-insulin-dependent (Type II) diabetes mellitus (previously referred to as adult onset type), where there is a combination of impaired insulin secretion plus insulin resistance due to a decrease in insulin receptors. Finally, 5% of diabetics have the condition secondary to certain medical conditions, where insulin antagonists are produced in excess, e.g. acromegaly, Cushing's syndrome, or associated with drugs that oppose the effects of insulin, e.g. steroids, contraceptive pills.

The consequence of this failure of insulin secretion or action is diabetes mellitus, with a variable spectrum from asymptomatic glycosuria to life-threatening keto-acidosis. The results of this insulin deficiency can be summarized as follows:

1. A reduced tissue uptake of glucose from the extracellular fluid; after the ingestion of carbohydrate foods the hepatic uptake of glucose is diminished and this is a major factor in the production of post-prandial hyperglycaemia.
2. An increase, sometimes by a factor of two, in gluconeogenesis in the liver. This makes an important contribution to the fasting hyperglycaemia of diabetes mellitus.
3. An increase in glycogenolysis in the liver, which further contributes to fasting hyperglycaemia. Insulin antagonizes the glycogenolytic effects of glucagon and the catecholamines.

All the above processes produce hyperglycaemia, and when the plasma glucose is sufficient to exceed the renal tubular transport maximum for glucose reabsorption, which is approximately 10 mmol/l or 180 mg per 100 ml (the 'renal threshold'), glycosuria ensues, promoting an osmotic diuresis with losses of water, sodium, potassium and other electrolytes.

4. An increase in lipolysis, with excessive triglyceride breakdown resulting in a high level of free fatty acids in the blood. These free fatty acids are converted in the liver to acetoacetate and beta-hydroxybutyrate ('ketone bodies') and when these ketoacids can no longer be metabolized by extrahepatic tissues, ketosis and acidosis may occur.
5. Decreased amino-acid uptake and protein synthesis resulting from insulin insufficiency contributes to the increased availability of amino-acid precursors for gluconeogenesis. Decreased protein synthesis is evident as a negative nitrogen balance and tissue wasting.

Diabetics show all the above features in varying degrees of severity. Insulin given by injection will correct these abnormalities in nearly all cases. However, dietary restriction alone will often be sufficient in 40% of diabetics, diet in combination with an oral hypoglycaemic agent in a further 35%; only 25% of diabetics will need insulin therapy.

TREATMENT OF DIABETES MELLITUS

INSULIN-DEPENDENT DIABETES MELLITUS

In insulin-dependent diabetes there is an almost complete lack of endogenous insulin and without insulin treatment ketoacidosis may arise at any time. Education of the diabetic in self-regulation is important, with instruction in diet, syringe care, the technique of s.c. insulin injection and the understanding of the causes and symptoms of hypoglycaemia. A deliberate hypoglycaemic reaction should be induced so that the patient can recognize the early symptoms and take quickly absorbed oral glucose tablets. Insulin is given by deep s.c. injection once or twice daily, depending on the age of the patient and the degree of control required. In very unstable ('brittle') diabetics there is increasing use of continuous s.c. insulin infusion using portable minipump devices. In diabetic ketoacidosis it is necessary to give insulin by continuous i.v. infusion.

The object of the treatment is to relieve hyperglycaemic symptoms, correct hyperglycaemia, ketonuria and hyperlipidaemia, to establish and maintain an ideal body weight and, in children, normal growth and development and to avoid ketosis and hypoglycaemia — the diabetic should be taught how to increase insulin dosage when ill and to decrease it when hypoglycaemia occurs. The long-term aim is to establish the best control possible in order to prevent or delay the onset of the long-term complications of diabetes. Urine tests for glucose, such as Diastix or Clinitest, and for ketones, e.g. Ketostix, have been the mainstay of assessing diabetic control, but in many insulin-dependent diabetics there is increasing use of self-monitoring of blood glucose at home using a test-strip read by eye, e.g. 'BM-Test Glycemie 20–800' (Boehringer Corp. Ltd), or by a small portable meter, e.g. 'Dextrostix' read in a 'Glucometer' (Ames). The aim of this treatment is to try to maintain pre-prandial blood glucose values at less than 10.0 mmol/l and if possible between 4.4 and 6.7 mmol/l (80–120 mg per 100 ml).

Insulin Preparations

Insulin preparations can be classified into four types according to the duration of action (Table 10.3). In the UK and Europe insulin has been available as 40 strength and 80 strength, i.e. 40 or 80 units/ml. There is also a 20 strength soluble insulin BP available for occasional patients requiring very small doses of insulin. In 1983 100 strength insulin ('U100') was introduced into the UK, the intention being to gradually establish this as the only insulin strength

Table 10.3 *Time actions of various types of insulins*

Type	Onset of action (hours)	Peak effect (hours)	Duration of action (hours)
Short-acting	$^1/_3$–$^1/_2$	4–6	8–10
Intermediate-acting	4	6–10	8–16
Long-acting	6	10–18	24–32
Insulin mixtures	Variable actions depending on predetermined proportions of short/intermediate- or intermediate/long-acting insulins.		

available to be injected, using suitably graduated insulin syringes with marks corresponding to the number of units of insulin — a method similar to that existing in North America and Australia.

There is a multiplicity of different insulin preparations. Table 10.4 lists the

Table 10.4 *Conventional bovine insulin preparations available in the UK**

Generic name	Other name	Duration of action
Insulin injection, BP	Soluble	Short
Isophane insulin, BP	Neutral protamine Hagedorn (NPH)	Intermediate
Insulin zinc suspension (amorphous), BP	Semilente	Intermediate
Protamine zinc insulin, BP (PZI)		Long
Insulin zinc suspension (crystalline), BP	Ultralente	Long
Insulin zinc suspension, BP	Lente (30% semilente, 70% ultralente)	Intermediate/long

* These insulins are being gradually withdrawn and replaced by purified bovine preparations. (See Table 10.5.)

conventional bovine insulin preparations available, but these are now being used less as many doctors prefer to start newly diagnosed insulin-dependent diabetics, especially children and young adults, on the more recently introduced purified or highly purified insulins which are less antigenic (Table 10.5). There is little justification in changing the type of insulin in those patients already established and well controlled, some for many years, on the conventional bovine insulins. However, it has been shown that diabetics treated with such insulins have antibodies to proinsulin, polymers of insulin and various other pancreatic polypeptides such as glucagon, somatostatin, pancreatic polypeptide and vasoactive intestinal polypeptide. All of these are immunogenic and may lead to the production of insulin-binding antibodies. Insulin extracted from pigs is less antigenic than that extracted from bovine sources. It is at present not certain whether this immune response is harmful in the long-term, but there is a definite trend to phasing out conventional bovine insulin and presenting insulin as purified or highly purified preparations. There is no exact definition of 'purified' or 'highly purified', but insulin

Table 10.5 *New purified and highly purified insulins available in the UK*

Proprietary name	Animal source	Equivalent conventional bovine preparation	Duration of action
Actrapid MC	Pork	Soluble	Short
Velosulin	Pork	Soluble	Short
Neusulin	Beef	Soluble	Short
Hypurin Neutral	Beef	Soluble	Short
Insulatard	Pork	Isophane	Intermediate
Neuphane	Beef	Isophane	Intermediate
Hypurin Isophane	Beef	Isophane	Intermediate
Semitard MC	Pork	Semilente	Intermediate
Hypurin protamine zinc insulin	Beef	PZI	Long
Ultratard MC	Beef	Ultralente	Long
Rapitard MC*	Beef and Pork		Short/intermediate
Mixtard (30% Velosulin, 70% Insulatard)	Pork		Short/intermediate
Initard (50% Velosulin, 50% Insulatard)	Pork		Short/intermediate
Monotard MC	Pork	Lente	Intermediate/long
Hypurin Lente	Beef	Lente	Intermediate/long
Lentard MC†	Beef and Pork	Lente	Intermediate/long

MC is the manufacturer's abbreviation for 'Monocomponent'.
* Rapitard MC comprises 25% Actrapid MC and 75% MC crystalline bovine insulin (biphasic insulin).
† Lentard MC comprises 30% amorphous MC porcine insulin and 70% crystalline MC bovine insulin.

manufacturers use the terms according to whether they feel the product has had some or almost all of the impurities removed. In clinical practice there is probably no marked difference between them. 'Human' insulin is now being manufactured either by the genetic manipulation of *Escherichia coli* (recombinant or biosynthetic human insulin) or by the chemical manipulation of porcine insulin (semi-synthetic human insulin).

Table 10.6 *'Human' insulins available in the UK*

Proprietary name	Source	Equivalent conventional bovine preparation	Duration of action
Humulin S	Recombinant DNA technology from *E. coli* (bio-synthetic human insulins)	Soluble	Short
Humulin I		Isophane	Intermediate
Human Actrapid	Biochemical conversion of porcine to human insulin (semi-synthetic human insulins)	Soluble	Short
Human Monotard		Lente	Intermediate/long

In the preparation of insulin by genetic manipulation, the genes for the insulin chains are produced by chemically synthesizing DNA from a known base sequence or by copying back to DNA from messenger RNA. The genes are then introduced into the host *E. coli* by using plasmids. Plasmids are rings of DNA extracted from bacterial cells and they can be cleaved chemically so that the necessary gene may be inserted. The plasmid with the new gene is then closed, using a ligating enzyme. An important point is that the plasmids are *extra-chromosomal* self-replicating elements in the bacteria, and so, inside the host cells, the reprogrammed plasmids resume replication without using the chromosomal mechanism. The *E. coli* are cultured by fermentation to produce large quantities of the insulin chains.

As yet, there is no evidence that the source of insulin improves control, but in time it may be shown that the best insulin to give is that which is most like the natural hormone.

Advantages of Highly Purified or Human Insulins

1. Fat atrophy does not occur at the injection site. If it has already occurred with conventional insulins the atrophy will resolve in 6–9 months after changing to highly purified or human insulin which may continue to be injected into the affected area.
2. Localized red itchy patches are less common and a generalized allergy is extremely rare.
3. Insulin resistance, an uncommon condition where the daily insulin dose exceeds 200 units, will respond to lower doses of highly purified or human insulin if the resistance is due to high insulin antibody titres. In clinical practice many poorly controlled ('brittle') diabetics, often with a daily insulin dose in excess of 100 units, are changed to highly purified or human preparations empirically in case antibodies to bovine insulin are the cause of the unsatisfactory control.
4. Patients needing insulin temporarily, e.g. in pregnancy, during acute illness or after major surgery, should be given highly purified or human insulin to minimize the development of insulin allergy in later years should insulin be required again. Women with gestational diabetes are most appropriately treated with a highly purified preparation to prevent the transplacental passage of insulin antibodies, although there is no evidence at present that these are harmful to the fetus.

As the highly purified and human preparations are less antigenic, if a diabetic is changed from a conventional insulin to a highly purified or human one, there may be a fall in the dosage of 30–40%, and occasionally even more, in the first 3–4 weeks. It is usual practice, if the previous daily insulin dose exceeds 40 units, for the initial dose of highly purified or human insulin to be reduced immediately by 20%, further adjustments being made as necessary.

Insulin Regimens

With the vast choice of insulins available, treatment obviously varies from centre to centre, but basically the insulin regimen is determined by the age of the patient and the degree of control required.

1. Young diabetics. Most insulin-dependent diabetics who want to achieve very good control will require twice daily injections using a combination of short and intermediate acting preparations, e.g. Velosulin and Insulatard, Actrapid MC and Monotard MC or Neusulin and Neuphane, injected before breakfast, with a second injection before the main evening meal.
2. Elderly diabetics. In older patients or those with poor intelligence or motivation, strict control may result in troublesome hypoglycaemia, especially at night, and this can be a danger for elderly diabetics living alone. As the primary aim is to relieve symptoms, a single morning injection of one of the intermediate/long-acting insulins, e.g. Monotard MC, Lentard MC.

Adverse Effects

Hypoglycaemia is the major adverse reaction. It is caused by excessive insulin dosage, a missed or late meal or by excessive exercise. The diabetic should therefore always carry quick-acting oral glucose tablets. The unconscious patient should be given 20 ml of 50% dextrose i.v., together with glucagon (p. 401). Prolonged severe hypoglycaemic reactions may require 10–20% dextrose infusions over 24–48 hours or longer, together with high-dose steroids, e.g. dexamethasone, 2 mg i.m. 4 hourly and 20 ml of 20% mannitol i.v. over 20 minutes, to prevent cerebral oedema. Unfortunately, particularly if treatment is delayed, some diabetics may develop irreversible brain damage and death may occur.

Other adverse reactions to insulin include local fat atrophy, local skin allergy and insulin resistance. These have already been discussed.

NON-INSULIN-DEPENDENT DIABETES MELLITUS

Approximately 75% of diabetic patients are controlled without the use of insulin. The mainstay of treatment in this group, the so-called Type II diabetics, is diet, but about half of these patients require an oral hypoglycaemic agent in addition.

Oral Hypoglycaemic Agents

There are two groups of oral hypoglycaemic agents, the sulphonylureas and the biguanides, differing in chemical structure, pharamacology and therapeutic indications.

Sulphonylureas

Sulphonylureas are related to the sulphonamides and were discovered by chance from the observation in 1942 that some patients treated with a sulphonamide for typhoid fever developed symptoms of hypoglycaemia. The modification of the sulphonamide molecule led to the development of the sulphonylureas (Figure 10.1). Their main action is to stimulate insulin secretion from pancreatic beta-cells, but in addition they have two other extrapancreatic actions: in the liver they decrease hepatic gluconeogenesis and reduce hepatic insulin degradation, and in peripheral tissues such as muscle and fat cells they enhance the peripheral utilization of glucose by increasing insulin receptor binding sites.

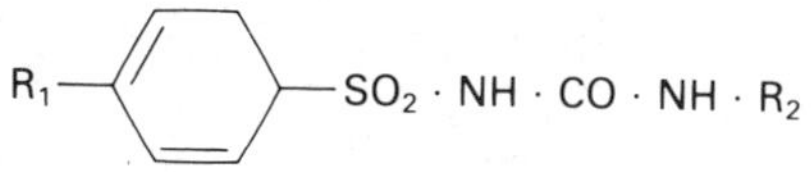

$$R_1 - \langle \rangle - SO_2 \cdot NH \cdot CO \cdot NH \cdot R_2$$

Figure 10.1 Basic structure of the sulphonylureas.

The sulphonylureas are rapidly absorbed from the gastrointestinal tract and are transported in the blood, bound to proteins. They are only able to exert their effect as they are released from these protein complexes. Their hepatic metabolism and renal excretion vary, resulting in different plasma half-lives (Tables 10.7 and 10.8). The available preparations are usually divided into two groups:

1. First generation (Table 10.7) — tolbutamide, chlorpropamide, acetohexamide, tolazamide, glymidine.
2. Second generation (Table 10.8) — glibenclamide, glibornuride, glipizide, gliquidone, gliclazide.

The first generation drugs were introduced between 1956 and the early 1960s. The second generation group became available from 1969 onwards and have a different chemical structure which was obtained by modifying R_1 and R_2 groupings (see Figure 10.1). They are more active at lower dose levels but are not more potent in terms of hypoglycaemic action and are still liable to produce side-effects, as described below. The choice of sulphonylurea is largely a matter of personal preference. The second generation drugs are more expensive, but have no real proven advantage so far as clinical effectiveness is concerned. Tables 10.7 and 10.8, show the daily maintenance dose, i.e. the dose required to achieve relief of symptoms and control of glycosuria with random plasma glucose values of 6–10 mmol/l (110–180 mg/dl), of the various preparations. Those diabetics with day-time glycosuria but no overnight glycosuria should be treated with a shorter acting drug such as tolbutamide, since this will reduce the risk of nocturnal hypoglycaemia, which is especially dangerous in the elderly.

Indications

Sulphonylureas are indicated for use in non-obese non-insulin-dependent

Table 10.7 The first generation sulphonylureas

Sulphonylurea (Tablet size, mg)	Plasma half-life (hours)	Duration of hypoglycaemic activity (hours)	Mode of metabolism	Rate of renal excretion	Daily maintenance dose (g)
Tolbutamide (500)	4–10	6–12	liver metabolism, inactive metabolites	100% in 24 hours	1.0–3.0 (divided dose)
Chlorpropamide (100, 250)	24–40	up to 60	excreted intact by kidney	80–90% in 4 days	0.1–0.5 (single dose)
Acetohexamide (500)	4–10	12–24	liver metabolism, active metabolites	>50% in 24 hours	0.25–1.5 (single or divided dose)
Tolazamide (100, 250)	7	12–24	liver metabolism, active metabolites	85% in 24 hours	0.1–1 (single or divided dose)
Glymidine* (500)	4	4–12	liver metabolism active metabolites	90% in 48 hours	0.5–2.0 (single or divided dose)

* Sulphapyrimidine derivative, generally included with first generation sulphonylurea drugs.

Table 10.8 *The second generation sulphonylureas*

Sulphonylurea (Tablet size, mg)	Plasma half-life (hours)	Duration of hypoglycaemic activity (hours)	Mode of metabolism	Rate of renal excretion	Daily maintenance dose (mg)
Glibenclamide (2.5, 5)	10–16	up to 24	liver metabolism inactive metabolites	50% in 5 days	2.5–15 (single or divided dose)
Glibornuride (25)	5–12	up to 24	liver metabolism inactive metabolites	70% in 3 days	12.5–75 (single or divided dose)
Glipizide (5)	3–7	up to 24	liver metabolism inactive metabolites	90% in 3 days	2.5–30 (single or divided dose)
Gliquidone (30)	1.4	up to 24	liver metabolism inactive metabolites	<5% in 24 hours	15–120 (single or divided dose)
Gliclazide* (80)	10–12	up to 24	liver metabolism inactive metabolites	<5% in 24 hours	40–320 (single or divided dose)

* Conventionally included with second generation sulphonylurea drugs but structurally different from all other first and second generation drugs by virtue of a nitrogen-containing heterocyclic ring.

patients whose symptoms persist despite dietary adherence. In some cases, a sulphonylurea may be commenced at the time of diagnosis in those patients unlikely to respond to diet alone because of severe hyperglycaemia and weight loss.

Adverse Effects

The sulphonylureas are a safe group of drugs with a low incidence of adverse effects. Although the University Group Diabetic Program (UGDP) reported from the USA that the sulphonylurea tolbutamide increased cardiovascular mortality, the study had various important shortcomings and its findings have not been confirmed. The following, however, are well-recognized side-effects.

Hypoglycaemia. Sulphonylurea-induced hypoglycaemia is less common than insulin-induced hypoglycaemia and is often wrongly diagnosed in elderly subjects as a cerebrovascular accident because the adrenergic component (sweating, tachycardia, etc.) of the hypoglycaemia is usually absent. Long-acting sulphonylureas (e.g. chlorpropamide, glibenclamide) should be avoided in elderly subjects who may miss a meal or inadvertently take an excessive dose of tablets. Liver disease and impaired renal function may also prolong the hypoglycaemic action of the sulphonylurea. Most sulphonylureas, apart from chlorpropamide, are metabolized in the liver before excretion by the kidney, but some may have active metabolites (see Tables 10.7 and 10.8). Less than 5% of gliquidone and gliclazide is excreted in the urine and these are the sulphonylureas of choice in patients with renal impairment, although other drugs with inactive metabolites, e.g. tolbutamide, glipizide, may also be used. Conversely, drugs which do not rely on hepatic metabolism (e.g. chlorpropamide) are indicated in patients with hepatic failure. Sulphonylurea-induced hypoglycaemia is often prolonged and requires a continuous i.v. infusion of glucose for 2–3 days or even longer.

Gastrointestinal side-effects. Less than 3% of patients complain of mild dyspeptic symptoms.

Cholestatic jaundice. Transient disturbances in liver function tests can occur in the first two months of treatment and are of no clinical significance. However, a hypersensitivity type of cholestatic jaundice, similar to that seen with chlorpromazine, may occur at any time and necessitate drug withdrawal.

Allergic skin reactions. The most common allergic skin reaction is a mild maculopapular rash, but others include photosensitivity and, rarely, severe exfoliative dermatitis and Stevens–Johnson syndrome. Glymidine does not cross-react with other sulphonylureas and may be useful if a rash has occurred with one of the other preparations.

Alcohol intolerance. A disulfiram-like ('Antabuse-like') effect may occur, with facial flushing after alcohol, in patients being treated with sulphonylureas, most commonly with chlorpropamide and rarely with the other preparations. It can occur after drinking even small amounts of alcohol and if it is upsetting then the patient may be changed to another sulphonylurea or alternatively treated with metformin. This so-called chlorpropamide-induced alcohol flush (CPAF) is a dominantly inherited trait, variably reported in 30–60% of non-insulin-dependent diabetics.

Effect on water excretion. Chlorpropamide and tolbutamide have an antidiuretic effect and occasionally may cause water intoxication, especially in elderly patients. Paradoxically, acetohexamide, tolazamide and gliben-clamide have a mild diuretic action which is rarely of clinical significance, although glibenclamide has been of benefit in a few cases of patients with the syndrome of inappropriate ADH secretion.

Interactions

Concurrent administration of other drugs which bind to plasma proteins will displace the sulphonylurea from the protein-binding site, thus increasing bioavailability and leading to unexpected hypoglycaemia in a previously well-controlled patient. This occurs with, for example, salicylates (high dose), barbiturates, MAOIs, phenylbutazone, sulphonamides, co-trimoxazole, phenytoin, clofibrate, and warfarin. The non-selective β-adrenoreceptor antagonists may mask the symptoms and signs of hypoglycaemia and in addition delay the recovery from hypoglycaemia by inhibiting gluco-neogenesis and glycogenolysis.

Diabetogenic drugs, e.g. thiazide diuretics, frusemide (but not bumetanide), corticosteroids, contraceptive pills and diazoxide may require an increase to be made in the dosage of sulphonylurea.

Biguanides

The biguanides are derived from the parent substance guanidine, which was shown in 1918 to have hypoglycaemic properties but was too toxic for clinical use. The basic structure of the biguanides is shown in Figure 10.2.

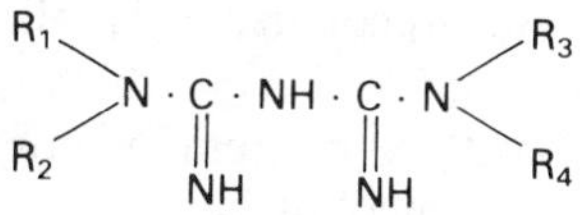

$$R_1 \diagdown \quad \diagup R_3$$
$$N \cdot C \cdot NH \cdot C \cdot N$$
$$R_2 \diagup \; \| \quad \| \; \diagdown R_4$$
$$\quad\;\; NH \quad NH$$

Figure 10.2 Basic structure of the biguanides. (With metformin, the formula is $(CH_3)_2N \cdot C \cdot NH \cdot C \cdot NH_2$.)

In the UK dimethylbiguanide (metformin) and phenethylbiguanide (phenformin) were introduced in the early 1960s. In 1982 phenformin was withdrawn from the UK market because of the risk of lactic acidosis. Metformin (Glucophage) is therefore the only biguanide now available in the UK. Butylbiguanide (Buformin) is available in some European countries.

Metformin has no pancreatic action and in order to be therapeutically effective requires the presence of endogenous insulin. Its hypoglycaemic effect is mediated through diminished glucose absorption, increased glucose uptake by muscle and decreased hepatic gluconeogenesis. In addition, recent studies have shown that metformin increases the number of insulin receptor sites on cell surface membranes, thus allowing for increased sensitivity of peripheral tissue to endogenous insulin. Unless taken in excessive dosage, metformin does not cause hypoglycaemia.

Metformin is rapidly absorbed from the gut, is not protein-bound in the plasma, is not metabolized to any degree by the liver and is excreted unchanged by the kidney within 24 hours. The mean plasma half-life is short at approximately 2–3 hours. Metformin is available as 500 mg and 850 mg tablets. The daily maintenance dose is 0.5–3.0 g in divided doses.

Indications for Metformin Treatment

Biguanides are the treatment of choice in obese diabetics uncontrolled by diet alone. They are preferable to sulphonylureas because they do not induce further weight gain. Metformin may also be used as an alternative in non-obese diet-failure diabetics, but in this group sulphonylureas are the first-choice therapy unless they produce adverse effects. It may be added into the drug regimen of patients uncontrolled by sulphonylureas and combined therapy with metformin and a sulphonylurea may give satisfactory control for several years and delay insulin therapy in elderly patients.

Adverse Effects

Gastrointestinal intolerance. Anorexia, nausea, vomiting, diarrhoea and a metallic taste in the mouth may occur, the last being due to a concentration of metformin by the salivary glands. The gastrointestinal effects are often transient and mild, and may be minimized by starting with a small dose, e.g. metformin 0.5 g twice daily, this being increased gradually. The drug should be taken after meals.

Lactic acidosis. This is a well-recognized complication of treatment with either phenformin or buformin (neither of which is available in the UK). It especially occurs in patients with co-existent liver or renal disease, circulatory failure, infections or excessive alcohol intake and is fatal in 50% of cases. Although treatment with metformin may cause a small elevation of plasma lactate, metformin-associated lactic acidosis is rare and the few reported cases have been in patients with renal failure or after i.v. pyelography. The risk of potential lactic acidosis can be minimized by restricting the use of metformin to patients with normal renal and liver function; during intercurrent illness metformin should be replaced by insulin and the drug avoided for 48 hours before an i.v. pyelogram.

Megaloblastic anaemia. Malabsorption of vitamin B$_{12}$ and, more rarely, folate depletion have been reported with metformin, but frank megaloblastic anaemia is extremely rare and is perhaps coincidental. However, it is advisable to check serum folic acid and B_{12} levels at yearly intervals.

Glucagon

Glucagon is a polypeptide hormone containing 29 amino acids (molecular weight 3485) produced by the alpha-cells in the pancreatic islets of Langerhans in response to hypoglycaemia. It is transported via the portal circulation to the liver, where the major portion is bound. Glucagon has a short half-life in the blood of 10–15 minutes. The main physiological action of glucagon is as a hyperglycaemic agent and it raises the blood sugar by stimulating glycogenolysis and gluconeogenesis; in addition, it accelerates lipolysis with free-fatty acid release from adipose tissue. Glucagon has been shown to have widespread actions on gastrointestinal activity, but the physiological significance of these is not entirely clear. These effects include the inhibition of gastric and duodenal activity and a decrease in gastric acid output, an increase in bile flow, decreased secretion of pancreatic digestive enzymes, and an inhibition in small and large intestinal motility. In addition to the effects on carbohydrate metabolism, other metabolic actions demonstrated experimentally using pharmacological doses, again of uncertain physiological significance in the human, include the release of pituitary hormone, the release of catecholamines from the adrenals, an increase of renal electrolyte loss and a lowering of plasma calcium levels, partly by its action on the kidney, partly by stimulation of calcitonin release, and partly by a direct effect on the skeleton, inhibiting bone resorption. Glucagon also has a positive inotropic action on the heart and can act as an antagonist to β-adrenoreceptor blocking agents (p. 278).

Preparations and Uses

Glucagon is available commercially under that name as a freeze-dried preparation in ampoules of 1 mg and should be dissolved in the accompanying diluent. Its main clinical use is the treatment of insulin-induced hypoglycaemic coma in diabetics, when 1–2 mg may be injected s.c., i.m. or i.v. if the patient is unconscious. This usually restores consciousness in 10–15 minutes and is useful in general practice or for relatives to use in an emergency. Although i.v. glucose is the treatment of choice for hypoglycaemia, both i.v. glucose and glucagon may be used in the same patient if necessary. Glucagon may be used in other forms of insulin hypoglycaemia, e.g. in patients with insulinoma, but it is ineffective in alcohol-induced fasting hypoglycaemia, since in this condition there are no hepatic glycogen stores.

Glucagon may also be used for endoscopy and radiography of the gastrointestinal tract, e.g. for hypotonic duodenography, where 1–2 mg i.v. will dilate the stomach and duodenum and inhibit motility. Utilizing some of the other pharmacological effects mentioned above, glucagon has been tried in the treatment of acute pancreatitis, diverticular disease of the colon, Paget's disease, cardiac failure and cardiogenic shock, but the excessive doses that have to be given, together with the short half-life of the drug, caused unacceptable nausea and vomiting, electrolyte disturbances and hyperglycaemia. Thus glucagon has only gained general acceptance for the treatment of hypoglycaemic coma and as an adjuvant to gastrointestinal endoscopy and radiography.

ADRENOCORTICAL HORMONES

The adrenal cortex secretes several hormones which have profound effects on water, electrolyte, fat, protein and carbohydrate metabolism. They are necessary for life and enable the body to react to stress. Addison, in 1855, was the first to describe the effects of destruction of the adrenal glands, but it was not until 1952 that the most recently isolated adrenal steroid (aldosterone) was discovered.

Adrenocortical hormones are all steroids, with the basic cyclopentanoperhydrophenanthrene nucleus shown below.

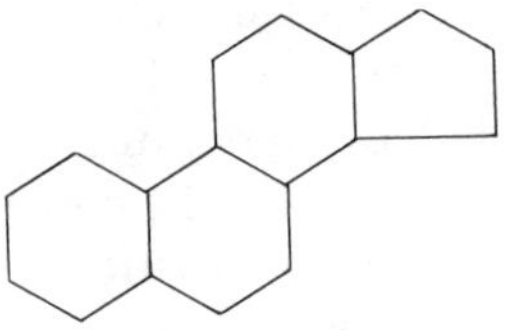

THE CYCLOPENTANOPERHYDROPHENANTHRENE
NUCLEUS

There are two chemical types of adrenocortical hormones: the corticosteroids, which contain 21 carbon atoms, and the androgens, which contain 19 carbon atoms. The corticosteroids are further divided on the basis of function into glucocorticoids and mineralocorticoids.

Synthesis
All adrenocortical hormones are synthesized from cholesterol in a reaction which involves the consumption of adrenal ascorbic acid; a scheme for the synthesis is shown in Figure 10.3. Only small amounts are stored, and the rate of synthesis is extremely rapid.

Many steroids have been artificially synthesized in an attempt to produce drugs that have predominantly glucocorticoid or mineralocorticoid activity, the natural hormones having both effects.

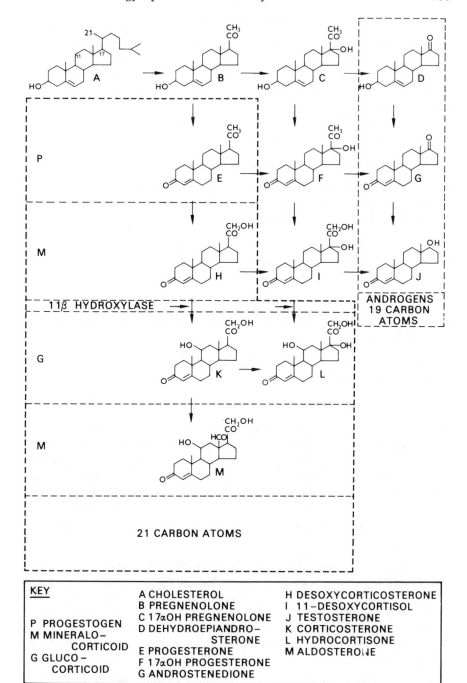

Figure 10.3 The biosynthesis of steroid hormones.

Glucocorticoids

The major glucocorticoids produced by the adrenal cortex are hydrocortisone (cortisol) and corticosterone, formed in the zona fasciculata and zona reticularis under the stimulus of ACTH (corticotrophin). As their concentration in the blood rises, the secretion of ACTH is inhibited by negative feedback.

The actions of glucocorticoids are predominantly on carbohydrate, protein, and fat metabolism.

Carbohydrate metabolism. Glucocorticoids cause:

1. Inhibition of the tissue oxidation of glucose (anti-insulin effect).
2. Increased glucose synthesis from protein catabolism.
3. Increased liver and muscle glycogen stores.

If food is continuously available, blood sugar and glycogen stores are maintained in the absence of glucocorticoids. In starvation, hypoglycaemia occurs and glycogen stores are rapidly depleted.

Protein metabolism. Protein catabolism is increased.

Fat metabolism. Lipolysis is increased (this requires growth hormone and thyroxine), and fat mobilization and redistribution enhanced.

Electrolyte and water metabolism. Glucocorticoids have weak mineralocorticoid activity (p. 408).

Disorders of Production

Overproduction. Cushing's syndrome is the term given to the clinical features resulting from prolonged tissue exposure to inappropriately high levels of plasma free cortisol or synthetic glucocorticoids. The causes are pituitary-dependent bilateral adrenal hyperplasia (Cushing's disease), adrenocortical adenoma or carcinoma, ectopic ACTH secretion (usually by small cell cancer of the lung) and treatment with corticosteroids or ACTH. In Cushing's syndrome the normal effects of corticosteroids are exaggerated with:

1. Increased blood sugar and liver glycogen (secondary diabetes).
2. Increased protein breakdown, leading to muscle wasting, osteoporosis, and increased capillary fragility in the skin (producing striae and bruising).
3. Increased lipolysis and a characteristic redistribution of fat, which is laid down in the face (moon face), abdomen, and back (buffalo hump).
4. Increased mineralocorticoid activity (p. 408), leading to hypertension.
5. Hirsutism.

Additional effects of large amounts of circulating glucocorticoids are:

1. Suppression of secretion of ACTH by the pituitary, leading to atrophy of the zona fasciculata and reticularis.

2. Suppression of the inflammatory response, leading to poor healing of wounds and lowered resistance to infection.
3. Suppression of antibody formation, reducing immunological responses.
4. A reduction in the number of circulating eosinophils and lymphocytes (lympholytic action).
5. Involution of lymphoid tissue.
6. Growth suppression in children.
7. The precipitation of psychotic episodes.
8. Activation (and perhaps production) of peptic ulcers.

Underproduction. Primary adrenocortical insufficiency most commonly results from autoimmune or tuberculous destruction of the adrenal cortex. The resultant clinical picture, known as Addison's disease, is characterized by excessive pigmentation due to raised plasma levels of ACTH and β-LPH (p. 368), and postural hypotension, weight loss, weakness, nausea and abdominal pain due to lack of corticosteroid secretion. Secondary adrenocortical insufficiency results from failure of secretion of CRF or ACTH in the presence of potentially normal adrenocortical function. It occurs in patients with pituitary or hypothalamic disease (e.g. pituitary tumour or craniopharyngioma), and also following the withdrawal of chronic administration of supraphysiological doses of corticosteroids or ACTH. In primary adrenocortical insufficiency there is deficiency of both glucocorticoids and mineralocorticoids, whereas in the secondary form, aldosterone secretion is maintained as it is largely independent of ACTH.

Natural glucocorticoids

Hydrocortisone (cortisol). The structure and actions of hydrocortisone are described above. Normal secretion is at the rate of about 20 mg/day, the blood levels showing a diurnal variation (8–26 μg/100 ml or 220–720 nmol/l at 08.00 h; < 10 μg/100 ml or < 275 nmol/l at 22.00 h). It is 90% bound to globulin (transcortin) and albumin, the globulin having low capacity but high affinity, the albumin the reverse. Pregnancy increases transcortin levels, with a resultant increase in total plasma hydrocortisone. Seventy per cent of secreted hydrocortisone is metabolized in the liver and then excreted by the kidney as glucuronide and sulphate conjugates. The 17-OH steroid excretion can be used as an index of glucocorticoid production.

Synthetic hydrocortisone is available as 10 mg and 20 mg tablets. Prolonged action may be achieved by the use of esters given parenterally.

Hydrocortisone sodium succinate injection, BP, is available in 100 mg and 500 mg doses. It can be given i.v., its peak effect being seen after about 8 hours, with noticeable effects after 1–2 hours. Efcortesol injection is a proprietary preparation with similar properties which is supplied made up in a stable solution.

Corticosterone. Corticosterone has less glucocorticoid but more mineralocorticoid activity than hydrocortisone. It is not used therapeutically.

Synthetic glucocorticoids

Synthetic glucocorticoids are used mainly for their anti-inflammatory activity, and vary in potency. Those in common use are listed in Table 10.9.

Table 10.9 *Synthetic glucocorticoids*

Drug	Activity relative to hydrocortisone		Equivalent dose (mg)
	Glucocorticoid	Mineralocorticoid	
Hydrocortisone	1	1	20
Cortisone	0.8	0.8	25
Prednisone	4	0.8	5
Prednisolone	4	0.8	5
Methylprednisolone	5	0.5	4
Triamcinolone	5	0	4
Betamethasone	25	0	0.75
Dexamethasone	25	0	0.75

Prednisone is converted to prednisolone, and cortisone to hydrocortisone, both in the liver. Both prednisone and cortisone are biologically inactive and should not be used topically.

Available Drugs

Many synthetic glucocorticoids are now available for systemic use, either alone or in combination with other drugs. They include hydrocortisone, cortisone, prednisone, prednisolone, methylprednisolone, triamcinolone, paramethasone, betamethasone, dexamethasone, deoxycortone and fluocortolone, all of which are marketed under many proprietary names. Some of these compounds are also produced in the form of enemas or rectal foam for use in ulcerative colitis or proctitis. Steroid creams and ointments are also commonly used for inflammatory skin diseases. Their potency varies with the dose of glucocorticoid used, and significant absorption may occur from inflamed surfaces or with enclosed dressings. Betamethasone and beclomethasone are also available, either in aerosol or powder form, for use in chronic asthma.

Uses of Glucocorticoids

Dosage depends on the condition and severity of the illness to be treated and the glucocorticoid used.

Replacement therapy. For an acute Addisonian crisis, hydrocortisone (as hydrocortisone sodium succinate) should be given i.v. in doses of up to

100 mg 6-hourly. Maintenance therapy in Addison's disease should be with hydrocortisone 20 mg in the morning and 10 mg in the evening, in combination with a mineralocorticoid. Alternatively the glucocorticoid can be given as cortisone acetate 25 mg and 12.5 mg, or as prednisolone 5 mg and 2.5 mg. In secondary adrenocortical insufficiency mineralocorticoid replacement is not necessary. It is essential that the dose of glucocorticoids is increased at times of intercurrent stress in all patients with adrenocortical insufficiency and the following dosage regimens are recommended:

Major surgery (e.g. cholecystectomy). Hydrocortisone sodium succinate is given with the premedication in a dose of 100 mg i.m. and 6-hourly thereafter for 3 days. The preoperative maintenance therapy is substituted from the fourth day if the clinical situation permits.

Minor surgery (e.g. herniorraphy). Hydrocortisone sodium succinate is given with the premedication in a dose of 100 mg i.m. and 6-hourly thereafter for 24 hours.

Other surgical procedures (e.g. dilatation and curettage). Hydrocortisone sodium succinate 100 mg i.m. with the premedication is all that is required.

Dental treatment under local anaesthesia. The morning dose of oral glucocorticoid should be doubled on the day of treatment.

Severe cold, influenza, etc. Patients should be advised to double the morning and evening dose of glucocorticoid for the 2–3 days' duration of the pyrexial illness. In the event of vomiting, hydrocortisone sodium succinate 100 mg i.m. should be given. For this purpose the patient should have a supply of ampoules of hydrocortisone, in addition to syringes and needles and should know how to use them. If the vomiting continues for longer than 12 hours, or if the intercurrent illness takes the form of prolonged severe diarrhoea or pyrexia, the patient should be transferred to hospital because of the risk of adrenal crisis.

Anti-inflammatory uses. Glucocorticoids given parenterally, orally or locally have marked anti-inflammatory activity. In the treatment of the connective tissue disorders (rheumatoid arthritis, systemic lupus erythematosus, scleroderma, dermatomyositis, polymyositis, cranial arteritis) prednisone or prednisolone may be given orally in divided doses up to a total of 60 mg daily. Many other conditions (sarcoidosis, nephrotic syndrome with 'minimal change' lesions, post-hepatic cirrhosis, bronchial asthma) may also require systemic glucocorticoids in high dosage. In ulcerative colitis and proctitis, systemic or local administration (cortisone, hydrocortisone or prednisolone enemas or foam) may be useful. Local application of glucocorticoids may prevent or remove scarring in infections or lesions of the cornea, or when injected into keloid (triamcinolone). Local injections of hydrocortisone acetate, which is insoluble and poorly absorbed, can be used in inflammatory conditions affecting joints or bursae. Application of glucocorticoids to the skin (betamethasone) may be useful in eczematous conditions, but systemic absorption may occur, especially with prolonged application or enclosed dressings. Beclomethasone dipropionate or betamethasone valerate is administered to asthmatics by aerosol and is said not to be absorbed to a significant extent.

Allergic conditions. As they suppress the immune response, glucocorticoids can be used systemically in the treatment of acquired haemolytic anaemia, thrombocytopenic purpura, serum sickness and angioneurotic oedema. Prednisolone is usually used. Hydrocortisone is usually given for anaphylactoid reactions, but its action is slow.

High doses (up to 60 mg daily) of prednisolone may be used, in combination with antimetabolites such as azathioprine, to suppress the rejection phenomenon after renal, cardiac or liver transplantation.

Reticuloses and leukaemias. Because of their lympholytic activity, systemic glucocorticoids in high dosage may be used in the treatment of Hodgkin's disease and lymphatic leukaemia. They are usually given with chemotherapeutic agents (p. 515). In myeloma they are used to treat the hypercalcaemia which can occur.

Miscellaneous uses. In shock due to Gram-negative bacteraemia, i.v. hydrocortisone in doses up to 2 g 6-hourly may be beneficial when used as an adjunct to antibacterial chemotherapy.

In raised intracranial pressure, i.v. dexamethasone in doses of 4 mg 6-hourly may reduce symptoms by relieving cerebral oedema.

Administration

High or prolonged dosage produces the abnormalities of Cushing's syndrome mentioned above. Important points to remember are:

1. A large single dose or short course of glucocorticoids is unlikely to produce adverse effects. In life-threatening situations (status asthmaticus, necrotizing vasculitis) the potential benefits of glucocorticoid therapy far outweigh the risks. Prolonged dosage causes suppression of the pituitary–adrenal axis, leading to adrenocortical insufficiency if the glucocorticoid is suddenly withdrawn. Hence, under those conditions, the dosage of steroid should be reduced gradually over several weeks or months.
2. Topical application (by enema, inhalation or local application to skin) may be associated with significant absorption, which can result in suppression of the pituitary–adrenal axis.

Mineralocorticoids

The major mineralocorticoid produced by the adrenal cortex is aldosterone, which is formed in the zona glomerulosa. Desoxycorticosterone also has significant mineralocorticoid activity.

Actions

Mineralocorticoids control electrolyte and water metabolism by their action on the kidney. They act on the distal convoluted tubule, causing reabsorption of Na^+ (and Cl^-) in exchange for K^+ and H^+ ions, probably by interfering with the synthesis of the enzymes normally concerned with ionic transport. Because of the increased retention of Na^+, water is retained by the body (osmotic effect), and in the presence of excessive mineralocorticoid activity, the extracellular fluid (ECF) volume is increased and hypokalaemia and alkalosis are found. This leads to hypertension, oedema, an inability to excrete a water load, and the neuromuscular and cardiac effects of hypokalaemia.

Disorders of Production

Overproduction may be primary (Conn's syndrome, due to the hypersecretion of aldosterone) or secondary (due to other causes of disturbed water and electrolyte metabolism). The effects are described above. Treatment is by removal of the cause of hypersecretion, or the use of an aldosterone antagonist (spironolactone).

Underproduction is seen in Addison's disease (p. 405) and leads to renal sodium loss and potassium retention, causing dehydration, hypotension, and hyperkalaemia. Treatment is by mineralocorticoid replacement.

Natural mineralocorticoids

Aldosterone. The structure and synthesis of aldosterone are described above. Aldosterone secretion is not under the control of ACTH under normal conditions and suppression of ACTH secretion does not lead to atrophy of the zona glomerulosa. The juxta-glomerular apparatus of the kidney, in response to changes in the ECF volume, secretes the hormone renin. Renin causes the formation of angiotensin I from angiotensinogen I (a glycoprotein) in the blood, and the decapeptide angiotensin I is then converted to the octapeptide angiotensin II, which stimulates the synthesis and release of aldosterone. The feedback control of this system is by the interaction of ECF volume with renin secretion.

In contrast to the glucocorticoids, aldosterone in plasma is not bound to protein. It is rapidly metabolized in the liver and conjugated before excretion.

Desoxycorticosterone. Desoxycorticosterone is a powerful natural mineralocorticoid which is rapidly metabolized, especially by the liver. It is ineffective if given orally, and parenteral preparations are available.

Preparations

Desoxycorticosterone acetate. This is an oily suspension, which is given in a dose of 2–5 mg i.m. daily.

Desoxycorticosterone trimethylacetate. This is a crystalline suspension, which is injected i.m. in 25 mg doses. This is said to release 1 mg daily for 25 days.

Fused deoxycortone pellets. These may be implanted, releasing 1 mg per day for 3–6 months.

Synthetic mineralocorticoids

Fludrocortisone, which is effective given orally, has largely superseded desoxycorticosterone. It is given in a daily dose of 0.1–0.2 mg, and has weak glucocorticoid activity.

Mineralocorticoid activity is summarized in Table 10.10.

Table 10.10 *Synthetic mineralocorticoids*

Drug	Activity relative to hydrocortisone	
	Glucocorticoid	*Mineralocorticoid*
Hydrocortisone	1	1
Desoxycorticosterone	0	100
Aldosterone	0.3	3000
Fludrocortisone	10	125

Uses of Mineralocorticoids
Mineralocorticoids are used only for replacement therapy, in the dosage stated. The only adverse effects are due to overdosage, as described.

ABNORMALITIES OF CORTICOSTEROID PRODUCTION

One or more of the enzymes required for the complete synthetic pathway shown in Fig. 10.3 may be congenitally absent. The most common deficiency is that of 11β-hydroxylase, which prevents the formation of cortisol and corticosterone. This removes the feedback inhibition of these compounds on ACTH production, and the high levels of ACTH produced cause excess corticosteroid synthesis, rerouted to produce androgens. High androgen levels in infancy cause the adrenogenital syndrome, characterized by precocious puberty in boys and virilization in girls. Treatment is by suppression of ACTH production with low doses of prednisolone.

Drugs that Interfere with Corticosteroid Synthesis

Metyrapone

Metyrapone (Metopirone) inhibits the action of 11β-hydroxylase and is used to reduce plasma cortisol levels in patients with Cushing's syndrome prior to pituitary or adrenal surgery, thereby reducing operative morbidity. The initial dose is 250 mg twice daily and is increased until plasma cortisol levels are reduced to 300–400 nmol/l. It may be necessary to increase the dose to 1 g every six hours. The only adverse effects are nausea and vomiting, which can be largely controlled if the drug is taken with food.

Trilostane

Trilostane (Modrenal) blocks the conversion of pregnenolone into progesterone by inhibiting the 3β-hydroxysteroid dehydrogenase and isomerase system. It is an alternative to metyrapone in the management of Cushing's syndrome, but has also been used successfully in the medical treatment of Conn's syndrome. The initial dose is 60 mg orally four times daily, but as much as 960 mg daily may be necessary to achieve a satisfactory reduction in plasma cortisol levels. Trilostane appears to be better tolerated than metyrapone, but adverse effects include flushing and palatal oedema.

Aminoglutethimide

Aminoglutethimide blocks the conversion of cholesterol into pregnenolone and has been used in the palliative treatment of adrenal carcinoma. Adverse effects, mainly rashes and nausea, are common, occurring in up to 40% of patients.

Drugs that Interfere with Mineralocorticoid Action

Spironolactone

Spironolactone (Aldactone, Diatensec, Spiroctan) competitively antagonizes the action of aldosterone on the renal tubule. It is of value in situations such as severe cardiac failure or hepatic cirrhosis with oedema where there is an element of secondary hyperaldosteronism. It may be used in the long-term treatment of Conn's syndrome as an alternative to surgery.

SEX HORMONES

Gonadotrophins

The gonadotrophins, luteinizing hormone (LH) and follicle-stimulating hormone (FSH), are secreted by the anterior pituitary in response to hypothalamic gonadotrophin-releasing hormone (Gn-RH). In the female, LH and FSH, as their names imply, control the ovarian cycle. In the male, LH stimulates testicular androgen production, while FSH stimulates spermatogenesis. Chorionic gonadotrophin (HCG) is secreted by the syncytiotrophoblast in pregnancy. Its actions are mainly those of LH and it maintains the corpus luteum until placental steroidogenesis is established.

Human gonadotrophins are available as menopausal gonadotrophin (HMG), which is prepared from the urine of post-menopausal women and contains both LH and FSH, and chorionic gonadotrophin, which is prepared from the urine of pregnant women.

Indications

HMG and HCG are used in the induction of ovulation (p. 429). In the male they are used to induce fertility in hypogonadotrophic hypogonadism. They are of no use if there is primary testicular failure or mechanical blockage in the epididymis or vas deferens. If testosterone replacement is already being given, it is discontinued and replaced by, for example, HCG (1500 iU) plus HMG (75 iu of both LH and FSH), both given three times weekly by i.m. injection for at least six months.

HCG can be used on its own to induce the changes of puberty in males who suffer from delayed puberty in association with low gonadotrophin levels. When this is due to hypopituitarism, long-term therapy will be required and this is more conveniently given as testosterone (p. 413). However, it may be difficult to distinguish between an isolated deficiency of Gn-RH or gonadotrophins and constitutional delayed puberty. In the latter condition puberty will eventually occur spontaneously, but before this happens treatment may be indicated for psychological reasons. Therapy with HCG rather than testosterone is considered to be more physiological, since the patient's own testosterone production is stimulated and has the advantage of promoting testicular enlargement. A suggested regimen is to give 12-week courses of 1500 iu three times weekly i.m., separated by intervals of 12 weeks during which no treatment is given. The treatment-free periods may minimize the danger of inducing disproportionate skeletal advancement. More importantly, they allow assessment to be made as to whether the patient is entering puberty spontaneously, in which case treatment can be discontinued. If there is no lasting benefit after three courses, it is likely that long-term testosterone replacement will be required. Finally, HCG is used to induce testicular descent in patients with cryptorchidism, although its value remains uncertain.

Gn-RH is synthesized for intranasal application. However, it is not yet generally available and its place in the management of hypothalamic disorders remains to be established.

Androgens

Androgens are the predominant sex hormones in the male. The major source of androgens is testicular tissue and the most important androgen produced by the testes is testosterone.

Testosterone

Testosterone is converted in most target tissues to the more active dihydrotestosterone by a 5α-reductase. The synthesis and secretion of testosterone by the Leydig cells of the testes is stimulated by LH.

Actions

Testosterone promotes growth of the genitalia and the development of male secondary sex characteristics. It is necessary for the maintenance of libido and potency and its presence within the seminiferous tubules is required for spermatogenesis. Circulating testosterone, on the other hand, inhibits gonadotrophin production by the anterior pituitary, so that suppression of spermatogenesis is a side-effect of testosterone therapy. Androgens also have an anabolic action, promoting growth in height until they fuse the epiphyses, developing and maintaining muscle mass and preventing osteoporosis.

Preparations

Oral. Oral preparations of testosterone and its synthetic analogues are only weakly active because of hepatic breakdown. However, fluoxymesterone 10–20 mg per day may suffice in the middle-aged or elderly to alleviate minor symptoms and prevent osteoporosis.

Intramuscular. Testosterone oenanthate 250 mg every 2–3 weeks or Sustanon 250 (a combination of testosterone esters) in a dosage of one ampoule every 3–4 weeks is given by i.m. injection.

Implants. Testosterone pellets 400–600 mg every 4–6 months are inserted s.c. into the anterior abdominal wall by means of a trocar and cannula under local anaesthesia.

Indications

The main use of testosterone is in the treatment of male hypogonadism, the clinical syndrome which results from reduced testosterone secretion. If this occurs before puberty, then puberty is delayed and there may be associated short stature. Caution is then required, since the effect of testosterone on epiphyseal closure may result in the stunting of growth. For this reason no more than half the adult replacement dose should be used for the first year. If there is co-existing growth hormone deficiency, testosterone should be withheld until an acceptable height has been obtained with human growth hormone.

The aims of testosterone replacement therapy are not only to induce and maintain secondary sex characteristics and potency, but also to alleviate minor symptoms of testosterone deficiency (e.g. tiredness, lack of concentration and depression) and, in the longer term, to prevent osteoporosis.

In hypergonadotrophic hypogonadism there is primary testicular failure and infertility which is irreversible. With the exception of male Turner's syndrome, these patients are commonly of average or above average height before the usual age of puberty, so the concern that ultimate height may be prejudiced does not arise. In hypogonadotrophic hypogonadism, testicular failure is secondary to hypothalamic or anterior pituitary dysfunction. However, diminished testosterone secretion results in failure of spermatogenesis, so there is associated infertility. If hyalinization of the seminiferous tubules has occurred as a result of a long-standing reduction in gonadotrophin secretion, then the infertility will be irreversible. In any event, testosterone replacement will not restore fertility. When fertility is desired, therefore, testosterone is replaced by gonadotrophin therapy (p. 411) to stimulate spermatogenesis as well as androgen production.

Finally, testosterone replacement will not restore potency in the presence of hyperprolactinaemia, which may be present, e.g. when the cause of the hypogonadism is a pituitary tumour. In this situation, treatment with bromocriptine will also be required.

Adverse Effects
Side-effects of testosterone therapy are salt and water retention, hypertension, cholestatic jaundice (especially with methyltestosterone and fluoxymesterone), polycythaemia (due to stimulation of erythropoiesis) and premature closure of the epiphyses if given in early puberty. Priapism and gynaecomastia may occur at the onset of treatment. Androgens are contraindicated in the presence of prostatic carcinoma or breast carcinoma in men. They produce virilization in women and suppress spermatogenesis in men.

Anabolic steroids

Anabolic steroids are synthetic androgens which were developed to have a less virilizing effect while retaining their protein-building property. In practice they have only limited application and they all have some androgenic activity. They are used in the treatment of some aplastic anaemias for their stimulant effect on erythropoiesis and in the palliative treatment of breast carcinoma. Oxymetholone and nandrolone are two examples, but there are several different compounds.

Small doses of anabolic steroids have been used to promote growth in cases of delayed puberty where lack of height is the major problem. Theoretically they should be particularly useful in girls, since oestrogen replacement produces only a slight acceleration in growth. In practice, however, their value is limited by their virilizing effects and their effect on epiphyseal closure.

Cyproterone acetate

Cyproterone acetate is a synthetic progestogen which has a potent anti-androgenic effect and mild glucocorticoid activity. It competes with testosterone and dihydrotestosterone for the androgen receptor in target organs including hair follicles. In addition, it suppresses pituitary LH and ACTH secretion, thereby reducing androgen production from both the ovaries and the adrenal glands.

Cyproterone acetate is used in the treatment of severe hirsutism in women. It crosses the placenta and may cause feminization of a male fetus. To avoid this risk it is combined with ethinyl oestradiol, which ensures effective contraception as well as regular menstrual bleeding. Cyproterone acetate 50 mg is given twice daily for days 5–14 of the cycle, with ethinyloestradiol 50 μg daily for days 5–25. The cyproterone acetate is given in the first half of the cycle only because of its long half-life, which is produced by a depot effect in adipose tissue. If given in the second half of the cycle, irregular bleeding occurs. No effect can be expected before six months, but it is claimed that the rate of hair growth is reduced in 75% of patients after 9–12 months. Side-effects are weight gain, hypertension and loss of libido and there is a theoretical risk of hypoadrenalism due to the suppression of ACTH. However, the latter is unlikely when the drug is given intermittently in this way. Treatment has to be continued indefinitely but the hazards of long-term therapy are as yet unknown. These hazards will presumably include, at least, those of long-term oestrogen therapy (p. 421) and for mild hirsutism cosmetic methods of treatment are to be preferred.

Cyproterone acetate has also been used in the treatment of precocious puberty.

Oestrogens

Oestrogens and progestogens are the predominant sex hormones in the female. The ovaries are the major source of oestrogens and the most important oestrogen produced by the ovaries is oestradiol. Oestradiol is partly converted by the liver to the less active oestrone and oestriol. As a result of hepatic metabolism, the natural oestrogens, although well absorbed, are relatively inactive when given orally. Synthetic oestrogens on the other hand (e.g. ethinyloestradiol, mestranol and stilboestrol), are both well absorbed and active orally.

Actions
Oestrogens are responsible for the development of female secondary sex characteristics including development of the breasts and female distribution of body fat and pubic hair. They produce myometrial hypertrophy, endometrial hyperplasia and vaginal keratinization, and their sudden withdrawal causes menstrual bleeding. Together with progesterone, they are responsible for the cyclical changes that occur in the endometrium. Their secretion is stimulated predominantly by FSH during the follicular phase, and predominantly by LH during the luteal phase. In turn, they exert both negative and positive feedback effects on gonadotrophin secretion (p. 428).

Physiologically, these effects are important in the control of the menstrual cycle, and pharmacologically, the negative feedback effect is used to suppress ovulation.

Indications

Oral contraception. The commonest use of oestrogens is in oral contraception, when they are given in combination with a progestogen.

Dysfunctional uterine haemorrhage. This term refers to irregular cyclical bleeding, often heavy and prolonged, that is not due to localized or systemic disease. A combined oestrogen–progestogen preparation, given from the 5th to the 26th day, regulates the cycle and reduces menstrual loss. Blind hormone therapy without proper investigation may be dangerous in masking malignancy. Oestrogen has also been given i.v. to control acute severe bleeding.

Endometriosis. Oestrogen alone induces proliferation of the endometrium, but continuous therapy with oestrogen plus progestogen for 9–12 months produces decidual change, followed by necrosis and involution. Extensive endometriosis may require surgery or a combination of surgery and hormone treatment.

Primary dysmenorrhoea. Primary dysmenorrhoea seems to occur only in ovulatory cycles. A combined oestrogen–progestogen preparation can be given cyclically to suppress ovulation.

Use of oestrogens in post-menopausal women. Oestrogens may be used to treat those symptoms that occur after the menopause as a consequence of natural loss of ovarian function. A case has also been put for their widespread prophylactic use in postmenopausal women, but this remains controversial.

Vasomotor symptoms. If symptoms such as hot flushes and night sweats are severe enough to merit treatment, this can be begun with, for example, 0.625 mg of conjugated oestrogen or 10 μg of ethinyloestradiol daily for three weeks out of four, increasing the dose as necessary. The symptoms tend to improve with time, whether treatment is given or not, and periodic attempts should be made to reduce the dose and finally to stop treatment. Most patients can be weaned off therapy after 18–24 months.

Lower genital tract atrophy. Atrophy of the vulva, vagina and urethra can cause dyspareunia, apareunia and the urethral syndrome. Treatment can be given orally or as oestrogen cream applied topically. The doses of oestrogen required are usually lower than those necessary to control vasomotor symptoms. However, treatment may have to be long term and it is important to realize that topical oestrogen is well absorbed, so the same precautions are required as with oral therapy.

Prophylactic oestrogen therapy. While the administration of oestrogens in the doses employed in the combined contraceptive pill has an adverse effect on the incidence of circulatory disease, it has been suggested that oestrogens in physiological amounts protect the female against atherosclerosis. This may be important in the young oestrogen-deficient patient, but oestrogen replacement has no obvious protective effect beyond the age of 50. The main argument for prophylactic oestrogen after the menopause is in the prevention of osteoporosis. Loss of bone mass is retarded and the incidence of fractures is reduced. However, when treatment is stopped, bone loss accelerates for a period, so treated patients may eventually be no better off. For maximal effect replacement has to be started as soon as possible after the menopause and continued long term. Against the possible benefits, therefore, must be placed the risks of long-term oestrogen therapy in this age group. The two major concerns are the risk of endometrial carcinoma and circulatory disease (pp. 421, 422). The former can be prevented by combining oestrogen with a cyclical progestogen, e.g. norethisterone acetate, 5 mg per day for the last five days of each 21 day course of oestrogen. Unless the patient has had a hysterectomy, cyclical progestogen should be added whenever oestrogens are given for longer than six months, irrespective of the indication. The risk of circulatory disease is related to the dose of oestrogen employed and this is usually less than half that used in the 50 μg contraceptive pill. However, it would seem wise to employ the same selection criteria (with the exception of age) as are used in deciding on the suitability of patients for combined oral contraception.

Oestrogen replacement should be considered after the menopause when there is a strong family history of osteoporosis, and can be given for premature menopause or early castration.

Treatment of female hypogonadism. Oestrogen replacement is indicated to induce female secondary sex characteristics and to prevent the long-term sequelae of oestrogen deficiency. The sudden introduction of large doses may produce unsightly nipple pigmentation and cosmetically poor breast development, and, as with testosterone replacement, disproportionate skeletal maturation. Treatment is, therefore, begun with small doses, e.g. ethinyloestradiol, 10 μg per day given continuously for six months, followed by a combined contraceptive pill, containing firstly 20 μg and later 30 μg of oestrogen, administered cyclically to induce withdrawal bleeding.

Suppression of lactation. The use of oestrogen to suppress lactation has now been superseded by bromocriptine (p. 371).

Treatment of malignant disease. Oestrogens may be of benefit in the treatment of some cases of carcinoma of the breast and prostate. Their use in the male causes feminization.

Treatment of hirsutism. The combined contraceptive pill (preferably employing a progestogen with low androgenic activity, e.g. ethynodiol diacetate) can be used to treat hirsutism. Prednisolone may be added so as to suppress both gonadotrophins and ACTH and thus both ovarian and adrenal androgen secretion. In addition, the oestrogen increases sex-hormone binding globulin and so decreases circulating free androgen. In practice only the minority of patients gain significant benefit.

Adverse Effects
Side-effects of oestrogens include nausea, vomiting, weight gain, oedema and breast enlargement and tenderness. Other side-effects and contraindications are discussed on p. 421.

Anti-oestrogens

Tamoxifen

Tamoxifen is an anti-oestrogen which may act by blocking receptor sites in target organs. It is used in the palliative treatment of breast carcinoma. Its side-effects are similar to, but less severe than those of oestrogens.

Clomiphene

See p. 428.

Progestogens

There are two groups of progestogens: first, derivatives of progesterone (e.g. hydroxyprogesterone), which is the main natural progestogen secreted by the corpus luteum; and secondly, derivatives of testosterone (e.g. norethisterone), which have more androgenic activity. Progestogens act mainly on the same tissues as oestrogens, modifying their effects. Progesterone limits oestrogen-induced proliferation of the endometrium and converts the abundant watery secretion of oestrogen-stimulated endocervical glands to a scant viscid material. It stimulates the secretion of a glycogen-rich mucus by the endometrial glands and loosens the underlying stroma, so preparing the uterus for implantation. The abrupt decline in the output of progesterone as well as oestrogen at the end of the cycle leads to menstruation.

Progesterone itself, like the natural oestrogens, is relatively inactive when administered orally, because it is rapidly metabolized by the liver.

Indications

Oral contraception. Progestogens are used alone or in combination with oestrogen in contraception (pp. 420, 427).

Dysfunctional uterine bleeding. This condition may be associated with failure of formation of the corpus luteum (anovulatory menorrhagia) or with an inadequate luteal phase. In either case, progesterone output during the second half of the cycle is inadequate and menorrhagia may result from the unopposed proliferative effect of oestrogen on the endometrium. The administration of a progestogen alone, e.g. norethisterone, 10 mg daily for ten days from the 15th day of the cycle, may achieve control. Alternatively, a combined oestrogen–progestogen preparation may be given as described above. In acute severe bleeding, large doses, e.g. up to 30 mg daily of norethisterone, can be given to arrest bleeding within 48 hours. When treatment is stopped, withdrawal bleeding occurs, but this is usually less severe. Thereafter cyclical hormone therapy can be commenced.

Endometriosis. Continuous therapy with progestogen alone does not cause decidualization and necrosis of endometrial growths, which requires oestrogen as well, but yields an atrophic endometrium. Breakthrough bleeding may occur owing to the suppression of gonadotrophins and, therefore, of oestrogen production, and a low dose of oestrogen may have to be added to stabilize the endometrium. Therapy with danazol may be more effective in producing endometrial atrophy and freer from side-effects than regimens employing oestrogen.

Primary dysmenorrhoea. Cyclical treatment with progestogen alone is less likely to be effective than treatment with a combined oestrogen–progestogen preparation.

Habitual abortion. Progestogens have been used in the treatment of habitual abortion, but their efficacy is in doubt.

Treatment of malignant disease. Progestogens have been used in the treatment of carcinoma of the uterus, breast, prostate and, rarely, kidney and testis.

Adverse Effects

Side-effects of progestogens include nausea, weight gain, altered libido, menstrual irregularity, acne, urticaria, virilization of the fetus and gynaecomastia. Side-effects of combined oestrogen-progestozen therapy are discussed on p. 421.

Danazol

Danazol is a synthetic derivative of ethisterone. It has mild androgenic activity, which may inhibit synthesis or release of gonadotrophins, but it may act directly on the endometrium to produce atrophy. It has been used in the treatment of endometriosis, dysfunctional uterine bleeding, mammary dysplasia, gynaecomastia and precocious puberty. Side-effects are weight gain, fluid retention, gastrointestinal upset, acne, oily skin, exacerbation of hirsutism and a mild worsening of carbohydrate tolerance in diabetes mellitus.

ORAL CONTRACEPTION

Hormonal contraception is the most effective and for many the most aesthetically acceptable form of contraception.

The Combined Oestrogen–Progestogen Pill

Mode of Action
Pituitary gonadotrophins are suppressed (negative feedback effect). As a result, follicular maturation is impaired and ovulation is inhibited. The effect is dose related, so occasional ovulation is more likely with 20–30 μg oestrogen pills than with 50 μg pills. In addition, there are peripheral effects on cervical mucus, rendering it relatively impenetrable to sperm, and on the endometrium, rendering it unfavourable to implantation. There may also be effects on ciliogenesis and on mucus in the fallopian tubes, which impair gametal transport.

Composition
The oestrogen is either ethinyloestradiol (20–50 μg) or mestranol (50 μg) which is demethylated in the liver to ethinyloestradiol, and various synthetic progestogens are used, as indicated in Table 10.11.

Table 10.11 *Synthetic progestogens used in the combined oestrogen–progestogen pill*

Progestogen	Dose (mg)
Norethisterone acetate	1–4
Norethisterone	0.5–1
Ethynodiol diacetate	0.5–2
Levonorgestrel	0.15–0.25
Norgestrel	0.5
Lynoestrenol	2.5

Apart from the considerations of total doses employed, there is as yet no proof that one combined pill is superior to another in respect of effectiveness or side-effects. One tablet is taken daily for 21 days, followed by a 7-day interval during which withdrawal bleeding occurs. The suppression of gonadotrophin secretion usually persists for about five days after the taking of the pill has ceased, so there is no follicular development during the treatment free period. It is usually recommended that the first course is started on the 5th day of the cycle, but ovulation may not be inhibited during the first cycle unless the pill is commenced on the first day.

Efficacy
The combined pill has a failure rate of 1–4 per 1000 women years. Failures probably result mainly from patient error.

Pharmacokinetics

The steroids used in the combined pill are well absorbed and peak plasma concentrations occur within two hours of administration. After an initial rapid fall (distribution), there is a slower decline in plasma concentrations (elimination), with detectable levels still present at 24 hours. There is, however, a wide range of plasma concentration in blood samples taken about 12 hours after administration, owing to interindividual variation in the rates of metabolism. With the relatively low dose of both oestrogen and progestogen now used, this may be important, with the possibility of failure of contraception occurring due to patient error, intercurrent illness or drug interactions. It is recommended that the pill be taken regularly at the same time each day. If vomiting occurs within two hours after administration (i.e. during the absorption phase) the dose should be repeated and back-up methods of contraception should be used during episodes of diarrhoea and vomiting or during concurrent therapy with a broad-spectrum antibiotic, as discussed below.

Adverse Effects

Thrombo-embolism. There is an increased risk of deep venous thrombosis and pulmonary embolism. The risk is related to the dose of oestrogen, so pills containing more than 50 μg of oestrogen are no longer employed. The combined pill should not be started during the first two weeks postpartum and it should be discontinued for one month before and two months after elective surgery, because of the increased risk of thrombosis during these times. Alternative contraception should be used if necessary perioperatively until the pill can be restarted.

Stroke and myocardial infarction. There is also an increased risk of stroke, both thrombotic and haemorrhagic, and of myocardial infarction. These conditions account for most of the excess mortality in pill users.

Hypertension. Hypertension occurs in about 5% of users after 5 years. It appears to be related to the length of usage, so arterial pressure has to be monitored indefinitely in women taking the pill. Any increase in arterial pressure or the development of hypertension during use is an indication for withdrawal. Fortunately, the elevation is usually relatively mild and almost always reverts to normal when the pill is stopped. The pathogenesis may involve the renin–angiotensin system and the effect is probably mediated by oestrogens with progestogens having a synergistic effect.

Pill-related mortality. In a study carried out by the Royal College of General Practitioners, pill users had a 40% higher death rate than non-users. Virtually all the excess mortality was due to disease of the circulatory system (mostly ischaemic heart disease and subarachnoid haemorrhage). The two major factors affecting the risk were age and cigarette smoking. Thus the excess annual death rate ranged from 1 per 77000 in non-smokers under the age of

35 to 1 per 500 in smokers over the age of 45. From these and other studies it is obvious that the combined pill should only be prescribed to patients who have an acceptable profile of risk factors for circulatory disease. It should probably not be given to women over the age of 35 years and heavy smoking (more than 15 cigarettes per day) should lower the prohibitive age to 30 years. Other risk factors (see under contraindications) must also be taken into account and during follow-up the risk–benefit equation should be reviewed periodically.

Liver and gall-bladder disease. Increased plasma conjugated bilirubin and alkaline phosphatase occur in up to 2% of patients. Both oestrogens and progestogens may be involved. Clinical jaundice probably only occurs in women who have pre-existing defective hepatic excretory function, e.g. Dubin–Johnson and Rotor's syndromes, or recurrent cholestasis of pregnancy. It almost invariably becomes manifest during the first three cycles of treatment.

The pill should not be given in the presence of acute or chronic liver disease, not only because of the risk of jaundice but also because the steroids are metabolized in the liver. Following an attack of acute hepatitis, the combined pill can be restarted if liver function has returned to normal.

The pill increases biliary cholesterol saturation and causes a slight reduction in bile-acid concentrations. Gallstones occur about twice as commonly in women using the pill.

Finally, the incidence of benign liver tumours appears to be increased in pill users. The risk is small, but increases with the duration of use.

Neoplasia. There is evidence that long-term use of the combined pill may increase the risk of carcinoma of the breast and cervix, but not ovary. Although this evidence is not conclusive it is recommended that long-term users should have regular cervical cytology examination. The progestogen component appears to protect against the risk of endometrial carcinoma, which is known to occur with unopposed chronic oestrogen therapy. The incidence of benign breast disease is decreased and uterine fibroids may enlarge during oral contraceptive use.

Carbohydrate intolerance. The pill may impair carbohydrate tolerance. This effect can occur with progestogen alone, but does not occur with oestrogen alone. However, the combination of oestrogen and progestogen has a greater effect than progestogen alone and the effect diminishes as the oestrogen dose is lowered. Clinically, the pill may unmask latent diabetes or result in an increased insulin requirement in the established diabetic. This can be overcome by increasing the dose of insulin, but there are reports of retinopathy and nephropathy having progressed while the pill was being used and there is concern that the pill may add to the risk of cardiovascular and cerebrovascular disease in diabetics. For these reasons close supervision is required and the pill should be used for as short a period as possible. When no further pregnancies are planned consideration should be given to sterilization.

Nausea and vomiting. Nausea, if it occurs, is usually found when the pill is first taken and may subside with continued use. It may be avoided by taking the pill at bedtime or after a meal or by changing to a pill of lower oestrogen content. Rarely is it necessary to stop the pill.

Breakthrough bleeding. Almost 50% of patients experience breakthrough bleeding at some stage in the course of treatment. It is due to failure of the synthetic hormones to maintain the endometrium and is more common with low oestrogen preparations. When it occurs during the initial months of use, however, it will resolve spontaneously in approximately 50% of patients without their having to resort to a higher dose preparation. Failure to take the pill at the same time each day, missing out doses altogether, drug interaction and impaired absorption should all be considered. When it occurs after several months of use, arbitrarily switching to another low-dose preparation may be effective. As a last resort a higher dose oestrogen pill can be used, temporarily if possible. Failure to respond to these simple measures should raise the suspicion of coincidental cervical, uterine or ovarian pathology.

Absence of withdrawal bleeding. Unlike the normal menstrual cycle, the proliferative effect of oestrogen on the endometrium during oral contraceptive use is always inhibited by progestogen. Perhaps for this reason bleeding on withdrawal tends to be less and in some women may cease entirely. Like breakthrough bleeding, this effect is more common with low-oestrogen pills. Although hardly an undesirable effect in itself, it causes concern about potential pregnancy and this must obviously be excluded. Otherwise, management consists of excluding factors that may lower blood oestrogen concentrations, as already discussed, and reassurance. If bleeding is still desired, giving a higher oestrogen pill can be considered.

Weight gain and fluid retention. Acyclic weight gain is thought to be due to progestogen-induced increase in appetite and a pill of lower progestogen content may be tried. Cyclic weight gain is thought to be due to oestrogen-induced fluid retention and a lower oestrogen content pill may be tried. Corneal oedema is another rare manifestation of fluid retention, but may be a nuisance to women using contact lenses.

Migraine. Migraine may be precipitated or aggravated, unchanged or sometimes even improved. When there is an exacerbation the pill should be stopped, since there is concern that some patients may go on to develop cerebrovascular lesions.

Depression. Depression may be more common in pill users, but it is unclear whether this has a psychological or biochemical basis. It is more likely to occur in the presence of a previous history of depression or of the 'premenstrual tension syndrome'. When it occurs alternative contraception should be recommended.

Epilepsy. The pill may increase the frequency of fits, particularly if these have been related to premenstrual tension, and some patients develop epilepsy for the first time on the pill. The possibility of contraceptive failure due to the enzyme-inducing properties of anticonvulsants is discussed on p. 425.

Asthma. Asthma may be aggravated during pregnancy or premenstrually and caution should, therefore, be exercised in prescribing the pill to asthmatics.

Infection. The pill may double the carriage rate of *Candida albicans* in the female genital tract and thus predispose to symptomatic candidiasis. The incidence of urinary tract infection appears to be increased in women taking the pill. This could be due to progestogen-induced ureteral dilatation or possibly to increased sexual activity.

Porphyria. The combined pill may precipitate an acute attack in acute intermittent porphyria and a hepatotoxic reaction with increased skin blistering in variegate porphyria.

Other adverse effects. Other side-effects include breast fullness and tenderness, chloasma, hirsutism and rarely skin lesions resembling herpes gestationis. Libido may be impaired, unchanged or increased.

Effects on Pregnancy, Lactation and Subsequent Reproductive Function
There is no increase in abortion or congenital abnormalities in ex-pill users, but there is debate as to whether there is an increase in congenital abnormalities following inadvertent pregnancy while on the pill (p. 562).

Established lactation is not affected by the pill and there is no evidence that low-dose preparations have any adverse effect on the infant. However, introduction of the pill is usually delayed until feeding is established.

There is usually a prompt return of fertility on discontinuing the pill, except for a temporary delay for the first two months. A small percentage of women have prolonged amenorrhoea, but this does not appear to differ from spontaneous secondary amenorrhoea occurring in the absence of previous oral contraception and a causal relationship is not certain. The usual causes of secondary amenorrhoea should, therefore, be sought.

Effects on Laboratory Function Tests
Oestrogen-containing pills increase the hepatic synthesis of a variety of transport proteins, e.g. transcortin, thyroxine-binding globulin, sex-hormone binding globulin, transferrin and caeruloplasmin. This increases the total plasma concentration of the relevant compounds, but free levels are usually unaffected. Free testosterone, however, may be decreased, since this

compound is more avidly bound to its carrier protein and this effect is exploited in the use of the pill to treat hirsutism.

Plasma fibrinogen and plasminogen levels are raised, so an elevated erythrocyte sedimentation rate (ESR) may occur. The rates of synthesis of albumin and haptoglobulin, on the other hand, are decreased.

The combined pill produces changes in clotting factors and lipids which presumably contribute to the risk of vascular disease. It is not certain how many coagulation factors are involved, but it has been suggested by various workers that fibrinogen, factors II, VII, VIII, IX and X are increased, while antithrombin III is decreased. Fasting serum triglycerides and low-density lipoproteins are increased and cholesterol is slightly increased. Pills containing levonorgestrel and norethisterone reduce high-density lipoproteins. Rarely the pill may induce hyperlipidaemic crises in women with familial hyperlipidaemia.

Finally, there is an increased incidence of positive antinuclear factor and rheumatoid factor.

Beneficial Effects

In addition to the primary effect of contraception, menstrual flow is diminished and regulated. Dysmenorrhoea and premenstrual tension are usually alleviated and acne may be improved. There is a decreased incidence of benign breast disease.

Interactions

There is little convincing clinical evidence that 'the pill' interferes with the response to other drugs. It may prolong the half-life of phenylbutazone and pethidine and impair the response to tricyclic antidepressants. A variable effect has been reported with anticoagulants, but in view of the known effect of oestrogens on clotting factors, treatment with warfarin should be carefully monitored during oral contraceptive therapy.

The major concern is that other drugs may cause failure of oral contraception.

Rifampicin. Rifampicin increases the rate of metabolism of both oestrogen and progestogen, presumably by inducing hepatic microsomal enzymes. Increasing the dose of oestrogen may not be sufficient to overcome this effect and alternative methods of contraception should be used.

Anticonvulsants. Phenytoin, phenobarbitone, primidone and carbamazepine are all inducers of microsomal enzymes. In addition, these drugs increase the binding of progestogens to sex-hormone binding globulin, thereby lowering the 'free' concentration of steroids. Patients taking anticonvulsants should either use alternative methods of contraception or take a relatively high steroid dose. In most cases a preparation containing 50 μg of ethinyloestradiol will suffice. If breakthrough bleeding occurs, indicating inadequate oestrogen levels, a preparation containing 30 μg of ethinyloestradiol can be added to give a total daily dose of 80 μg. If anticonvulsant therapy is discontinued, the oestrogen dose should be reduced to 30 μg per day.

Broad-spectrum antibiotics. Synthetic oestrogens and progestogens are extensively excreted in the bile as glucuronide and sulphate conjugates. In the gut lumen the glucuronide conjugates are hydrolysed by bacteria to liberate the original compound which is reabsorbed. Broad-spectrum antibiotics may interfere with this enterohepatic circulation by killing bacteria, although the latter may rapidly develop resistance. This is unlikely to be important in the case of progestogens, which are reduced prior to conjugation and probably undergo enterohepatic circulation only as the inactive metabolites. However, plasma concentrations of ethinyloestradiol could be reduced as a result of such therapy. The importance of this interaction clinically remains uncertain, but many women on the pill receive antibiotics, e.g. for cystitis, and it seems wise to recommend back-up methods of contraception while treatment lasts.

Contraindications

The patients for whom these drugs are prescribed are young and predominantly healthy. The possibility of serious side-effects, however rare, is therefore less acceptable than in other situations in therapeutics. Having read the foregoing, the reader may wonder whether the pill should ever be prescribed. Firstly, the serious side-effects are related to the oestrogen content of the pill and the introduction of preparations containing low doses of oestrogen has probably resulted in a decrease in pill-related mortality during recent years. (In view of the known effect of progestogens in modifying the actions of oestrogens it may be that the dose and type of progestogen is also important and this will probably receive more attention in the future.) Secondly, the proper selection of patients with low-risk profiles minimizes the risks. For the high-risk patients non-hormonal methods or the progestogen-only pill may offer acceptable alternatives. Finally, against the risks of the pill must be balanced the risks of pregnancy itself. Properly prescribed and with adequate supervision, the combined pill is as safe as other forms of birth control and safer than none at all.

The contraindications to combined oral contraceptives are summarized below.

Absolute contraindications.
1. Carcinoma of the breast or uterus.
2. Undiagnosed abnormal genital bleeding.
3. Present or previous history of:
   myocardial infarction;
   thrombotic or haemorrhagic stroke and subarachnoid haemorrhage;
   arterial or venous thrombosis and thrombo-embolism.
4. Acute or chronic liver disease.
5. Hyperlipidaemia.

6. Pregnancy.

Relative contraindications.
1. Age.
2. Smoking.
3. Hypertension.
4. Diabetes mellitus.
5. Obesity.
6. Migraine.
7. Uterine fibroids.

Triphasic Formulations

The triphasic pill attempts to mimic more closely the normal menstrual cycle. Three different combined pills containing varying doses of progestogen and oestrogen are employed at different times in the cycle. In practice the advantages are not obvious and they are less convenient to take.

The Progestogen-only Pill

With the progestogen-only pill, contraception relies on the effects of progestogen on the endometrium and cervical mucus. A much lower dose of progestogen is used than in the combined pill, so ovulation is not regularly inhibited and the woman menstruates spontaneously. The pill is started on the first day of the cycle and taken every day without any interval between cycles. The failure rate is higher than with the combined pill, the efficacy being similar to that of intra-uterine devices. Also, there is a tendency for irregular bleeding to occur; especially during the early months. However, it appears to be free from serious adverse effects and may, therefore, offer a suitable alternative when the combined pill is contraindicated. It does not suppress lactation and may be preferred in nursing mothers (in whom fertility is in any case reduced).

Progestogen can also be given as a depot injection (medroxyprogesterone acetate, Depo-Provera) for short-term interim contraception.

POST-COITAL CONTRACEPTION

Post-coital contraception is not generally employed, but may be used in special situations, e.g. following sexual assault. Two combined pills (each containing, for example, $50 \mu g$ of ethinyloestradiol and $250 \mu g$ of levonorgestrel) are taken immediately, followed by a further two pills twelve hours later. This form of contraception should only be used between presumed fertilization and presumed implantation, i.e. not after day 18 in a 28-day cycle and within 72 hours of unprotected coitus. It is said to be about 98% effective. Side-effects are nausea and vomiting.

DRUGS USED TO INDUCE OVULATION

CONTROL OF OVULATION

At the end of the luteal phase, as oestrogen and progesterone levels fall, gonadotrophin secretion begins to increase (negative feedback effect). The rise in FSH stimulates the development of a number of ovarian follicles, which secrete oestradiol, which again suppresses FSH production. The synthesis of FSH receptors on the granulosa cells is stimulated by oestradiol and the follicle which produces the most oestradiol develops the largest number of receptors. It is only this follicle which is able to continue to develop in the face of the declining production of FSH and most of the remainder become atretic. By this mechanism the most active follicle is selected for ovulation. This intra-ovarian autoregulation can be overridden when supraphysiological amounts of gonadotrophins are administered therapeutically to induce ovulation with resulting multiple ovulation and conception.

When blood levels of oestradiol reach a critical level before mid-cycle, there is a brief but massive surge of LH (positive feedback effect). This results in ovulation and the formation of the corpus luteum. The latter secretes oestradiol and progesterone, and gonadotrophin secretion is again inhibited. If pregnancy does not occur, the corpus luteum involutes. The resulting fall in steroid production causes menstruation and initiates the next cycle.

Anovulation may occur if there is inadequate FSH stimulation during the follicular phase. The resulting oestradiol output then fails to trigger the LH surge. Alternatively, there may be a failure of the positive feedback mechanism, in which case the LH surge does not occur despite a normal oestradiol rise.

Clomiphene

Clomiphene, which is distantly related to diethylstilboestrol, acts as an antioestrogen by competing for oestrogen-receptor binding sites. It is able to inhibit the negative feedback of gonadal steroids on the hypothalamus, stimulating pituitary FSH release and thus initiating the ovulatory cycle.

Indications
Clomiphene is used in the infertile female to treat absent or infrequent ovulation when this is not due to disorders that require specific treatment, e.g. thyroid disease, anorexia nervosa or hyperprolactinaemia. As can be predicted from its mode of action, patients with low endogenous oestrogen levels are unlikely to respond. The drug is given in a dose of 50 mg per day starting on the 2nd or 3rd day of the cycle and continuing for five days. The plasma progesterone level 12–14 days after finishing the course can be used to assess whether ovulation has occurred. If it has not occurred during the first three cycles, then the dose can be increased by 50 mg per day at two monthly intervals up to a maximum dose of 200 mg per day.

If ovulation fails to occur despite a good oestrogen response to clomiphene (failure of positive feedback mechanism), a single i.m. injection of HCG 5000 iu 7 days after the last clomiphene tablets may be tried for a few cycles before accepting the failure of the treatment.

Adverse Effects
Side-effects include vasomotor flushes and abdominal distension, bloating or pain. More rarely, nausea, vomiting, breast discomfort and visual symptoms may occur. The latter include blurring of vision, scotoma and abnormal perception, but they disappear when the drug is discontinued. Ovarian hyperstimulation is rare with the above doses and almost all multiple births have been twins.

Gonadotrophins

Gonadotrophins (p. 411) are used in the treatment of anovulatory infertility that has failed to respond to clomiphene and when other potential infertility factors have been excluded. This form of treatment is restricted to specialized centres. HMG (which contains FSH and LH) is given to stimulate follicular growth and maturation and bring oestrogen levels into the optimum range for ovulation. HCG is then given to stimulate ovulation. There is a risk of multiple pregnancy and the abortion rate may be higher than with pregnancy following spontaneous ovulation. Hyperstimulation of the ovaries causes ovarian enlargement and if severe, ascites, pleural effusion, electrolyte imbalance and hypovolaemia.

DRUGS ACTING ON THE UTERUS

Myometrial Stimulants

Myometrial stimulants include oxytocin, ergometrine and the prostaglandins.

Oxytocin

Oxytocin is an octapeptide released from nerve terminals in the posterior pituitary. Its physiological role in man is not well defined, but in pharmacological doses it stimulates contractions of the pregnant uterus. Given in low doses by slow i.v. infusion (2–5 milliunits per minute), it is used to induce or augment labour. Uterine activity must be monitored to avoid overstimulation, causing rupture of the uterus and fetal asphyxiation. Other side-effects are hypotension, fluid retention and fetal dysrhythmias. In the management of atonic post-partum haemorrhage large doses are used to induce tetanic contraction of the uterus and so control haemorrhage from the placental site. I.m. oxytocin, in combination with ergometrine, as described below, is now commonly given for prophylaxis of post-partum haemorrhage.

430 Clinical Pharmacology

Ergometrine

Ergometrine is an ergot alkaloid. These substances are produced by the fungus *Claviceps purpurea*. Poisoning with ergot alkaloids used to occur when rye contaminated with the fungus was used in baking. The condition, known as St Anthony's Fire, caused tingling of the hands and feet and gangrene of the digits. This was caused by spasm of blood vessels due to a direct action of the ergot alkaloids on vascular smooth muscle.

Ergometrine causes long-sustained and powerful contractions of the uterine fundus in later pregnancy and these are likely to result in fetal death and uterine rupture. It has no place, therefore, in the induction of labour, but can be given i.v. in a dose of 125–250 μg to control atonic post-partum haemorrhage or bleeding due to incomplete abortion. It can also be given at or after delivery of the anterior shoulder as prophylaxis of post-partum haemorrhage or at the time of surgical evacuation of the uterus to minimize post-operative blood loss. Side-effects are nausea, vomiting and, due to peripheral vasoconstriction, hypertension and gangrene of the extremities.

Syntometrine

Syntometrine is the proprietary name for a combination of 5 units of oxytocin and 500 μg of ergometrine. It is given i.m. at or after delivery of the anterior shoulder for prevention and control of post-partum haemorrhage. Owing to the rapid absorption of the oxytocin, it produces a powerful contraction of the uterus within two minutes. As this effect wears off, the ergometrine starts to exert its long-sustained effect.

Prostaglandins

Prostaglandins, which are also discussed elsewhere (p. 106), play a major part in reproduction. They stimulate or augment uterine contractions and cause structural alterations in the cervix which soften and 'ripen' it. They are also concerned with ovulation and the control of menstruation.

Prostaglandins are rapidly metabolized and inactivated in the blood stream. This causes problems in achieving effective concentrations at the site of action, without producing troublesome systemic effects, and has led to attempts to administer the compounds locally.

There are at least 14 related natural prostaglandins of which only PGE_2 (dinoprostone) and $PGF_{2\alpha}$ (dinoprost) are important clinically. In the future, improved synthetic analogues with an enhanced duration of action and fewer side-effects may become available.

Uses of Prostaglandins in Obstetrics

Cervical priming and induction of labour.
Oral. Oral PGE_2 is given hourly in doses of 0.5 mg, increasing in a stepwise

fashion to 2 mg. Gastrointestinal side-effects (vomiting and diarrhoea) are common. This method is chiefly used in combination with amniotomy in multiparous women who have favourable induction prospects.

Vaginal. Vaginal PGE_2, as a gel or pessaries, can be given to ripen or prime the cervix. The doses required are relatively low, so gastrointestinal side-effects and uterine overstimulation are uncommon. Depending on the parity of the patient and on the state of the cervix prior to treatment, labour may follow priming without the need for formal induction in from 40–90% of patients. Even if formal induction with amniotomy or oxytocin is still required, the duration of labour is shortened, analgesic requirements are reduced and Caesarian section or forceps delivery are less likely to be required.

Second-trimester termination. Larger doses are required than for the induction of labour. Oral administration is ineffective and systemic administration produces unacceptable side-effects. Vaginal administration also produces side-effects and is not consistently successful. The intra-uterine route has, therefore, been used. Two-hourly extra-amniotic installation or the continuous infusion of PGE_2 or $PGF_{2\alpha}$ via a catheter through the cervix results in an abortion within 48 hours in 90% of cases. Intra-amniotic injection has also been employed.

First-trimester termination. Prostaglandins may be used to prime the cervix before surgical termination by vacuum aspiration. The aim is to reduce the risk of injury and haemorrhage during the procedure and to prevent subsequent cervical incompetence.

Adverse Effects
The side-effects of prostaglandins are dose-related and more common after i.v. administration. They are nausea, vomiting, diarrhoea, intestinal colic, flushing, shivering, headache, dizziness, pyrexia and erythema at the site of infusion. $PGF_{2\alpha}$ should be avoided in asthmatics because it is a bronchoconstrictor.

Myometrial Relaxants

β_2-adrenoreceptor stimulants, e.g. ritodrine, terbutaline and salbutamol, relax uterine muscle and may be used in selected cases to inhibit premature labour. They have also been used to relieve fetal distress due to excessive uterine activity while awaiting operative delivery, and in the treatment of hypertonus due to myometrial stimulants. Side-effects are nausea, vomiting, flushing, sweating, tremor, tachycardia and hypotension. Since these drugs enhance glycolysis and lipolysis, they may induce ketoacidosis when used in pregnant diabetics.

Prostaglandin-synthetase Inhibitors

Many patients with primary dysmenorrhoea have increased endometrial synthesis of prostaglandins. This is thought to cause inco-ordinate uterine hyperactivity resulting in muscle ischaemia and pain. Many of the non-steroidal anti-inflammatory agents, e.g. aspirin, naproxen and mefenamic acid, are prostaglandin-synthetase inhibitors and should, theoretically, be particularly suited to the treatment of this condition.

FURTHER READING

Dempsey A. T. (1980) The stimulation of ovulation. *Br. J. Hosp. Med.*, 24: 48.

Drife J. (1983) Which pill? *Br. med. J.*, 287: 1397.

Embrey M. P. (1981) Prostaglandins in human reproduction. *Br. med. J.*, 283: 1563.

Keen H., Glynn E. A., Pickup J. C., Viberti J. C., Bilous R. W., Jarrett R. J. & Marsden R. (1980) Human insulin produced by recombinant DNA technology: safety and hypoglycaemic potency in healthy men. *Lancet*, ii: 398.

Leading article (1982) Prolactinomas: bromocriptine rules O.K.? *Lancet*, i: 430.

Quigley M. M. (1981) Post-menopausal oestrogen replacement therapy: an appraisal of risks and benefits. *Drugs*, 22: 153.

Review (1981) Update on oral contraception. *Clin. Obstet. Gynec.*, 24: 867.

Royal College of General Practitioners Oral Contraception Study — further analyses of mortality in oral contraceptive users (1981). *Lancet*, i: 541.

Toft A. D., Campbell, I. W. & Seth, J. (1981) *Diagnosis and Management of Endocrine Diseases*. Oxford: Blackwell Scientific Publications.

Utiger R. D. (1978) Treatment of Graves' disease. *New Engl. J. Med.*, 298: 681.

Wass J. A. H., Williams J., Charlesworth M., Kingsley D. P. E., Halliday A. M., Doniach I., Rees L. H., McDonald W. I. & Besser G. M. (1982) Bromocriptine in management of large pituitary tumours. *Br. med. J.*, 284: 1908.

11   Vitamins

R. H. Girdwood

The term 'vitamin' was introduced because it was believed that the presence of certain amines in the diet was necessary for life to continue. In fact, the substances now known as vitamins are not amines, and not all of them have been shown to have a role as therapeutic agents in deficiency states in man. In some developing countries vitamin depletion is very common; in other parts of the world it is so rare that the medical student may not encounter an example during his undergraduate years. In the UK a primary deficiency of ascorbic acid, calciferol or folic acid may be found, and under special circumstances there may be a depletion of vitamin B_{12} or vitamin K; other forms of vitamin deficiency are rarely encountered. It should be said, however, that claims have been made that neural tube defects in the fetus are less likely to occur if the mother takes vitamin supplements. It is not certain whether this is true; if it is, it is not clear whether folic acid is the substance that is important in this respect.

VITAMIN A

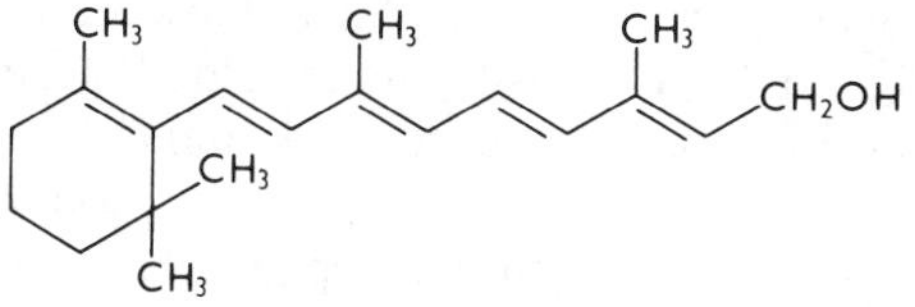

RETINOL (VITAMIN A₁)

Vitamin A_1 is known as retinol, and vitamin A_2, which is found in many fish liver oils, is 3-dehydroretinol. Retinol is a pale yellow substance which is fat-soluble. The main sources of retinol in the diet vary from country to country, but include fish liver oils, butter, eggs, cheese and liver. Margarine may be fortified with vitamin A. However, there are certain hydrocarbon pigments, the β-carotenes, which man and certain other mammals can absorb and convert to vitamin A. These provitamins are found in green vegetables, carrots, sweet potatoes (red and yellow varieties), tomatoes and bananas. Red palm oil is a concentrated source. Vitamin A is a complex primary alcohol.

433

The optimal daily intake for the adult is about 750 retinol equivalents (RE); in pregnancy and lactation the requirement is about 1000 RE, and at 6–12 months of age 300 RE is needed. One RE is taken to represent 1 μg of retinol. One International Unit (IU) for vitamin A is the specific biological activity of 0.3 μg of retinol, which is equivalent to that of 0.6 μg of β-carotene, so one might expect 1 RE to be equal to 2 μg of β-carotene. However, because of the poor dietary utilization of β-carotene, 1 RE is equal to 6 μg of β-carotene or 12 μg of other provitamin A carotenoids.

Metabolism

So far as carotenes are concerned, the level of dietary fat appears to be important, since if it is low, absorption is poor. With vitamin A itself the retinyl ester is hydrolysed in the lumen of the small intestine and retinol passes into the mucosal cell, where it is re-esterified. Retinyl palmitate is formed and makes its way in chylomicrons by the thoracic duct to the blood stream, which then carries it to the liver. Here it is stored to be available when required. In normal individuals the stores are sufficient to last 1–2 years.

Much of the provitamin is converted into retinol in the small intestinal mucosal cell, but the conversion also occurs in other tissues. On leaving the liver the hepatic retinol ester is hydrolysed and the retinol becomes associated with a retinol-binding protein (an α-globulin). A fall in plasma levels means that stores are exhausted. In kwashiorkor or other forms of protein deficiency there will be insufficient retinol-binding protein in plasma to carry vitamin A to the sites where it is needed.

Functions

Retinol is oxidized to retinal (vitamin A aldehyde). In the retina there are rods which are particularly sensitive to light of low intensity and cones which are sensitive to light of high intensity and to colours. Retinal is the prosthetic group of photosensitive pigments in the rods and cones. The visual pigment operative in low-intensity vision is known as rhodopsin. A number of pigments are involved in day vision. These pigments are lipoproteins united to retinal, the aldehyde entering into combination with amino groups of the former. Light falling on rods or cones causes an energy exchange from alterations in the pigments and this leads to potential differences which cause the nervous impulses that give visual impressions. Night blindness is an early symptom of vitamin A deficiency, because visual purple cannot be regenerated.

Other roles for vitamin A are less certain, but it seems to be needed for the formation of mucus-secreting cells which synthesize glycoproteins. In vitamin A deficiency there are hyperkeratinization, xerophthalmia (dryness of the conjunctivae followed by hyperkeratinization), squamous metaplasia of the mucosa of the upper respiratory tract, bone deformities, retarded growth and impairment of reproductive activity. Many of these abnormalities suggest that vitamin A has a role in mucoprotein synthesis. If there is xerophthalmia, the eye may become infected and sight destroyed (keratomalacia).

Stability
Vitamin A and carotene are stable to mild cooking and to processing, but they are unstable at high temperatures in the presence of oxygen. They are destroyed in conditions that lead to the oxidation of fats and are protected by antioxidants found in many foodstuffs. Losses are small during canning, but in dehydrated carrots degradation products of carotene give an unpleasant flavour. In Eastern countries it is important to remember that frying causes a considerable loss of vitamin A from ghee. Rancid fats have a catalytic effect on vitamin A destruction. Light accelerates the destruction of vitamin A, hence fish liver oils should be kept in amber-coloured bottles.

Clinical Importance
Reference to the possible lesions has been made above. Apart from anaemia, it is likely that protein malnutrition and vitamin A deficiency are the two most common nutritional diseases in the world. If protein is given to patients with kwashiorkor, vitamin A must also be given to avoid using up the last reserve of the latter.

Preparations
Halibut liver oil capsules, BP, contain the equivalent of 4000–5250 units of vitamin A activity and also a variable amount of vitamin D. The dose is one to three capsules daily. Concentrated vitamin A solution (BPC) contains 50 000 units in 1 g. There are vitamin A capsules (BPC) with 4500 units of activity and strong vitamin A capsules (BNF) with 50 000 units of activity. Ro-A-Vit tablets contain 50 000 units as the acetate and there are 1 ml ampoules for deep i.m. injection containing 300 000 units as the palmitate. This is approximately 165 mg.

Indications
In many countries there is no need to give additional vitamin A, but in others the administration of vitamin supplements, including vitamin A, to expectant or nursing mothers and infants is advisable. In deficiency states high dosage (25 000–200 000 units daily) is desirable temporarily. In kwashiorkor, half an ampoule may be given once weekly to a child, but after six weeks there should be a delay of at least two weeks before further treatment with vitamin A is given, lest there should be features of overdosage.

Overdosage
It is usual to quote the remote possibility of the eating of large amounts of polar bear liver as a cause of acute intoxication with malaise, drowsiness, vomiting and headache. There is increased intracranial pressure. Chronic poisoning is more likely and is usually due to mothers thinking that unusually

high daily doses of cod liver oil or, worse, halibut liver oil will be beneficial to children. Other features of overdosage are anorexia, irritability, sparse hair, painful tender swellings of the bones and possibly liver enlargement.

The taking of high doses of vitamin A in pregnancy may cause fetal abnormalities. Under normal circumstances, not more than 7500 units should be taken daily by pregnant women.

Vitamin A Acid

This vitamin A derivative (retinoic acid) is available in some countries as a cream, solution or gel for the topical treatment of acne. The comedo of acne is a mass of horny cells which accumulate in a follicle, and vitamin A acid may prevent its formation by inhibiting the formation of the cement substance that binds horny layer cells together.

VITAMIN D AND CALCIUM METABOLISM

Certain sterols can prevent the development of rickets because, with irradiation, the molecular structure alters to give a form of vitamin D. Cleavage of the carbon-to-carbon bond between C9 and C10 is the essential alteration caused by the photochemical action and with some sterols this change gives antirachitic activity.

Vitamin D_1, which was described at an early stage of knowledge of the subject, can be ignored as it is an impure mixture of sterols.

Vitamin D_2 is *ergocalciferol*. It is formed by the irradiation of ergosterol, which is present in certain yeasts, fungi, vegetable oils and, to a lesser extent, milk, and it is the vitamin-D constituent of a number of commercial vitamin preparations. It is absorbed in the jejunum and upper ileum and is carried to the liver where 25-hydroxyergocalciferol (25-hydroxyvitamin D_2) is formed, and apparently converted to 25-hydroxyvitamin D_3.

Vitamin D_3 is *cholecalciferol*. It is a natural substance formed from 7-dehydrocholesterol in the oily secretions of mammalian skin by the action of ultra-violet light. In man there is no significant difference between the

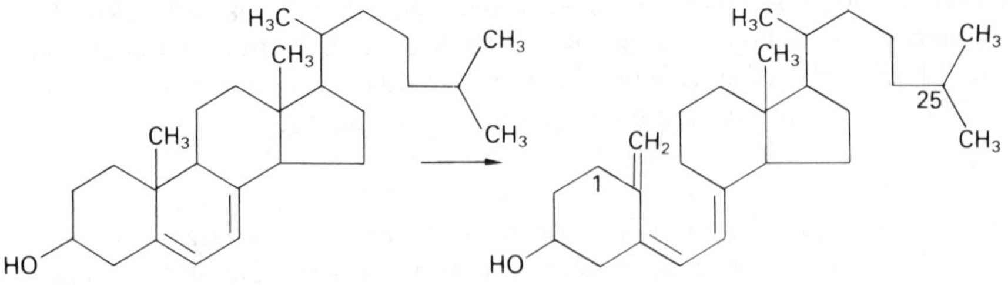

7-DEHYDROCHOLESTEROL   CHOLECALCIFEROL

actions of vitamin D₂ and D₃, and the structural difference is that ergosterol and ergocalciferol both have a double bond between C22 and C23, and a methyl group at C25.

It follows that, because it is in animal fats, vitamin D₃ will be found in certain foodstuffs. One or other of the two forms of vitamin D occur in fatty fish and their oils, in eggs, butter, and vitaminized margarine, usually being greater in quantity in the latter than in butter. There is some in cheese and only very little in meat or white fish.

25-hydroxycholecalciferol

Cholecalciferol is absorbed from the same areas of the intestine as ergocalciferol and it, too, is taken to the liver, where it is metabolized to 25-hydroxycholecalciferol (25-hydroxyvitamin D₃, 25-(OH)D₃ or calcifediol). It then enters the blood stream and circulates in association with a vitamin-D binding globulin.

Calcitriol

This, the natural active substance, is 1,25-dihydroxycholecalciferol (1,25-dihydroxyvitamin D₃ or 1,25-(OH)₂D₃) and it is formed from 25-hydroxyvitamin D₃ by the action of 25-OHD₃-1α-hydroxylase, which is situated in the mitochondria of kidney cells. The activity of this renal enzyme is believed to be increased by a fall in the levels of calcium and perhaps phosphate in plasma or by a dietary deficiency of vitamin D, but to be increased by a high intake of the vitamin. It is also known that its activity is stimulated by parathyroid hormone (pp. 386, 438), and that this may be the main stimulus to its production. In birds there is stimulation by prolactin and by oestrogens. It has been suggested that, if calcitriol is taken by mouth, a type of messenger RNA is formed in the nuclei of intestinal cells and that this directs the synthesis of a calcium binding protein which transfers calcium across to the plasma. Possibly, however, this is too simple an explanation. It must be borne in mind that, whereas calcitriol promotes calcium absorption within 2–6 hours, vitamin D takes nearly 24 hours, presumably because it has to be converted into 1,25-dihydroxyvitamin D₃.

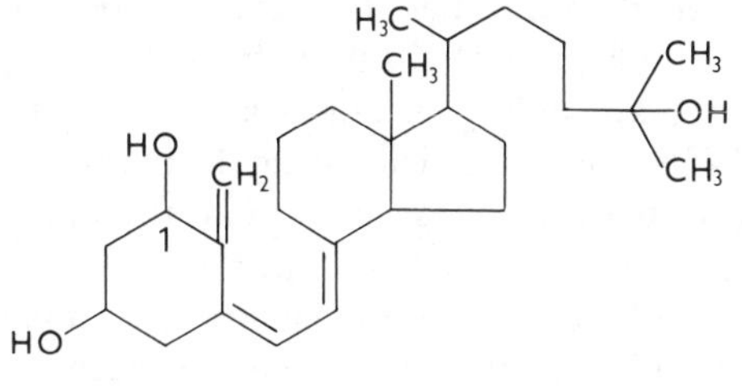

1,25–DIHYDROXYCHOLECALCIFEROL (CALCITRIOL)

It is thought that a deficiency of 1,25-dihydroxyvitamin D₃ is the reason for osteomalacia and hyperparathyroidism in renal failure. A low level of calcium causes an increase in parathormone by a feedback mechanism. Conversely, in hypoparathyroidism there is a low level of 1,25-dihydroxyvitamin D₃ and hence a low level of calcium in the blood.

A synthetic preparation of calcitriol (Rocaltrol) is available and has the greatest biological activity of known vitamin D metabolites. It will act even if there is severe renal failure, but is expensive and may readily cause hypercalcaemia. It is *not* a commercial substitute for the more usual vitamin D preparations. Its therapeutic use and that of another commercially available product, 1α-hydroxyvitamin D₃, is considered on p. 441.

24,25-dihydroxycholecalciferol

The role of this natural metabolite of vitamin D is uncertain, but a simple view is that it, rather than a more active substance, is formed when requirements for calcium are decreased. It does not stimulate intestinal absorption of calcium.

Functions of Vitamin D
The active metabolite of vitamin D (calcitriol) promotes the absorption from the intestine of calcium and possibly magnesium and other elements in group II of the periodic table. The transport of calcium through the intestinal cell is an active process, as has already been stated, and vitamin D also promotes the absorption of phosphorus by a separate mechanism from that of calcium and is believed to stimulate the synthesis of alkaline phosphatase in the intestinal mucosa. At the growing points of bones calcium comes into contact with inorganic phosphates liberated from organic phosphates by enzymes. Osteoblasts utilize calcium phosphate to make new bone. In growing bone new cartilage is formed at the epiphyses, while at the diaphyseal end the cartilage degenerates, being invaded by capillaries and osteoblasts. Here there is a need for calcium phosphate. When there is no more new cartilage the epiphysis and diaphysis fuse. It does not seem that vitamin D has an active role in bone formation, but rather that it ensures that calcium and phosphate are available when required. The action of parathormone (pp. 386, 437) has to be taken into account.

In the absence of vitamin D there is an excess of osteoid tissue, but normal calcification cannot occur. Calcification beneath the periosteum is also impeded. Epiphyses are enlarged, bones are softened, and there may be tetany because of a lack of ionized calcium in the plasma. The serum inorganic phosphorus is low, perhaps because the parathyroid glands increase the excretion of phosphorus by the kidneys if the serum calcium level falls (p. 386). An earlier index of vitamin D deficiency is a raised serum alkaline phosphatase level. This enzyme is formed by the accumulated osteoblasts in the osteoid tissue referred to above. Vitamin D helps to retain calcium and phosphate by enhancing their reabsorption in the proximal tubules of the kidney.

It is possible that the colour of the skin of man, which depends on latitude, minimizes the synthesis of excessive amounts of vitamin D in equatorial regions, but it follows that a coloured person is more likely to suffer from rickets if there is insufficient vitamin D in the diet in a temperate country.

To complete the picture it should be added that the concentration of ionized calcium in the blood regulates the secretion of parathormone (p. 386). A low level of calcium causes an increase of parathormone and hence an augmented production of 1,25-dihydroxyvitamin D_3. This increases the absorption of calcium and phosphate from the intestine. Parathormone acts on bone to increase the rate of resorption of calcium and phosphate, especially in the stable, older areas, where the osteoclasts and osteocytes are stimulated. The synthesis of collagen, a substance required for maintenance of the bony matrix in bone, is inhibited. In the kidneys, parathormone increases tubular *reabsorption* of calcium at a distal site, but increases the renal *excretion* of inorganic phosphate in all segments proximal to the collecting duct.

Human Requirements

One International unit (IU) is equivalent to the specific biological activity of 0.025 μg of vitamin D_3, i.e. 1 mg equals 40 000 IU. The normal average daily dietary intake is said to be 400 IU (10 μg) at the age of 6 months, 600 IU at 3 years and 800 IU later in childhood. Apart from pregnancy and lactation, when 400 IU is appropriate, the adult needs only about 100 IU. Most of the required vitamin D activity is obtained from the effects of sunlight.

The prolonged taking of barbiturates or anticonvulsant drugs may give biochemical evidence of an increased need for vitamin D. This may be because of increased hepatic microsomal activity and impaired conversion to 25-hydroxyvitamin D_3.

Stability

Vitamin D is very stable and there is little loss from processing or storing. When vitamin-D enriched milk is dried, there may be some loss of content.

Deficiency States

1. Deficiency of vitamin D leads to rickets in the infant or child, and osteomalacia in the adult. In the UK there is sometimes a problem of deficiency in the elderly.
2. After partial gastrectomy there may be impaired absorption of vitamin D and of calcium. It is uncommon in gluten enteropathy.
3. In idiopathic or post-surgical hypoparathyroidism there is hyperphosphataemia, hypocalcaemia and a low serum concentration of 1,25-dihydroxyvitamin D_3.

4. In chronic renal failure there is impaired formation of the active 1,25-dihydroxyvitamin D₃. The resulting condition is renal osteodystrophy (renal rickets). Sometimes, as a result, the hypocalcaemia that ensues causes the parathyroid glands to become overactive, so that there is hyperplasia of all four glands, with a low plasma and urinary calcium (secondary hyperparathyroidism). There may be osteomalacia due to the action of parathormone, but also metastatic calcification. A further stage that is occasionally seen is tertiary hyperparathyroidism, where parathyroid hyperplasia has been followed by the appearance of autonomous parathyroid adenomata and a rise in the plasma calcium level.

5. With repeated haemodialyses unusual forms of osteomalacia have occurred. In addition to deficiency of 1,25-dihydroxyvitamin D₃ and phosphorus retention, there may be other confusing issues such as excess of aluminium in the dialysate solution. Efforts are being made internationally to control the purity of such fluids. A dialysate solution free of phosphate can cause osteomalacia.

6. Renal calcium leak. There is a defect in renal tubular reabsorption of calcium and plasma 1,25-dihydroxyvitamin D₃ levels may be raised. The normal subject excretes less calcium in winter.

7. Hyperabsorption of calcium. In a few patients there is, for no obvious reason, an excess of 1,25-dihydroxyvitamin D₃, and increased calcium absorption.

8. Lack of 1α-hydroxylase enzyme activity. This is an autosomal recessive condition where vitamin-D resistant rickets occurs. There is a response to 1α-hydroxyvitamin D₃ (p. 441) or to 1,25-dihydroxyvitamin D₃, but it is not yet certain that the genetic defect is simply a block in the synthesis of 1,25-dihydroxyvitamin D₃.

9. Hypophosphataemic vitamin-D resistant rickets. This is more commonly found and is inherited as an X-linked dominant genetic defect. There is rickets or osteomalacia, stunted growth and hypophosphataemia. The defect is a high renal tubular clearance of phosphate with no other renal abnormality. The bony changes are secondary to the hypophosphataemia.

10. Fanconi's syndrome. This is a heterogeneous group of disorders which can be idiopathic or acquired (e.g. in multiple myeloma). Again, there is hypophosphataemia as part of the syndrome and hence there may be rickets or osteomalacia.

Preparations

Calciferol injection, *BPC*, contains 600 000 IU in 2 ml. Where high dosage is required, this is used.

Calciferol tablets, *strong*, *BP*. Each tablet contains 1.25 mg, equivalent to 50 000 IU of antirachitic activity. In the treatment of hypoparathyroidism one to four tablets are given daily. These tablets are sometimes used for a period in malabsorptive states and in renal osteodystrophy, but should not be used otherwise.

Calcium with vitamin D tablets, *BPC*, contain calcium sodium lactate 450 mg, calcium phosphate 150 mg and calciferol 12.5 μg. Each tablet has approximately 500 IU of antirachitic activity. The dose given is commonly one tablet daily.

Halibut liver capsules, *BP* (p. 435) have a variable amount of vitamin D activity.

Vitamin A and D capsules, *BPC*. Each capsule contains 4500 IU of vitamin A activity and 450 IU of vitamin D.

Vitamin capsules, *BPC*, have vitamin A activity (2500 IU), vitamin D (300 IU), thiamine hydrochloride 1 mg, riboflavine 0.5 mg, nicotinamide 7.5 mg and ascorbic acid 15 mg. One or two are taken daily.

Dihydrotachysterol (Tachyrol, AT10). The substance initially used was, in fact, a mixture of sterols obtained from tachysterol, itself a product of irradiation of ergosterol. Its potency varied, but crystalline dihydrotachysterol was later obtained. Its structure is related to that of alfacalcidol, but it has to be converted in the liver to 25-dihydrotachysterol. It has antirachitic properties and raises the plasma calcium concentration by its action on the intestinal transport of calcium and phosphorus. The crystalline substance marketed as Tachyrol is promoted for the treatment of rickets or osteomalacia resistant to vitamin D, for renal osteodystrophy and for idiopathic or postoperative hypoparathyroidism. The initial dose is 0.2 mg daily. The alternative preparation, AT10, contains 0.25 mg/ml of dihydrotachysterol in an oily solution for oral administration and is recommended by the marketing company for use in the acute, chronic and latent forms of hypocalcaemic tetany due to hypoparathyroidism, and also for skin lesions such as pemphigus and impetigo herpetiformis which are associated with hypoparathyroidism.

Alfacalcidol (1α-hydroxyvitamin D_3 or 1α-OHD$_3$). This is available as One-Alpha in 1 μg or 0.25 μg capsules. It is converted rapidly in the liver to 1,25-(OH)$_2$D$_3$. The indications for its use are renal bone disease, hypoparathyroidism, pre- and postoperative management of hyperparathyroidism (to prevent hypocalcaemia, a recommendation that has been challenged as regards its efficacy), rickets associated with a lack of 1α-hydroxylase, and hypophosphataemic vitamin D resistant rickets or osteomalacia. The initial adult dose is 1 μg daily. For children over 20 kg this dose is also correct, but under 20 kg the initial dose is 0.05 μg/kg per day.

In renal bone disease there may be tertiary hyperparathyroidism (p. 440) and lack of response to 1 α-OHD$_3$. When treatment with this preparation is given in renal disease it may be necessary to use phosphate binding agents to prevent metastatic calcification. Capsules of 475 mg dried aluminium hydroxide gel, BP, are marketed as Alu-Cap. In the gut, aluminium hydroxide absorbs phosphate ions.

Calcitriol (1,25-dihydroxyvitamin D_3). This is available as Rocaltrol in 0.25 μg or 0.5 μg capsules. As has already been indicated (p. 438), it has the greatest biological activity of all available vitamin-D metabolites. This synthetic preparation is promoted for the correction of abnormalities of calcium and phosphate metabolism in patients with renal osteodystrophy. It is a very active substance and the dosage for use in children has not yet been established. In the adult, treatment should start with two to four 0.5 μg capsules daily and the serum calcium concentration should be monitored at least weekly. No other vitamin D preparations should be given simultaneously, and, as with alfacalcidol, phosphate binders may be required. The treatment of overdosage is referred to below.

In the Asian community in the UK rickets is not uncommon. The difference in synthesis of vitamin D_3 when the skin is dark may be a factor, and another problem is that margarine (which is fortified with vitamin D) is not eaten. It has been suggested that chappati flour might be fortified with the vitamin.

Overdosage

Mothers may give infants far too much concentrated calciferol, or doctors may erroneously give enormous doses for excessively long periods when there has been evidence of deficiency. Particular care has to be taken when calcitriol (p. 438), alfacalcidol (p. 441) or dihydrotachysterol (p. 441) are used, plasma calcium levels and other appropriate biochemical measurements being done regularly as advised by the marketing companies.

The toxic factor in vitamin D overdosage is now taken to be 25-hydroxyvitamin D_3 and not 1,25-dihydroxyvitamin D_3. The concentration of the latter is normally about 20 to 45 pg/ml, whereas that of the former is usually about a thousand times as much. This is because the 1-hydroxylation reaction in the kidneys is carefully controlled to give a narrow range of concentration of the active substance, whereas 25-$(OH)D_3$ formation by the liver depends on the quantity of vitamin D supplied to that organ. Vitamin D not so converted is inactivated and excreted in the bile.

As a result of overdosage there may be loss of appetite, nausea, vomiting, constipation and stupor. Metastatic calcification occurs in the renal tubules, arteries and elsewhere. The plasma calcium level is raised. Renal calculi may be formed. Patients with sarcoidosis cannot tolerate vitamin D.

Where there is severe hypercalcaemia, high doses of synthetic salmon calcitonin (Calsynar) are advised (p. 444). Initially 400 IU should be given 6- or 8-hourly. Administration of the offending source of vitamin D should be terminated. A loop diuretic and i.v. fluids may be given. In acute overdosage of calcitriol or alfacalcidol, gastric lavage may be required.

In sarcoidosis or metastatic bone disease, hypercalcaemia is better treated with corticosteroids.

Drugs Affecting Calcium Metabolism

Calcium

Calcium lactate or gluconate may be used with calciferol in the treatment of rickets, osteomalacia, or hypocalcaemic tetany.

Calcium gluconate injection, BP, is prepared in 5 ml ampoules containing 10% w/v, equivalent to 0.9% w/v of calcium.

Calcium gluconate tablets, BPC, contain 600 mg of calcium gluconate (dose one to ten tablets).

Calcium gluconate effervescent tablets, BPC, contain calcium gluconate 1 g.

Calcium lactate tablets, BP, contain 300 mg (dose 1–5 g).

Mention should be made here of the importance of calcium at the cellular level. A hormone or a nerve impulse acts as a first messenger outside the cell, while cyclic adenosine monophosphate (cyclic AMP) has for a number of years been accepted as a second messenger in the cell, initiating various reactions. It was next accepted that intracellular calcium is also of crucial importance. There followed the discovery that a calcium-dependent regulator, to which the name *calmodulin* has been given, is also required. This is a heat-stable acidic protein of 16 700 daltons, and its molecule has four calcium-binding sites. Calmodulin, calcium and cyclic AMP are inextricably linked in the regulation of a wide range of essential cell processes. For instance, calmodulin activates adenylate cyclase and phosphodiesterase, which hydrolyse ATP and cyclic AMP respectively, and also activates the calcium pump which returns a raised intracellular calcium level to its resting value. Some of the calcium influx blocking agents used in cardiovascular disease may act by inhibiting calmodulin, and it and calcium are of supreme importance in many cellular activities.

Prednisolone

The many actions of corticosteroids are dealt with elsewhere (p. 404). In certain diseases affecting the bones, such as multiple myelomatosis and metastatic bone disease, there may be excessive release of calcium into the blood stream from bone, and this may have adverse effects, including the causation of renal failure. Prednisolone (or prednisone), usually given in combination with a cytotoxic drug (p. 514), may cause a fall in the blood calcium level, possibly by preventing the release of calcium from osseous tissue.

Disodium edetate

Disodium edetate forms calcium sodium edetate in the body, because it forms a poorly dissociable chelate complex (p. 525) with the calcium. The rapid i.v. administration of disodium edetate causes hypocalcaemic tetany. If it is administered slowly over a period of days, calcium is mobilized from bone and excreted in the urine, with little alteration of the plasma calcium level. Therefore it has little therapeutic application.

Phosphates

Phosphates are sometimes given for the treatment of hypercalcaemia associated with hyperparathyroidism (p. 386), multiple myelomatosis or metastatic bone disease. It seems likely that calcium phosphate is formed and, hence, it might be undesirable to give i.v. sodium phosphate, as has been suggested. An oral preparation (Phosphate-Sandoz) contains elemental phosphorus 500 mg, sodium 487 mg and potassium 123 mg in a tablet. The recommended dose is up to six tablets daily.

Calcitonin

Calcitonin is a single-chain polypeptide hormone, of molecular weight 3600, which contains 32 amino acids and is secreted by the parafollicular cells (C cells) of the thyroid gland. It is obtained for clinical use from porcine thyroid. There are human, porcine, and salmon calcitonins with slightly different structures, and there is a synthetic substitute for salmon calcitonin, known as salcatonin. The effects of calcitonins are the opposite of those produced by parathormone (p. 387).

Calcitonin is secreted in increased amounts when the serum calcium concentration rises. Its mode of action is uncertain, but it may decrease the permeability of cells to calcium. There is decreased bone reabsorption and increased bone formation. This results in a decrease in the urinary output of calcium, magnesium and hydroxyproline. The plasma calcium level falls. Calcitonin is available commercially as porcine calcitonin in vials containing 160 IU, and may be given s.c. or i.m. Salcatonin is available in multidose vials containing 400 IU in 2 ml (Calsynar). As an example, clinical and biochemical improvement has been observed in Paget's disease of bone with dosage regimens ranging from 50 IU of salcatonin three times a week to 100 IU daily in single or divided doses. There may be relief of bone pain or nerve compression. Deafness does not usually respond to calcitonin. High doses of calcitonin are used in patients with severe hypercalcaemia, but corticosteroids may be more effective in sarcoidosis or metastatic malignant disease of bone. If there is a history of allergy, a scratch (or intradermal) test should be done before calcitonin is given. Calcitonin from porcine thyroid is available as Calcitare.

Disodium etidronate

Disodium etidronate (Didronel) is a diphosphonate and is marketed for the treatment of Paget's disease, particularly in patients with polyostotic Paget's disease with symptoms of pain and clinically significant elevation of urinary hydroxyproline and serum alkaline phosphatase. It may also be tried if there is extensive involvement of the skull or spine with the prospect of irreversible neurological damage or when there is involvement of a weight-bearing bone.

Diphosphonates are stable analogues of pyrophosphate and they are resistant to enzymatic and chemical hydrolysis. It is thought that in bone they make the mineral phase unavailable for normal osteoclast activation and function. In untreated Paget's disease there is excessive osteoclastic resorption. When this drug is given there is inhibition of calcification of bones and teeth and a decrease in circulating concentrations of 1,25-dihydroxyvitamin D_3. Nearly three-quarters of the patients treated with this substance have a decrease in pain and an improvement in biochemical parameters after about six weeks of treatment. If this therapy is continued for six months, the improvement may be maintained for a considerable time. Unfortunately, if large doses are given, the mineralization of newly formed bone is impaired, and osteomalacia occurs. Sometimes bone pain becomes worse and pathological fractures may take place. The recommended dose is 5 mg/kg body weight per day by mouth for a period up to six months, and further treatment should not be given for at least three months.

Trials of other diphosphonates are under way.

VITAMIN K

Fat-soluble vitamin K is referred to on p. 472.

VITAMIN E

Vitamin E has been isolated from the unsaponified fraction of wheat germ oil and named tocopherol. In vitamin E-deficient rats there is increased oxidation of polyunsaturated fatty acids, with muscle weakness and degeneration. Many claims for the therapeutic use of vitamin E have been made, but there is no clear evidence that vitamin E deficiency occurs in man, except for a suggestion that a form of normochromic normocytic anaemia may occur in premature infants because of tocopherol deficiency in the maternal diet.

Vitamin E may play a part in inhibiting platelet aggregation.

ASCORBIC ACID

In man ascorbic acid is a vitamin, but apart from other primates, guinea-pigs, the red-vented bulbul bird and the fruit-eating bat, animals can synthesize vitamin C. It might be argued that all mankind has an inborn error of metabolism in that the enzyme that converts L-gulono-γ-lactone to ascorbic acid is missing. Most animals synthesize ascorbic acid from glucose via glucuronic acid and this substance.

Ascorbic acid is a simple sugar and is the most active reducing agent known to occur naturally in living tissues. It is easily oxidized to dehydroascorbic acid and is in equilibrium with this.

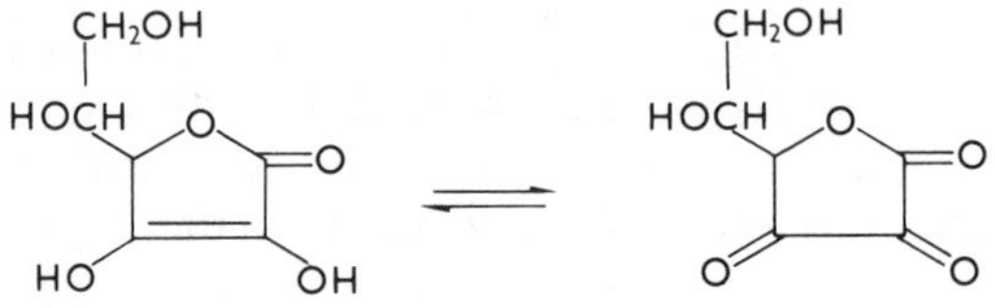

ASCORBIC ACID   DEHYDROASCORBIC ACID

Ascorbic acid is a white crystalline substance that is very soluble in water and easily oxidized. The largest concentrations in the body are in the adrenal glands, the liver, the spleen and the brain. It is present in leucocytes and in plasma.

The main sources are fruits, potatoes, other vegetables, milk and nuts. It is found in liver and in fish roe. Dried pulses and cereals do not contain ascorbic acid, but they form the vitamin on germination. The actual content in potatoes is not so very high, but this is an important source of the vitamin in the UK. Human milk usually contains three or four times as much vitamin C as does cows' milk. In the UK it is believed that a daily intake of 30 mg of ascorbic acid is needed, but in the USA the authorities consider that full saturation is desirable and recommend 60 mg.

Metabolism

Two points which may be mentioned are that damage to the tissues such as a burn or surgical operation causes loss of ascorbic acid from the body and that injections of ACTH cause a quantitative loss from the adrenal cortex.

Functions

Collagen has a high content of hydroxyproline. When proline is incorporated by cellular ribosomes into a protein unit, ascorbic acid and oxygen are needed to add a hydroxyl group to carbon-4 of the proline to allow collagen to be formed. In the absence of vitamin C, normal fibrous collagen is replaced by a non-fibrous precursor. Because of its reducing or antioxidant effect, ascorbic acid may assist in the utilization of iron and it may decrease the requirements of certain other vitamins. Those on a low intake of ascorbic acid cannot utilize tyrosine normally. Since there are many enzymes in living cells, some being reduced by ascorbic acid and others oxidized by dehydroascorbic acid, it is obvious that there is need for a normal amount of vitamin C throughout the tissues of the body. Large doses of ascorbic acid improve absorption of iron from the small intestine (p. 457). Although anaemia develops in scurvy, this seems to be due to haemolysis. It is easier to understand why wound healing is impaired when collagen formation is faulty.

Stability
Vitamin C is very labile in foodstuffs. The greatest losses in the preparation of food are from leaching into the processing water. With bruised and wilted vegetables ascorbic acid oxidase destroys the vitamin. Leafy vegetables should not be stored below freezing point in the open, but losses are less in prepared frozen foods. Vitamin C is stable in fruits or vegetables in cans or bottles if protected from air, but once these are opened the content soon falls. Some fruit juices or fruit-flavoured drinks are very deficient in vitamin C content. Dehydrated potatoes, when reconstituted, may have lost most of their vitamin C and in large institutions the preparation and serving of foodstuffs in bulk may result in the recipient receiving negligible amounts of ascorbic acid.

Clinical Importance
Lack of ascorbic acid causes scurvy. In deficiency, the plasma concentration of vitamin C falls; then there is decreased tissue and leucocyte concentration. The patient becomes weak and tired, anaemic and prone to infection, has swollen bleeding gums, and develops haemorrhages. Scurvy is sometimes seen in infants; in the adult it is most commonly found in the elderly. In the past it was much more prevalent. The normal body stores about 1500 mg of ascorbic acid and this will last about three months if the intake ceases.

Preparations

Ascorbic acid tablets, *BP*, are available in 25, 50, 100, 200 and 500 mg strengths. The therapeutic dose is not less than 250 mg daily in divided doses.

It is likely that other deficiencies will also be present and it may be necessary to give ferrous sulphate (p. 458) or other vitamins simultaneously.

Indications
The prevention and treatment of scurvy is the main indication. Some authorities believe that large doses will reduce the number of attacks of the common cold, but the evidence for this is poor and there is no need for expensive compounds of analgesics with ascorbic acid. Large doses of vitamin C will improve the absorption of ferrous sulphate, but this is seldom of

practical importance. Very large doses of several grams a day over a long period may lead to oxalate stones in the urine.

In the condition known as methaemoglobinaemia a substantial proportion of the circulating haemoglobin is in a form that cannot transport oxygen. This may be caused in certain people by drugs such as acetanilide or phenacetin and is due to an excessive rate of methaemoglobin formation. The drugs should be stopped, and ascorbic acid can be given. There are also congenital forms and in some of these treatment with ascorbic acid is satisfactory. This is due to this reducing agent reacting directly with methaemoglobin. An alternative method of treatment if there is a serious problem is to give methylene blue i.v. (1–2 mg/kg body weight). It seems to enable methaemoglobin to be reduced by enzyme systems that are normally unable to do this.

ENERGY RELEASE IN THE BODY CELLS

Chemical energy from foodstuffs reaches the cells as glucose, fatty acids and amino acids. It is released by oxidative processes in the cells and the stages are complex. Acetyl coenzyme A is required for the synthesis of new carbohydrate, fat and protein, and coenzyme A contains the vitamin pantothenic acid. The various reactions involve five known vitamins — thiamine, riboflavine, nicotinic acid, pyridoxine and pantothenic acid. Brief reference will now be made to each of these.

THIAMINE

THIAMINE

Thiamine, or vitamin B_1, was at one time known as aneurine. It has a pyrimidine ring joined by a methylene bridge to a thiazole moiety. It is the only compound produced by living matter that has a thiazole ring. The main sources of thiamine are yeasts and the germs and pericarp tissues of cereals, but in the British diet it is obtained largely from cereals, meats, potatoes, milk and vegetables other than potatoes. Most mammals depend on their dietary intake. It is convenient to remember that the normal adult requirement of vitamin B_1 is about 1 mg, but more correct to suggest 0.5 mg for every 1000 kcal of intake. Deficiency leads to beriberi (p. 449), and this may occur in rice-eaters who take polished rice. In the last century the march of industry into underdeveloped countries led to polished rice (with the thiamine thus largely removed) becoming available at about the same cost as home-pounded rice, and the results were disastrous. In developing countries where other cereals are now being highly milled, similar problems may develop. Those reading about such matters should realize that in the USA the word 'corn' is short for Indian corn, also known as maize, and that in England corn means wheat, whereas in Scotland it means oats.

Functions

In the form of its pyrophosphate, thiamine acts as the coenzyme of carboxylase. When glucose breaks down, an important step is the formation of pyruvic acid, which, in the absence of oxygen, is reduced to lactic acid. During exercise, lactic acid accumulates in muscle and goes into the body fluids, but with a supply of oxygen the lactic acid is oxidized back to pyruvic acid. Pyruvic acid accumulates in the body, however, unless it is oxidatively decarboxylated to acetyl coenzyme A, an essential compound in metabolism. This decarboxylation requires thiamine pyrophosphate, coenzyme A, nicotinamide adenine nucleotide and lipoic acid.

Thiamine pyrophosphate is also needed for the oxidative decarboxylation of α-ketoglutaric acid and is required in the transketolase reaction.

It is not certain why the features of beriberi or other conditions associated with thiamine deficiency result from pyruvic acid accumulation or other disturbances that might be expected from interference with these functions.

Stability

B₁ is one of the more labile of the vitamins. Quite apart from the problems of milling, referred to above, much can be lost in food processing, mainly from leaching into water. When rice gruel is prepared, losses are very great, and this is important in many countries. There is considerable loss in baking if alkaline baking powders are used, and there is loss from toasting bread, adding sulphur dioxide to mince, or cooking fish or meats.

Clinical Importance

Deficiency causes dry beriberi (a form of polyneuropathy), wet beriberi (with cardiac failure), Wernicke's encephalopathy (with ocular signs and mental changes), and Korsakoff's psychosis (with mental disturbances). It was common in Japanese prisoner-of-war camps, may be found occasionally with malabsorption, and occurs in alcoholics.

Preparations

Thiamine hydrochloride tablets, BP, are available in various strengths up to 300 mg, but 3 mg tablets are frequently used for prophylaxis. For treatment 25–100 mg is given daily.

Thiamine hydrochloride is also available for i.m. or i.v. injection.

Usually there is deficiency of more than one vitamin. Preparations that are available to treat this include: *vitamin B compound tablets*, *BPC*, containing thiamine hydrochloride 1 mg, riboflavine 1 mg and nicotinamide 15 mg; and *vitamin B compound tablets, strong, BPC*, containing thiamine hydrochloride 5 mg, riboflavine 2 mg, nicotinamide 20 mg and pyridoxine hydrochloride 2 mg.

Overdose is not a problem.

Indications
The conditions are referred to above, but there is controversy about the true value of treating dry beriberi with thiamine hydrochloride. Certainly in wet beriberi the patient must be kept in bed in case of heart failure and given 50–100 mg i.v. slowly. In all cases other vitamins of the B complex should also be given, as an excess of one may make matters worse in relation to others that are marginally deficient.

RIBOFLAVINE

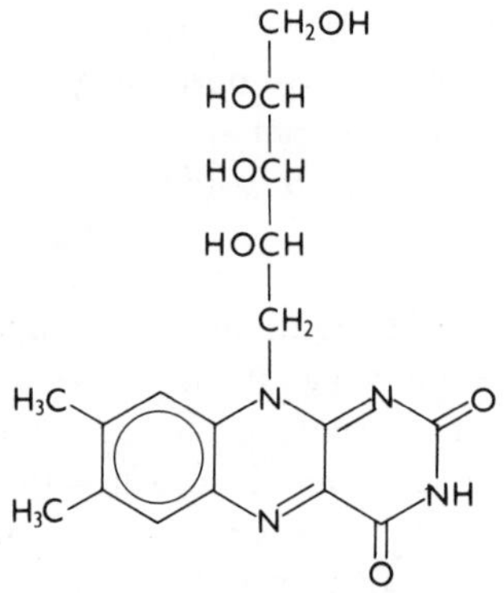

RIBOFLAVINE

Riboflavine (termed riboflavin in the USA) used to be known as vitamin B_2. It is a yellow crystalline substance that is not fat-soluble but dissolves slightly in water. It has an alloxazine ring structure linked to an alcohol derived from ribose.

In animal and plant tissues riboflavine is linked with phosphoric acid to give flavin mononucleotide (FMN). This combines with certain proteins to form flavoproteins (yellow enzymes), which are capable of reversible oxidation and reduction However, in some flavoproteins the linkage is with adenosine, to give flavin adenine dinucleotide (FAD). The riboflavine requirement is 2 mg, or more correctly, according to some, 0.55 mg/1000 kcal. The main sources of riboflavine in the UK are milk, meats, cereals, potatoes, other vegetables, fruit and fish. It is also found in eggs. Rice and maize meal are poor sources.

Functions
Riboflavine acts as an active prosthetic group of the flavoproteins required for tissue oxidation in the control of cellular energy processes (p. 448).

Stability
Riboflavine is stable to oxygen and to acid conditions, but not to light or alkali. In milk, exposure to light may be particularly harmful, and the lumiflavine which is produced may destroy vitamin C. Heat alone is not harmful.

Clinical Importance
Since deficiency of riboflavine interferes with cellular energy processes, it is surprising that deficiency leads only to an odd assortment of clinical abnormalities, viz. angular stomatitis, cheilosis, nasolabial seborrhoea, scrotal dermatitis, glossitis (a magenta tongue, due to capillary dilatation and a sluggish blood flow), and invasion of the cornea by capillary blood vessels. Photophobia and corneal opacities may develop. The 'burning feet syndrome' which occurred in Japanese POW camps may have been due to riboflavine deficiency.

Preparations
Riboflavine may be given in 5 mg tablets three times daily, or one of the vitamin B compound tablets (p. 450) may be used.

Indications
It is only in exceptional circumstances that riboflavine deficiency occurs, and other deficiencies will almost certainly be present. Angular stomatitis is usually due to other causes in the UK.

NICOTINIC ACID

NICOTINIC ACID   NICOTINAMIDE

Nicotinic acid is a simple derivative of pyridine, and its amide is its natural form in the body. The term niacin is a generic one used to include nicotinic acid and its amide together with other derivatives that can become biologically active in the body. In the USA the term niacin is often used for nicotinic acid itself.

In man, nicotinic acid can be synthesized from tryptophan. The importance of this is uncertain because nutritional deficiencies of nicotinic acid are so frequently associated with a coincidental deficiency of tryptophan.

In cellular oxidation the dehydrogenase system responsible for oxidations in the citric acid cycle requires three intermediate carrier stages before molecular oxygen affects the final step, which is the conversion of the hydrogen to water. Thus, starting with citric acid, electrons are picked up and passed through three linked stages.

1. Nicotinamide adenine dinucleotide (NAD) picks them up, giving NADH$_2$. NAD is:

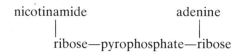

2. FAD (p. 450) is then reduced to FADH$_2$ from transfer of hydrogen, with re-formation of NAD.
3. The iron-containing substance cytochrome (p. 456) is converted to a reduced form by hydrogen transfer, and FAD is re-formed.
4. Ferrous iron in reduced cytochrome (p. 456) is oxidized to the ferric form by cytochrome oxidase in the presence of oxygen.

In general, NAD is used by most oxidative reactions in energy-yielding metabolism, but most reductive reactions such as the hexose monophosphate shunt utilize nicotinamide adenine dinucleotide phosphate (NADP) in a reduced form (NADPH) as the hydrogen donor.

Nicotinic acid is widely distributed in foodstuffs, and in the British diet the main sources are meats, cereals, potatoes, other vegetables, fish and milk. In many cereals, particularly maize, it is mainly in a bound form that is biologically unavailable.

Stability
This is one of the most stable of the B group of vitamins. There may be loss from leaching into processing water. Heat releases it from maize and other foods in which it is bound, but, unfortunately, this does not occur markedly with rice.

Some nicotinamide is synthesized in the body from tryptophan.

Clinical Importance
Pellagra is a deficiency state which still occurs in maize-eaters, particularly when refined maize flour has been introduced. This is because nicotinic acid is bound and reduced in amount. It is also found in those eating sorghum (jowar), possibly because the leucine in it interferes with tryptophan and nicotinic acid metabolism. It has been found in alcoholics and rarely in malabsorptive states. There are erythema, dermatitis, glossitis, diarrhoea, mental disorder, and peripheral neuropathy in severe cases.

Treatment with isoniazid (*iso*-nicotinic acid hydrazide) may block the action of kynureninase, a pyridoxal-dependent enzyme in the pathway of nicotinamide synthesis from tryptophan. This may give a pellagra-like dermatitis.

In the rare hereditary condition of Hartnup disease, in which there is renal amino-aciduria and also malabsorption of amino acids, a pellagra-like rash may occur because of tryptophan deficiency.

The carcinoid syndrome may manifest itself as pellagra because carcinoid tumours synthesize large amounts of 5- hydroxytryptophan and 5-hydroxytryptamine, diverting tryptophan required for the synthesis of nicotinic acid ribonucleotide.

Preparations

Nicotinic acid itself causes flushing, and nicotinamide tablets, BPC, are used. These contain 50 or 500 mg. For prophylaxis 15–30 mg is given daily, and for treatment, 50–250 mg. It is likely that multiple deficiencies will require attention (p. 449). Ampoules containing a mixture of vitamins including nicotinamide are available for i.m. or i.v. use. The i.v. injection of nicotinic acid itself causes an increase in the plasma concentration of unconjugated bilirubin.

Indications

Nicotinic acid is used in the prevention and treatment of pellagra. It is also sometimes tried for the treatment of chilblains and of Meniere's syndrome.

PYRIDOXINE

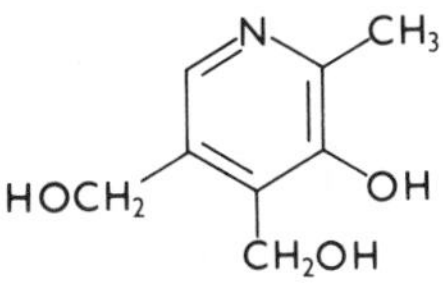

PYRIDOXOL 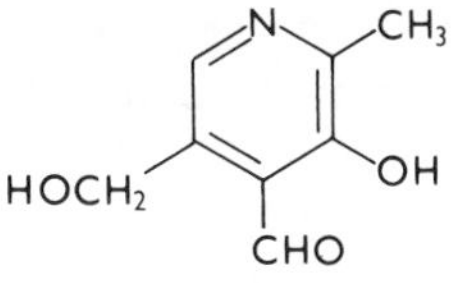   PYRIDOXAL 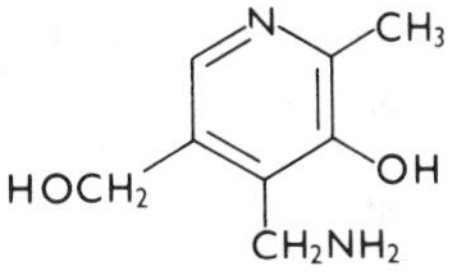   PYRIDOXAMINE

The term 'pyridoxine' or 'vitamin B6' is given to the closely related chemical substances pyridoxol, pyridoxal and pyridoxamine. The active forms are phosphates.

Amino acids can be metabolized in various ways, one of which is transamination, where an amino group is transferred to a keto acid, with the formation of another amino acid that can be used to synthesize new proteins. Thus pyridoxol can take up an amino group and form pyridoxamine, but it then transfers this group to a keto acid.

True pyridoxine deficiency is so uncommon that it is rarely considered as a clinical entity, but it has been reported in children given unusual artificial feeding, and leads to irritability and convulsions. There have been claims that depression associated with the taking of oral contraceptives can be prevented by pyridoxine. Familial defects of vitamin B₆ metabolism have been described, including a form of anaemia that responds to treatment with pyridoxine. In homocystinuria, which is an inborn error of metabolism, the patient is deficient in an enzyme that is activated by pyridoxine. Folate deficiency may also be present.

Isoniazid (p. 34) in excessive dosage may cause a peripheral neuropathy by interfering with the activity of pyridoxine, and if high doses of isoniazid are used, pyridoxine should also be given. Isoniazid forms a hydrazone with pyridoxal phosphate and this is metabolically inactive. Pyridoxine interferes with the therapeutic action of levodopa (p. 237). It has been said that the impairment of glucose tolerance frequently seen in non-diabetic pregnant women may be controlled by the administration of pyridoxine. If so, the reason for this is not clear.

Pyridoxine tablets, *BPC*, are prepared in 10, 20 or 50 mg strengths. In pyridoxine-deficiency anaemia 50–100 mg is given daily. For pyridoxine-deficiency convulsions in infants 4 mg/kg body weight is given for short periods. A controlled-release tablet containing 100 mg of pyridoxine hydrochloride is marketed under the brand name Comploment Continus for deficiency of vitamin B₆ caused by usage of the contraceptive pill.

An injectable preparation is also available. Injections of pyridoxal-5-phosphate have been used in the treatment of sideroblastic anaemia.

PANTOTHENIC ACID

There is no definite evidence of a disease entity from lack of this substance, which is widely distributed in natural foodstuffs.

FURTHER READING

Bender D. A. (1980) Vitamin D. In: Barker B. M. & Bender D. A. (eds) *Vitamins in Medicine*, 4th edn, pp. 42–146. London: Heinemann.

Bennink H. J. T. C. & Schreurs W. H. P. (1975) Improvement of oral glucose tolerance test in gestational diabetes by pyridoxine. *Br. med. J.*, 3:13.

Dallman P. R. (1974) Iron, vitamin E and folate in the preterm infant. *J. Pediat.*, 85: 742.

Department of Health and Social Security (1970) *Interim Report on Vitamin D by the Panel on Child Nutrition and First Report by the Panel on Nutrition of the Elderly*. Report No. 123. London: HMSO.

Dixon A. St. J. (1983) Non-hormonal treatment of osteoporosis. *Br. med. J.*, 286: 999.

Editorial (1979) Vitamin C, disease and surgical trauma. *Br. med. J.*, i: 437.

Editorial (1982) Calmodulin — ubiquitous cell regulator. *Lancet*, ii: 192.

Editorial (1982) Vitamins to prevent neural tube defects. *Lancet*, ii: 1255.

Elomaa I., Blomgvist C., Gröhn P., Porkka L., Kairento A-L., Selander K., Lamberg-Allardt C. & Holmström T. (1983) Long-term controlled trial with diphosphonate in patients with osteolytic bone metastases. *Lancet*, i: 146.

Heath D. A., Van't Hoff W., Barnes A. D. & Gray J. G. (1979) Value of 1-alpha-hydroxyvitamin

D₃ in treatment of primary hyperparathyroidism before parathyroidectomy. *Br. med. J.*, i: 450.

Huang W. Y., Cohn D. V. & Hamilton J. (1975) Calcium-binding protein of bovine intestine: the complete aminoacid sequence. *J. biol. Chem.*, 250: 7647.

LeQuesne P. M. (1983) Persisting nutritional neuropathy in former war prisoners. *Br. med. J.*, 286: 917.

Long R. G. Varghese Z., Meinhard E. A., Skinner R. K., Mills M. R. & Sherlock S. (1978) Parenteral 1,25-dihydroxycholecalciferol in hepatic osteomalacia. *Br. med. J.*, i: 75.

Miller L. T., Benson E. M., Edwards M. A. & Young J. (1974) Vitamin B₆ metabolism in women using oral contraceptives. *Am. J. clin. Nutr.*, 27: 797.

Mundy G. R. & Raisz L. G. (1981) Recent advances in the drug therapy of disorders of calcium and bone metabolism. In: *Year Book of Drug Therapy*, Hollister L. E. & Lasagna L. (eds) Chicago: Year Book Medical Publishers.

Ritchie J. F., Fish M. B., McMasters V. & Grossman M. (1968) Edema and haemolytic anaemia in premature infants — a vitamin E deficiency syndrome. *New Engl. J. Med.*, 279: 1185.

Stevenson J. C. & Whitehead M. I. (1982) Postmenopausal osteoporosis. *Br. med. J.*, 285: 585.

Venkataswamy G., Krishnamurthy K. A., Chandra P., Kabir S. A. & Pirie A. (1976) A nutrition rehabilitation centre for children with xerophthalmia. *Lancet*, i: 1120.

12   Haematinics

R. H. Girdwood

There are many causes of anaemia and various reasons for deficiency of haemopoietic factors. Sometimes there is an underlying illness or abnormality that can be dealt with, or, if there is primary malnutrition, there may be social and/or economic reasons for its having occurred. Particular consideration will be given here to three groups of haematinics, viz. iron preparations, cobalamins and folates.

IRON

Iron is an essential constituent of the human body, the total content being 3–5 g in the adult. Of this, about two-thirds is present in the red cells in the oxygen-transport pigment, haemoglobin, being released and utilized again when the red cell is destroyed after about 120 days. Most of the remainder is in stores in marrow, spleen or liver, as ferritin or haemosiderin. The haemosiderin granule contains ferritin and also other forms of iron. Iron also occurs in the oxygen-storage pigment, myoglobin, of skeletal muscle, and in cytochromes, which are located chiefly in mitochondria and take part in the final stages of aerobic respiration by reversible oxidation and reduction of iron atoms (p. 452). The oxidation and reduction of iron is also a vital reaction in the functioning of the enzymes succinic dehydrogenase and xanthine oxidase.

The iron requirements are usually believed to be 0.5–1.0 mg daily for adult males and postmenopausal women, the loss being mainly by desquamation of cells from the gut and dermis. There are traces of iron in sweat. The output in the urine is negligible but may be increased in proteinuria or where there is iron overload. Most of the iron released from red cells is reconverted into haemoglobin. Menstruating women and adolescents require to absorb 1.0–2.0 mg daily and in pregnancy the requirements are 1.5–4.5 mg.

INTAKE AND ABSORPTION

Iron is widely distributed in foodstuffs, occurring in organ meats, pulses, leafy

456

vegetables, oysters, chocolate, wheat, oatmeal, muscle meats, eggs and many other substances. Milk and milk products, however, are a poor source. Cooking practices may be important. Whole rice contains about 5 mg/100 g, whereas polished rice after cooking may contain as little as 0.2 mg/100 g, and this may be of considerable importance in certain tropical countries, particularly if hookworm infestation is rife. It is said that iron is more readily absorbed from animal foods than from vegetable sources. It is believed that the normal European or North American diet provides about 10–20 mg daily, but of this only about 5–10 per cent is absorbed. In iron deficiency the proportion absorbed is greater, and this is also true when there is increased erythropoiesis.

Iron is largely in the ferric form in foodstuffs, but is mostly easily absorbed as ferrous iron. Gastric acid favours the reduction of the former to the latter and there is evidence for the view that achlorhydria impairs iron absorption. The iron stores are usually well filled in pernicious anaemia, despite the fact that in this condition labelled ferrous iron given with bread is not as well absorbed as in subjects with gastric acid. Various factors may influence the extent of absorption. Thus phytates form non-absorbable salts with iron, only about 5% of wheat iron being available, and phosphates and calcium also reduce iron absorption. Fructose, on the other hand, increases it, perhaps by forming a stable iron chelate. Large quantities of ascorbic acid increase the absorption of food iron. It has been suggested that pancreatic exocrine secretion contains a substance that inhibits iron absorption, and there is conflicting evidence about various non-acid gastric secretions that may either improve or impair the degree of absorption of dietetic iron.

The cells of the small intestine are responsible for both absorption and excretion of iron. In the mucosal cell ferrous iron passes to the blood stream, excessive amounts being converted within the cell into ferric iron; this combines with a protein named apoferritin to give ferritin, and when the effete mucosal cell is exfoliated into the gut lumen, the excess iron is carried out in the faeces. However, this control mechanism cannot deal with a large excess of iron. The Bantu of Africa may have a daily dietary intake of as much as 100–150 mg of iron, partly derived from cooking utensils, and excess iron is deposited in stores, giving the condition named siderosis (or, less correctly, haemosiderosis). Some persons have a genetically determined abnormality of iron absorption, so that even with a normal intake by mouth an excess is absorbed, and to this condition the name 'haemochromatosis' is given. It is possible for an excessive amount of a therapeutic iron preparation to be given over a long period to a normal person with detrimental effects from excessive absorption, or, more commonly, for excessive deposition of iron in the tissues to follow repeated blood transfusion.

After the iron reaches the blood stream it is transported by a glycoprotein β_1-globulin termed transferrin and in due course reaches the bone marrow, where it is incorporated into haemoglobin.

Preparations of Iron Used in Therapy

Iron is usually given by mouth, there being little need for injections, but, where necessary, it can be given in a suitable form i.m. or i.v.

Oral Therapy

Preparations

Tablet preparations are ferrous sulphate, ferrous gluconate and ferrous fumarate.

Liquid preparations are ferrous fumarate syrup and sodium ironedetate. Of the ferrous salts available, the cheapest is ferrous sulphate, and this is usually tolerated without difficulty. Any iron preparation taken orally may be said by some patients to cause nausea, diarrhoea or constipation, and it is sometimes found that this can be overcome by taking a very small dose (one tablet) for the first two or three days, two tablets for a further few days, and then going on with the usual therapeutic dose of one tablet three times daily. Alternatively, another iron preparation may be tried. Iron is best absorbed if the tablets are taken between meals, but gastrointestinal disturbance is less if the dose is taken just after food. The haematological response usually begins 5–10 days after therapy is started.

Three ferrous sulphate tablets daily (a total of 600 mg of ferrous sulphate) provides 180 mg of iron, while three ferrous fumarate tablets (each containing 200 mg) provides the same amount of iron, but three ferrous gluconate tablets (each of 300 mg) gives 108 mg of iron. Occasionally a patient is unable to swallow tablets and then a liquid preparation such as ferrous fumarate syrup (140 mg, equivalent to 45 mg of iron in 5 ml) may be prescribed. This form of therapy may also be preferable in postgastrectomy iron deficiency.

There are many proprietary preparations containing iron together with other haematinics or with alleged tonics. In pregnancy it is reasonable to give iron together with folic acid, in order to prevent anaemia. For a non-anaemic pregnant woman a preparation giving approximately 100 mg of elemental iron and 350 μg of folic acid daily should be satisfactory.

Some manufacturers provide delayed-release ferrous sulphate preparations. These tend to be expensive, but might be justified where there is claimed to be intolerance to other forms of oral iron therapy.

Adverse Effects

Reference has already been made to gastrointestinal disturbances. Liquid preparations may stain the teeth black. Children may ingest a large number of tablets, thinking they are sweets, and this can cause an acute illness with gastroenteritis, shock, and even death from circulatory failure. Iron preparations should not be given within four hours of the taking of a tetracycline, as the two bind to each other with consequent impaired absorption of both.

Parenteral Therapy

Iron dextran and iron sorbitol (known as iron sorbitex in the USA) are used.

The use of injectable forms of iron does not necessarily result in a speedier rise in the haemoglobin level than when iron is given by mouth. However, it is justifiable to give such injections when loss of blood is greater than can be offset by the oral administration of iron, when a patient is unwilling or unable to take iron by mouth, or when there is disease of the alimentary tract of such an extent that oral iron preparations cannot be tolerated (e.g. some cases of ulcerative colitis or regional enteritis). Occasionally, in the anaemia of rheumatoid arthritis, the response to i.m. iron injections is good, and Jehovah's Witnesses who refuse blood transfusions may, on occasion, be treated by i.v. iron infusions.

Iron dextran injection

Iron dextran injection (Imferon, Ironorm) was first introduced for i.m. use, but there were reports of sarcomatous change in rats and rabbits receiving very large i.m. doses of the substance. There has been little evidence to show that this is a possible danger in man. Indeed, it has been calculated that over 100 million doses of iron dextran have been given since it was first marketed more than 25 years ago without there being any increased incidence of buttock tumours. Nevertheless, iron dextran is more commonly given i.v. in a suitable vehicle (sterile normal saline or 5% glucose to make a solution not exceeding 5% iron dextran v/v) as a total dose infusion.

Iron dextran injection contains 50 mg of iron per ml of solution and is available in 2, 5 and 20 ml ampoules. If administered i.m., it is given by deep injection into the upper and outer quadrant of the buttock. The total dose is calculated from a formula based on the weight of the patient and the degree of anaemia, and this is provided in the manufacturer's literature. It is usual to give a 25 mg test dose the first day and to follow this with 50 mg the next day and then 100 mg every second day or weekly until the total dose is given. If the compound is to be given i.v., the initial test dose should be 25 mg given slow, diluted with the patient's own blood. In small or underweight adults and in children a lesser dose should be employed. Most of the iron dextran is absorbed by lymphatics from the muscle and passes into the blood stream. The dextran is metabolized in the liver and the iron combines with protein to form normal storage forms of iron. If an excessive amount is given, siderosis will result.

When total dose infusion is employed, it is started at the rate of 5 drops/min. for 10 minutes under strict medical observation. If all is well, the rate may be increased to between 45 and 60 drops/min. The amount to be given is again calculated from the manufacturer's instructions.

Adverse Effects

When iron dextran is injected, hypersensitivity reactions may occur. Thus there may be urticaria, back pain, fever, arthralgia and lymphadenopathy. Alarming reactions and even death may occur after total dose infusion, so this method of treatment must be terminated immediately if there is the least sign of an abnormal response. Patients with a history of bronchial asthma should not receive iron dextran by the i.v. route and, if possible, the preparation should not be given to those with a history of allergy. Injectable antihistamines and hydrocortisone should be at hand when it is used. If despite a history of allergy other than asthma it is still felt that the preparation must be used, antihistamines should be given well before the start of treatment and throughout the period of administration of the compound. Total dose infusion should be avoided if the patient has rheumatoid arthritis because in that condition there is a high incidence of arthralgia. It is unwise to use total dose infusion in the first trimester of pregnancy.

Iron sorbitol injection

Iron sorbitol citric acid complex, BP, used for injection contains 50 mg of elemental iron per ml. It can only be given i.m., and must *not* be given i.v. It is obtained in 2 ml ampoules or 2 ml cartridges with a disposable syringe. It is injected deeply into the buttock as is iron dextran, the usual single dose being 1.5 mg/kg body weight. The dose for adults weighing 60 kg or more is 100 mg and the daily dose should not exceed this. For the first injection a trial dose of one-half the calculated amount should be administered. The total number of injections in a course is usually 10–24.

Adverse Effects

There may be minor problems such as pain at the injection site, flushing, myalgia or arthralgia. If minor reactions occur, the treatment should be discontinued. More serious adverse effects are dizziness, nausea, vomiting, hypotension, syncope and even death. If a patient is taking iron by mouth, this will increase the tendency to reactions, because transferrin is unable to take up the injected iron. Accordingly, iron should not be given by mouth simultaneously, or for two days before treatment starts. Where there is serious liver or kidney disease, the danger of reactions is greater. Patients receiving iron sorbitol should be warned that the urine may become dark on standing, from the formation of iron sulphide.

Lack of response to iron therapy may be because of some other defect in haem synthesis such as pyridoxine deficiency or lead poisoning. There may be impaired formation of globin, as in thalassaemia or the haemoglobinopathies. In chronic infections or uraemia the response to iron therapy may be poor.

Desferrioxamine Mesylate (Deferoxamine Mesylate, USP)

Desferrioxamine mesylate is a highly specific iron-chelating agent obtained from *Streptomyces pilosus*. It combines with ferric iron to form the non-toxic ferrioxamine, which is excreted in the urine. Desferrioxamine can be used in acute iron poisoning, but in conjunction with other essential measures. In an adult the treatment includes the following:

1. Give 2 g i.m. When administered parenterally the contents of one vial of the proprietary preparation Desferal which contains 500 mg of desferrioxamine mesylate can be dissolved in 5 ml of distilled water. It can be given i.m. or s.c., even if slightly opalescent. For i.v. infusion it can be further diluted with saline or glucose, but only clear solutions should then be employed.
2. After gastric lavage using a solution of desferrioxamine 2 g in 1 litre of water, leave 10 g of desferrioxamine in 50 ml of fluid in the stomach.
3. Infuse desferrioxamine i.v. at a rate of not more than 15 mg/kg body weight per hour to a maximal dose of 80 mg/kg body weight in 24 hours.
4. Give 2 g i.m. 12-hourly until the clinical condition is satisfactory and the serum iron level less than 500 μg per 100 ml.

Raw egg and milk can be given until the desferrioxamine is obtained, and gastric lavage carried out with 1% sodium bicarbonate solution.

In acute iron poisoning in children it is suggested that, in the first instance, 2 g should be given i.m. and 5 g by mouth after gastric lavage. Theoretically 100 mg can chelate about 8.5 mg of iron, so 5 g can chelate the iron contained in 10 tablets of ferrous sulphate.

Desferrioxamine is also used in the management of haemochromatosis, but is least satisfactory in the primary form. Venesection is more useful. The most iron that can be removed from the body by desferrioxamine in haemochromatosis is 10–50 mg daily, but it may be of some benefit when the excessive iron deposition follows repeated blood transfusions. Excretion is impaired in renal failure. Some children with thalassaemia are dependent on regular blood transfusions. It has been found that the build-up of iron in tissues and organs may perhaps be prevented if desferrioxamine is given by s.c. infusion rather than i.m. injection.

Adverse Effects

If desferrioxamine is given rapidly i.v., it may cause hypotension, urticaria or tachycardia. There may be pain at the site of s.c. or i.m. injection, and long-term treatment may give blurred vision, diarrhoea or leg cramps. Cataracts may form after prolonged treatment.

COBALAMINS

The name 'vitamin B_{12}' is used to describe the various forms of cobalamins that occur in nature. They are water soluble cobalt-containing compounds of considerable complexity that are produced by bacteria and required by man in trace amounts. The absence of cobalamins leads to megaloblastic anaemia only in man, but in some animals it causes a wasting disease. It seems that vitamin B_{12} has to be synthesized by micro-organisms and that it occurs in the tissues and organs of animals because it is either formed by bacteria in the alimentary tract or taken in the diet. It does not occur in plants unless they are contaminated by micro-organisms. There are live micro-organisms in the nodules of legumes and precursors of vitamin B_{12} are present in algae. In man any effective bacterial synthesis occurs in the large intestine, but the vitamin B_{12} formed there is excreted in the faeces. Man obtains vitamin B_{12} from animal products in his diet, and from sea food, egg yolk, milk and cheese. Bacterial contamination of vegetables or even of well water may be a source.

The cobalamins bound to protein are freed by the digestive process and in man these combine with intrinsic factor, a glycoprotein with a molecular weight of about 50 000 that is secreted by the parietal cells of the stomach. The vitamin B_{12}–intrinsic factor complex passes through the cells of the ileum, intrinsic factor is separated off and vitamin B_{12} becomes attached to a B_{12}-binding β-globulin known as transcobalamin II. There is also a storage protein, transcobalamin I, which is an α-globulin. Vitamin B_{12} is finally deposited in the liver, mainly as 5′-deoxyadenosylcobalamin but partly as hydroxocobalamin, and the stores are sufficient to last for 2 or 3 years. Most of the plasma vitamin B_{12} is methylcobalamin. Large doses of vitamin B_{12} taken by mouth may enter the blood stream independent of intrinsic factor, probably by diffusion, but this is not a physiological mechanism. The normal daily requirement is 2–5 μg and there is a limit to the amount that intrinsic factor can transfer across the ileal mucosa, the maximum probably being about twice the daily requirement.

The functions of the active form of vitamin B_{12} have excited interest for many years, but the observation that the anaesthetic gas, nitrous oxide, produces megaloblastic changes in the marrow has confirmed some beliefs and explained other puzzling features. The complexities of the situation and possible explanations can be taken step by step as follows:

1. Nitrous oxide inhibits methionine synthetase and hence the formation of methionine from homocysteine cannot occur.
2. Vitamin B_{12} and folic acid are cofactors in the formation of methionine from homocysteine. One suggestion about the effect of nitrous oxide is that it oxidizes biologically active methylcob (I) alamin to biologically inactive methylcob (III) alamin, and methylcob (II) alamin forms. The methyl donor is methyltetrahydrofolate.
3. If methionine is not available, formate cannot be formed.
4. If formate is not available, 5-10 methylene tetrahydrofolate ($5,10,CH_2$-H_4 Pte Glu) cannot be produced, as this step involves the interaction of tetrahydrofolate (p. 465) with formate.

5. If 5,10-CH$_2$-H$_4$ Pte Glu is not available, the methylation of deoxyuridine to deoxythymidine cannot take place normally.
6. If thymidine is not available, DNA cannot be formed normally.
7. If DNA is not formed normally, abnormal red cell precursors are formed. These are megaloblasts. Changes also can be found in the nuclei of epithelial cells.
8. In animals much less of the thymidine methyl comes from formate, so megaloblastic change does not occur.

(Much of this was foreseen in the early days of vitamin B$_{12}$ research and it is difficult to see why it was found necessary to give as much as 1–2 g of thymidine to obtain a response in pernicious anaemia, something that was tried the year after vitamin B$_{12}$ was first isolated.)

The lack of methionine is believed to affect the nervous system for a different reason. In the brain and spinal cord there is an active methionine synthetase system which is believed to be inactivated both by nitrous oxide and by vitamin B$_{12}$ deficiency. Apparently there is no need for thymidine or for DNA synthesis in nervous tissue.

Preparations

Parenteral preparations include hydroxocobalamin, cyanocobalamin and liver extract fortified with vitamin B$_{12}$. Oral preparations include cyanocobalamin and cyanocobalamin with intrinsic factor.

An oral preparation will be of value only if it can be absorbed. It is true that some vitamin B$_{12}$ is absorbed by mass action if a very large dose (e.g. 3 mg) is given and that if the problem is one of dietary deficiency, the patient's intrinsic factor will promote the absorption of vitamin B$_{12}$. Usually, however, it is necessary to give injections, which can be s.c. or i.m. Occasionally a patient will refuse to have injections and then can be treated with the oral preparation of vitamin B$_{12}$ with intrinsic factor derived from animal stomach. In time, however, antibodies to this intrinsic factor may develop. There is no real place for liver injections in therapeutics and although depot preparations of cobalamins have been produced and also forms to be used as snuff or by inhalation, the best treatment is that of injecting hydroxocobalamin.

Hydroxocobalamin. When a cobalamin is given by injection, much of it is excreted in the urine almost at once. It so happens that when vitamin B$_{12}$ was first isolated from liver, a cyano group was attached to the cobalt atom, but this was derived from charcoal columns used in the isolation procedure. Accordingly, the name 'cyanocobalamin' was used for the therapeutic substance first employed. If the –CN group is replaced by –H$_2$O, this gives aquacobalamin, or vitamin B$_{12b}$. The anhydrous form of this is hydroxocobalamin (Neo-Cytamen), or vitamin B$_{12a}$. The latter is the therapeutic agent of choice, as it is a stable form that is more readily bound to plasma protein than is cyanocobalamin. Hence injections can be given less frequently. According to one calculation, the body's requirements could be met by three injections of 1000 μg of hydroxocobalamin annually, whereas eleven injections of 1000 μg of cyanocobalamin would be required.

In practice, however, it is usual to start treatment with 1000 μg two or three times a week until there is a remission, and then to give a maintenance dose of 1000 μg every 6–8 weeks. The patient with Addisonian pernicious anaemia should be warned that treatment must continue for life. In pernicious anaemia the amount of iron stored in the body is usually high, but soon after treatment commences these stores may become depleted and hence a supplementation of ferrous sulphate by mouth may be needed. Very occasionally the body stores of folate are depleted and folic acid has to be given simultaneously before there is an adequate response to hydroxocobalamin therapy. If anaemia is very severe, it may be necessary to infuse red cells at the commencement of treatment and, to avoid circulatory overloading of a weakened heart, to give frusemide at the same time. It has been claimed, but not substantiated, that hypokalaemia may develop at the peak of the initial response to vitamin B_{12} therapy.

Cyanocobalamin. There is no good reason for using cyanocobalamin instead of hydroxocobalamin. If it is employed, the maintenance dose should be 1000 μg monthly. It is used for the Schilling test. When the term 'vitamin B_{12}' is applied to a single therapeutic agent rather than to a whole group of cobalamins, it refers to cyanocobalamin.

Indications
The four main indications are:

1. Lack of intrinsic factor, as in Addisonian pernicious anaemia or after gastrectomy operations.
2. Malabsorptive disorders or operations involving the lower ileum.
3. Severe dietary deficiency over a long period, as in the Vegans, who are a dedicated group of extreme vegetarians. Some Indian vegetarians have developed features of vitamin B_{12} deficiency.
4. Bacteria in stagnant areas of abnormal small intestine or, in some areas around the Baltic, the fish tapeworm, deviating vitamin B_{12} from the host.

The treatment may involve removing the cause of the trouble but in (1), (2) and possibly (4), vitamin B_{12} has to be given by injection. There are very rare causes of deficiency such as congenital intrinsic factor deficiency, congenital malabsorption of vitamin B_{12} and deficiency of transcobalamin II. There is little evidence of the value of vitamin B_{12} in the treatment of any other condition, except that in tobacco amblyopia, where the disturbance of vision may be due to the effect of cyanide on the optic nerve, the administration of hydroxocobalamin may be helpful, because it is converted to cyanocobalamin.

For some reason that has not been explained, corticosteroids can convert the megaloblastic marrow of untreated pernicious anaemia to a normoblastic marrow and confuse the diagnosis.

Adverse Effects

No serious toxic effects have been reported from either hydroxocobalamin or cyanocobalamin. It is hydroxocobalamin, not cyanocobalamin, that should be used in cyanide intoxication or tobacco amblyopia. Cyanocobalamin would make matters worse.

FOLATES

Widely distributed in foodstuffs of both vegetable and animal origin are derivatives of pteroylglutamic acid, the formula of which is shown below.

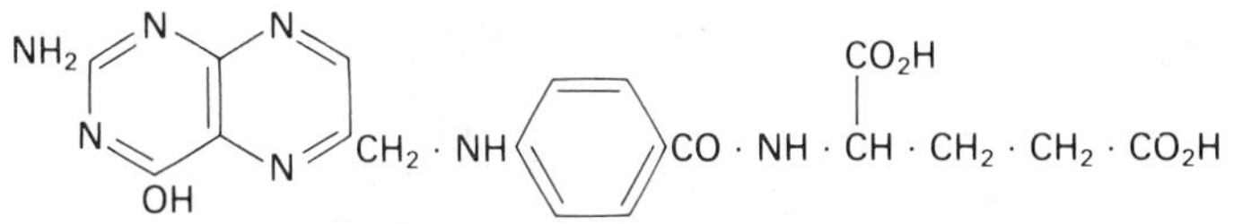

Frequently these occur in the diet as conjugates with amino acid residues attached in peptide linkage. It is believed that more than 90% of the folate derivatives in food are in reduced forms, being dihydro or tetrahydro derivatives. In addition, they are polyglutamates with a number of glutamic acid residues attached to the γ-carboxyl group. To add to the complexity, they are mostly methyl or formyl derivatives of the reduced polyglutamates. In the course of digestion, the polyglutamates are believed to enter the epithelial cells of the villi in the small intestine, and it is possibly there that an enzyme named γ-glutamyl carboxypeptidase or, more commonly, *folate conjugase* removes the peptide chains. Before that the normal processes of digestion may have removed extra glutamic acid residues to yield pteroylglutamic acid, and the substances are no longer in the reduced form. Accordingly, the next stage is the reduction of monoglutamates to the dihydro and then tetrahydro forms. It is not entirely clear where this happens, but it may occur in the cells of the small intestine. The enzyme is known as *folate reductase* or, alternatively, dihydrofolate reductase.

As a result of these and other processes, the form of folate that is found as a storage form is a 5-methyl reduced polyglutamate (5-methyl H_4 Pte Glu$_x$) (Fig. 12.1). It is found in plasma and red cells largely as 5-methyl-tetrahydrofolate (5-methyl H_4 Pte Glu) and can be measured by microbiological assay with *Lactobacillus casei* as the test organism. There is no free movement of folate from viable red cells back to the plasma.

So far as its functions in bodily metabolic processes are concerned, reduced forms of folate are needed for the production of purines and pyrimidines. Thus, 5,10-methenyl H_4 Pte Glu is needed for the introduction of a carbon unit into the purine ring in the 8 position and then 10-formyl-7,8,H_4 Pte Glu is needed for the introduction of a second carbon

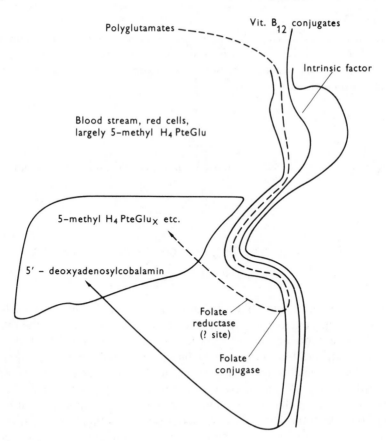

Figure 12.1 Folate absorption and storage.

unit, which is required to close the ring at the 2 position. As regards pyrimidines, 5,10-methylene H_4 Pte Glu is needed for the methylation of deoxyuridine to deoxythymidine. If there is folate depletion, DNA formation is impaired and megaloblasts appear in the bone marrow. Accordingly, just as with vitamin B_{12} depletion, deficiency of folate leads to megaloblastic anaemia. This time, however, the body stores are not so abundant, and if a normal subject is deprived of folate for about 18 weeks, megaloblastic anaemia will develop.

Reference has already been made to methionine synthesis (p. 463), for which it is probable that a polyglutamate is required. Deficiency of folate does not lead to subacute combined degeneration of the spinal cord. When a patient has pernicious anaemia or another cause of vitamin B_{12} depletion, the giving of folic acid will cause a haematological remission. This form of therapy *must not* be used in vitamin B_{12} deficiency, since, perhaps because of the utilization of remaining traces of cobalamin in the body, the features of cord degeneration are increased. Additionally, the response to folic acid treatment may be only transient. A reduced form of folate is required for the conversion of histidine to glutamic acid in the body, and in folate deficiency formiminoglutamic acid is excreted instead of glutamic acid in the urine.

Human Requirements

The amount of pteroylglutamic acid required is about 50–200 μg/day, and possibly 200–400 μg in pregnancy. Not all the folate in the diet may be absorbed, and there is a lack of agreement about how best to measure the folate in foodstuffs. A commonly used way to estimate folate is to use a solution of it as a growth factor for *L. casei*, but some of that present in foodstuffs may be degraded in its preparation for assay and since one of the factors determining the content of available folate is the method of cooking, there is little value in considering details of the quantity in foodstuffs at the time of purchase.

Certain drugs cause folate deficiency and megaloblastic anaemia by interfering with folate metabolism. With some the mechanism is clear. Thus, pyrimethamine (p. 75), which interferes with the folate reductase mechanism in malaria parasites, also does so in man, but to a much lesser extent. Trimethoprim (p. 50) interferes with folate reductase in certain bacteria, but is 50 000 times more active against bacterial folate reductase than it is against that of man and is unlikely to constitute a practical hazard except when a person is already folate-depleted. Aminopterin has an amino group in the 4 position of the pteroylglutamic acid molecule, and methotrexate (p. 503) is 4-amino-10-methylpteroylglutamic acid. Both bind the human folate reductase very firmly. With some drugs that cause folate deficiency (e.g. phenytoin or primidone), the mechanism is not understood, but it is known not to be similar to the one just described. Alcoholics may have megaloblastic anaemia, because of a reduced folate intake, but some workers believe that another little-understood mechanism may be involved. It has even been said that megaloblastic change may be produced by alcohol in patients with normal stores of folate and vitamin B_{12}. Alcohol given i.v. for nutritional purposes may cause acute folate depletion. It has been claimed that i.v. amino acids may also do this.

Certain drugs used to treat malignancies (e.g. cytarabine, fluorouracil, azauridine) block DNA synthesis and cause megaloblastic change. Oral contraceptive pills have been said to induce megaloblastic anaemia, possibly in women who are already folate-deficient. Many workers deny that this occurs and if it does happen, one would expect to see it more often. If it does occur, the mechanism is unknown.

Preparations

Oral preparations include folic acid (pteroylglutamic acid). Parenteral preparations include folate sodium and, as an alternative for special purposes, folinic acid (calcium leucovorin injection).

Folic acid is available as such, usually in 5 mg tablets, or combined with iron salts in a variety of combinations of doses. For therapeutic purposes it is usual to start with 15 mg daily by mouth, but if there is a malabsorptive condition, it is better to give the first doses s.c. or i.m. Mention has already been made (p. 458) of the use of folic acid together with an iron preparation in the prevention of anaemia in pregnancy. In severe megaloblastic anaemia of pregnancy or in malabsorptive states, blood transfusion may be required at the commencement of treatment. The possibility that folic acid given during pregnancy by itself or with other vitamins may diminish the incidence of neural tube defects is mentioned on p. 433. If this is true, the quantity required is not known.

The only need for folinic acid is in the treatment of megaloblastic anaemia caused by drugs that inhibit the dihydrofolate reductase mechanism. Folinic acid is 5-formyl-5,6,7,8-tetrahydropteroylglutamic acid (5-formyl H_4 Pte Glu), and it acts beyond the stage blocked by pyrimethamine or methotrexate; in theory, at least, folic acid will not be effective in treating this anaemia. If leukaemia is being treated by a drug that acts as a folic acid antagonist in relation to white cell division, it is likely that folinic acid will make the primary disease relapse again. Where a drug such as phenytoin is causing megaloblastic anaemia by a different mechanism, it is possible to treat it with folic acid and to continue the anticonvulsant therapy as before. If there is concern about possible folate deficiency in those receiving trimethoprim, it is reassuring to know that folic or folinic acid given to the patient is not available to bacteria.

Indications

The main causes of folate depletion are (1) malnutrition, including the taking of goat's milk in infancy and the overcooking of vegetables; (2) excessive demands, as in pregnancy; (3) malabsorption, as in gluten enteropathy or tropical sprue; and (4) interference with metabolic pathways as described above.

Inborn errors of folate metabolism because of enzyme deficiency states are rare. Folate depletion can occur in haemolytic anaemia if the intake is low, in myelofibrosis and in leukaemia, perhaps because of competition of cells for folate. There may be folate depletion in dermatitis herpetiformis, perhaps because of associated gluten enteropathy. Haemodialysis can lead to a fall in the serum folate level, but the red cell folate, a better measure of stores, is not affected, so supplementary folic acid may not be necessary.

Adverse Effects

Folic acid must not be used alone in the treatment of vitamin B_{12} deficiency, and it is important to remember that a patient with undiagnosed pernicious anaemia might, because of general weakness, buy a vitamin preparation containing folic acid and develop subacute combined degeneration of the cord without anaemia as a result.

Other Anaemias

Reference will be made later made to various drug induced anaemias (p. 564). Attention will also be drawn to the possibility of using monoclonal antibodies (p. 553) where marrow grafting is being used to treat aplastic anaemia.

FURTHER READING

Amess J. A. L., Burman J. F., Nancekievill D. G. & Mollin D. L. (1978) Megaloblastic haemopoiesis in patients receiving nitrous oxide. *Lancet*, ii: 339.

Arnstein H. R. V. & Wrighton R. J. (eds) (1971) *The Cobalamins*. Edinburgh: Churchill Livingstone.

Blakley R. L. (1969) *The Biochemistry of Folic Acid and Related Pteridines*. Amsterdam: North-Holland.

Broquist H. P., Butterworth C. E. & Wagner C. (eds) (1977) *Folic Acid. Biochemistry and Physiology in Relation to the Human Nutrition Requirement*. Washington, DC: National Academy of Sciences.

Chanarin I., Deacon R., Perry J. & Lumb M. (1981) How vitamin B_{12} acts. *Br. J. Haematol.*, 47: 487.

Cunningham J., Sharman V. L., Goodwin F. J. & Marsh F. P. (1981) Do patients receiving haemodialysis need folic acid supplements? *Br. med. J.*, 282: 1582.

Editorial (1978) Alcohol and the blood. *Br. med. J.*, ii: 1504.

Editorial (1982) Vitamins to prevent neural tube defects. *Lancet*, ii: 1255.

Girdwood R. H. (1973) Drug induced megaloblastic anaemia. In: Girdwood R. H. (ed.) *Blood Disorders Due to Drugs and Other Agents*, p. 49. Amsterdam: Excerpta Medica.

Gross F. (ed.) (1964) *Iron Metabolism*. Berlin: Springer-Verlag.

Hallberg L., Harwerth H. G. & Vannotti A. (1970) *Iron Deficiency: Pathogenesis, Clinical Aspects, Therapy*. London: Academic Press.

Hausmann K. (1949) Liver extracts, vitamin B_{12} and thymidine. *Lancet*, ii: 962.

Layzer R. B. (1978) Myeloneuropathy after prolonged exposure to nitrous oxide. *Lancet*, ii: 1227.

Nunn J. F., Gorehein H., Sharer N. M., Jones J. A. & Wickramasinghe S. N. (1982) Megaloblastic haemopoiesis after multiple short-term exposure to nitrous oxide. *Lancet*, i: 1379.

Pippard M. J., Letsky E. A., Callender S. T. & Weatherall D. J. (1978) Prevention of iron loading in transfusion-dependent thalassaemia. *Lancet*, i: 1178.

Wardrop C. A. J., Lewis M. H., Tennant G. B., Williams R. H. P. & Hughes L. E. (1977) Acute folate deficiency associated with intravenous nutrition with aminoacid–sorbitol–ethanol: prophylaxis with intravenous folic acid. *Br. J. Haematol.*, 37: 521.

Weinbren K., Salm R. & Greenberg G. (1978) Intramuscular injections of iron compounds and oncogenesis in man. *Br. med. J.*, 1: 683.

13 Anticoagulant Drugs and Related Substances

R. H. Girdwood

The process of blood coagulation is a matter of great complexity, and although anticoagulant drugs are used for the treatment of thromboses in blood vessels, the product of blood coagulation has structural differences from those of a thrombus, particularly if it is in an artery.

BLOOD COAGULATION

In blood coagulation many substances, frequently designated by numbers, are involved. The end product is the formation of insoluble strands of fibrin derived from fibrinogen and this conversion is brought about by thrombin. The strands of fibrin enmesh erythrocytes and leucocytes.

There are two mechanisms by which the process may be initiated. As will be seen from Fig. 13.1, there is an intrinsic system where various factors are converted to an active state and these then initiate the next stage of coagulation. The active factors are themselves quickly destroyed. The process may be started in vitro by contact with glass, whereas in the body it may be the contact of factor XII with collagen of a damaged vessel that is the starting point, this itself being a complex matter that need not be discussed here. Calcium ions and platelet factor 3 play an essential role in clotting. There are other platelet factors, but their function is uncertain.

There is also an 'extrinsic system' of coagulation, so called because it is activated by tissue fluid, this being 'extrinsic' to the blood vessels, but present in most tissues. The final steps of the process are the same from the stage where factor X is activated to Xa. However, the *initiation* of this step is not by factor VIII, but rather by a system involving an entirely different factor, viz. factor VII. This is a globulin that can be found in plasma, and the activation of factor X in the extrinsic system of clotting is triggered off by a complex that is formed between tissue factor, factor VII and calcium ions. When a vessel wall is injured, it is likely that tissue fluid activates the extrinsic system and, at the same time, factor XII comes in contact with collagen and activates the intrinsic system. Bleeding ceases because blood vessels contract and a platelet plug is formed in the capillaries, while in larger vessels fibrin is formed and in it both red cells and leucocytes are trapped. The formation of a large

470

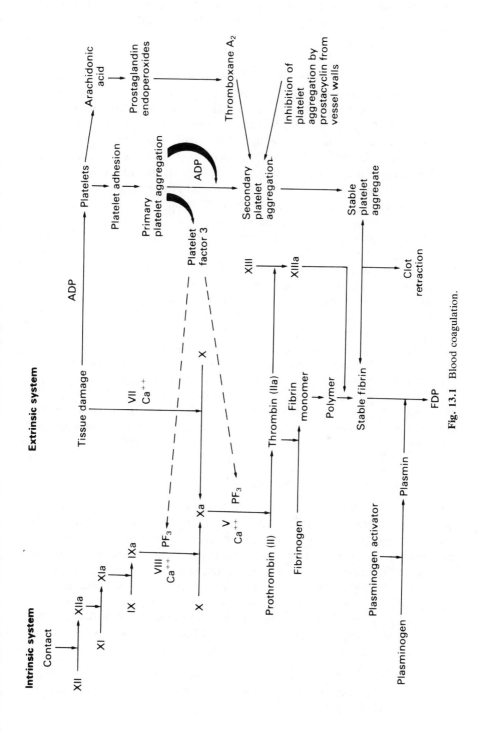

Fig. 13.1 Blood coagulation.

thrombus in an artery is another matter (p. 474), and the use of anticoagulant drugs to treat this type of thrombus is not entirely logical.

FIBRINOLYSIS

Under certain pathological circumstances the blood may coagulate extensively in the body (p. 477); it is possible that some fibrin is normally deposited on the vascular endothelium to repair deficiencies. The process is little understood, but there is in the body a mechanism to cause a lysis of clots, including those formed at the sites of injury. The balance is a delicate one.

Plasminogen is a β-globulin with a molecular weight of about 90 000, and plasmin is a trypsin-like endopeptidase. The latter attacks fibrin, and in excess can act on fibrinogen. The end products of fibrin digestion are shown in Fig. 13.1 as FDP (fibrin degradation products).

Plasminogen activators are present in many tissues, in the circulating blood and in urine. One cellular localization of plasminogen activator in man is the endothelium of veins and venules. There is an increase of activator in tissues undergoing repair (e.g. healing myocardial infarcts). Plasminogen activators used as therapeutic agents are referred to on p. 485.

Plasminogen inhibitors (which are not shown in Fig. 15.1) are usually non-specific proteinase inhibitors which are present in blood, tissues, urine and other body fluids. Blood plasma contains high concentrations of inhibitors which may be active against both plasminogen and plasmin. These include an α_1-trypsin inhibitor and an α_2 macroglobulin. Any tendency of the blood to clot is counterbalanced by the action of these inhibitors and by prostacyclin (p. 483) and antithrombin III (p. 476). At a point of injury the action of the activated clotting process is so great that the inhibitors are overwhelmed. Synthetic inhibitors are referred to on p. 486.

Vitamin K

Vitamin K is a fat-soluble vitamin which is required for the formation of coagulation factors II, VII, IX and X in the liver. Its precise function is uncertain, but it is not a constituent of any of these factors. After their polypeptide chains are formed, there seems to be a vitamin-K-dependent step in which a prosthetic group is attached to the polypeptide chain or an amino acid is modified. There are various forms of vitamin K, but those that occur in nature are K_1, which is widely distributed in plants, and K_2, which is synthesized by intestinal bacteria. Bile is needed for the absorption of the vitamin, and if the liver is diseased, the formation of clotting factors is impaired. The causes of vitamin K deficiency in man are:

1. A deficiency state in the newborn before the bowel is colonized by bacteria. The neonate thus becomes deficient in prothrombin and in factors VII, IX and X.

2. Rarely, a similar condition to that in (1) in those receiving long-term treatment with sulphonamides or antibiotics.
3. Obstructive jaundice, with consequent lack of bile salts in the small intestine.
4. Malabsorptive disorders, such as gluten enteropathy.

All these may lead to bleeding, and in liver failure the formation of coagulation factors from vitamin K may be impaired. The actions of orally administered anticoagulant drugs are discussed on p. 479.

Preparations

Phytomenadione (Vitamin K_1, Konakion) is fat-soluble and is available in 10 mg tablets or as a water-miscible solution in ampoules containing either 1 mg in 0.5 ml or 10 mg in 1 ml. There is also a water-soluble preparation, menadiol sodium diphosphate (Synkavit), which is available in 10 mg tablets or in ampoules containing either 10 mg in 1 ml or 100 mg in 2 ml.

Indications

The causes of hypoprothrombinaemia are indicated above and these are also indications for the use of members of the vitamin K group. These compounds are also used as antidotes to oral anticoagulants. In an emergency in the adult 10–25 mg of phytomenadione should be given i.v. The oral dose is 10–20 mg daily. If there is reason to fear hypoprothrombinaemia in the newborn, the mother can be given 5–10 mg of phytomenadione. In treating a newborn infant the dose should be 1 mg i.m., repeated at 8-hourly intervals if necessary. It is important to know that water-soluble analogues may cause haemolysis in the newborn, giving hyperbilirubinaemia. Moreover, a high dosage of the water-soluble analogue or of a fat-soluble preparation named menadione may lead to haemolysis in anyone suffering from glucose-6-phosphate dehydrogenase deficiency (p. 564). In high dosage, haemolysis may occur with these in normal adults. Accordingly, the safest preparation to use is phytomenadione.

If a patient has an overdose of a coumarin type of anticoagulant or of phenindione (p. 479), the treatment is to give phytomenadione 10–25 mg slowly i.v. The prothrombin level should show improvement in 3 hours, when, if this is not sufficient, a further dose may be given, but not more than 40 mg should be administered i.v. in 24 hours. Naturally, the anticoagulant should not be given during this time.

A fat-soluble analogue, acetomenaphthone (7 mg), is available for the treatment of chilblains in a tablet with 25 mg of nicotinic acid (Pernivit). Nicotinic acid causes vasodilatation, but it is not clear what beneficial action a vitamin K analogue can have.

Adverse Effects

If phytomenadione is given too rapidly i.v., there may be flushing, sweating, constriction in the chest, cyanosis and collapse.

THROMBOSIS

DEEP VENOUS THROMBOSIS

As has already been said, when blood vessels undergo trauma, a platelet plug is formed in capillaries, whereas in larger vessels coagulation occurs, with consequent formation of fibrin as a remedial event. In a deep vein in the leg, stasis may occur and a thrombus develop by activation of the coagulation mechanism, although just how this occurs is uncertain. There is some aggregation of platelets, but it seems to be formed fibrin that anchors the thrombus to the wall of the vein. Once it starts to form, it may rapidly extend even to 50 cm or more in length. Venous thrombosis sometimes occurs where there is lack of movement in the legs because the subject has been in bed for several days or has travelled a long distance by air. There is an increased tendency to venous thrombosis in pregnancy and after operations on the pelvis. Contraceptive pills, particularly those of high oestrogen content, may lead to thrombosis. The exact mechanism of this is unknown, although there may be some acceleration of the clotting of procoagulants in the intrinsic and extrinsic systems as well as reduction of antithrombin III levels (p. 476). It is reasonable to use heparin, oral anticoagulants or possibly streptokinase in deep venous thrombosis in order to stop any extension of the thrombus and to prevent clots from breaking off. These might cause pulmonary emboli and lead to pulmonary infarction.

ARTERIAL THROMBOSIS

It may be asked why thrombosis does not occur more frequently in both arteries and veins. Quite apart from the flow of the blood, it must be realized that normal endothelium is a rich source of plasminogen activator and that there are antithrombins in the blood stream. However, if the endothelium is damaged, platelets adhere to collagen and this stimulates them to aggregate, despite the fact that prostacyclin (p. 483) in normal vessel walls seems to prevent platelet aggregation. The actions of prostacyclin and its possible therapeutic uses are considered later (p. 484).

If some thrombin is formed, it, together with collagen, acts to release adenosine diphosphate (ADP) from intracellular storage granules in platelets. This causes platelet aggregation, provided calcium ions and fibrinogen are present. Platelets take up and store serotonin, adrenaline and noradrenaline from plasma, but release these from storage granules at the same time as ADP. These substances, in turn, also have an action as platelet aggregators.

When this release reaction happens, thromboxanes and prostaglandins are synthesized in platelets (p. 124), arachidonic acid being released from membrane phospholipids and acted upon by the cyclo-oxygenase enzyme to give prostaglandin endoperoxide (PGG_2). This is converted to PGH_2 and isomerized enzymatically or non-enzymatically to the stable substances PGE$_2$, PGF$_{2\alpha}$ and PGD$_2$, but enzymatically to the unstable prostacyclin and thromboxane A$_2$ (Fig. 13.2) Thromboxane A$_2$ is a powerful stimulator of platelet aggregation. Other granules release a factor involved in clotting (Fig. 13.1) and also fibrinogen, so the process is obviously complex.

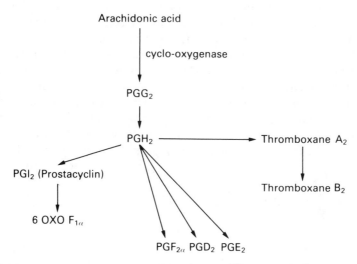

Fig. 13.2 Metabolism of arachidonic acid by the cyclo-oxygenase pathway (after Vane, 1982).

An arterial thrombus may commence to form by platelet adhesion and then aggregation at an atheromatous plaque. The structure of the established thrombus differs from that of a blood coagulum in that it has a 'white head', consisting mainly of aggregated platelets, and a 'red tail', composed of a fibrin mesh which entangles platelets, erythrocytes and leucocytes. None of the anticoagulants described in this chapter has any pronounced influence on this type of thrombus.

Arachidonic acid is eicosatetraenoic acid, and it has been suggested that the Eskimos have a low incidence of myocardial infarction because their diet contains the related substance eicosapentaenoic acid, which does not have platelet-aggregating properties. It is transformed by platelet microsomes into thromboxane A$_3$, which does not aggregate platelets, and in vessel walls it can be used to synthesize an anti-aggregating agent. This discovery may or may not be shown to be of clinical significance.

ANTICOAGULANTS

The anticoagulant drugs commonly used are heparin, which is given by injection and is quick-acting, and drugs of the coumarin or indanedione type, which are given by mouth and act more slowly.

Heparin

Heparin consists of a heterogeneous group of straight-chain anionic mucopolysaccharides of molecular weights that average 15 000. Commercial heparin consists of polymers of two repeating disaccharide units. These are D-glucosamine-L-iduronic acid and D-glucosamine-D-glucuronic acid. Heparin is strongly acidic because of its content of covalently linked sulphate and carboxylic groups. It occurs in mast cells and in liver and lung, but it does not seem to be free in the plasma and hence its natural function in the body is unknown. It has a strong electronegative charge and, perhaps for this reason, it forms in plasma a 'clearing factor' which acts as a lipase in hydrolysing the triglycerides of chylomicra, thus releasing free fatty acids. Whether this has any bearing on natural processes is unknown. Heparin does not cross the placenta in pharmacologically significant amounts and does not appear in maternal milk. However, it should not be used if there is a threatened abortion. Its half-life after a 'bolus' given i.v. is 1–2 hours. It is metabolized in the liver by the enzyme heparinase and a partially degraded form known as uroheparin appears in the urine.

Commercial preparations of heparin are extracted from bovine lungs by a process of digestion.

Actions

Heparin inhibits blood coagulation not only in the body, but also in vitro. In the blood there are proteins that are antithrombins and heparin requires antithrombin III as a cofactor. Antithrombin III is believed to be part of a natural defence mechanism of the body against thromboses and there are families whose members are deficient in it and have thrombotic incidents when they reach maturity. It is an α_2-globulin and a protease inhibitor that neutralizes the activated forms of factors IXa, Xa, XIa and XIIa and also the fibrin stabilizing factor (factor XIII). Antithrombin III also forms irreversible complexes with thrombin so that both these proteins are inactivated. A complex is formed between heparin, antithrombin III and the activated clotting factors. This increases the velocity of the activity of antithrombin III, particularly against factor Xa and against thrombin. However, high doses of heparin could deplete the body of antithrombin III and hence increase the thrombotic tendency. This appears to be more likely if the compound is given i.v. Platelet factor 4, the physiological role of which is unknown, can bind heparin locally and interfere with its action. Heparin may cause slight vasodilatation and hence have a beneficial effect in arterial embolism, including the giving of some pain relief.

Preparations

Heparin sodium can be given i.m. in a depot form, but causes painful haematomas. It is therefore administered i.v. either intermittently or by drip infusion. The potency of various preparations varies, and hence the dose is usually prescribed in units (10 000 units is approximately 100 mg). In the BP preparation, ampoules of 1 ml contain 12 500 units. There are 5 ml vials containing 1000, 5000, 25 000 or 125 000 units. Sodium heparin and calcium heparin prepared in lower dosage forms for s.c. use are available (e.g. Calciparine, Minihep, Minihep Calcium, Uniparin) in 0.2 ml vials containing 5000 units and are used to prevent deep-vein thrombosis or thrombo-embolic events. When heparin is used in high dosage, as in open-heart surgery or haemodialysis, it is important to remember that the usual commercial preparations contain preservatives such as parachlorometacresol and that it is advisable to obtain a special preparation without preservative, because of possible adverse effects. There are heparin preparations containing from 10 to 100 units per ml for clearing intravascular cannulae.

Indications

Heparin is used to depress clotting during the first 36 hours of anticoagulant therapy or may be employed as the sole anticoagulant for longer periods. It is used to prevent clotting in open-heart surgery and in haemodialysis. Low-dosage heparin has a significant effect in preventing postoperative deep venous thrombosis and pulmonary embolism. Self-administration has been used during pregnancy and the puerperium, being continued in those with a high risk of thrombosis for 5–6 weeks after delivery.

In the condition known as disseminated intravascular coagulation the entry into the circulation of a tissue thromboplastin or of a substance starting off the process of coagulation may have disastrous results for the patient. This can occur with massive haemolysis, and from amniotic fluid embolism, abruptio placentae, septicaemia, snake bite and a variety of other causes.

What may result then is shown in Fig. 13.3.

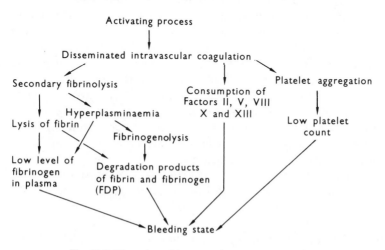

Fig. 13.3 Disseminated intravascular system coagulation.

Here many factors lead to generalized bleeding, and a clue to the occurrence of disseminated intravascular coagulation is a combination of a low platelet count with fragmented red cells, a very low plasma fibrinogen level and a high level of fibrin degradation products. The treatment is to remove the cause if possible, give heparin therapy to block further activation of the clotting system and, if fibrinogen levels are very low, give a preparation of fibrinogen or plasma and possibly platelet concentrates. This treatment, which can involve giving an anticoagulant to a patient who is bleeding, requires the careful attention of specialists, particularly as the condition may be confused with the even rarer one of primary fibrinolysis, which is *not* treated with heparin.

Heparin is administered intraperitoneally during peritoneal dialysis, but may lose its anticoagulant activity locally because of a loss of antithrombin III activity.

Administration
If given intermittently i.v., the dose for the adult is 5000–6000 units 4-hourly, or 10 000 units every 6 hours. Action is rapid, taking place in about 10 minutes. It is the practice in many centres to give heparin for the first 36 hours after a coronary thrombosis and to start anticoagulants by mouth at the same time. When heparin is given by infusion, a suitable dose is 20 000 units in 1 litre of 5% dextrose or 0.9% sodium chloride over a 12 hour period. This can be given for 36 hours until oral anticoagulants are effective, or in certain conditions it is given alone by a small continuous drip infusion pump. Sodium chloride is preferable to dextrose as a vehicle. It is given s.c. as a dose of 5000 units two hours before operation, followed by 5000 units 8-hourly for 7–14 days. If the patient is still confined to bed, this should be continued until ambulation is possible, provided this time is not excessive. The injection should be into the s.c. tissue of the lateral abdominal wall.

The whole blood clotting time measured by a standardized method can be used to control the dose of heparin given i.m. or i.v. and it should be maintained at two to three times the control value. When heparin is given continuously i.v., this should ideally be done every 2 hours, which makes this method of administration a difficult one to control optimally.

The British Committee for Standardization in Haematology advises daily monitoring, preferably at the same time each day. It suggests that the best control is achieved by using an actuated partial thromboplastin time technique, maintaining 1.5–2.5 times the control reading. An alternative is to measure the thrombin time, which can be very sensitive to low levels of heparin but is only linear over a narrow therapeutic range. The calcium thrombin time, which is a modification, is preferred by the Committee because it is linear over a wider range. This test is not prolonged by oral anticoagulant drugs.

With intermittent injections over 48 hours or less many clinicians do not undertake tests of coagulation.

Adverse Effects

An overdose may cause bleeding. Those who do not use heparin in the initial stage of treatment of coronary thrombosis claim that it may cause cardiac irregularities. Transient alopecia and diarrhoea have been reported. Urticaria, asthma and anaphylactic shock (p. 549) have occurred. No other drugs should be added to an infusion fluid containing heparin. Osteoporosis and spontaneous fractures can occur if treatment is continued for several months.

Toxicity.

Antidotes. Protamines are low molecular proteins found in the sperm of certain fish. Protamine sulphate in a 1 % solution is given slowly i.v. to combat heparin overdosage. For each 1 mg of heparin, 1 mg of protein sulphate is required, except that, if half an hour has passed, the dose should be reduced by half. An overdose of protamine sulphate may in itself inhibit blood clotting.

Coumarins and Indanediones

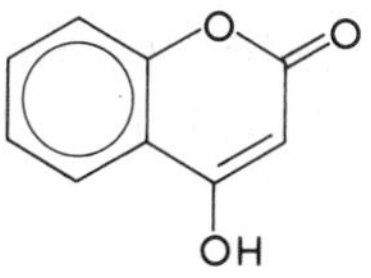

4–HYDROXYCOUMARIN 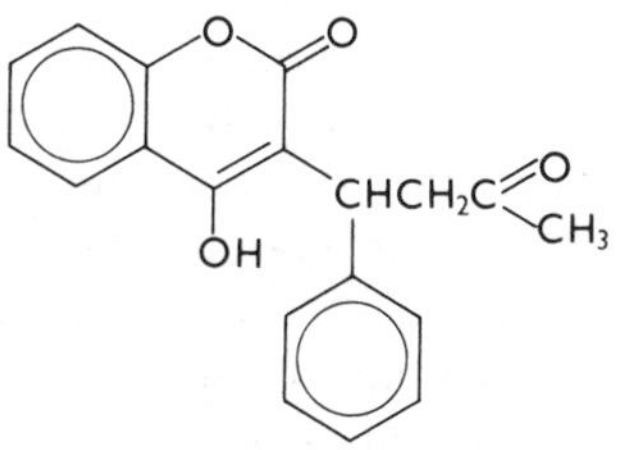   WARFARIN 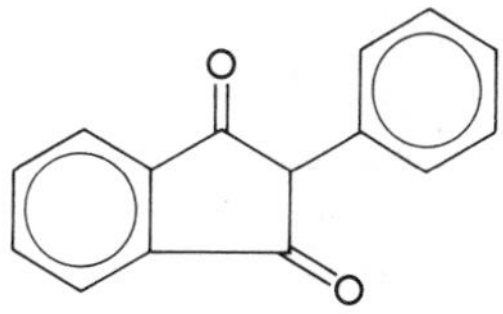   PHENINDIONE

Coumarins and indanediones, which are derivatives of 4-hydroxycoumarin and indane-1,3-dione respectively, are given by mouth. To have anti-coagulant activity, a coumarin requires to have a hydroxyl group in the 4 position and a carbon residue or hydrogen atom in the 3 position.

These substances are not active in vitro, but interfere with blood coagulation when taken by mouth. Quite a number have been produced and they differ mainly in their speed of onset and duration of action.

Mode of Action

Coumarins and indanediones prevent the formation of the vitamin-K-dependent factors II (prothrombin), VII, IX and X in the liver. Proteins are produced which are antigenically similar to these factors but do not have their normal procoagulant activities. The half-lives of these clotting factors in the circulation are said to be, respectively, 60, 6, 24 and 40 hours, so the initial anticoagulant effect is on factor VII, and of the four factors affected, the prothrombin content is the last to be depressed. The anticoagulant effect takes 36–48 hours to be significant and this is why heparin is so often used for initial action.

Pharmacokinetics

These substances are well absorbed when given by mouth and peak levels occur in 2–3 hours. They are largely bound to plasma protein and become concentrated in the liver, which is the main site of their action. The maximal anticoagulant effect of a single dose may be 1–2 days after administration, and various preparations differ in the duration of their action. Thus it may be 4–7 days before warfarin sodium ceases to have an effect. There are genetically determined differences between individuals in their ability to metabolize this group of drugs. The half-life of phenindione is 5–10 hours, and it is said that the half-life of warfarin may vary within the range of 15–70 hours. The drugs are detoxicated in the liver, but there is great variation between individuals in the rate of this process. Warfarin is metabolized in the liver and its metabolites excreted in the urine. The substance available commercially is a racemic mixture, the S form being more potent but more rapidly excreted. The principal metabolic product of S warfarin is 7-hydroxywarfarin, whereas that of R warfarin is a warfarin alcohol. The metabolism of phenindione also occurs in the liver. When phenindione is given, it causes a reddish discoloration of the urine, and this may be mistaken for haematuria. Enzymes that degrade the oral anticoagulants in the liver may be inhibited or enhanced by other drugs and it is of the greatest practical importance to be aware of this. The 'oral anticoagulants' cross the placenta and predispose to fetal and neonatal bleeding. They may also cause fetal abnormalities in early pregnancy. Many obstetricians prefer to use heparin in the first 12 weeks of pregnancy, but have found warfarin or phenindione to be safe between the 13th and 36th weeks. When a mother is breast feeding, heparin is to be preferred.

Preparations

There are many preparations, but it is probably sufficient to mention *warfarin tablets*, *BP*, which are available in strengths of 1, 3 and 5 mg, and *phenindione*, which can be obtained as tablets of 10, 25 and 50 mg. *Warfarin sodium* is also available for i.m. or i.v. use, but this is seldom employed.

Indications

Acute myocardial infarction. There are some who consider that the most important part of treatment is to get the patient sitting at his bedside within 3 days to prevent venous thrombosis through being in bed, but certainly some patients are too ill to leave bed at this early stage. It is a common policy to give oral anticoagulants for about 3 weeks to patients under 60 years, with a first infarct. When thrombosis occurs in an artery, including a coronary vessel, platelets are more likely to be of importance than is fibrin (p. 470), and oral anticoagulants have little effect on platelets. However, deep vein thrombosis or mural thrombosis may be prevented.

Arterial thrombosis. The value of anticoagulants in this condition is uncertain. If surgery is not being carried out, a heparin drip may be of more value than oral anticoagulants.

Deep venous thrombosis and pulmonary embolism. These conditions are more common than is generally realized and it has been shown by sophisticated tests that about one-third of those patients kept in bed after surgical operation develop venous thrombosis within a few days. The same is said to be true in patients with myocardial infarction, and in both groups the danger is greater in older persons. Beneficial effects from oral anticoagulants are more likely in venous thrombosis than when the blockage occurs in an artery, and the danger of pulmonary embolism is considerable. Some would give either low-dosage heparin (p. 477) or oral anticoagulants to all older persons who are immobilized by operation unless there is some contraindication.

Superficial venous thrombosis. This does not usually require anticoagulant therapy.

Cerebrovascular disease. If there is thrombosis of intracranial venous sinuses (a rare condition), anticoagulants may be used unless there is evidence of haemorrhagic infarction of the brain. It is sometimes difficult to differentiate between cerebral arterial thrombosis or embolism, on the one hand, and cerebral haemorrhage, on the other, and hence anticoagulants should not usually be given in such conditions. Occasionally there are repeated transient ischaemic attacks, and there is some evidence that anticoagulants give benefit, particularly if it is the vertebrobasilar system that is affected. They may be withdrawn cautiously after a year, but continued again if another attack ensues.

Atrial fibrillation. Patients with atrial fibrillation who have had pulmonary or systemic embolism may benefit from long-term anticoagulant therapy.

Cardiac surgery. When artificial heart valves have been inserted, anticoagulants reduce the incidence of thromboembolism.

Administration
A loading dose is given initially and this may be at the same time as the commencement of heparin therapy. The initial dose of warfarin sodium is 30–50 mg. When phenindione is used, the corresponding dose is 200–300 mg. On the second day 10 mg of warfarin or 100 mg of phenindione may be administered, and thereafter the daily dose, usually 5–12 mg of the former or 25–100 mg of the latter, is decided from day to day by a suitable test of blood clotting.

Since a patient may bleed and yet have a normal coagulation time by the ordinary method of measurement, it is necessary to use more sophisticated methods. The one most commonly employed is the so-called 'one-stage prothrombin time' (see below), which is really a 'brain thromboplastin time', measuring the deficiency of factors II, V, VII and X. Heparin interferes with this test. One problem is that the oral anticoagulants cause depression of factors II, VII, IX and X, so this method of assay does not show factor IX depression. Another difficulty is that the results of the test vary between different laboratories and that they can be expressed as prothrombin time, index or ratio, or can be based on a graph drawn from dilutions of normal plasma. Although a patient sometimes bleeds from factor IX deficiency because the assay does not show this up, in many centres the 'one-stage prothrombin time' is used, the ratio of the prothrombin time of the patient's plasma to the prothrombin time of the control plasma being kept at 2.0–2.5. Alternatively, control can be by the 'prothrombin and proconvertin method', which does not show factor V deficiency, or by the 'Thrombotest', which is available commercially in a standardized form. This meaures the deficiencies produced by oral anticoagulants, including that of factor IX. The therapeutic range to be aimed at is 8–15%. Capillary or venous blood can be used with this test.

Adverse Effects

Bleeding may occur from an overdose or for the reasons given above. Other adverse reactions have been reported, more commonly after phenindione than following warfarin administration. These include skin rashes, blood dyscrasias, jaundice, pyrexia, nausea and vomiting. Nephrosis is said to occur on occasion after phenindione administration. Warfarin and other oral anticoagulants are contraindicated during pregnancy and labour, and in lactating women it may affect prothrombin levels in breast-fed babies.

Toxicity.

Antidotes. Phytomenadione (p. 473) may be used as an antidote.

Interactions

Very many interactions have been suggested, but there is doubt about the practical significance of some. Nevertheless, the likelihood of interactions must be taken very seriously, since death may occur from bleeding after an unfortunate combination of therapeutic agents. It is not possible to construct a complete list, but there is evidence for the following:

Increased Sensitivity to Oral Anticoagulants

1. Displacement of anticoagulant from its binding to plasma protein.
   Phenylbutazone and numerous non-steroidal anti-inflammatory agents
   Sulphonamides, co-trimoxazole
   Oral anti-diabetic agents
   Ethacrynic acid
   Mefenamic acid

Nalidixic acid

Aspirin and numerous non-steroidal anti-inflammatory agents may also interfere with platelet function (p. 124) and prolong the bleeding time.

2. Inhibition of microsomal enzymes or competition for them.
   Alcohol
   Disulfiram
   Chloramphenicol
3. Depression of the formation of factors II, VII, IX and X (i.e. vitamin K-dependent factors) in the liver.
   Quinine, quinidine, cincophen
   Thyroxine
4. Causation of hepatic dysfunction.
   Anabolic steroids
5. Reduction of vitamin K production by intestinal bacteria.
   Tetracyclines
6. Reduction of vitamin K absorption.
   Liquid paraffin
7. Uncertain
   Cimetidine causes increased sensitivity to warfarin
   Clofibrate probably causes reduced platelet function and a more rapid turnover of the vitamin-K-dependent clotting factors.
8. Renal damage.
9. Acute illness, weight loss or decreased intake of vitamin K.

It should be noted that there will be increased sensitivity to oral anticoagulants if there is hepatic dysfunction or if the patient has vitamin K deficiency from other causes. *Most importantly*, the stopping of drugs that induce hepatic microsomal enzymes (e.g. barbiturates) without a reduction in the dosage of the warfarin or phenindione may cause serious bleeding. Heparin administration increases the bleeding tendency if it is given with an oral anticoagulant.

Decreased Sensitivity to Oral Anticoagulants

1. Genetic variation. Hereditary resistance may be a dominant trait.
2. Induction of hepatic microsomal enzymes by a number of drugs, including:
   Barbiturates
   Phenytoin
   Dichloralphenazone
   Ethchlorvynol
   Glutethimide
   Halperidol
   Griseofulvin
   Mercaptopurine
   Rifampicin
   It is believed that nitrazepam, diazepam and flurazepam do not have this effect.
3. Reduction of antithrombin III level and a possible rise in the levels of factor VII, IX or X.
   Oral contraceptives
   Oestrogens
4. Increased excretion in the faeces.
   Cholestyramine

Stopping the administration of a drug that *increases* sensitivity will, of course, lead to a decrease in sensitivity to anticoagulants.

Prostacyclin (Epoprostenol)

Prostacyclin (PGI$_2$; Flolan) is formed enzymatically from the prostaglandin endoperoxide (PGH$_2$) by blood vessel microsomes or fresh vascular tissue. It is the main product of arachidonic acid (p. 106) in the walls of arteries and veins, and it seems that the vessel wall can also form prostacyclin from prostaglandin endoperoxides released by platelets. It may be regarded as a form of natural anticoagulant. It has been given the approved name epoprostenol. In contrast to thromboxane A_2 (p. 124), prostacyclin is the most potent known inhibitor of platelet aggregation, being about a thousand times more active in this respect than adenosine. In experimental work it has been shown to inhibit thrombus formation and it is known that its ability to prevent platelet aggregation is by stimulation of adenylate cyclase. This leads to an increase in cyclic AMP concentration in the platelets. Prostacyclin has a short half-life of 2–3 minutes, but possibly it is more stable in plasma. Unlike certain other prostaglandins, it is not inactivated by passing through the pulmonary circulation. In addition to its effects on platelets, it is a vasodilator.

Prostacyclin and thromboxane A_2 can be thought of as a brake and an accelerator in platelet aggregation, and it may be that an unexplained tendency to thrombosis in certain conditions may be due to an imbalance of the two factors.

Reference has already been made (p. 124) to the fact that aspirin and certain non-steroidal anti-inflammatory agents can prevent the production of either thromboxane A_2 or prostacyclin, depending on the concentration of the drug in the blood. This is achieved by the inhibition of cyclo-oxygenase in platelets and remains throughout their lifespan. It was shown in one study that a single dose of 300 mg of aspirin would inhibit the production of both prostacyclin and thromboxane A_2, whereas a single dose of 40 mg inhibited only thromboxane A_2 synthesis. Accordingly, a dose of aspirin as low as this may be of value in preventing venous thrombosis. However, aspirin only inhibits one pathway of platelet aggregation and does not affect ADP- or thrombin-induced aggregation (p. 474).

Prostacyclin generation by atherosclerotic arterial tissue is lower than that by normal tissue and experimentation has suggested that low-density lipoproteins inhibit prostacyclin synthesis and high-density lipoproteins stimulate it.

The possible therapeutic applications of this basic knowledge include the development of one or other of the following:

1. Prostacyclin analogues infused i.v. Unfortunately, these cause headache, nausea and stomach cramps and lower the diastolic blood pressure and peripheral resistance.
2. Thromboxane synthetase inhibitors. One, known at present as UK-37, 248-01, has been tried in volunteers, with slow but transient rises in the bleeding time but no change in the clotting time.
3. Selective antagonists of thromboxane. The practical use of these in man has yet to be established. They are competitive antagonists and around an athenomatous plaque they will be overcome by an excess of thromboxane.

Possible uses of chemically synthesized epoprostenol sodium (or an alternative prostacyclin analogue when marketed) include the preservation of platelets during cardiopulmonary bypass, renal dialysis and charcoal haemoperfusion. Prostacyclin prevents activation of platelets by the artificial surfaces and reduces platelet losses in the machines. It may be, too, that prostacyclin will be of use in syndromes likely to be associated with a deficiency of endogenous prostacyclin (haemolytic uraemic syndrome and thrombotic thrombocytopenic purpura). There may be a place for prostacyclin analogues in the prevention of arterial thrombosis in atheroma.

Platelet Aggregation Inhibitors

The use of aspirin, other non-steroidal anti-inflammatory agents and sulphinpyrazone is referred to on pp. 124 and 125. Dipyridamole (Persantin) inhibits phosphodiesterase and stimulates adenyl cyclase formation. It is said to inhibit the formation of thromboxane A_2. Dipyridamole is available in 100 mg tablets and the recommended adult dose is 300–600 mg daily in divided doses. It has been used, frequently together with aspirin, for transient ischaemic attacks, in cardiac surgery, for deep venous thrombosis and to prevent secondary myocardial infarction. One difficulty is that the dose of aspirin given has usually been sufficiently high to interfere with prostacyclin formation, and further studies are needed using aspirin in smaller quantities.

Various Related Therapeutic Agents

Ancrod

Ancrod (Arvin) is derived from the venom of *Agkistrodon rhodostoma*, the Malayan pit viper. It has a coagulant effect on fibrinogen similar to that of thrombin. Thrombin clots fibrinogen by splitting fibrinopeptides A and B, but this preparation releases only fibrinopeptide A. Hence, a fibrin is formed that is much more susceptible to proteolysis. Ancrod can be used as an anticoagulant that acts in about 4–6 hours. It is given i.v. and monitored by measuring the fibrinogen level. This ingenious use of the substance to promote controlled defibrination so that the blood is incoagulable without either obvious clotting or bleeding is still under trial.

Streptokinase

Streptokinase (Kabikinase, Streptase) is so called because it is derived from certain strains of streptococci, and it acts as a plasminogen activator (Fig. 13.1), possibly affecting plasminogen absorbed on to fibrin. Accordingly, fibrinolysis occurs. It is not employed more because of the likelihood of reactions such as pyrexia, problems of haemorrhage, the necessity for strict laboratory control of dosage and the cost of the product. It can be used in deep venous thrombosis, pulmonary embolism or central retinal vein thrombosis. In deep venous thrombosis partial or complete lysis of thrombi up to 3 days old can be anticipated in two-thirds of patients given adequate dosage. It has also been employed in treating the recurrence of thrombosis after vascular surgery and in thrombosis of haemodialysis shunts. It is being used in myocardial infarction, by injection into coronary arteries, but only experienced workers should attempt to use this technique.

Streptokinase is administered slowly by i.v. infusion after an initial dose given in 30 minutes. The initial injection has to be sufficient to neutralize antibodies to the drug in the circulation, and a streptokinase resistance test can be done. The dosage varies from individual to individual, but is of the order of 500 000 units for a loading dose (covered by 100 mg of hydrocortisone i.v. because of possible reactions), followed by an infusion of 100 000 units hourly, preferably using an infusion pump. In deep vein thrombosis this may be continued for 5 days. The test most commonly used for the control of therapy is the thrombin time test, which is maintained at two to four times the normal value.

Streptokinase should not be used unless the manufacturer's literature is at hand, and, in order to be able to treat haemorrhage if it occurs, aminocaproic acid should be available for i.v. infusion (20–50 ml of a 10% solution) or tranexamic acid (10 mg/kg body weight). Concurrent administration of an anticoagulant or a drug that interferes with platelet aggregation should be avoided.

Urokinase is a physiological substance related to streptokinase that can be isolated from human urine. The purified product is very expensive.

Aminocaproic acid

Aminocaproic acid (Epsikapron) is a monoamino carboxylic acid which inhibits competitively the activation of plasminogen to plasmin. It can be given as an i.v. infusion or injection, or by mouth as an effervescent powder or a syrup. In the rare condition of *primary* fibrinolysis (p. 478), where, for example, plasminogen activator may be released at a site of operation, its use is indicated. However, in disseminated intravascular coagulation (p. 477), *secondary* fibrinolysis is a dangerous protection against thrombosis, and aminocaproic acid will potentiate this tendency. In some such cases, however, it is used cautiously after the patient is well heparinized.

Aminocaproic acid is used to reverse the action of streptokinase, as it renders the plasminogen molecule incapable of interacting with the latter. There are conditions of local fibrinolysis which can be treated with aminocaproic acid and it is sometimes used in haemophilia to control bleeding.

Tranexamic acid

Tranexamic acid (4-aminomethylcyclohexane carboxylic acid; Cyklokapron) acts in a similar way to aminocaproic acid and the indications for its use are the same. It can be administered as an i.v. infusion or injection, can be used topically as a bladder rinse or on a tampon inserted into a dental alveolus, and is available in tablet form. There is the same danger of using it in disseminated intravascular coagulation as with aminocaproic acid.

Aprotinin

Aprotinin (Trasylol) is a polypeptide proteinase inhibitor that can inhibit streptokinase and has also been used in acute pancreatitis, since it has an antitrypsin effect. Release of trypsins into the blood stream may be a serious consequence of acute pancreatitis. Aprotinin is also used for hyperfibrinolytic haemorrhage. Each 5 ml ampoule contains 100 000 kallikrein inactivator units.

Anabolic steroids

Fibrinolysis can be stimulated by certain anabolic steroids. One such compound is the 17α-alkyl anabolic steroid, stanozolol (Stromba). It increases the levels of plasminogen, augments plasminogen activity by a vascular activator and at the same time reduces plasmin inhibitors and fibrinogen levels. It is used in the control of the vascular symptoms of cutaneous vasculitis, Raynaud's phenomena in patients with scleroderma, in the rare Behçet's disease and perhaps in patients with genetically determined antithrombin III deficiency. The dose is 5 mg twice daily. Another method of enhancing fibrinolysis is with ethyloestrenol, an anabolic steroid not to be confused with ethinyloestradiol (p. 420).

Clofibrate

Clofibrate (Atromid-S), a branched-chain fatty acid, may prolong blood coagulation time and necessitate a reduction in the dose of oral anticoagulants if given to a patient receiving them. Its main effect, however, is to reduce very low density lipoproteins. It has been disappointing in trials to reduce the incidence of coronary thrombosis and may lead to the development of gallstones, so should not be used in patients with gallbladder disease. There are now considered to be five types of hyperlipidaemia in man. Clofibrate is effective in lowering the plasma triglyceride level in type III, and it has an effect in type IV, although strict diet therapy is probably better. It is not of value in type I, and is of limited value in type IIb. It may be of value in the treatment of xanthomata if they are associated with hyperlipoproteinaemia. Some workers think that it is of use in treating exudative diabetic retinopathy. It is given by mouth in a dose of 20–30 mg/kg body weight daily in 2 or 3 divided doses. Clofibrate is available in capsules containing 500 mg.

Probucol

Probucol (Lurselle) is available in 250 mg tablets for hypercholesterolaemia.

Cholestyramine resin

Cholestyramine resin (Questran) is an anion exchange resin which is given by mouth and binds bile acids in the gut. These are necessary for cholesterol absorption. It is highly effective in type II hyperlipoproteinaemias (high plasma cholesterol with normal or slightly elevated triglycerides), but is contraindicated in types III, IV and V, as in them it may raise triglyceride levels. It may relieve diarrhoea associated with ileal resection, Crohn's disease, vagotomy and diabetic vagal neuropathy. It may relieve pruritus in partial (not complete) biliary obstruction, and can be of value in radiation-induced diarrhoea. It may interfere with the normal absorption of fat or fat-soluble vitamins. Each sachet contains the equivalent of 4 g of anhydrous cholestyramine, and 3–6 sachets daily may be needed to reduce cholesterol levels.

Desmopressin

Desmopressin (DDAVP) is desamino-cys-1-8-D-arginine vasopressin. Given i.v., it causes a marked and sustained increase in factor VIII levels in patients with mild haemophilia. The reason for this is uncertain, but the preparation can be used to enable minor surgery to be carried out in patients with haemophilia or von Willebrand's disease without the use of factor VIII concentrate. Care has to be taken to avoid water intoxication, and tranexamic acid should be available because of possible enhancement of fibrinolysis.

FURTHER READING

Aspenström G. and other members of an international group (1970) Collaborative analysis of long-term anticoagulant administration after acute myocardial infarction. *Lancet*, i: 203.

Barrowcliffe T. W., Johnson E. A. & Thomas D. (1978) Antithrombin III and heparin. *Br. med. Bull.*, 34: 143.

Beitz J. & Förster W. (1980) Influence of human low density and high density lipoprotein cholesterol on the *in vitro* prostaglandin I_2 synthetase activity. *Biochem. Biophys. Acta*, 620: 352.

Belch J., McKay A., McArdle B., Leiberman P., Pollock J. G., Lowe G. D. O., Forbes C. D. & Prentice C. R. M. (1983) Epoprostenol (prostacyclin) and severe arterial disease. *Lancet*, i: 315.

Belch J., Newman P., Drury J. K., McKenzie F., Capell H., Leiberman P., Forbes C. D. & Prentice C. R. M. (1983) Intermittent epoprostenol (prostacyclin) infusion in patients with Raynaud's syndrome. *Lancet*, i: 313.

Editorial (1971) Anticoagulant interactions. *Br. med. J.*, 4: 128.

Editorial (1981) Prostacyclin in therapeutics. *Lancet*, i: 643.

Editorial (1983) Dazoxiben *Lancet*, i: 627.

European Cooperative Study Group for Streptokinase Treatment of Myocardial Infarction (1979) Streptokinase in acute myocardial infarction. *New Engl. J. Med.*, 301: 797.

Feinstein D. I. (1982) Diagnosis and management of disseminated intravascular coagulation: the role of heparin therapy. *Blood*, 60: 284.

Forbes C. D., Barr R. D., Reid G., Thomson C., Prentice C. R. M., McNicol G. P. & Douglas A. S. (1972) Tranexamic acid in control of haemorrhage after dental extraction in haemophilia and Christmas disease. *Br. med. J.*, ii: 311.

Furman K. I., Comferts E. D. & Hockley J. (1978) Activity of intraperitoneal heparin during peritoneal dialysis. *Clin. Nephrol.*, 9: 15.

Gimson A. E. S., Hughes R. D., Mellon P. J., Woods H. F., Langley P. G., Canalese J., Williams R. & Weston M. J. (1980) Prostacyclin to prevent platelet activation during charcoal haemoperfusion in fulminant hepatic failure. *Lancet*, i: 173.

Hanley S. P., Bevan J., Cockbill S. R. & Heptinstall S. (1981) Differential inhibition by low dose aspirin of human venous prostacyclin synthesis and platelet thromboxane synthesis. *Lancet*, i: 969.

Kakkar V. V., Bentley P. G., Scully M. F., MacGregor I. R., Jones N. A. G. & Webb P. J. (1980) Antithrombin III and heparin. *Lancet*, i: 103.

Kakkar V. V., Flac C., Howe C. T., O'Shea M. & Flute P. T. (1969) Treatment of deep vein thrombosis. A trial of heparin, streptokinase and arvin. *Br. med. J.*, i: 806, 810.

Kakkar V. V., Nicolaides A. N., Field E. S., Flute P. T., Wessler S. & Yin E. T. (1971) Low doses of heparin in prevention of deep-vein thrombosis. *Lancet*, ii: 669.

Kiil J., Kiil J., Axelsen F. & Anderson D. (1978) Prophylaxis against postoperative pulmonary embolism and deep-vein thrombosis by low-dose heparin. *Lancet*, i: 1115.

Mackie M., Bennett B., Ogston D. & Douglas A. S. (1978) Familial thrombosis: inherited deficiency of antithrombin III. *Br. med. J.*, i: 136.

Moncada S. & Vane J. R. (1981) Prostacyclin and blood coagulation. *Drugs*, 21: 430.

Nilsson I. M. (1974) *Haemorrhagic and Thrombotic Diseases*. London, New York, Sydney, Toronto: Wiley.

Pitney W. R. (1971) Disseminated intravascular coagulation. *Semin. Hematol.*, 8: 65.

Ritter J. M., Barrow S. E., Blair I. A. & Pollery C. T. (1983) Release of prostacyclin in vivo and its role in man. *Lancet*, i: 317.

Robertson B. R., Nilsson I. M., Nylander G. & Olow B. (1967) Effect of streptokinase and heparin on patients with deep venous thromboses. A coded examination. *Acta chir. Scand.*, 133; 205.

Standing Advisory Committee for Haematology of the Royal College of Pathologists (1982) Drug interaction with coumarin derivative anticoagulants. *Br. med. J.*, 285: 274.

Tyler H. M., Saxton C. A. P. D. & Parry M. J. (1981) Administration to man of UK-37, 248-01, a selective inhibitor of thromboxane synthetase. *Lancet*, i: 629.

Vane J. R. (1982) *Prostacyclin in Health and Disease*. Publication No. 58, Royal College of Physicians, 9 Queen Street, Edinburgh, EH2 1JQ.

Walker I. D. (1981) Anabolic steroid therapy in arterial disease: a review. *Scot. med. J.*, S85.

14   Chemotherapy of Malignant Disease

J. G. McVie

Cancer medicine is a fast-expanding speciality owing to the increasing scope and complexity of cytotoxic drugs. Ten years ago only the leukaemias and lymphoproliferative tumours, along with rare solid tumours such as choriocarcinoma, were within the scope of drug therapy. Over the past decade a host of tumour types in adults and children have been shown to be chemosensitive. Several new drugs have been developed which are active, and new combinations of drugs have evolved. The physician planning cancer care is now much more aware of the pharmacokinetics of the drugs he uses and also of their possible interactions with one another and with other cancer treatments such as radiation. Other important considerations are the nutritional status of the patient, because it affects his tolerance to treatment, and his immune status, since it is so frequently unbalanced by the malignant tissue or the treatment. Of more profound significance, however, has been the change in emphasis of the role of chemotherapy in conjunction with local treatments for cancer, such as radiation and surgery. The emergence of the concept of adjuvant chemotherapy for micrometastatic disease is as exciting as it is challenging. Few patients with breast cancer or small-cell carcinoma of the lung have truly localized disease. This is clear from the patterns of relapse after adequate treatment directed to the locally obvious disease. Blind treatment for dormant nests of metastatic cells is therefore under trial not only in those conditions, but also in a variety of other solid tumours. Adjuvant chemotherapy is already clearly of value in several tumours of children, such as Wilms' tumour and Ewing's tumour, and in a variety of sarcomas, including osteosarcoma and lymphoma. In adults one of the major thrusts has been in the area of 'early' breast cancer. Two controlled clinical trials have clearly shown the value of postoperative chemotherapy in delaying recurrence and improving survival in premenopausal women. In postmenopausal women using the same drug protocols, delay in recurrence has been observed, but no statistically significant improvement in survival has as yet accrued. Further trials in this and other tumours involve not only the use of cytotoxic drugs, but also the use of other agents such as hormones.

Treatment of acute lymphatic leukaemia in children has provided the pointer to more successful chemotherapy in other tumour types. For instance, certain drugs, such as vincristine, prednisolone and colaspase, have been found to be of clear value in inducing remission. These drugs, however, are less useful in the maintenance of such remissions, and other drugs, such as methotrexate, mercaptopurine and cyclophosphamide, have been brought into protocols on a cyclical basis as consolidation manoeuvres.

Early long-term successes in the treatment of leukaemia were marred by the late development of central nervous system involvement and this brought home the problem of distribution of the available drugs to all leukaemic cells. It was obvious that none of the agents used reached cells in the cerebrospinal fluid, so the intrathecal route of administration was then successfully exploited. Survival for 5 years after the diagnosis of acute leukaemia is now a startling reality.

Studies of animal leukaemia have shown that the transplantation of a single leukaemic cell into a suitable recipient will result in the death of the animal from leukaemia at a fairly constant time after the transplant. This points to the main target that clinicians have to hit if they are to find a true cure for malignant disease, viz. the eradication of every tumour cell. To accomplish this without inflicting damage to the normal host tissues is not an easy matter, since the therapeutic index of most antimitotic drugs is low. As they mainly attack cells in division, normal tissue, such as marrow, gut, hair follicle, ovary and testis, may be damaged by circulating drug almost to the same degree as the tumour cells. The main limiting toxicity is marrow suppression, although the development of ancillary aids to treatment, such as platelet, red and white cell transfusion products, bone marrow infusion and sterile laminar flow rooms, have improved the support of affected patients.

Drugs that have side-effects on different cell systems have been used in combination so that additive toxicity may be avoided. Choice of agents has

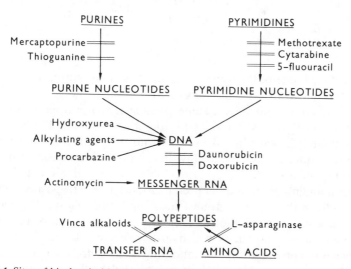

Fig. 14.1 Sites of biochemical inhibition of protein synthesis by some agents used to treat malignancy.

also been facilitated by an understanding of the biochemical mechanism of their action. Certain drugs inhibit DNA synthesis alone (Figure 14.1) and thus only injure actively dividing cells, while others act irrespective of the tumour cell cycle and may, indeed, kill resting cells. The latter make up a varying percentage of a given malignancy. Generally, the number rises in advanced disease and is notably lower in tumours known to be particularly sensitive to chemotherapy, such as Burkitt's lymphoma or choriocarcinoma.

Tumour resistance to antimitotic drugs occurs almost as readily as resistance to antibiotics occurs with certain bacteria. High doses of a single agent may lessen the emergence of resistance but the mechanisms of resistance are widely variable and often extremely subtle. Some cells are able to block the transfer of a drug over their membranes, whereas others increase the concentrations of enzymes that inactivate the drug, or else lessen the availability of activating enzymes. It is also possible for damaged cell chromosomes to be repaired by appropriate deletion. Generally, malignant cells are not as efficient at repairing drug-induced defects as are normal cells. A rest period is therefore included in anticancer protocols, so that haemopoietic tissue, for example, may recover while the tumour that is being treated has less potential to do so.

ALKYLATING AGENTS

Mustine Hydrochloride

$$CH_3\ N\underset{CH_2\ CH_2\ Cl}{\overset{CH_2\ CH_2\ Cl}{\diagdown}} \bullet HCl$$

MUSTINE HYDROCHLORIDE

In World War I, one of the weapons used was sulphur mustard, a gas which burned the body, affected the lungs and bone marrow and pierced both clothing and equipment. It was some years later that nitrogen mustard, or mustine hydrochloride was developed from it and was found to be useful in the treatment of leukaemia. Like most cytotoxic agents, it is dangerous and difficult to administer therapeutically. In solution it is an unstable molecule which splits off a halide ion and goes on to form a highly reactive cyclic ethyleneimonium compound. The end product is electropositive and will react rapidly with negative groups, including thiol, phosphate, hydroxyl, amino, carboxyl, and imidazoles. Curiously, administration of ready-made ethyleneimonium compounds which are widely employed in the textile industry has not provided any substance that is more efficacious than mustine in its antineoplastic properties. Only one, triethylene thiophosphoramide, is used therapeutically, particularly in the treatment of malignant effusions.

Mode of Action

Mustine serves as a model for all the alkylating agents, the remainder differing marginally in their mechanism of alkylation. The main chemical reaction is the formation of a covalent bond between a side-limb of the drug and the 7-nitrogen group of guanine. As most alkylating agents have two side-chains, adjacent guanine groupings may be linked and, indeed, fixed through the intermediate drug. If the aforementioned guanines are in parallel strands of the DNA helix, division of the helix, a prerequisite of cell mitosis, is hindered. If the strands are split at all, they may reunite in an imperfect and impotent form, encouraging disorganization of the chromosomal material and, hence, cell death. This mechanism of action of mustine and its derivatives is called 'cross-linking of DNA'.

The alkylation reaction is not limited to biguanine links, but may occur between guanine of DNA and that of another protein, or between two adjacent proteins. Guanine has also been found to associate with other bases — for instance, thymine. The result of this alliance is disruption and miscoding of base pairs essential to protein synthesis. Whereas only 20% of the molecules of mustine form double bonds (the remainder alkylate only a single side-chain), drugs that are totally monofunctional are relatively ineffective cell poisons. This emphasizes the importance of the double-edged interaction and explains the prolonged search for less toxic derivatives modelled on the structure of mustine.

The above concepts apply to some extent in all cell systems exposed to alkylating agents, in that indiscriminate damage occurs on administration to a patient. As the prime effect is on dividing cells, normal tissues which divide as fast as or faster than tumour cells may be injured, and, hence, dosage is limited by side-effects as life-threatening as the presence of the tumour itself. Bone marrow hypoplasia may be fatal because of either agranulocytosis and overwhelming infection or thrombocytopenia and catastrophic bleeding.

Pharmacokinetics

Mustine hydrochloride must be given i.v., since it causes tissue necrosis on direct contact. It is rapidly bound to the tissues and altered as described above. Instillation into the pleural and peritoneal cavities is possible, but care must be taken that the drug is, in fact, being injected into the serous cavity and not through it. If a large amount of fluid is present in the cavity, the drug may be diluted too much to be effective. On the other hand, if a high concentration is achieved, considerable pain may be provoked at the injection site. Little or no absorption of drug takes place from such serous cavities, so that distant side-effects such as bone marrow suppression are not a problem.

Preparations

Mustine hydrochloride. 10 mg ampoules are marketed to be dissolved in 10 ml saline or water immediately prior to injection.

Indications

The outstanding contribution that mustine has made is in the treatment of advanced Hodgkin's disease, a tumour of lymphoid tissue. Used alone, it induces complete remission in 13% of patients, but, in association with three other drugs given in a cyclical intermittent programme, the remission rate leaps to 80%. Injections of mustine and vinblastine (p. 509) are given twice in the first fortnight of a cycle. For those two weeks prednisolone (p. 514) and procarbazine (p. 514) are given daily by mouth. Two weeks' rest from all drugs follows, and the cycle is then repeated. During that respite the patient's bone marrow will usually recover, so the drugs of the next cycle do not have a cumulative toxicity.

I.v. mustine or cyclophosphamide in high dosage may be used in superior mediastinal compression due to lung cancer or lymphoma. This would normally be followed by radiotherapy or further appropriate chemotherapy.

Administration

The recommended technique of injection is directly into the tubing of an i.v. giving set. Physiological saline or dextrose injection, BP, 5% should be allowed to run through the set as fast as the cannula permits. Even with great care, some extravasation of drug may happen from time to time, leading to pain at that site. Slow infusion of mustine diluted in 500 ml of physiological saline leads to phlebitis at the relevant area and occlusion of the vein. Mustine can be given intra-arterially, as rapid local tissue fixation occurs and very little drug reaches distant sites. Regional perfusion is a technique that extends the use of intra-arterial injection, since it employs temporary bypass of the affected section of the circulation. This cuts down even further the risk of toxicity to tissues out of the region perfused by the drug. Mustine may be applied topically to skin lesions, but is of doubtful value except perhaps to improve cosmetic appearances in a disfiguring condition such as mycosis fungoides.

Control of Dosage

As with most cytotoxic agents, the dose of mustine is given on a basis of either body weight or surface area. The dose depends critically on the depression of blood counts produced as a side-effect. Further, as the drug is most often used in combination with others, some of which are also injurious to bone marrow, attention must be paid to the possibility of additive toxicity and quantities administered lowered accordingly. An accepted weekly dose of mustine in such a combination is 0.1 mg/kg body weight, whereas if it is used alone, 0.4 mg/kg body weight is tolerable.

Adverse Effects

A legion of toxic effects has been the main stimulus in the search for better-tolerated alkylating agents. As well as the damage wrought at the site of injection, nausea and vomiting are an almost constant accompaniment of mustine. A few patients are improved by prophylactic antiemetics, but the majority will feel miserable for at least 8 hours following therapy. The main haemopoietic toxicity is the development of leucopenia and thrombocytopenia. Recovery commences around 2–3 weeks after exposure to the drug.

Temporary sterility and interference with the ovulatory cycle is usual, although permanent amenorrhea is only occasional. High doses of mustine have produced convulsions in some patients. As hyperuricaemia may follow the rapid breakdown of dying tumour cells, allopurinol may be required to avert the development of gout. Skin rashes and diarrhoea are rare side-effects.

Contraindications

Mustine is mutagenic and teratogenic, so pregnancy is an absolute contraindication to treatment.

Cyclophosphamide

CYCLOPHOSPHAMIDE

As is evident from the formula above, cyclophosphamide (Endoxana) is a derivative of mustine and predictably acts by alkylation. It has a wide spectrum of antitumour activity in animals and is an extremely useful drug in clinical oncology. It has a greater therapeutic index than its parent drug and is cytotoxic in many more human cancers.

Mode of Action

No drug activity whatever is demonstrable in tissue cultures of any tumour mixed with cyclophosphamide. This is due to the fact that in clinical use cyclophosphamide is metabolized in the liver to the active form of the compound, probably phosphoramide mustard. If the drug is pretreated by phosphatases or phosphoramidases, it will then kill cultures of tumour cells. As several tumours contain high levels of these enzymes, it was proposed that cyclophosphamide might be harmless, except in the tumour, where its toxic metabolites were enzymatically formed and, hence, it killed the growth. In practice, however, the ideal model does not appear to be reproduced, as metabolized cyclophosphamide circulates widely from the liver to all tissues, including the tumour. Hence, as with all cytotoxic agents, side-effects are the main limiting feature in the administration of cyclophosphamide in doses lethal to the target lesion.

Pharmacokinetics
Oral administration is feasible, as absorption from the gut is good. Maximum plasma levels are reached in an hour, and distribution in the tissues is rapid. About one-fifth of the drug is excreted unchanged in the urine, half is protein bound, and the remainder is metabolized.

Preparations
Cyclophosphamide tablets, BP. Tablets of 10 mg and 50 mg, and a white powder for solution in 100, 200, 500 and 1000 mg vials are produced. The powder should be refrigerated until used, and care must be taken over preparation with sterile water, as it is rather slow to dissolve.

Indications
Many human tumours are sensitive to some degree to the alkylating action of cyclophosphamide. The drug is mainly used in combination with other drugs in the induction of remission. Lymphomas and tumours of ovary, lung or breast may regress completely in a combination high-dose intermittent regimen with drugs such as doxorubicin (p. 511), methotrexate (p. 503) and fluorouracil (p. 507). Multiple myeloma has been shown to respond equally to cyclophosphamide and melphalan. Better results are gained when prednisolone is added to either drug. Development of resistance to an alkylating agent and response to a different member of its family have been particularly evident in myeloma. For this reason, alkylating agents plus vincristine are now being used in combination to treat the disease on the same basis as three antibiotics are used to prevent the emergence of drug resistance in tuberculosis. The results of such an approach are considerably better than those obtained from single drugs.

The other group of tumours which respond very well to cyclophosphamide are solid tumours such as rhabdomyosarcoma, Ewing's sarcoma, and neuroblastoma in children.

Administration
The principal routes of administration are by mouth or i.v. 'bolus'. Different tumours have been shown to require a variation in the drug regimens. Low-dose continuous therapy using 2–7.5 mg/kg body weight daily has been partially effective in leukaemia, myeloma and ovarian cancer, but toxicity is common.

High doses, 1–1.5 g/m^2 (i.e. based on surface area) given intermittently i.v., in contrast, induce useful remissions and prolongation of life in at least half the patients treated. A lower-dose (0.6–1 g/m^2) regimen may be incorporated in a combination schedule, commonly with vincristine and prednisolone, to successfully treat lymphomas, including Hodgkin's disease.

Adverse Effects
Depression of the white cell count, usually after 10 days, is the principal

dose-limiting consequence of cyclophosphamide treatment. For some reason platelets are spared to a greater extent than white cells. Alopecia is a sequel in over a third of patients receiving the drug, but it is temporary. It is advisable to warn of the possibility and to match the existing hair with a wig at the earliest sign of hair loss. Sterile haemorrhagic cystitis is due to direct bladder irritation by acrolein, a metabolite of cyclophosphamide. It can be avoided by ensuring an adequate fluid intake over the period of therapy or by the co-administration of mesna (2-mercaptoethane sulphonate sodium). This compound provides an excess of sulphydryl groups which neutralize acrolein and inactivate it. Owing to the rapid excretion of mesna into the urine, no impairment of antitumour effect has been reported from the combination of drugs. Minor problems are rashes, impairment of fertility, retarded growth of the finger nails, skin hyperpigmentation and occasional anorexia, nausea, stomatitis, vomiting and diarrhoea.

Contraindications
The drug should not be administered in pregnancy, since all alkylating agents are likely to have a teratogenic effect.

Chlorambucil

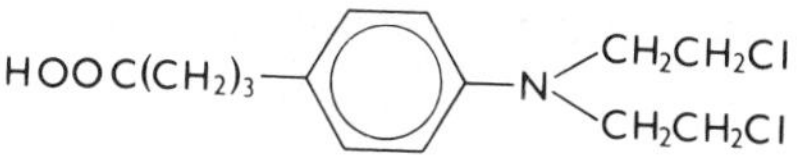

$$HOOC(CH_2)_3 - \text{\Large $\bigcirc$} - N \underset{CH_2CH_2Cl}{\overset{CH_2CH_2Cl}{<}}$$

CHLORAMBUCIL

The phenylbutyric acid mustard, chlorambucil (Leukeran), was developed in an attempt to improve the solubility of mustine. The product proved to be water-soluble and fat-soluble, and therefore is a surface-active compound. It is absorbed quickly and efficiently on to cells and remains an alkylator after adhesion. It is particularly useful in chronic lymphatic leukaemia and lymphoma.

Mode of Action
As with mustine, internal molecular cyclization must occur prior to alkylation. Unlike the parent, chlorambucil shows an affinity towards lymphocytes, and damage to other tissues is not common.

Pharmacokinetics
Absorption after oral ingestion is good. I.v. administration is possible, but no gain over mustine is achieved. Modes of metabolism and excretion of the drug have not been adequately researched.

Preparations
Chlorambucil tablets, BP. Tablets containing 2 and 5 mg are available.

An oral dose of 0.2 mg/kg body weight per day for 1–2 weeks is commonly prescribed, repeated at fortnightly intervals.

Indications
No other drug has shown a comparable role in the control of chronic lymphatic leukaemia. Over 60% of patients respond with a fall in white cell count and an improvement in symptomatology. Waldenström's macroglobulinaemia commonly improves after chlorambucil therapy in a similar fashion. Ovarian carcinoma and non-Hodgkin's lymphoma are the other indications for using the drug. In the latter condition, an improvement in the remission rate and survival are reported when prednisolone is given in addition to chlorambucil in an intermittent regimen, and lately the successful substitution of chlorambucil for mustine in the treatment of Hodgkin's disease has been reported.

Adverse Effects
Lymphopenia and sometimes granulocytopenia may be expected after exposure to chlorambucil. Occasional rashes, diarrhoea and hepatitis have been reported.

Contraindications
Pregnancy is a contraindication, as mentioned on p. 497.

Melphalan

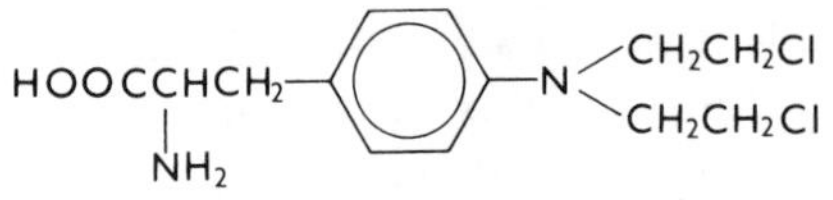

MELPHALAN

Phenylalanine mustard, or melphalan (Alkeran), is a derivative of the L-isomer of phenylalanine. The equivalent D-form is inactive against cancer cells, which is surprising, as the alkylating groups are unaltered in each isomer. Melphalan is active in the treatment of myeloma and breast cancer and, if given in very high doses, melanoma may respond. It is an alkylating agent similar to its parent mustine.

Pharmacokinetics
Absorption of the oral preparation is good, as its solubility is very high. It starts to disappear from the blood after 6 hours and is metabolized extensively in the tissues. Excretion is partly in urine and partly in bile.

Preparations
Melphalan tablets, BP. Melphalan is given in the form of 2 mg or 5 mg tablets

in a variable dose of up to 16 mg daily for 1–20 days. A respite of 2–4 weeks is generally required for the recovery of marrow function, particularly in multiple myeloma when the marrow is filled with tumour. Melphalan is available for i.v. or intra-arterial use in high-potency ampoules of 100 mg powder with diluent supplied.

Indications
Melphalan in combination with prednisolone, other alkylating agents and vincristine is frequently used to treat multiple myeloma; over half of all patients show marked improvement in skeletal metastases, renal function and plasma protein levels. Median survival time is prolonged to beyond 2 years; the survival duration is about 1 year if the patient is untreated. It has been shown to be active in delaying recurrence and prolonging survival of premenopausal women when given as adjuvant therapy after mastectomy for early breast cancer.

Adverse Effects
Myelosuppression and nausea, anorexia, and vomiting are the main consequences of therapy.

Contraindications
Pregnancy is a contraindication to treatment with melphalan.

Busulphan

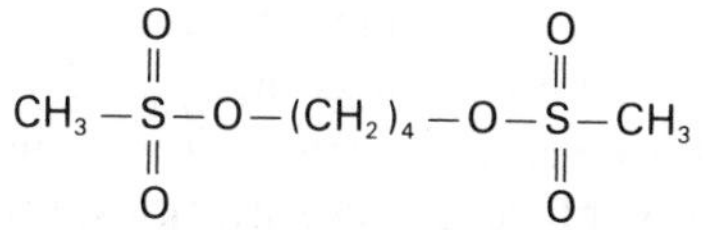

$$CH_3-\underset{\underset{O}{\|}}{\overset{\overset{O}{\|}}{S}}-O-(CH_2)_4-O-\underset{\underset{O}{\|}}{\overset{\overset{O}{\|}}{S}}-CH_3$$

BUSULPHAN

Busulphan (Myleran) is a dimethane sulphonate chemically similar to several other compounds, but it alone possesses antineoplastic properties. It has been the drug of choice in chronic myeloid leukaemia for many years, but is not as widely used owing to its incrimination as a cause of late second malignancy.

Mode of Action
The two arms of the busulphan molecule appear to be the critical distance apart, around 0.8 nm, thus having the best effect in cross-linking DNA strands through alkylation. The majority of busulphan, however, is not fixed to tissues in the fashion of mustine but is excreted as a metabolite in the urine.

Pharmacokinetics
Busulphan is given by mouth and is well absorbed despite low solubility. It

disappears quickly from the blood, even after i.v. infusion and is excreted in the urine as methane-sulphonic acid.

Preparations

Busulphan tablets, BP. Tablets of 0.5 and 2 mg are available and are prescribed in a daily dose of 1–6 mg. Therapy may continue on a long-term low-dose plan or else in 4–6 week courses with appropriate rests to allow marrow recovery.

Indications
Complete remission is achieved in over 90% of patients with chronic myeloid leukaemia. Survival time is not convincingly prolonged, however, and death due to 'blast' crisis is the rule after 2–3 years. Hydroxyurea with or without thioguanine is now preferred to busulphan, because of the more likely occurrence of acute leukaemia after administration of this drug. Polycythaemia and thrombocythaemia may be satisfactorily controlled by busulphan, but it is usually reserved for cases refractory to radioactive phosphorus, a safer and more efficacious drug in these two disorders (p. 519).

Adverse Effects
Thrombocytopenia is more readily induced by busulphan than by chlorambucil. Furthermore, recovery tends to take a considerable time. Hyperuricaemia is often a sequel to a successful reduction of a high granulocyte count. Amenorrhoea is frequent, and impotence in the male slightly less so. On prolonged exposure, three effects must be expected. Uniform hyperpigmentation, including involvement of the skin creases and excluding the oral cavity, may be accompanied by a 'wasting syndrome' comparable to Addison's disease. Levels of steroid in the plasma and urine, also electrolytes and blood glucose concentrations, however, remain normal. The other long-term hazard is a pneumonitis due to the deposition of intra-alveolar fibrin and a subsequent fibrosis.

Contraindications
Pregnancy and pulmonary impairment are contraindications to busulphan therapy.

Nitrosoureas

1,3-Bis(2-chloroethyl)-1-nitrosourea, or carmustine, is one of a family of nitrosourea compounds which act as alkylating agents. It acts on the synthesis of DNA and has one main advantage over its rivals. It is lipid-soluble and reaches the brain, so lesions there may at least be reached if not destroyed. It is potent in the treatment of myeloma and certain brain tumours, but has serious late toxicity on marrow, liver and kidney. Lomustine and semustine are similar less toxic derivatives under study at present, especially in the treatment of gut malignancies. They both cause nausea and vomiting, and the results of treatment have been uniformly disappointing.

Two new nitrosoureas, streptozocin and chlorozotocin, are of considerable interest because they have no myelosuppressive effect, yet retain an antitumour effect in certain systems. Streptozocin, in particular, is of importance in the treatment of tumours of the islet cells of the pancreas, such as malignant insulinoma and the malignant Zollinger-Ellison syndrome. This drug appears to be particularly toxic to the beta cells of the pancreas, and very favourable responses have been achieved either when it has been used by weekly i.v. injection (1 g) or by infusion through a hepatic artery catheter. It is disappointing in trials against adenocarcinoma of the pancreas, a relatively common tumour which is notoriously insensitive to cytotoxic drugs.

Preparations

Carmustine (BiCNU) is provided as a powder in a 100 mg vial with diluent.

Lomustine (CCNU, CeeNU) capsules of 10, 40 and 100 mg are marketed, whereas *semustine* (methyl CCNU) is only available for experimental use.

Streptozocin has lately become available commercially in some countries in 1 g vials, but *chlorozotocin* remains on the experimental list of the National Cancer Institute of the USA.

Other Drugs

Ifosfamide

Ifosfamide or isophosphamide (Mitoxana) is an oxazaphosphorine related to cyclophosphamide which appears to give less myelotoxicity and more urothelial toxicity. The two drugs are metabolized in a similar fashion and, in countries where it is available, mesna (p. 497) may also be given. Ifosfamide is supplied as a powder for reconstitution in vials of 500 mg, 1 g and 2 g, and the instructions supplied by the marketing company should be adhered to, mesna also being given if available. It is indicated for the same tumours as cyclophosphamide, but seems to be particularly active in soft tissue sarcoma in adults or children where responses have been reported after failure of treatment with cyclophosphamide. Caution must be exercised because of myelosuppression, and the drug is likely to be teratogenic and mutagenic.

Treosulfan

This is a bifunctional alkylating agent which can be taken by mouth in the dose of 1 g daily. The tablet size is 250 mg and its principal use to date has been the treatment of ovarian cancer. However, it is similar to chlorambucil in its activities and like that drug has been implicated in the pathogenesis of second malignancies.

Dacarbazine

Dacarbazine (DTIC) is a triazene compound which requires metabolic activation in liver before forming an active alkylating agent. Its principal use has been in the treatment of malignant melanoma, where it is claimed to be effective in 20% of cases. It has also been included in several combinations in the treatment of Hodgkin's disease. It almost invariably causes nausea and vomiting, and other side-effects include myelosuppression and hepatotoxicity. The dose is 3–4 mg/kg body weight daily for 5 days by the i.v. route. It is available in vials of 100 and 200 mg as a powder for reconstitution. It should be protected from light when administered.

Cisplatin

Cisplatin (Neoplatin) was discovered as a product of electrolysis from a platinum electrode and was noted to be bactericidal against *Escherichia coli*. It is a potent anti-tumour alkylating agent, the exact mode of action of which, however, is not clear. Being a heavy metal, its principal toxicity is in the kidney, but ototoxicity and neuropathy are also common. Nausea and vomiting is invariable and frequently shows resistance to antiemetics. Provided it is infused with care after a fluid load including mannitol, cisplatin is an extremely effective agent in the treatment of testicular teratoma and cancer involving the ovary, lung, cervix, bladder and head and neck. The dosage is variable according to the frequency of administration and the concomitant drugs in the protocol. It is commonly given as a short infusion of 20 mg/m^2 daily for five days. Vials of 10 and 50 mg powder are supplied. Several analogues are under trial in Europe and the USA in order to find a less toxic drug with equal or better cytotoxic effect.

Mitobronitol

Mitobronitol (Myelobromol) has recently been registered for treatment of chronic myeloid leukaemia. It is supplied in tablets of 125 mg, and the recommended dose is 250 mg daily, dependent on the degree of myelosuppression produced.

Estramustine

Estramustine phosphate (Estracyt) is a molecule resembling a fusion of mustine and an oestrogen. Capsules of 140 mg of the phosphate salt are available for treatment of oestrogen-resistant prostatic cancer in a dose of three capsules daily, this being adjusted according to the degree of gastrointestinal and bone marrow toxicity.

Thiotepa (Triethylene thiophosphoramide)

The principal indication for thiotepa is local treatment of intracavitary effusion or early bladder cancer. It can also be considered as an i.v. drug for the treatment of systemic cancers sensitive to alkylating agents. Thiotepa powder is available in a 15 mg vial for reconstitution with sodium chloride and bicarbonate. Side-effects are those common to other alkylating agents, mainly myelosuppression, mucositis and teratogenesis.

Ethoglucid

A 1% solution of ethoglucid (Epodyl) is recommended for instillation in the bladder as a treatment for early bladder cancer. It is supplied as a liquid in 1 ml ampoules containing 1.13 grams, and should not be drawn into plastic syringes.

ANTIMETABOLITES

Antimetabolites discussed are analogues of folic acid, of purines and of pyrimidines.

Analogues of Folic Acid

METHOTREXATE

Methotrexate was the second drug to prove of use in acute leukaemia in children, the first being aminopterin (4-aminopteroylglutamic acid). The formula should be compared with that of folic acid (p. 465). Over 30 years ago, dramatic complete remissions were reported following treatment with methotrexate and other folate analogues. The remissions were temporary, but can now be prolonged with the help of other maintenance drugs. Methotrexate remains the drug of choice in cerebral leukaemia, given either intrathecally or in high dosage i.v., and is active against a wide variety of solid tumours. It is available as Methotrexate (Lederle) or Emtexate (Nordic).

Mode of Action
Methotrexate is bound intracellularly to dihydrofolate reductase in the same fashion as folate. The latter normally is reduced by dihydrofolate reductase to tetrahydrofolate. Hence, inhibition of the enzyme leads to depletion of

tetrahydrofolate and consequent diminution of thymidylate, purine synthesis and DNA synthesis. Cells have been known to resist the effect of the drug, either by limiting its transport across the cell membrane or by 'switching on' additional dihydrofolate reductase synthesis. Both modes of resistance are overcome by an increased concentration of methotrexate, but concomitant side-effects due to normal cell damage are restrictive.

A technique known as 'rescue' has evolved from the discovery that folinic acid, given a short time after methotrexate infusion, saved normal cells from damage, whereas malignant cells continued to die. It is a feature of such cells that they recover poorly from insult and that their repair mechanisms are far less efficient than those of non-malignant tissue. Folinic acid rescue has been used clinically with success and has allowed very high doses of methotrexate to be administered without the appropriate predicted toxicity, in previously resistant tumours of head and neck or bone. Rescue may also be achieved by thymidine or the enzyme carboxypeptidase.

Pharmacokinetics

Administration may be by the oral, i.v., intra-arterial, or intrathecal route. Absorption from the gut is fair: over 40% of the drug appears in the urine within 8 hours of ingestion. If a large dose is given in an i.v. 'bolus', 90% is excreted in that time. A slow infusion is very effective in maintaining plasma and tissue levels for many hours. Indeed, the kidney and liver may retain a small amount for months. Ninety per cent of the drug in the plasma compartment is protein bound and may be displaced by other protein-bound substances, such as sulphonamides, salicylates and tetracyclines, given concomitantly. Around 10% of a 'bolus' of methotrexate is actively excreted in bile and lost in faeces.

Preparations

Methotrexate tablets, *BP*, containing 2.5 mg or 10 mg of methotrexate are available. They should be kept in a dark bottle. Ampoules of powder are available in quantities of either 5 or 50 mg, and this must be dissolved in sterile water. This preparation contains parabens which may be neurotoxic. For high-dose i.v. use, vials of 2.5, 5, 25, 50, 500, 1000 and 5000 mg are available. A special preparation not containing parabens or any other preservative must be used for intrathecal or intraventricular administration.

Indications

Methotrexate given by mouth or i.v. remains a useful induction agent for acute lymphoblastic leukaemia, especially in combination with prednisolone, although most protocols employ it weekly as maintenance treatment.

Tumours of breast, bladder and head and neck respond well to methotrexate, as does osteosarcoma. Intra-arterial regional perfusion can also be used to treat localized tumours. Choriocarcinoma, a rare tumour of the trophoblast, is peculiarly sensitive to methotrexate, and many complete cures have been recorded when it has been used alone or with other drugs. The use of methotrexate is not confined to the treatment of malignant disease, as it has some effect in psoriasis and has potent immunosuppressive effects which have been utilized in organ transplantation. It is routinely used after a bone marrow transplant, to prevent graft versus host disease.

Adverse Effects

Megaloblastic change in the bone marrow, oral ulceration and diarrhoea associated with malabsorption are common and may be avoided by folinic acid rescue and appropriate monitoring of the dose of drug. More serious marrow depression may occur, and occasionally gastrointestinal haemorrhage or perforation. Dermatitis, photosensitivity, alopecia and depigmentation of skin are troublesome in a few patients. Reports of hepatic fibrosis due to chronic low-dose therapy have recently been challenged, and, certainly, impaired liver function tests are not in themselves a signal to stop the drug.

Toxicity.

Antidotes. Folinic acid is mentioned above as an agent that may lessen the toxicity of certain aspects of methotrexate overdose provided it is given within 24 hours after the cytotoxic drug. Thymidine is available also, but carboxypeptidase remains experimental.

Contraindications

Abortion and fetal abnormalities have followed exposure to methotrexate during early pregnancy. Some patients receiving the drug in late pregnancy have delivered normal children. Renal impairment leads to failure of excretion and consequent increased toxicity.

Analogues of Purines

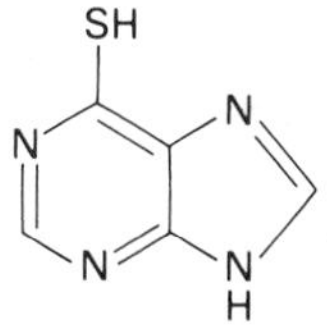

6-MERCAPTOPURINE

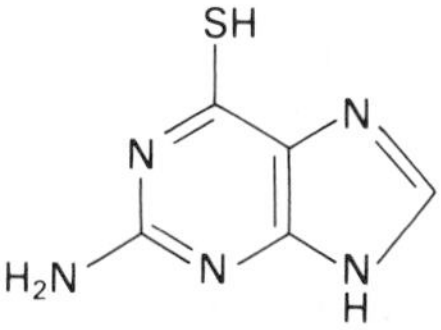

6-THIOGUANINE

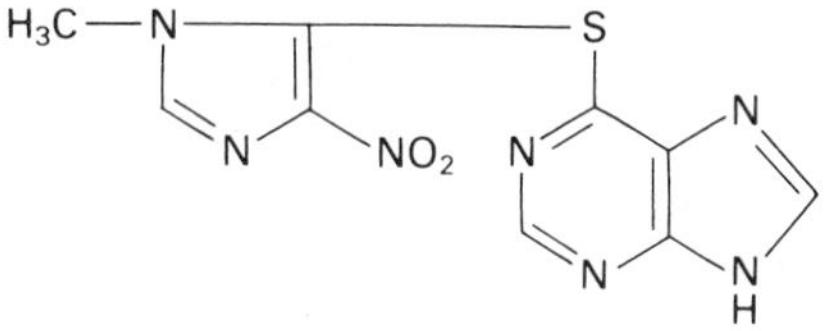

AZATHIOPRINE

The sulphydryl analogues of adenine and guanine, mercaptopurine and thioguanine respectively, are mainly used in antileukaemic protocols. Cross-resistance exists between the two drugs. Azathioprine has similar, less marked activity and is commonly used as an immunosuppressive agent in connective tissue disorders and in the prevention of transplant rejection.

Mode of Action
The purine analogues are activated in the cell to form the appropriate ribonucleotide, 6-thioinosinic acid. This compound inhibits synthesis of adenylic and guanylic acid from inosinic acid. Further, it stimulates a feedback mechanism which suppresses *de novo* purine synthesis. Lastly, it prevents interconversion among precursors of purine synthesis. The net result is a paralysis of cell division due to inadequate DNA synthesis.

Pharmacokinetics
All three drugs are absorbed from the gut after oral ingestion in the fasting state. Some mercaptopurine is metabolized by xanthine oxidase in the liver to a harmless metabolite and the remaining drug is methylated at the sulphydryl group. The sulphur radicals are excreted in the urine. Thioguanine is similarly methylated and the product 2-amino-6-methylthiopurine appears in the urine several hours later. Azathioprine differs only in that 10% of it reaches the urine unchanged.

Preparations

Mercaptopurine tablets, BP (Puri-Nethol). Light-sensitive tablets, containing 50 mg, are standard.

Thioguanine tablets (Lanvis). These contain 40 mg.

Azathioprine tablets, BP (Imuran). These tablets contain 50 mg, and this compound should be protected from the light. A vial containing 50 mg of powder which should be dissolved for injection is also manufactured.

Indications
Many protocols for the treatment of acute lymphatic leukaemia utilize mercaptopurine (2–3 mg/kg body weight per day) in the phase of consolidation which follows successful induction of remission. Thioguanine is useful in that role also, but is more often used in the treatment of acute myeloid leukaemia in adults, either in induction or in maintenance. In both cases the drug is given in combination, commonly with other drugs in a dose of 2 mg/kg body weight per day. Occasional cases of chronic myeloid leukaemia refractory to busulphan respond to mercaptopurine. Azathioprine is prescribed in a dose of 1–4 mg/kg body weight per day, mainly for immunosuppression.

Adverse Effects

All the purine analogues depress the bone marrow, cause diarrhoea, and occasionally produce jaundice.

Interactions

Allopurinol blocks the enzyme xanthine oxidase, which breaks down purines, as mentioned above. If allopurinol is given with mercaptopurine or azathioprine, the dose of the latter drugs need only be a third of that usually employed. Failure to lower the dose leads to accumulation of the drug which would normally be inactivated by xanthine oxidase and to serious toxic effects. Thioguanine can safely be given with allopurinol, as it is not metabolized by oxidation.

Contraindications

Pregnancy is a contraindication owing to the possible teratogenicity of the antimetabolites.

Analogues of Pyrimidines

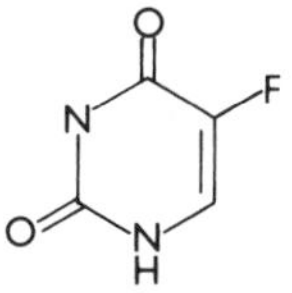

5-FLUOROURACIL

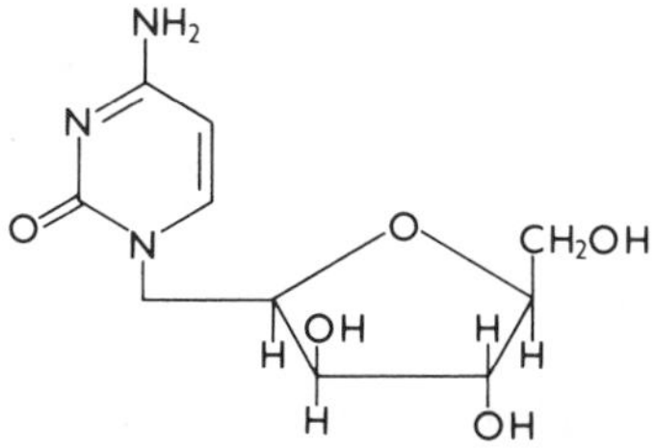

CYTARABINE

The two analogues to be discussed are a fluorine-substituted variant of 5-fluorouracil and a cytidine nucleoside, cytarabine, which has arabinose in place of ribose. Both compounds were intentionally manipulated in attempts to design antimetabolites that might either inhibit synthesis of DNA or else become incorporated in DNA, with consequent disorganization of protein manufacture. Fluorouracil is widely accepted to be the most active agent in gastrointestinal tumours. It has also been approved in the treatment of breast and ovary cancer. Cytarabine, in contrast, is an antileukaemic agent which is less effective against solid tumours.

Mode of Action

Fluorouracil is inactive until converted, like uracil, to a ribonucleotide. None of the halogenated uracils, except the fluorine forms, are cytotoxic, yet fluorouracil is the only member that does not become incorporated into DNA. Instead, it acts on DNA synthesis by blocking the formation of thymidylic acid, which is a crucial precursor of DNA. The mechanism is known to be adherence to and inhibition of the catalytic enzyme thymidylate synthetase. The fluorine ribonucleotide has an affinity for the enzyme many hundred times greater than has the natural substrate, deoxyuridylic acid. An additional toxic effect is incorporation into RNA and thus interference with further RNA synthesis.

Cytarabine, like fluorouracil, does not become incorporated into DNA, but, unlike it, does not appear in RNA either. It seems to become phosphorylated in vivo, and the triphosphorylated drug then prevents DNA polymerase completing the ultimate step in the assembly of DNA. Partial inhibition of other enzymes has been shown in vitro, but it is unclear how relevant these actions are in man.

Pharmacokinetics

Fluorouracil may be given by mouth, but, as it is inconsistently absorbed, particularly when used in gastrointestinal malignancy, the i.v. route is preferable. Degradation takes place principally in the liver, although 10–20% appears unchanged in the urine. The main end product is carbon dioxide, which is expired in the lungs.

Cytarabine is administered either i.v. or s.c. and is deaminated rapidly in the liver and kidneys; the metabolite formed, uracil arabinoside, is then excreted in the urine. The drug cannot be traced in the plasma half an hour after the injection of a 'bolus', so lengthy infusion techniques have been attempted.

Preparations

Fluorouracil is available in ampoules of 250 mg in 5 ml; also available are a topical preparation in the form of a 5% cream (Efudix) for the treatment of malignant skin conditions, and capsules of 250 mg.

Cytarabine injection (Cytosar) is available as a freeze-dried preparation, packaged with accompanying diluent in vials of 100 mg.

Indications

Malignancies of the stomach, colon, rectum and breast show a 30% response rate to 15 mg/kg body weight per day of fluorouracil over several days each month. The response is never complete and can be improved and prolonged if other drugs or radiotherapy are employed in synchrony. Intra-arterial perfusion of hepatic metastases has met with limited success, although a very useful reduction in liver capsule pain is common. The dose used is about 250–500 mg/day. As noted before, cytarabine is most efficacious in the induction of remission in acute myeloid leukaemia. Synergism exists between it and daunorubicin (p. 511), and when they are used together, more than half of all patients enter complete remission. The usual dose of cytarabine is 2 mg/kg body weight per day, but lately up to 6 g/m² have been shown to be successful in refractory leukaemia. As toxicity is dose related, such patients must be treated in cancer centres only.

Adverse Effects
Both drugs are myelotoxic and irritant to the gastrointestinal tract. Fluorouracil also interferes with growth of nails and hair and rarely may produce cerebellar signs and cardiotoxicity.

Toxicity.
Antidotes. Theoretically, uridine and deoxycytidine should reverse the effects of fluorouracil and cytarabine respectively. As yet, no clinical evidence has emerged to support the in vitro work.

Contraindications
Neither drug should be prescribed in pregnancy.

VINCA ALKALOIDS

The periwinkle, *Vinca rosea*, has proved to be the source of two active antimitotic drugs, vincristine and vinblastine. Their main clinical applications have proved to be in the treatment of leukaemias and lymphomas. The drugs are similar dimeric alkaloids, differing in only one respect, a methyl group in vinblastine which takes the place of a formyl group in the vincristine molecule. A third drug, vindesine, has recently been approved.

Mode of Action
The drugs act like colchicine (p. 138), another plant product, on the mitotic spindle of dividing cell nuclei. They arrest fission at the metaphase by disrupting microtubules. Whether such a property leads to significant cell death is not certain; one result is definite and that is that the cells become synchronized for a short time in their division cycle.

Pharmacokinetics
I.v. administration is advisable, as the alkaloids are irritant if given i.m. or s.c. Instillation into a serous cavity is feasible, but rarely indicated. Oral preparations have been proved inadequate owing to unpredictable absorption and frequent diarrhoea. Clearance from the plasma to the tissues is rapid, and the main pathway of excretion is in bile.

Preparations

Vincristine injection, *BP* (Oncovin) is available as ampoules of 1 and 5 mg of vincristine sulphate powder with lactose, accompanied by 10 ml vials of diluent. They should be kept in a refrigerator, and when constituted the solution should be used within 24 hours.

Vinblastine injection, BP (Velbe) is available in 10 mg vials of the powdered sulphate with lactose and diluent and should be stored and dispensed in similar conditions to those used for vincristine.

Vindesine sulphate, BP (Eldisine) is available as powder (with mannitol) for reconstitution in 5 mg vials with diluent.

Indications

Nine out of ten children may recover from acute lymphatic leukaemia under the influence of prednisolone and vincristine. Remission is prolonged to over 5 years by intensive consolidation with other drugs. Vinblastine is surprisingly ineffective in leukaemia when the similarity of structure and pharmacology of the two drugs is considered. The difference in tumour specificity is more marked when the relative toxicities against lymphoma are appraised. Vinblastine is used in Hodgkin's disease as part of the established quadruple combination in a dose of 10 mg weekly. Vincristine is also active in quadruple regimens, but vincristine is preferred in the treatment of non-Hodgkin's lymphomas. The usual dose is 0.15 mg/kg body weight weekly, with an upper limit of 2 mg per injection. Vincristine, too, is active in combinations prescribed for cancer of the breast and for several sarcomas in children. Vinblastine is less useful in these tumours, but, when given in a high dose with bleomycin and cisplatin (p. 502), dramatic remissions are seen in advanced teratoma of the testis. Vindesine is active in leukaemia, lymphoma and non-small cell cancer of the lung (particularly in combination with cisplatin).

Adverse Effects

Neurotoxicity is common to these drugs but more pronounced after vincristine. Paraesthesiae, loss of tendon reflexes, jaw pain, foot drop, ptosis, sensory loss and convulsions have been reported. Constipation is common, so that a stool-softening agent is often prescribed in conjunction with vinca therapy. Alopecia and hyponatraemia are more frequently noticed following vincristine than after vinblastine. The latter drug, however, is the more toxic to marrow, and low blood counts can be expected about 10 days after administration. Vincristine, by contrast, may actually increase the platelet count.

Contraindications

In animal studies the vinca alkaloids are teratogenic, although no clinical reports have appeared.

ANTITUMOUR ANTIBIOTICS

A variety of antimitotic substances have been isolated from the *Streptomyces* genus. Two are anthracyclines, daunorubicin and 14-hydroxydaunorubicin or doxorubicin; bleomycin is a group of sulphur-containing polypeptides, and actinomycin D consists of two similar cyclic polypeptide chains linked by a phenoxazone complex. Mitomycin C is the most potent of a family which share a quinone ring, an indole group, an aziridine ring and a methoxyformamide side-chain. It is not listed in *British Approved Names 1981*. There are few malignancies which do not respond in some measure to at least one of these drugs.

Mode of Action

The principal binding site for the interaction of the antibiotics and cell nuclei is DNA itself. Actinomycin D and daunorubicin intercalate between the strands of the DNA helix, probably attached by hydrogen bonds to guanine bases. DNA synthesis is thereby impeded and the binding sites which form a template for RNA synthesis are preferentially blocked. Doxorubicin intercalates between DNA nucleotides by forming a bridge from its electropositive amino-sugar group to negative phosphate moieties on the DNA helix. The strands of intercalated DNA are then unable to separate in mitosis. Although bleomycin also binds to DNA, it is not clear at what receptor site or what the outcome is in terms of cell damage. In tissue culture, single-strand scission of DNA has been reported, as has also been noted after mitomycin. The latter also alkylates DNA, mostly at 0–6 residues of guanine.

Pharmacokinetics

Absorption from the gut is variable and, accordingly, i.v. administration is necessary. Bleomycin is an exception, as it may be given i.m., but there is subsequent pain at the injection site. The antibiotics disappear quickly into the tissues from the plasma. Doxorubicin and daunorubicin are metabolized after active membrane transport and are concentrated fiftyfold in the cell nuclei. The other drugs are metabolized or tissue bound and only 10% of any of the antibiotics appears in the urine. High concentrations of bleomycin are detected in skin and lungs.

Preparations

Daunorubicin hydrochloride (Cerubidin) is available in vials containing 20 mg of powder for solution in 20 ml of normal saline. Injection of the resulting red fluid is best done in a fast-running i.v. saline infusion.

Doxorubicin (Adriamycin) is also a red powder supplied in vials of 10 mg or 50 mg, together with vials of water for injection. Injection into a fast-running drip is desirable. Infusion into an intra-arterial catheter is possible.

Actinomycin D (*Dactinomycin*, Cosmegen Lyovac) is available in vials of 0.5 mg of powder plus mannitol for dissolving in a dilute solution of normal saline.

Bleomycin sulphate is available as a freeze-dried powder, equivalent to 15 mg of the drug, presented in ampoules. It is stable at room temperature for 2 years. Solutions may be made up with water or normal saline, or 1% lignocaine for i.m. use.

Mitomycin C injection is a blue powder reconstituted from a 2 or 10 mg vial.

Indications

Daunorubicin in a dose of 2–3 mg/kg body weight, accompanied by cytarabine, is the standard treatment for acute myeloid leukaemia. A total dose of 20 mg/kg body weight should not be exceeded. Doxorubicin is also active in the therapy of leukaemia but, unlike its parent, also has many other valuable roles. It has achieved remissions alone and in combination at a dose range of 40–80 mg/m² 3-weekly to a maximum total of 500 mg/m² in lymphomas, breast, lung, bladder and thyroid cancers, and varied sarcomas of soft tissue origin. Actinomycin D has transformed the prognosis of Wilms' tumour in children. It has mainly been used as an adjuvant to surgery and/or radiotherapy. The usual dose is 15 μg/kg body weight per day for 5 days. Other tumours which respond well to the drug are choriocarcinoma and sarcomas in children, and it has been used for transplantation crises.

In contrast with the first three drugs, bleomycin has a particular effect in squamous tumours of skin, head and neck, external genitalia, cervix and oesophagus.

Bleomycin given by infusion for 5 days has been lately included in protocols for the treatment of testicular teratoma, together with vinblastine and cisplatin. Complete remission rates are of the order of 70–80%.

Optimal dosage has not been fully explored, the common practice being to give 15 mg i.m. or i.v. once or twice weekly, to a total dose of 300 mg. Each of the antibiotics to which reference has been made has a recommended dosage ceiling and therefore each is of limited value in long-term maintenance therapy. Mitomycin can be used as a single agent in breast cancer (dose 10 mg/m² every 4–6 weeks) or in combination chemotherapy at a lower dose. A particular combination with doxorubicin and fluorouracil has become the standard treatment for advanced stomach cancer in some countries, and results in a consistent remission rate of 40%.

Adverse Effects

Daunorubicin and doxorubicin are limited in total dose to prevent cardiac toxicity. Like actinomycin D, they cause marrow suppression and have irritant properties at the site of injection and in the gastrointestinal tract. Nausea, vomiting and diarrhoea frequently follow infusion. Doxorubicin invariably induces alopecia, whereas this is rare with the other members of the group. Bleomycin distinctively spares the marrow, but causes stomatitis and dermatitis, and is limited in total dose by interstitial pneumonitis. This may be detected early by abnormal lung function tests, which are an indication to stop treatment. Failure to do so may lead to fatal pulmonary fibrosis analogous to the effect of long-term treatment with busulphan. Mitomycin leads to late myelosuppression, around 3–5 weeks after administration.

Contraindications

Cardiac impairment is a contraindication to the use of daunorubicin and doxorubicin, whereas respiratory disease precludes bleomycin. As doxorubicin is partly excreted in bile, diminution of liver function may increase the drug-associated toxicity. It is occasionally possible to adjust the drug dose to avoid such danger. Pregnancy is an absolute contraindication to any of the antitumour antibiotics, as teratogenicity may be expected.

EPIPODOPHYLLOTOXINS

Podophyllotoxin is a tubulin binding agent derived from the mandrake plant. Two semi-synthetic analogues, etoposide (VP 16 213) and teniposide (VM 26), have been under clinical trial in Europe for ten years and are only now finding their respective roles.

They are glycosidic derivatives, which irreversibly arrest cells before mitosis. Etoposide can be given by mouth as bioavailability is around 50%, but it is usually given by short i.v. infusion of 60–100 mg/m^2 daily for up to 7 days. A clear schedule dependence has been proved in favour of a five-day schedule over a single dose in the treatment of small-cell lung cancer. It is probably the most active drug in this disease and is now accepted as a drug to be considered in the first-line combination in the treatment of teratoma. It is also active in ovarian cancer and Hodgkin's disease. Teniposide has not been so widely tested but is used by specialists in certain European countries as a first choice in non-Hodgkin's lymphoma and has use in leukaemia, bladder cancer and malignant glioma in a dose of 50–100 mg/m^2 by infusion each two to three weeks.

Etoposide (Vepesid) is available as 100 mg capsules or a 5 ml ampoule, 20 mg/ml for further dilution. Teniposide is only available on a 'named patient' basis until licensed for general use.

ENZYMES

L-asparaginase has a distinctive role in the induction of remission in acute leukaemia. Some tumour cells depend on the amino acid L-asparagine for nutrition and growth. L-asparaginase catalyses its hydrolysis to L-aspartic acid and ammonia, thus depriving the affected cells of the amino acid and causing the possibly detrimental accumulation of aspartic acid. Dosages have varied widely in clinical practice, but commonly 10 000 units/m^2 i.v. daily for 10 days has been tried in leukaemia. Toxicity is frequent, ranging from hypersensitivity reactions to hepatitis, uraemia, pancreatitis, marrow suppression and central nervous system disturbances. The approved name for L-asparaginase is colaspase.

METHYL HYDRAZINES

Many of the derivatives of methyl hydrazine have antileukaemic properties. *Procarbazine* (Natulan) is the only one to reach clinical acceptance. It acts rather like irradiation, as it breaks up single strands of DNA, prolongs the interphase of mitosis and inhibits the repair of the damage which it has wrought in the chromatid. It is given orally in a dose of 50–75 mg twice daily and is excreted by the kidney. It causes nausea and vomiting, and depresses the marrow. It is a monoamine oxidase inhibitor and interacts with several drugs, particularly the phenothiazines and alcohol. Heinz-body haemolytic anaemia and hepatitis are sometimes provoked. The outstanding indication for procarbazine is in the quadruple protocol described earlier, which has been so dramatic in the treatment of Hodgkin's disease, although the drug is also useful in lung and brain tumours.

UREA DERIVATIVES

The simple drug *hydroxyurea* (Hydrea) specifically inhibits DNA synthesis by impairing the enzyme ribonucleotide reductase. It is administered orally in 500 mg capsules and, because of its short half-life, may best be given on a chronic low-dose basis. Most trials, however, have employed a high dose, 80 mg/kg body weight twice weekly. It has clinical applications in the treatment of chronic myeloid (granulocytic) leukaemia and solid tumours such as lung or breast. The main side-effects are marrow depression, vomiting, rashes and alopecia.

GLUCOCORTICOIDS

Prednisolone is used in the treatment of acute and chronic lymphatic leukaemia because of its lympholytic action (p. 408). In the former disease it can be given to initiate or maintain remission, but it is best employed in combination with the chemotherapeutic agents already discussed. It should be used alone only if other drugs are ineffective or producing severe adverse effects. It gives some benefit in the combination therapy of acute myeloblastic leukaemia and there are several schemes of treatment of lymphadenoma and of other lymphomas which involve the use of prednisolone. Where the disease processes just referred to are accompanied by haemolytic anaemia or thrombocytopenia, corticosteroids may help to control these complications. In multiple myeloma they may prevent the release of calcium from osseous tissue, a complication that can lead to renal failure. Prednisolone adds to the efficacy of several breast cancer combinations, such as that of methotrexate, fluorouracil and cyclophosphamide.

COMBINATION CHEMOTHERAPY

Table 14.1 lists a variety of drugs that have been shown to be useful as single agents or in combinations in the treatment of a variety of malignant conditions. There are thousands of possible combinations of the forty or so active cytotoxic drugs, and to list them would be both tedious and pointless. Progress in the field of trials of combination chemotherapy has come from careful clinical research, which, up until recently, was based on pragmatism rather than science. The development of drug assays for certain cytotoxic agents has improved the understanding of individual drug disposition in patients, drug interactions within combinations, and the dependence on biochemical parameters such as plasma albumin levels for optimum exposure of the tumour to the drug. Lately, too, there have commenced drug-testing systems in vitro, which, if developed, might give the clinician useful clues to the sensitivity of tumour clones to a battery of cytotoxic drugs displayed singly or in combination. Moreover, much attention is now being paid to the scheduling of drugs with respect to the growth kinetics of the individual tumour, after the realization that many tumours consist of cells that are not actively dividing and which are therefore relatively immune to the effect of most cytotoxic drugs. There are several theoretical manipulations which might coax arresting cells into the division cycle (Fig. 14.2) at which time they may be synchronized by a drug such as hydroxyurea or a vinca alkaloid and then killed by a cell cycle specific agent.

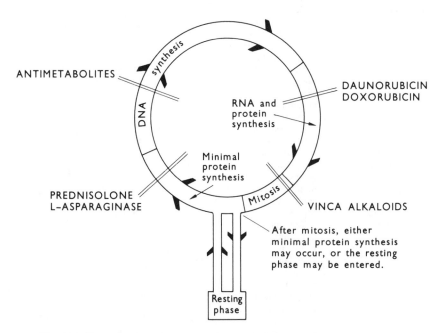

Fig. 14.2 Sites of action of agents with specific effects on phases of the cell cycle.

Table 14.1 *Response to chemotherapeutic agents for malignant conditions*

Disease	Drugs of value	Response	Survival	Percentage showing prolonged survival
Acute lymphoblastic leukaemia	Combinations such as that of vincristine, prednisolone, mercaptopurine and methotrexate *or* alternatives	Good	Prolonged	90
Chorio-carcinoma	Methotrexate, cisplatin, etoposide, cyclophosphamide, mercaptopurine	Good	Prolonged	90
Lymphadenoma (Hodgkin's disease)	Combinations such as that of mustine, vinca alkaloids, procarbazine and prednisolone Also doxorubicin, carmustine, bleomycin etoposide and dacarbazine	Good	Prolonged	90
Lymphoma (excluding lymphadenoma)	Combination of cyclophosphamide, vincristine, and prednisolone Also doxorubicin bleomycin, teniposide and nitrosoureas	Good	Prolonged	70
Chronic lymphatic leukaemia	No treatment in many, as illness slight Chlorambucil Prenisolone, if haemolysis	Good	Prolonged	50
Acute myeloblastic leukaemia	Daunorubicin, cytarabine and thioguanine, followed by other maintenance combinations	Good	Prolonged	70
Chronic myeloid leukaemia	Hydroxyurea *with* thioguanine Mitobronitol Busulphan	Good	Prolonged	70
Multiple myeloma	Melphalan Carmustine Vincristine Cyclophosphamide Prednisolone (in various combinations)	Good	Prolonged	70

Table 14.1 continued

Disease	Drugs of value	Response	Survival	Percentage showing prolonged survival
Ovarian carcinoma	Chlorambucil, hexamethyl-melamine, cisplatin, cyclophosphamide and doxorubicin	Good	Prolonged	80
Breast carcinoma	Doxorubicin, fluorouracil, cyclophosphamide, vincristine, methotrexate and prednisolone in combinations Aminoglutethimide, mitomycin and tamoxifen	Good	Slight	60
Bronchogenic carcinoma (small cell)	Combination from cyclophosphamide, doxorubicin, methotrexate, procarbazine, vincristine, etoposide	Good	Prolonged	40
Astrocytoma	Nitrosoureas Procarbazine	Fair	Slight	20
Wilms' tumour	Actinomycin and vincristine	Good	Prolonged	80
Sarcomas in children	Actinomycin and vincristine Doxorubicin, cyclophosphamide	Good	Prolonged	80
Burkitt's lymphoma	Cyclophosphamide	Good	Prolonged	70
Teratoma of testis	Vinblastine Cisplatin Bleomycin Actinomycin Methotrexate Etoposide	Good	Prolonged	90

The importance of developing safe effective combinations of cytotoxic drugs is emphasized by the recent expansion of the role of chemotherapy into the treatment of 'early' cancer. In the treatment of advanced cancer the therapeutic aim may well be palliation (p. 490) along with limited prolongation of survival; in the adjuvant setting avoidance of toxicity is paramount, and prolongation of survival is essential to counterbalance the potentially mutagenic and carcinogenic side-effects of cytotoxic drugs.

SEX HORMONES

The use of androgens in metastatic carcinoma of the breast is referred to on p. 414, and of oestrogens in prostatic carcinoma on p. 417. Oestrogens may stimulate the growth of metastatic breast carcinoma in premenopausal women or those who have just passed the menopause, but later in life they may give benefit if there are metastatic deposits from the breast. There is controversy as to whether contraceptive pills of high progestogen activity may cause some increase of breast carcinoma. It has been claimed in the USA that oestrogen therapy during pregnancy may lead to vaginal adenocarcinoma years later in female offspring.

Tamoxifen

Tamoxifen is an interesting compound which has oestrogenic properties in the mouse, but anti-oestrogenic properties in the rat and human. It is of considerable value in the hormonal management of patients with breast cancer. It is available in 10 mg and 20 mg tablets, and in a dose of 20 mg twice daily continuously has been shown to produce remissions in advanced breast cancer in 30% of patients. There is a strong correlation between response to tamoxifen and the presence of oestrogen receptors in the cytoplasm and nucleus of primary breast cancer tissue. Side-effects of the drug are minimal, almost totally confined to nausea and vomiting. Several clinical trials are in progress to investigate the value of combinations of tamoxifen with conventional combination chemotherapy protocols in early and advanced breast cancer. A proprietary name is Nolvadex.

Aminoglutethimide

Aminoglutethimide (Orimeten) is an inhibitor of adrenal steroidogenesis. When combined with hydrocortisone (as a supplementary glucocorticoid) it achieves responses in metastatic breast cancer and to a lesser extent prostate cancer. A dose of one tablet (250 mg) 2–4 times daily is advised. Side-effects include drowsiness, skin rash and occasional ataxia; caution must be exercised in the co-administration of drugs metabolized in the liver, such as dexamethasone, oral anticoagulants or oral hypoglycaemics, since such metabolism may be accelerated by aminoglutethimide.

RADIOACTIVE ISOTOPES

Only a few radioactive isotopes are employed in therapy. They should not be used in women of child-bearing age.

Radioactive Phosphorus

There is a radioactive isotope of phosphorus, ^{32}P, which can be taken by mouth or, preferably, may be given i.v. It is used in the treatment of polycythaemia vera; alternative agents being busulphan (p. 499) or pyrimethamine (p. 76). The isotope is concentrated in the bone marrow, and it has a half-life of 14.3 days. It emits β radiation, but no γ rays.

Radioactive Iodine

The use of radioactive iodine in hyperthyroidism and carcinoma of the thyroid has been referred to on p. 384. The isotopes usually given are ^{131}I, which has a half-life of 8.04 days, and ^{132}I, with a half-life of 2.26 hours. Each emits both β and γ rays. Iodine seeds have been locally implanted in small inoperable tumours such as those of the pancreas.

Radioactive Gold

An isotope of gold, ^{198}Au, is concentrated in the liver and has been used to treat various abdominal tumours. It has also been instilled into the pleural cavity in carcinoma of the lung and into the peripheral lymphatics in malignant melanoma. Its half-life is 2.69 days and it emits β and γ rays.

IMMUNOSUPPRESSANTS

Immunosuppression is a specialized field and it is perhaps sufficient to state here that the therapeutic agents available are (1) glucocorticosteroids, (2) antimetabolites such as azathioprine which destroy cells of lymphoid tissue that play a part in antibody-mediated and cell-mediated immune responses, and (3) antilymphocytic serum. Unfortunately, reactions may be severe. Cyclosporin is an exciting new drug, first listed in *British Approved Names* in November 1982. It has important immunosuppressive properties with an action on T lymphocytes (p. 549). It is a neutral cyclic endecapeptide obtained from the fermentation broth of the fungus *Trichoderma polysporum*, and is highly effective in preventing acute allograft rejection in man, hence its use in transplant units.

MISCELLANEOUS USES OF CERTAIN ANTI-TUMOUR AGENTS

In certain intractable medical conditions, it is sometimes possible to obtain a response from azathioprine, methotrexate, cyclophosphamide or actinomycin when other methods of treatment have failed. Certainly, in some instances this appears to be a form of immunosuppression. The conditions include active chronic hepatitis, idiopathic acquired haemolytic anaemia, primary biliary cirrhosis, regional ileitis, systemic lupus erythematosus and ulcerative colitis. Less convincing is their use in membranous glomerulonephritis, minimal-lesion glomerulonephritis, rheumatoid arthritis and idiopathic thrombocytopenic purpura. Vincristine has a supportive role in this last, due to its thrombopoietic effect.

FURTHER READING

Ansfield F., Klotz J., Nealon Th., Ramirez G., Minton J., Hill G., Wilson W., Davis H. Jr & Cornell G. (1977) A phase III study comparing the clinical utility of four regimens of 5-fluorouracil, *Cancer*, 39: 34.

Bagley ChM. Jr, Bostick F. W. & Devita V. T., Jr (1973) Clinical pharmacology of cyclophosphamide, *Cancer Res.*, 33: 226.

Bender R. A., Zwelling L. A., Doroshow J. H., Locker G. Y., Hands K. R., Murinson D. S., Cohen M., Myers C. E. & Chabner B. A. (1978) Anti neoplastic drugs: clinical pharmacology and therapeutics, *Drugs*, 16: 46.

Cavalli F., Sonntag R. W., Jungi F., Senn H. J. & Brunner K. W. (1978) VP 16–213 monotherapy for remission induction of small cell lung cancer, *Cancer Treat. Rep.,* 62: 473.

Chabner B. (1982) *Pharmacologic Principles of Cancer Treatment*. Philadelphia: Saunders.

Ehrlichman C., Donehower R. C. & Chabner B. A. (1980) The practical benefits of pharmacokinetics in the use of antineoplastic agents, *Cancer Chemother. Pharmacol.*, 4: 139.

Frei E., III, Canellos G. P. (1980) Dose: a critical factor in cancer chemotherapy, *Am. J. Med.*, 69: 585.

McVie J. G., Stuart J. F. B., Calman K. C. & Steele W. S. (1981) Pharmacology of high dose oral methotrexate, *Cancer Treat. Rep.*, 65: Suppl. 1, 141.

Nebert D. W. (1981) Possible clinical importance of genetic difference in drug metabolism, *Br. Med. J.*, 283: 531

Powis G., Ames M. M. & Kovach J. S. (1981) Dose-dependent pharmacokinetics and cancer chemotherapy, *Cancer Chemother. Pharmacol.*, 6: 1.

Rossi A., Bonadonna G., Valagussa P. & Veronesi U. (1981) Multimodal treatment in operable breast cancer: five-year results of the CMF programme, *Br. Med. J.*, 282: 1427.

15 Heavy Metals; Chelating Agents; Antidotes; Resins

J. A. J. H. Critchley

HEAVY METALS

There are three main categories of metals which are of interest for their therapeutic or toxic potential. Firstly, sodium, potassium, calcium and magnesium are the main body cations and are integral to cell membrane regulation. Other cations such as lithium, barium and strontium exert pharmacological effects by replacing them. Secondly, transition metals (chromium, manganese, iron, cobalt, nickel, copper, zinc and molybdenum) are fundamental to the activity of various enzymes because they can readily change their valency in redox reactions. Although this reactivity renders them essential in trace amounts for cell function, they can be highly toxic in excess.

Thirdly, there are the heavy metals. This term is often used loosely in medical literature but in this chapter it is defined as those metals with atomic numbers of 47 (silver) or higher (cadmium, gold, mercury, lead and bismuth). They readily form co-ordinate (i.e., dative) bonds with the functional groups on protein molecules which act as ligands. In particular, these are $-OH$, $-SH$ and $-NH_2$ groups in which the oxygen, sulphur or nitrogen atom donates the lone pair of electrons for the co-ordinate bond. Heavy metals have a particular affinity for $-SH$ (sulphydryl or thiol) groups which are ubiquitous constituents of amino acids (cysteine and methionine), peptides, proteins, enzymes and coenzymes.

The secondary structure of proteins is maintained by disulphide bonds between cysteine residues. The bonding of metals to the thiol groups of enzymes causes structural and other changes which can on one the hand be vital for their function but, on the other, highly disruptive. In particular, the coenzymes involved in acetylation and oxidative decarboxylation are very vulnerable to metal poisoning.

Heavy metals were more commonly used in medicine before the discovery of much less toxic drugs, for example, in the chemotherapy of syphilis. They are, however, still used in a variety of industrial processes and, despite increasing awareness of their potential toxicity, poisoning on both an individual and community scale still occurs. Although legislation supported by industrial inspection is reducing the incidence of such toxicity, it is essential that the medical profession remains alert to heavy metal poisoning because its early clinical features are not specific.

Gold

Gold compounds were used for centuries as antipruritics. Now chrysotherapy ($\chi\rho\upsilon\sigma\acute{o}s$, gold) is only used for rheumatoid arthritis. Effective preparations have monovalent (aurous) gold associated with an organic radical containing a sulphydryl group. The two parenteral forms, sodium aurothiomalate and aurothioglucose, of which the former is more commonly used, are a solution and a suspension in oil, respectively. Both are water-soluble. After intramuscular injection rapid breakdown occurs with the gold binding principally to the sulphydryl groups of serum albumin, while the thiol-containing radical is mainly taken up by cellular membranes in the tissues. The recently introduced oral preparation, auranofin, contains a triethylphosphine ligand which aids absorption of a thioglucose gold-containing complex.

Gold can persist for decades in the lysosomes of synovial cells and macrophages. One hypothesis regarding its mode of action is that phagocytosis and lysosomal enzyme action are inhibited by thiol-monovalent gold interactions. A contrasting suggestion is that gold compounds act as prodrugs supplying active thiol-bearing ligands. The similarity in the clinical response to gold salts with that of levamisole and D-penicillamine is interesting. Penicillamine contains a sulphydryl group and levamisole has a sulphur-containing ring which can be hydrolysed to form a sulphydryl group.

Twenty-five to fifty per cent of patients receiving gold therapy have toxic or allergic reactions that are partly due to the solvent/suspension vehicles of the parenteral preparations. The skin and mucous membranes are most commonly involved but haematopoiesis, the central and peripheral nervous systems, liver and kidneys can also be affected. Thus gold therapy is contraindicated in renal failure and a wide range of other conditions. There should be careful patient selection and supervision including regular urinalysis and blood counts.

Silver

Silver ions have a very disruptive action on bacterial cell walls. Silver nitrate solution and silver sulphadiazine ointment are used in the dressing of burns. Silver sulphadiazine is very effective against *Pseudomonas* and other Gram-negative organisms and by virtue of its lower solubility, does not have the potential of the nitrate to precipitate significant amounts of chloride or protein. Thus hypochloraemia and increased adherence of eschars to dressings is avoided. It was used extensively in the 1982 South Atlantic conflict. Silver nitrate solution (1 per cent) is still used for the prophylaxis of ophthalmia neonatorum because it is less likely than penicillin to produce sensitization and resistant strains of the gonococcus. Silver salts can precipitate proteins by ligand interactions and so have astringent and caustic properties. These are exploited in the use of silver nitrate pencils ('lunar caustic') to remove warts and granulation tissue. Prolonged use of silver-containing ointments may cause a slate-grey skin discoloration (argyria) which usually resolves with time.

Lead

Lead toxicity (plumbism or saturnism) was known in antiquity. Features include a metallic taste, constipation, abdominal colic, neuropathy (wrist and foot drop), encephalopathy, renal damage and anaemia caused by inhibition of haem synthesis. Its widespread use in industry (e.g. batteries, shipbuilding, print type and glazing) is now controlled, and restrictions on the composition of household paints have greatly reduced childhood poisoning. However, there is evidence that environmental exposure to, for example, tetraethyl lead, the 'antiknock' petrol additive, is associated with intellectual impairment in children. There are plans to reduce the permitted lead level in British petrol from 0.4 to 0.15 g/l, and there are compelling arguments to prohibit it altogether. Another hazard is that lead can be leached out of old water pipes in soft water areas, and cooking utensils.

Mercury, bismuth and cadmium

Prior to the 1920s, mercury was the main remedy for syphilis, hence the old adage 'a night with Venus results in a lifetime with Mercury'. Mercurial diuretics are also obsolete (p. 354). The presence of mercury in purgatives (calomel) or teething powders is considered dangerous, but it persists in several antiseptics. Elemental mercury is absorbed percutaneously or by inhalation, but when acutely swallowed (broken thermometers) it is rarely toxic. However, acute ingestion of soluble salts is corrosive to the intestine. Features of chronic poisoning include gingivitis, skin disorders, nephrotoxicity and neurological disorders such as tremor and erethism (abnormal shyness with blushing). The phrase 'mad as a hatter' comes from the use of mercury salts in the felt hat industry.

Manifestations of mercury toxicity depend on its distribution. Renal toxicity predominates with inorganic salts which do not readily enter neural tissue. Organic mercurials (methyl and other alkyl derivatives) are much more lipid-soluble. They are well absorbed and less corrosive, and can cause severe neurological toxicity without renal effects. The inhaled element is rapidly oxidized to the ionic form but not before some can cross the blood–brain barrier. Although frank poisoning is now rare, tragedies still occur, especially with methylmercury. The notorious Minamata disease was due to industrial effluent being discharged near a Japanese fishing village.

Parenteral bismuth was introduced in 1921, supplanting mercury in the treatment of syphilis until the penicillin era. Bismuth toxicity is similar to that of mercury. Insoluble bismuth chelate (De-Nol; tripotassium dicitratobis-muthate) is effective oral therapy for peptic ulceration (p. 336) and is non-toxic since it is not absorbed.

Cadmium toxicity is causing concern because of its increasing use in industry (e.g., in batteries and corrosion resistant alloys). Like inorganic mercurials, it accumulates in the kidney, bound to the protein, metallothionein.

Arsenic and antimony

Arsenic has features in common with the heavy metals. The thiol coenzyme, α-lipoic acid, which is essential for oxidative decarboxylation, is particularly sensitive to trivalent arsenic. Both penta and trivalent organic arsenicals are used to treat trypanosomiasis, although the pentavalent form is much less toxic and is probably reduced to the trivalent form in the parasite. Organic arsenicals, once adjuncts to bismuth therapy for syphilis, are used in pesticides, rodenticides and fungicides.

Arsenic is used in industry (e.g., electroplating, dyeing and cosmetics). Acute poisoning with inorganic arsenic results in severe abdominal pain, vomiting, diarrhoea, muscle cramps, renal failure, convulsions and often death. Hence its use in homicide. With chronic exposure, multisystem involvement occurs and may include malignancy. Organic arsenicals are much less toxic. The lipid-soluble arsenical gas, lewisite, penetrates the skin and causes blistering.

Antimony poisoning mimics that of arsenic. Trivalent antimonals are used in schistosomiasis, and pentavalent compounds are used to treat leishmaniasis.

Miscellaneous metallic elements

Drugs containing the heavy metal, platinum, are used in cancer chemotherapy (p. 502).

Various zinc salts are used in topical preparations for psoriasis, eczema and acne because of their antiseptic/astringent properties. Alum sticks stop minor haemorrhage (e.g., shaving cuts). Aluminium hydroxide is an antacid (p. 333) and aluminium silicate is the main component of kaolin (p. 347).

The soluble salts of the metalloid, selenium, are highly toxic, but traces of the element are essential for the function of glutathione peroxidase and the cytochrome P_{450} enzyme system. Selenium sulphide has antimitotic properties that are employed topically to control seborrhoeic dermatitis and dandruff.

Thallium is highly toxic, especially to the nervous system, but was formerly used as a depilatory. Its use in rodenticides and insecticides is strictly controlled in most countries.

CHELATING AGENTS

Compounds with two or more ligands can form complexes with metals which involve the production of a heterocyclic ring. These complexes are known as chelates ($\chi\eta\lambda\acute{\eta}$, claw). They tend to be very stable, and so pluck metals away from bonds with endogenous ligands. Chelating agents are therefore useful in the treatment of poisoning. The affinity of a chelating agent for a particular heavy metal depends on the types of ligand involved and the stereochemical arrangement of the co-ordinate bonds around the metal ion. However, no chelating agent is entirely specific for a particular metal ion and all have the potential disadvantage of removing important endogenous ions, such as calcium.

Clinically useful chelating agents must be able to penetrate into the sites of heavy metal accumulation, as well as to form complexes that are more stable than those that exist between the metal and the great excess of endogenous ligands. They should also be relatively resistant to metabolism and sufficiently water-soluble to be readily excreted in the urine. Obviously, the chelates themselves should be non-toxic. Chelating agents are concentrated in the kidney where liberation of toxic metals or removal of trace elements may damage tubular cells.

CALCIUM DISODIUM EDETATE

EDTA derivatives

Therapeutic chelating agents should have a low affinity for calcium in order to prevent problems from hypocalcaemia. Thus the disodium salt of the powerful chelating agent, EDTA (ethylene diamine tetra-acetic acid), which causes hypocalcaemic tetany and coagulation abnormalities, cannot be used systemically.

Its calcium chelate (calcium disodium edetate) does not cause significant hypocalcaemia or other toxicity, and it chelates all metals (e.g., lead and zinc) which can displace the calcium. It is a large ionic complex that does not readily cross cell membranes. Consequently, its access into tissues is limited and parenteral administration is necessary because of poor absorption. Its efficacy depends on chelation of the heavy metal in body fluids followed by redistribution of the tissue-bound metal.

DTPA derivatives

Diethylene triamine penta-acetic acid is structurally similar to EDTA but has greater affinity for most heavy metals. However, it is often no more effective because, like EDTA, efficacy is limited by access to sites of metal storage rather than binding capacity. Again, it is the calcium disodium chelate which is used clinically.

Other chelating agents

$$H - \underset{\underset{\text{SH}}{|}}{\overset{\overset{\text{H}}{|}}{C}} - \underset{\underset{\text{NH}_2}{|}}{\overset{\overset{\text{H}}{|}}{C}} - COOH$$

CYSTEINE

$$H_3C - \underset{\underset{\text{SH}}{|}}{\overset{\overset{\text{CH}_3}{|}}{C}} - \underset{\underset{\text{NH}_2}{|}}{\overset{\overset{\text{H}}{|}}{C}} - COOH$$

PENICILLAMINE

$$H - \underset{\underset{\text{SH}}{|}}{\overset{\overset{\text{H}}{|}}{C}} - \underset{\underset{\text{SH}}{|}}{\overset{\overset{\text{H}}{|}}{C}} - CH_2OH$$

DIMERCAPROL

A number of chelating agents have close similarities to the ligand-providing amino acid, cysteine, but are metabolized much more slowly. They are smaller and less ionized molecules than the EDTA derivatives, and have far better access to sites of metal deposition. One-to-one complexes involving two co-ordinate bonds are readily formed between chelating agent and metal ion. In the case of penicillamine, the metal ion binds to the sulphur and nitrogen atoms. The dimercaprol complex involves the two sulphydryl groups.

Penicillamine (dimethyl cysteine). This is a breakdown product of penicillin. It is active orally as well as parenterally. It chelates copper, lead, mercury and zinc in vivo. The L-isomer inhibits pyridoxine-dependent enzymes. The toxicity and allergic reactions observed with older preparations are mostly avoided by using pure D-penicillamine. In Wilson's disease there is a deficiency of caeruloplasmin. Deposition of toxic amounts of copper occurs and results in hepatic cirrhosis and extrapyramidal neuronal damage. Penicillamine is prophylactic and can even reverse this damage by copper mobilization. It is also used in rheumatoid arthritis (p. 136) and to prevent nephrolithiasis in cystinuria. Here, excessive cystine (cysteine–cysteine disulphide) excretion causes renal calculi. Penicillamine–cysteine disulphide is fifty times more soluble, and calculi may eventually be dissolved completely.

Dimercaprol (2,3-dimercaptopropanol, BAL) was introduced as an antidote to the arsenical war gas, lewisite (hence 'British anti-lewisite'). It is a foul-smelling oily fluid that is dissolved in vegetable oil because it is unstable in aqueous solution. Administration is by deep (painful) intramuscular injection and 50 per cent of individuals have side-effects. These tend to be more alarming than hazardous, but include transient hypertension with tachycardia, nausea, unusual burning sensations, increased secretions and even convulsions. With mercury, arsenic and cadmium, it forms stable 1:1, and even more stable and soluble 2:1, chelates. Dimercaprol chelates other metals (e.g., lead and copper) and is used in Wilson's disease.

Dimercaptosuccinic acid (DMSA) and **2,3-dimercapto-l-propanesulphonic acid, sodium salt** (DMPS), are similar but much less toxic and can be given orally. They are effective treatment for arsenic, lead and mercury poisoning and have been studied extensively in the USSR and China.

TREATMENT OF HEAVY METAL POISONING

Prompt diagnosis is important and prevention of further exposure is mandatory. Acute ingestion of heavy metal salts may have corrosive and other florid systemic actions, while the effects of chronic intoxication are usually more insidious. Supportive and symptomatic measures are important. The enzyme inhibition and other cellular damage are often initially reversible, but tend to become irreversible with time. Thus any treatment should be commenced as early as possible. Except in exceptional circumstances, heavy metal concentrations should be monitored if chelating agents are to be used because they are potentially toxic and their administration is often unpleasant (e.g., painful i.m. injections).

Gold poisoning is usually treated with dimercaprol. When chronic silver poisoning occurs the majority of the metal is in the elemental form and chelating agents are ineffective. Local sodium thiosulphate injections may reduce argyria.

Lead poisoning is particularly dangerous in small children. Children are usually given both calcium disodium edetate and dimercaprol, parenterally. A course of these can be followed by penicillamine administration which is inferior in accelerating lead excretion, but can be given orally. Adults are often treated by calcium disodium edetate alone, which is given in short courses separated by a few days to allow redistribution of the lead. Unfortunately, the non-ionic lead in the tetraethyl derivative is relatively inaccessible to chelating agents.

Outbreaks of mercury poisoning are usually misdiagnosed for months or even years, because of the vague and insidious early clinical features. Dimercaprol, dimercaptosuccinic acid and DMPS effectively protect against renal damage from inorganic mercury salts. Protection against neurological damage is much less satisfactory. Penicillamine does increase mercury excretion after exposure to the vapour or alkyl (e.g., methyl) derivatives but the clinical efficacy of treatment may not be impressive.

Bismuth, arsenic and antimony poisoning are treated with dimercaprol or penicillamine. Chelating agents are relatively ineffective against selenium intoxication because it involves oxidation of sulphydryl enzymes rather than ligand binding. Thallium poisoning has been treated with the highly toxic chelating agents, dithizone and dithiocarb, but clinical experience is limited and there is no consensus regarding their efficacy.

The radioactive heavy metals, radium and ^{90}Sr are extremely difficult to remove from the body because of their chemical similarity to calcium.

Chelating agents tend to be ineffective because very little of their calcium is replaced by the radioactive metals. These are sequestered in bone and become imprisoned because ionizing radiation destroys the surrounding capillaries. However, DTPA does effectively chelate ^{239}Pu.

ANTIDOTES

ROLE OF ANTIDOTES IN THE GENERAL MANAGEMENT OF ACUTE POISONING

The management of poisoning is based on the principles of intensive supportive care, backed up by specific treatment when necessary. Otherwise medical intervention should be kept to a minimum. A few maxims should be emphasized. All but a small minority of unconscious poisoned patients recover with supportive care alone. A clear airway is imperative; improving the airway alone may improve ventilation, blood pressure and level of consciousness. Methods to enhance drug elimination are only clinically useful in a few situations. The important ones are urinary alkalinization for aspirin poisoning (p. 126) and haemoperfusion with activated charcoal or ion-exchange resin columns for very severe barbiturate poisoning.

Antidotes are available for a very small number of poisons, of which only a few are commonly encountered in clinical practice, but nevertheless may be life-saving. Agonist–antagonist interactions at drug receptors are theoretically of value. Cholinergic and anticholinergic drugs (p. 208), alpha and beta adrenoreceptor agonists and antagonists (p. 230), histamines and antihistamines (p. 556) and opiates and naloxone (p. 114) are considered elsewhere. However, apart from naloxone, these are rarely required in practice.

Poisoning with opiates, including dextropropoxyphene, pentazocine and dihydrocodeine, should always be considered when the combination of coma and constricted pupils is encountered. The resulting respiratory depression can be fatal. When given in time, naloxone is life-saving. An intravenous dose of at least 0.8–1.2 mg is usually necessary to reverse coma. Furthermore, naloxone has a shorter duration of action than many opiates so patients need close observation, and repeated doses are often necessary.

Vitamin K$_1$ and protamine reverse the actions of oral anticoagulants and heparin, respectively (p. 473). Oximes, such as pralidoxine, reactivate cholinesterases that have been phosphorylated by organophosphorus compounds (p. 203).

Iron poisoning

Parenteral desferrioxamine should be administered if there is coma or shock, and should be seriously considered in any patient with a serum iron concentration that is above 5 mg/l. Desferrioxamine (deferoxamine) mesylate is a chelating agent that forms very stable 1:1 complexes with inorganic iron and can remove inorganic iron from ferritin and transferrin, but not from haemoglobin or cytochromes. The complexes are non-toxic and are eliminated renally. Its affinity for iron is thirty times that for calcium.

DESFERRIOXAMINE –IRON CHELATE

Absorption after oral administration is very poor. Gastric lavage with desferrioxamine is an extremely expensive and usually unnecessary method of removing ingested iron. Sodium bicarbonate (5 per cent solution) is a far cheaper alternative. Desferrioxamine may be of value in haemosiderosis and thalassaemia (p. 461).

Paracetamol poisoning

The liver metabolizes the majority of a therapeutic dose of paracetamol (acetaminophen or *N*-acetyl-*p*-aminophenol) to non-toxic glucuronide or sulphate conjugates. A small fraction (usually less than 10 per cent) is converted by microsomal cytochrome P_{450} to a potentially toxic, highly reactive, electrophilic, intermediate metabolite that is neutralized by the thiol groups of hepatic glutathione. However, paracetamol overdosage may deplete the liver of reduced glutathione. The reactive metabolite is then free to react with liver cell macromolecules and by a similar mechanism causes renal damage. The thiol-containing amino acids, *N*-acetylcysteine, cysteamine and methionine, are effective antidotes if given within 8–12 hours of the overdose. They probably act as glutathione precursors or by combining directly with the reactive metabolite. *N*-acetylcysteine is the treatment of choice because it can be given intravenously and is remarkably free from side-effects (p. 129).

Cyanide poisoning

Cyanides are widely used in industry but with such strict precautions that poisoning is extremely rare. Sodium cyanide is available for pest control.

Hydrogen cyanide is formed in the combustion of polyurethane foam. Gastric hydrochloric acid reacts with sodium or potassium cyanide to form hydrogen cyanide which is more readily absorbed than the cyanide ion itself. Small amounts of cyanide cause hyperventilation because it is a potent stimulator of the peripheral arterial chemoreceptors and inhibits cellular respiration by binding to the ferric component of cytochrome oxidase. As oxygen utilization is much reduced, patients may not be cyanosed, despite profound cellular hypoxia.

Contrary to popular belief, most patients do not die within minutes of cyanide poisoning. Many survive with no more than supportive measures such as the maintenance of adequate ventilation with a highly oxygen-enriched mixture. Antidotes have a complementary role and because they are potentially dangerous, should only be given when the diagnosis of severe poisoning is certain. The one of choice is i.v. dicobalt edetate (Kelocyanor — 600 mg, initially) which forms a readily excreted, non-toxic chelate with cyanide ions.

The older treatment is to oxidize haemoglobin to methaemoglobin thus creating an excess of ferric ions which compete for the cyanide. Intravenous sodium nitrite (10 ml of 3 per cent solution over three minutes) is usually effective. However, to produce sufficient methaemoglobin by the 'first aid' remedy of amyl nitrite inhalation would probably cause severe hypotension and cannot be recommended. After sodium nitrite, sodium thiosulphate (50 ml of 25 per cent solution over 10 minutes) should be given to accelerate the endogenous elimination of cyanide by non-toxic thiocyanate formation. Oxygen therapy appears to greatly potentiate the protective effects of this sodium nitrite/thiosulphate combination.

Drugs causing methaemoglobinaemia

Certain drugs and oxidizing agents (in particular, chlorates, used as weed killers) can cause methaemoglobinaemia. This is treated by reducing the methaemoglobin with methylene blue. Ascorbic acid is of no clinical value.

Poisoning by substrate analogues

Some poisoning is due to the compound being enzymatically converted to a toxic metabolite (p. 588). This is put to beneficial use in some cancer chemotherapy (p. 490). Fluoroacetate (a rodenticide) is metabolized to fluorocitrate thus inhibiting the Krebs cycle. Poisoning by ethylene glycol (e.g., in 'anti-freeze') and methanol (methyl alcohol) are due to their conversion by alcohol dehydrogenase to acetaldehyde and formaldehyde, respectively. By giving excess of the normal substrate of the enzyme, the formation of toxic metabolite is competitively inhibited. Thus large amounts of acetate protect against fluoroacetate and ethanol (ethyl alcohol) protects against ethylene glycol or methanol poisoning. Treatment consists of maintaining a plasma ethanol concentration of 100–200 mg/100 ml.

Alkylating agents and free radicals

Sulphydryl groups and other ligands can be inactivated by covalent bonding with alkylating agents and oxidation by free radicals. Alkylating agents have been used as riot control agents and by the military. Exposure to their vapour causes lacrimation, respiratory irritation and blistering.

Free radicals participate in toxic processes ranging from radiation damage to halogenated hydrocarbon hepatotoxicity and paraquat pulmonary toxicity. Glutathione, and in particular, the more freely diffusible sulphydryl group donors such as *N*-acetylcysteine, may have a potential protective role by neutralizing these free radicals.

Interruption of enterohepatic circulation

The oral administration of ion-exchange resins or activated charcoal has been used to enhance the elimination of drugs, such as digitoxin, which undergo substantial enterohepatic recirculation.

RESINS USED IN THERAPEUTICS

The ion-exchange resins used in therapeutics are high molecular weight polymers that are insoluble in water. Their cation- or anion-exchange sites render them hydrophilic and are provided by either inorganic acid radicals or quaternary amino groups, respectively. Given orally, they are not affected by digestive enzymes nor absorbed into the bloodstream, so they function by binding ions which diffuse freely or are secreted into the gut lumen.

Cation-exchange resins

Sodium cellulose phosphate is taken orally to reduce calcium absorption in patients with idiopathic hypercalciuria.

Sodium polystyrene sulphonate or **calcium polystyrene sulphonate** are administered orally or rectally in the treatment of hyperkalaemia. The sodium or calcium exchanges with potassium in the gut lumen which is in equilibrium with plasma potassium. In the presence of cardiac failure the calcium form is more suitable but it is contraindicated in patients with hypercalcaemia.

With all cation-exchange resins, careful monitoring is essential to prevent hypokalaemia, hypernatraemia or hypercalcaemia.

Anion-exchange resins

The chloride salts of the anion-exchange resins, cholestyramine (Questran) and colestipol (Colestid), have a high affinity for bile acids. They relieve pruritus secondary to bile acid accumulation in primary biliary cirrhosis and obstructive jaundice. They also alleviate the diarrhoea that follows ileal resection, when bile acids reach the colon.

There is a strong positive correlation between the risk of coronary heart disease and plasma concentrations of cholesterol or its main transport lipoprotein, low-density lipoprotein (LDL). When bile acids are bound by cholestyramine or colestipol, removal of negative feedback control increases hepatic cholesterol metabolism thus lowering plasma cholesterol and LDL. Patients with familial hypercholesterolaemia (Type II) have excess LDL and respond well to therapy with anion-exchange resins, together with a low cholesterol diet. However, these resins are not beneficial in other hyperlipoproteinaemias. Long-term prospective studies are in progress to elucidate whether cholestyramine reduces the risk of coronary heart disease in normal individuals.

Cholestyramine and colestipol are usually given to adults in doses of 8–16 g/day and are not without their side-effects. Their consistency and sheer bulk are unpalatable and cause gastrointestinal upsets. Steatorrhoea and impaired absorption of fat-soluble vitamins may occur. The resins release chloride resulting in hyperchloraemic acidosis. They bind acidic drugs, so several hours should elapse between giving resin and any acidic drug.

Extracorporeal haemoperfusion with anion-exchange resin columns has been used to treat severe barbiturate and other poisoning (p. 157). Unfortunately, the procedure removes physiologically important blood components, such as platelets, as well as the intoxicating drug. This illustrates the important therapeutic maxim that before using a treatment, its necessity and potential benefits should be weighed carefully against any possible harmful effects.

FURTHER READING

Aposhian H. V. (1983) DMSA and DMPS – Water soluble antidotes for heavy metal poisoning. *Ann. Rev. Pharmacol. Toxicol.*, 23: 193.

De Bruin A. (1977) *Biochemical Toxicology of Environmental Agents*, p. 879. Amsterdam: Elsevier.

Klaassen C. D. (1980) Heavy metals and heavy-metal antagonists. In Gilman A. G., Goodman L. S. & Gilman A. (eds) *The Pharmacological Basis of Therapeutics*, p. 1615. London: Baillière Tindall.

Perrin D. D. & Whitehouse M. W. (1981) Metal ion therapy: some fundamental considerations. In Rainsford D. K., Brune K. & Whitehouse M. W. (eds) *Trace Elements in the Pathogenesis and Treatment of Inflammation*, p. 261. Agents and Actions Supplements, Vol. 8. Basel: Birkhauser Verlag.

Proudfoot A. T. (1982) *Acute Poisoning*. Oxford: Blackwell Scientific.

Prescott L. F. (1979) Drug overdosage and poisoning. In Avery G. S. (ed.) *Drug Treatment;*

Principles and Practice of Clinical Pharmacology and Therapeutics, 2nd Ed. p. 263. Sydney: ADIS.

Prescott L. F. & Critchley J. A. J. H. (1983) The treatment of acetaminophen poisoning. *Ann. Rev. Pharmacol. Toxicol.*, 23: 87.

16   The Principles of Drug Therapy in Skin Disorders

R. C. Heading

To many physicians and to undergraduate students, the treatment of skin disorders sometimes appears to be irrational or empirical, and possibly more appropriate to the practices of a former age. While it must be admitted that smearing diseased skin with ointments containing zinc oxide and castor oil, or coal tar and salicylic acid, may initially seem to be unscientific to the contemporary student of pharmacology, the principles which underlie the drug treatment of skin disorders are, of course, no different from those relating to any other organ or system. However, the skin differs from most other organs in being readily accessible and visible. Thus, the topical application of drugs to areas of diseased skin forms a major part of the therapeutics of dermatology, and the response to such treatment is easily observed. It is perhaps in this field of topical therapy that the physician who is more familiar with 'internal' medicine may be uncertain of the nature and actions of the drugs that are available.

It is not the purpose of this chapter to provide a guide to the treatment of the various skin diseases, as this is more appropriately considered in a textbook of treatment, but some of the principles and objectives of drug therapy in dermatology will be considered.

TOPICAL PREPARATIONS

Preparations for topical application and their absorption from the skin will be discussed.

Vehicles (Bases)

Preparations for topical application to the skin consist of 'vehicles' (lotions, creams, ointments, etc.) in which active drugs may be dissolved or suspended. The term 'base' is widely used as a synonym for 'vehicle', and should not be confused with a 'base' in chemical terminology, the opposite of an acid. Although the constituents of a vehicle are normally inactive pharmacologically, they often have physical actions of major therapeutic value. Moreover, the results of therapy with pharmacologically active drugs may be very much affected by the nature of the vehicle used.

Lotions

These are solutions of active drugs in water or water–alcohol mixtures. Quite apart from the actions of the active drug it contains, a lotion will cool inflamed skin by evaporation of the aqueous phase, and the resulting vasoconstriction helps to reduce the discomfort of inflammation. Lotions are, therefore, used to cool and soothe inflammatory skin lesions.

Creams

These are emulsions, either oil in water or water in oil. They also cool inflamed skin by evaporation of the water component, although the water-in-oil emulsions (cold creams) are more effective in this respect than oil-in-water systems (vanishing creams). With both types, the oily component which remains after such evaporation may act as a barrier to the passage of water through it and thus may serve to impede water evaporation from the skin (helpful for dry skin) or protect it from external moisture (e.g., 'nappy creams', to protect an infant's perineal skin from irritation by urine).

The oily component of creams may serve as a vehicle for lipid-soluble drugs.

Ointments

These generally have no aqueous component. There are three types:

1. Water-soluble ointments are mixtures of glycols, particularly polyethylene glycols.
2. Emulsifying ointments contain paraffins with an emulsifying wax (e.g., cetostearyl alcohol and sodium lauryl sulphate) or an emulsifying fat, such as lanolin.
3. Non-emulsifying ointments contain paraffins or other long-chain hydrocarbon substances which are immiscible with water.

The oils, fats and greases which are pharmacologically inactive constituents of creams and ointments are alternatively termed 'emollients'. These substances are immiscible with water, and, as described above, will reduce water evaporation from the skin. However, because of their immiscibility, oils and greases cannot be effectively applied to exuding skin lesions, and such lesions therefore require a water-based application. The general principle 'wet lesion – wet dressing' is fundamental to the treatment of skin diseases.

In certain circumstances, an ointment or cream has to be diluted to reduce the concentration of a pharmacologically active agent it contains. Creams are diluted with the continuous phase of the emulsion — that is, water for oil-in-water emulsions or oil for water-in-oil emulsions. The dilution of ointments is undertaken by the same general principles, and thus polyethylene glycols might be used to dilute a water-soluble ointment, whereas soft white paraffin would be more appropriate for a greasy ointment. Specific recommendations regarding diluents for a particular ointment are generally provided by its manufacturers.

Powders
These are used for two purposes. They may act as a dry lubricant between opposing skin surfaces where friction occurs; talc (a hydrated magnesium silicate) is particularly effective for this purpose. Alternatively, powders which absorb water readily (e.g., starch or zinc oxide) may be used to increase the evaporating surface of a moist skin lesion and thus will act as drying agents.

Shake lotions
These are aqueous suspensions of insoluble powders and therefore combine the cooling effect of a lotion with the drying action of a powder. They are used on inflamed and exuding skin lesions. Calamine lotion, which contains powdered zinc carbonate, is one of the best-known.

Pastes
These are ointments containing insoluble powders. They may be sufficiently thick to provide physical protection of a healing lesion against abrasion.

ABSORPTION FROM TOPICAL PREPARATIONS

When a pharmacologically active substance is applied to the skin, its absorption is principally impeded by the superficial layer of keratin. In some respects, this layer acts as a simple physical barrier in that absorption through it proceeds in accordance with the physicochemical laws of diffusion. Penetration is dependent on temperature and on the concentration of the drug in the preparation applied. It is also dependent on the thickness of the keratin layer, and for this reason, the skin of the palm, which is particularly thick, is more resistant to penetration than the skin on the forearm or chest. Of course, the thickness of the keratin layer may be increased by skin disease, but it may then also be functionally abnormal. For example, excessive and abnormal keratinization occurs in chronic psoriasis, but this keratin is less effective as a barrier than the thinner keratin layer of healthy skin.

There are some aspects of absorption through the skin which indicate that the barrier is more complex than an inert semipermeable membrane. For example, rates of absorption are not releated in any simple fashion to the molecular weights of the substances being absorbed. In addition, some drugs may be concentrated in the keratin layer, which then acts as a reservoir. There are, therefore, few general rules by which absorption of a given drug may be reliably predicted, but four general points relating to absorption may be made:

1. Ionized substances tend to be poorly absorbed.
2. When an active drug is dissolved in a vehicle which is itself absorbed, absorption of the drug usually proceeds in parallel with absorption of the vehicle.
3. The physicochemical laws of partition apply to drug absorption from non-absorbable vehicles. Thus, a drug which is highly soluble in such a vehicle may be poorly absorbed, whereas it will be more readily absorbed from another vehicle in which it is less soluble.
4. The absorption of many topically applied drugs may be enhanced by *occlusion*. This consists of covering the treated skin with an impermeable plastic or polythene sheet which prevents water evaporation. The keratin layer then becomes softer and less effective as a barrier, so absorption of the drug is facilitated. An occlusive effect is also obtained by the use of thick greasy ointments.

Certain industrial solvents, notably dimethyl sulphoxide and dimethylacetamide, are known to produce marked impairment of the barrier function of keratin without disrupting its structural integrity. At present these substances are not much used, because of possible toxicity, but occasionally they may provide a means of enhancing the absorption of other drugs.

Pharmacologically Active Agents Applied to the Skin

In general, topical preparations are an appropriate means of drug administration to the epidermis while dermal disorders are often better treated by systemic routes of administration. This should not be taken to imply that topical application does not lead to systemic absorption, since, with some drugs, an undesired degree of such absorption may occur. Other drugs may sometimes be administered systemically from a controlled release 'patch' preparation that is applied to the skin. For example, glyceryl trinitrate may be given in this manner (p. 308). Nevertheless, the majority of agents used topically have their actions on various aspects of epidermal growth and integrity, and thus act on the cells (keratinocytes), on their connections (desmosomes), on keratin itself, or on infections of the epidermis.

Coal tar

Coal tar inhibits epidermal cell mitoses and abnormal keratinization. In psoriasis, where epidermal cell proliferation is increased and keratinization is disorganized (parakeratosis), coal tar minimizes the abnormality and facilitates restoration of the normal growth process. Coal tar is incorporated in various ointments and pastes, and concentrations of 3–5 per cent are appropriate for most purposes (e.g., coal tar and salicylic acid ointment, BPC or coal tar paste, BPC). Greater concentrations of tar are also available (e.g., coal tar paint, BPC, zinc and coal tar paste, BPC). The choice of preparation is determined by the nature, site and chronicity of the lesion being treated, and also by the suitability of the preparation for a particular patient's circumstances. Thick messy applications are usually not appropriate for a patient at home, and thus the use of zinc and coal tar paste, for example, is virtually limited to hospital practice.

Ichthammol*

Ichthammol is an almost black viscous liquid with a strong characteristic odour. It consists of the ammonium salts of the sulphonic acids of an oily substance prepared by the destructive distillation of a bituminous schist (shale), together with ammonium sulphate. It used to be considered as being similar to, but less potent than, coal tar in its actions. This is now much less certain since the realization that epidermal cell division is inhibited by a bland ointment alone (i.e., one without a pharmacologically active constituent). Ichthammol is used in the treatment of chronic eczemas, usually as an ointment or paste containing 1% of the drug. Bandages impregnated with ichthammol are sometimes a convenient way to treat and protect diseased skin.

Salicylic acid

Salicylic acid is a keratolytic agent which softens keratin and promotes desquamation. It is used to remove the excess scaly keratin found in psoriasis, chronic eczemas and some other conditions. Salicylic acid is incorporated in creams and ointments at various concentrations, but is usually used at strengths of 2–3%. At higher concentrations, more substantial desquamation of the epidermis is produced, and injudicious use is liable to cause ulceration. Systemic absorption of the drug may be a hazard if it is applied to large areas of skin.

Dithranol

Dithranol is used in the treatment of psoriasis. Its mechanism of action is uncertain, but may involve inhibition of epidermal cell division by the formation of complexes with DNA. Dithranol is normally used at concentrations of between 0.1 and 1% in zinc and salicylic acid paste for the treatment of severely thickened areas of long-standing psoriasis. Unfortunately, the drug both burns and discolours uninvolved skin as well as staining clothing or bed linen, and its application must, therefore, be strictly limited to the diseased area. For this reason, the use of dithranol is usually restricted to patients admitted to hospital.

*It has various other names, including bituminol and ichthyol. The latter is from the Greek word for a fish, possibly since the bituminous rocks from which it is distilled contain the fossilized remains of fish.

Benzoyl peroxide

Benzoyl peroxide is an antibacterial agent with mild keratolytic properties used in the treatment of acne. Lotions and creams, containing 5 or 10% of the drug, are available.

Antibiotics

The uses of antibiotics are considered in Chapter 1. The topical application of antibiotics is appropriate in the treatment of skin lesions that are perpetuated or complicated by secondary infection by bacteria and in the treatment of primary infections that are sufficiently superficial to justify this route of administration (e.g., some cases of impetigo). Topical application of antibiotics to deep-seated infections, such as boils, is quite useless.

Although the choice of antibiotic may depend to some extent on the infecting organism, gentamicin, framycetin, gramicidin, neomycin, bacitracin, and polymyxin B are incorporated in a variety of preparations for topical use. Sodium fusidate ointment may be of particular value in staphylococcal infections. Chlortetracycline ointment is now less valuable than it used to be, because of the increasing frequency of infections by resistant organisms.

Antifungal agents

Fungal infections of the skin are often responsive to appropriate topical therapy, and this is discussed on page 55. The term 'fungicide' tends to be applied rather indiscriminately to antifungal drugs, but the majority probably serve to impair fungal growth rather than actually kill the organism in situ. However, the fungal hyphae are then incapable of invading the newly forming layers of the epidermis and thus are eventually shed by desquamation.

Benzoic acid in a lotion or ointment and **undecenoic acid** (often as zinc undecenoate) in powder or ointment form impair fungal growth.

Tolnaftate is an antifungal agent used topically as a 1% solution or cream.

Clotrimazole, econazole and **miconazole** are imidazole drugs with antifungal and antiyeast activity. Creams containing 1% clotrimazole or econazole, or 2% miconazole are used.

Nystatin and amphotericin are effective against superficial infection with *Candida*, but have no activity against dermatophyte infections. Nystatin ointment, BPC, contains 100 000 units/g in a polyethylene and liquid paraffin gel base.

Dyes

The aniline dyes have an important place in the history of antibacterial chemotherapy, since it was recognition of their antibacterial properties that led to the development of sulphonamides. Several of these dyes are still occasionally useful as paints or lotions for topical application.

Aqueous eosin (2%) is antibacterial and weakly antifungal. It may be used on inflamed and ulcerated skin lesions.

Castellani's paint (magenta paint, BPC) has a broad spectrum of antibacterial and antifungal activity.

Gentian violet (crystal violet paint, BPC) may also be used, especially for the treatment of superficial *Candida* infections.

Antiparasitic agents

Benzyl benzoate is highly effective in the treatment of scabies (infestation with *Sarcoptes scabiei*). The drug is applied as an emulsion and two or three applications at intervals of 24 hours are usual.

Crotamiton (Eurax), as a 10% lotion or ointment, is used in the treatment of scabies. The drug has antipruritic properties as well as killing the sarcoptes parasite, and therefore provides good relief of symptoms.

Gamma benzene hexachloride (Quellada) is effective in the treatment of scabies and pediculosis. It is usually applied as a cream or lotion, and has the advantage that one application is usually adequate. It is a chlorinated insecticide, larvicide and acaricide.

Malathion (Prioderm) is effective in dealing with head or pubic lice if used as a 0.5% lotion. This is an organophosphorus insecticide that is also used as an agricultural and horticultural pesticide.

Astringents

Astringents are substances that are applied to wet (i.e., exuding) lesions to precipitate and coagulate the protein of the exudate. They 'dry' the lesion. Astringents are generally incorporated in aqueous solutions and are applied as soaks or are painted on. Aluminium acetate, zinc sulphate and potassium permanganate are used in this way. Lead acetate is also effective, but there is concern about possible systemic absorption.

Silver nitrate (0.5–1% solution) is a potent astringent. At higher concentrations it is caustic.

Corticosteroids

The corticosteroids are used in the treatment of many skin disorders, and, as in various other situations, the pharmacological basis of their beneficial actions is often uncertain. Probably their best-known role is in the treatment of eczema, where they are highly effective in promoting healing, probably by virtue of inhibiting allergic responses, reducing inflammation and retarding epidermal cell division. Hydrocortisone (1% ointment) is effective in many situations, but the potent fluorinated steroids, betamethasone, fluocinolone and clobetasol, are widely used. The fluorinated forms will make acne rosacea worse. Since topical application of corticosteroids will inevitably impair the skin's natural defences againt infection, many steroid preparations include an antibacterial agent. This is especially desirable in the treatment of lesions that are liable to infection, such as infected or seborrhoeic eczemas.

Unfortunately, prolonged use of the fluorinated steroids leads to skin atrophy, with development of striae, telangiectasia and an increased liability to bruising. Hirsutism is also likely. Accordingly, these drugs should not be used on a long-term basis unless the ointments that are normally employed are diluted to reduce the steroid concentration. The side-effects are then much less frequent. If long-term local steroid therapy is necessary mild preparations may be preferred.

Systemic absorption of topically applied steroids undoubtedly occurs, but the risk of clinically significant pituitary and adrenal suppression has probably been exaggerated. It is, nevertheless, a complication which should be borne in mind, especially in infants, and in adults if large areas of skin are being treated for long periods. Absorption of steroids is much enhanced by the use of occlusive dressings.

Drugs used in the treatment of photosensitivity

Sunburn is an inflammatory response of normal skin to light of ultraviolet wavelengths in the 290–320 nm range.

Para-aminobenzoic acid and mexenone (Uvistat) absorb light of these wavelengths, and therefore provide an effective barrier against sunburn when applied as a cream. They may also be effective in cases of skin photosensitivity (an abnormal response induced by disease or drugs), but this may also be due to light of longer wavelengths, and a physical barrier to light is then necessary. Preparations for this purpose are mostly ointments containing zinc oxide or titanium dioxide to make them opaque, and are usually tinted for cosmetic acceptability.

Chloroquine or hydroxychloroquine when given systemically is concentrated in the basal layer of the epidermis, and provides an effective internal barrier to light. However, its toxicity, particularly to the retina (p. 70), implies that it should only be used for this purpose in severely afflicted patients in whom the more conventional means of protection are inadequate or impractical. Courses of treatment should not exceed six months.

PUVA

This acronym refers to a form of treatment based on the interaction of methoxsalen (8-methoxypsoralen) and long-wave ultraviolet light. Two hours after oral administration of methoxsalen the patient is exposed to ultraviolet light of 320–400 nm wavelength. This causes the substance or a derivative to combine with pyrimidine bases in DNA, resulting in an inhibition of cell division.

PUVA treatment appears to be very effective in psoriasis and also in mycosis fungoides. However, because of the theoretical possibility of chromosomal damage or even the induction of epidermal malignancy, PUVA treatment in the UK is at present subject to careful monitoring.

DRUGS GIVEN SYSTEMICALLY

Most of the drugs administered systemically for the treatment of dermatological disorders are also used for other purposes and have been fully described in these contexts.

Accordingly, only a brief reference to some drug actions that have particular relevance to the skin will be made here.

Antihistamines (H1 antagonists; p. 555) have an exaggerated reputation as effective antipruritics. They are of undoubted value in the treatment of urticaria, but a primary role for histamine in mediating other causes of itching is less certain. The sedative properties of many antihistamine drugs may be the basis of much of their apparent success as antipruritics.

Antibiotics (Chapter 1) may be administered systemically for deep infections of the skin or when deep or widespread extension of infection from a superficial lesion is suspected (e.g., streptococcal cellulitis, which may develop from infection of an apparently trivial skin lesion).

Griseofulvin (p. 60) is used for systemic treatment of many fungal (dermatophyte) infections of the skin. Prolonged therapy is usually necessary.

Ketoconazole (p. 58) is effective against superficial (i.e., mucocutaneous) and systemic fungal and yeast infections. It may also be used in the treatment of fungal infections of the finger or toe nails, but prolonged therapy is needed. It is available in 200 mg tablets.

Etretinate (Tigason) is a synthetic derivative of vitamin A and is a relatively new agent that is of value in the treatment of hyperkeratotic and dyskeratotic disorders, including congenital ichthyosis and severe psoriasis that is refractory to other therapy. The drug is said to be teratogenic and therefore its use in women who have child-bearing potential may be hazardous. It is available to hospitals in the UK in 10 and 25 mg capsules.

13-*cis*-Retinoic acid is also a derivative of vitamin A and may be used in a dose of up to 1 mg/kg body weight per day to treat severe acne. It is also potentially teratogenic.

Tretinoin (Retin-A) should not be confused with 13-*cis*-retinoic acid. It is available for topical use in forms of acne in which comedones, papules and pustules predominate, and is supplied as a 0.025% lotion or gel, or a 0.05% cream.

Antimalarials (p. 69), particularly chloroquine and hydroxychloroquine, are valuable in the treatment of discoid lupus erythematosus. Their mode of action in this condition has not been satisfactorily defined, but it appears that their property of minimizing photosensitivity is not a sufficient explanation. They may interfere with an abnormal immunological process that is thought to occur in the skin as a result of activity by a 'forbidden clone' of lymphoid cells.

The usual dose of chloroquine or hydroxychloroquine is 300 mg, daily, initially, with a maintenance dose of 1 g/week. Toxic effects (p. 70) must be borne in mind and are a major problem with chloroquine.

Dapsone is used in the treatment of dermatitis herpetiformis. It is remarkably effective, but the mechanism of action is unknown. The dose required varies from 50–300 mg, daily. Minor haemolysis is frequently induced, especially at the higher doses; clinically significant methaemoglobinaemia, neutropenia and haemolytic anaemia can occur.

Corticosteroids are given systemically in the treatment of many skin disorders, including severe erythema multiforme (Stevens–Johnson syndrome), exfoliative dermatitis, pemphigus, pemphigoid, dermatomyositis, pyoderma gangrenosum and severe drug eruptions. The increased risk of secondary infection of a skin lesion is an inevitable accompaniment of corticosteroid therapy. The general properties, actions and side-effects of corticosteroids have been described elsewhere (pp. 404–7).

Methotrexate (p. 503) is of value in occasional cases of severe psoriasis. An intermittent dosage regimen is usually employed to minimize the risk of hepatic fibrosis.

DRUG SENSITIVITY AND THE SKIN

The involvement of the skin in adverse reactions to many drugs is discussed in Chapter 17, and therefore will not be repeated here. However, it is perhaps appropriate to re-emphasize that sensitivity reactions are no less frequent when preparations are given topically than after systemic routes of administration have been employed, and that the risk of such a reaction is a factor to be considered when choosing therapy. For example, sensitivity to the topical application of neomycin is not unusual, whereas such a response is very infrequent with chlortetracycline. Unfortunately, the frequency with which a particular drug gives rise to sensitivity reactions when administered systemically is a poor guide to the risk of reactions to topical application.

The topical use of antihistamines is now virtually obsolete, because of a high risk of sensitivity, although this is rare with systemic administration. Similarly, sensitivity is frequently encountered with topically applied local anaesthetics, whereas it is much less frequent if they are given by injection. It should be self-evident that, in general, the occurrence of a sensitivity reaction to a drug, whatever the route of its administration, is a contraindication to further use of that drug. For example, a patient who has suffered from aplastic anaemia as a result of taking chloramphenicol (p. 18), and has been fortunate enough to survive, should not have it applied to the skin.

FURTHER READING

Abel E. A. & Farber E. M. (1980) Photochemotherapy. In: Rook A. & Savin J. (eds) *Recent Advances in Dermatology*, pp. 259–283, Edinburgh: Churchill Livingstone.

British National Formulary, Number 6 (1983) Drugs acting on the skin, pp. 332–364. London: British Medical Association/The Pharmaceutical Society of Great Britain.

Champion R. H. (1981) Psoriasis and its treatment. *Br. med J.*, 282: 343.

Cunliffe W. J. (1980) Acne vulgaris: pathogenesis and treatment. *Br. med. J.*, 280: 1394.

Editorial (1981) Retinoids in dermatology. *Lancet*, i: 537.

Hay R. (1982) Ketoconazole. *Br. med J.*, 285: 584.

Hemseler T., Honigsmann H., Wolff K. & Christophers E. (1981) Oral 8-methyoxypsoralen photochemotherapy of psoriasis. *Lancet*, i: 851.

Ive A. & Comaish S. (1980) Topical therapy. In: Rook A. & Savin J. (eds) *Recent Advances in Dermatology*, pp. 285–315, Edinburgh: Churchill Livingstone.

Jones H., Blanc D. & Cunliffe W. J. (1980) 13-*cis*-retinoic acid and acne. *Lancet*, ii: 1048.

Mills O. H. & Kligman A. M. (1983) Drugs that are ineffective in the treatment of acne vulgaris. *Br. med J.*,, 108, 371.

17 Adverse Drug Reactions

R. H. Girdwood

Appendix I refers to genetic variations in man that may lead to unexpected reactions to drugs; haemolytic anaemia occurs in those deficient in glucose-6-phosphate dehydrogenase (p. 564). Overdosage with certain substances may cause illness or death, and drug interactions, although sometimes beneficial, are more often likely to cause trouble to the patient (p. 598).

Public attention was drawn to the possible dangers of new medications on 26 November 1961, when the newspaper *Welt am Sonntag* published an article disclosing the suspicions of certain physicians that the recently introduced hypnotic thalidomide could cause fetal deformities if given during pregnancy. In the UK this led to the setting up in 1963 of the Committee on Safety of Drugs. The drug industry agreed neither to organize clinical trials nor to market a new preparation without the approval of this group of advisers.

Meanwhile, comprehensive legislation was being prepared, and this led to the passing of the Medicines Act of 1968. One of the provisions of the Act was the formation of a Committee on Safety of Medicines, a statutory body to replace the voluntary one; it was established to evaluate the evidence submitted by pharmaceutical companies about their products and to advise the Licensing Authority as to whether or not a new drug should be accepted.

Doctors in the UK are asked to notify suspected toxicity or side-effects, preferably on an official card, to the Medical Assessor (Adverse Reactions), Committees on Safety of Medicines and Dental and Surgical Materials, Market Towers, 1 Nine Elms Lane, London SW8 5BR. For all drugs, serious or unusual reactions should be reported. For new drugs, all reactions should be recorded. Some may be selected for monitoring by a post-marketing surveillance scheme to ensure that adverse reactions are quickly identified.

When a drug is promoted, the manufacturers must by law produce to doctors in the UK a data sheet in a standard form, and the Association of the British Pharmaceutical Industry, 12 Whitehall, London SW1A 2DY, which co-operates readily with members of the medical profession, has bound many of the data sheets in a volume named the ABPI Data Sheet Compendium, which appears regularly. The data sheets include for each preparation a note about contraindications and warnings; this includes known side-effects and precautions to be observed in taking the drug, alone or in combination, and also information about the effects of overdosage and how to treat them. The Committee on Review of Medicines is studying the safety and efficacy of drugs that were available before the Medicines Act of 1968 was passed and which were granted a Licence of Right.

Some drug companies provide an information service to which doctors may refer by letter or telephone and adverse reactions reported to the companies must be conveyed by them to the Committee on Safety of Medicines. Most countries have some measure of control over the marketing of new drugs, but in some developing countries drugs are promoted without due regard to their efficacy or adequate warning about their possible adverse effects. Not only do many countries have a body that keeps an adverse reactions register, but also a composite one is maintained by the World Health Organization. However, it has to be stated that the standard of reporting is poor in most countries. Sometimes this is because of the doctor's fear of litigation, and for this reason the information given to any such Committee must be treated by it as strictly confidential.

The fact that a drug is alleged to have caused a reaction is not proof that this is correct. The giving of a substance and the development of an illness may be coincidental, or several drugs may have been given simultaneously. If an adverse reaction is then reported, each drug should be mentioned. Aplastic anaemia sometimes follows the taking, simultaneously, of three non-narcotic analgesics. Any one of them may be the cause, a combination of two or more may be the reason, or the incident may be coincidental. Nevertheless, as there is uncertainty, aplastic anaemia must then be shown in a register against each of the three analgesics that have been given. If at the same time the patient is reported as having been given sodium chloride, it would not be sensible to list in a register that sodium chloride may cause aplastic anaemia. However, when there is any doubt about possible cause and effect, the substance must be included.

Every effort is made to avoid the marketing of drugs that will cause adverse reactions and a promising new product may have to be abandoned after years of preliminary work because of some unexpected development even at the stage of clinical trials. It has been stated that for every drug that is marketed preliminary work has been carried out on 8000. Such figures cannot be precise, but they indicate the problems facing research workers in the drug industry.

Tests on animals, including teratogenicity trials, are carried out with substances that are promising, but often the only way to know what will happen when a drug is given to humans is to administer it to them. In the first instance, a new substance that has passed all preliminary screening tests and is likely to be of therapeutic value is commonly given to volunteers (*not* patients) before it is taken to the Committee on Safety of Medicines. The volunteers are frequently workers in the drug industry and it is obvious that problems must arise at this stage of organization. Indeed, despite the fact that it was the thalidomide tragedy that led to the present system of drug monitoring, it would not be correct to suggest that an entirely new hypnotic could be guaranteed to be absolutely safe if given early in pregnancy even after having been screened on a few animal species (p. 562). To this problem there seems to be no complete solution.

EXPECTED ADVERSE REACTIONS

With some medications the beneficial effects are so obvious that the drug must be made available despite the fact that adverse reactions are predictable. Throughout this book reference has been made to the known adverse effects of certain drugs, many of which have been in use for years. It should be noted that side-effects are not always adverse effects; they can be beneficial.

PROPRIETARY NAMES

Throughout this book approved names have been used whenever possible. The British Pharmacopoeia Commission, acting on behalf of the Medicines Commission, regularly publishes a list of approved names. Thus in 1981 the latest edition of a list of the names issued after 1948, together with those issued earlier for substances that had not become the subject of monographs in the *British Pharmacopoeia*, was published. Communications relating to approved names are dealt with by the Secretary and Scientific Director, British Pharmacopoeia Commission, Market Towers, 1 Nine Elms Lane, London SW8 5NQ. The booklet *British Approved Names, 1981* * is valuable because it includes a guide to their pronunciation and gives a list of proprietary names with the approved equivalent. The *British Pharmacopoeia* was last published in 1980.

The relevance of this information to the subject of adverse drug reactions may be questioned. The matter is considered at this stage because so many substances have a number of proprietary names with no relation to one another or to the approved name, and the practitioner may be in doubt as to what he is prescribing. Frequently even the approved name gives no indication of the chemical structure of a substance, but usually it is helpful.

Problems of nomenclature are frequently encountered. Thus dipyridamole (p. 485) is easily confused with disopyramide (p. 299), particularly since both may be used to treat patients with cardiac disorders. The

---

*British Approved Names 1981 is published by Her Majesty's Stationery Office at a cost of £6.95. It is available from Government Bookshops in the UK at 49 High Holborn, London WC1V 6HB; 13a Castle Street, Edinburgh EH2 3AR; 41 The Hayes, Cardiff CF1 1JW; Brazennose Street, Manchester M60 8AS; Southey House, Wine Street, Bristol BS1 2BQ; 258 Broad Street, Birmingham B1 2HE; 80 Chichester Street, Belfast BT1 4JY.

proprietary names Ceporin, Ceporex, Kefadol, Keflex, Keflin and Kefzol are confusing, but, unfortunately, *British Approved Names 1981* lists 24 cephalosporin or cephamycin antibiotics whose names commence with cef or ceph. The only way a doctor or student can manage this type of problem is by knowing the names, uses and dosages of two or three of the alternatives and by keeping up to date as newer, more effective substances with fewer adverse effects are marketed.

It is not practicable to ask medical students to remember a variety of proprietary names for the same substance and it is important for a doctor or nurse to be sure just what is being used, particularly in relation to adverse reactions. The argument in *favour* of using proprietary names is that various preparations of the same substance may differ in their availability and, hence, may not be equivalent in therapeutic efficacy. Moreover, in some countries there are laws that may be invoked when a patient takes legal action following an alleged adverse reaction following the administration of a drug. If a proprietary name has not been used this may transfer the liability from the manufacturer to the prescriber or pharmacist.

ALLERGIC RESPONSES

HYPERSENSITIVITY AND IDIOSYNCRASY

Apart from recognized genetic variations which may be familial and lead to an abnormal response to a drug, there may be an unexpected reaction in an individual. * This is frequently known as an *idiosyncrasy*. Sometimes the term *hypersensitivity* is used; this may be an unexpected event after the first dose, or, in its more common usage, a reaction on a subsequent occasion. *Hypersusceptibility* means a greater than normal response of the expected kind to the ordinary dose of a drug and to avoid confusion the term 'hypersensitivity' should not be used as a synonym for this.

The term *drug allergy* is used in a very vague sense, having different meanings to different authorities. It really should be limited to situations in which there is evidence that an abnormal response is due to an antigen–antibody type of reaction, though frequently the mechanism is not certain. The word 'allergy' is derived from the Greek 'ἄλλος (other, different)

---

*There is a non-profit making organization known as the Medic-Alert Foundation, 9 Hanover Street, London W1R 9HF; telephone no. 01-499 2261. It has a small life-membership fee and provides a metal bracelet or necklace indicating sensitivity to penicillin or other medical products. A central file is kept and additional information is available to authorized persons about the medical abnormality of the member. A stamped addressed envelope should be enclosed. This is a world-wide organization founded by a Californian doctor whose daughter nearly died after being given an antitetanus injection, as it had not been realized that she was allergic to this antitoxin. In the USA and Canada the telephone number is 209-634-4917 and in South Africa it is 43-7003.

together with ἔργον (work), and was first used to mean the altered state produced by a sensitizing dose of foreign material.

Anaphylaxis means extreme sensitivity to the introduction of foreign matter into the body. However, the term 'anaphylaxis' or *anaphylactic shock* is used if it is an antigen–antibody reaction, and 'anaphylactoid' if no immunological mechanism is known to be involved.

It must be admitted that the terminology is confused, confusing and not always used correctly.

The Immunological System

B cells

Lymphocytes differentiate from precursor bone marrow cells into two main types. About 25% are B cells, which leave the marrow to localize in the lymphoid tissues of the gut, spleen and elsewhere. They are so called because of analogies with lymphocytes derived from the bursa of Fabricius in birds. These cells are recognizable by the presence of membrane-bound immunoglobulin (Ig) on their cell surface. Plasma cells are derived from B cells and they can synthesize immunoglobulin.

T cells

About 25% of peripheral blood lymphocytes are T cells, so called because they require the presence of the thymus to mature normally. They are involved in delayed sensitivity reactions and in homograft rejection, and the thymus seems to direct the differentiation of those lymphocyte cells that come within its influence, rendering them immunologically competent and able to react appropriately with an antigen. A cell-mediated antibody response is one where, following stimulation by an antigen, the antibody that is formed is not free, but is bound to the surface of the lymphocytes, which are then said to be sensitized. Unlike the B lymphocytes or the plasma cells which rapidly synthesize an antibody and release it, the T lymphocytes, when sensitized, undergo morphological changes, becoming larger, with more basophil cytoplasm and nuclear changes. Advantage can be taken of this alteration when attempts are being made to identify T cells because similar changes can be produced in them by various plant mitogens, such as phytohaemagglutinin derived from the kidney bean. This is referred to as lymphocyte transformation. Moreover, sheep erythrocytes can form a rosette around T cells (the active rosette test) and there is a further form of recognition in that T lymphocytes react with anti-T lymphocyte antisera.

So far as the action of sensitized T cells is concerned, there are two main subsets, as has been shown by using monoclonal antibodies (p. 552) to cell surface antigens. Some 40–50% of peripheral blood lymphocytes are T cells of a *helper–inducer* subset and these have a 62 000 dalton surface protein.

They assist in the activation of B cells, as can be seen by the development of the latter into plasma cells in culture conditions with stimulation by pokeweed, and they also help the other main subset of T cells to develop cytotoxic properties.

This second subset, the cells of which are identified by antibodies to a 32 000–43 000 dalton surface protein, includes *suppressor* T cells which inhibit the induction of Ig synthesis in B lymphocytes and also cytotoxic T cells. Such cell populations may be involved in defence against viral infections. The fact that one subset of T cells helps B cells to participate in an immune response whereas another suppresses it means that there is a mechanism to clamp down a continuing response. There is an accelerator and a brake.

A number of active T-cell products are already being produced in the laboratory and in the future may well have a place in the treatment of immunological disorders.

Immunoglobulins

Immunoglobulins are the proteins that have antibody activity. They are secreted by B lymphocytes in the later stages of their development into plasma cells. There are five classes, designated immunoglobulin IgG, IgA, IgM, IgE, and IgD. Each has a basic structure of four linked polypeptide chains, designated heavy and light chains. The classes differ from one another both in the heavy chain structure and in the way the chains are linked. One end of the Ig molecule (termed the Fab, or fragment antibody binding end) carries the site that combines with a specific antigen. The other end (the Fc, or fragment crystallizable end) determines many of the biological properties characteristic of a given Ig class. For example, IgG (the major immunoglobulin in the serum and extravascular fluids) has the ability to activate the complement system, and this is especially important in immune complex disorders. The only class to be transported across the placenta is IgG. In contrast, IgA does not activate complement, but a form of IgA is the main immunoglobulin of external secretions. Little is known about IgD, but IgE, which is present in the serum in very small concentration, has the ability to bind to mast cells by its Fc end. Subsequent binding of antigen triggers the release of inflammatory products from the mast cells, and this may lead to an anaphylactic reaction. IgM is the immunoglobulin with the highest molecular weight and is particularly effective in activating complement to cause lysis of cells.

The complement system consists of a series of plasma proteins which can be activated in a cascade sequence. During activation, a variety of inflammatory substances are produced, including potent chemo-attractants for neutrophils, and activated complement proteins may lyse cells. Complexes of antigen and antibody can activate the complement cascade.

Immunological Mechanisms Involved in Allergic Drug Reactions

To elicit an immunological response, a drug requires to have a molecular weight greater than 5000 daltons or else it must be firmly bound to another molecule of larger size. In the latter relatively common situation, the low molecular drug is termed a *hapten*, and the large molecule, the *carrier*. This may be a normal plasma protein, a denatured protein in the event of injury, or a bacterial product if there is infection.

Conditions associated with IgE antibodies include anaphylaxis, bronchial asthma, allergic rhinitis and urticaria. In case of penicillin allergy, there may be specific serum IgE antibodies against the penicilloyl conjugate. In some other instances of IgE-mediated drug reaction, it is likely that the antibody is directed against a contaminant or carrier rather than against the drug itself. The IgE system is under T cell control, and defects in suppressor T cell function may predispose to the development of IgE-mediated allergy.

Cytotoxic antibodies, which are usually IgG, may react with a drug such as penicillin bound to red cells. These antibodies, although directed against the drug, can lead to lysis of the cell either by activating the complement system or by sensitizing the erythrocyte to destruction by mononuclear cells. A different mechanism of red cell destruction is caused by methyldopa, which may induce the production of an IgG autoantibody directed against Rh antigens.

Antigen–antibody complexes are involved in a variety of allergic drug responses. The complexes may bind to the red cell surface and activate complement, the result being lysis. This commonly occurs with the IgM class of antibodies, whereas complexes involving IgG tend to lead to *platelet* destruction, because platelets have a surface receptor which binds IgG complexes. Various antigen–antibody complexes may bind to granulocytes and induce granulocytopenia.

The syndrome of serum sickness also involves antigen–antibody complexes which circulate, activate complement, and produce effects in small vessels, especially in skin and kidney. The complement activation products attract neutrophils which cause tissue damage. A similar mechanism is involved in extrinsic allergic alveolitis, when an inhaled antigen reacts with antibody in the tissue fluids, leading to a localized inflammatory reaction in the lungs.

Cell-mediated allergic reactions, involving the contact of antigen with sensitized T cells, are commonly involved in skin-contact allergies, but rarely occur after the systemic administration of drugs. The skin lesions are infiltrated with lymphocytes, plasma cells and mononuclear phagocytes. It has been shown by studies in vitro that the patient's T lymphocytes produce lymphokines in response to the sensitizing drug. These are soluble biologically active materials and include skin reactive factors.

It has been the practice to refer to four types of reaction. *Type I* is due to IgE antibodies and includes anaphylaxis after penicillin. *Type II*, usually due to IgG or IgM antibodies, includes drug-induced haemolytic anaemia and thrombocytopenia. Serum sickness is a *Type III* reaction, whereas skin contact allergies are of the *Type IV* variety.

MONOCLONAL ANTIBODIES

It is convenient to refer here to monoclonal antibodies and the therapeutic implications of their development.

To act against a specific antigen it is necessary to have a specific antibody, but in the natural immune system, thousands of antibodies are present. However, it has been found that by fusing two kinds of cells, antibodies of remarkable specificity can be made. The basic technique is to fuse the lymphocytes that make the required antibody but cannot be augmented in a laboratory with myeloma cells that have lost the ability to secrete antibodies but grow readily in the laboratory. Thus there are formed immortal hybrid myelomas (hybridomas), which secrete what are now named monoclonal antibodies, and these react with a specific antigen. For instance, a tumour possessing a particular antigen could be tagged by a monoclonal antibody grown in culture in the laboratory, and killer cells of the immune system could attack these marked cells. Antibody molecules might even be able to carry potent drugs to the site where tumour cells were being attacked. Further possibilities are referred to on p. 553.

One method of production of monoclonal antibodies is by immunizing mice with a human antigen (such as a specific protein, hormone or cell type). The mice become immunized and produce specific antibody. The mouse spleens are removed and a suspension of spleen cells is prepared. Mouse myeloma cells originating from other animals and maintained as a stable cell line are fused with these immune spleen cells to form a hybridoma, non-fused myeloma cells and spleen cells being eliminated by growing the cells in a selective medium that permits only the hybrids to survive. Hybridoma cells producing specific antibodies are thus produced, and these are cloned and recloned. A clone producing antibody of the desired specificity and immunoglobulin isotype is maintained by intraperitoneal injection into histocompatible or immunosuppressed mice, in which the hybridoma cells grow as an ascites tumour. Ascitic fluid develops, the mice are sacrificed and the fluid stored after removal of cells. The ascitic fluid containing monoclonal antibody is purified and tested to ensure that it is sterile and virus free. The cell line can continue to be cultured in vitro and propagated in larger scale culture.

A second approach for producing monoclonal antibodies perhaps holds greater potential for therapy. It is possible to obtain human myeloma cell lines and fuse these with B lymphocytes from the peripheral blood of immunized human donors. Although it is at an early stage, this method holds the promise of producing monoclonal *human* immunoglobulin molecules directed against specified antigens. These agents would avoid the allergic problems that may arise in the use of immunoglobulins derived from mouse cells.

Indications

One example of the therapeutic application of mouse monoclonal antibody is the use of antibody to human T lymphocytes in the treatment of renal transplant rejection. The failure of renal transplants is largely due to immunological reactions and it is to be hoped that this type of fluid given i.v. into humans will prevent the onward development of acute renal rejection. An anti-T monoclonal antibody of IgG_2 class, known as OKT3, has been used with encouraging results in a few patients.

A method of treatment of certain lymphatic leukaemias and lymphomas (p. 491) is to use chemotherapy and radiation treatment, followed by bone marrow transplantation using donors who are histocompatible. These donors are difficult to find, but a monoclonal antibody such as OKT3 could, in theory, be used to eliminate T cells (which cause graft-versus-host disease) in donor bone marrow prior to transplantation, even if the histocompatibility is not complete. It is thought that the monoclonal antibody binds human T cells and renders them inactive, while activating complement to assist in T cell lysis. The treated marrow is given i.v. through a standard blood-giving set. The use of this technique is also under trial in myeloid leukaemia and aplastic anaemia.

Monoclonal antibodies directed against cancer cells and malaria parasites have been developed and others have been used to purify interferon (p. 62). So far as tumours are concerned, the problem is to produce an antibody that is specifically cytotoxic for, or specifically opsonizes the target cells without damaging essential normal tissues. An alternative approach is to attach a very toxic agent (such as ricin or diphtheria toxin) to monoclonal antibodies raised to specific tumour cell markers, thus using the antibody to carry the lethal toxin direct to the tumour.

In relation to autoimmune diseases, there are prospects for the future, but the procedures are complex and experimental, possibly involving the development of hybridomas that develop monoclonal antibodies active against other monoclonal antibodies. This is possible because antibody specificity depends on the shape of a combining site on the antibody where it combines with the antigen. Because of its characteristic shape, the antibody can, in turn, act as an antigenic determinant to generate other antibodies which recognize the uniqueness of the first one. The body is a factory which can generate a huge number of different antibody specificities and the promise for future therapeutic developments is great. Already the possibility of immunological contraception is being explored.

DRUG TREATMENT OF ALLERGIC REACTIONS

Histamine and Antihistamines

Histamine

Histamine is widely distributed and has protean effects on the systems of the body. However, its exact role in normal body function remains obscure, and it has no therapeutic uses.

Histamine, or β-imidazolethylamine, is formed by the decarboxylation of histidine in virtually all tissues. The greatest amounts are found in mast cells, skin, lung and intestine. In the mast cell, histamine is stored, bound to heparin.

Given orally, histamine is rapidly metabolized by the intestinal flora and on passage through the intestinal wall. Given parenterally, its action is rapid and transient.

Actions

Histamine is thought to interact with two specific receptors, designated H_1 and H_2, and competitive antagonism can be demonstrated in vitro with specific antagonists. All the effects of histamine, except those on gastric secretion (and in animals some effects on blood pressure), are attributed to the H_1 receptor. Certain preparations prevent the action of histamine on gastric secretion, which is attributed to the H_2 receptor. These are discussed elsewhere (p. 335).

Actions on the Cardiovascular System

Histamine causes marked vasoconstriction of arteries and veins, but marked dilatation of capillaries, the latter being the most prominent action in man (the major effect, with corresponding changes in blood pressure, differs in different species). Its effects are due to a direct action on smooth muscle receptors. Capillary permeability is also increased and relaxation of precapillary sphincters occurs. The histamine is derived from local mast cells. The cerebral vessels respond to histamine with dilatation, causing headache. In man the blood pressure generally falls. Histamine has no direct action on the heart.

Actions on Smooth Muscle

Histamine causes contraction of the smooth muscle of the uterus and bronchioles. Other substances including 5-hydroxytryptamine (5-HT) may also be implicated in the production of asthma. The term 'autocoid' is sometimes given to histamine, 5-HT, angiotensin, kinins and prostaglandins. They all have pharmacological activity and are normally present in the body or may be formed there, but are not hormones.

Actions on Exocrine Glands

Histamine, acting on the H_2 receptor, causes the secretion of large quantities of gastric juice rich in acid and pepsin. Gastrin may act through the release of histamine, as the actions of both are blocked by H_2-receptor antagonists.

Actions on Skin

Acting on cutaneous nerve endings, histamine causes itching when introduced into the skin. The triple response (localized red spot, followed by surrounding 'flare' or blush, followed by wheal) is due to capillary dilatation, a localized arteriolar dilatation caused by an axonal reflex, and oedema due to increased capillary permeability. The triple response is identical with the reaction produced by firm stroking of the skin with a sharp instrument (exaggerated in dermographia), suggesting that local histamine release may be responsible for the latter.

Actions on Endocrine Glands

Large doses of histamine provoke the secretion of catecholamines from the adrenal medulla.

Actions on the Central Nervous System

Large amounts of histamine are found in various central nervous system structures, and histamine may function as a neurotransmitter.

Inflammation

In an acute inflammatory response, histamine may initiate early changes such as the axon reflex and allergic responses.

Anaphylactic Shock

As has already been mentioned (p. 551), anaphylaxis is associated with the production of an IgE antibody. The antibody coats mast cells, and subsequent antigen–antibody interaction disrupts the cell, releasing vasoactive amines, particularly histamine. This can occur on second exposure to drugs (penicillin, iodine-containing contrast media, etc.; p. 10), insect stings, or any foreign protein. The effects include hypotension and bronchoconstriction, and the condition can be fatal. Treatment should consist of rapid i.v. injection of an antihistamine and hydrocortisone, together with i.m. or s.c. adrenaline if necessary. The release of the vasoactive amines may be prevented by pretreatment with disodium cromoglycate (p. 558).

Morphine, tubocurarine, dextrans and antihistamines may cause histamine release with a transient fall in blood pressure.

Indications

Histamine has no therapeutic use. In tests of gastric secretory function, it has been superseded by pentagastrin.

Antihistamines

All antihistamines are competitive antagonists at the histamine receptor.

H₁-receptor antagonists. A large number of H₁-receptor antagonists are available. As histamine antagonists, their clinical use is disappointing. They are most effective in preventing increases in capillary permeability, but, because of the nature of the histamine response, they are usually only effective if given before histamine is liberated.

Actions
Ideally, H₁ antagonists should prevent bronchoconstriction, smooth muscle contraction, catecholamine release from the adrenal medulla, and the vascular effects described above. They do not prevent histamine release, and, as bronchoconstriction in asthma is probably due to the release of other natural substances in addition to histamine, their effects are disappointing. Antihistamines may have local anaesthetic, sedative and anticholinergic effects, and are often powerful antiemetics.

Pharmacokinetics
Antihistamines are all well absorbed if given orally, the rapidity of onset and duration of action varying with the preparation. Those that have been investigated in detail have been shown to be metabolized in the liver. Antihistamines should be used with caution in patients with liver disease.

Preparations
Five distinct groups of preparations are available: alkylamines, phenothiazines, piperazines, ethylenediamines and ethanolamines.

Alkylamines. Chlorpheniramine (Piriton) is commonly used. It is available in 5 mg tablets, 8 mg Duolets, 12 mg Spandets and 10 mg doses for injection. Other alkylamines include doxylamine (p. 564) and triprolidine, pheniramine and dimethindene.

Phenothiazines. Promethazine (Phenergan) has prolonged action and is available for oral or parenteral use. The dose is 20–50 mg. It may cause photosensitivity. Mepyramine, dimethothiazine and trimeprazine are some alternatives. Other phenothiazines are described on p. 164.

Piperazines. Chlorcyclizine and cyclizine (Marzine) are available in 50 mg tablets. Both cause sedation. Meclozine (p. 340) and buclizine are extremely long-acting and cause marked sedation. Piperazine compounds may cause choreoathetotic symptoms. They are very effective antiemetics.

Ethylenediamines. Tripelennamine, pyrilamine and antazoline are representative.

Ethanolamines. Diphenhydramine and dimenhydrinate (Dramamine, Gravol) cause sedation and are effective hypnotics. The latter is used to prevent motion sickness.

Other H₁-receptor antagonists include cyproheptadine, mebhydrolin, meclastine and phenindamine.

Diphenhydramine, phenindamine and orphenadrine are useful anti-Parkinsonian agents (p. 240).

Some antihistamines are listed in Table 17.1. A number of them are also available as syrups or elixirs. The table does not include antihistamines primarily intended to prevent nausea, vomiting or motion sickness.

Indications

Allergic conditions. Given prophylactically, antihistamines may prevent the symptoms of hay fever, allergic rhinitis, and acute urticaria. Chronic urticaria responds less well and non-urticarial drug eruptions may even become worse. Anaphylaxis is more effectively treated by the physiological antagonist adrenaline, 1 ml of adrenaline injection, BP, being given i.m. At the same time 100 mg of hydrocortisone should be given i.v. and 10 mg of chlorpheniramine i.v. may give some benefit. Allergic reactions to drugs and blood products may be prevented if they have been anticipated. There is no protection against haemolytic responses.

Motion sickness. The antiemetic effects of antihistamines are often very useful in motion sickness.

Table 17.1 *Some antihistamines (H₁-receptor antagonists) used in allergic disorders, including urticaria*

Compound	Some proprietary names	Tablet/ capsule (mg)	Injection
Astemizole	Hismanal	10	
Azatadine	Optimine	1	
Brompheniramine	Dimotane LA	12	
Chlorpheniramine	Piriton	4, 8	10
Clemastine	Tavegil	1	2
Cyproheptadine	Periactin	4	
Dimethindene	Fenostil retard	2.5	
Dimethothiozine	Banistyl	20	
Diphenhydramine	Benadryl	25, 50	
Diphenylpyraline	Histryl, Lergoban	5	
Ketotifen	Zaditen	1	
Mebhydrolin	Fabahistin	50	
Mepyramine	Anthisan	50, 100	50
Mequitazine	Primalan	5	
Phenindamine	Thephorin	25	
Pheniramine	Daneral SA	75	
Promethazine	Phenergan	10, 25	25
Terfenadine	Triludan	60	
Trimeprazine	Vallergan	10	
Triprolidine	Actidil, Pro-Actidil	2.5, 10	

Nausea and vomiting. Nausea and vomiting in pregnancy, and in other circumstances (e.g. radiation sickness), may be relieved by antihistamines. Their value must be weighed against possible teratogenicity if they are used in the first trimester of pregnancy (p. 561).

Anti-Parkinsonian effects. Some antihistamines, particularly those with anticholinergic activity, are useful in the treatment of tremor and rigidity associated with Parkinsonian syndromes.

Sedatives. Many antihistamines cause drowsiness, which is dangerous if patients drive or operate machinery. This effect can be useful for preoperative sedation and sedation in children.

Side-effects

Drowsiness is the major side-effect, and synergistic effects are seen with hypnotics or alcohol. Dizziness, tinnitus, lassitude, diplopia, gastrointestinal upsets and allergic dermatitis are common, the last particularly with topical use. Some antihistamines liberate histamine. Blood dyscrasias are very rare. Because large doses cause excitement and even convulsions, antihistamines should not be given to epileptics. Anticholinergic effects (blurring of vision, dry mouth, urinary retention, constipation) may occur and are usually prominent in overdosage. They may slow the absorption of other drugs by delaying gastric emptying. Piperazine compounds are teratogenic in animals and should not be used during pregnancy. The treatment of overdosage is symptomatic.

H_2-receptor antagonists These are discussed elsewhere (p. 335).

Substances other than Antihistamines used to deal with Allergic Reactions

Corticosteroids

Hydrocortisone sodium succinate, BP (p. 406) is used to treat allergic reactions; its mode of action is uncertain. It should be given i.v. to treat an acute allergic reaction to a drug.

Adrenaline

Adrenaline injection, BP (p. 222) contains adrenaline acid tartrate 1.8 mg/ml, equivalent to adrenaline 1 in 1000. In an emergency it should be given i.m. or s.c. It is more rapidly active by the former route. It must not be given i.v. as it may cause cardiac irregularities and even death.

Sodium cromoglycate

This product inhibits the release from mast cells of histamine, leukotrienes (slow reacting substances of anaphylaxis, SRS-A) and chemotactic factors which mediate allergic reactions. In the lungs sodium cromoglycate (Intal) prevents the immediate and late immunological responses (Type I and Type III responses) to immunological stimuli. It also prevents the bronchoconstriction caused by exercise, cold air and chemical irritants. In food allergy (once adequate investigations have been performed to determine sensitivity to one or more ingested allergens) it can be used in conjunction with restriction of the main causative allergens. For this purpose it is marketed under the name Nalcrom. Patients who are unable to avoid allergenic foods under certain circumstances (e.g. in restaurants) may receive some protection by taking a single dose of 100 mg about 15 minutes before the meal. Release of histamines or kinins from the gastrointestinal tract into the circulation has been suggested as the cause of urticaria in food-sensitive subjects. Sometimes the problem is due to sodium benzoate as a preservative, or to tartrazine or other colouring materials. Protection may be afforded by the taking of sodium cromoglycate. Claims have not been made for protection against drug-induced allergic responses.

DESENSITIZATION

When a patient has an allergy to a drug, it is better that he should avoid that drug and other substances that are chemically closely related to it. It is sometimes possible to densensitize the patient by giving him very small amounts of the drug by injection where this is possible and gradually increasing the amount until a normal dose is tolerated. Corticosteroids and adrenaline should be available and the doctor must be prepared to deal with a medical emergency if the procedure is unsuccessful. It is obviously better to use a different type of drug, but the Medic-Alert warning bracelet or necklace is useful in case the patient should be unconscious when treated (p. 548).

CROSS-REACTIONS

Unfortunately, when a patient develops a sensitivity to one drug, there may be sensitivity reactions when drugs that are chemically related are used, or even when entirely different substances are given. In an extreme case, a patient may have an adverse reaction to every known drug used to treat tuberculosis (p. 31), even though their chemical structures are so different.

EFFECTS OF AGE, SEX, RACE AND OTHER FACTORS

Reference will be made elsewhere to individual variations in the response to drugs (p. 595) and to the effects of disease (p. 596). The age, sex and race of the patient may also be important. Thus, the elderly person is readily confused by tranquillizers or hypnotics; androgens cause virilization in women; atropine does not dilate the pupil as much in dark-skinned races as in those with fair skins. The weight of the patient and general state of nutrition may be important, in that a normal dose for a heavy patient may be a toxic dose for an underweight person. Not only does a feverish illness sometimes modify drug reactions, but also the environmental temperature may be important. Atropine (p. 206) inhibits sweating and should therefore not be used in very hot climates. An abnormal reaction to a drug may be familial, and this is particularly important with certain anaesthetics.

INFECTION

An important matter to bear in mind is the danger of infection when a drug is injected, or given i.v. in an infusion. It is necessary to avoid bacterial contamination, and manufacturers may be able to prevent this by adding small amounts of a bacteriostatic agent such as chlorocresol (0.05–0.15%) to aqueous injections issued in multidose containers. Such containers should be avoided, single-dose ampoules being preferred.

Bacteriostatic agents may occasionally cause problems, since most doctors overlook the possibility of preservatives causing adverse reactions when large amounts of a sterile solution are used in complex procedures.

Particularly where blood or blood products are in use, the danger of viral hepatitis has to be borne in mind. Such products may be made from pooled plasma and should be tested for hepatitis B surface antigen before being used.

More recently, the possible spread of the little understood acquired immuno-deficiency syndrome (AIDS) by blood or blood products has caused much concern, particularly in the USA, where the mortality rate in those affected has been about 40%.

DEATH AFTER TAKING DRUGS

Many people would consider that the most serious possible adverse effect that can occur after taking a drug is death. This can be from an overdose, but may occur quite unexpectedly from a therapeutic dose. For several years the most frequent reports to the UK Committee on Safety of Medicines of deaths after the taking of drugs were those resulting from thomboembolic disease after the use of high-oestrogen-content contraceptive pills. More recently the Swedish experience has been that lowering the oestrogen content has diminished the morbidity rate but not mortality because, although there has been a reduction in venous thromboses, the frequency of arterial complications has remained constant. In Britain, however, it is considered that less arterial thrombo-embolic incidents also have occurred since the oestrogen content was lowered. It is considered that more requires to be known about the influence of the progestogen content.

PROBLEMS FROM USING DRUGS IN PREGNANCY

Teratogenic (Dysmorphogenic) Effects

The unfortunate term 'teratogenic' is derived from the Greek words τέρας and γένεσις, meaning monster-producing. A better adjective is 'dysmorphogenic' ('causing a derangement in form'). A great deal of disquiet arose from the unexpected thalidomide disaster (p. 545). However, only a very small number of drugs have been shown with certainty to cause any form of fetal deformity if given to a pregnant mother. There is a great difference in the effects of drugs given to pregnant animals of various species so far as their offspring are concerned, so there is no way of producing a screening programme in animals that will definitely ensure that a new drug will not be dysmorphogenic in humans. Equally, a drug may have this effect in animals but not in man. Thus, salicylates may cause the malformation of ribs and vertebrae in mice, and although thalidomide causes severe abnormalities in the offspring of New Zealand strains of rabbits and in some strains of mice, it does not lead to congenital malformations if given to Silver Grey strains of rabbits or to hamsters, most strains of rats or some strains of mice.

So far as new drugs are concerned, the situation is so obscure that in a data sheet the manufacturer, having no clear evidence of danger and yet being unable to guarantee safety, may include some warning such as: 'In the light of present knowledge and uncertainties about possible teratogenic agents, current authoritative opinion is that no drug should be taken by a pregnant woman, especially during the first four months of pregnancy, except under medical supervision.'

Stages in pregnancy when drugs may have dysmorphogenic effects

In the preimplantation period the blastocyst is free in the uterus and obtains nutrition from uterine secretions. At this stage there is no evidence that exogenous agents might cause congenital abnormalities. After implantation has occurred, however, the period of real danger commences. In the earlier stages there may be embryonic death or the induction of major malformations. It is later that minor malformations are possible. Accordingly, it is in the embryonic stage of the first 56 days that serious trouble may ensue, but it is at the *end* of this time that the woman may realize that pregnancy has occurred. After 8 weeks, there is the fetal period. The major differentiation of organs has already occurred, but differentiation of the external genitalia, development of the central nervous system and closure of the palate is occurring. During this time, drugs might cause abnormalities of the brain, impaired palatal closure or pseudohermaphroditism.

The drugs may have a direct action on the fetus (e.g. thalidomide) or may modify maternal metabolism (e.g. hypoglycaemic agents). Many drugs or their metabolites can cross the placenta, but the fetal liver lacks many of the enzymes available to the mother. This may enable certain substances to diffuse back unchanged into the maternal circulation when the drug has been excreted or metabolized by the mother.

It should be realized that it is not only drugs that may affect the fetus, but that there may be hazards from excessive alcohol intake, infections (especially if viral), metabolic disorders and nutritional deficiency states. Excessive intake of vitamin A in pregnancy may cause fetal abnormalities (p. 436).

Choice of animal species for tests of drug danger in pregnancy

There is no satisfactory single animal species available for testing and, as has already been indicated (p. 547), different species or even strains are needed for different drugs. It is not really sufficient to use only rodents. In many instances, primates would seem to be the ideal animal, but the supply of the monkey species is not sufficient for this to be practicable. It can be said that with new drugs such precautions as are possible are being taken, but they cannot ever replace trials on humans.

There is no evidence that drugs given to males may cause fetal abnormalities. A number of substances, including alkylating compounds (p. 492) and nitrofurantoin (p. 53), may interfere with male fertility.

Drugs that are known to affect the fetus

Thalidomide was reported to have caused abnormalities of limbs, skull, ears, heart, liver, gastrointestinal tract, kidneys, uterus and lungs. It was claimed that even a single tablet taken at a particular stage of early pregnancy might cause abnormalities. The reason for this action is not clear. Drugs with a closely related chemical structure do not have the same effects in species of animal affected by thalidomide.

Folate antagonists and drugs used in cancer chemotherapy. Aminopterin (p. 503), a folate antagonist, was unwisely tried as an abortifacient in women; in a few cases where it failed, congenital abnormalities were produced. Any such folate antagonist or cytotoxic agent should be avoided in pregnancy. There have been suggestions that a slight hazard exists with antiepileptic drugs (p. 250), but it is important to give adequate antiepileptic treatment to a pregnant epileptic woman. It has been suggested that epilepsy in the mother is more related to malformation in a child than is the form of treatment that she takes.

Sex hormones. Although contraceptive pills have until recently been considered not to pose a problem, possibly because of low dosage, there is doubt as to whether they are completely safe. Androgens and progestogens are well known to cause virilization of the female fetus. This has been reported with norethisterone (p. 418) when used in 10–40 mg doses daily in an attempt to prevent abortion. Such a dose is greater than that in contraceptive pills. Ethisterone also has this effect, as, of course, has testosterone (p. 412). The giving of exogenous sex hormones or perhaps oral contraceptives may cause fetal abnormalities. In the latter instance the problem could arise in a breakthrough pregnancy when the patient was taking an oral contraceptive, though in 1981 a WHO group concluded that oral contraceptives used in the month before conception probably do not affect the fetus. Administration of progestogens to prevent abortion is unwise and of doubtful value.

A further problem is that vaginal cancer has been reported in young women whose mothers had been treated with stilboestrol for threatened abortion in early pregnancy. This form of therapy is not now employed.

Corticosteroids. There have been reports of cleft palate being produced by corticosteroids, but coincidence cannot be ruled out. If a pregnant patient is receiving them for a chronic disease such as systemic lupus erythematosus, the administration of corticosteroids should be continued, although it may be possible to reduce the dosage. Unfortunately, intrauterine growth retardation may occur.

Sulphonylureas. Sulphonylureas (chlorpropamide, tolbutamide; p. 395) cause fetal abnormalities in rats and mice and there has been a fear that they may do so in humans.

Sulphonamides. Sulphonamides are structurally related to sulphonylureas and so there is a certain amount of worry as to whether they might injure the fetus. Just before labour these compounds should be avoided, as they displace bilirubin from plasma protein. Co-trimoxazole and co-trifamole contain a folate antagonist (pp. 51–2) and should be avoided in the first trimester. Even in later months it is wise to give folic acid with these drugs. Sulphonamides should be avoided in glucose-6-phosphate dehydrogenase (G-6-PD) deficiency (p. 564).

Tetracyclines. If a mother takes tetracyclines after the third month, her child may have dental hypoplasia and staining of the tooth enamel.

Analgesics. The use of modern non-steroidal anti-inflammatory agents (p. 107) should be avoided in pregnancy because of the inhibition of prostaglandin synthesis that they cause. If prostaglandins are inhibited in the fetus, there may be premature closure of the ductus arteriosus.

Streptomycin. Deafness may be caused by the effect of streptomycin on the auditory apparatus of the fetus and it should therefore not be given in pregnancy. It is advisable also to avoid *gentamicin* and *kanamycin* unless they have to be given as life-saving drugs. It is said that *quinine* and *chloroquine* may also cause deafness. The latter is also concentrated in the eye of the fetus.

Other problems are that fetal goitre may be caused by iodide or antithyroid drugs, and that haemorrhage may be induced by oral anticoagulants in the later months. It is also possible that warfarin and related substances taken early in pregnancy cause fetal abnormalities.

Chloramphenicol. Chloramphenicol should not be given before labour, as fatal chloramphenicol toxicity may develop in neonates. This is because the liver of the newborn does not contain sufficient glucuronyl transferase for the conjugation of chloramphenicol with glucuronic acid to occur and there is inadequate renal excretion.

Drugs that may affect the fetus

Preparations to prevent nausea or vomiting. Most manufacturers advise against the use of their products in the early stages of pregnancy, but for a preparation of meclozine with pyridoxine (Ancolozin) which has been in use for many years, the statement made is 'Whilst drug therapy is undesirable during the first trimester of pregnancy, the administration of Ancoloxin may be warranted if vomiting is severe'.

A great deal has been written about Debendox as a possible cause of congenital abnormalities, and litigation has ensued in the USA. This combination of substances was marketed for the prevention or treatment of nausea and vomiting of pregnancy, and hence it was certain that some mothers who were going to have abnormal babies would take the preparation; there was no firm evidence that it caused deformities. The original preparation consisted of dicyclomine (an antispasmodic), doxylamine (an antihistamine) and pyridoxine (a vitamin). In the USA, where it was marketed as Bendectin, the antispasmodic component was dropped, after claims about teratogenicity had been made by a few mothers, and then a similar step was taken in the UK. The manufacturers then stated 'There have been a large number of epidemiological studies of Debendox. Although there have been some reports of congenital abnormalities associated with its administration in early pregnancy, a causal relationship has not been established. For no medicinal product can a small risk of teratogenic effect be excluded with absolute certainty and so the use of any drug during pregnancy should be avoided if at all possible'.

This is true, and any company that markets a substance, however harmless, for use in early pregnancy renders itself liable to litigation. No matter which product a pregnant woman may remember having taken, she is liable to think that this was the cause of a deformed baby. Inevitably, production of Debendox ceased in June 1983 despite the fact that the substance had been used widely for 27 years.

Antihypertensive drugs. There is some concern about the possibility that β-adrenergic blocking drugs may inhibit the fetal heart response to hypoxia in late pregnancy, hence methyldopa is commonly used for the treatment of hypertension in pregnancy. Hydralazine can be used in acute hypertensive crises. Diazoxide may cause fetal hypotonia and hypoglycaemia.

Drug allergies in the mother may sometimes affect the fetus, and drugs that depress respiration may cause fetal distress if given during labour. For instance, compounds containing dextropropoxyphene (p. 119) should be avoided, and diazepam and similar substances (p. 150) may depress respiration in the newborn if the mother receives relatively large doses before delivery.

Specific Adverse Reactions

It is possible to mention some well-recognized dangers, but a complete list of all reported reactions would occupy more than the whole of this book. The important thing is that clinicians should always be ready to suspect that an illness is drug-induced, and this is not unreasonable when in more than one survey it has been shown that about 15% of patients admitted to hospital either have a reaction of some sort at the time of admission or develop it in hospital. Moreover, in addition to this, in one of the major teaching hospitals in the UK, some 10% of acute medical admissions are due to the taking of an overdose of drugs. The management of drug overdosage is dealt with in specialized texts.

Blood disorders

Over a thousand drugs that are currently in use have been reported to have caused adverse reactions involving the formed elements of the blood or their precursors.

Haemolytic anaemia. Some drugs can provoke antibody formation that can lead to increased destruction of a person's own red cells. There are two main possibilities.

In what is sometimes called drug-induced immune haemolytic anaemia, antibodies are formed in the body and act against the drug, but cannot be shown in the serum in vitro unless the drug is present. This is not very common, but is found with penicillin (p. 10). A similar mechanism has been described with some cephalosporins and cephamycins, quinine, rifampicin, sulphonamides, insulin, stibophen, chlorpropamide, chlorpromazine and a few other drugs.

The second type of reaction is what is sometimes known as a drug-induced 'autoimmune' haemolytic anaemia. Antibodies that are formed are directed against intrinsic red cell antigens, and they can be detected in the patient's serum in vitro without adding the drug. This can occur with methyldopa, chlorpromazine, hydantoins, methysergide, levodopa and mefenamic acid. How any drug stimulates antibody formation is uncertain.

Reference has already been made to the production of haemolytic anaemia where there is deficiency of G-6-PD. The mechanism is complex, but if G-6-PD is not acting normally, the red cell is not protected against oxidant damage and is destroyed prematurely. Here the development of haemolysis is predictable if the patient is known to have this genetic defect and is given certain drugs, including chloroquine, primaquine, sulphonamides, sulphones, or nitrofurantoin. Sometimes a drug will only produce haemolysis if there is concurrent infection, and this anaemia may then be precipitated by aspirin, chloroquine, etc. (p. 70). There are a number of variants of the normal G-6-PD and, hence, racial and geographical differences in the drugs that may lead to haemolysis.

Megaloblastic anaemia. Megaloblastic anaemia is referred to elsewhere (p. 467). With some drugs, such as methotrexate, the mechanism is understood, whereas with others, such as phenytoin or primidone, it is not.

Aplastic anaemia. The haematological terminology is confused in that the term 'aplastic anaemia' is sometimes used to mean aplasia of the erythrocyte-forming tissue alone, but more commonly to indicate that the precursors of red cells, granulocytes and platelets, have all been injured. To this serious condition the name 'pancytopenia' may also be applied. It would not be possible to give a complete list of reported causes, but aplastic anaemia, with all these cell lines affected, is most commonly reported in the UK as being due to phenylbutazone and oxyphenbutazone, and as new non-steroidal anti-inflammatory substances are marketed (p. 120), the list of possible causative agents increases. Perusal of a list of these in 1983 shows that three-quarters of the preparations available in the UK had been reported to cause blood dyscrasias at least in a few people and that almost every one had been said on occasion to cause alimentary bleeding from mucosal irritation. At one time the main cause was chloramphenicol (p. 18). Naturally enough, drugs used in the treatment of leukaemia may cause aplastic anaemia, but this is an expected effect of vigorous therapy.

Causes other than the substances mentioned include heavy metals, benzol compounds, chlordiazepoxide, chlorpropamide, colchicine, indomethacin, mepacrine, meprobamate, potassium perchlorate, streptomycin, sulphonamides, tolbutamide and troxidone. In countries where amidopyrine is still used, this is a prominent cause; it is not employed in the UK as an analgesic, because of this danger.

The mechanism is not certain, but it is possible that chloramphenicol may produce anaemia in two different ways. The matter is discussed further on p. 20.

Oxymetholone. Oxymetholone is an anabolic androgen (p. 414) used to treat aplastic anaemia. It is given by mouth in a dose of 2–5 mg/kg body weight for adults for 6 months or until a response is seen. Its mode of action is uncertain, but it may stimulate the production of erythropoietin, which, in turn, acts on primitive stem cells in the marrow.

Agranulocytosis. Certain drugs may cause granulocytopenia in some individuals, but thrombocytopenia, aplastic anaemia or even haemolytic anaemia, in others. Apart from cytotoxic agents (p. 490), the main causes of granulocytopenia in the UK are the non-steroidal anti-inflammatory agents (p. 120). Agranulocytosis or granulocytopenia has been reported with over a hundred drugs, including amidopyrine, arsphenamine, benoxaprofen, captopril, cefoxitin, chloramphenicol, chlordiazepoxide, chlorothiazide, chlorpheniramine, chlorpromazine, chlorpropamide, frusemide, imipramine, mepacrine, meprobamate, oxyphenbutazone, perphenazine, phenindione, phenylbutazone, prochlorperazine, promazine, promethazine, pyrimethamine, streptomycin, sulphonamides, thiouracils, tolbutamide and troxidone. There is no purpose in attempting to memorize such lists, which, in any case, are incomplete. In addition, a patient who develops agranulocytosis may have been affected by a chemical in some other way, such as in a hair rinse or an insecticide.

It has been suggested that there are two types of agranulocytosis, one of an immunological nature and the other a failure in cell division involving DNA synthesis, but there is uncertainty about this. The haematologist, however, recognizes two morphological types, which may merge into each other. In one there is a maturation arrest, so that myeloblasts and early myelocytes are readily found in the bone marrow. In the other, even the early precursors of granulocytes are eliminated. Most workers feel that the maturation arrest type is less serious and that recovery can be expected if the offending drug is withdrawn.

Thrombocytopenia. Again, cytotoxic drugs and other agents used to treat disorders such as leukaemia can be expected to cause a profound fall in platelets. In addition, however, there are a large number of drugs which may, in certain individuals, have this effect. Drugs reported as having caused thrombocytopenia include acetazolamide, amidopyrine, ampicillin, apronal, arsenicals, cephalosporins, chloramphenicol, chlorothiazide, chlorpromazine, chlorpropamide, co-trimoxazole, ergot, frusemide, gold, isoniazid, meprobamate, methyldopa, many non-steroidal anti-inflammatory agents, oestrogens, *para*-aminosalicylic acid, paracetamol, penicillins, penicillamine, phenindione, phenobarbitone, prednisone, prochlorperazine, potassium perchlorate, quinidine, quinine, salicylates, streptomycin, sulphonamides, tolbutamide and troxidone. A person sensitive in this way to quinine may develop thrombocytopenia from drinking a 'gin and tonic', since the tonic water contains quinine. In other individuals, capillary purpura may be produced by quinine (p. 73).

The mechanism of action varies with different drugs. Some have a toxic effect on megakaryocytes in the bone marrow; more rarely, there may be disintegration of platelets at the periphery, something clearly shown only with the antimicrobial substance ristocetin, which is seldom used because of its toxic effects. Thrombocytopenia may be produced by an immunological mechanism acting on the peripheral blood (p. 551). Another possible site of an immunological reaction is the marrow, and it has been suggested that thiazide diuretics might cause thrombocytopenia by some form of sensitivity reaction involving megakaryocytes.

Unlikely possibilities have sometimes to be considered: thrombocytopenia following a blood transfusion might be due to a drug taken by the donor to which the recipient is sensitive. Neonatal thrombocytopenia may follow the antepartum administration of drugs such as thiazide diuretics, quinine and even aspirin.

Non-thrombocytopenic purpura. Many drugs have been reported to cause capillary purpura without a reduction in platelets. A drug might combine with a capillary cell and lead to damage, with consequent small local haemorrhage. One substance that causes capillary purpura, apparently by some form of immunological mechanism, is carbromal, a hypnotic that is seldom used. Some drugs, such as quinine, may cause thrombocytopenic purpura in one person and non-thrombocytopenic purpura in another.

Coagulation abnormalities. These are referred to elsewhere (p. 482).

Sideroblastic anaemia. In this condition, some of the red cell precursors in the marrow contain a perinuclear ring of iron-staining granules in the cytoplasm. This is sometimes due to drugs interfering with haem synthesis, and these include isoniazid, cycloserine, pyrazinamide and chloramphenicol.

Leukaemia. It has been claimed that chloramphenicol and phenylbutazone may cause acute myeloblastic leukaemia, but this is unproven. Immunosuppressive therapy, particularly after renal transplantation, is associated with an increased incidence of leukaemia or lymphomatous disease. Perhaps malignant clones of the cells can emerge, or it may be that oncogenic viruses can invade cells or escape from immunological control.

Thrombosis. The association between thrombosis and the taking of the contraceptive pill is referred to on pp. 421 and 474.

Skin reactions

The possibilities are so many that it would serve little purpose to go into detail. A drug eruption may be due to topical application (contact dermatitis) or to the ingestion of a substance. Drug eruptions of the latter type tend to be abrupt in onset and symmetrical in distribution. There may be cross-reactions between various drugs, so a person with sensitivity to penicillins may also be sensitive to cephalosporins (p. 11). It is convenient to describe drug reactions as toxic, allergic or associated with sensitivity to light.

Toxic eruptions can be acne-form (anticonvulsants, oral contraceptives, corticosteroids, ethambutol, isoniazid, lithium, rifampicin), vesicular or bullous (barbiturates, including barbiturate intoxication, frusemide, sulphonamides, topical application of benzyl benzoate), lichenoid (chloroquine, methyldopa, *para*-aminosalicylic acid), leading to pigmentation (busulphan, griseofulvin, mepacrine) or verrucous (bromides, iodides).

Allergic responses may be of the following types: eczematous (allopurinol, warfarin), exfoliative dermatitis (cimetidine, gold salts, oxyphenbutazone, phenylbutazone, phenytoin), erythema multiforme (barbiturates, salicylates), erythema nodosum (barbiturates, sulphonamides), exanthematic (ampicillin, phenindione), fixed (phenolphthalein, sulphonamides); causing the Stevens–Johnson syndrome, a severe form of erythema multiforme (phenylbutazone, sulphonamides), systemic lupus erythematosus (griseofulvin, hydralazine, sulphonamides), toxic epidermal necrolysis (various non-steroidal anti-inflammatory agents, sulphonamides); and urticarial (benoxaprofen, cephalosporins, cephamycins, griseofulvin, imipramine, penicillin). Psoriasis may be precipitated by a drug (β-blocking drugs, chloroquine, lithium).

Light-sensitivity reactions give an exaggerated response to sunlight and may be distressing; they may seriously interfere with holidays. They can occur with various drugs, including antihistamines, benoxaprofen, chlorpromazine, griseofulvin, sulphonamides, sulphonylureas and tetracyclines.

Alopecia. This is common with cytotoxic drugs, but may also occur with carbimazole, oral contraceptives, gold, heparin, lithium, methyldopa, propranolol, warfarin and several other drugs.

Further information about the types of reaction mentioned and the many other drugs involved can be obtained from textbooks of skin diseases and of drug reactions.

Gastrointestinal disturbances

Very many drugs may cause gastrointestinal disturbances such as indigestion, nausea, vomiting, diarrhoea or constipation. Sometimes a measure of relief is obtained by giving the drug with food. On occasion a patient may feel nauseated on taking alcohol when being treated with a drug (e.g. rifampicin; p. 36). There may be serious disturbance of the small intestinal mucosa from folate antagonists such as methotrexate. Many anti-inflammatory drugs may cause gastritis, activation of gastric ulcers, ulceration of the small intestinal mucosa, or gastrointestinal bleeding. This is a hazard with almost all non-steroidal anti-inflammatory agents from aspirin to the most recently introduced preparations, and bleeding may also occur from the giving of corticosteroids or be caused by various other drugs. Potassium chloride tablets can cause small intestinal perforation unless specially prepared to avoid prolonged contact with any particular area of small bowel. The lodging of these or various other preparations in a hiatus hernia must be avoided. It is possible that an attack of acute pancreatitis may be precipitated by certain drugs, including corticosteroids, rifampicin and perhaps contraceptive pills.

Liver disorders

A variety of liver disorders may be induced by drugs. The disease may be acute or chronic, and, in the most severe reactions, death may occur.

Acute hepatic injury. In the most intense form of cytotoxic injury, there is *necrosis*, whereas in the milder form there is *fatty change*, but the picture may be a mixed one. Some drugs may cause damage by a direct action, perhaps only if a large dose is given; for example, carbon tetrachloride, which used to be used as a treatment for ancylostomiasis, may cause peroxidation and denaturation of the hepatocyte. Chloroform is still employed by some as an anaesthetic, and it, too, may be toxic to the cell.

On the other hand, damage to the main hepatic cells may be more indirect, by interference with certain metabolic pathways there. This can occur with mercaptopurine, methotrexate, asparaginase, large doses of tetracycline (particularly if given i.v.), severe overdosage with paracetamol, or the taking of excess of alcohol. With paracetamol, the injury is from a toxic metabolite which is normally inactivated by glutathione if the dose is not excessive.

Another variety of acute hepatic injury is the *cholestatic* form. The mechanism for this is uncertain. However, the clinical and biochemical features resemble those of obstructive jaundice, so there must be interference with the excretion of bile, with the hepatic transport of bilirubin, or with its conjugation. Steroids which do not have a methyl radical in the C19 position (19-norsteroids) are liable to cause cholestatic jaundice. Substitution in the 17α position with an alkyl or other group may also lead to this propensity. Thus methyltestosterone, which has an alkyl group in that position, causes cholestatic jaundice, whereas testosterone, which lacks this group, does not do so. The progestogens used in oral contraceptives are synthetic 19-norsteroids and they may also be 17-substituted (norethisterone, norethynodrel, ethynodiol and lynoestrenol). The oestrogen components ethinyloestradiol and mestranol are 17-substituted 19-norsteroids. Hence women taking oral contraceptives may have a transient rise in the serum transaminase when they first take these substances. Jaundice itself is rare. It is particularly apt to happen in women who have had idiopathic recurrent cholestasis of pregnancy. The synthetic progestogen, megestrol, is not a 17-substituted 19-norsteroid. Rifampicin interferes with the clearance of bilirubin from the liver by competitive inhibition. Novobiocin may interfere with the conjugation of bilirubin.

So far, reference has been made to drugs that may have hepatotoxic effects in anyone who takes them, but many more drugs are injurious to a small percentage of those who are given them, and often these effects are not dose related. It is difficult to be sure whether, with a given drug, the condition is true hypersensitivity (p. 548) or whether there may be a variation in the catabolism of the substance, with production of hepatotoxic metabolites. In a few individuals, halothane produces a hepatocellular type of jaundice, which is particularly liable to have serious consequences if, after recovery, the anaesthetic is again administered. There may be direct toxicity, but possibly also an immunological response to a toxic metabolite. Unexplained pyrexia or jaundice occurring after an administration of halothane (p. 265) should be regarded as a contraindication to its further use unless it is clear that there is a totally different reason for this. A second exposure to this anaesthetic within four weeks is always to be avoided. Chlorpromazine is a well-recognized cause of hepatocanalicular jaundice in some, as also is erythromycin estolate. Some agents, including chlorpromazine, may produce both hepatocellular and canalicular types of jaundice. If other systemic features, such as a rash, fever or eosinophilia occur, then it is more likely that a hypersensitivity type of reaction is being produced, and this is often the case in the small proportion of patients who develop jaundice after taking chlorpromazine. Phenylbutazone, indomethacin, ibuprofen and certain related drugs may give a hypersensitivity type of hepatocellular damage, as may ketoconazole (p. 58).

Tests of liver function may give abnormal results when a variety of drugs are taken.

Chronic hepatic disease.

Chronic active hepatitis may be due to viral infection, but a similar clinical picture may be caused by drugs, including oxyphenisatin (formerly used to treat constipation), methyldopa, paracetamol, sulphonamides and isoniazid. Where clinical effects are more rapid, the term 'subacute hepatic necrosis' is sometimes used.

Hepatic cirrhosis may occur from the long-term taking of ethyl alcohol or inorganic arsenicals, and cirrhosis may follow upon chronic active hepatitis. Up to 50% of patients receiving long-term treatment for psoriasis with methotrexate may develop periportal inflammation with fibrosis, and this sometimes progresses to cirrhosis.

Hepatic vein thrombosis. This may be consequent upon the taking of contraceptive pills (pp. 421, 474).

Hepatic tumours. It is fairly clear that there is a small increase in the incidence of benign liver tumours in women taking contraceptive pills over a long period, but in 1977 a WHO scientific group concluded that there was no clear indication of a relationship between using the oestrogen–progestogen combined pill and the occurrence of any form of cancer.

Cholelithiasis. The use of clofibrate as a lipid-lowering substance (p. 487) has been found to cause an increased incidence of gallstones.

Adverse effects of drugs on the kidneys

Most drugs or their metabolites are excreted by the kidneys, and it is therefore not surprising that these organs may be the targets for adverse reactions. A complete list cannot be given, but some of the toxic effects will be described.

Acute renal damage. Drugs may have adverse effects on various sites in the kidneys, and some may affect more than one site.

Glomerulonephritis. Glomerular damage may be caused by hydralazine, phenylbutazone or sulphonamides. In this last case, the lesion occurs more commonly if the drug is one of the long-acting variety. There may be focal necrotizing glomerulonephritis or a diffuse proliferative and exudative form.

Acute tubular necrosis. Gentamicin, streptomycin and, indeed, all aminoglycoside antibiotics are potentially nephrotoxic, the damage being to the proximal tubules, in particular. Deafness may occur because of ototoxicity and impaired renal function. The antifungal agent, amphotericin, may produce proximal or distal tubular lesions. Cephaloridine and cephalothin can cause proximal tubular damage, particularly if frusemide is given simultaneously. In place of these, newer 'second' or 'third generation' cephalosporins or, alternatively, cephamycins should be used.

Acute tubular necrosis follows overdosage with paracetamol.

Acute interstitial nephritis. This is rare but many follow treatment with sulphonamides, co-trimoxazole, rifampicin, fenoprofen, ibuprofen, phenyl-butazone, phenindione, thiazide diuretics and various other drugs. It is regarded as a hypersensitivity reaction and there may be an associated skin rash, fever, eosinophilia, arthralgia or liver dysfunction. In the kidneys, there is an interstitial infiltrate of mononuclear cells and eosinophils. Tubular degeneration occurs, but the glomeruli are spread.

Acute vasculitis with renal involvement. This is a rare hypersensitivity reaction. Cutaneous angiitis is rarely associated with renal lesions, but this may occur with allopurinol, sulphonamides and thiazide diuretics. Perhaps the protein-bound drug acts as a hapten and this causes antibody formation directed against the blood vessel walls.

Non-acute renal damage.

Nephrotic syndrome. Gold injections may have a direct action on the renal tubules, and penicillamine possibly causes the nephrotic syndrome by a mechanism that involves the deposition of immune complexes and complement in the basement membrane of glomerular capillaries. The nephrotic syndrome may also be caused by mercurials, penicillamine, phenindione, probenecid, tolbutamide, troxidone and various other unrelated substances. The condition is usually reversible.

Analgesic nephropathy. There is papillary necrosis, possibly because of ischaemia, which is caused by damage of the vasa recta. Renal tubules passing into necrotic papillae are obstructed and undergo atrophy. The radiographic appearances are well recognized. The condition is caused by taking large doses of phenacetin, a drug which is no longer used in the UK, for a long period. Paracetamol is the principal metabolite of phenacetin, and many patients with analgesic nephropathy have taken paracetamol or aspirin for long periods in addition to the phenacetin. There is evidence to suggest that normal doses of paracetamol do not cause kidney damage, but some experts consider that there may be a danger from the long-term use of aspirin.

Lupus erythematosus. Disseminated lupus erythematosus may be caused by a number of drugs, including hydralazine, isoniazid, nitrofurantoin and procainamide. The kidney may be involved. The mechanism is uncertain, but if administration of the drug ceases, the patient usually recovers.

Retroperitoneal fibrosis. This curious condition is found, particularly after the taking of methysergide, but, very occasionally, other drugs have been blamed. The fibrosis may cause ureteral obstruction.

Renal stones. Calcium-containing stones may be found after excessive consumption of mixtures containing alkali with calcium, together with milk, for the treatment of duodenal ulceration. They also occur when excessive amounts of vitamin D are given, after prolonged therapy with corticosteroids, or when skeletal cancer or myeloma is treated with chemotherapeutic agents.

Crystalluria. Urates may be released by the breakdown of nucleoprotein when malignant conditions are treated with chemotherapeutic substances. Urates are produced in large amounts and may be precipitated in the renal tubules. To prevent this, allopurinol (p. 140) is used. Crystalluria occurs with the less soluble sulphonamides, such as sulphathiazole and sulphadiazine. Crystals may also form if acetazolamide is used. It was formerly given as a diuretic but is now used only in the management of glaucoma.

Pulmonary disorders

The lungs are involved in the metabolic transformation of certain drugs. In paraquat poisoning, this substance or metabolites may accumulate, bringing about pulmonary fibrosis and frequently death. Fibrosis may also be caused by a few drugs, including busulphan, nitrofurantoin and methysergide. A syndrome resembling systemic lupus erythematosus, sometimes associated with a pleural effusion, may occur with penicillin, hydralazine, procainamide, isoniazid and phenytoin.

Bronchoconstriction may be caused by β-receptor blocking agents, particularly in asthmatics, but an allergic form of asthma may be precipitated by a number of substances, including penicillin, streptomycin, iron-dextran infusions, anaesthetic induction agents in combination with a muscle relaxant, and even sodium cromoglycate. In asthma, there is thought to be an imbalance between cyclic AMP and cyclic GMP. The former leads to bronchodilation and the latter to bronchoconstriction. Prostaglandin $F_{2\alpha}$, used for therapeutic abortions tips the balance towards cyclic GMP and may cause bronchoconstriction. Drugs, including aspirin, that inhibit the enzyme prostaglandin synthetase, may alter the ratio of prostaglandins, $F_{2\alpha}$ and E_1, and hence cause bronchospasm.

Pulmonary oedema may occur from overloading with i.v. fluids, and can also follow the i.v. administration of diamorphine. This latter occurrence may be a form of hypersensitivity. Pulmonary eosinophilia, due to a hypersensitivity reaction in the alveolar walls, may be caused by sulphonamides, penicillin, tetracycline, imipramine and a few other drugs. Pulmonary alveolitis may occur when amiodarone (p. 305) is given.

Cardiovascular disorders

The effects of drugs on the heart rate need not be discussed here, although the claim that the slowing of the heart caused by β-receptor blocking agents may be beneficial in times of stress is of interest. It has been suggested that those who might receive this benefit include airline pilots, racing drivers, musicians and surgeons.

When prazosin was introduced for the treatment of hypertension, it was found that, unless a very small dose was given in the first instance, there was dizziness, hypotension, collapse and even loss of consciousness.

Gynaecomastia

Abnormal development of the breasts occurs in males who are given oestrogens. For some reason that is not clear, this may also occur from taking digoxin, methyldopa or spironolactone.

Ocular changes

These may be due to prolonged use of carbromal, chloroquine, ergot or phenothiazines. With this last group, there may be pigmentary retinal changes, diplopia, allergic reactions in the conjunctivae or lids, oculogyric crises or lenticular opacities. Corticosteroids may cause elevation of intraocular pressure and, with prolonged use, posterior subcapsular cataracts. Quinine may cause a disturbance of vision and it is not certain whether this is a direct effect on the optic nerve or whether it is secondary to vascular spasm. Ethambutol may cause optic neuritis. Where there is a visual abnormality, treatment with the offending drug must cease at once.

As is now well known, practolol was found to cause serious ocular damage in a number of patients. The features ranged from a gritty feeling to photophobia, panconjunctivitis, absence of tears, subconjunctival fibrosis, entropion, corneal ulceration and blindness. The reason for this is not clear. Some patients developed a rash that was described as psoriasiform, although this was not a precise description. Others had ulceration of the nasal or oral mucosa, hearing impairment or sclerosing serositis. Other beta-blockers have not done this, but have caused reversible dry eye symptoms and also rashes.

In Japan, clioquinol has caused subacute myelo-optic neuropathy in many patients.

Central nervous system disorders

A Parkinson type of syndrome may be produced by large doses of chlorpromazine or other phenothiazines. Even in small doses, prochlorperazine can cause extrapyramidal side-effects and there may be a curious jerking movement of the neck. Presumably, there is a disturbance of the balance between cholinergic and dopaminergic effects in the extrapyramidal structures. The adverse effects are not permanent and in any case can be overcome by the use of anticholinergic drugs such as benzhexol.

Tardive dyskinesia is a choreiform syndrome with repetitive purposeless involuntary movements. It is a serious and sometimes irreversible side-effect that is occasionally seen in those with schizophrenia or other psychiatric disorders, who have been given long-term treatment, particularly with phenothiazines or butyrophenones. It differs from Parkinsonism in that there is no muscular rigidity.

Other disorders

An unexplained febrile reaction may be found to be due to a drug, while hypothermia may be produced by chlorpromazine or nitrazepam, particularly in the elderly.

Those who drive cars, or work with machinery or in dangerous situations should remember that not only alcohol but also drugs, including hypnotics and tranquillizers, can cause accidents. Various drugs, particularly some aminoglycosides (p. 15) are ototoxic.

The administration of a drug may interfere with the diagnosis of a disease. For example, co-trimoxazole may delay the diagnosis of malaria.

When a drug is undergoing tests in animals prior to use in humans, tests for carcinogenicity are carried out where the substance has a chemical structure that suggests carcinogenic potential, where it is to be used for long periods in humans, where there is concern because of some special aspect of its biological action or if some previous study suggests that there may be a problem. From time to time, there has been concern about possible carcinogenicity from the long-term use of certain oestrogens or progestogens.

Genetically determined adverse reactions, such as porphyria or malignant hyperthermia after anaesthesia, are discussed on pages 255–9.

The possible dangers of inoculations must be considered by the clinician, but do not come within the scope of this chapter.

FURTHER READING

Announcement (1983) Production of Debendox to stop. *Lancet*, i: 1395.

Antunes C. M. F., Stolley P. D., Rosenhein N. B., Davies J. L., Tonascia J. A., Brown C., Burnett L., Rutledge A., Pokempner M. & Garcia R. (1979) Endometrial cancer and estrogen use. *New Engl. J. Med.*, 300: 9.

Bramble M. G. & Record C. O. (1978) Drug-induced gastrointestinal disease. *Drugs*, 15: 451.

Chan T. K., Todd D. & Tso S. C. (1976) Drug-induced haemolysis in glucose-6-phosphate dehydrogenase deficiency. *Br. Med. J.*, 2: 1227.

Cooke A. R. (1976) Drugs and gastric damage. *Drugs*, 11: 36.

Curtis J. R. (1979) Drug-induced renal disease. *Drugs*, 18: 377.

D'Arcy P. F. & Griffin J. P. (1979) *Iatrogenic Diseases*, 2nd edn. London: Oxford University Press.

Davies D. M. (ed) (1981) *Textbook of Adverse Drug Reactions*, 2nd edn. London: Oxford University Press.

Denz C., El-Awar N., Cicciarelli J., Terasaki P. I., Billing R. & Lagasse L. (1981) Cytotoxic monoclonal antibody to a human leiomyosarcoma. *Lancet* i: 403.

Dillman R. O., Shawler D. L., Sobol R. E., Collins H. A., Beauregard J. C., Wormsley S. B. & Royston I. (1982) Murine monoclonal antibody therapy in two patients with chronic lymphocytic leukemia. *Blood*, 59: 1036.

Editorial (1974) Halothane and liver damage. *Br. med. J.*, 3: 589.

Editorial (1982*a*) T lymphocytes. *Lancet*, i: 778.

Editorial (1982*b*) Valproate and malformations. *Lancet*, ii: 1313.

Editorial (1983) Drug targeting in cancer. *Lancet*, i: 512.

Filipovich A., McGlave P. B., Ramsay N., Goldstein G., Warkentin P. & Kersey J. H. (1982) Pretreatment of donor bone marrow with monoclonal antibody OKT3 for prevention of acute graft-versus-host disease in allogeneic histocompatible bone-marrow transplantation. *Lancet*, i: 1266.

Fleming D. M., Knox J. D. E. & Crombie D. L. (1981) Debendox in early pregnancy and fetal malformation. *Br. med. J.*, 283: 99.

Girdwood R. H. (ed) (1973) *Blood Disorders Due to Drugs and Other Agents*. Amsterdam: Excerpta Medica.

Girdwood, R. H. (1974) Death after taking medicaments. *Br. med. J.*, i: 501.

Gordon-Smith E. C. (ed) (1980) Haematological effects of drug therapy. *Clinics in Haematology*, 9: 453.

Greenberg G., Inman W. H. W., Weatherall J. A. C., Adelstein A. M. & Haskey J. C. (1977) Maternal drug histories and congenital abnormalities. *Br. med. J.*, ii: 853.

Griffin J. P. & D'Arcy P. F. (1979) *A Manual of Adverse Drug Interactions*, 2nd edn. Bristol: John Wright.

Inman W. H. W. (1977) Study of fatal bone marrow depression with special reference to phenylbutazone and oxyphenbutazone. *Br. med. J.*, i: 1500.

Janossy G., Ganeshaguru K. & Hoffbrand A. V. (1982) Leukaemia and lymphoma: recent immunological and biochemical developments (including information about monoclonal antibodies). *Recent Advances in Haematology*, 3, 207.

Kohler G. & Milstein C. (1975) Continuous cultures of fused cells secreting antibody of predefined specificity. *Nature*, 256: 495.

McGregor A. M. (1981) Monoclonal antibodies: production and use. *Br. med. J.*, 283: 1143.

McNulty H. & Spurr P. (1979) Drug names that look or sound alike. *Br. med. J.*, ii: 836.

Medical Research Council Working Party on Mild to Moderate Hypertension (1981) Adverse reactions to bendrofluazide and propranolol for the treatment of mild hypertension. *Lancet*, ii: 539.

Medico-Pharmaceutical Forum (1978) Publication No. 7. *Post-marketing Surveillance of Adverse Reactions to New Medicines*. London: 1 Wimpole Street, London, W1M 8AE.

Morelock S., Hingson R., Kayne H., Dooling E., Zuckerman B., Day N., Alpert J. J. & Flowerdew G. (1982) Bendectin and fetal development. *Am. J. Obstet. Gynaec.*, 142: 209.

Prescott L. F. (1973) Clinically important drug interactions. *Drugs*, 5: 161.

Rao J. M. & Arulappi R. (1981) Drug use in pregnancy: how to avoid problems. *Drugs*, 22: 409.

Robson J. M., Sullivan F. M. & Smith R. L. (ed) (1965) *Embryopathic Activity of Drugs*. London: Churchill.

Roitt I. M., Male D. K., Guarrotta G., de Carvalho L. P., Cooke A., Hay F. C., Lydyara P. M., Thanavala Y. & Ivanyi J. (1981) Idiotypic networks and their possible exploitation for manipulation of the immune response. *Lancet*, i: 1041.

Sher P. P. (1982) Drug interferences with clinical laboratory tests. *Drugs*, 24: 24.

Sjöström H. & Nilsson R. (1972) *Thalidomide and the Power of the Drug Companies*. London: Penguin Books.

Smith R. (1981) Compensation for drug injury: problems on both sides of the Atlantic. *Br. med. J.*, 282: 1443.

Smith R. (1981) Product liability all dressed up American style. *Br. med. J.*, 282: 1535.

Smith R. (1981) Two solutions to an insoluble problem. *Br. med. J.*, 282: 1610.

Smithells R. W. & Sheppard S. (1978) Teratogenicity testing in humans: a method demonstrating safety of Bendectin. *Teratology*, 17: 31.

Stockley I. (1974) *Drug Interactions and Their Mechanisms*. London: The Pharmaceutical Press.

Venning G. R. (1983) Identification of adverse reactions to new drugs. I: What have been the important adverse reactions since thalidomide? *Br. med. J.*, 286: 199.

Venning G. R. (1983) Identification of adverse reactions to new drugs. II: How were 18 important adverse reactions discovered and with what delays? *Br. med. J.*, 286: 289, 365.

Venning G. R. (1983) Identification of adverse reactions to new drugs. III: Alerting processes and early warning systems. *Br. med. J.*, 286: 458.

Venning G. R. (1983) Identification of adverse reactions to new drugs. IV: Verification of suspected adverse reactions. *Br. med. J.*, 286: 544.

Vessey M. P. (1978) Contraceptive methods: risks and benefits. *Br. med. J.*, ii: 721.

Volans G. N., Mitchell G. M., Proudfoot A. T., Shanks R. G. R. & Woodcock J. A. (1981) National poisons information services: report and comment, 1980. *Br. med. J.*, 282: 1613.

Williams G. R., Law T. L., Kennedy D. H. & Love W. C. (1982) Delayed diagnosis of malaria. *Br. med. J.*, 284: 1616.

Yudkin J. S. (1978) Provision of medicines in a developing country. *Lancet*, i: 810.

Zimmerman H. J. (1978) Drug-induced liver disease. *Drugs*, 16: 25.

Appendix 1
General Aspects of Drug Action

A. Pottage

INDIVIDUAL VARIATION IN DRUG RESPONSE

Knowledge of a drug's actions, dosage, appropriate routes of administration and likely toxicity is the minimum requirement for safe prescribing. This information is readily available in the manufacturer's information on the product or the national formulary and these should always be consulted before unfamiliar drugs are prescribed. Even when such advice is followed, however, some patients will show either little response or exaggerated toxicity with 'standard' dosage, and some will develop unexpected adverse reactions. These problems occur because of inter-patient variation. 'Recommended' dosage is merely the dose or dose range which is appropriate for the majority of the population. Some patients will require more and some will require less, to achieve the optimum balance between desired response and toxicity. The spectrum of adverse reactions known to occur with the drug can only include those noted, and reported, in the population already treated. With new drugs this population may be surprisingly small. For these reasons, the prescribing information can serve only as a guide to generally appropriate dosage for initiation of therapy and to the more common adverse reactions. If the response is inappropriate or unexpected, dosage modification or a change of drug should be considered.

Within-patient variation also produces problems, particularly with respect to dosage. A change in the patient's clinical condition such as the development of hepatic, renal or cardiac failure may significantly alter drug disposition and lead to toxicity if dosage is not reduced. Drug dosage may need to be adjusted as patients get older and, if drug interactions occur, when a number of drugs are prescribed simultaneously. For these reasons, safe long-term drug therapy requires continual reassessment of dosage and the need for the drug. This is particularly important when drugs that are known to interact with other agents are added to or deleted from a stable treatment regimen.

When an unexpected response to a drug occurs, an attempt should be made to identify the cause as it may also result in abnormal responses to other drugs. For this purpose, a guide to the evaluation of abnormal drug responses is given below. More general background information is given in the sections which follow.

578

EVALUATION OF AN ABNORMAL DRUG RESPONSE

Possible Causes of an Abnormal Drug Response
The following possibilities should be explored.

Wrong drug.
  Name of drug. Some drug names are confusingly similar, e.g. chlorpromazine, chlorpropamide. Confirm that the correct drug has been prescribed and that the prescribed drug has been given.
  Known actions. Examples of these include: microbial sensitivity to different antibiotics varies; glucagon does not increase blood sugar if liver glycogen is depleted; and oral hypoglycaemics are ineffective in juvenile onset diabetics. Confirm drug actions using the manufacturer's information on the product or the national formulary.
  Suitability for patient. Examples of this include: tetracyclines discolour dentition in children; many psychoactive drugs cause confusion in the elderly; anticholinergics precipitate urinary retention; non-selective β-blockers precipitate bronchospasm in asthmatics and interfere with diabetic control; and aminoglycosides produce muscle weakness in myasthenics. Check product information or national formulary for contraindications and warnings. Avoid unnecessary prescribing in pregnancy. Consider genetic variation between ethnic groups.
  Suitability for clinical condition. If the drug requires metabolism for activation or elimination, then this may be impaired in liver disease. If the drug is eliminated in an unchanged state by the kidney, then this may be impaired in renal disease. If the drug has active metabolites, then the possibility of failure of formation in liver disease and accumulation in renal disease should be considered.

Wrong route of administration.
  Suitability for clinical condition. Oral drug absorption is unreliable with pyloric stenosis, vomiting and shock. Oral absorption is delayed by narcotics and pain. Absorption from intramuscular injections is delayed if tissue perfusion is poor (e.g. in shock). Check for interactions with other drugs that might interfere with absorption.
  Suitability for therapeutic aims. Oral administration is relatively safe but gives a slow response. Intravenous (i.v.) administration gives a rapid response but is potentially dangerous. Give i.v. injections slowly. Consider if the route is appropriate to the urgency of the clinical situation.

Wrong dose.
  Recommended dosage regimen. Confirm the dose level (i.e., tablet strength and ampoule content) and the dosing frequency using the manufacturer's information on the product or the national formulary. If the drug has a long half-life, the onset of action is delayed unless a loading dose is given. If the

half-life is very short, frequent administration or constant rate infusion is necessary to produce steady levels.

Compliance. Confirm that the prescribed dosage has been taken.

Suitability for patient. Dosage modification may be necessary at extremes of age and weight. Consider the extremes of normal inter-patient variation and possible genetic variation in drug disposition.

Suitability for clinical condition. Dose reduction may be necessary if elimination is impaired because of liver disease, renal disease or cardiac failure. Absorption of drugs with high first-pass metabolism may increase with liver/small bowel disease. Drug replacement may be necessary after dialysis, bypass surgery or diuresis.

Drug interaction. Consider the effects of added or deleted therapy on absorption, distribution, elimination, desired response, etc. Monitor the effects of therapy repeatedly during the transition, and alter dosage accordingly.

Plasma drug concentration. Measure the peak and trough (pre-dose) concentrations at steady state (>3 half-lives from the start of therapy). If the values are low, look for causes of impaired absorption, increased distribution or increased elimination. If the values are high, look for causes of increased absorption, impaired distribution or impaired elimination. If the clinical condition is stable, make proportional adjustment to dose rate.

Even when the cause is known, serious or unexpected adverse reactions to drugs should be reported promptly to:

1. The government body responsible for monitoring adverse drug reactions
2. The drug manufacturer.

Follow-up information should be supplied when requested. Information on known adverse reactions and the effects of accidental or deliberate over-dosage can be obtained from the manufacturer, or, in an emergency, from a Poisons Information Centre. In the British Isles, these are located at:

1. The Poisons Unit, New Cross Hospital, Avonley Road, London SE14 5ER.
   Telephone 01-407-7600.
2. Scottish Poisons Information Bureau, Royal Infirmary, Edinburgh EH3 9YW.
   Telephone 031-229-2477.
3. Poisons Information Centre, Cardiff Royal Infirmary, Cardiff CF2 1S2.
   Telephone 0222-492233.
4. Royal Victoria Hospital, Grosvenor Road, Belfast BT12 6BB.
   Telephone 0232-40503, ext. 704.
5. The Poisons Information Centre, Jervis Street Hospital, Dublin 1.
   Telephone 01-45588. (If dialling from the UK, precede the number by 00.)

DRUG DISPOSITION

Passage Through Membranes

In order to enter and pass through the body, drugs must cross cell membranes. These consist of a lipid layer with a protein layer on each side and behave as though they contain small water-filled channels. Drugs cross cell membranes by:

1. *Diffusion*. This is the most common way. As most drugs are too large to pass through the water-filled channels, they diffuse through the lipid. The rate of diffusion is determined by concentration gradient and lipid solubility. If the drug is bound on one side of the membrane, or cleared rapidly by blood or lymph, the concentration gradient towards that side is increased. Lipid solubility is determined by chemical structure and degree of ionization. Ionized drugs are more water-soluble, whereas unionized drugs more lipid soluble, and as most drugs are weak acids or bases, their degree of ionization is determined by the surrounding pH. Acidic drugs are mainly in the unionized form at pH values *below* their pKa, whereas basic drugs are mainly unionized at pH values *above* their pKb.

2. *Active transport*. Many natural substances are carried across membranes by an energy-requiring transport system, which can work against a concentration gradient. Drugs that are analogues of the natural substance may compete for the carrier.

3. *Filtration*. Small molecules (mol. wt. <150) can cross membranes by filtration through the water-filled channels. Some membranes, such as those of glomerular cells and capillary endothelial cells, allow larger molecules (mol. wt. up to 60 000) to cross. The direction of travel is with the concentration gradient, unless molecules are carried through by 'bulk flow' of water. The passage of charged molecules is influenced by the potential difference across the membrane.

Distribution Across Membranes

Concentration gradient and lipid solubility determine the *rate* at which a drug can cross the cell membrane. Differences in pH between two compartments separated by a membrane can influence the *distribution* of drug between the compartments at equilibrium. If the pH in one compartment is such that the drug exists mainly in the ionized, poorly lipid-soluble form, it cannot diffuse out of the compartment and is 'trapped'. Ion trapping that results from pH differences across membranes is often described, but is of limited importance because equilibrium conditions rarely occur in vivo. Usually, the equilibrium is disturbed by changing drug concentrations on both sides of the membrane as a result of clearance by blood flow, excretion or metabolism.

DRUG ABSORPTION

Oral Administration

Most drugs are given by mouth and absorption can occur through the buccal, gastric or intestinal mucosa. In tablet or capsule form, drugs bypass the buccal mucosa and enter the stomach and small intestine. Absorption from these sites is determined by:

1. *Surface area.* The surface area of the gastric mucosa is small, and little drug absorption takes place in the stomach. Absorption is rapid from the small intestine because of its much larger surface area. The rate of gastric emptying determines the rate of drug entry to the small intestine, and therefore determines the speed of onset of absorption. Pyloric stenosis, pylorospasm, drugs with anticholinergic effects and narcotics delay gastric emptying and drug absorption. Metoclopramide accelerates gastric emptying and drug absorption.

2. *Gut motility.* Hypomotility reduces the rate at which capsules and tablets dissolve and the speed at which drugs go into solution. This usually reduces the rate of absorption. Although in theory, the extent of absorption may increase if hypomotility allows the drug to remain at a specific absorptive site for a longer time, this is uncommon. However, increased gut motility can reduce the extent of absorption of drugs at specific sites.

3. *Intraluminal pH.* The pH within the gut lumen controls the degree of ionization of weak acids and bases. Acids should be absorbed best in the stomach, and bases absorbed best in the small intestine. In practice this is much less important than the effects of gut motility and surface area. Intraluminal pH influences drug solubility, the rate of dissolution of tablets and capsules, and drug stability. Aspirin is insoluble at low pH, and many compounds are destroyed by acid in the stomach.

4. *Mucosal blood flow.* Mucosal blood and lymph flow clears the drug from the mucosa and maintains the concentration gradient that is necessary for absorption. Blood flow increases after meals, thus increasing the concentration gradient. It decreases on standing, with exercise and in 'shock', thus reducing the concentration gradient.

5. *Mucosal metabolism.* The gut mucosa can metabolize a number of drugs. This reduces the amount of unchanged drug entering the body (the 'bioavailability'). If mucosal metabolism is reduced by mucosal disease (coeliac disease) or drugs such as monoamine oxidase inhibitors, the amount of unchanged drug entering the body increases, the effect being the same as an increase in dose.

6. *Hepatic metabolism.* All drugs absorbed from the stomach, the small and large intestine, and the upper rectum are transported to the liver by the portal venous system. If the drug undergoes hepatic metabolism, a proportion will be metabolized before the drug enters the systemic circulation. This again reduces the amount of unchanged drug entering the body (the 'bioavailability'). If metabolism is impaired by liver disease or by other drugs which reduce rates of hepatic metabolism (e.g. cimetidine) the amount of unchanged drug entering the systemic circulation can increase, the effect again being the same as an increase in dose. Mucosal or hepatic

metabolism immediately after absorption is called pre-systemic or 'first-pass' elimination.

7. *Interactions with substances in the gut lumen.* These can also result in a change in 'bioavailability'. Food may delay absorption by delaying gastric emptying. Food reduces the amount of iron, phenoxymethylpenicillin, propantheline, tetracyclines, rifampin, levodopa and isoniazid that is absorbed, but increases the absorption of phenytoin, spironolactone, lithium and nitrofurantoin. Griseofulvin absorption is enhanced by a fatty meal. Tetracyclines bind to antacids, and to calcium and ferric salts and are poorly absorbed. Antacids influence absorption by changing the rate of gastric emptying and intraluminal pH, as well as binding to drugs. Acid-binding resins reduce the absorption of acidic drugs.

8. *Pharmaceutical formulation.* Most drugs for oral use are dispensed as tablets or capsules which dissolve rapidly in the gastric contents. Thereafter, absorption is determined by the factors described above. If drugs are unstable in acid, or produce gastric irritation, they may be made up in 'enteric coated' or 'positioned release' formulations, enclosed in a coating which only dissolves at high pH, i.e., when the tablet has left the stomach. Alternatively, drugs that are rapidly eliminated from the body and require frequent dosing throughout the day to maintain steady blood levels may be made up in 'controlled release' formulations. In these, a large amount of drug is enclosed in a poorly soluble or insoluble matrix, or is surrounded by an impermeable membrane with a minute hole in it. Small quantities of the drug are released over long periods, thus prolonging the duration of action of each dose. As absorption from these formulations is slow, they may also be used for drugs that produce side-effects because of high plasma concentrations after rapid absorption.

Rate versus extent of absorption. Delayed gastric emptying and controlled release pharmaceutical formulations delay the *rate* of drug absorption, but if all of the drug is eventually absorbed, the extent of absorption is unchanged. If the rate of absorption is reduced, there will be a delay in the onset of drug effect at the start of treatment, but after repeated doses, the mean plasma concentration at steady state, and the response, will be unaffected. Binding of the drug in the gut, incomplete absorption for other reasons and changes in pre-systemic elimination (reduced or increased bioavailability) alter the *extent* of drug absorption, and essentially change the dose given. The mean plasma concentration achieved at steady state, and the response, will change accordingly.

Sublingual Administration
Although the surface area of the buccal mucosa is small, it is highly vascular. Lipid-soluble compounds are rapidly absorbed when allowed to dissolve in the mouth and enter the systemic circulation directly, thus avoiding pre-systemic elimination. The route is most useful for tasteless drugs that are

effective in small doses. If the drug undergoes extensive pre-systemic elimination, absorption can be terminated by swallowing the tablet.

Rectal Administration
The rectal mucosa is highly vascular and absorption from the lower part avoids pre-systemic elimination. The route is most useful for drugs causing upper gastrointestinal irritation, for unconscious or vomiting patients, and for infants.

Intramuscular Injection
Injection of high concentrations results in a large concentration gradient between injection site and local blood vessels and rapid absorption should occur. Irritation from high concentrations of drug is a practical limitation and the absorption of some compounds (e.g. diazepam and phenytoin) is so unreliable that intramuscular injection is best avoided. Aqueous solutions are usually rapidly absorbed, but suspensions, oily solutions or 'depot' preparations are slowly absorbed. Absorption rates are higher in muscles with high blood flow (e.g. deltoid) than in those with low blood flow (e.g. gluteus). The rate of absorption can be increased by massaging or heating the site of injection, or reduced by cooling the site of injection or using vasoconstrictor agents (e.g. adrenaline). Absorption from intramuscular injections will be delayed if peripheral perfusion is poor, e.g. in 'shock'. The above factors also determine the rate of absorption from intradermal and s.c. injections.

Topical Administration to Skin or Mucosa
The rate of absorption is directly proportional to the concentration applied, the lipid solubility of the drug and the skin or mucosal blood flow, but inversely proportional to the degree of keratinization. The increased blood flow that occurs with inflammation increases absorption, as do occlusive dressings.

Topical Administration to Lungs
The lungs provide a large surface for absorption of lipid-soluble compounds, which rapidly enter the systemic circulation because of the high pulmonary blood flow. This is clearly an advantage with inhaled gaseous anaesthetics, but it is a disadvantage with inhaled adrenergic bronchodilators which produce systemic cardiovascular effects. If powders or aerosols are inhaled, most of the particles are deposited in the oropharynx and the drug is swallowed and absorbed. Only particles of $<2\ \mu$m usually reach the alveoli.

Intravenous Injection
Drugs injected intravenously enter the systemic circulation directly, passing sequentially through the right heart and lungs before they are distributed to tissues by the arterial circulation. Many basic drugs are taken up into the lungs, initially reducing the arterial concentration. As pre-systemic hepatic

and mucosal elimination is avoided, the bioavailability of drugs given intravenously is always complete (100 per cent).

DRUG DISTRIBUTION

On entering the systemic circulation, drugs are transported to the tissues in plasma, bound to plasma proteins. The rate at which they are transported to different tissues depends on tissue blood flow. Drugs acting on the brain, heart, lungs, liver and kidney usually produce effects more quickly than drugs acting on tissues that have a smaller blood supply.

Drug distribution between different tissues is determined by lipid solubility, tissue uptake and plasma protein binding. At equilibrium, drugs are partitioned between plasma water, plasma protein and the different tissues. Binding to plasma protein and the extent of distribution to other tissues determines the amount of free drug that is available in plasma water to produce the effect.

Lipid Solubility

Lipid-soluble drugs enter cells readily and may be stored in fat. They are usually widely distributed and only a small proportion of drug in the body remains in the plasma, unless plasma protein binding is extensive. The elimination of widely distributed drugs is usually slow, because clearance from the plasma removes only a small proportion of the body content in any given time. The converse applies to water-soluble drugs which are generally poorly distributed, exist in large amounts in plasma or extracellular fluid and can be cleared rapidly by liver, kidney or haemodialysis.

Tissue Uptake

Lipid-soluble drugs enter most cells and fat readily by diffusion. Considerable amounts of the drug may be stored in body tissues such as fat or muscle, where it produces no pharmacological effect. If access to these 'stores' is restricted by reduced tissue blood flow (in cardiac failure or 'shock'), the drug cannot be distributed fully from the plasma, and hence plasma concentrations rise, with a resultant increase in drug effects. The increase in plasma concentration is likely to be proportionately greater with lipid-soluble drugs as these are mainly distributed to extravascular sites under normal conditions.

Distribution of water-soluble compounds to the brain is usually restricted by the 'blood–brain barrier': lipid-soluble compounds enter and leave readily by diffusion. The 'blood–brain barrier' becomes less selective with meningeal inflammation. Water-soluble compounds leave the brain by filtration through arachnoid villi.

Lipid-soluble compounds of mol. wt. $< 1\,000$ cross the placenta easily and enter the fetus: water-soluble compounds diffuse across slowly, if at all. At equilibrium, there may be comparable concentrations of lipid-soluble drugs in maternal and fetal plasma. As fetal drug elimination systems will be immature, the effects of a given drug concentration on the fetus will be more prolonged.

Plasma Protein Binding

Drugs differ in their degree of plasma protein binding. Extensive binding tends to reduce drug distribution, because the drug is held in plasma. In the absence of protein binding, lipid-soluble drugs cannot be carried in plasma because of their poor water-solubility, while basic drugs are poorly absorbed because the plasma pH prevents the development of a concentration gradient across cell–plasma boundaries. The binding is reversible and influenced by drug and protein ionization and therefore by the plasma pH. With most drugs, the binding is independent of drug concentration in the plasma. However, if concentrations increase to high levels the proportion that is bound may decrease. This occurs at therapeutic concentrations with disopyramide.

Plasma protein binding is one factor determining the free (active) drug concentration in the plasma, and therefore the response. Drugs may be displaced from their binding sites by other drugs or by acidic metabolic products in renal failure. Alternatively, the total amount of protein that is available for binding may be reduced in liver disease. This results in an increase in free drug concentration. With widely distributed lipid-soluble drugs the displaced free drug is rapidly distributed to extravascular sites, the free concentration in the plasma showing little change. Poorly distributed, water-soluble compounds cannot enter tissues so readily and the free concentration in the plasma may increase significantly.

As plasma protein binding is reversible, free drug cleared from the plasma by the liver or kidney is rapidly replaced by dissociation from plasma proteins. Because of this, plasma protein binding does not usually delay elimination. If tissue distribution is not extensive, much of the drug in the body will be in plasma and overall elimination will be rapid. If the drug is widely distributed, however, overall elimination will be slow because even rapid clearance of free drug in plasma will only remove a small fraction of the total amount present in the body in a given time.

DRUG ELIMINATION

The major routes of drug elimination are metabolism by the liver or excretion by the kidney. Drug metabolites are usually excreted directly by the kidney, although some may be secreted the bile and then reabsorbed. Drugs excreted in the bile and also those first eliminated by the salivary glands, stomach and small intestine can be reabsorbed, and this recycling prolongs drug activity. Drug secretion into milk or sweat results in elimination.

Drug Metabolism

The liver is quantitatively the most important site of drug metabolism, although some occurs in bowel mucosa and kidney. In the absence of metabolism, elimination of lipid-soluble drugs would be very slow. Because they are widely distributed, only a small proportion of drug in the body is found in plasma, and renal clearance only removes a small fraction of the body content in a given time. Furthermore, lipid-soluble drugs are easily reabsorbed in the renal tubule and returned to the body. Metabolism converts lipid-soluble compounds to polar, more water-soluble compounds. These are more rapidly excreted by the kidney because of their reduced distribution volume and rate of tubular reabsorption.

Metabolism in the liver occurs in two stages. Stage I reactions are oxidations, reductions or hydrolyses which make the compound more polar, but not necessarily inactive. The enzymes (mixed function oxidases) that are responsible for this use cytochrome P-450 as a cofactor. In the Stage II reactions, the drug or metabolite is conjugated to an organic acid or other group, the resulting metabolite being highly water-soluble as well as pharmacologically inactive.

Factors influencing hepatic metabolism include:

1. *Liver disease.* In liver disease, drug elimination is highly unpredictable. Drug clearance may be impaired if liver blood flow is reduced or shunting occurs. Metabolism may be reduced if the functional liver cell mass decreases, or enzyme activity is reduced. As the relative contribution of these factors to hepatic function in the individual patient is usually unknown, it is safest to assume that drug elimination will be impaired in liver disease and it is wise to reduce the dosage or monitor plasma concentrations accordingly. Liver disease can alter drug distribution as well as reduce the rate of drug elimination. It can also increase the amount of drug absorbed if bioavailability is usually low because of pre-systemic elimination. Impaired elimination and increased absorption both result in increased plasma concentrations from any given dose.
2. *Enzyme induction.* Many drugs, insecticides and other environmental pollutants are enzyme-inducing agents and they produce increased amounts of drug metabolizing enzymes in the liver. This process can occur very rapidly and persist for several weeks after the last exposure to the inducing agent. The increased enzyme activity accelerates the metabolism of the inducing agent, and any other drug metabolized by the same route. Drug dosage may need to be increased during enzyme induction to avoid treatment failure and to be reduced on terminating exposure to the inducing agent in order to avoid toxicity. Some drugs producing enzyme induction are described on page 599.
3. *Competition.* A number of drugs impair the metabolism of other drugs given simultaneously, either by competing for the metabolic pathway or binding to cytochrome P-450. The result is a delay in the elimination of the drug with the least affinity for the system and this leads to higher plasma concentrations than expected with any given dose. The effects of drug

competition disappear rapidly on discontinuation of the offending drug. Some drugs known to compete for metabolism are described on page 599.

Hepatic clearance. Metabolized drugs are cleared by the liver at different rates (Table A1.1). Those with high hepatic clearance have relatively short half-lives and low bioavailability because of pre-systemic elimination. Their rate of elimination is determined primarily by liver blood flow while changes in enzyme activity have a lesser effect. Factors which influence blood flow (e.g. posture, exercise, cardiac failure and shock) change their rate of elimination more than enzyme-inducing agents. Drugs with low hepatic clearance have relatively long half-lives and show little pre-systemic elimination. Their clearance is determined primarily by enzyme activity, rather than blood flow, and enzyme-inducing agents can have substantial effects on the rate of elimination.

Table A1.1 *Intrinsic hepatic clearance*

High	Low
Hydrocortisone	Diazepam
Lignocaine	Phenylbutazone
Pethidine	Phenytoin
Propranolol	Tolbutamide
Tricyclic antidepressants	Warfarin

Drug metabolites. Although drug metabolites are less lipid soluble than their parent drugs, they are not necessarily less active. Many drugs (e.g. cyclophosphamide, prednisone, cortisone, imipramine and codeine) require metabolism for activation. Alternatively, drug metabolites may have a similar spectrum of activity to the parent drug. Since metabolite concentrations in plasma may approach or even exceed parent drug concentrations at steady state (as a result of their reduced distribution volume), active metabolite concentrations should be taken into account when plasma concentrations are monitored.

Renal Excretion

Unbound drug in plasma is filtered in the glomerulus and enters the renal tubule. Lipid-soluble compounds then diffuse through the tubular epithelium and return to the body. Ionized or water-soluble compounds are retained in the tubule and excreted. The elimination of some weak acids (e.g. phenobarbitone, salicylate) can be increased if the urine is made alkaline because the drug is then ionized in the renal tubule and reabsorption is inhibited. Acidification of the urine has similar effects with weak bases such as amphetamine, quinidine and strychnine. Physiological variation in urine pH usually has little effect on the rate of drug excretion unless renal excretion of unchanged drug is the major route of elimination and the pK value lies between 6.5 and 10.

Other factors influencing renal excretion include:

1. *Renal disease*. Renal blood flow, glomerular filtration and tubular secretion may be abnormal in renal disease and, in general, their function declines in parallel. If renal excretion of unchanged drug is the major route of elimination then accumulation will occur in renal disease and the dose rate should be reduced to avoid toxicity. A fall in creatinine clearance gives an estimate of the severity of renal impairment, but drug clearance may not fall in parallel. Plasma concentration monitoring of the drug and of active metabolites, which will also accumulate, can be used to adjust dosage. Drug distribution may also be abnormal in renal disease.
2. *Competition*. Some strong acids and bases are actively secreted into and out of the renal tubular lumen and competition can occur for active transport systems. Probenecid competes with penicillin for secretion into the tubule, thus delaying its excretion. It impairs the reabsorption of uric acid, thus enhancing its elimination. Other similar drug interactions are described on page 600.

PHARMACOKINETICS, DOSAGE REGIMENS AND PLASMA CONCENTRATION MONITORING

PHARMACOKINETICS

The rate of most pharmacokinetic processes in the body is proportional to the mass of drug that is available to take part. With 'first-order' kinetics, the rate of the process decreases as the mass of drug available decreases. If the drug concentration is plotted against time, it declines exponentially. If log drug concentration is plotted against time, it declines linearly. Although the rate of the process changes, the proportion of drug removed in a given time is constant, and the time taken to remove 50 per cent (the half-life) gives a measure of the velocity of the process. With 'zero-order' kinetics, the rate is constant and independent of the mass of drug present. Zero-order kinetics occur when a rate-limiting process is saturated above a certain drug concentration.

Various parameters are used to describe drug kinetics and those of clinical relevance are given below. It is important to remember that values for these parameters which have been obtained in healthy subjects may not be applicable to patients.

Volume of Distribution
The apparent volume of distribution is the theoretical volume in which a

known amount of drug would have to be uniformly dispersed in order to produce a measured plasma concentration. If the apparent volume of distribution is large, only a small fraction of drug in the body remains in the plasma. If the apparent volume of distribution is small, more of the body content is found in the plasma. In general, lipid-soluble compounds and those with little plasma protein binding have ready access to extravascular tissues and large distribution volumes, whereas water-soluble compounds and those extensively bound to plasma proteins have small distribution volumes.

Clearance

Unbound drug in plasma is cleared by hepatic metabolism, renal excretion, etc., the total plasma clearance (systemic clearance) being the arithmetic sum of the renal clearance, hepatic clearance and other clearance processes. If renal or hepatic clearance decreases, the total clearance declines by the same amount. Clearance gives a better estimate of the rate of drug elimination than half-life for the reasons given below.

Half-life

The half-life of a drug in the body, plasma, urine, etc., is the time taken for drug concentrations to decline by 50 per cent. If the half-life is two hours and the starting concentration is 8 mg/l, the concentration at 2 hours will be 4 mg/l, at four hours, 2 mg/l, and at six hours 1 mg/l, etc. The half-life is inversely proportional to clearance and directly proportional to distribution volume. If distribution volume stays constant, an increase in clearance shortens the half-life and a decrease in clearance prolongs the half-life. If clearance stays constant, an increase in distribution volume prolongs the half-life and a decrease in distribution volume shortens it. As liver disease, renal disease and drug interactions can influence both distribution and clearance simultaneously, their effects on half-life are not always predictable.

DOSAGE REGIMENS FOR LONG-TERM TREATMENT

The aim of drug therapy is to produce an effective drug concentration at the site of action. At equilibrium, this correlates with the plasma concentration, which can often be measured. The optimum plasma concentration is that which produces the maximum response with the minimum toxicity. As the concentration increases, the response may increase further, or more patients may respond, but toxicity may increase or more patients complain of adverse effects. In practice, a concentration range is usually established (therapeutic range) in which most individuals will respond and few will show toxicity. Standard dosage regimens are designed to produce plasma concentrations within the therapeutic range in the majority of patients. Modified regimens may be available for patients with hepatic, renal or cardiac failure.

Loading Dose

The loading dose required to produce any given plasma concentration is determined by the volume of distribution.

Loading dose (mg) = Desired plasma concentration (mg/l) × Distribution volume (l)

If the distribution volume is large, the dose will be large and it may be necessary to give it in several small increments to avoid toxicity because excessively high plasma concentrations can occur before distribution to extravascular sites. Once the loading dose has been given, the drug should show equilibrium or 'steady-state' behaviour, and the desired plasma concentration can be maintained with regular dosage. Even though 'effective' plasma concentrations are achieved rapidly with loading doses, the response may be delayed if distribution from the plasma to the site of action is slow. Cardiac and central nervous system effects usually occur rapidly.

Maintenance Dosage

At equilibrium or 'steady state', the rate of drug input and the rate of elimination are the same. The dose required to produce any desired plasma concentration is determined only by the total clearance.

Maintenance dose rate (mg/h) = Desired plasma concentration (mg/l) × Total clearance (l/h)

If the clearance stays constant, doubling the dose rate will double the plasma concentration. If the clearance falls by 50 per cent, the dose rate must be reduced by 50 per cent to maintain the same concentration.

Dosage Interval and Steady-state Behaviour

If a drug is given by intravenous infusion at a constant rate, the plasma concentration will increase progressively until equilibrium is achieved and the rate of excretion equals the rate of input. At this time, the plasma concentration becomes steady and 'steady-state' conditions exist. The time taken to reach full steady state is approximately five times the drug half-life. A similar period is required to achieve new steady-state conditions when dose rates are changed. Hence the maximum effect of any drug given repeatedly, or of any change in dose rate, will not be apparent until five half-lives have passed. However, this only applies when drugs are given at a constant rate throughout. A loading dose given at the start of therapy or when increasing the dose rate will reduce the time necessary to achieve steady state. (Figure A1.1). Because drugs with very short half-lives reach steady-state conditions rapidly, loading doses are not necessary unless the clinical situation is urgent (e.g. treatment of dysrhythmias, convulsions, etc.).

Constant rate infusions produce constant plasma concentrations at steady state. However, most drugs are given intermittently and under these circumstances the clearance only determines the mean plasma concentration. With intermittent dosing, plasma concentrations increase to a peak soon after drug administration, and then decline to a trough value just before the next

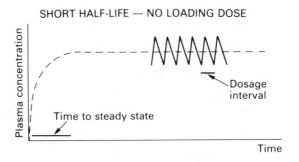

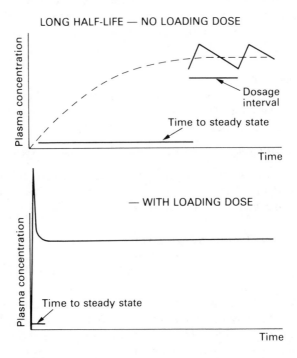

Figure A1.1 Plasma concentration profiles with repeated (oral—) or continuous (i.v.---) drug administration. The half-life determines the time taken to achieve steady state and the oral dosage interval. The total clearance and the dose rate determine the steady-state concentration. A loading dose reduces the time taken to reach steady state, irrespective of half-life.

dose. The degree of fluctuation between doses is also determined by the half-life. If this is short, plasma concentrations increase and decline rapidly. If the half-life is long, fluctuation in plasma concentration between doses is much less. Toxicity can occur if the peak plasma concentration exceeds the upper limit of the therapeutic range, and failure of therapy if the trough (pre-dose) concentration falls below the lower limit. To keep both peak and trough concentrations within these limits, drugs with short half-lives must be given either continuously (constant rate i.v. infusion), or frequently (short dosage interval), or in a controlled release formulation in which small quantities of drug are released continuously over a long period. The last reduces the peak concentration after administration and, by prolonging the absorption period, maintains plasma concentrations up to the time of the next dose. Drugs with long half-lives can be given much less frequently and do not normally require controlled release formulation.

PLASMA CONCENTRATION MONITORING

If an assay is available to measure plasma drug concentrations, and if the 'therapeutic' concentration range is known, plasma concentration monitoring can be used to optimize therapy in individual patients for long-term treatment. Concentrations should always be measured at the same time after drug intake, and one to two hours after a dose (peak) or just before the next dose (trough) give the extremes. Concentrations should only be measured at steady state (in practice, > 3 half-lives from the start or change of dosage) because the relationship between dose rate and concentration achieved is complex at other times.

'Recommended' dosage regimens are based on drug clearance values found in the majority of the population normally treated. For various reasons (e.g., liver disease, renal disease, cardiac failure, extremes of age) the clearance in an individual may be different and the recommended dose rate will produce concentrations that are either too high or too low. If a drug is given at a constant rate until steady-state conditions are achieved and the plasma concentration is measured, the dose rate required to produce any other plasma concentration can be calculated from the following equation.

$$\text{New dose rate} = \frac{\text{Desired concentration} \times \text{Old dose rate}}{\text{Measured concentration}}$$

Alternatively, the concentration achieved can be plotted against dose rate, and the dose rate required to produce any new concentration can be derived graphically (Figure A1.2). If peak concentrations are measured, these methods will calculate the new peaks; if trough concentrations are measured, new troughs will result. In addition, the methods calculate the dose rate, i.e., the dose given divided by the dosage interval. If the clearance is half the normal, the dose rate should be halved, and this can be achieved either by halving the dose or by doubling the dosage interval. As a reduced clearance usually results in a longer half-life, doubling the dosage interval and keeping the dose constant may be the more appropriate.

The above principles only apply to drugs showing first-order kinetics. Some drugs, notably phenytoin and aspirin, show zero-order kinetic behaviour at therapeutic dose levels, and with these the relationship between dose rate and plasma concentration is not linear (see Figure A1.2). Plasma concentrations increase disproportionately as dosage is increased. When

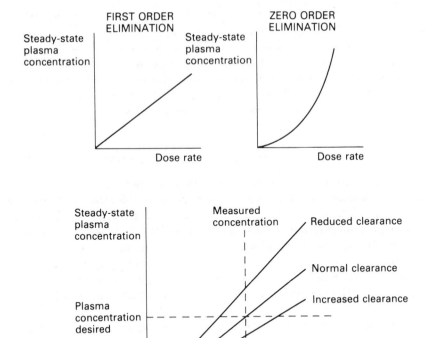

Figure A1.2 Relationship between steady-state plasma concentration and dose rate for drugs showing first-order and zero-order elimination. With drugs showing first-order elimination, the optimum dose rate for patients with abnormal drug clearance can be derived by measuring a steady-state plasma concentration and plotting this value against the dose rate given.

adjusting dosage, progressively smaller changes should be made as dosage is increased.

Plasma concentration monitoring can be very useful, but interpretation of the results may be difficult. Random plasma concentrations give little information other than whether or not the patient has taken the drug. If a plasma concentration is unusually low, the patient may have missed a recent dose. As a result of inter-patient variation in response to a given plasma drug concentration, the recommended 'therapeutic range' is not universal. If plasma concentrations within the recommended range result in no therapeutic or adverse effects, the dose rate may be increased. If 'therapeutic' plasma concentrations result in unacceptable toxicity, the dose rate should be reduced.

FACTORS INFLUENCING DRUG ACTION IN INDIVIDUALS

COMPLIANCE

Failure of compliance is failure to take drugs in the manner recommended. Doses may be forgotten, drug courses terminated prematurely, or drug regimens inadvertently exchanged if a number of drugs are prescribed simultaneously. Compliance is likely to be poor if the patient feels well, if the drugs make the patient feel worse, if many different drugs are prescribed simultaneously or if little time is spent explaining the different drug regimens and aims of therapy. Prepacked dispensers holding a week's supply of drug in compartments corresponding to the different dosing times can be useful for the elderly. Clearly written dosing instructions are useful for all patients.

INDIVIDUAL VARIATION

Age
Children and some elderly patients may require reduced drug dosage because of their small size. In infants, drug elimination systems are immature, and in the elderly, there is a progressive loss of drug metabolizing capacity and renal function. Dosage should initially be low and, if necessary, increased with caution.

Height/weight
Body mass and the ratio between the amounts of 'lean' and 'fat' tissue determine drug distribution, and hence, the plasma concentration resulting from any given dose. With lipid-soluble drugs in particular, higher than usual doses may be necessary in large or fat individuals, and smaller doses may be required in small or thin individuals.

Sex
Women may require smaller doses than men because of their smaller size. Drugs which have secondary endocrine effects may produce hirsutism, deepening of the voice, etc., in females, and gynaecomastia in males. With women of childbearing potential, the effects of a drug on a possible pregnancy should always be considered and unnecessary prescribing should be avoided. Lipid-soluble drugs cross the placenta easily, and they are only slowly metabolized by the fetus, if at all. Acidic drugs (e.g., antithyroid agents) may be secreted into milk.

Genetic Variation
Rates of drug metabolism vary between individuals and, for most drugs, the interindividual variation is continuous, i.e., it shows a normal distribution. Hence, approximately two per cent of the normal population will have a rate of metabolism more than two standard deviations from the mean, while

another two per cent will have a rate that is less than two standard deviations from the mean.

Drugs showing discontinuous variation in *rates of metabolism* are less common, although the genetic trait that is responsible may be widespread. Examples include:

1. *Acetylator status.* The population is divided into fast and slow acetylators, the proportion varying between ethnic groups. Drugs acetylated before elimination include hydralazine, procainamide and some sulphonamides. Slow acetylators are more likely to show drug accumulation and toxicity, while fast acetylators are likely to demonstrate a failure to respond.
2. *Plasma cholinesterase deficiency.* Inactive plasma cholinesterase is found in one patient in 3000. Such patients fail to metabolize the neuromuscular blocking agent, suxamethonium, and prolonged paralysis results from normal dosage. A plasma cholinesterase with increased activity is much less common.
3. *Vitamin D resistance.* Patients with this trait fail to metabolize vitamin D to the active form and develop vitamin D resistant rickets.

Examples of discontinuous variation in *response to drugs* include:

1. *Glucose-6-phosphate dehydrogenase (G-6-PD) deficiency.* G-6-PD deficiency which is common in negroes, can result in acute haemolysis with a variety of drugs, including sulphonamides, sulphones, nitrofurantoin, phenazone, aspirin, probenecid, quinine, primaquine, pamaquin and chloroquine.
2. *Acute intermittent porphyria.* Acute porphyria can be precipitated in susceptible individuals by barbiturates and other enzyme-inducing agents, sulphonamides, pentazocine, meprobamate, glutethimide, tolbutamide, methyldopa, thiopentone, Althesin, alcohol, griseofulvin and contraceptive medication. Increased activity of δ-amino-laevulinic acid synthetase is the cause.
3. *Malignant hyperpyrexia.* This is rare, but a rapid and often fatal increase in body temperature occurs in sensitive individuals given halothane and/or suxamethonium.
4. *Methaemoglobinaemia.* In individuals lacking the enzyme methaemoglobin reductase, oxidizing agents (sulphonamides, phenacetin, nitrates and quinones) produce methaemoglobinaemia.
5. *Warfarin resistance.* This is very rare, but affected patients show resistance to all coumarin anticoagulants, although they are absorbed and metabolized normally.

Disease

Effects on absorption. Drug absorption after oral administration may be delayed by conditions that cause a slowing of gastric emptying (e.g., nausea, pain, pylorospasm or pyloric stenosis) or hypomotility. This reduces the speed of onset of drug action at the start of therapy. Drug absorption may be increased with small bowel or liver disease if first-pass elimination is reduced. The effect is the same as increasing the dose. Absorption after intramuscular injection may be delayed if the peripheral circulation is poor.

Effects on distribution. Distribution may be abnormal if plasma protein binding changes occur in liver or renal disease, or if tissue access is reduced by poor peripheral perfusion (e.g., in cardiac failure or shock). Changes in protein binding may alter the free drug concentration in the plasma, and hence the effect. Impaired tissue distribution increases the total drug concentration in the plasma and usually increases the effect.

Effects on elimination. The effects of liver and renal disease on drug elimination are largely unpredictable in the individual. With both conditions it is wise to assume that clearance will be reduced. The half-life of a drug usually increases, although it may not if the condition results in a fall in distribution volume (e.g., as seen with tolbutamide). Low dosage should be used initially, and dosage increases made with caution. Plasma concentration monitoring at steady state may be helpful, although it should be remembered that if the half-life is prolonged, steady-state conditions will take longer than normal to achieve. Metabolites, active or otherwise, may not be formed in normal amounts in liver disease, and may accumulate significantly in renal disease. The rate of metabolism of high clearance drugs (e.g., lignocaine) may be reduced in cardiac failure, because of changes in liver blood flow.

Abnormal Sensitivity to Drug Effects

Asthma. Asthmatic attacks may be precipitated by histamine, cholinergic drugs and β-receptor antagonists.

Respiratory insufficiency. Drugs causing respiratory depression (e.g., narcotics, barbiturates, benzodiazepines, glutethimide and other hypnotics) can precipitate respiratory failure in patients with little functional reserve.

Prostatic hypertrophy. Acute urinary retention may occur with potent diuretics or drugs which reduce bladder tone (e.g., anticholinergics).

Thyroid disease. Hyperthyroid patients are abnormally sensitive to adrenaline, and may be resistant to morphine.

Myasthenia. Myasthenic patients show an exaggerated response to competitive neuromuscular blocking agents, and drugs with only weak neuromuscular blocking activity (e.g., aminoglycosides, quinine and quinidine) can produce paralysis.

Electrolyte imbalance. Hypokalaemia potentiates the effects of digitalis and of competitive neuromuscular blocking agents. It antagonizes the antidys-rhythmic effects of lignocaine, quinidine, procainamide, disopyramide, mexiletine, tocainide and phenytoin.

TOLERANCE

In a patient with a stable clinical condition, the development of tolerance means that increasing doses of drug are required to maintain a given response, or that the response declines during continuous treatment. This may be due either to a change in receptor sensitivity (e.g., with narcotics) in which case cross-tolerance to other similar drugs may occur, or to depletion of neurotransmitter stores with drugs acting indirectly (e.g., with ephedrine and the amphetamines). Enzyme induction resulting in accelerated drug elimination produces effects similar to the development of tolerance because increased dosage is necessary to maintain an effect.

DRUG INTERACTIONS

Drugs can interact at any point from the time of manufacture to the process of elimination. The possibility of an interaction should always be considered when drugs are added to, or deleted from, a stable therapeutic regimen.

Pharmacodynamic Interactions

Agonists and antagonists acting at a specific receptor will interact if given together. If the antagonist is competitive, its effects can be overcome by increasing the concentration of the agonist, and vice versa. The effects of non-competitive antagonists are not surmountable by increasing agonist concentration. If different drugs produce the same response by different mechanisms, they may be effective in combination at lower dosage than would be necessary if they were used alone. This serves to minimize adverse effects, and combinations of antibiotics, antihypertensive drugs and cytotoxic agents are often given for this purpose. Antibiotic combinations also delay the development of resistant organisms.

Pharmacokinetic Interactions

Absorption. Drugs that delay gastric emptying (e.g., narcotics and anticholinergics) delay drug absorption. Drugs that accelerate gastric emptying (e.g., metoclopramide) accelerate absorption. Calcium or ferric salts bind tetracyclines, cholestyramine binds acidic drugs and kaolin binds many drugs, thus reducing absorption. Neomycin or colchicine, which damage the small bowel mucosa, can also reduce absorption. The effects of antacids are complex because different compounds increase or decrease gastric emptying rate. Reduced absorption caused by binding may also occur.

Distribution. Drugs can compete for plasma protein binding; the drug with the highest affinity displaces the other. Free concentrations of displaced drug are increased and this may produce increased effects. Warfarin and tolbutamide are displaced by phenylbutazone, clofibrate, frusemide, ethacrynic acid and salicylate. Phenytoin is displaced by phenylbutazone and salicylate. Displacement interactions are only clinically important when the displaced drug has a narrow therapeutic plasma concentration range and a small volume of distribution. If the distribution volume is large, displaced drug is rapidly distributed to extravascular tissues, and the free concentration in plasma shows little change.

Antihypertensive drugs, such as guanethidine, bethanidine or debrisoquin, require uptake into the adrenergic nerve terminal to produce their effects. Chlorpromazine, sympathomimetics and tricyclic antidepressants prevent their uptake, thus reducing their hypotensive activity.

Metabolism. Inducing agents increase the activity of the drug metabolizing systems in the liver, which accelerates their own metabolism and that of other metabolized drugs that are given simultaneously. If pre-systemic elimination occurs, it will also increase, and the bioavailability will fall. Increased dosage is required to maintain an effect. In contrast, enzyme induction potentiates the activity of drugs metabolized to an active form, and increases the toxicity of drugs with toxic metabolites. Drugs known to cause enzyme induction include barbiturates, phenylbutazone, phenytoin, glutethimide, meprobamate, phenazone, dichloralphenazone, griseofulvin, methaqualone, ethchlorvynol, rifampicin and halothane.

Some drugs inhibit the metabolism of other compounds, either by a direct action on the enzyme system (e.g., cimetidine binding to cytochrome P-450) or by competition for a metabolic pathway. Some examples are shown in Table A1.2. Many more probably occur. If metabolism is inhibited, the drug will accumulate with repeated dosing and dosage reduction may be necessary to avoid toxicity.

Table A1.2 *Drug interactions — inhibition of hepatic metabolism*

Metabolism inhibited	Causative agents
Tolbutamide	Dicoumarol, chloramphenicol, phenylbutazone
Warfarin	Cimetidine, ethanol, tricyclic antidepressants, quinidine
Phenytoin	Cimetidine, diazepam, dicoumarol, isoniazid, PAS, phenylbutazone, sulthiame
Nortriptyline	Perphenazine, hydrocortisone

Specific metabolic interactions occur with the following:

Monoamine oxidase (MAO). MAO breaks down endogenous monoamines (e.g., adrenaline and noradrenaline) and those ingested in food (e.g., tyramine). MAO inhibitors result in the accumulation of large amounts of adrenaline and noradrenaline in nerve endings. Headache and severe hypertension may occur if these large stores are released by indirect sympathomimetics, such as amphetamine, ephedrine or the compounds in many proprietary nasal decongestants. Tyramine, found in cheese and certain meat extracts, is usually destroyed by MAO in the gut wall. MAO inhibitors prevent this destruction, allowing tyramine access to the body where it releases the increased amounts of adrenaline and noradrenaline described above ('cheese reaction'). MAO inhibitors may also potentiate the effects of antihypertensive agents, insulin and sulphonylureas. Unpredictable reactions, including hypotension, convulsions and coma can occur with pethidine, tricyclic antidepressants and general anaesthetics.

Plasma cholinesterase. Suxamethonium, procaine, propanidid and physostigmine are metabolized by plasma cholinesterase. Anticholinesterases such as neostigmine prevent their breakdown.

Xanthine oxidase. Azathioprine, mercaptopurine and procarbazine are metabolized by xanthine oxidase. Their dosage should be reduced if given with the xanthine oxidase inhibitor, allopurinol.

Alcohol dehydrogenase. This enzyme converts ethanol to acetic acid via acetaldehyde. Disulfiram and citrated calcium carbamide inhibit the enzyme and produce unpleasant effects from accumulation of acetaldehyde if alcohol is taken. Sulphonylureas, metronidazole and procarbazine can also inhibit the enzyme, producing the same effects with alcohol.

MAO inhibitors, disulfiram and allopurinol may not be as specific in their actions as the above would suggest, and impaired metabolism of a number of other compounds has been reported.

Excretion. A number of drugs compete for active secretion into and out of the renal tubules. Some examples are given in Table A1.3. The drug with the greatest affinity for the secretory system will delay the excretion of the other. If excretion is delayed, the drug will accumulate with repeated dosing, and dosage reduction may be necessary to avoid toxicity.

Table A1.3 *Drug interactions — inhibition of renal tubular secretion*

Delayed excretion of	Causative agents
Cephalexin, cephalothin, dapsone, indomethacin, PAS, penicillins, sulphinpyrazone	Probenecid
Chlorpropamide	Dicoumarol, phenylbutazone
Methotrexate	Salicylate, sulphonamides

Pharmaceutical Interactions
Tablets, capsules and solutions for injection may contain a variety of substances (e.g., stabilizers, antiseptics, buffers and bulking agents) in addition to active drug. These are usually carefully chosen by the manufacturer to have predictable effects on the pharmacokinetics or activity of that particular drug. Effects on other drugs given simultaneously will be less

predictable. Clinically, pharmaceutical incompatibilities are only likely to occur if solutions are mixed in syringes or bottles before injection. Protamine zinc insulin (PZI) converts soluble insulin to more PZI, kanamycin inactivates methicillin, and hydrocortisone interacts with penicillin and heparin. Many more interactions are known. Any of the substances present in the drug solution may interact, and a precipitate may or may not form. Drugs in solution should be injected separately, and if given intravenously by infusion, the tubing should be flushed through with saline between injections.

Effects of Drug Interactions
Many drug interactions are theoretically possible but all are not equally serious. The effects of MAO inhibitors, sudden loss of hypertensive control with tricyclics and delayed excretion of cytotoxic drugs with allopurinol, are undoubtedly dangerous. Other pharmacokinetic interactions are usually less dramatic. A delay in the rate of absorption reduces the speed of onset of effect with the first few doses, but has little effect on mean plasma concentration or response at steady state. This is only reduced if the dose rate is reduced (impaired absorption), or elimination is increased (enzyme induction). Increased plasma concentrations and response at steady state result from protein binding displacement (water-soluble drugs) or delayed elimination

Table A1.4 *Approximate drug half-lives*

< 2 hours	2–5 hours	5–10 hours	24–36 hours
ACTH	Atropine	Atenolol	Carbamazepine
Acetylsalicylic acid	Chloramphenicol	Chlordiazepoxide	Chlorpromazine
Amikacin	Cimetidine	Clonidine	Diazoxide
Amoxycillin	Clindamycin	Disopyramide	Nitrazepam
Ampicillin	Erythromycin	Methotrexate	Nortriptyline
Benzylpenicillin	Ethambutol	Phenformin	*Phenytoin
Carbenicillin	*Ethanol	Primidone	
Cephalosporins	Hydralazine	Quinidine	
Chlorothiazide	Hydrochlorothiazide	Sulphonamides	> 36 hours
Cloxacillin	Indomethacin	Tetracyclines	Amiodarone
Frusemide	†Isoniazid	Theophylline	Chlorpropamide
Gentamicin	Kanamycin	Tolbutamide	Chlorthalidone
Heparin	Lincomycin		Diazepam
Isosorbide dinitrate	Metoprolol	10–24 hours	Digitoxin
Levodopa	Paracetamol	Amitriptyline	Digoxin
Lignocaine	Pethidine	Clofibrate	Phenobarbitone
Methicillin	Prazosin	Desipramine	Thyroxine
Methyldopa	Prednisolone	Doxepin	Warfarin
Naloxone	Prednisone	Doxycycline	
Nitroglycerin	†Procainamide	Imipramine	
PAS	Propranolol	Lithium	
Rifampicin	Ranitidine	Lorazepam	
	Salbutamol	Mexiletine	
	*Salicylate	Practolol	
	Streptomycin	Tocainide	
	Triamterene	Trimethoprim	
	Tubocurarine	Valproic acid	

*Zero order elimination; †Polymorphic acetylation.

(competition for metabolic pathway or renal excretion). Serious toxicity or failure of therapy is most likely if plasma concentrations need to be finely controlled, as with phenytoin, oral anticoagulants, oral hypoglycaemics and antidysrhythmics. The greatest risk is during the period immediately after an interacting drug is added to, or deleted from, a stable therapeutic regimen. Drug effects and, if necessary, plasma concentrations should be monitored repeatedly until new steady-state conditions are achieved.

In Table A1.4 guidance is given on the half-lives of a number of the commoner drugs.

FURTHER READING

Drug Disposition
Barber H. E. & Petrie J. C. (1981) Elimination of drugs. *Br. Med. J.*, 282: 809–810.
Brater D. C. (1980) The pharmacological role of the kidney. *Drugs*, 19: 31–48.
Lindop W. E. & Orme McL.E. (1981) Plasma protein binding of drugs. *Br. Med. J.*, 282: 212–214.
Scott A. K. & Hawksworth G. M. (1981) Drug absorption. *Br. Med. J.*, 282: 462–463.

Prescribing
Bliss M. R. (1981) Prescribing for the elderly. *Br. Med. J.*, 283: 203–206.
O'Hanrahan M. & O'Malley K. (1981) Compliance with drug treatment. *Br. Med. J.*, 283: 298–300.
Ramsay L. E. & Tucker G. E. (1981) Drugs and the elderly. *Br. Med. J.*, 282: 125–127.
Rao J. M. & Arulappu R. (1981) Drug use in pregnancy: how to avoid problems. *Drugs*, 22: 409–414.
Rylance G. (1981) Drugs in children. *Br. Med. J.*, 282: 50–51.
Shaw P. G. (1982) Common pitfalls in geriatric drug prescribing. *Drugs*, 23: 324–328.

Pharmacokinetics
Greenblatt D. J. & Koch-Weser J. (1975) Clinical Pharmacokinetics I. *New Engl. J. Med.*, 293: 702–705.
Greenblatt D. J. & Koch-Weser J. (1975) Clinical Pharmacokinetics II. *New Engl. J. Med.*, 293: 964–970.
Mawer G. E. (1982) Dosage adjustment in renal insufficiency. *Br. J. Clin. Pharmac.*, 13: No. 2, 145–153.
Rowland M. & Tozer T. N. (1980) *Clinical Pharmacokinetics — Concepts and Applications*. Philadelphia: Lea and Febiger.

Drug Interactions and Adverse Reactions
Aronson J. K. & Grahame-Smith D. G. (1981) Adverse drug interactions. *Br. med. J.*, 282: 288–291.
Rawlins M. D. (1981) Adverse reactions to drugs. *Br. Med. J.*, 282: 974–976.
Stackley I. (1981) *Drug Interactions*. Oxford: Blackwell.

Appendix 2
A Short List of Drugs

R. H. Girdwood

A book of this type must necessarily give an account of a large number of drugs, and many readers have indicated that they would appreciate some guide as to how best to shorten the list when faced with practical therapeutics. It is not possible to produce a selection which will satisfy everybody. The substances that are preferred vary not only in different countries and in individual towns, but there may be a divergence of views amongst consultants in the same city or even within a single hospital.

There follows a list which was prepared after discussion with numerous consultant physicians in an Edinburgh teaching hospital and with the authors of chapters in this book. It is intended primarily to indicate the drugs of first choice in medical wards in a large teaching hospital in the UK, but, of course, other medicinal agents are commonly used there. No effort has been made to include drugs employed in special units or for skilled specialized procedures, such as the chemotherapy of malignant disease or the treatment of skin disorders. Any list, such as the present one, requires constant revision, both additions and deletions being necessary as knowledge advances.

I am grateful to all the doctors who give their opinions about the list, and particularly to the members of the staff of the Pharmacy of the Royal Infirmary of Edinburgh for the trouble they have taken in merging the opinions of so many clinical colleagues and making available the benefit of their experience. In particular, I would like to thank Mrs Dorothy Anderson, the Information Pharmacist, for the great deal of trouble she has taken to make this list possible.

It should be noted that this Appendix does not include information about precautions that must be taken when any of the substances are administered. The dosage is given to indicate what is most commonly obtained from a hospital pharmacy in order to treat adult inpatients, but does not necessarily indicate what a patient should receive or allow for variations in dose that may be necessary to meet particular needs or situations.

BNF Ref.*	Drug	Route of administration if not given orally
1	**DRUGS ACTING ON THE GASTROINTESTINAL SYSTEM**	
1.1	**Antacids**	
1.1.1	*Alu-Cap* Aluminium hydroxide gel BP Magnesium trisilicate mixture BPC	
1.1.2	*Gaviscon* liquid *Gastrocote* tablets *Maalox* tablets	

1.2	**Antispasmodics (or drugs interfering with motility)**
	Mebeverine hydrochloride 135 mg
	Metoclopramide — tablets 10 mg
	                      — syrup 5 mg/5 ml
	                      — injection 10 mg/2 ml
	Propantheline bromide — tablets 15 mg
	                      — injection 30 mg
		
		i.m. or i.v.
		
		i.m. or i.v.

1.3	**Ulcer-healing drugs**
	Cimetidine (*Tagamet*) — tablets 200 mg
	                    — injection 200 mg/2 ml
	Ranitidine (*Zantac*) — tablets 150 mg
	                    — injection 25 mg/ml
		
		i.m. or iv.
		
		i.v.

1.4	**Antidiarrhoeal drugs**	
1.4.2	Codeine phosphate tablets 30 mg Diphenoxylate and atropine tablets (*Lomotil*) Kaolin and morphine mixture	
1.5	Sulphasalazine tablets 500 mg	
1.6	**Laxatives**	
1.6.1	Bran Ispaghula (*Isogel* granules)	
1.6.2	Danthron and poloxamer '188' (*Dorbanex* liquid) *Senokot* tablets *X-Prep* liquid	
1.6.4	Lactulose — *Duphalac* syrup Magnesium sulphate mixture	
1.6.5	Glycerol suppositories Phosphate enemas *Beogex* suppositories	p.r. p.r. p.r.
1.7	**Rectal and colonic drugs**	
1.7.2	Hydrocortisone acetate 10% foam (*Colifoam*)	p.r.
1.7.3	*Anusol-HC* suppositories *Proctosedyl* ointment	p.r. topically

*The reference is to the relevant section of the *British National Formulary* No. 5 (1983), published jointly by the British Medical Association and the Pharmaceutical Society of Great Britain.

BNF Ref.	Drug	Route of administration if not given orally
2	**TREATMENT OF DISEASES OF THE CARDIOVASCULAR SYSTEM**	
2.1	**Cardiac glycosides**	
	Digoxin—tablets — 62.6 μg	
	— 125 μg	
	— 250 μg	
	— injection 250 μg/ml	i.v.
2.2	**Diuretics**	
2.2.1	Bendrofluazide tablets 5 mg	
2.2.2	Frusemide — tablets — 40 mg	
	— 500 mg	
	— injection — 20 mg/2 ml	i.m. or i.v.
	— 50 mg/5 ml	i.v.
	— 250 mg/25 ml	i.v.
	Bumetanide — tablets 1 mg	
	— injection 0.5 mg/ml	i.m. or i.v.
2.2.3	*Moduretic* tablets (amiloride 5 mg; hydrochlorothiazide 50 mg)	
2.2.4	Spironolactone tablets — 25 mg	
	— 100 mg	
2.2.8	*Navidrex K* tablets (cyclopenthiazide 0.25 mg; potassium chloride 600 mg)	
2.3	**Anti-arrhythmic drugs (anti-dysrhythmic)**	
2.3.2	Atropine sulphate injection 600 μg/ml	i.v.
	Verapamil — tablets 40 mg	
	— injection 2.5 mg/ml	i.v.
2.3.3	Disopyramide — capsules 100 mg	
	— injection 10 mg/ml	i.v.
	Lignocaine (*Xylocard*) injection 20 mg/ml	i.v.
	Lignocaine (*Xylocard*) 200 mg/ml	i.v. infusion
	Mexiletine — capsules — 50 mg	
	— 200 mg	
	— injection 250 mg/10 ml	i.v.
	Phenytoin sodium injection 50 mg/ml	i.v.
	Practolol injection 2 mg/ml	i.v.
2.4	**Beta-adrenoreceptor blocking drugs**	
	Propranolol tablets — 10 mg	
	— 40 mg	
	— 80 mg	
	Metoprolol tartrate tablets — 50 mg	
	— 100 mg	
2.5	**Anti-hypertensive drugs**	
2.5.1	Diazoxide injection 15 mg/ml	i.v.
	Hydralazine tablets — 25 mg	
	— 50 mg	
	— injection 20 mg in powder form	i.v.

BNF Ref.	Drug	Route of administration if not given orally
	Prazosin tablets — 0.5 mg, 1 mg — 2 mg, 5 mg	
2.5.2	Methyldopa — tablets 250 mg — injection 50 mg/ml	i.v.
2.5.5	Captopril tablets — 25 mg — 50 mg — 100 mg	
2.6 2.6.1	**Vasodilators** Glyceryl trinitrate tablets 500 μg Isosorbide dinitrate tablets — 5 mg — 10 mg Nifedipine capsules 10 mg	s.l. s.l.
2.7 2.7.1	**Sympathomimetics** Dopamine injection 40 mg/ ml Isoprenaline injection 2 mg/2 ml	i.v. i.v.
2.8 2.8.1	**Anticoagulants and protamine** Heparin injection 1000, 5000 and 25 000 units/ml	i.v.
2.8.2	Warfarin tablets 1, 3, and 5 mg	
2.8.3	Protamine sulphate injection 1%	i.v.
2.9	**Antiplatelet drugs** Dipyridamole tablets — 25 mg — 100 mg	
2.11	**Antifibrinolytic drugs** Tranexamic acid — injection 500 mg/5 ml — tablets 500 mg	i.v.
2.12	**Drugs used in the treatment of hyperlipidaemia** Cholestyramine (*Questran*) sachets 4 g	
3 3.1 3.1.1	**TREATMENT OF DISEASES OF THE RESPIRATORY SYSTEM** **Bronchodilators** Salbutamol (*Ventolin*) — respirator solution 5 mg/ml — inhaler 100 μg dose Terbutaline (*Bricanyl*) — respirator solution 10 mg/ml — inhaler 250 μg/dose	 inhalation inhalation inhalation
3.1.1.2	Adrenaline injection 1 in 1000	s.c. or i.m.
3.1.2	Ipratropium bromide (*Atrovent*) inhaler 18 μg/dose	inhalation
3.1.3	Aminophylline — injection 250 mg/10 ml — suppositories 360 mg	i.v. p.r.

BNF Ref.	Drug	Route of administration if not given orally
	Choline theophyllinate (*Choledyl*) — tablets 200 mg — syrup 62.5 mg/5 ml	
3.2	**Corticosteroids** Beclomethasone (*Becotide*) inhaler 50 μg/dose	inhalation
3.3	**Prophylaxis of asthma** Sodium cromoglycate (*Intal*) *spincaps* 20 mg	for insufflation
3.4 3.4.1	**Allergic disorders** Chlorpheniramine — tablets 4 mg — injection 10 mg	s.c., i.m. or i.v.
3.5	**Respiratory stimulants** Doxapram i.v. infusion 2 mg/ml	i.v.
3.9	**Cough medicines** Codeine linctus 15 mg codeine/5 ml Methadone linctus 2 mg methadone/5 ml Simple linctus	
4 4.1 4.1.1	**DRUGS ACTING ON THE CENTRAL NERVOUS SYSTEM** **Hypnotics, sedatives and anxiolytics** Dichloralphenazone (*Welldorm*) capsules 650 mg Nitrazepam tablets 5 mg Triclofos elixir 500 mg/5 ml	
4.1.2	Diazepam tablets 2 mg, 5 mg and 10 mg	
4.2 4.2.1	**Drugs used in psychoses and related disorders** Chlorpromazine — tablets 25 mg — syrup 25 mg/5 ml — (*Largactil*) injection 50 mg/2 ml Thioridazine (*Melleril*) syrup 25 mg/5 ml Haloperidol injection 5 mg/ml	i.m. i.m. or i.v.
4.3 4.3.1	**Antidepressant drugs** Amitriptyline tablets 25 mg Imipramine tablets 25 mg	
4.6	**Drugs used in nausea and vertigo** Cyclizine (*Valoid*) — tablets 50 mg — injection 50 mg/ml Metoclopramide — tablets 10 mg — injection 10 mg/2 ml Prochlorperazine — tablets 5 mg — injection 12.5 mg/ml	i.m. or i.v. i.m. or i.v. i.m.
4.7 4.7.1.1 (see also 10.1.1)	**Analgesics** Aspirin (soluble) tablets 300 mg Paracetamol tablets 500 mg	

BNF Ref.	Drug	Route of administration if not given orally
4.7.1.2	NARCOTIC ANALGESICS USED FOR MILD TO MODERATE PAIN	
	Dihydrocodeine — tablets 30 mg	
	— injection 50 mg/ml	s.c., i.m.
	Pentazocine (*Fortral*) — tablets 25 mg	
	— injection 30 mg/ml	s.c., i.m. or i.v.
	COMPOUND ANALGESICS	
4.7.1.3	Paracetamol 500 mg and codeine phosphate 8 mg	
	Paracodol dispersible tablets	
4.7.2	NARCOTIC AND OTHER ANALGESICS USED FOR SEVERE PAIN	
	Morphine sulphate injection 10 mg/ml	s.c., i.m. or i.v.
	Morphine 10 mg and cyclizine 50 mg	
	(*Cyclimorph 10*)	s.c., i.m. or i.v.
	Diamorphine hydrochloride injection 5 mg	s.c., i.m. or i.v.
	Dipipanone 10 mg and cyclizine 30 mg	
	(*Diconal* tablets)	
	Pethidine tablets 50 mg	
	Pethidine injection 100 mg/2 ml	s.c. or i.m.
	Morphine or Diamorphine oral mixture	
(see also 15.1.7)	NARCOTIC ANTAGONIST	
	Naloxone injection 0.4 mg/ml	s.c., i.m. or i.v.
4.8	**Antiepileptics**	
4.8.1	Carbamazepine (*Tegretol*) tablets — 100 mg	
	— 200 mg	
	Ethosuximide capsules 250 mg	
	Phenobarbitone sodium — tablets 30 mg	
	— injection 200 mg	s.c., i.m. or i.v.
	Phenytoin sodium (*Epanutin*) capsules — 25 mg	
	— 50 mg	
	— 100 mg	
	Primidone (*Mysoline*) tablets 250 mg	
	Sodium valproate (*Epilim*) tablets — 200 mg	
	— 500 mg	
4.8.2	Diazepam injection 10 mg/2 ml	i.v.
4.9	**Drugs used in parkinsonism and related disorders**	
4.9.1	Levodopa and carbidopa (*Sinemet* 110 and 275) tablets	
4.9.2	Benzhexol tablets 2 mg	
5	**TREATMENT OF INFECTIONS**	
5.1	**Antibacterial drugs**	
5.1.1	PENICILLINS	
5.1.1.1	Benzylpenicillin (*Crystapen*) injection 600 mg	i.m. or i.v.
	Phenoxymethylpenicillin potassium tablets 250 mg	
5.1.1.2	Flucloxacillin (*Floxapen*) — capsules 250 mg	
	— injection 500 mg	i.m. or i.v.

BNF Ref.	Drug	Route of administration if not given orally
5.1.1.3	Ampicillin — capsules 500 mg	
	— injection 500 mg	i.m. or i.v.
	Mezlocillin injection 5 g	i.v. infusion
5.1.1.4	Azlocillin (*Securopen*) injection 5 g	i.v. infusion
	Ticarcillin (*Ticar*) injection 5 g	i.v. infusion
5.1.2	CEPHALOSPORINS AND CEPHAMYCINS	
	Cefotaxime injection 1 g	i.m. or i.v.
	Cefoxitin injection 1 g	i.m. or i.v.
	Cefuroxime injection 750 mg	i.m. or i.v.
	Cephalexin tablets 500 mg	
5.1.3	TETRACYCLINES	
	Oxytetracycline tablets 250 mg	
5.1.4	AMINOGLYCOSIDES	
	Gentamicin injection 40 mg/ml	i.m. or i.v.
	Amikacin (*Amikin*) injection 500 mg/2 ml	i.m. or i.v.
	Neomycin (*Nivemycin*) tablets 500 mg	
	Neomycin elixir 100 mg/5 ml	
	Netilmicin (*Netillin*) injection 50 mg/ml	i.m. or i.v.
5.1.5	MACROLIDES	
	Erythromycin — tablets 250 mg	
	— (*Erythrocin*) injection 300 mg	i.v.
5.1.6	Clindamycin (*Dalacin-C*) — capsules 150 mg	
	— injection 150 mg/ml	i.m. or i.v.
5.1.7	OTHER ANTIBIOTICS	
	Chloramphenicol — capsules 250 mg	
	— injection 1.2 g	i.m. or i.v.
	Sodium fusidate (*Fucidin*) — capsules 250 mg	
	— injection 580 mg	i.v. by infusion
	Vancomycin solution 500 mg of lyophilized material reconstituted in 15–30 ml water	by mouth
5.1.8	Co-trimoxazole — tablets	
	— suspension	
	— injection	i.v.
	Trimethoprim tablets 100 mg	
5.1.9	ANTITUBERCULOUS DRUGS	
	Ethambutol (*Myambutol*) tablets 100 mg, 400 mg	
	Isoniazid tablets 100 mg	
	Rifampicin capsules 300 mg	
	Rifampicin 150 mg and isoniazid 100 mg tablets	
	Rifampicin 300 mg and isoniazid 150 mg tablets	
	Streptomycin sulphate injection 1 g	i.m.
	Pyrazinamide tablets 500 mg	
5.1.11	OTHER ANTIMICROBIAL DRUGS	
	Metronidazole — tablets 200 mg	
	— injection 500 mg	i.v.
	— suppositories 1 g	p.r.

BNF Ref.	Drug	Route of administration if not given orally

5.2 · **Antifungal drugs**
Amphotericin (*Fungilin*) lozenges
Flucytosine tablets 500 mg
Ketoconazole (*Nizoral*) tablets 200 mg
Miconazole (*Daktarin*) — tablets 250 mg
 — injection 10 mg/ml · i.v. infusion
Nystatin mixture 100 000 units/ml

5.3
(see also
11, 12) · **Antiviral drugs**
Idoxuridine — ophthalmic preparations
 — topical applications
 — paint for oral lesions
Acyclovir — eye ointment
 — tablets 200 mg
 — intravenous infusion · i.v.

6 · **TREATMENT OF DISORDERS OF THE ENDOCRINE SYSTEM**
6.1 · **Drugs used in diabetes**
6.1.1 · Insulin · s.c., i.m. or i.v.

6.1.2 · ORAL HYPOGLYCAEMIC DRUGS
6.1.2.1 · Chlorpropamide tablets — 100 mg
 — 250 mg
Glipizide tablets 5 mg

6.1.2.2 · Metformin (*Glucophage*) tablets 500 mg

6.1.4 · TREATMENT OF HYPOGLYCAEMIA
Glucagon injection 1 mg · s.c., i.m. or i.v.
(see also
9.2.2) · Dextrose injection 50% · i.v.
Dextrose monohydrate powders 50 g

6.2 · **Thyroid and antithyroid drugs**
6.2.1 · Thyroxine sodium tablets — 25 μg
 — 50 μg
 — 100 μg

6.2.2
(see also
6.7.2) · Carbimazole (*Neo-mercazole*) tablets 5 mg
TRH (Thyrotrophin releasing hormone), injection
 200 μg TRH in 2 ml (protirelin) · i.v.

6.3 · **Corticosteroids**
Cortisone acetate tablets 25 mg
Hydrocortisone tablets — 10 mg
 — 20 mg
Hydrocortisone sodium succinate injection
 100 mg · i.m. or i.v.
Prednisolone — tablets 5 mg, 25 mg
 — enteric coated tablets 2.5 mg, 5 mg
Fludrocortisone acetate tablets 100 μg

6.5 · **Hypothalamic and pituitary hormones**
6.5.1 · Tetracosactrin (*Synacthen*) — injection 250 μg/ml · i.m. or i.v.
 — depot injection
 1 mg/ml, with zinc
phosphate complex · i.m.

BNF Ref.	Drug	Route of administration if not given orally
6.5.2	Desmopressin (*DDAVP*) — injection 4 µg/ml	i.m. or i.v.
	— solution 100 µg/ml	intranasal
	Vasopressin (*Pitressin*) injection 20 units/ml	s.c. or i.m.
6.7	**Other endocrine drugs**	
6.7.1	Bromocriptine (*Parlodel*) — tablets 2.5 mg	
	— capsules 10 mg	
9	**DRUGS AFFECTING NUTRITION AND BLOOD**	
9.1	**Drugs used in iron deficiency**	
9.1.1	Ferrous sulphate tablets 200 mg	
	Ferrous fumarate (*Fersamal*) syrup 140 mg/5 ml	
9.1.2	DRUGS USED IN MEGALOBLASTIC ANAEMIAS	
	Hydroxocobalamin injection 1 mg/ml	i.m.
	Folic acid tablets 5 mg	
	Folic acid injection 15 mg	i.m.
	Cyanocobalamin injection — 1 mg/ml	i.m. ⎱ Schilling
	— 250 µg/ml	i.m. ⎰ test only
9.2	**Electrolyte and water replacement**	
9.2.1.1	Potassium chloride (*Slow K*) tablets 600 mg	
	Potassium chloride (*Sando K*) effervescent tablets	
	HYPERKALAEMIA	
	Calcium polystyrene sulphonate powder	
	(*Calcium Resonium*) 15 g dose	
	also enema (*Calcium Resonium*) 30 g/100 ml	p.r.
9.2.2	Potassium chloride 0.3% and dextrose 5%	infusion
	Sodium chloride infusion 0.9%	infusion
	Sodium chloride (*hypertonic*) 5%	infusion
	Potassium chloride 0.3% and sodium chloride 0.9%	infusion
	Sodium chloride 0.45% and dextrose 5%	
	Sodium chloride 0.18% and dextrose 4%	infusion
	Sodium bicarbonate — 8.4%	infusion
	— 1.26%	infusion
	Potassium chloride solution, strong 1.5 in 10 ml	i.v. *and must be diluted*
	Dextrose i.v. infusion — 5%	infusion
	— 10%	infusion
	— 20%	infusion
9.5	**Calcium and phosphorus**	
9.5.1	Calcium gluconate injection 10%	i.m. or i.v.
	Calcium effervescent tablets (*Sandocal*)	
9.6	**Vitamins**	
	Vitamin B tablets, compound, strong	
	Vitamin B$_1$ (thiamine) injection 100 mg/ml	i.m. or i.v.
	Parentrovite injection — IMM or IMHP	i.m.
	Pyridoxine hydrochloride tablets 50 mg	
	Orovite tablets	
	Ascorbic acid tablets (Vitamin C) 50 mg	
	Calcium with vitamin D tablets	
	Calciferol injection 300 000 units	i.m
	Phytomenadione (*Konakion*) injection 10 mg	i.m. or i.v.

BNF Ref.	Drug	Route of administration if not given orally

10	**TREATMENT OF MUSCULOSKELETAL AND JOINT DISEASES**	
10.1	**Drugs used in rheumatic diseases and gout**	
10.1.1	ANTI-INFLAMMATORY ANALGESICS	
	Aspirin (soluble) tablets 300 mg	
	Aspirin (*Nu Seals*) enteric coated 600 mg	
	Ibuprofen tablets 200 mg and 400 mg	
	Indomethacin — capsules 25 mg	
	— suppositories 100 mg	
10.1.4	DRUGS USED IN THE TREATMENT OF GOUT	
	Indomethacin capsules 25 mg	
	Allopurinol tablets 100 mg, 300 mg	
	Colchicine tablets 250 μg	
10.2	**Drugs used in other musculoskeletal disorders**	
10.2.1	Neostigmine — tablets 15 mg	
	— injection 500 μg/ml	s.c., i.m. or i.v.
	Pyridostigmine bromide (*Mestinon*) tablets 60 mg	
11	**DRUGS ACTING ON THE EYE**	
11.3	**Anti-infective preparations**	
	Chloramphenicol — eye drops 0.5%	
	— eye-ointment	
	(See also antiviral drugs)	
11.5	**Mydriatics and cycloplegics**	
	Atropine sulphate eye-drops 1%	
	Cyclopentolate hydrochloride 1%	
11.6	**Treatment of glaucoma**	
	Acetazolamide tablets 250 mg	
	Adrenaline eye-drops (*Eppy*) 1%	
	Pilocarpine nitrate eye-drops 1%, 2%	
11.8	**Miscellaneous ophthalmic preparations**	
	Hypromellose eye-drops 0.3%	
12	**TREATMENT OF DISEASES OF THE EAR, NOSE AND OROPHARYNX**	
12.1	**Drugs acting on the ear**	
12.1.3	Docusate sodium 5%	
	(*Waxsol*) ear-drops	
12.3	**Drugs acting on the oropharynx**	
	Benzocaine lozenges, compound	
15	**ANAESTHESIA**	
15.1.3	ANTICHOLINERGIC PRE-MEDICATION AGENTS	
	Atropine sulphate injection 600 μg/ml	i.m. or i.v.
15.1.4	SEDATIVE AND ANALGESIC PERIOPERATIVE DRUGS	
	Diazepam tablets 10 mg	
	Droperidol (*Droleptan*) injection 5 mg/ml	i.m. or i.v.

BNF Ref.	*Drug*	*Route of administration if not given orally*
15.2	**Local anaesthesia** Lignocaine 1% 20 ml vial Lignocaine 2% 20 ml vial	
	MISCELLANEOUS Acetylcysteine (*Parvolex*) injection Desferrioxamine (*Desferal*) injection	i.v. s.c. or i.v.

Index

614